Using Quattro® PRO

Stephen Cobb

Osborne **McGraw-Hill**

Berkeley New York St. Louis San Francisco
Auckland Bogotá Hamburg London Madrid
Mexico City Milan Montreal New Delhi Panama City
Paris São Paulo Singapore Sydney
Tokyo Toronto

Osborne **McGraw-Hill**
2600 Tenth Street
Berkeley, California 94710
U.S.A.

For information on translations and book distributors outside of the U.S.A.,
please write to Osborne **McGraw-Hill** at the above address.

A complete list of trademarks appears on page 831.

Using Quattro® PRO

4567890 DOC 99876543210

ISBN 0-07-881546-0

CONTENTS

Foreword

Quattro PRO is the spreadsheet users have been waiting for, providing them more features in less computer memory than any other PC spreadsheet ever developed. No longer are users forced to choose between multi-page consolidation and advanced publishing; they can have both. In addition, users have Lotus 1-2-3 compatibility, full mouse support, connectivity to Paradox, dBASE, and Reflex, and a host of advanced features. In short, Quattro PRO provides powerful spreadsheet capability without requiring expensive hardware.

Now Borland-Osborne/McGraw-Hill presents *Using Quattro PRO* to help our users derive full benefit from Quattro PRO. Beginning users and experienced spreadsheet veterans alike will find that this book unlocks the incredible power, flexibility, and functionality of this state-of-the-art program. Author Stephen Cobb leads readers from an introduction to spreadsheet technology and commands, to consideration of statistical tools and charting options, to Quattro PRO's powerful programmable application development environment.

We are extremely proud to add *Using Quattro PRO* to the Borland-Osborne/McGraw-Hill Business Series of books. We know readers will find it is an authoritative and comprehensive guide to help them take full advantage of the powerful functions and high performance of Quattro PRO.

Philippe Kahn
President
Borland International, Inc.

Acknowledgments

Many thanks to my patient editors at Osborne, Liz Fisher and Ilene Shapera, who stuck with this project across the months and across the miles to Scotland. Thanks also to Lisa Biow for her watchful eye and to Nan and Scott in Scotts Valley for their valuable assistance. To Chey, Erin, Dorothy, and Briah go my thanks for the endless encouragement and unconditional good cheer.

Introduction

This book is a complete guide to Quattro PRO, the greatly enhanced electronic spreadsheet from Borland International. The Quattro PRO user enjoys numerous state-of-the-art features, such as multiple spreadsheets with dynamic linking between them and sophisticated graphing capabilities, including a variety of high-quality fonts and a complete drawing facility. There are also such helpful features as an on-screen listing of functions; the ability to undo the last command entered; complete support for mouse users; and a single-key delete feature. In learning to use Quattro PRO, you will be mastering one of the best implementations of desktop computer power.

About This Book

If you are new to electronic spreadsheets, the best approach is to read this book chapter-by-chapter. By following the examples, learning Quattro PRO is made easy. Users experienced in other spreadsheets can probably skim the first chapter. If you just want to read about certain topics, you may first want to survey the book to learn about Quattro PRO's features and examine the examples to see how Quattro PRO is applied to typical spreadsheet tasks. Users of 1-2-3 may want to review Appendix B before getting started. The comprehensive index allows you to use the book as a complete reference to Quattro PRO's commands and features.

With this book and Quattro PRO you can tackle such tasks as budget projection, financial recordkeeping, scientific data analysis, graphing statistical information, and custom applications development, and do so through a system of commands that can be learned quickly and customized easily. Because of the ease with which Quattro PRO reads and writes data to and from a variety of popular formats, it is the ideal program for today's office.

How This Book Is Organized

This book will introduce you to Quattro PRO's features and capabilities, providing practical applications that you can easily adapt to your own needs. Chapter 1 introduces you to the basics of spreadsheets and discusses Quattro PRO in relation to other spreadsheets, pointing out important capabilities and features. You are also introduced to the basic concepts of the program's operation, such as entering data and using the menu system. Chapter 2 demonstrates the operation of the main spreadsheet commands, and Chapter 3 discusses database management.

The real breadth of Quattro PRO's capabilities becomes apparent in Chapter 4, where you will find a detailed examination of how to establish and edit formulas and utilize the built-in @functions. In Chapter 5 a comprehensive spreadsheet-building exercise brings together and reviews elements from earlier chapters as well as Quattro PRO's printing and preview features. The chapter then explores techniques for developing presentation-quality spreadsheets with visual enhancement. Chapter 6 demonstrates many of the customizable aspects of the program, such as international currency, date formatting, and color display. Chapter 7 discusses data storage in detail, proceeding from the basics of disk storage to such advanced topics as password file protection. Handling multiple windows and spreadsheet linking is discussed in depth. You will also see how Quattro PRO's File Manager simplifies hard disk management. The program's ability to read data from such programs as 1-2-3, Reflex, dBASE, and Paradox is also described.

Chapter 8 presents an in-depth discussion of Quattro PRO's extensive graphics capabilities with numerous tips for effective chart making. Chapter 9 explains how to manipulate date- and time-related information. It also describes advanced techniques for regression analysis, matrix arithmetic, frequency distribution, and what-if tables, and demonstrates the use of XY graphs. Quattro PRO commands for transforming text data into paragraphs and values are illustrated with numerous examples in Chapter 10, which covers the string functions and parse feature.

For users seeking to streamline their work, Chapter 11 provides tips on the use of Quattro PRO Shortcuts. The simple techniques of recording keystrokes in macros is described along with other methods of macro creation. Step-by-step examples lead you through each method. Chapter 12 shows how to automate tasks with special macros. The command language of Quattro PRO is discussed with examples of how it can be used to create worksheet-specific menus. You will also find tips on creating and modifying user interfaces and developing linked spreadsheet applications. In Chapter 13 you will find a variety of examples of Quattro PRO's unique features, including the graph annotator, showing how they can be applied to typical office tasks.

Appendix A offers ideas for setting up Quattro PRO on a hard disk system. Appendix B offers tips for users of 1-2-3 and other spreadsheets working with Quattro PRO. Appendix C offers tips for problem solving and support and includes common questions and answers about using Quattro PRO.

About Quattro PRO

At the end of 1987 Borland International introduced the first version of Quattro. This program offered significant improvements over the very popular spreadsheet from Lotus Development, 1-2-3 Release 2A. In addition to intelligent background calculation of numeric information, powerful database and graphics commands, and sophisticated macro capabilities, the first version of Quattro offered a highly flexible user interface. This ability to extensively customize the program, along with such practical features as macro recording, cell deleting with the DELETE key, and the use of shortcuts to invoke menu items with a single key, led to a series of rave reviews in the computer press.

While the initial success of Quattro established it firmly in the marketplace, Borland was well aware that Lotus had plans for a major overhaul of 1-2-3 and that Microsoft was gaining market share with its Windows-based spreadsheet called Excel. Both the improved 1-2-3 and Excel offered multiple worksheets. The appeal of linking separate spreadsheets together lies in the ability to mimic classic accounting practices where figures are broken down into manageable schedules which can then be summarized. Multiple worksheets mean that your work on the computer can more closely imitate the way you used to work on paper. In 1988 Borland acquired Surpass, a rival spreadsheet much-acclaimed for its windowing and linking abilities. Meanwhile the graphing abilities of Quattro were being enhanced for incorporation into Paradox, Borland's powerful relational database. At the same time Borland was refining a program design feature called VROOMM for Virtual Real-time Object-

Oriented Memory Management. This is a method of loading a program into memory in small units as needed. Since you are only using a few parts of a program at any one time, VROOMM makes it possible to load large spreadsheets in a limited memory area and still provide a considerable number of desirable features.

Quattro PRO combines the basics of the original Quattro, the technology of Surpass, a full range of drawing and graphing tools, and VROOMM. All of these elements were combined and then refined through an extensive test program. Quattro PRO runs on a wider range of equipment than either 1-2-3 Release 3 or Excel, and yet provides a comparable set of features. By providing both character and graphic modes of display, Quattro PRO offers the user a unique combination of high-speed operation and presentation-quality output.

In addition to the features of the original Quattro, users of Quattro PRO will find multiple worksheets and windows, an even greater variety of graphs, as well as a complete drawing facility to annotate graphs. Graphs and drawings can be placed directly into worksheets and both text and graphics can be printed in high resolution. Throughout the program there is built-in support for both keyboard and mouse users. The appearance of even the most basic spreadsheets can be improved through the use of multiple fonts, line drawing, and shading. Quattro PRO comes with an impressive range of fonts, including Bitstream Dutch and Swiss styles in a wide range of sizes. Also included in the program is the SQZ! facility for compressing files on disk and the File Manager, a complete system for listing, organizing and moving disk files.

While all this might sound complicated, much of the program's power lies in its ease of use and its ability to keep pace with ever-expanding information-processing needs. Using the column and row format of the spreadsheet to collect, organize, and manipulate information, Quattro PRO allows you to perform everything from the simplest arithmetic to complex calculations such as regression. You can also sort information and search for specific data. You can do statistical analysis and draw a graph of just about any set of data. In addition, you can tell Quattro PRO to remember a series of instructions and then repeat them at will. These can be simple steps you frequently repeat or complex instructions that you are simplifying for others who are using the program.

Conventions Used in This Book

One of Quattro PRO's hallmarks is the ability it gives to the user to alter the program's operation and appearance. To better illustrate Quattro PRO's numerous interface options, the look of the screens in this book do vary. For this reason, you will occasionally note differences between your screen and the screen shown in the book. Some of the screens in the book use Quattro PRO's graphics display system to show visual elements, such as combined charts and data, more clearly. Occasional screens feature a high-resolution mode to include more data than the normal 80 characters by 25 lines. In some cases the mouse palette, part of Quattro PRO's built-in mouse support, is displayed in the figures as it appears down the right of the screen when a mouse is in use. Users who do not have a mouse connected will not see this palette.

Quattro PRO has intelligent menu positioning so that, whenever practical, a menu you have selected is positioned on the screen in such a way as to avoid obscuring the current cell in the underlying work area. This may mean that illustrations show menus in slightly different positions from the way they appear on your screen. Also, Quattro PRO stacks menus with submenus, or child menus, appearing below parent menus. The initial chapters show the full set of menus while later in the book the submenu alone may be shown. Note that many menus are illustrated with the "drop shadow" option, an effective way of clarifying separate menus when more than one is on the screen at a time. The expanded versions of menus are used in most of the figures with narrow versions used on occasions when a particular point in the underlying spreadsheet needs to be illustrated. The narrow versions of the menus reveal more of the work area, while the expanded versions show more clearly the user's progress through the menu system and the current settings. The intent throughout is to give you a strong sense of how the flexibility of Quattro PRO adds to both its power and ease of use.

Additional Help from Osborne/McGraw-Hill

Osborne/McGraw-Hill provides top-quality books for computer users at every level of computing experience. To help you build your skills, we suggest that you look at the books in the following Osborne/McGraw-Hill series that best address your needs.

The "Teach Yourself" series is perfect for people who have never used a computer before or who want to gain confidence in using program basics. These books provide a simple, slow-paced introduction to the fundamental uses of popular software packages and programming languages. The "Master Skills Check" format ensures that you understand concepts thoroughly before you progress to new material. Plenty of examples and exercises (with answers at the back of the book) are used throughout the text.

The "Made Easy" series is also for beginners or users who may need a refresher on the new features of an upgraded product. These in-depth introductions guide users step-by-step from the program basics to intermediate-level usage. Plenty of "hands-on" exercises and examples are used in every chapter.

The "Using" series presents fast-paced guides that cover beginning concepts quickly and move on to intermediate-level techniques and some advanced topics. These books are written for users already familiar with computers and software who want to get up to speed fast with a certain product.

The "Advanced" series assumes that the reader is a user who has reached at least an intermediate skill level and is ready to learn more sophisticated techniques and refinements.

The "Complete Reference" series provides handy desktop references for popular software and programming languages that list every command, feature, and function of the product along with brief but detailed descriptions of how they are used. Books are fully indexed and often include tear-out command cards. "The Complete Reference" series is ideal for both beginners and pros.

"The Pocket Reference" series is a pocket-sized, shorter version of "The Complete Reference" series. It provides the essential commands, features, and functions of software and porgramming languages for users at every level who need a quick reminder.

The "Secrets, Solutions, Shortcuts" series is written for beginning users who are already somewhat familiar with the software and for experienced users at intermediate and advanced levels. This series provides clever tips, points out shortcuts for using the software to greater advantage, and indicates traps to avoid.

Osborne/McGraw-Hill also publishes many fine books that are not included in the series described here. If you have questions about which Osborne/McGraw-Hill books are right for you, ask the salesperson at your local book or computer store, or call us toll-free at 1-800-262-4729.

Other Osborne/McGraw-Hill Books of Interest to You

We hope that *Using Quattro PRO* will assist you in mastering this popular super spreadsheet, and will also peak your interest in learning more about other ways to better use your computer.

If you're interested in expanding your skills so that you can be even more "computer efficient", be sure to take advantage of Osborne/McGraw-Hill's large selection of top-quality computer books that cover all varieties of popular hardware, software, programming languages, and operating systems. While we cannot list every title here that may relate to Quattro and to your special computing needs, here are just a few related books that complement *Using Quattro PRO*.

Paradox 3 Made Easy takes you through all the basics of working with Release 3, Borland's new upgrade of their relational database. From beginning concepts to intermediate techniques, you'll learn Paradox 3 as you follow "hands-on" lessons filled with examples and exercises. Also see *Paradox Made Easy* for Release 2.0.

Paradox 3: The Complete Reference is an ideal desktop encyclopedia for all Paradox users from beginners who know some basics to veteran users. This book provides brief, yet in-depth descriptions of every Paradox Release 3.0 command, function, and feature. If you have Paradox Release 2.0, see *Paradox: The Complete Reference*.

If you are just starting out with DOS, look for *DOS Made Easy,* a step-by-step, in-depth introduction to PC-DOS and MS-DOS through version 3.3, or see *DOS 4 Made Easy* if you use PC-DOS or MS-DOS version 4.0.

If you're looking for an intermediate-level book, see *Using MS-DOS* (covering all versions through 3.3), a fast-paced, hands-on guide organized into 15-minute sessions that quickly covers basics, before discussing intermediate techniques and even some advanced topics. If you have DOS version 4, see *Using DOS 4.*

Why This Book Is for You

If you want to get the most out of Quattro PRO, this book is for you whether or not you have worked with other computer programs. Chapter 1 explains how to get started with Quattro PRO, even if you have never used an electronic spreadsheet before. You are introduced to the basic concepts of the program's operation, such as entering data and using the menu system. Simple but practical examples are used to show how easily the power of Quattro PRO can be applied to typical problems and tasks.

If you are familiar with other spreadsheet programs, such as 1-2-3 and Microsoft Excel, you will find that this book is written with an understanding of the features and limitations of these other programs. Chapter 1 examines Quattro PRO in relation to other spreadsheet products, pointing out Quattro PRO's special features. Examples throughout the book show the particular power of Quattro PRO and highlight the exciting techniques that it offers you for tackling common spreadsheet assignments.

Building from the basics and proceeding through a thorough documentation of the program's features, this book will lead you to master increasingly sophisticated applications of Quattro PRO's unique abilities. You will be able to tackle your work with new and imaginative techniques that represent the state of the art in electronic spreadsheeting.

Learn More about Quattro

Here is an excellent selection of other Borland-Osborne/McGraw-Hill books on Quattro that will help you build your skills and maximize the power of this widely used spreadsheet.

If you are just starting out with Quattro 1.0, look for *Quattro Made Easy,* a step-by-step, in-depth introduction to Borland's spreadsheet. If you're looking for an intermediate-level book on Quattro 1.0, see *Using Quattro:*

The Professional Spreadsheet, a fast-paced, hands-on guide that quickly covers basics, before discussing intermediate techniques and even some advanced topics. If you have DOS version 4, see *Using DOS 4*.

For all Quattro 1.0 users (from beginners who are somewhat familiar with the program to veteran users), see *Quattro: Secrets, Solutions, Shortcuts*. This book provides clever tips and points out shortcuts for using Quattro to greater advantage. Traps to avoid are also mentioned. Also see *Quattro: The Complete Reference,* a handy desktop encyclopedia that lists all the Quattro 1.0 commands, features, and functions.

Quattro PRO is the spreadsheet users have been waiting for, providing them more features in less computer memory than any other PC spreadsheet ever developed. No longer are users forced to choose between multi-page consolidation and advanced publishing; they can have both. In addition, users have Lotus 1-2-3 compatibility, full mouse support and connectivity to Paradox, dBASE, and Reflex, and a host of advanced features. In short, Quattro PRO provides powerful spreadsheet capability without requiring expensive hardware.

Now Borland-Osborne/McGraw-Hill presents Using Quattro PRO to help our users derive full benefit from Quattro PRO. Beginning users and experienced spreadsheet veterans alike will find that this book unlocks the incredible power, flexibility and functionality of this state-of-the-art progam. Author Stephen Cobb leads readers from an introduction to spreadsheet technology and commands, to consideration of statistical tools and charting options, to Quattro PRO's powerful programmable application development environment.

We are extremely proud to add *Using Quattro PRO* to the Borland-Osborne/McGraw-Hill Business Series of books. We know readers will find it is an authoritative and comprehensive guide to help them take full advantage of the powerful functions and high performance of Quattro PRO.

1 *Getting Started*

This chapter tells you what Quattro PRO is, how it compares with other software, how to load it into your computer, and how to start using Quattro PRO for a variety of tasks. In the process, you will learn the basic concepts of Quattro PRO and build a foundation for the many features you will learn about in the rest of this book.

This chapter also compares Quattro PRO with other electronic spreadsheet programs. There is a section that compares and contrasts Quattro PRO with Lotus 1-2-3 and Microsoft Excel. This discussion will be of interest to those of you who want to know what distinguishes Quattro PRO from these other programs. The section entitled "Starting Quattro PRO" outlines the procedures for getting Quattro PRO up and running on your PC. The "Spreadsheet Concepts" section explains basic spreadsheet operations and provides information about the keyboard and menus.

What Is Quattro PRO?

Quattro PRO is a spreadsheet program with integrated database and graphics capabilities. The terms spreadsheet, database, and graphics refer to ways of organizing and analyzing information. If you are not familiar with these terms, you should refer to the introduction of this book, which discusses the development of personal computers and popular software packages and their relationship to typical office tasks.

Electronic Spreadsheets

Although not essential to your use of the program, a short account of Quattro PRO's forerunners provides an interesting perspective from which to view both the Quattro PRO program and some of the competing products you may have used. In many respects Quattro PRO is a lot like earlier programs such as 1-2-3 Release 2.01 from Lotus, SuperCalc 4 from Computer Associates, and the original version of Quattro itself. However, in other very important respects, Quattro PRO is quite different from its predecessors.

Early Favorites

Lotus 1-2-3 has become a standard for spreadsheet software. It has been at the top of the best-seller list for several years. However, before 1-2-3 was introduced in 1982, another program held that position. That program literally created the spreadsheet genre and popularized the concepts upon which 1-2-3 and Quattro PRO are based. The program was VisiCalc, developed by Software Arts, which was the first spreadsheet for microcomputers. It was introduced in 1978 for the pioneering Apple II computer.

VisiCalc introduced the column and row format that forms a grid, or *matrix,* for numbers and words. You can see the column and row arrangement on the Quattro PRO screen shown in Figure 1-1. VisiCalc also provided a simple but effective system of commands that controlled basic procedures like storing and printing the information. In addition, VisiCalc established the syntax for writing the instructions, or *formulas,* that perform calculations on the numbers in the spreadsheet cells. An example of this syntax is **100+B5** shown at the top of Figure 1-1. The overall design of 1-2-3 and Quattro PRO, including such details as the syntax of the commands, is based on the conventions first used by VisiCalc.

Another spreadsheet program, SuperCalc, was introduced in 1980 for computers that ran on the CP/M operating system. SuperCalc was quickly upgraded to run on the IBM PC when the PC came on the market in 1982. There are still a substantial number of SuperCalc users today. The latest version of the program, SuperCalc 5, offers some features that are similar to those found in Quattro PRO (including linked spreadsheets).

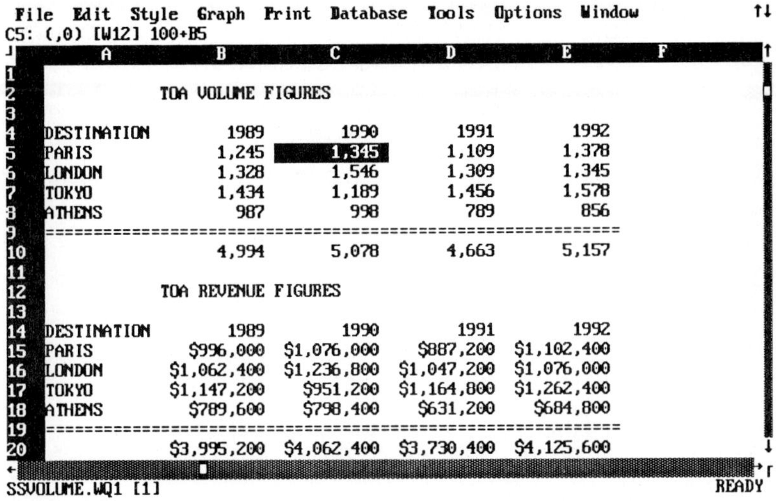

Figure 1-1. *Sample Quattro PRO screen*

Menu and Help Systems

In 1-2-3, commands are organized into an easy-to-use menu structure that provides brief explanations of the commands. The 1-2-3 menu system is activated by the slash (/), the same key that always precedes VisiCalc commands. You can choose commands either by entering their first letter, which is the system used by VisiCalc, or by pointing with the arrow keys and picking highlighted options. Many programs now use a similar method for selecting menu items. This method is sometimes referred to as a *point-and-shoot* interface. 1-2-3 users can also request help, and the program responds with information appropriate to the command being carried out. This context-sensitive help feature is also widely used in other software programs.

Quattro PRO's menu system provides a point-and-shoot interface with *pull-down menus* that temporarily cover part of the work area. The main menu items are always listed across the top of the screen (see Figure 1-2). An explanation of the highlighted item appears on the bottom line of the screen, whenever the menu is activated (by using / or F3).

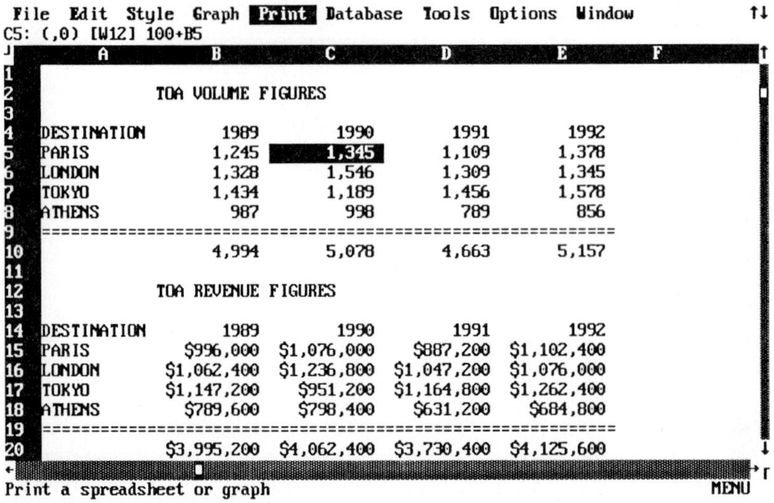

```
 File  Edit  Style  Graph  Print  Database  Tools  Options  Window        ↑↓
C5: (,0) [W12] 100+B5
⌐          A            B            C            D            E         F      ↑
1
2                 TOA VOLUME FIGURES
3
4  DESTINATION         1989         1990         1991         1992
5  PARIS              1,245        1,345        1,109        1,378
6  LONDON             1,328        1,546        1,309        1,345
7  TOKYO              1,434        1,189        1,456        1,578
8  ATHENS               987          998          789          856
9  ================================================================
10                     4,994        5,078        4,663        5,157
11
12                TOA REVENUE FIGURES
13
14 DESTINATION         1989         1990         1991         1992
15 PARIS            $996,000   $1,076,000     $887,200   $1,102,400
16 LONDON         $1,062,400   $1,236,800   $1,047,200   $1,076,000
17 TOKYO          $1,147,200     $951,200   $1,164,800   $1,262,400
18 ATHENS           $789,600     $798,400     $631,200     $684,800
19 ================================================================
20               $3,995,200   $4,062,400   $3,730,400   $4,125,600      ↓
Print a spreadsheet or graph                                        MENU
```

Figure 1-2.   *The Quattro PRO menu bar*

Pull-down menus take advantage of the fact that you do not need to see the entire work area when you are using a menu. These menus are not limited to a few lines and can thus be fairly extensive. In fact, Quattro PRO presents expanded versions of many menus on demand, allowing you to get complete information about each option. Figure 1-3 shows a menu that lists worksheet files that are available to be retrieved from drive A. You can browse through this list to find the file you want. By typing **+** you will see a wider version with more details about the files. This expanded menu is shown in Figure 1-4. As soon as a menu is no longer needed, you can put it away and return to the full work area.

Database Commands

The developers of 1-2-3 realized that many of the lists that users were compiling with spreadsheets would be more manageable if they could be sorted, and that much of the information in spreadsheets could also be considered a database. Because of this, they added several features that gave 1-2-3 database-management capabilities. With such a capability, a

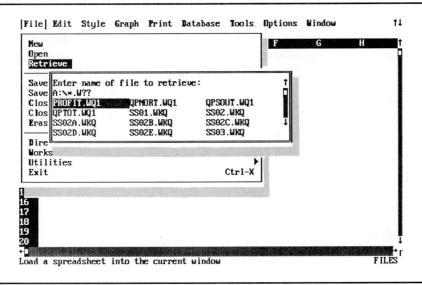

Figure 1-3. *The File Retrieve list*

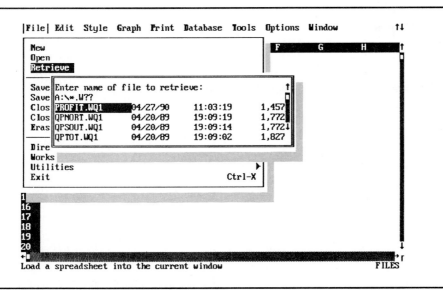

Figure 1-4. *Wide version of File Retrieve list*

File Edit Style Graph Print Database Tools Options Window   ↑↓
C3: [W27]

	A	B	C	D	E	F
1			Take Over Airlines			
2			Repair Shop Inventory Listing			
3						
4	Item#	Back?	Description	Cost	Price	On Hand
5	110002	N	Cone Machelle, Right	1,340.56	1,675.70	23
6	110011	N	Wheel Brackets, Wing Right	876.87	1,096.09	16
7	110007	N	Cover Clamp	5.75	7.19	24
8	110003	Y	Forward Bulkhead Unit	342.45	428.06	2
9	110010	N	Wheel Brackets, Clip	45.89	57.36	4
10	110001	N	Cone Machelle, Left	1,340.56	1,675.70	34
11	110014	Y	Wheel Brackets, Valve Rod	132.56	165.70	27
12	110013	N	Wheel Brackets, Wing Left	978.56	1,223.20	4
13	110005	N	Cone Machelle, Lower	1,340.56	1,675.70	9
14	110006	N	Machelle, Retaining Flange	56.98	71.23	5
15	110009	Y	Wheel Brackets, Rear	980.67	1,225.84	7
16	110012	N	Wheel Brackets, Valve Stem	3.50	4.38	8
17	110008	N	Wheel Brackets, Front	897.89	1,122.36	21
18	110016	N	Wheel Rim Seals	3.50	4.38	32
19	110004	Y	Cone Machelle, Upper	1,340.56	1,675.70	5
20	110015	N	Wheel Brackets, Seal	23.67	29.59	34

SSINVENT.WQ1 [1]   READY

Figure 1-5.   *A list of inventory items*

list of inventory items, such as the one shown in Figure 1-5, can be sorted
in many different ways. For example, sorting by the number of items on
hand quickly reveals which items need reordering. You can also ask 1-2-3
for a separate list of selected items, such as those on back order. In effect,
this ability to *query* allows the user to frame questions like "Find me all
items in the inventory that are priced over $1000," which involves a search
of the data using criteria such as "price greater than 1000."

In Quattro PRO the database commands have been streamlined. You
can establish search criteria as simple formulas and perform as many as
five levels of sort at once. Information can be extracted into a spreadsheet
directly from a database programs such as dBASE IV and Paradox. You
can even perform search-and-replace actions in a spreadsheet. For example, with one command you could change all of the Wheel Brackets in
the inventory in Figure 1-5 to Axle Struts.

Graphics Capability

If the 1 and the 2 of 1-2-3 are spreadsheet and database, then what is the
3? The 3 is the ability to draw charts based on the information in the

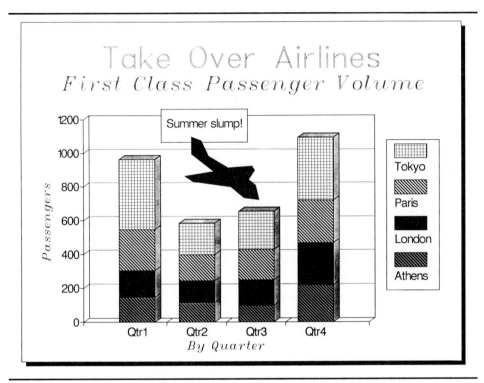

Figure 1-6.   *A Quattro PRO graph*

spreadsheet (a task that had previously required a separate program). Using the same spreadsheet menus and command structure, you can generate graphs that are linked to your data. The ability to produce charts without having to re-enter the numbers they are based on is a boon for many business applications.

Since 1-2-3 was introduced there has been a strong growth of interest in business graphics and users have sought increasingly sophisticated chart-making capabilities. As you can see from the example in Figure 1-6, Quattro PRO now provides most of the features found in stand-alone charting programs, including free-floating text and drawing elements, and provides direct access to them from the spreadsheet. Indeed, Quattro PRO allows you to insert graphs into spreadsheets. This means that you can use Quattro PRO to assemble documents that combine data with graphs. An example is shown in Figure 1-7.

	Qtr1	Qtr2	Qtr3	Qtr4	Total
Athens	149	115	97	219	580
London	159	132	153	248	692
Paris	241	153	178	257	829
Tokyo	418	187	229	374	1208
Totals	967	587	657	1098	3309

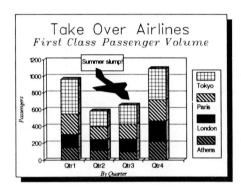

Figure 1-7.   *Combined data and graph*

Macros

In addition to expanding the range of tasks performed by an electronic spreadsheet, 1-2-3 provided the ability to type a series of commands and then replay them at will. Originally called the *typing alternative,* this feature was like the *macro* keys being used by some word processing programs. The replay feature proved very popular, especially among those who were preparing spreadsheets for use by others less skilled in the use of the program. A considerable degree of automation can be achieved with macros, and they have developed into an important applications development tool.

As you might expect in a product from a company known for its programming languages and software development tools, Quattro PRO has a complete macro facility. In column A of Figure 1-8 you can see a simple

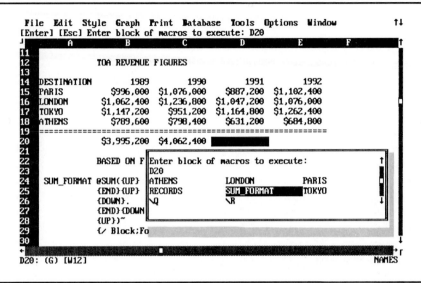

File Edit Style Graph Print Database Tools Options Window
[Enter] [Esc] Enter block of macros to execute: D20

	A	B	C	D	E	F
11						
12		TOA REVENUE FIGURES				
13						
14	DESTINATION	1989	1990	1991	1992	
15	PARIS	$996,000	$1,076,000	$887,200	$1,102,400	
16	LONDON	$1,062,400	$1,236,800	$1,047,200	$1,076,000	
17	TOKYO	$1,147,200	$951,200	$1,164,800	$1,262,400	
18	ATHENS	$789,600	$798,400	$631,200	$684,800	
19	===					
20		$3,995,200	$4,062,400			
21						
22		BASED ON F				
23						
24	SUM_FORMAT	@SUM({UP}				
25		{END}{UP}				
26		{DOWN}.				
27		{END}{DOWN				
28		{UP})~				
29		{/ Block:Fo				
30						

Enter block of macros to execute:
D20
ATHENS   LONDON   PARIS
RECORDS   SUM_FORMAT   TOKYO
\Q   \R

D20: (G) [W12]   NAMES

Figure 1-8. *A recorded macro*

macro that was recorded to sum up a column of numbers and format the answer. The user is about to execute the macro under the numbers in column D. You can see that Quattro PRO automatically lists your macros, making them easier to choose. Macros are covered in detail in Chapter 11, where you will see that Quattro PRO provides a complete debugging environment. This means that you can watch a macro execute while you follow the code and use such techniques as trace variables and conditional cells to troubleshoot problems. One very convenient feature of Quattro PRO is the ability to store macros in a *library* that is accessible to multiple spreadsheets.

Versions

Like most popular software programs, the original version of 1-2-3 has been through several revisions. Each revision expanded the program's capabilities, but also increased the demands that the software placed on the hardware, requiring more memory and faster machines. Over the years the community of 1-2-3 users has grown and numerous add-on programs have been developed to enhance the program's built-in features. To address the diverse needs of such a large group of users, Lotus decided to release two versions of the program—one runs on older hardware, and the other is optimized for newer machines. Consequently, there is now 1-2-3 Release 2.2, an enhanced version of the previous release that is designed with earlier systems in mind, plus a largely rewritten program called Release 3 which takes advantage of more powerful processors and larger memory capacities.

The story of Quattro PRO is slightly different. First introduced in the fall of 1987 as Quattro 1.0, the program had been under development for several years. The developers' goal was first to design a spreadsheet that allowed users to do everything they could already do with other products—but to do it faster and easier—and then to provide what might otherwise be add-on features as part of the program itself. Many of the ideas that went into the first version of Quattro, and probably accounted for its early success, came from research into what spreadsheet users really wanted from their software. Of course, not everything that users wanted could be included all at once. After all, every release of a piece of software is a compromise between the need to get the product to market and the desire to meet as many needs as possible while remaining easy to use and within the limits of the hardware.

Some of the features that users had sought, such as better graphics, were only partly met by the first version of Quattro. Other features, such as the ability to work with several spreadsheets at the same time, were not addressed at all. After releasing Quattro 1.0, Borland continued developing the technology to meet these needs.

Sophisticated memory-management techniques were developed to work around the structural limitations of DOS and to make possible much larger spreadsheets. A system for creating charts and managing fonts and graphics, called the *Borland Graphic Interface,* or *BGI,* was further refined to give greater creative freedom and presentation-quality images. In 1988, Borland International acquired Surpass Software Systems, makers of Surpass, an impressive program that featured advanced spreadsheet linking. This technology, along with such features as automatic column adjustment and a visual file manager, was incorporated into Quattro PRO.

The end result is a program of great power that is surprisingly easy to use. Furthermore, it is a program that will run on a wide variety of equipment. Of course, for those situations where the hardware needs of Quattro PRO are too much, there is still the original version of Quattro, itself a powerful improvement on 1-2-3 Release 2.0. Quattro PRO can read and write original Quattro files and offers a menu interface that matches the earlier version. For such situations as sales persons using small laptops while in the field, the original Quattro fits the bill perfectly as it is capable of running from a single 720K drive. Back at the office, dozens of separate Quattro files can be consolidated on a desktop system running Quattro PRO with its spreadsheet-linking feature.

New and Improved: Quattro PRO

If you are familiar with Quattro from its earlier version or conversant with trends in spreadsheet technology, you may want to know what is fresh in Quattro PRO. The following sections present some of the more important new features.

Spreadsheet Power

Although Quattro PRO retains the 8192 rows and 256 columns of its predecessor, it offers far greater capacity. This is achieved through the ability to link multiple spreadsheets and by innovative memory-management techniques. The spreadsheet interface is considerably altered from the original Quattro with a menu bar that is permanently displayed.

Windows upon Windows   Quattro PRO permits up to 32 spreadsheet windows to be open at once, providing tremendous ability to view and compare information. You can copy and move data between windows. You can *tile* windows, as shown in Figure 1-9, so that many are visible at once. Alternatively, you can *stack* windows on top of each other. You can *zoom* any window to fill the screen.

Spreadsheets That Relate   You can link together up to 63 spreadsheets. Several spreadsheets can supply information to a consolidated sheet. An example is shown in Figure 1-10, where revenue from three offices is consolidated in one master spreadsheet. You can update data in several files simultaneously, make quick comparisons between spreadsheets, and even chart data from separate spreadsheets in one graph. The linked files can be located in memory or on disk.

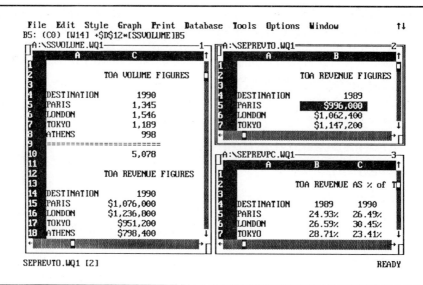

Figure 1-9. *Tiled spreadsheet windows*

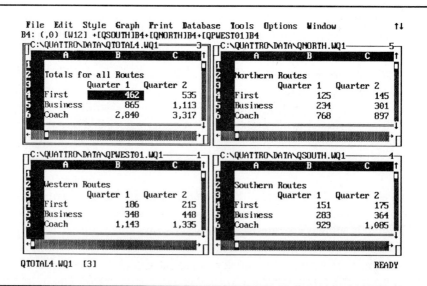

Figure 1-10. *Consolidating spreadsheets*

Recalculation in the Background   The intelligent recalculation feature of the original Quattro has been improved. Recalculation now works in the background, avoiding the need to pause for spreadsheet recalculation.

Removable Row and Column Headings   For cleaner-looking models you can now hide the row numbering and column lettering. This enhances Quattro PRO's ability to build custom applications, such as data entry forms. An example is shown in Figure 1-11.

The Undo Key   In addition to the Transcript feature for disaster recovery, Quattro PRO has a simple Undo command that can reverse many kinds of mistakes made when working with spreadsheets, graphs, and even files, including accidental deletion.

Self-Setting Column Widths   Do you get tired of setting and resetting column widths? Quattro PRO can determine column width automatically, based on a column's longest entry, plus a specified number of spaces. Furthermore, groups of columns can now be adjusted in one step.

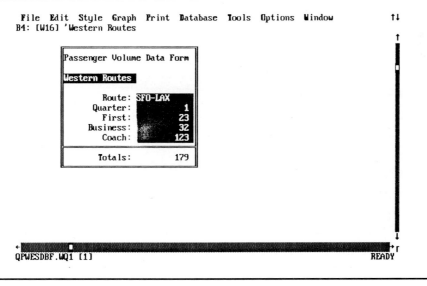

Figure 1-11.   *Data entry form*

Presentation-Quality Spreadsheets   Quattro PRO offers you a variety of new options to enhance the appearance of spreadsheets, including bullet characters, lines around cell blocks, cell shading, and a choice of fonts. In Figure 1-12 you can see a printed example of what can be accomplished with these features.

Linear Programming   There is now a set of linear programming commands for automatically finding the best spreadsheet solutions within given constraints. You can use the commands to optimize data without resorting to add-in modules.

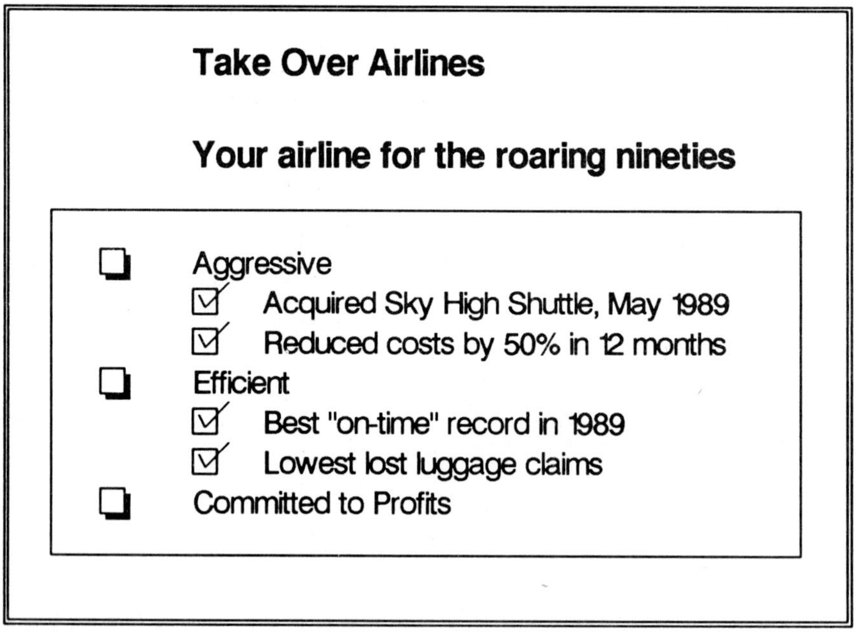

Take Over Airlines

Your airline for the roaring nineties

- ☐ Aggressive
  - ☑ Acquired Sky High Shuttle, May 1989
  - ☑ Reduced costs by 50% in 12 months
- ☐ Efficient
  - ☑ Best "on-time" record in 1989
  - ☑ Lowest lost luggage claims
- ☐ Committed to Profits

Figure 1-12.   *Presentation-quality features*

New @function Commands   Quattro PRO offers 13 new @function commands, as well as an improved version of @NPV. The new @functions are

@DSTDS, @DVARS, @FVAL, @IPAYMT, @IRATE, @NPER, @PAYMT, @PPAYMT, @PVAL, @STDS, @SUMPRODUCT, @VARS , and @VERSION

Graphics Power

Building upon the improved graphics that the original Quattro brought to traditional spreadsheet software, Quattro PRO offers several further refinements. Perhaps the most notable of these is the ability to combine graphs and data in one document.

Types of Graphs   The number of graph types has been increased with the addition of column and high-low charts. You can create custom designs such as dual y-axis and logarithmic graphs. Three-dimensional style is available for many graph types. You can adjust bar width, legend position, graph framing, and use new graph text options to enrich graphs.

Graph Insertion   You can now insert graphs directly into the spreadsheet, viewing and printing the graph on the same page. Inserted graphs are updated automatically when spreadsheet data changes. You can see an example of this in Figure 1-13.

Annotation   A new graph annotation utility allows you to draw lines, arrows, boxes, circles, and other shapes directly onto a graph. You can add explanatory text in a variety of fonts, styles, and sizes, as shown in Figure 1-14, which is a printout of the spreadsheet in Figure 1-13.

Text Fonts   Quattro PRO includes a variety of fonts for printing and displaying graphs. Both Hershey and high-quality bitstream fonts are supported. The latter were used in printing Figure 1-14.

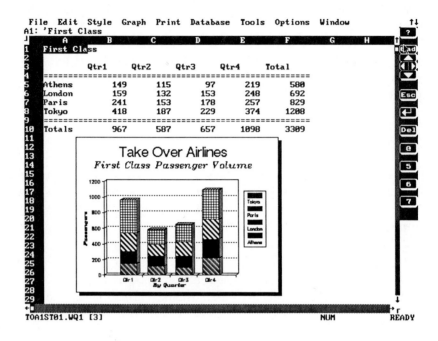

Figure 1-13. *Graph inserted in spreadsheet*

Database Power

In the original version of Quattro there were several refinements to database operations, including provision for up to five sort keys. Quattro PRO continues to refine database capability.

Controlling Data Entry The type of data that is entered into a spreadsheet can be controlled, as can the area into which it is entered. To improve the accuracy of data entry, Quattro PRO can distinguish between numbers, labels, and dates.

Adding to Existing Databases   You can add records from a Quattro PRO spreadsheet database directly to an existing database created by another program (such as Paradox).

Selective Retrieval   You can use selection criteria in Quattro PRO to extract specific records from a database created by another program.

User Power

Some of the new features in Quattro PRO provide benefits that are not confined to one particular area. These include mouse support and high-resolution modes that display more columns and rows on your screen.

First Class

	Qtr1	Qtr2	Qtr3	Qtr4	Total
Athens	149	115	97	219	580
London	159	132	153	248	692
Paris	241	153	178	257	829
Tokyo	418	187	229	374	1208
Totals	967	587	657	1098	3309

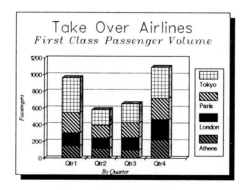

Figure 1-14.   *Printed spreadsheet*

Use of the Screen Many of today's monitors are capable of high-resolution graphics. Quattro PRO detects such capability in your system and offers several ways to use it to your advantage. For example, in Figure 1-15 you can see that more than the usual number of columns and rows are visible. When you create graphs with Quattro PRO and want to include them in spreadsheets, as seen earlier in Figure 1-13, you can use the graphics mode to view both the data and the chart at the same time. The default mode of Quattro PRO is still the character mode that is supported by every PC monitor there is, so you do not have to upgrade your display system to use Quattro PRO. However, if your monitor supports graphics mode you can switch to it at any time, or even make it the permanent default.

Use of the Mouse Support for the use of a mouse, a convenient pointing device, is built into Quattro PRO. You can use your mouse to choose menu commands, select files, mark cell blocks, scroll rows and columns, and so on. If you are using a mouse, a mouse palette is provided along the right edge of your screen, as shown in Figure 1-15 (and earlier in Figure 1-13).

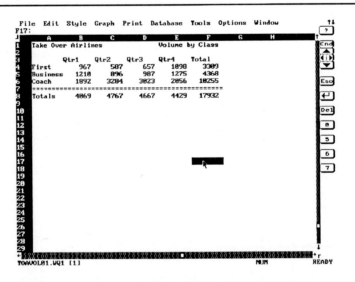

Figure 1-15. *Expanded view in graphics mode*

This gives the mouse a wide range of functions. Note that the palette is available in character mode as well as graphics mode.

Managing Files   Quattro PRO gives you sophisticated access to disk files without your having to exit the program and use DOS commands. With the File Manager, you can open, copy, move, rename, and delete files, and create directories. The File Manager's directory tree, shown in Figure 1-16, provides a visual presentation of the directories and subdirectories on your hard disk.

Using Extra Memory   Quattro PRO autodetects and uses expanded memory beyond 640K. You can use this area to store all parts of your spreadsheet, which means that you may never have to worry about creating a spreadsheet too large to fit into memory. Quattro PRO not only uses this memory, but uses it wisely, storing only one copy of identical formulas or labels in a spreadsheet, thus minimizing the memory space needed for your spreadsheets.

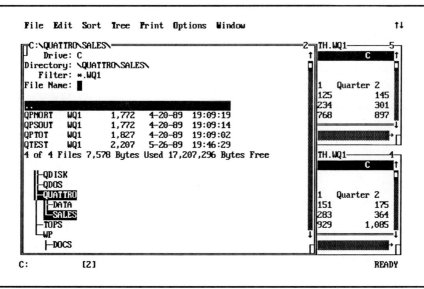

Figure 1-16.   *Directory tree in File Manager*

Mapping the Spreadsheet   As spreadsheets increase in size it becomes more difficult to keep track of the layout of information. Quattro PRO provides a *Map view* of your spreadsheet, showing which areas are occupied and what kind of data they contain. There is an example of this view in Figure 1-17.

Macro Libraries   You can now store macros in a separate spreadsheet, called a macro library, which you can access from any other spreadsheet. You can create multiple libraries and have them open at the same time. If you execute a macro that is not located in the current spreadsheet, Quattro PRO searches through the libraries until it finds the macro. Quattro PRO also has several new macro commands: {GRAPHCHARS}, {MESSAGE}, {STEPON}, and {STEPOFF}.

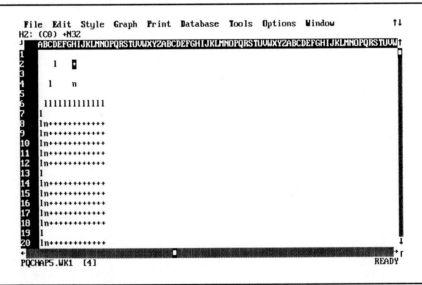

Figure 1-17.   *Map view of spreadsheet*

Quattro PRO and the Competition

The purpose of this book is to show you how to use Quattro PRO and not to get into a "features war." Claims of "49 standard features" versus "48 standard features," are too often dependent upon the definition of "standard," and as technology develops, yesterday's special features become today's standards. Yet it is worthwhile to make some comparisons between Quattro PRO, its competitors, and its predecessors, particularly if you are familiar with such standards as 1-2-3 Release 2.01 and want to know in what ways Quattro PRO is different.

Users of 1-2-3 Release 2.01 have a choice between upgrading to newer versions of the same program, or switching to such rivals as Quattro PRO and Microsoft Excel.

Borland designed Quattro PRO so that it would preserve much of the investment of time and effort put into spreadsheet development by 1-2-3 Release 2.01 users. Quattro PRO reads and writes 1-2-3 worksheets, as well as several other popular formats, and can even be set up to look like 1-2-3 for those who are used to that arrangement of menu items. Quattro PRO is similar to Microsoft Excel 2.1 but does some things that Excel does not and requires less hardware to do it. Quattro PRO runs on a wider range of hardware than Excel, is faster, and offers comparable features without the need to invest in the Windows operating environment.

Speed of Execution

Faster than 1-2-3 Release 2.01 and Excel 2.1, Quattro PRO gets you into and out of the program quickly. You will also spend less time waiting for the program to catch up with you, especially as you develop large and sophisticated applications. Since you will wait seconds rather than minutes for results, you are more inclined to try "what if" scenarios. Although speed for its own sake is not necessarily a worthwhile goal, speed that translates into faster answers is a valuable asset, one that you will value highly as you find more and more tasks for Quattro PRO.

Self-Contained Design

All of the parts of Quattro PRO—the spreadsheet, database, graphics, file management and translation—are accessible from the main spreadsheet menu. There is no separate access system or DOS shell to work through, so you can get to your task promptly. Like Excel, you can save workspaces and load files from the DOS prompt.

Graphics Features

Although word processing is still the leading application for microcomputers, anyone who has read microcomputer magazines over the last five years knows that articles and advertisements alike seldom miss an opportunity to show PCs displaying graphs. Apart from simply wanting to show something more visually exciting than a screenful of words, many of these illustrations reflect business's fascination with graphics—a fascination that is now emerging as a serious field of application. However, the graphics abilities of 1-2-3 Release 2.01 fall short of the emerging standards in presentation graphics. Quattro PRO provides a wider range of chart options and rivals many stand-alone graphics packages. Quattro PRO also prints its graphs directly from the spreadsheet environment, offers a preview mode similar to Excel's, and can place graphs within a spreadsheet (which Excel cannot do).

Custom User Interface

The standard Quattro PRO menus use the pull-down technique to provide easy-to-read menus from which to pick commands. As in 1-2-3, you can select with the arrow keys and then press the ENTER key, or you can type the first letter of the command. However, Quattro PRO can remember your last choices, which makes repetitive operations quicker, and you can use a *Shortcuts* feature to assign any menu item to a one- or two-key *control sequence*. Thus, for example, the command File Save can be accomplished by pressing CTRL-S. Quattro PRO enables you to customize the entire menu structure. You can use menus that provide the same arrangement of commands used in 1-2-3, or you can design your own menus. Customizing the menus allows you to remove potentially disastrous commands, like Erase, in order to make the program safer for less experienced users.

Automatic File Translation

You can load a 1-2-3 worksheet or dBASE database directly into Quattro PRO. You can save a Quattro PRO worksheet directly to several different file formats. You can even extract specific records from a database file created by another program.

Enhanced Macro Capability

To make macros easier to create, Quattro PRO has a RECORD mode that automatically stores a sequence of keystrokes. To increase the number of possible macros and manage them better, the program has a *macro list* feature that lets you run named macros by pointing and selecting. To make complex macros easier to work with, Quattro PRO has a sophisticated debugging feature that lets you watch the macro in action. One nice touch is that menu choices are not recorded as single letters but are automatically converted to the name of the menu item. For example, instead of seeing just /PG you will see { / Print;Go}. Quattro PRO also runs macros originally written for 1-2-3.

Formulas and Functions

Quattro PRO offers all of the built-in formulas and functions that you find in 1-2-3 Release 2.01, and adds some more that are very useful.

Running Quattro PRO

For all its power and versatility, Quattro PRO is surprisingly easy to use. Although its impressive array of features might lead you to expect that Quattro PRO requires the very latest PC technology, it has modest minimum hardware requirements.

The program is largely memory resident, which means that, once loaded, it seldom needs to read from the disk. Quattro PRO can be used with a wide range of popular PCs, as long as they have at least 512K of RAM. While every computer model cannot be discussed here, the following guidelines will help you determine your equipment needs for using the program. Preparing the program for use on any system is very easy.

Memory Size

As just mentioned, to run Quattro PRO a computer will need at least 512K of random access memory (RAM). To learn how much RAM is in your computer, use the Check Disk command (CHKDSK) from the disk operating system disk, as described in Appendix A.

Depending upon market conditions, RAM can be a fairly inexpensive commodity and it is definitely worth upgrading to at least 640K. The benefits in speed and capacity will be reflected beyond your use of Quattro PRO. With 512K of RAM in your PC, Quattro PRO will be able to handle modest spreadsheets. This capacity increases when you have 640K, depending on your operating system and other programs you might be using. Due to the different types of information that go to make up spreadsheets—including values, calculations, and formatting—it is not really possible to give an upper limit to spreadsheet size with Quattro PRO.

Quattro PRO can work better with even more memory. There are basically two ways to add more memory beyond 640K: expanded memory, and extended memory. Expanded memory cards, like AST RAMpage!, Intel Above Board, and Quadram Liberty, that conform to the Lotus/Intel Expanded Memory Specification can increase RAM to 8000K, or 8 megabytes. Quattro PRO can use this area to extend spreadsheet size dramatically. As long as you install the memory board and its software correctly, Quattro PRO will automatically detect and use the added space. The investment in such cards is more than returned, since enhanced memory enables you to apply the power of Quattro PRO to much larger collections of information.

If you have an 80286 or 80386 system, such as an IBM PC AT or a COMPAQ 386, you can also use Extended memory for Quattro PRO. *Extended memory* is memory beyond 640K that is counted and checked by your system when it is powered up. Your system thinks of this memory as simply an extension of the basic 640K but DOS cannot recognize it as such. Fortunately, although Quattro PRO cannot directly recognize this memory there are programs like 386MAX from Qualitas and the HI386 from RYBS that can make this Extended memory look like Expanded memory, allowing Quattro PRO to use it. (See Appendix A for more about memory expansion.)

Disks and Drives

Quattro PRO comes on several floppy disks, the number depending upon the disk size. To ensure that it can be loaded by a wide range of systems, the program is available on 360K 5 1/4-inch disks and on the newer 3 1/2-inch floppy disks used by the IBM PS/2 models and laptop systems like the Toshiba T1200. These drives can hold 720K or more, which is very convenient for Quattro PRO use.

Quattro PRO requires a hard disk for proper operation. The continuing decline in the price of hard disk drives make them an increasingly attractive proposition for anyone who makes more than occasional use of a computer. The advantages of a hard disk drive are faster access to files on the disk, more room for larger files, and the ability to store all of the parts of a program like Quattro PRO on one disk. Many different programs can be placed on the hard disk to make movement between them quick and easy. (Appendix A provides some pointers on hard disk installation and organization for the Quattro PRO user.)

Display Systems

If you have a system with graphics display capability, you will be able to see the graphs drawn by Quattro PRO. This graphics capability is provided by a combination of a suitable display card/adapter and an appropriate monitor.

Computers present images on the screen in two ways. The first is referred to as character or text mode. This mode uses a set of characters (A through Z, numbers, symbols and shapes) to display information that is mainly text, but which can also include simple drawings and designs. This mode is the default mode used by Quattro PRO to display the spreadsheet. The other display technique is referred to as graphics. In the graphics mode the display uses a series of dots to show everything from simple letters and numbers to complex shapes and a wide variety of character sizes and styles. This is how Quattro PRO displays graphs. Note that even if your system cannot display graphs, it can create them for printing.

If you have only an IBM monochrome monitor and an IBM monochrome display adapter, you will not be able to see Quattro PRO graphs without upgrading in some way. This upgrade can be relatively inexpensive as monochrome graphics cards are fairly cheap and enable even the old IBM monochrome monitors to show graphics. Color is more expensive, but EGA or VGA cards coupled with high-resolution monitors enable Quattro PRO to really shine, displaying all of its graphics features to good advantage. You can then set Quattro PRO to run in graphics mode all the time, viewing more than the normal number of columns and rows at once. (More details on graphics are provided in Chapter 8.)

Printing and Plotting

Quattro PRO can produce hard copy of your information on paper in a number of different ways. The three options described here are Print Spreadsheet, Print Graph Print, and printing from the screen. Given this flexibility of print options, Quattro PRO works well with a variety of printers. Just about any printer can use the Print Spreadsheet method. Graph Print and printing from the screen are limited to specific combinations of hardware and software.

Print Spreadsheet   When you are working with text and numbers in the spreadsheet, Quattro PRO has a print option on the menu bar. When you select this option, you can send text reports to your printer and set print factors like paper size and margins, as well as send special messages or codes about the type of print you want. These codes are called *setup strings,* and they are different for each printer model. (Chapter 5 covers setup strings in detail, and Appendix B contains lists of codes for several printers.)

Graph Print   Since graphic images are more complex than text reports, some spreadsheet programs require special procedures to print them. However, with Quattro PRO you simply select a graph print option from the Print menu. You do not have to save the graph in a special file. You can chose from a variety of printers and plotting devices, a complete list of which is provided in Appendix A. If you have a color device such as the HP

Colorpro, you can assign colors to the various parts of the graph. If you are using a color monitor, you can have the graph print as it is displayed.

Screen Print When using Quattro PRO, the information that you want to print is sometimes only what is on the screen. During a Quattro PRO spreadsheet session in character mode you can print whatever is on the screen at any time by using the Print Screen (PRTSC) key on your keyboard. You cannot print from the graphics mode in this way unless you have a special program (such as InSet by Inset Systems, Inc.). Details on how to obtain and use InSet with Quattro PRO are given in Appendix A.

Input: The Keyboard

Quattro PRO's response to typed commands is usually immediate; the results are quickly displayed. There are several different PC keyboard layouts. As you can see in Figure 1-18, the basic differences are in the placement of the cursor and function keys. These differences should not be a problem when learning or using Quattro PRO. While it might be annoying

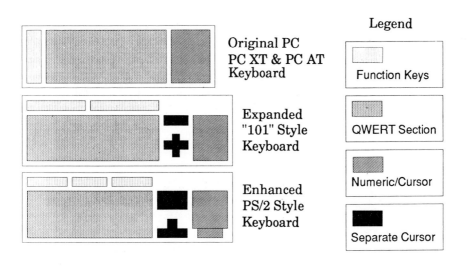

Figure 1-18. *Alternative keyboard layouts*

to adjust from one keyboard to another, you should realize that all the keys are the same, even if their locations are different. For this reason, in this book the keys will be referred to by the names that are on them, rather than by their location.

For example, the key marked ESC or ESCAPE may be on the left or the right side of the keyboard. However, pressing ESCAPE does the same thing whether the location is left or right. Quattro PRO uses the ESCAPE key the same way many other programs do, to let you change your mind. After you have selected an option from a menu, pressing ESCAPE lets you deselect the option. Keys used extensively by Quattro PRO are shown in Table 1-1.

Quattro PRO uses the cursor-movement keys extensively for highlighting options and moving around the screen. These are the arrow keys: UP, DOWN, LEFT, and RIGHT. These keys may be found in a separate group or may share keys with the numeric keypad. When you turn on your computer the arrow/number keys are set to arrows, just like the alphabet keys are set to lowercase. Use the SHIFT key to produce numbers instead of arrows, or lock in numbers by tapping the NUM LOCK key. This process is the same as using either SHIFT for the capital letters *A* through *Z* or locking in capital letters with the CAPS LOCK key. Full use of the cursor-movement keys is discussed when you begin working the first example in this chapter.

Quattro PRO makes effective use of the function keys, labeled F1, F2, and so on. These keys are either down the left side or across the top of the keyboard, depending on the layout. The function keys as used in Quattro PRO are listed in Table 1-2, and they will be explained as they are used in the examples. The command card at the back of this book lists the function keys, as does the keyboard template in the Quattro PRO manual. Diagrams of the function keys for both horizontal and vertical layouts also are shown later in this chapter. Keeping one of these diagrams or templates handy while using the program can reduce the amount of time you spend looking up the keys in a text.

Input: The Mouse

If you have a mouse attached to your PC and properly installed, Quattro PRO will automatically detect it, presenting a mouse pointer on the screen, together with a mouse palette down the right hand side of the spreadsheet display. This mouse palette can be customized, as will be described in Chapter 9.

Key	Purpose
ENTER	Enter data into worksheets; select highlighted menu items; confirm block coordinates and other settings
ESCAPE	Cancel changes on the edit line; take you out of menus; return you to READY mode; unlock block coordinates
BACKSPACE	Remove characters to the left on the edit line; unlock block coordinates; return beginning coordinate to current cell
DELETE	Delete cell contents; remove current character from edit line
INS	Control OVERSTRIKE mode when editing
SHIFT	Used to get the upper half of any key, including capitals *A* through *Z*, symbols such as $, and numbers on the numeric keypad
CAPS LOCK	Type *A* through *Z* as capital letters without shifting; does not affect any other keys
NUM LOCK	Lock numeric pad into numbers; lock out cursor movement with those keys
SCROLL LOCK	Switch between Move and Size when adjusting windows
CTRL	Used with certain keys to execute commands, such as CTRL-BREAK, which stops macro execution, CTRL-D, which prepares cell for data entry, and CTRL-ENTER, which assigns shortcuts
ALT	Used with - to record keystrokes for macros and with selected keys to execute macros
PRINT SCREEN	Print current screen; this key will not print graphs
@	Precedes built-in formulas, the @functions
/	In READY mode activates the menu; in formulas used for division
\	Used as cell fill command to repeat characters; also used in naming instant macros
+	Both plus keys are used to begin formulas and perform addition. The plus key on the numeric keypad expands menus
#	Used for multiplication sign
–	Used for subtraction

Table 1-1. *Keys Frequently Used in Quattro*

	Regular	**Alt**	**Shift**
F1	Help	Previous Help	
F2	Edit	Macro Menu	Debug
F3	Menu/Choice	Function List	Macro Commands
F4	Absolute		
F5	Goto	Undo	Pick Window
F6	Pane	Zoom	Next Window
F7	Query	All Select	Select
F8	Table		Move (in File Manager)
F9	Calc		Copy (in File Manager)
F10	Graph		Paste (in File Manager)

Note also ALT-N, which selects window N.

Table 1-2.   *Function Keys*

Starting Quattro PRO

A great deal of effort went into making Quattro PRO an easy program to start on almost any computer. There are two steps: installing the program and issuing the command that begins the program. Most hard disk drive systems have a hard disk drive that is called C and a floppy disk drive that is called A. To install Quattro PRO you place disk 1 of the program disk into drive A and *log on* to that drive. This means that you make drive A the *active drive,* which is done by typing **A :** and pressing ENTER at the DOS prompt. The DOS prompt will probably look like C or C:\ and then change to A or A:\ when you execute this command.

With drive A active, type **INSTALL** and press ENTER to initiate the installation process. When the program files are copied onto the hard disk you will need to answer some questions about your system. Having answered these, Quattro PRO will be installed and ready to use. To load Quattro PRO from the DOS prompt, type **Q** and press ENTER when you are in the Q2 directory. You will see a screen like the one shown in Figure 1-19. You are now ready to start working with the program. Next time you use your system, type **CD\Q2** followed by **Q** to run the program.

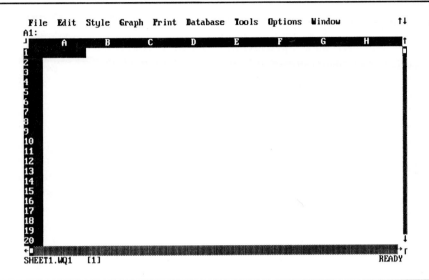

Figure 1-19. *Opening screen*

Startup Problems

If you do not know what the DOS prompt is or how to get to it, or if you have difficulty following the installation process described here, or if you do not get the screen shown in Figure 1-19, you should consult Appendix A. If you want to customize such things as the way Quattro PRO handles your screen or the menu structure, consult Chapter 6, "Dealing with Defaults."

Starting and Leaving Quattro PRO

As you have seen, you can start Quattro PRO by typing **Q** at the DOS prompt. This is the basic method of starting the program on a hard disk. The command can be incorporated into a menu system on a hard disk system, or Quattro PRO can be started automatically, as soon as your system is turned on or reset. The procedures for setting up these methods are explained in Appendix A. You can instruct Quattro PRO to load a worksheet as soon as the program loads. Commands for doing so are explained in Chapter 6.

When you type **Q** and press ENTER the program loads into memory. This takes from two to ten seconds, depending on the type of hardware you are using. You are then presented with the opening screen (shown in Figure 1-19). Leaving the program can be done in several ways and is described in the section "Saving and Ending" later in this chapter. Normally, you will want to store the work you have done in a file on disk. However, if you do not need to store any of your work, you can simply turn off the computer or restart it. If you want to go directly back to the DOS prompt, you can type / followed by **F** for **F**ile and then **x** for E**x**it. If you have done any work that has not been saved on disk, you will be prompted to confirm the Exit command.

Spreadsheet Concepts

This section introduces the basic concepts of spreadsheets and prepares you for the next chapter. Some brief examples demonstrate how to enter and calculate numbers with Quattro PRO and familiarize you with the special keys and the menu system.

The Worksheet Area

When you first load Quattro PRO you have an empty electronic work space called a *worksheet* in which to place numbers, words, and instructions (formulas and calculations). As you can see in Figure 1-19, there is a line of letters near the top of the screen and a list of numbers down the side. The letters represent a series of columns and the numbers a series of rows. The intersection of each column and row forms a rectangle, a box into which you put information. These boxes are called *cells*. One of them is highlighted when you start the program. This highlighted cell is called A1 because it is in column A on row 1. Every cell has a name based on its location, or *coordinates,* just like a map. You move from cell to cell to lay out information. When you first start Quattro PRO you are in cell A1. If you were to enter information at this point, it would be placed in cell A1. The cell you are in is called the *current cell.*

The highlighting that marks the cell you are in is called the *cell selector*. It can be moved with the cursor keys or the arrow keys. When you move the cell selector, the horizontal and vertical borders indicate which column and row you are in, using reverse highlighting. Your exact location is recorded at the bottom left of the screen.

Worksheet Size

The worksheet is very large; the columns continue off the side of the screen through column Z. Farther columns are numbered AA through AZ, then BA through BZ, and so on. After repeating the alphabet nine and a half times, you get to the last column, IV, a total of 256 columns. The rows go beyond 20 down to 8192. Multiplying the columns and rows together gives you a total of over two million cells. Obviously your monitor can show you only a small portion of this huge work area at a time, as you can see from the diagram in Figure 1-20. Since the monitor can only show you about 1/400th of the total area of the worksheet, the screen acts like a cockpit

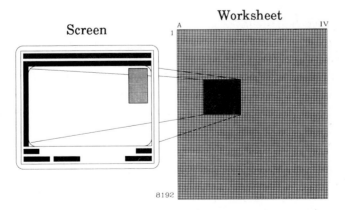

Figure 1-20. *Viewing the spreadsheet*

window, showing you different parts of the worksheet as you move the cell selector around.

Quattro PRO provides important information around the edge of the screen, as shown in Figure 1-21. When you are using Quattro PRO, the horizontal and vertical borders, the top menu bar and command line, and the bottom status area work like a dashboard or control panel. They display important information and messages. The status of the CAPS LOCK, NUM LOCK, and SCROLL LOCK keys is shown at the bottom of the screen. Error messages are displayed to help you when you make a mistake. The *mode indicator* shows you a variety of messages about the current task. The *cell identifier* shows the contents of the current cell, its display format, and its width setting. More detailed functions of the various parts of this control panel are shown in Figure 1-22, which shows a menu in the upper part of the screen.

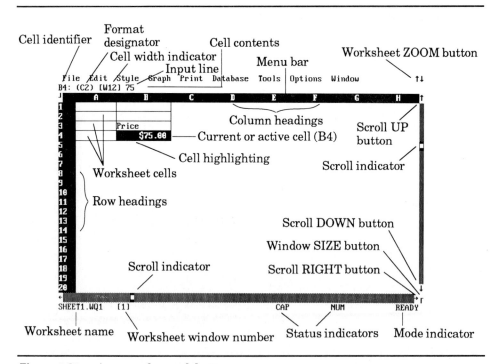

Figure 1-21.   *Annotated spreadsheet screen*

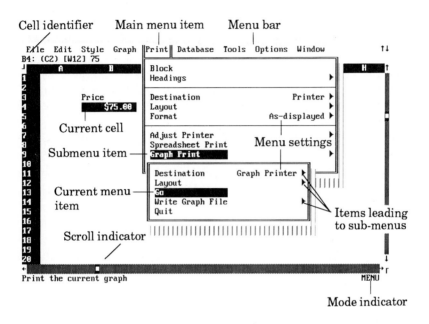

Figure 1-22. *Further details of the screen*

Movement Keys

To explore the work area, press the RIGHT ARROW key once. You will see the highlighting move to the next cell to the right, B1. You are now in cell B1. Press the DOWN ARROW key once and you will be in cell B2. Notice that in the bottom-left corner your current location is being monitored. This indication is very helpful, since eyeballing your location is notably prone to error, particularly after several hours at the screen.

Your keyboard has the ability to repeat keystrokes and will do so if you lean on, rather than just tap, a key. Throughout the rest of this book you should take the term *press* to mean lightly tap rather than push and hold down. To see the keyboard repeat feature in action, press the DOWN ARROW key and hold it for two seconds. You will see the cell indicator move quickly down the screen and the numbers at the left will scroll by rapidly. You can see that you are dragging the screen with you to view a different area of the spreadsheet. Now try pressing the HOME key. It takes you back to A1.

The full range of cursor movement keys can be seen in Figure 1-23. The UP, DOWN, LEFT, and RIGHT ARROW keys move you one cell in each of their respective directions. Used with the CTRL key, the RIGHT and LEFT ARROW keys move a screen at a time across the worksheet. A similar effect can be achieved with the TAB and SHIFT TAB keys, respectively. The PAGE UP and PAGE DOWN keys move you 20 lines at a time up and down the worksheet. The HOME key always places you in A1 (unless you are using locked titles, described in the next chapter). The END key followed by the UP, DOWN, LEFT, or RIGHT ARROW key takes you to the last cell in that direction. The last cell means the last occupied cell in a row or column and the first occupied cell if the next cell is empty. Do not use the END key like the CTRL key; you press END and then the arrow key.

The INSERT and DELETE keys are often grouped with the cursor keys. Pressing DELETE removes the contents of the current cell. Pressing INSERT changes the way that the EDIT mode works and allows you to add text to the middle of a value or label without typing over other characters.

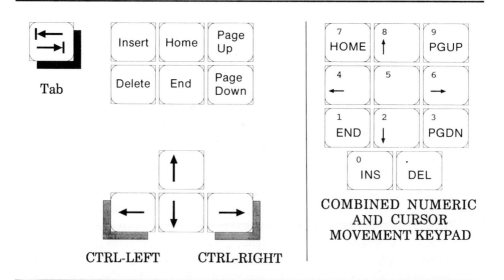

Figure 1-23.   *Cursor movement keys*

Types of Information

Quattro PRO categorizes all information into one of two types of data: values or labels. To oversimplify, values are numbers and calculations, and labels are words or text. Quattro PRO treats the two categories of data differently. By looking at the first character of each new entry into the worksheet, Quattro PRO determines the appropriate category for that data—value or label.

Values

To see how to enter information into Quattro PRO and how the program recognizes values, try the following exercise. With the cell indicator in cell A1, type **789** from the row of numbers at the top of the keyboard. Do *not* press ENTER or any other key; just observe what has happened. Notice that the number 789 has not yet been placed into the worksheet. Instead, it is on the top command line, which is now acting as the edit line. The cursor is flashing after the number 9. At this point you can either continue to type or use the BACKSPACE key to erase what you have typed. Also notice that a change has taken place in the bottom status area. The mode indicator now says VALUE. This tells you that Quattro PRO is reading what you have typed as a value. If you pressed the ENTER key prematurely or otherwise caused the number to leave the top line of the screen, just type **789** again and observe what happens before you press ENTER.

Mode Indicator

You can now place the number 789 into the worksheet. To do so, press the ENTER key and observe that the number disappears from the edit line and is placed into the worksheet in the cell you are highlighting. The cell identifier in the top status area now lists the contents of the cell. While the cell identifier might seem like a duplication of effort, you will see in a moment that what Quattro PRO shows you in the cell identifier is sometimes different from what it displays in the worksheet. The cell identifier shows the exact content of the cell as Quattro PRO reads it.

When you have pressed ENTER you will also see that the mode indicator returns to READY. Notice that the numbers you have entered are placed on the right-hand side of the cell. Quattro PRO normally aligns numbers evenly with the right of the column. This is referred to as *flush-right alignment*.

Locking Capitals

Now that you are back in the READY mode, you can move to another cell. Press the RIGHT ARROW key once and you will be in cell B1. Here you will enter a label. Before you type, take a look at your keyboard and locate the CAPS LOCK key. This key allows you to type in capital letters without using the SHIFT key. Many people find it convenient to type labels all in capitals. Press the CAPS LOCK key once and notice the bottom status area reflects this change with the message CAPS. When you are locked into capitals, the letters *A* through *Z* are automatically typed as capitals. However, you must still use the SHIFT key to access symbols and commands that are on the upper half of the keys.

Labels

In a moment you are going to type the word *BASE* because you will use Quattro PRO to figure out the full price of a car from, among other things, the base price. When you type the letter **B**, notice that the mode indicator says LABEL. Also notice that the word is being typed on the edit line so you can change it with the BACKSPACE key if you make an error. Type **BASE**, press ENTER, and observe the cell identifier at the bottom of the screen. In front of the word you typed is an apostrophe ('). The apostrophe was automatically placed there by Quattro PRO as a reminder that this is a label. Although you are not likely to confuse this particular label with a number, later you will encounter instructions that look like labels but are in fact values.

The apostrophe not only tells you that this is a label but also signifies that this is a left-aligned label. Labels can either be left-aligned, right-aligned, or centered in the column. Right-aligned labels are preceded by a quotation mark ("). Centered labels begin with a caret (^), which is the shifted 6 on the keyboard. Rather than make you type one of the three label align characters (', ", or ^) before every label, Quattro PRO will assume one of them. This is the *default label alignment* and, as you can see, it is left-aligned. Later you can change the default or change the alignment of a block of labels. To enter a label aligned differently from the default, just type the desired alignment before the text of the label. If you want the label to begin with one of the alignment characters, use two of them. Thus, entering " "**Right On**" will actually produce a right-aligned label that reads "Right On".

Entering with Arrows

You will now enter another label directly below "BASE." This will be the word PREP, for dealer preparation costs, but you will use a slightly different method to enter it into the cell. First press DOWN ARROW to move to cell B2, and then type **PREP**. It will appear on the edit line like the numbers **789** and **BASE** did before. Now press the DOWN ARROW key again. Doing so enters the label and moves you down to the next row. This can be a very useful feature if you want to enter a series of labels or numbers. The direction keys will enter what you are typing and move you in a particular direction with one keystroke. For this reason it is important not to press the cursor keys when you are entering information into an empty cell. Practice this method of entering by typing **TAX** and then pressing the DOWN ARROW key, followed by **TOTAL** and the DOWN ARROW key. The results will look like Figure 1-24.

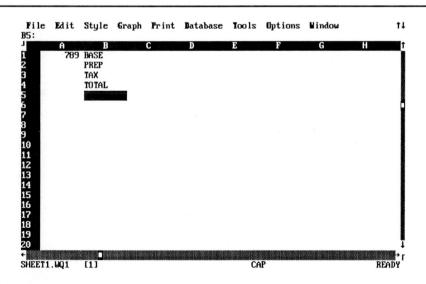

Figure 1-24. *Entered data*

Editing Cells

Changing worksheet entries and correcting mistakes is one of the most important procedures you will need to know. In this example, 789 is a ridiculously low price for a car, so you need to change it. Press HOME; you will be highlighting cell A1 and the number 789. To change a cell entry completely, just type a new entry. Type **8000** and press ENTER. Do *not* put commas in the thousands when entering numbers in Quattro PRO; they will be put in later. The new number completely replaces the old one.

What if you want to modify the contents of the cell, rather than completely replace them? For example, you might want to change 8000 to 8095 to reflect a price increase. When you do not need to completely change a cell, you can change part of it using the Edit key, F2. In this case, you press F2 while your cell selector is in A1. When you do so, the contents of the cell are returned to the edit line.

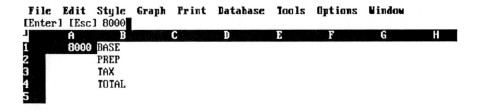

Press BACKSPACE to back over the last two zeroes, and type **95**. Now press ENTER to see the modified contents returned to the cell.

Suppose you now want to add a figure for dealer preparation costs to the worksheet. First press DOWN ARROW once. You will be in cell A2. Type the number **567**, and enter it into the cell by pressing the DOWN ARROW key. You are now in cell A3 and ready to do some math with Quattro PRO.

Instructions and Formulas

In cell A3 you want a figure for the tax that must be paid on the base price of the car. Assume that the tax rate is 10% or 0.1. The figure you want in cell A3 is 8095×0.1. You want Quattro PRO to calculate this for you, so you are going to type an instruction into cell A3 that will tell the program to multiply the number in cell A1 by 0.1 and place the answer in cell A3. Note that you are not going to tell the program simply to multiply the number 8095 by 0.1. Quattro PRO can do that, but that is not the true power of a spreadsheet. What you want to do is establish a relationship between the cells so that, even if the number in A1 changes, the relationship will remain and A3 will continue to give you 0.1 times the content of A1. The instruction will be entered as **.1*A1** . Quattro PRO uses the asterisk for a multiplication sign. Although the instruction contains a letter as well as numbers, the program considers the decimal point to be a *value indicator* and so reads what follows it as a value. Type **.1*A1** and press ENTER. You will immediately see the tax figure calculated.

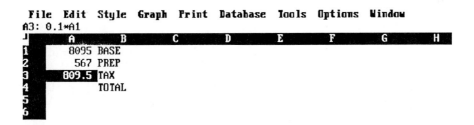

Look at the cell identifier in the second line of the screen. It should look like this:

```
 File  Edit  Style  Graph  Print  Database
A3: 0.1*A1
        A        B        C        D
```

Notice that Quattro PRO is not concerned about the actual number in cell A3. It simply records the relationship between the two cells. This will remain the same, whatever number is in cell A1.

Suppose that the base price goes up. Press HOME to move to 8095 in cell A1. Change it by typing **8900**, the new price, and pressing ENTER. Instantly, Quattro PRO updates cell A3. If you move the cell indicator down to cell A3 and look at the cell identifier, you will see that the cell contents have not changed. They are still the same formula you entered before.

Now you want to calculate a total price for the car including the base price, preparation costs, and tax. You will need to add several cells together. To do this, first place the cell selector in the cell that is to contain the answer—in this case, cell A4. Now you will type an instruction that tells Quattro PRO that this cell will contain the sum of cells A1, A2, and A3. You might think that you could type **A1+A2+A3**, and this is almost correct. However, instructions involving only cell references need special treatment because Quattro PRO will read the letter *A* as a label. To get around this and to make sure that Quattro PRO knows that what you are typing is a value, type a plus sign first and then the cell reference. Make sure the cell selector is in A4, and then type the formula **+A1+A2+A3** and press ENTER.

The Function Instruction

If you decided to take out a loan to finance the full price of this car, you might want to calculate how big a monthly payment you would have to make. A loan payment calculation involves three pieces of information. Labels for these three items will be typed into column D, starting in D1. Move the cell selector to D1. Then, using the DOWN ARROW key to enter them, type the three labels **PRINCIPAL**, **INTEREST**, and **TERM**. Also type one more label, **PAYMENT**, and then move back up to cell E1 where you will enter the principal amount. Your screen should look like this:

```
 File  Edit  Style  Graph  Print  Database  Tools  Options  Window
E1:
     A         B        C       D        E      F       G       H
1    8900  BASE             PRINCIPAL
2     567  PREP             INTEREST
3     890  TAX              TERM
4   10357  TOTAL            PAYMENT
5
```

The amount you want to finance is the total price from cell A4. Instead of typing the number again, simply type **+A4** and press ENTER. This establishes a relationship between these two cells so that whatever is in cell A4 is also in cell E1.

Now move the cell selector to E2. Here you want to enter the rate of interest you will pay. This needs to be expressed as a rate per period of the loan. Suppose you are going to make monthly payments. You need to enter the amount of interest you will pay in one month. If the bank is charging 12% per annum (A.P.R.), the rate is 0.01, or 1%, per month. Type **.01** in cell E2 and press DOWN ARROW to go to cell E3. In this cell type the term, the number of months for the loan, say **36**, and press DOWN ARROW.

A formula for the payment will be entered in cell E4. You do not need to know the actual formula. Quattro PRO knows exactly how to calculate a loan payment if it is given the principal, interest, and term because it has a special built-in function. In fact there are dozens of built-in functions covering most common calculations. Press the Function Choices key, ALT-F3, and you will see a list of these pop up over the worksheet, as in Figure 1-25. Press PAGE DOWN and you will see more of these formulas. Press PAGE DOWN until you see the function you need, @PMT. Highlighting the @PMT function and press ENTER. The function will be typed on the edit

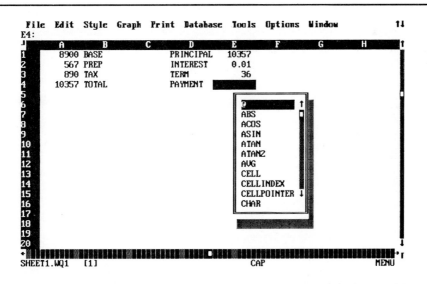

Figure 1-25. *Function list*

line for you and the menu of choices will disappear. Notice that the name of the function is preceded by the @ sign (shifted number 2 on the keyboard). This is a special code that helps Quattro PRO distinguish functions from other entries. This gives rise to the term *@functions* for the built-in formulas that use this code.

The @PMT function needs to know the amounts for principal, interest, and term of the loan. This information is presented to the function within parentheses so the open parenthesis character is typed for you. Now type **E1,E2,E3)** *Note:* leave in closed paren and press ENTER. These three entries are called *arguments* — cell numbers in this case. Most functions require some sort of argument to operate.

You do not have to use the Function Choices key to create this formula. You can press ESCAPE to remove the Choices menu and return to the READY mode. With the cell selector in E4, you could simply type the entire formula **@PMT(E1,E2,E3)** and press ENTER to place it into the cell. Either method is acceptable and produces the monthly payment, as shown in Figure 1-26.

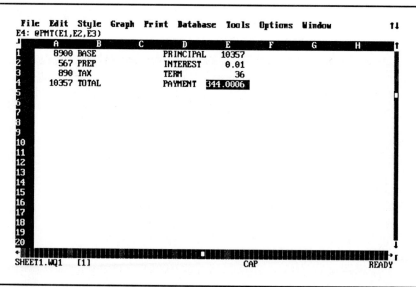

Figure 1-26.   *The monthly payment*

To give you an idea of how flexible a spreadsheet can be, you can now try some changes to the assumptions that produce the answer in E4. For example, if you were considering a more expensive model you could type the new price in A1 and immediately see the new payment in E4. To make payments less expensive each month, type in a longer term, such as 48 months, into E2.

Using the Menu System

The manipulation of facts and figures in cells is only part of the power of Quattro PRO. A whole range of commands arranged in a series of menus and submenus can be accessed through the menu bar at the top of the screen by pressing the MENU key, which is the forward slash key. Type /, and you will see that the menu bar is activated, with the first option, File, highlighted. You can use the RIGHT ARROW key to highlight Edit, and continue across the bar to highlight each of the items in turn. Notice that the word MENU appears in the mode indicator at the lower right of the screen. An explanation of what each of the items does is given on the bottom row of the screen.

Now type **F** or DOWN ARROW and the first menu, File, will be pulled down, as shown in Figure 1-27. The items you see listed in the box are the categories of file operation that Quattro PRO offers. The words across the bottom of the screen tell you what the option on the menu does. For example, in Figure 1-27 the item "New" is highlighted. You can see that this opens a new spreadsheet window. You can pull down each of the menus in turn by pressing the RIGHT ARROW key with the File menu visible. If you keep pressing RIGHT ARROW or LEFT ARROW you will return to the File menu.

You can select any item on a menu by typing the highlighted letter, which is usually the first letter. Alternatively, you can first press DOWN ARROW to put the menu bar on the desired option and then press ENTER. Try moving the highlight to the word Utilities and you will see the message "Access DOS, the file manager, for settings for compressing files." Notice that this menu item has a small triangle next to it. This means that a submenu will appear when this item is selected. Select the Utilities option and you will see DOS Shell, File Manager, and SQZ! Press CTRL-BREAK to go back one step in the menu system. You leave the menu completely by pressing ESCAPE until you are back in the READY mode.

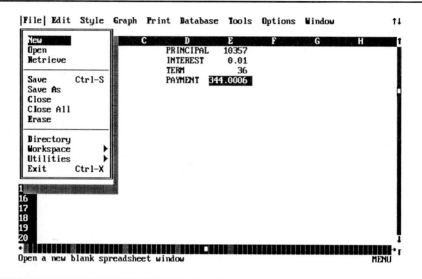

Figure 1-27.   *The File menu*

Saving and Ending

Having completed this series of calculations, you may decide to take a break. You need to think about where the information you have created is located. So far, all of the work you have been doing is in the computer's memory. The only problem with this is that the memory is only as good as the power to your computer. If you accidentally pull the plug or suffer an electrical failure, the memory's contents are lost. You must transfer the data to permanent storage on disk. This has to be done on a regular basis and should always be done before you leave your PC unattended.

Type / to bring up the menu and then type **F** for File. Now type **S** for Save and you will see a prompt like the one in Figure 1-28. You can type in a name for the file into which you want Quattro PRO to store this worksheet. The name can be any eight letters or numbers, like QLOAN101, but no spaces are allowed within the name (QLOAN_MY is acceptable). Although you can use some punctuation in file names, not all punctuation characters are valid in file names. For this reason, it is best to avoid punctuation when naming files. For complete details on file naming, see Chapter 7. When you have typed the name, press ENTER.

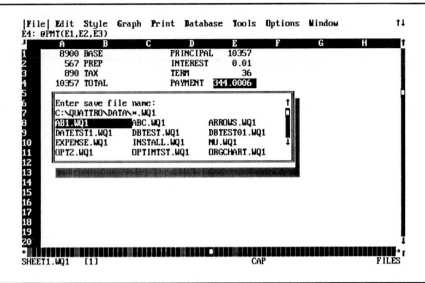

Figure 1-28. *The File Save prompt*

Note that the first time you save a spreadsheet the program will suggest storing it on the same drive and directory you started the program from, typically C:\Q2 or C:\QUATTRO. You may want to avoid storing data files among program files. To change this before saving the file, select Directory from the File menu and type the name of a data file directory for a hard drive system. Then press ENTER. From now on until you restart the program, Quattro PRO will save spreadsheets to this directory rather than to the directory occupied by the program files.

To make this change permanent, you can type / and select Options, Start-up, and then Directory. Enter the desired drive and directory and press ENTER, and then press ESCAPE to return to the Options menu. Now select Update, which will place your choice in a small file on the disk. Quattro PRO refers to this configuration file every time you load the program.

Now that you have saved your work, you can either turn off your system or return to DOS by typing / to activate the menu and selecting File followed by Exit. Quattro PRO knows if you have not saved changes to your work and, if this is the case, will prompt you to confirm the Exit command. If you do not want to stop working with Quattro PRO but want to begin a fresh file after saving the last one, you can clear the worksheet area by typing /, selecting File, and then Erase. Again, Quattro PRO will prompt for confirmation of this choice if you have not saved changes to the worksheet on the screen. For more information on file saving, see Chapter 7.

Entry, Movement, and Menu Selection with a Mouse

So far the instructions given have assumed that you are using the keyboard to communicate with Quattro. With the excellent mouse interface built in to Quattro PRO and the increasing popularity of these devices you may well want to try using your mouse to select cells, commands, and actions. The first step is to make sure that your mouse and mouse driver are installed correctly. If the mouse is installed, then Quattro PRO will place a *mouse pointer* on the screen for you. This is a small rectangle if you are displaying Quattro PRO in character mode, or a small arrow if you are using graphics mode. If you are having trouble seeing the mouse pointer, just move the mouse and you should see the pointer move on the screen. If a mouse pointer fails to appear, check the installation instructions that came with the mouse and the mouse notes in Appendix A of this book.

In Figure 1-29 you can see the mouse palette on the right of the screen. This is the way it appears in character mode. Clicking on Esc is the same as pressing ESCAPE, and clicking on the crooked arrow is the same as pressing ENTER. Mouse actions consist of pointing, clicking, and dragging. *Pointing* means placing the mouse pointer over a specific object on the screen. *Clicking* means pressing and then quickly releasing the mouse button when you are pointing to an object. Quattro PRO uses just one mouse button; if your mouse has more than one button, use the button on the left. *Dragging* means pointing to an object and then holding down the mouse button while moving the mouse. For example, you can point to cell B2 and then drag the mouse pointer to cell D10 to highlight cells B2 through D10. When you release the mouse button the cells remain selected.

The mouse can be very powerful when using Quattro PRO. For example, to delete the contents of a cell you can click on the cell, and then click on Del in the mouse palette to pick Delete. To erase a group of cells you can drag the highlight across the cells in question and then click on Del. You can use the mouse to pick menu items by clicking on the item you want. Any command that requires a group of cells to be selected will accept cells

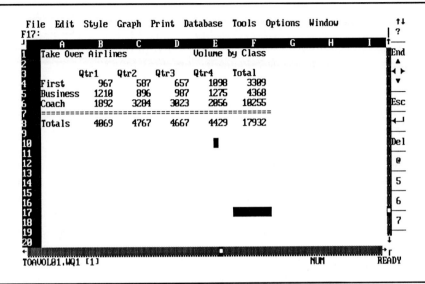

Figure 1-29.   *The mouse palette*

highlighted by dragging with the mouse. To dismiss a pull-down menu you do not have to press ESCAPE—you can just click anywhere on the worksheet.

Quattro PRO allows you to preselect cells for some commands such as formatting. Thus you can highlight a block of cells using the mouse, and then use the Style Numeric Format command to assign a format to all of the cells. The selected cells are automatically assumed to be the ones to which you want to apply the command.

Parts of Quattro PRO consist of lists, which you can navigate with the mouse. You can see a list *scroll bar* on the right of the function list in Figure 1-25. The worksheet scroll bars and the rest of the mouse palette will be discussed in the next chapter. In general this book assumes that mouse users are among the more adventurous and will probably discover for themselves what the mouse can do. In order to avoid the book getting too long and unwieldy there are not separate mouse instructions for every activity. However, when the mouse has a particularly useful or important role to play, then appropriate references are made and the palette is displayed.

Spreadsheet Practice

To practice data entry, you can type in the values and labels shown in Figure 1-30. This set of figures is called a *model*. A model shows a numerical picture of a set of values. This particular model is a record of passenger volume figures for Take Over Airlines, Inc., over a four-year period. Four main destinations are served by Take Over Airlines (TOA) and the volume figures are listed by destination.

In a new worksheet, move down to A4 where you will enter the title CITY. Type **CITY** and press RIGHT ARROW to enter this label and prepare to type the first year of the model in cell B4. Later in this book you will learn several different ways of handling dates and calendar information in Quattro PRO, including sophisticated date arithmetic. In this situation you can simply type **1989** and press RIGHT ARROW to enter it and move to C4 for the next year.

However, instead of typing 1990, this time you will create the year by adding one to the previous year. This is the formula $1 + B4$, whic does not need an additional plus sign in front of it because 1 is a value indicator. Type **1 + B4** and press RIGHT ARROW. Now type **1 + C4** and again press RIGHT ARROW. Then type **1 + D4**, and this time press ENTER. You can return to B4, update that cell to 1990, and see the other years change automat-

File Edit Style Graph Print Database Tools Options Window						1↕
A2: [W12]						
A	B	C	D	E	F	
1						
2		TOA VOLUME FIGURES				
3						
4 DESTINATION	1989	1990	1991	1992		
5 PARIS	1245	1345	1109	1378		
6 LONDON	1328	1546	1309	1345		
7 TOKYO	1434	1189	1456	1578		
8 ATHENS	987	998	789	856		
9						
10						

Figure 1-30.   *The TOA volume figures*

ically. In the next chapter you will see that there are shortcuts to entering a series of similar formulas such as the ones used here for the years.

Now go to cell A4 and enter the city names. The DOWN ARROW key will work well for this. Follow the city names with the numbers shown in Figure 1-30. These numbers will be used in several later examples. When you are done entering all of the cities and their data, save this information in a file named QNEW.WQ1. You will then be able to recall the file for later use in Chapter 2.

Database Concepts

As mentioned in the introduction of the book, people who made extensive use of spreadsheets soon found that much of the information they were recording in the columns and rows of a worksheet for the purposes of calculation were actually lists. Collections of facts and figures like inventory records, personnel files, and sales receipts were originally put in a spreadsheet so that users could perform analysis on them with the powerful formulas of spreadsheet software. However, users also wanted to sort such information. They wanted quick ways of finding selected items within their spreadsheet's growing collections of facts and figures.

For example, when using the spreadsheet to total a day's sales figures, which begin as a stack of receipts, you would probably enter them in numerical order to check that they were all accounted for. Then you might like to know how many of which items had been sold, for which you would sort the list by product name. You might also want to look at the major sales of the day, sorting them by amount of sale. The facilities for performing these kinds of tasks are called *database management*.

A *database* can be defined as a collection of information organized in a meaningful way. The telephone book, for example, is a database. A database-management program provides for entering, storing, and manipulating data. Much of the information you deal with on a daily basis comes from a database. The company personnel records, your customer account files, and the TOA volume figures used earlier are all typical examples of information that can be considered a database.

Database Basics

There are two basic elements in a database. Each category of information is called a field. Thus, the telephone book has three fields: name, address, phone number. Each set of information (for example, Doe, John/13 Elm Street/555-4321) is called a *record.*

Two basic arrangements are used for tracking data. The telephone book is a *tabular database.* The information is arranged in a table of columns and rows, as shown in Figure 1-31. The vertical columns—Name, Address, and Phone—are the fields. The horizontal rows are records. This can also be called a *list format*; the information is simply arranged in a list. The same information can be arranged differently, as in a business card file, which is a *form-oriented* database. The form in Figure 1-31 shows the same information as the table, but each record is on a separate form. To see all of the records you have to page through all of the forms. This is usually the case with such databases as medical records and index cards.

The form-oriented database offers a fill-in-the-blanks approach to data entry. This is a familiar interface and for this reason it is popular with

Phone Book as Tabular Database

Name	Address	Phone
Sith,R	123 Bryant	555-3454
Sith,S	20 Rosalie	555-7868
Soot,A	3543 Ellis	555-5325

Phone Numbers as Forms

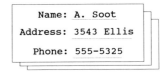

Spreadsheet Database

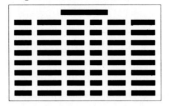

Form-oriented Database

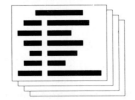

Figure 1-31.   *Diagram of forms / tables*

high-volume users and people doing extensive data entry. The tabular database lets you see all of your data laid out in the same area and, in the case of Quattro PRO, provides outstanding math and calculation facilities.

Quattro PRO as a Database Manager

In addition to calculating numbers, Quattro PRO does indeed work as a database-management program. It can sort and select from collections of information using simple menu commands. As you might imagine, Quattro PRO uses the tabular approach to storing data. However, you can use a command called the Input Form to make entering information easier and closer to the style used in a form-oriented database. Quattro PRO has a technical limit of 8191 separate records, each with as many as 256 fields.

Example

You can regard the volume figures for TOA as a small database. Suppose that the boss at TOA wants the volume figures rearranged. The instruction to "rearrange this list in alphabetical order" sounds simple enough, but as anyone who has had to type lists on a typewriter knows, you might as well say "do this over again." In Figure 1-32 you can see the volume numbers

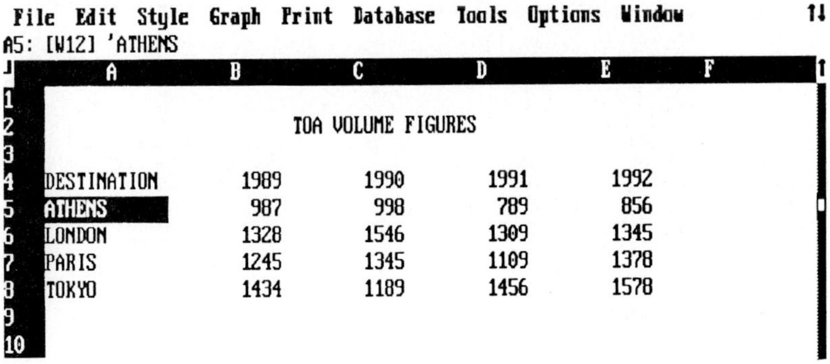

```
 File  Edit  Style  Graph  Print  Database  Tools  Options  Window          1↓
A5: [W12] 'ATHENS
↓         A          B          C          D          E          F           ↑
1
2                        TOA VOLUME FIGURES
3
4    DESTINATION      1989       1990       1991       1992
5    ATHENS            987        998        789        856                    □
6    LONDON           1328       1546       1309       1345
7    PARIS            1245       1345       1109       1378
8    TOKYO            1434       1189       1456       1578
9
10
```

Figure 1-32. *The TOA figures sorted*

for TOA, shown earlier in Figure 1-30, now rearranged into an alphabetical list by city. None of the figures are in the same place they started out. With Quattro PRO this kind of sort can be done quickly and easily. In Chapter 3 you will read how to use the database commands and apply them to a wide range of tasks.

Graphics Concepts

Few trends in business practice have been more apparent than the move toward graphic representations of information—the profusion of bar

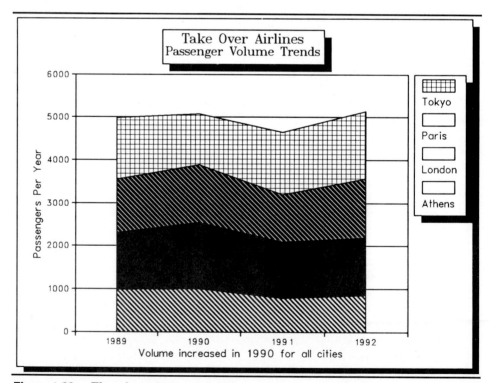

Figure 1-33. *The volume figures graphed*

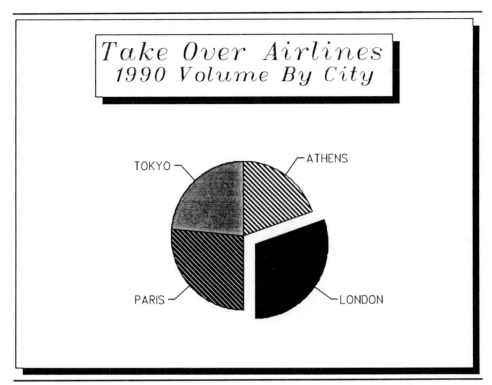

Figure 1-34. *A pie chart*

charts and pie charts in magazines, newspapers, newscasts, and even presidential addresses. This is a result of the information explosion, itself a consequence of an increasingly literate world. As the sheer volume of information to which we are exposed rises, faster means of assimilating the key points are needed. It is generally accepted that presenting facts as pictures helps achieve this goal. The person who uses a picture may well make a quicker and more lasting impression. Furthermore, when figures are shown as shapes, patterns of information are easier to detect.

An increasing number of programs are designed to graph information. Many can accept data straight from the keyboard or grab it from another program. Some spreadsheet programs can generate graphs from their own data. However, Quattro PRO has made graphs a more integral part of the program. Using Quattro PRO you can graph chosen elements of your data with exceptional speed. Changes to the data are immediately reflected in the graph.

The volume figures for TOA, seen earlier in Figure 1-30, are charted in Figure 1-33. The numbers by themselves were uninspiring and made the overall performance hard to gauge. The graph shows a clearer picture. In Figure 1-34 you can see a pie chart that shows how the total volume for 1990 was broken down among cities. London's performance is shown exploded from the rest of the pie for emphasis. In Chapter 4 you will learn how to use the graphics commands to produce presentation-quality charts and to analyze data.

2 *Spreadsheet Commands*

Chapter 1 introduced the Quattro PRO spreadsheet and told you how it can be used. In the example at the end of that chapter you saw how the Quattro PRO screen acts like a pilot's control panel, providing you with valuable information and status reports as you navigate around the huge worksheet. You also experimented with the basics of entering data and saved your work to a disk file for later retrieval. In this chapter you will find spreadsheet commands explored in depth with practical examples.

Starting a Spreadsheet Session

When you load Quattro PRO you are presented with a worksheet *window,* called window [1]. This window contains an empty worksheet that is a grid of more than two million cells. You can enter new information into this blank worksheet, or if you have already stored a spreadsheet, you can retrieve it from disk. The empty worksheet that is presented when you first load Quattro PRO is called SHEET 1. Its file name is SHEET1.WQ1. The worksheet name appears in the status line at the bottom-left corner of the screen, as you can see in Figure 2-1. This is the default name—the name that Quattro PRO will use unless you issue instructions to the contrary.

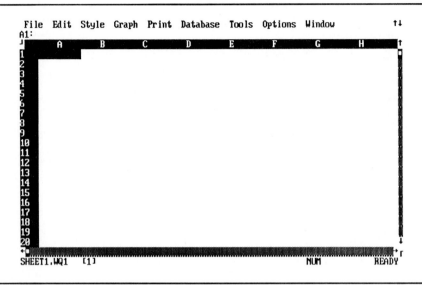

Figure 2-1. *The opening screen*

Multiple Windows

An important distinction to bear in mind when using Quattro PRO is between worksheets and worksheet windows. In Figure 2-2 you can see four different worksheets: SHEET1.WQ1, REVENUE.WQ1, EXPENSE.WQ1, and PROFIT.WQ1. Each worksheet is in a separate worksheet window: SHEET1.WQ1 is in window [1], REVENUE.WQ1 is in window [2], EXPENSE.WQ1 is in window [3], and PROFIT.WQ1 is in window [4]. However, it is important to distinguish between the window and the worksheet that occupies it. For example, PROFIT.WQ1 could just as easily appear in window [2], with REVENUE.WQ1 in window [4]. The number of the window in which a particular worksheet appears is determined by the order in which the worksheets were created or read from disk.

This distinction becomes clearer as you consider a typical work session with Quattro PRO, which begins by opening window [1] and filling it with a fresh SHEET 1. At any time during your work on SHEET 1, you can use the File New command, to open up a second worksheet window containing a second empty worksheet. This second worksheet is initially called

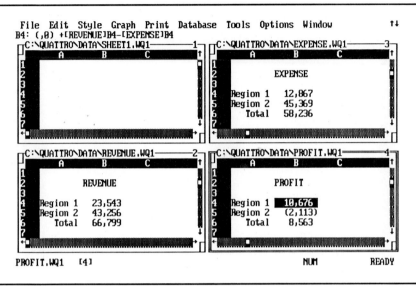

Figure 2-2. *Several worksheets*

SHEET2.WQ1, and it appears without your having to close the first. The second worksheet is as large as the first, and it is positioned over the top of the first, obscuring it like a document placed on top of another in a pile, as shown in Figure 2-3. Note the number 2 in square brackets on the status line, which is telling you that this is the second worksheet window that you have open.

When you have several worksheet windows open, you can display them all on the screen at once by using the Window Tile command. The effect was shown in Figure 2-2 and can also be seen in Figure 2-4, where two windows are open. This arrangement is referred to as *tiling*. An alternative method of showing that more than one window is open is to use *stacking*. You can see the effect of the Window Stack command in Figure 2-5.

Only one worksheet window at a time can be the *current window*, which is the one you are actively using. This window contains the worksheet or document that will be affected by the commands you issue, and its name appears on the lower left of the screen. The current worksheet window is also marked by double lines around it, instead of single, so you can see that QSOUTH.WQ1 is the active document and window [1] the active window in Figures 2-4 and 2-5.

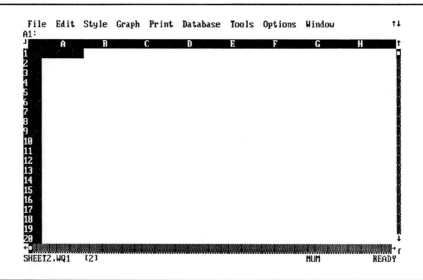

Figure 2-3. *Second worksheet on top of first*

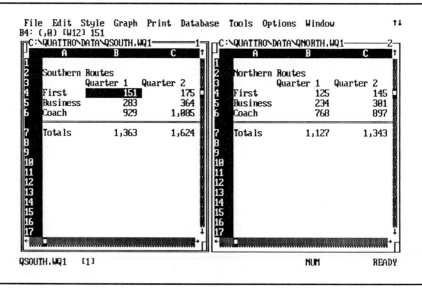

Figure 2-4. *Two windows tiled*

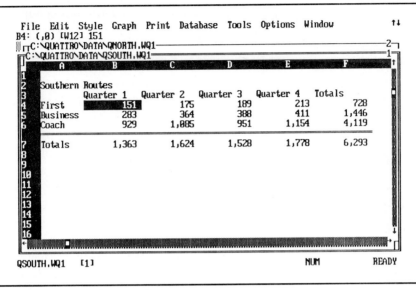

Figure 2-5. *Two windows stacked*

Bringing Back Stored Files

When you use the File New command to create a fresh worksheet, you open a new document, and the contents of those documents that are already open are not affected. If you want to work on a spreadsheet that you have already stored on disk you have two commands to choose from: File Open and File Retrieve.

Opening Files The File Open command opens up a new worksheet window and reads a file from disk into it. Because this command does not affect any of the other windows or their contents it is a safe way to read existing files from disk. However, there are disadvantages to reckless use of File Open. If you open too many new windows without closing ones you are not using, you will burden your computer unnecessarily. Not only will you notice that your system response time slows down, but opening more windows than you really need makes it difficult to keep track of your work.

Retrieving Files   When you use the File Retrieve command to read a worksheet file from disk, you bring it into the current worksheet window, replacing all two million cells of the worksheet that is already occupying the current window. This means you erase anything that was entered into the current worksheet prior to the File Retrieve command being issued. For this reason, you should be sure to save any work in progress before performing the retrieval operation. When working on one spreadsheet you may decide that you would like to see a different spreadsheet. Fortunately, Quattro PRO is keeping track of your work and will prompt you before overwriting the current worksheet, as shown in Figure 2-6.

The Transcript Feature   In addition to prompting before overwriting or erasing data, Quattro PRO has a "disaster recovery" facility called *Transcript*. This feature keeps track of your keystrokes—both data entries and commands—and stores them in a special log file on disk. If you suffer

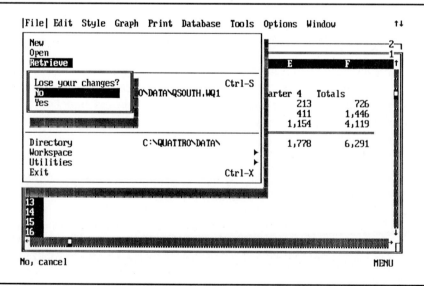

Figure 2-6.   *Lose changes prompt*

a power loss or if you accidentally delete some data, as in the case of a hasty retrieval of another worksheet, you can recall the lost data by replaying your actions from the Transcript log. Refer to Chapter 7 for details on using Transcript.

Using the File List

Suppose that you have started Quattro PRO and decide to retrieve a worksheet stored on disk. You do this by typing / to activate the menu and pressing ENTER to select File. When you select Retrieve from the File menu, a list of previously saved worksheet files appears as shown in Figure 2-7. This is an alphabetical list that grows as you add more files. The maximum number of files you can see is 12. Any more files must be scrolled into view with the cursor-movement keys or mouse manipulation of the scroll bar on the right of the box.

You pick one of these files by using the cursor-movement keys to highlight the name and then pressing ENTER. Alternatively, you can type the file name and press ENTER.

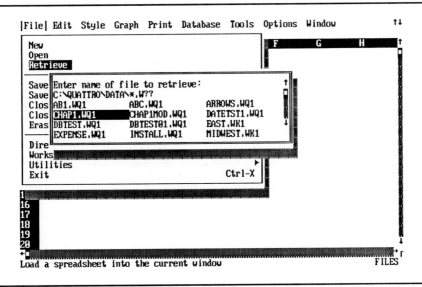

Figure 2-7. *File Retrieve command*

A copy of the file is read from the disk into the computer's memory. In Figure 2-8 you can see the retrieved TOA worksheet from Chapter 1. Notice that the cell selector is on the same cell on which you left it when the file was stored to disk. This feature allows you to return to the point where you left off. If you leave the cell selector on the fringe of your worksheet and then retrieve the file some time later, you may be confused about the location of the cell selector. For this reason, some people prefer to press HOME before saving their work so that the worksheet looks familiar when they retrieve it.

Resaving Files

Once you begin to make changes to a worksheet, you should save the file on a regular basis. You do this because the copy of the worksheet that you have in memory disappears if the power to your PC is turned off. Although Quattro PRO can recover your work using its Transcript feature, it is still a good idea to save your files regularly, perhaps every 15 minutes. This decreases the amount of rebuilding that Transcript has to do should you suffer a loss of power.

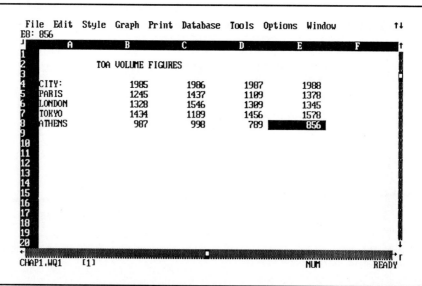

Figure 2-8. *Retrieved worksheet*

Automatic File Save   When you save a worksheet you must decide
whether to overwrite the old version of the worksheet with the new version
or to put the new version in a new file and give it a different name. To save
a worksheet over the top of the original version you type / and then select
File and Save (**/FS**). Quattro PRO uses the file name that appears in the
lower left of the screen, which is the default file name.

Prompted File Save As   To save the current worksheet to a new file
name, you use File Save As (**/FA**). A prompt will appear asking you for the
file name to use. The existing, or default, name from the lower left of the
screen is displayed, as shown in Figure 2-9. At this point you can accept
the name by pressing ENTER or by clicking the mouse button.

Accepting the default name might seem like the same action as using
the File Save command. However, with both File Save and File Save As,
Quattro PRO will check to see whether a file of the same name exists on
disk. If it does, then you will be prompted as shown in Figure 2-10. Your
choices are Cancel, Replace, and Backup. Generally you will want to
replace the older version until the worksheet design is complete. Then you
may want to save different sets of numbers in different files, in which case
you pick Cancel and repeat the File Save As command, entering a new
name instead of the default name.

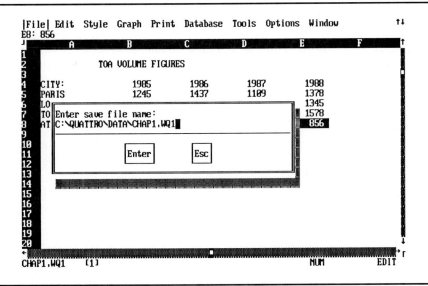

Figure 2-9. *File Save As command*

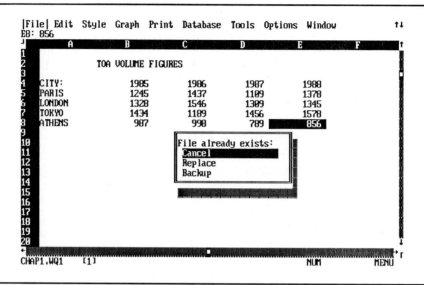

Figure 2-10.   *"File already exists" prompt*

To change the default file name in the save file prompt you can just type the name you want. This will automatically replace what is already there. Alternatively, you can edit the default file name by pressing the Edit key (F2), followed by other editing keys to change the name. The keys that you can use are listed in Table 2-1. When the name is typed correctly you can press ENTER or click the mouse button to confirm the name.

Erasing Worksheets and Closing Windows

When you have saved a spreadsheet and want to build a new one, you can either use the File Erase command to clear the entire worksheet window, or you can open a fresh worksheet window with the File New command. To clear the worksheet window, type / and select File followed by Erase. If there has been no change to the worksheet since you saved it, you will get a clean work area immediately. If there are unsaved changes, you are asked to confirm that you want to erase, as shown in Figure 2-11. Quattro PRO asks for confirmation of several commands like this one that could

Key	Action
LEFT ARROW	Moves cursor 1 character left
RIGHT ARROW	Moves cursor 1 character right
HOME	Moves cursor to first character
END	Moves cursor to the right of last character
TAB	Moves cursor 5 character to the right
CRTL-RIGHT ARROW	Moves cursor 5 characters to the right
SHIFT-TAB	Moves cursor 5 characters to the left
CTRL-LEFT ARROW	Moves cursor 5 characters to the left
DELETE	Deletes character at cursor
INSERT	Toggles between INSERT and OVERSTRIKE modes
BACKSPACE	Deletes character to left of cursor
ESCAPE	Cancels editing
ENTER	Enters contents of edited cell
DOWN ARROW	Enters contents of edited cell
UP ARROW	Enters contents of edited cell
PAGE DOWN	Enters contents of edited cell
PAGE UP	Enters contents of edited cell

NOTE: If you add a math sign to the end of a formula in EDIT mode, you can use the cursor-movement keys or mouse for the pointing method of formula writing. You can do this after typing a math sign in the middle of a formula if you press F2 before pointing.

Table 2-1.   *Role of Keys in EDIT Mode*

have a drastic effect. In this case the File Erase command erases all two million cells from memory. Note that the File Erase command does not affect files that are stored on disk. To delete files from disk you use the File Utilities command described in Chapter 7.

When you use File Erase to clear a worksheet window, you do not close the window. The window remains open and the file name in the lower-left corner of the screen remains as it was before the File Erase command was issued. The command to close a window is File Close. This actually reduces the number of open windows by closing the current window. For example, in Figure 2-1 the File Close command would close PROFIT.WQ1, leaving three windows open. When you give the File Close command and you have unsaved changes in the worksheet currently occupying the window, Quattro PRO will ask you for confirmation before carrying out the command.

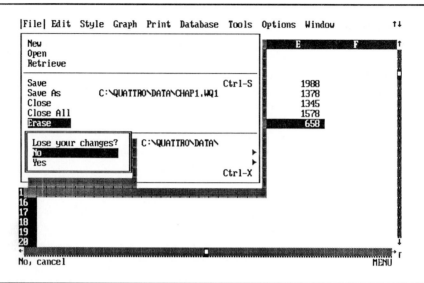

Figure 2-11.   *File Erase prompt*

Getting Down to Work

Now that you know how Quattro PRO handles opening and closing your work area, the next few sections discuss the ways in which the program handles worksheet defaults and data entry.

Worksheet Defaults

In a program as flexible as Quattro PRO, you can change many aspects of the way the program works. For example, the columns can be from 1 to 254 characters wide. However, the program gives a new worksheet some basic settings known as the *defaults*. A default is what the program does, or assumes, unless you tell it differently. For example, you have seen that the name of the worksheet in the current worksheet window is referred to as the default file name.

In a new worksheet the default columns are wide enough to accommodate nine characters; labels are aligned on the left; and the format for showing numbers is the *General format*. The General format shows numbers with no commas in the thousands and no decimal places (unless they are entered or calculated by a formula). A calculation resulting in many decimal places is shown in the General format with as many decimal places as will fit in the cell. (Changing the worksheet to other formats is described in detail later in this chapter in the section entitled "Format Commands.")

When you start working on a spreadsheet, you can change the default settings for that worksheet; for example, you can make all columns ten characters wide. (The commands for controlling columns are discussed later in this chapter.) You can also change the defaults permanently so that you always have columns that are ten characters wide. You can change other default settings of the program such as colors and displayed items. (Chapter 6 explains how to make these changes.)

Data Entry

As discussed in Chapter 1, there are two types of data in a spreadsheet: values and labels. There are also two methods of entering data into the spreadsheet, whether you are entering values or labels. You can either type your entry and press ENTER, which puts the data into the cell and leaves that cell highlighted; or you can type your entry and press a cursor-movement key, which enters the data and moves you in the direction of the key you pressed. In both cases, you put the cell selector on the cell where you want to enter the data before you begin typing. The labels and numbers in Figure 2-12 were entered by pointing to the first row of the column, typing the first entry, pressing DOWN ARROW, typing the next entry, pressing DOWN ARROW, and so on.

Canceling an Entry

At times you will need to change or cancel an entry as you type it. One common situation in which this occurs is when you start typing a piece of new data and realize that your cell selector is pointing to the wrong cell, possibly one that already has data in it. Data that you type first appears on the input line near the top of the screen. Pressing ENTER or an arrow key or clicking on Enter at this point will place the data from the input line into the wrong cell. If there is already data in the cell, the new data will replace the old, and you will have to re-enter the old data. If the cell is empty but is the wrong cell for the new data, you will have to remove the incorrect entry. Fortunately, Quattro PRO lets you change your mind before you enter what is on the input line. If you press ESCAPE or click on Escape, whatever you have typed is removed from the input line, and you are back in the READY mode. Then you can move the cell selector to the correct location.

If you start typing a new piece of data in the right place but make an error or a spelling mistake, use the BACKSPACE key to back the cursor over the data on the input line until you have erased the error, and then resume typing. Remember, you should *not* press the LEFT ARROW key to go back and correct mistakes while typing a new entry. Doing so will enter the data into the cell.

Cell Editing

After you have entered data, the data appears on the input line whenever the cell is selected. You can change the contents of a cell in several ways. Which method you use will depend upon the type of change you need to make. The following paragraphs explain the different ways of editing, using the data in Figure 2-12 as an example.

Re-Entry   When you re-enter data into a cell, the contents of the cell are changed. The simplest method of re-entry is to type the new data over the old, completely replacing it. For example, if you place the cell selector on the word *LONDON*, type **ROME**, and press ENTER, the entire word *LONDON* will disappear, not just the first four letters.

The Edit Key   If you want to change *LONDON* to *LONDON - HEATHROW*, you can avoid retyping the entire entry by using the Edit key (F2). When you place the cell selector on a cell and press F2, the contents of the cell are returned to the input line and the mode indicator displays EDIT. The status line at the bottom of the screen changes to show you what cell you are editing and what was in the cell before it was entered. With the cell contents back on the input line you can now add to the cell contents and place the revised entry back in the worksheet by pressing ENTER. (Mouse users can assign the Edit key to one of the three user-defined mouse buttons on the mouse palette, as described in Chapter 6.)

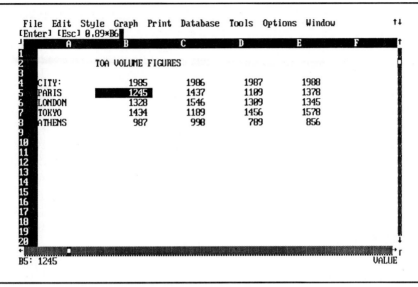

File Edit Style Graph Print Database Tools Options Window   ↑↓
[Enter] [Esc] 0.89*B6

	A	B	C	D	E	F
1						
2		TOA VOLUME FIGURES				
3						
4	CITY:	1985	1986	1987	1988	
5	PARIS	1245	1437	1189	1378	
6	LONDON	1328	1546	1389	1345	
7	TOKYO	1434	1189	1456	1578	
8	ATHENS	987	998	789	856	

B5: 1245   VALUE

Figure 2-12. *Entering data*

When you are in EDIT mode several keys perform differently. Pressing HOME moves the cursor to the left side of the entry. Pressing END places the cursor back on the right side. You can also move around the contents of the cell with the LEFT and RIGHT ARROW keys. Thus, if you mistakenly entered **LUNDON - EATHROW**, you could press F2 to edit the cell, press the LEFT ARROW key until your cursor is under the erroneous *U*, and then press the DELETE key to remove it, as in the following:

LUNDON - EATHROW to LNDON - EATHROW

You could then type **O** to insert it into the text to the left of the cursor.

LONDON - EATHROW

You would then move to the right with the RIGHT ARROW key to put the cursor under the *E*. There you would type **H** to complete the editing. You can press ENTER regardless of where your cursor is within the data, and the revised information will be placed back into the cell from the input line.

While you are editing a cell in EDIT mode, you are also in INSERT mode, where what you type is inserted into the text instead of replacing what was there before. However, you can get into OVERSTRIKE mode by pressing the INSERT key. When you press INSERT during editing, the message OVR appears in the status area at the bottom of the screen. Quattro PRO automatically reverts to INSERT mode when you leave EDIT mode. Table 2-1 lists the keys you can use in EDIT mode.

Cell Delete   There will be times when you will want to erase the entire contents of a cell. The correct way to clear out a cell is with the Cell Delete key, or DELETE. Simply put the cell selector in the cell you want to erase and press DELETE or click on Del in the mouse palette. If you want to erase a whole group of cells, you can use the Extend key (SHIFT-F7) and select the cells before pressing DELETE, as explained in the section "Worksheet Editing" toward the end of this chapter.

You may already know another method of erasing a cell that is used in other spreadsheet programs that do not have a Cell Delete key. You place the cell selector on the cell you want to delete and press the SPACEBAR and ENTER. With this method it appears that the cell has been emptied. But the cell identifier displays an apostrophe, which begins a label. You have replaced what was in the cell with a blank label. This method of cell deleting is a bad habit to get into, since the cell is not really emptied. It can also affect some calculations that include those cells. Blank cells are hard to find since there is nothing to see in them unless you first place the cell selector on one and observe the cell identifier. Consequently this method of blanking cells should be avoided.

Edit/Calc   When you enter a formula into a cell, what you see on the worksheet is the value that results from that formula. However, Quattro PRO records the formula and displays it in the cell identifier when you highlight the cell that contains the formula. The formula remains dynamic; that is, the value it displays will change when cells or functions referenced in the formula change. At times you will want to "freeze" the results of a formula and convert the formula to the value it created. One way to do this is to edit the cell. When you press F2 to edit a cell that contains a formula, the formula is placed on the input line. You press the Calc key (F9) to convert the formula to its result. You then press ENTER to place the value in the worksheet and replace the formula.

For example, suppose you are assembling passenger volume figures for TOA, and you are missing the number of passengers for Paris in the first year of the table. If you are in a hurry, you might decide to estimate the Paris number in Figure 2-12 by multiplying the numbers for London by a fraction. In cell B5 you enter **0.89*B6**. However, if you leave cell B5 dependent on B6, someone might see that it is a formula and not a real number. You simply highlight B5, press F9, and then press ENTER to replace the formula with the actual number it created. In Chapter 3 you will read how to convert whole blocks of formula cells into their values by using the Edit Values command.

Automatic Editing

If you enter data that Quattro PRO cannot read, pressing ENTER to place the data in a cell will result in a beep and possibly a message box on the screen. For example, Quattro PRO does not accept numbers that contain commas. In Figure 2-13 you can see the effect of entering **8,000**. The "Invalid character" message appears and the mode indicator has changed to ERROR. You can press ENTER or ESCAPE to remove the message. Quattro PRO will automatically place you in EDIT mode. It will also point out your error by placing the cursor at the first mistake it reads in what you have tried to enter. In this case, the program will place the cursor under the superfluous comma so that you can press DELETE to remove it. The corrected data can then be placed into the cell with ENTER. If you press ESCAPE three times at a data-entry error message, you will completely cancel the erroneous entry.

Quattro PRO not only tries to show you where the error lies, but gives you different error messages depending upon the type of error. For example, if were trying to calculate a loan payment (as was shown in Chapter 1) but you misspelled the @PMT function as **@PAYMENT**, you would get the "Unknown @-function" message. Many errors in data entry give rise to the "Invalid cell or block address" message, which indicates that the program is attempting to read what you have typed as a formula. This error arises when you want to enter an address, such as **123 Main St.**, a problem dealt with later in this chapter.

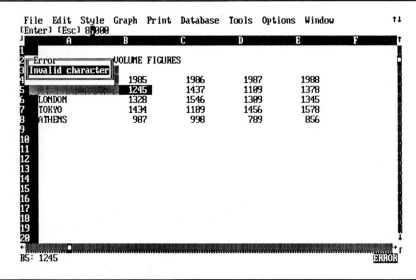

Figure 2-13.   *"Invalid character" error*

Format Commands

The difference between the numbers you see in the left and right halves of Figure 2-14 is a result of a change in the Numeric format. This feature determines how your numbers look. You will recall that Quattro PRO does not permit commas in numbers when you enter them. The commas, leading dollars signs, parentheses for negative numbers, and the number of decimal places shown in the figure are all functions of the Numeric format.

Numeric Formats

The appearance of numbers in the worksheet is controlled by the program through the Numeric format. In fact, the ability to change the way a number is displayed is a very powerful aspect of Quattro PRO, saving you

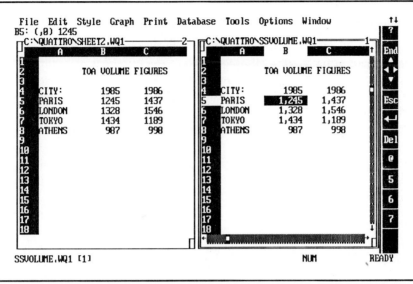

Figure 2-14. *Two formats*

a lot of typing and retyping. Quattro PRO initially uses the General format for numbers. This format shows decimal places only when you enter them or when you enter formulas that result in values with decimal places. The program calculates as many as 15 decimal places. When a formula creates a number with decimal places, the decimals are displayed until the complete number is shown or until the cell is filled, whichever comes first. For example, given the following cells, the General format will show cell D4 as **2.5**, cell D5 as **3.333333**, and cell D6 as **0.333333**.

B4: 5   C4: 2   D4: +B4/C4   =   2.5
B5: 10   C5: 3   D5: +B5/C5   =   1.333333
B6: 1   C6: 3   D6: +B6/C6   =   0.333333

Because this format results in the decimal place appearing at a different position in the column, you may want to use a different format for values such as dollars and cents.

Default Format

The Numeric format used by Quattro PRO can be changed for a part of the worksheet or for all of it. If all or most of the numbers in a worksheet are dollars, you might want to choose the Currency format as your default format. To change the overall, or *global*, format, type /, select Options, Formats, and then Numeric Format. The menu you see in Figure 2-15 shows all of the Numeric format choices. They are listed with examples in Table 2-2.

Some of the formats require that you indicate how many decimal places should be used. If you select such a format, a prompt automatically appears, as shown in Figure 2-16. As you can see, the options are from 0 to 15. Formats such as Fixed and Currency suggest two decimal places, but you can type your choice over this before pressing ENTER or clicking the Enter button to confirm the format selection.

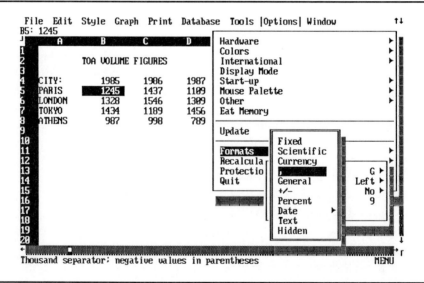

Figure 2-15.   *Numeric format choices*

Format Name	Description of Format
Fixed	No commas in 1000s, negatives in parentheses, user-defined decimal places: 2000.99 (2000.99)
Scientific	Exponential notation, negatives in parentheses, user-defined decimal places: 2.00E+03 (2.00E+03)
Currency	User-defined currency prefix, commas in 1,000s, negatives in parentheses, user-defined decimal places: 2,000.99 ($2,000.99)
, (Financial)	Commas in 1,000s, negatives in parentheses, user-defined decimal places: 2,000.99 (2,000.99)
General	Varies decimal places; uses exponential notation for large numbers; negatives preceded by minus sign (–)
+/–	Represents positive numbers as plus signs (+), negatives as minus sign (–) for simple bar charts
Percent	Divides contents by 100; uses % sign as suffix
Date	Various options, described in Chapter 9, including formats for time values
Text (Formulas)	Displays formulas in cells rather than their values

Table 2-2. *Format Choices*

Style and Numeric Format

Changing the default format affects the appearance of all values in the worksheet, except for those cells formatted with the Style Numeric Format command. In Figure 2-17 you can see the effect of changing the global format to Currency. Notice that the years, which are actually just numbers, are also changed to currency. Quattro PRO needs to be told that there is a block of cells that must be formatted differently. Cells formatted separately from the default format are not affected by changes to the default format.

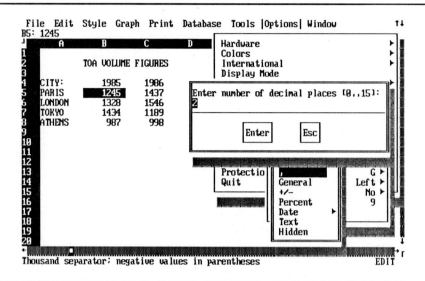

Figure 2-16.   *Decimal place prompt*

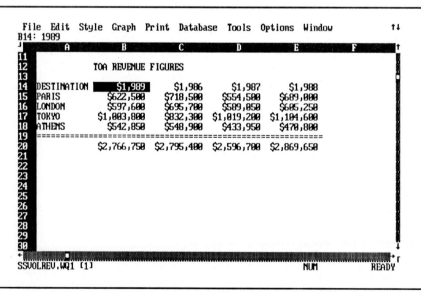

Figure 2-17.   *Global format change*

Formatting individual cells or groups of cells is the task of the Style commands, one of which is Numeric Format. This command allows you to specify a special format for one or more cells that is different from the whole worksheet. You normally begin a Style command by placing the cell selector on the cell you want to change or in the top-left corner of the group of cells if there is more than one cell to be worked on. When you type /, select Style, and then pick Numeric Format, you have the same format options as on the Default menu. There is one other item on this menu—the option to reset the format. You use this option when you want a manually formatted cell to revert to the default format.

The Fixed and General formats work well for entering years because they omit the commas. When you choose the Fixed format you must tell Quattro PRO that there are to be no (0) decimal places for these years. When you press ENTER to confirm the format, you will have to perform one more step: You must tell the program to which cells this format applies.

Quattro PRO assumes that when you enter the format command you want to format at least the cell where the cell selector is located when you start the command. In this case, this is referred to as block B14..B14, meaning all the cells from B14 to B14. To extend this range you use the cursor keys, pointing out the cells to be included. If you press END and then RIGHT ARROW, you can extend the highlight to the last active cell on the right, in this case E14. This is a very handy use of the END-arrow key combination. The highlighting extends over the cells and the block is now B14..E14. When you have told Quattro PRO the block to which the format applies, you press ENTER and, as you can see from Figure 2-18, all the cells within the block are changed. You can also type the coordinates of the cells you want to affect, rather than pointing them out. Notice that the input line tells you that cell B14 has a Fixed format with 0 decimal places assigned to it (F0). The full list of format identifiers is provided in Table 2-3.

Format Considerations

When a format change establishes the number of decimal places that can be displayed, Quattro PRO rounds the number for display purposes only. However, it remembers the number to 15 decimal places, even if the format says 0 decimal places are to be displayed. In Chapter 4 you will find a discussion of @ROUND function, which causes the program to round numbers permanently.

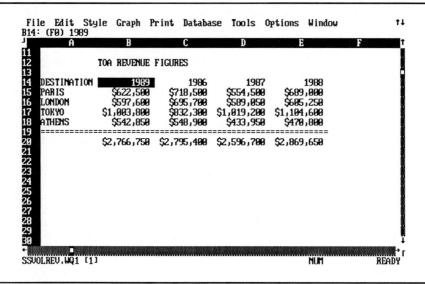

Figure 2-18. *Years formatted*

Code	Format
FO-F15	Fixed (0-15 decimal places)
SO-S15	Scientific (0-15 decimal places)
CO-C15	Currency (0-15 decimal places)
,0-,15	Comma/Financial (0-15 decimal places)
G	General (variable decimal places)
+	+/–
P1-P15	Percentage (0-15 decimal places)
D1-D5	Date formats
T	Text
D6-D9	Time formats
H	Hidden

Table 2-3. *Format Identifiers*

The default width of Quattro PRO columns is nine characters. To distinguish the numbers in adjacent cells and prevent them from appearing to run together, there is always a single character space to the right of a value entry. This means that a 9-character column can accept only eight digits. In Figure 2-19 you see what happens when you apply a default format that produces numbers longer than will fit into the 9-character columns. If you turn **1985** into **$1985.00**, the cell shows ********* to let you know you need to widen the column or change the format. Figure 2-20 shows the result of widening the columns. With wider columns the numbers reappear. (Widening columns is discussed later in this chapter.)

Use numeric formats to avoid worrying about the appearance of your numbers. In this way you can concentrate on building your spreadsheets and writing formulas. By setting the correct default format, you will not need to waste time changing the appearance of separate blocks of cells. When you do need to distinguish a group of cells from the whole, use the Style Numeric Format option. There are several other powerful options on the Style menu. The Style Alignment command is discussed later in this chapter, and the Style Line Drawing and Shading commands are discussed in Chapter 4.

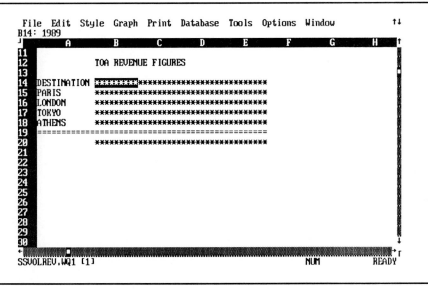

Figure 2-19. *Asterisk effect*

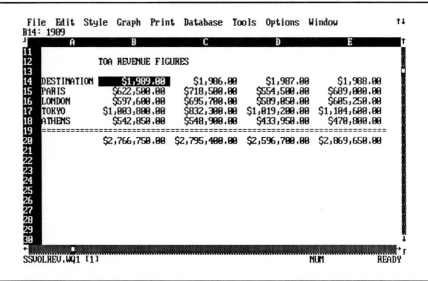

Figure 2-20.   *The effect of widening columns*

Values

You have already seen that Quattro PRO distinguishes between values and labels by the first character of a new cell entry. Anything that begins with one of the following characters is treated as a value:

0 through 9 . + - (@ # $

These items are called *value indicators*. If you do not begin an entry with one of these characters, the program will treat the entry as a label. Occasionally, you will need to enter data that looks like a number but is not. (Overcoming this problem is discussed in the "Wrong Numbers" section later in this chapter.)

Cell References

Whenever you enter instructions or formulas involving both numbers and cells, such as **1.1*A1**, the number can be typed first. This lets Quattro PRO know that what follows is a value. When formulas consist of cell references only, such as **A3+A4**, you obviously cannot do this; you must add a value indicator at the beginning of the entry. In the last chapter you saw that this can be a plus sign, as in **+A3+A4**. The plus sign does not alter the value of the cell reference it precedes. You can also use a parenthesis to begin a value entry, as in **(A3+A4)**. Parentheses are excellent value indicators when you need to control the order of calculation, as in **(A2+A3)*(B2+B3)**. However, for every opening parenthesis there *must* be a closing parenthesis. You may find it easier to use the single + for simple formulas. The + does not require that you use the SHIFT key.

Big Numbers

You will occasionally need to enter a large number into a Quattro PRO worksheet. Given the General display format and the default column width of nine characters (eight digits), entering the number **123456789** results in **1.2E+08** being displayed in the worksheet. The cell identifier lets you know that the number 123456789 is still stored. What you are seeing is the scientific notation (1.2×10 to the power of 8). Widening the column to ten characters will restore the number to its normal appearance. If you work with numbers in the millions and billions, you can set Exponential as the default format and see all of your numbers in the 1.0E+01 style. The Fixed, Currency, and Commas formats all show asterisks instead of converting a number too big for a cell into an exponential notation.

Wrong Numbers

Sometimes you need to work with numbers that are not values. For example, if you type a list of phone numbers into a spreadsheet and you type **555-1212** and press ENTER, you will get **-657** in the cell. This occurs because Quattro PRO reads the 5 as meaning a value is coming and performs math on the entry, reading it as *555 minus 1212*. To overcome this problem you must precede a wrong number with one of the label indicators described in the "Labels" section of this chapter. For example, the apostrophe is used to indicate a label aligned on the left of the cell. Thus **'555-1212** will enter the phone number as a left-justified label. To enter several numeric labels, you can use the Database Data Entry Labels command, described in Chapter 3.

Another common example of a wrong number is a street address, for example, *123 Main Street.* In this case, if you type **123 Main Street** without a label indicator in front of it, Quattro PRO will give you the error message "Invalid cell or block address" because it expects either a cell coordinate or a value since you began with the value 1. When you press ENTER, the program will cause a beep and will automatically switch you to EDIT mode so that you can correct the error. This often occurs when you type a formula or a number incorrectly; for example, if you omit a closing parenthesis or type a comma in a number.

When you are placed in EDIT mode, Quattro PRO places the cursor where it thinks the problem lies, which is usually the first character that caused the confusion. Thus, typing **1:00 A.M.** will cause Quattro PRO to put the cursor under the colon. In this case you can simply press HOME to place the cursor at the head of the entry to type the required label indicator. Remember that in EDIT mode you use ENTER to put the data into the cell. If you want to retype the entire entry, press ESCAPE to leave EDIT mode and return to READY mode.

Number Series

Quattro PRO provides several methods for entering a series of numbers— for example, 101, 102, 103, and so on. Such series are often needed to number consecutive columns and rows, as in the numbering of inventory items and their locations shown here:

Warehouse Number:

Item Number	101	102	103	104	105
30567	x				
30568			x		
30569		x			
30570					x

You can fill a group of cells with consecutive numbers automatically. You choose the starting number, the interval between numbers, and the ending number; for example, starting at 101, incrementing by 1, and ending at 105, as in the inventory item numbering. The command that performs this special form of value entry is called Edit Fill. This command is discussed in detail in Chapter 3.

Another method of numbering consecutively is achieved with formulas. Consider the row of years required in the table of volume numbers seen earlier in Figure 2-12. They appear as

1985 1986 1987 1988

These numbers can be created with a simple formula. If **1985** is in cell B4, then C4 can be **1+B4**. Cell D4 can be **1+C4** and cell E4 can be **1+D4**. You see

1985 1986 1987 1988

but the cells contain

1985 1+B4 1+C4 1+D4

When the years are entered this way, you need only type a new year over the top of **1985** and all the other years will adjust accordingly. For example, changing B4 to **1987** would produce the following:

1987 1988 1989 1990

In the section of this chapter entitled "Edit Copy" you will read how to copy formulas such as the ones used here to quickly create a series of related values.

Formulas

Much of the power of a spreadsheet lies in its formulas. When you are simply adding cells together or calculating internal rate of return on an investment, the ability to establish a relationship between cells gives you tremendous number-crunching ability. Quattro PRO's built-in formulas, such as the one used to calculate a loan payment in Chapter 1, are discussed in depth in Chapter 4. There you will learn how formulas are put together and entered in the spreadsheet.

Entering Formulas

So far you have seen formulas created by looking at the worksheet and deciding which cells are involved. For example, you know that the total of the three items shown here is going to be +A1+A2+A3:

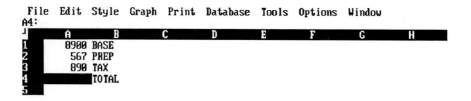

You might want to use this example to try the pointing method of entering formulas. This method begins with the plus sign or a value, if there is one in the formula. In VALUE mode, you use the arrow keys to highlight the first number you want in the formula. The program types the cell address for you.

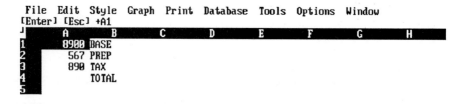

Now type the next math sign, another plus, and the cell selector moves back down to the cell in which you are building the formula. The basic procedure is math sign, point, math sign, point.

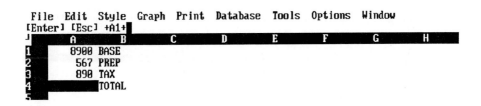

You can now point to the next cell that needs to go into the formula. It, too, is added on the edit line at the top of the screen as you build the formula.

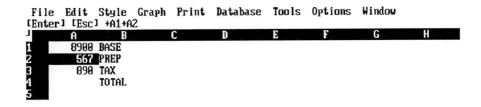

Type another math sign, **+** in this case, and the process is repeated for the third cell. The formula reads **+A1+A2+A3**. You now press ENTER to place it in the cell. This method is very useful when you have lots of cells scattered throughout the spreadsheet and you cannot remember the cell location of a particular number. The screen will look like the one in Figure 2-21 when a number is being pulled into a formula in B13 from B5.

The pointing method can be used effectively with formulas that involve functions, as in the case of the loan payment shown following, where the procedure is partially complete. The user placed the cell selector in E4, typed **@PMT(**, pressed the UP ARROW key to highlight E1, and then pressed a comma and moved the cell selector up to E2.

```
File  Edit  Style  Graph  Print  Database  Tools  Options  Window
[Enter] [Esc] @PMT(E1,E2
        A       B       C       D       E       F       G       H
1     8900  BASE                PRINCIPAL   10357
2      567  PREP                INTEREST    0.01
3      890  TAX                 TERM          48
4    10357  TOTAL               PAYMENT
5
```

File Edit Style Graph Print Database Tools Options Window   ↑↓
[Enter] [Esc] 500×B5

	A	B	C	D	E	F	G	H
1								
2		TOA VOLUME FIGURES						
3								
4	DESTINATION	1989	1990	1991	1992			
5	PARIS	1,245	1,437	1,189	1,378			
6	LONDON	1,328	1,546	1,309	1,345			
7	TOKYO	1,434	1,189	1,456	1,578			
8	ATHENS	987	998	789	856			
9								
10								
11								
12	DESTINATION	1989	1990	1991	1992			
13	PARIS							
14	LONDON							
15	TOKYO							
16	ATHENS							
17								
18								
19								
20								

B5: (,0) 1245   POINT

Figure 2-21. *Pointing method*

A second comma was pressed while E2 was highlighted, and the pointer moved to the third cell needed by the formula, E3. At E3 the closing parenthesis was typed to complete the formula. The ENTER key was then pressed to place the finished formula into the cell.

Mouse Formulas

You can use the mouse very effectively when building formulas. The basic procedure is to select the cell in which you want to create the formula, and then type a math character and click on the cell you want to place into the formula. You can then type the next math character, click another cell, and so on. You can click the Enter button to place the completed formula into the cell. When you need a formula to refer to a block of cells, you click on the top-left corner of the block and then drag the highlighting across to the lower-right corner.

Formula Errors

If you make what Quattro PRO considers to be an error when creating a formula, using either the typing or the pointing method, pressing ENTER to place the formula in a cell will result in a beep and an error message. Sometimes these can be quite specific, such as "Missing right paren" when you fail to close a pair of parentheses. Press ENTER at the message and the program will place you in EDIT mode and point out your error by placing the cursor at the first mistake it reads in what you have tried to enter. For example, entering **@PMT(E1,E2,E3,)** will cause the program to place the edit cursor under the superfluous third comma so that you can press DELETE to remove it. You can then re-enter the corrected formula.

Functions and Blocking

There is an alternative method of adding the three items in cells A1 through A3 one at a time, as with the formula +A1+A2+A3. The alternative is to consider these cells as part of a group, or *block*, and then apply a function that adds them to the block's contents. The function that does this is @SUM. Like the @PMT function, the @SUM function consists of the @ sign followed by the function name, SUM, followed by the parentheses containing the cells to which the function is applied. In this case, the block is made up of cells A1 through A3 inclusive. The completed formula is thus **@SUM(A1..A3)**. If you were to type this formula into a cell and press ENTER, you would see that Quattro PRO records this as **@SUM(A1.A3)**, but adds an extra period to make it easier to see. You never need to type the second period.

Instead of typing the formula you can use the pointing method. You place the cell selector in the cell that is to contain the formula and type **@SUM** and a left parenthesis, (. Then you point to the first cell in the block of cells to be summed, in this case, A1. While you are pointing to this first cell you type a period (.) to anchor this cell as the beginning of the block. The appearance of the double dots signifies that the cell reference is anchored, as shown in the following illustration.

```
File  Edit  Style  Graph  Print  Database  Tools  Options  Window
[Enter] [Esc] @SUM(A1..A3
J    A         B         C         D         E         F         G         H
1       8900 BASE                PRINCIPAL      0
2        567 PREP                INTEREST       0.01
3        890 TAX                 TERM           48
4            TOTAL               PAYMENT        0
5
```

Next you use the arrow keys to expand the highlighting to the other cells that are to be included in the block. This is sometimes referred to as *painting* the block. If you anchor the beginning of the block in the wrong cell, press ESCAPE to unlock that cell and move to another. When you have highlighted all the cells to be summed, type the closing parenthesis. The completed formula is placed in the original cell when you press ENTER. The completed formula in this case is @SUM(A1..A3), meaning the sum of all values in cells A1 through A3 inclusive.

The blocking method of formula writing works well for large areas of cells that need to be included in a formula like @SUM. Using a previous example, the total TOA volume figures can be summed by this blocking method:

```
File  Edit  Style  Graph  Print  Database  Tools  Options  Window            ↑↓
[Enter] [Esc] @SUM(B5..E8
J    A            B         C         D         E         F         G         H    ↑
1
2            TOA VOLUME FIGURES
3
4    DESTINATION    1989      1990      1991      1992
5    PARIS          1245      1437      1109      1378
6    LONDON         1328      1546      1309      1345
7    TOKYO          1434      1189      1456      1578
8    ATHENS          987       998       789       856
9
10           FOUR YEAR TOTAL =
```

There are some rules for blocking cells. The most important rule is that *the block must be rectangular*. The cell in which you anchor the beginning point of the block is usually the top cell in a column of cells or the left cell in a row. If the block includes cells from more than one column or row, you can begin the painting process in the top-left corner of the block, although any corner will do. The "Edit Commands" section of this chapter explains blocks in greater detail. That section also describes how to assign names to blocks of cells to make writing formulas even easier.

Labels

Although spreadsheets are thought of as number-crunching tools, the role played by labels is very important. Labels tell you and anyone else using the worksheets what the numbers mean. You should never fall into the trap of entering numbers and formulas without first placing appropriate labels to indicate what the numbers represent. Quattro PRO creates a label whenever a new cell entry begins with one of the following *label indicators:*

A through Z ' " ^ { [! / < > : ; ! ~ ? }] _) = & %

In addition to these characters, a space at the beginning of an entry also tells the program that you are typing a label. There is a special label character, the vertical bar, which can be used for printing instructions, as described in Chapter 5.

Aligning Labels

You have seen that by default Quattro PRO aligns labels on the left and puts an apostrophe in front of the text to remind you that this is a label. You can center a label in the column by starting the label with the caret sign (^), the symbol on the 6 key. You place a label flush right by preceding it with the double quotation mark ("). You can see left-, center-, and right-justified versions of the TOA city names in Figure 2-22.

The label-alignment characters can be inserted in several ways. You can make all labels right, left, or centered by default. Type / to activate the menu and pick Options, followed by Formats and Align Labels. Select the alignment you prefer. Once selected, this format remains in effect for the current session of Quattro PRO. You can also make this the permanent default by selecting the Update command from the Options menu.

To vary individual labels from the default label alignment setting, type the desired prefix preceding the text of the label. For example, if your default is left alignment, you can create a centered label as an exception by preceding it with the ^. To right-justify an individual label, type the double quote before the label text.

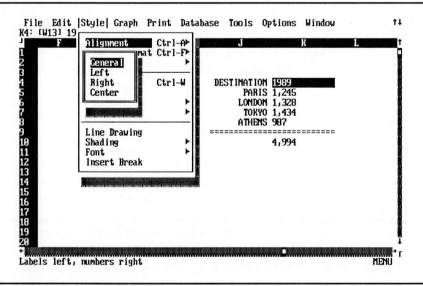

```
File  Edit  Style  Graph  Print  Database  Tools  Options  Window           ↑↓
02: [W11] ^Center
   ᴸ      L        M        N        O        P        Q        R           ↑
1
2                          Left     Center   Right
3                          PARIS    PARIS    PARIS
4                          LONDON   LONDON   LONDON
5                          TOKYO    TOKYO    TOKYO
6                          ATHENS   ATHENS   ATHENS
7
8
```

Figure 2-22.   *Alignment examples*

To vary a group of cells from the default alignment you use the Style Alignment command. This command also allows you to change the alignment of numbers, which can be positioned on the left or in the center of a column, as well as on the right where they normally appear. To change the alignment of a group of cells, type / to activate the menu and pick Style. Now select Alignment and you will see the four choices shown in Figure 2-23. When you

```
File  Edit  |Style|  Graph  Print  Database  Tools  Options  Window        ↑↓
K4: [W13] 19
   ᴸ      F      Alignment      Ctrl-A►            J         K        L      ↑
1                               mat Ctrl-F►
2                     ┌─────────┐
3                     │General  │
4                     │Left     │
5                     │Right    │   Ctrl-W     DESTINATION 1989
6                     │Center   │                   PARIS  1,245
7                     └─────────┘              ►   LONDON  1,328
8                                              ►    TOKYO  1,434
9                                                  ATHENS  987
10                    Line Drawing               =========================
11                    Shading      ►                   4,994
12                    Font         ►
13                    Insert Break
14
15
16
17
18
19
20
Labels left, numbers right                                            MENU
```

Figure 2-23.   *Alignment choices*

pick any of these you will be prompted to specify the block of cells you want to affect. After selecting the cells, press ENTER to confirm the change.

You can use General alignment to reinstate the usual alignment of labels on the left and numbers on the right. The Left, Center, and Right alignments apply to all values and numbers in the cells you select.

Long Labels

Quattro PRO labels can contain as many as 254 characters. You seldom need them this long, but you need to know how the program acts upon labels wider than one column. In Chapter 10 you will see wide labels wrapped into a rectangular area on the spreadsheet to let you compose text for letters, memos, and notations on spreadsheet models. For now, consider the labels in column A of Figure 2-20. These are city names that all fit neatly into a column with the default column width of nine characters. Suppose you want a title for this table that runs wider than the column. In the following you can see such a title typed in cell B2.

```
 File  Edit  Style  Graph  Print  Database  Tools  Options  Window        ↑↓
B2: ' TOA VOLUME FIGURES
        A         B         C         D         E         F         G         H      ↑
1
2            TOA VOLUME FIGURES
3
4    CITY:     1989      1990      1991      1992
5    PARIS     1245      1437      1109      1378
6    LONDON    1328      1546      1309      1345
7    TOKYO     1434      1189      1456      1578
8    ATHENS     987       998       789       856
```

When a label like this is entered, Quattro PRO gives no indication that it will exceed the 9-character width of the cell. However, when you press ENTER to put this label into the cell, you see that it does exceed the cell width. The label is still legible and will print when you print this worksheet. Looking at the status area you can see that all of the title is considered as the contents of cell B2.

Long labels simply borrow space from adjacent cells to display their contents. Placing the cell selector in C2 and referring to the cell indicator at the bottom of the screen will show you that there is nothing in this cell.

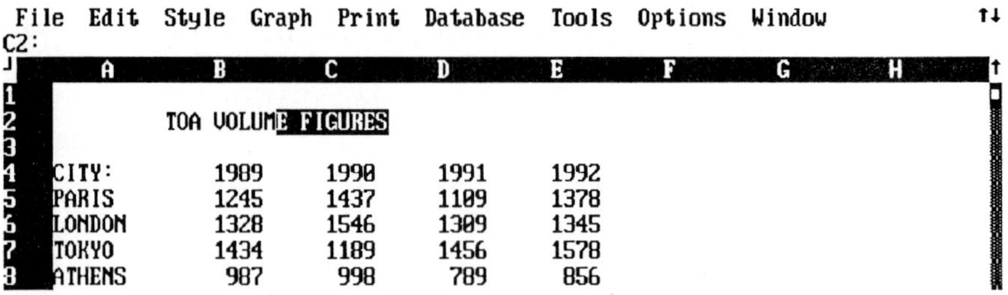

```
 File  Edit  Style  Graph  Print  Database  Tools  Options  Window        ↑↓
C2:
 J      A        B        C        D        E        F        G        H    ↑
 1
 2              TOA VOLUME FIGURES
 3
 4   CITY:      1989     1990     1991     1992
 5   PARIS      1245     1437     1189     1378
 6   LONDON     1328     1546     1309     1345
 7   TOKYO      1434     1189     1456     1578
 8   ATHENS      987      998      789      856
```

Cell C2 is empty. The contents of cell B2 simply flow over into that display area.

Unfortunately, this presents a problem when you want to enter a long label to the left of an occupied cell, as would be the case if you changed the label **CITY:** to **DESTINATION**. Figure 2-24 shows the effect of entering **DESTINATION** in cell A4. The cell to the right of A4 is occupied and Quattro PRO cannot display the full label. However, the missing letters are not lost, as you can see from the status line.

The solution to this problem is either to abbreviate the label, for example, change it back to **CITY:**, or to make the column wider. Normally, you will choose to widen the column using the column commands. There

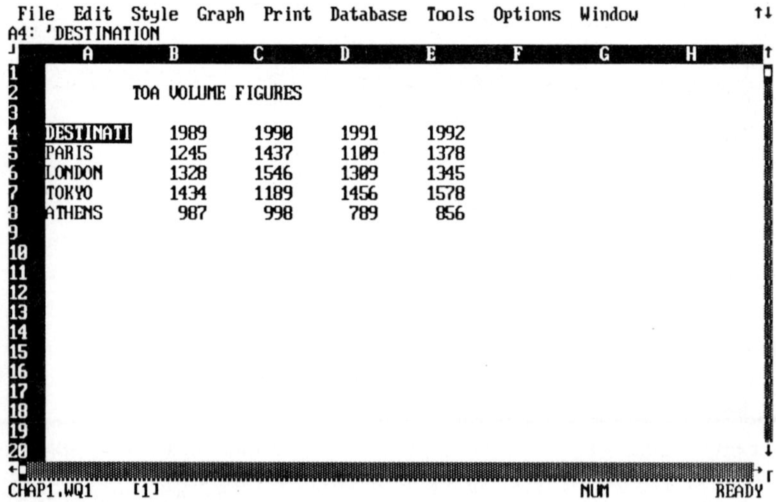

```
 File  Edit  Style  Graph  Print  Database  Tools  Options  Window        ↑↓
A4: 'DESTINATION
 J      A        B        C        D        E        F        G        H    ↑
 1
 2              TOA VOLUME FIGURES
 3
 4   DESTINATI   1989     1990     1991     1992
 5   PARIS       1245     1437     1189     1378
 6   LONDON      1328     1546     1309     1345
 7   TOKYO       1434     1189     1456     1578
 8   ATHENS       987      998      789      856
 9
10
11
12
13
14
15
16
17
18
19
20
CHAP1.WQ1    [1]                                     NUM        READY
```

Figure 2-24.   *Label overflow*

may be times when you will choose to shorten the label, particularly if you are trying to keep the worksheet small or if you want the entries in a column to be more consistent in width.

Underlines and Repeating Labels

Quattro PRO cannot underline labels. If you want to create the impression of a line beneath a label or across a spreadsheet as a visual divider, you can enter a line or lines into a separate row. Figure 2-25 shows equal signs used for a dividing line. To create this line, you must fill a cell with a single character, such as the equal sign or the hyphen. Instead of typing enough characters to fill the column, you use the backslash, which is the Cell Fill command. The \ is followed by the character you want to repeat. Thus, \= produces

=========

* produces

****

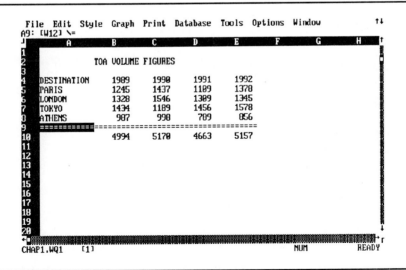

Figure 2-25. *The equal sign line*

and **\+=** produces

+=+=+=+=+

This technique is a lot quicker than manually entering a series of symbols. The Cell Fill command has an added advantage that when columns are altered in width: the command keeps the correct number of characters in the cell.

Alternatives to using repeating characters for underlining and dressing up your spreadsheet are the Style commands Line Drawing and Shading. These are described in Chapter 4.

Dates and Times

One category of information that deserves special attention is date and time calculations. Quattro PRO is very adept at handling dates and times and performing mathematics upon them. If you look at a date—for example, April 1, 1988—you can see that it is part text and part number. For a computer program to handle a date as something that has value, the date must be converted to a number. However for easy reading, a date has to be displayed as text.

If you were to type April 1, 1988 and press ENTER, you would have created a label, since the letter A is a label indicator. However, if you press CTRL-D before typing the date and then type the date in any of the following formats, Quattro PRO will convert the date to a number, but display it as a date:

	Date	**Format**
1.	01-Apr-88	DD-MMM-YY
2.	01-Apr	DD-MMM
3.	Apr-88	MMM-YY
4.	04/01/88	MM/DD/YY
5.	04/01	MM/DD

If you type the date using format 2 or 5, Quattro PRO assumes the current year. Format 3 assumes the first day of the month. A date entered in one of these styles preceded by CTRL-D will be recorded as a serial number, thus allowing you to perform date arithmetic with it. Quattro PRO does this by calculating the number of days between the date and the end of the last century. Using the first day of the century as day 1, any two dates can be compared and the difference calculated.

You can see the power of this function if you use Quattro PRO to answer the simple question: How many days have you been alive? In a new worksheet you can answer this question by following these steps:

1. In A1 press CTRL-D and then type your birth date in the form day, month, and year, using the appropriate one- or two-digit representation of dd/mm/yy, as in 12/25/52.

2. Press DOWN ARROW to enter the date and move down to the next cell.

3. In A2 press CTRL-D and then type today's date in the same format. Press DOWN ARROW to enter the date and move down to the next cell.

4. In A3 type **+A1-A2** and press ENTER. This is the number of days from your birth date to today.

If you look at the cell identifier while the cell selector is in cell A2, you will see a number. That number is the number of days from the turn of the century to the date in A2. In the next chapter you will see that many applications of Quattro PRO's database capabilities utilize date arithmetic. For a complete discussion of dates in Quattro PRO, refer to Chapter 9.

Working with Columns

There are several useful commands that you can apply to the columns from which the worksheet is built. You can add new columns, delete columns, and hide columns. You can also change the width of columns in several ways. You can issue a command that automatically adjusts column widths based on the data that you have entered in the columns.

Current Column Width

The column your cell selector is occupying is the current column. To widen the current column, type / to activate the menu and then select Style followed by Column Width. You are prompted for a width setting and reminded that the column can be from 1 to 254 characters wide. The current width is also shown, and you can see arrows in either side of the column letter, reminding you which column is being adjusted.

```
 File   Edit  |Style|  Graph   Print   Database   Tools   Options   Window
[Enter] [Esc] Alter the width of the current column [1..254]: 12
J          ←A→        B        C        D        E        F        G        H
1
2              TOA VOLUME FIGURES
3
4    DESTINATION      1989     1990     1991     1992
5    PARIS            1245     1437     1189     1378
6    LONDON           1328     1546     1309     1345
7    TOKYO            1434     1189     1456     1578
8    ATHENS            987      998      789      856
```

Initially, the default width of 9 is shown when you first enter this menu. You can either type the number of characters for the width, or press the RIGHT or LEFT ARROW key to widen or narrow the column on the screen. The width number changes as you do this. The arrow method lets you visually adjust the width until it is suitable. When the column is an appropriate width, in this case 12, press ENTER to confirm it and to return to READY mode. For the word *DESTINATION*, a column width setting of 12 is sufficient.

 The column width changes for the full length of the column. You cannot mix cells of varying widths within a column. When you have manually set the width of the current column, Quattro PRO shows you a width reminder in the cell identifier of any cell in the column. In this case the notation is [W12]. This is helpful if you change numerous columns in a worksheet.

Block Widths

In Figure 2-26 some changes have been made to the volume figures for the TOA example and the columns look cramped. In a case like this you do not need to set the width of each column. You can change the width of several columns at once by using the Block Widths option on the Column menu.

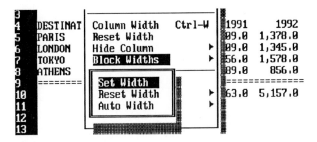

Picking this option gives you several options that affect a group of columns. You can pick Set Width, Reset Width, or Auto Width. If you select Set Width, the program prompts you for the location of the columns to be altered.

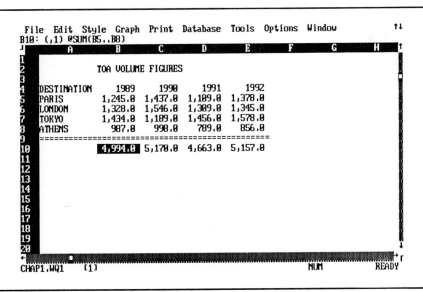

Figure 2-26. *Cramped columns*

```
File  Edit  |Style|  Graph  Print  Database  Tools  Options  Window
[Enter] [Esc] Enter block of columns: B10..B10
      A          B          C          D          E         F        G        H
1
2              TOA VOLUME FIGURES
3
4  DESTINATION    1989       1990       1991       1992
5  PARIS        1,245.0    1,437.0    1,109.0    1,378.0
6  LONDON       1,328.0    1,546.0    1,309.0    1,345.0
7  TOKYO        1,434.0    1,189.0    1,456.0    1,578.0
8  ATHENS         987.0      998.0      789.0      856.0
9  ======================================================
10             4,994.0    5,170.0    4,663.0    5,157.0
```

You indicate a block of columns in the same way that you mark blocks for other purposes: by extending the range with the cursor keys or the mouse. For example, here you can see that the RIGHT ARROW was used to increase the block:

```
File  Edit  |Style|  Graph  Print  Database  Tools  Options  Window
[Enter] [Esc] Enter block of columns: B10..E10
      A          B          C          D          E         F        G        H
1
2              TOA VOLUME FIGURES
3
4  DESTINATION    1989       1990       1991       1992
5  PARIS        1,245.0    1,437.0    1,109.0    1,378.0
6  LONDON       1,328.0    1,546.0    1,309.0    1,345.0
7  TOKYO        1,434.0    1,189.0    1,456.0    1,578.0
8  ATHENS         987.0      998.0      789.0      856.0
9  ======================================================
10             4,994.0    5,170.0    4,663.0    5,157.0
```

When the block is selected you press ENTER or click the Enter button, and the prompt changes to ask for a width. You can type the desired width setting as you do when using the regular Column Width command explained earlier.

```
 File  Edit |Style| Graph  Print  Database  Tools  Options  Window
[Enter] [Esc] Alter the width of columns [1..254]: 12
⌐        A      ←B→      ←C→       ←D→      ←E→      F       G       H
1
2              TOA VOLUME FIGURES
3
4  DESTINATION   1989     1990      1991     1992
5  PARIS       1,245.0  1,437.0  1,109.0  1,378.0
6  LONDON      1,328.0  1,546.0  1,309.0  1,345.0
7  TOKYO       1,434.0  1,189.0  1,456.0  1,578.0
8  ATHENS        987.0    998.0    789.0    856.0
9  =================================================
10             4,994.0  5,170.0  4,663.0  5,157.0
```

You can also use the LEFT and RIGHT ARROW keys to adjust the column width. Notice the arrows in the column heading reminding you which columns are being adjusted. When you press ENTER to confirm the width setting, all columns within the block (except any whose width has been set individually) will change to the new width.

The new width setting of the columns will appear in the input line, as in [W12] for 12 characters wide. If you want to change a group of columns back to the default column width you use the Reset option on the Block Width menu. This allows you to select a number of columns at once that need their individual width settings released.

Automatic Column Widths

Quattro PRO allows you to set up columns that adjust their width automatically to compensate for changes in the data entered. For example, a column of city names may look like it only needs 12 characters, but along comes Blue Ridge Summit and you need to change the width to at least 16. By using the Auto Width option on the Block Width menu you can alter the width of a column or group of columns to accommodate the widest entry plus a specific number of characters, from 0 to 40. Thus you can enter the number **2** to automatically expand or contract each column in the block so that each is two characters wider than the largest entry.

Global Width

You can assign specific widths to individual columns, either one at a time
or in groups, but you may want to change all of the column widths at once.
To make a global change to the column widths you type / and select Options,
Format, and then Global Width. Select the new width either by typing the
desired number of characters or by pressing the LEFT or RIGHT ARROW key.
Press ENTER or click the Enter button to confirm the setting.

   A default column width change does not change those columns that have
been set individually. For example, if column A was set to 12 it would
remain at 12 when you changed the global width, whatever global width
you chose. This is a very useful feature since it preserves the effort you
have made setting certain columns correctly. However, there may be times
when you want a column to revert to the global setting. To do this, place
the cell selector in the column you want to reset. Type / to activate the
menu, select Style and Reset Width. The column will now take its width
measurement from the default setting. Use the Reset Width command on
the Block Width menu to cause a group of columns to revert to the default
width.

Hiding and Exposing Columns

You can tell Quattro PRO to hide a column from display for purposes of
improved appearance or confidentiality. The formulas in the worksheet
operate as usual when a column is hidden. The full use of this feature is
covered in Chapter 5.

Inserting and Deleting Columns

At times you will have entered data only to find you need an extra column.
A new column is easy to create. Just pick Insert from the Edit menu and
you will be asked if you want to insert Rows or Columns. Pick Columns
and you will be asked to indicate the number of columns you want inserted.
Columns are added to the left of the current column. Press ENTER to insert
one column. Press the RIGHT ARROW key once for each additional column

you want to add, and then press ENTER. The new columns are added down all 8192 rows of the worksheet, so you should consider if there is any unseen data that will be affected at the time of the insert. You can press END, DOWN ARROW and END, UP ARROW while inserting a column in order to view lower and upper areas of the worksheet before you press ENTER to confirm the insertion.

Deleting columns works in the same way; you pick Delete from the Edit menu, and then Columns. Highlight the columns you want to delete. Deleting removes all the data in those columns and so it should be used with care. Check areas above and below the current screen for valuable data that might be deleted with the column. Note that the integrity of formulas in the worksheet is preserved whenever you insert columns or rows.

Working with Rows

You can use the Insert and Delete commands to manipulate spreadsheet rows. There will be times when you have entered data only to find you need an extra row. Just select Insert from the Edit menu, and then pick Rows. You will be asked to indicate the number of rows you want inserted. New rows are added above the current row. Press ENTER to insert one row. Press the DOWN ARROW key once for each additional row you want to add, and then press ENTER. New rows are added across all 256 columns of the worksheet, so you must consider if there is any unseen data that will be affected at the time of the insert. You can press CRTL-LEFT ARROW and CRTL-RIGHT ARROW while inserting a row in order to view other areas of the worksheet before you press ENTER to confirm the insertion.

The Delete command works the same way; you pick Delete from the Edit menu, followed by Rows. You then highlight the rows you want to remove. The Delete Rows command removes all the data in those rows across all 256 columns and so it should be used with care. Check the areas to the left and right of the current screen for valuable data that might be deleted with the rows.

Block Editing Commands

You have seen that the Insert and Delete commands on the Edit menu work with rows and columns. There are other Edit commands, such as Copy and Move, that are applied to a group of cells known as a block. These are among the most powerful and useful commands in the program and so it is important to be sure what constitutes a block. A block of cells is anchored in one cell and extended beyond that in any direction while maintaining a rectangular grouping to the cells. You can refer to a block of cells by any two diagonal coordinates. The diagram in Figure 2-27 shows what is and is not a block.

Edit Copy

One of the most useful abilities of a computer is its capacity for copying information. This capability is used in Quattro PRO to produce unlimited copies of standard worksheets, such as weekly expense report models, that have to be used again and again. The Edit Copy command as it applies to

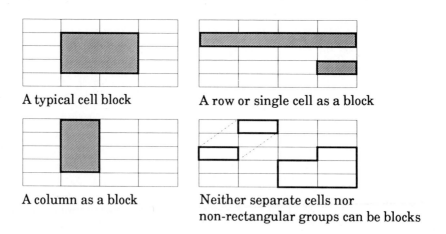

A typical cell block

A row or single cell as a block

A column as a block

Neither separate cells nor non-rectangular groups can be blocks

Figure 2-27.   *Blocks acceptable to Quattro PRO*

a block of cells is particularly useful when creating any model where the same labels, numbers, or formulas are used more than once.

Simple Copy   Consider the formulas mentioned earlier for producing a series of years by adding 1 to the previous year, starting with **1985** in cell B4:

	B	C	D	E
Row 4	1985	1+B4	1+C4	1+D4

When you create a formula like this in cell C4, which says **1+B4**, you are in effect telling Quattro PRO to add 1 to the cell on the left. The formulas **1+C4** and **1+D4** actually mean the same thing. You can copy the formula from C4 to D4 and E4. To do this, place the cell selector in the cell to be copied and pick Copy from the Edit menu. You will be prompted for the "Source block of cells," meaning "which group of cells do you want to copy?" Quattro PRO assumes you want to include the current cell and shows **C4..C4**. You can then do one of the following:

- Accept this cell reference by pressing ENTER.
- Reject it with BACKSPACE or ESCAPE.
- Use the cursor keys or mouse to highlight additional cells to be copied.
- Type the coordinates of the cell(s) you want to copy.

To copy C4, you can just press ENTER to accept that cell as the block to be copied. When you do this a new prompt appears: "Destination for cells." This prompt asks for the cells you are going to copy into, in this case **C4..E4**. You can indicate this by typing **C4.E4**. Alternatively you can type a period to anchor the beginning point of the block at C4 and then press RIGHT ARROW to include the other cells through to E4. (You could use **D4.E4** as the destination, but it does not matter if you copy the formula over the cell it is in. This is quicker when you are using the pointing method.) Having indicated the destination cells, press ENTER. Quattro PRO will copy the formula as instructed and convert each new formula relative to its location. This ability to address cells in a relative manner makes this kind of copying very useful. In Chapter 4 you will read about the difference between a relative cell address and an absolute one.

Large Copies   The Edit Copy command works for much larger groups of cells and for labels as well as values. In Figure 2-28 the example TOA figures are highlighted for copying. The cell selector was placed on A4 before the Edit Copy command was issued. The highlighting was then extended, or painted to E8. (The END-RIGHT ARROW and END-DOWN ARROW key combinations work well to paint a solid block of cells like this.) The arrangement of labels and years in A4 through E8 will be duplicated by the Edit Copy command in order to prepare for a revenue calculation for the same cities and years. Figure 2-29 shows the destination being pointed out. When the Edit Copy command is used to copy more than one source cell to one destination, you need only point out the upper-left cell of the destination. The command assumes that you have enough free cells to accommodate a block the size of the one you highlighted as the source.

Figure 2-30 shows the duplicated numbers being removed with Edit Erase Block, described in a moment. The empty cells will then be filled with calculations that determine revenue for TOA by multiplying the figures in the upper half by an average amount for each ticket. After a formula is written in B13, multiplying the volume figure in B5 by the

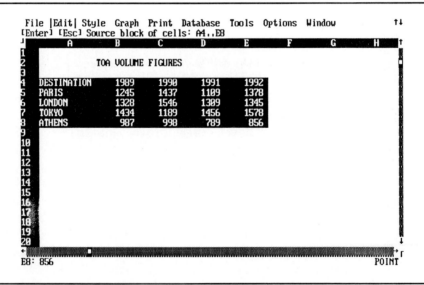

Figure 2-28.   Copying a block

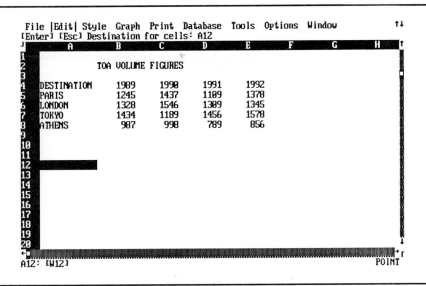

Figure 2-29. *Destination indicated*

```
File |Edit| Style  Graph  Print  Database  Tools  Options  Window        ↑↓
[Enter] [Esc] Block to be modified: B13..E16
J         A         B         C         D         E         F         G         H    ↑
1
2              TOA VOLUME FIGURES
3
4    DESTINATION    1989      1990      1991      1992
5    PARIS          1245      1437      1189      1378
6    LONDON         1328      1546      1309      1345
7    TOKYO          1434      1189      1456      1578
8    ATHENS          987       998       789       856
9
10
11
12   DESTINATION    1989      1990      1991      1992
13   PARIS          1245      1437      1189      1378
14   LONDON         1328      1546      1309      1345
15   TOKYO          1434      1189      1456      1578
16   ATHENS          987       998       789       856
17
18
19
20
E16: 856                                                              POINT
```

Figure 2-30. *Erasing a block*

amount of 500, the formula is copied across the whole row, as you can see in Figure 2-31. The results of a further series of formulas for London (450), Tokyo (700), and Athens (550) are highlighted in Figure 2-32. To copy this block to the other columns, you highlight it as the source of the copy and highlight **C14.E14** as the destination. When a column block is copied over several columns, you point out the top row of the new locations. Quattro PRO assumes you have space below that to accommodate the copied data.

The Copy Keys   You will use the Edit Copy command extensively when building spreadsheet models. The rhythm of the command keys will become second nature. To copy one cell to many cells, the pattern is Edit Copy (to pick the command), ENTER (to accept the current cell as the one to be copied), point (move the cell selector to select the upper-left cell of the destination block), anchor (type a period to lock in this coordinate), point (to select the rest of the destination block), and ENTER (to complete the command). To copy from many cells to one destination, use Edit Copy, point, ENTER, point, ENTER. When copying a block of several cells to multiple locations, use Edit Copy, point, ENTER, point, anchor, point,

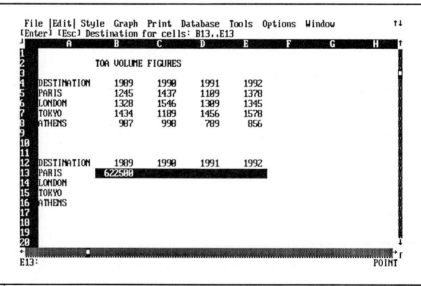

Figure 2-31.   Copying the formula

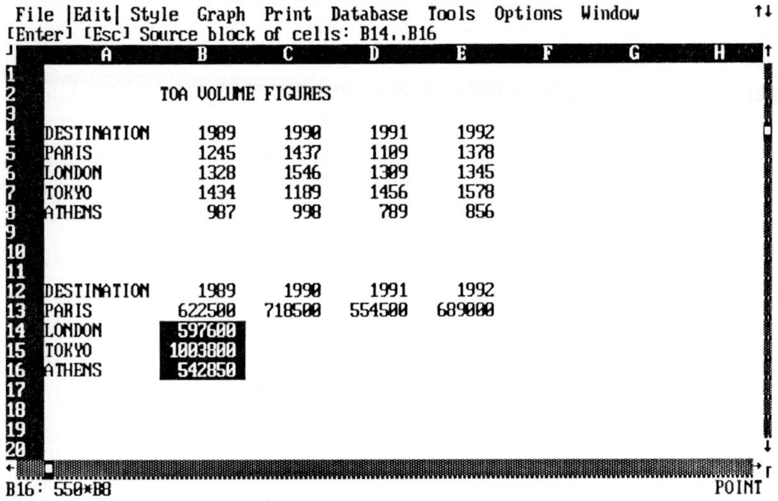

```
    File |Edit| Style  Graph  Print  Database  Tools  Options  Window          ↑↓
    [Enter] [Esc] Source block of cells: B14..B16
  ┌──────────A──────────B──────────C──────────D──────────E──────F──────G──────H──┐
  │1                                                                              │
  │2                   TOA VOLUME FIGURES                                         │
  │3                                                                              │
  │4    DESTINATION     1989      1990      1991      1992                        │
  │5    PARIS           1245      1437      1109      1378                        │
  │6    LONDON          1328      1546      1309      1345                        │
  │7    TOKYO           1434      1189      1456      1578                        │
  │8    ATHENS           987       998       789       856                        │
  │9                                                                              │
  │10                                                                             │
  │11                                                                             │
  │12   DESTINATION     1989      1990      1991      1992                        │
  │13   PARIS         622500    718500    554500    689000                        │
  │14   LONDON        597600                                                      │
  │15   TOKYO        1003800                                                      │
  │16   ATHENS        542850                                                      │
  │17                                                                             │
  │18                                                                             │
  │19                                                                             │
  │20                                                                             │
  └───────────────────────────────────────────────────────────────────────────────┘
    B16: 550*B8                                                            POINT
```

Figure 2-32. *The formulas blocked*

ENTER. To save you the trouble of selecting the Copy command from the Edit menu, Quattro PRO's shortcut feature has Edit Copy assigned to a single key combination, CTRL - C. You can therefore use CTRL - C as a quick way to commence the Copy command.

Always remember that the Edit Copy command does not check for existing data in the destination cells. You can actually lose data by inadvertently copying over it. Use caution the first few times you use Copy and always save the worksheet before performing large copy operations.

Erase Block

Use the Edit Erase Block command to delete the contents of more than one cell. The DELETE key is the best method for deleting single cells, but Edit Erase Block works effectively on large areas that need to be cleared. After picking the command, highlight the block to be modified (as shown earlier in Figure 2-30) and press ENTER. The contents of all selected cells are erased.

As an alternative to using the menu you can simply select the cells and then press DELETE. To select the cells with the mouse you just click on the top-left corner of the block and drag across to highlight them. With the keyboard, you press the Extend key (SHIFT-F7) and use the cursor keys to pick the area before pressing DELETE. Mouse users can also make use of the Extend key when selecting large areas. Click on the top-left corner cell of the block you want to select, and then press SHIFT-F7. Quattro PRO will extend the block to the next cell you click on. Although the program has an Undo key (ALT-F5), you should use the combination of cell selection and the DELETE key with care.

Search and Replace

Quattro PRO offers a very useful Edit command called Search & Replace. Normally associated with word processing programs, the term *search and replace* refers to a program's ability to search for every instance of one thing and replace it with another. For example, if you had used *NEW YORK* many times throughout a worksheet and were then told it should be *NEWARK*, you might think you had to move to each cell that says *NEW YORK* and type **NEWARK** over it. Instead, you can highlight the area of the worksheet containing the words you want to change and have Quattro PRO search and replace within that block to make the changes for you.

When you select Search & Replace from the Edit menu you get the special menu shown in Figure 2-33. In this example you are looking at an earnings report for commodity brokers and you want to increase the salary of all brokers making a Base of 25.00 to 28.00. From the Search & Replace menu you first choose Block to highlight the area of the spreadsheet to be searched. Include all cells that you need to change. In this case the block will be C4.C20. Then pick Search String to enter the characters you want Quattro PRO to search for. These can be letters, numbers, math signs within formulas, or any character or string of characters you have entered into the cells. In this case, 25 will work fine, since the rest of the number will remain the same. Pick Replace String to enter the characters to replace the ones you are searching for, in this case, 28. If you do not wish to replace the searched for item but rather delete it, leave this section blank. Such an operation would be appropriate if you wanted to change *LONDON HEATHROW* to plain *LONDON*, searching for *HEATHROW* and replacing with nothing. The Search & Replace options allow you to fine tune the operation. They are listed in Table 2-4.

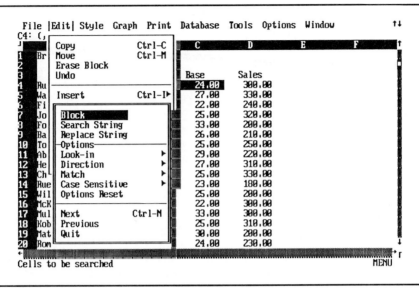

Figure 2-33.   *The Search & Replace menu*

To proceed with the search and replace operation, choose Next and Quattro PRO will highlight the first cell it finds that contains the characters you are searching for. You then must make a choice, as shown in Figure 2-34. You pick Yes to replace this instance of 25.00. Choosing No leaves this case as it is, for example, if there is an exception to the pay upgrade. Selecting All tells Quattro PRO to proceed with an automatic search and replace from this point on. Do not pick All unless you are certain about what will happen. If you are not careful about limiting the block to be searched, you could change instances of the search characters you did not anticipate.

The Edit option is a very handy one, allowing you to interrupt the search and replace to edit a particular cell that has been found, for example, if you wanted to use 29 for one of the entries. The Quit option tells Quattro PRO to stop the process before all instances have been changed. If you choose this option, the last cell found becomes the current cell. After the last instance of the search characters has been reached and your decision has been entered, Quattro PRO returns to the READY mode. The next time you use the Search & Replace command for this worksheet in this session, it will remember the settings that you entered. In fact, the Search &

Type	Option	Action
Look In:		
	Formula	Looks for search string within formulas, cell references, block names, and so on. A search for 2 finds 2*2, B2, B52s, and so on, but does not find 6*7.
	Value	Values the formula in each cell and looks for the search string in the result. Converts formula to value if result contains search string. Thus a search for 2 with 5 as a replace string will find 6*7 and convert it to 45.
	Condition	Allows you to set a condition in the search string, such as +B2>12, where B2 is the first cell in the search block. The search finds all cells with a value greater than 12.
Direction:		
	Row	Searches the block from the current cell proceeding row by row.
	Column	Searches the block from the current cell proceeding column by column.
Match:		
	Part	Searches for partial cell entries, so that a search string of **mar** would find **martian** and **market**.
	Whole	Requires that the match be the entire cell contents, except for the label indicator, so that a search string of **mar** would not locate a cell containing **mars**.
Case Sensitive:		
	Any-case	Does not require a match in cases, so that a search string of **erin** would find **Erin** and **ERIN**.
	Exact-case	Requires that the match be exact as far as case is concerned. A search string of **ERIN** would not find **Erin**.

Note: A search initiated with Next moves forward through the block from the current cell, whereas a search initiated with Previous moves backward. Both choices search the entire block.

Table 2-4. *Search & Replace Options*

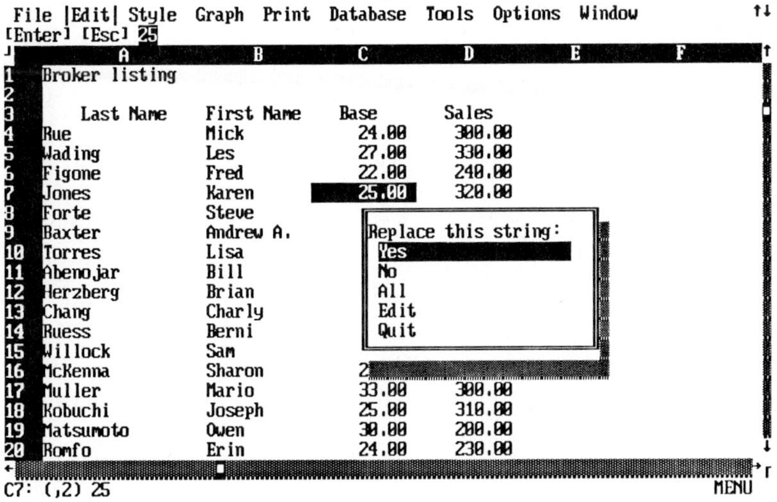

```
     File |Edit| Style  Graph  Print  Database  Tools  Options  Window      ↑↓
     [Enter] [Esc] 25
          A              B            C         D        E        F
  1 Broker listing
  2
  3      Last Name    First Name    Base      Sales
  4 Rue             Mick          24.00     300.00
  5 Wading          Les           27.00     330.00
  6 Figone          Fred          22.00     240.00
  7 Jones           Karen         25.00     320.00
  8 Forte           Steve
  9 Baxter          Andrew A.    ┌Replace this string:──────┐
 10 Torres          Lisa         │Yes                       │
 11 Abenojar        Bill         │No                        │
 12 Herzberg        Brian        │All                       │
 13 Chang           Charly       │Edit                      │
 14 Ruess           Berni        │Quit                      │
 15 Willock         Sam          └──────────────────────────┘
 16 McKenna         Sharon        2
 17 Muller          Mario         33.00     300.00
 18 Kobuchi         Joseph        25.00     310.00
 19 Matsumoto       Owen          30.00     200.00
 20 Romfo           Erin          24.00     230.00
 C7: (,2) 25                                              MENU
```

Figure 2-34. *Search choices*

Replace command will remember the settings even if you move to a different worksheet window, allowing you to repeat the same operation on similar spreadsheets, one after another. If you need to change the settings you can simply pick the Options Reset command.

Edit Move

You will occasionally need to move a group of cells from one location to another. If you need a few extra columns or rows in a spreadsheet, you can sometimes use the Edit Insert command to accomplish the changes you want. At other times you will be able to use the Edit Delete command to remove extra space, but these commands do not work well in crowded spreadsheets, and at times you will need to move a group of cells. The Edit Move command requires that you highlight the cells to be moved and then indicate their destination. Note that any cell entries within the area they are being moved to will be overwritten by the moved cells.

The Edit Move command preserves the integrity of the formulas within the block. Relative cell references are preserved correctly. Thus, the following line of cells moved from row 4 to row 6 would be adjusted as shown:

	B	C	D	E
Row 4	1985	1+B4	1+C4	1+D4
Row 6	1985	1+B6	1+C6	1+D6

There are some situations in which Edit Move does affect the way your formulas work. These are explained in Chapter 5. As a safety precaution, save your worksheet before a large block move so that you can retrieve the unchanged version if the effects of the move are not what you had anticipated. Large block moves will take several moments for the computer to complete. The mode indicator will flash WAIT until the operation is over.

Edit Names

If there is a block of cells that you work with frequently, you can save time by attaching a name to the block. For example, the figures for TOA passenger volume over the 4-year period may need to be totaled, and that total may then need to be used in several ways. By calling the cells in the block B4..E8 by the name TVF (for TOA Volume Figures), you can enter the formula **@SUM(TVF)** to get an immediate total for all the numbers in those cells. Likewise, you can use **@AVG(TVF)** to get the average volume. You can see these formulas at work in Figure 2-35. One of the great advantages to using these names is that you are less prone to error when writing formulas. It is easier to type **TVF** than **B4.E8**. If you typed **B5.E8** by mistake, Quattro PRO would not know you missed a line of numbers. But if you typed **TVD** by mistake, the program would beep and tell you that the name had not been found.

To name a block of cells, place the cell selector on the top-left cell of the group to be named, activate the main menu, select Edit, and then select Names. Select Create to assign a new name. Type the name at the prompt, as shown in Figure 2-36, and press ENTER. You will then be able to highlight the block of cells to be included, just as you do with other Edit commands. Press ENTER to complete the operation.

Once you have created a name, you can refer to it in formulas. Press the F3 key to show a list of Block Names, as shown in Figure 2-37. You can copy a name from the list into a formula by highlighting the name and

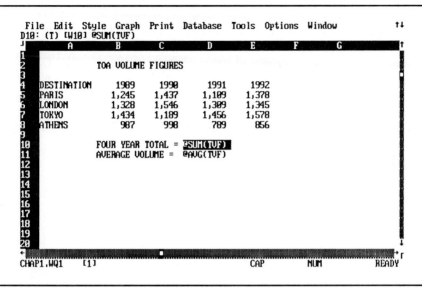

Figure 2-35. *The block name in use*

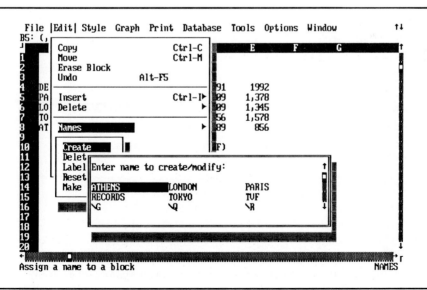

Figure 2-36. *Naming a block*

pressing ENTER. You can move to a named block by the Goto key (F5) and typing or inserting the name of the block and then pressing ENTER.

The next time you use the Edit Name Create command you will see the names that have been created listed alphabetically. Use the Delete command to delete redundant block names; that is, to remove the names from the cells. You do not actually delete the named cells. The Labels command allows you to assign names from labels in the spreadsheet, a technique described in Chapter 11. The Reset command deletes all block names at once. (Quattro PRO requires that you confirm this action with a Yes / No response in order to avoid accidental loss of names settings.) The Make Table command will print a list of the block names together with their cell coordinates in an area of the spreadsheet you designate. This task is best done in an area set aside for worksheet housekeeping, as described in Chapter 11.

As you might imagine, the names you use for blocks must follow certain rules. They can contain as many as 15 characters. You can use the letters *A* through *Z* and numbers 0 through 9 as well as punctuation characters. The names should bear some meaningful relationship to the contents of the cells, but at the same time they should not be too long. This would negate some of the convenience of using them. Block names should not be

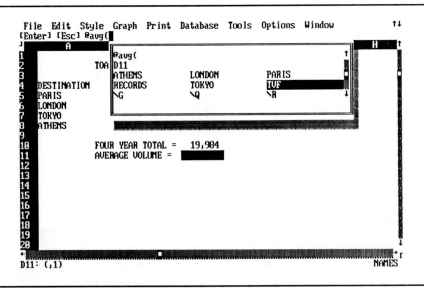

Figure 2-37. *Create Block Names list*

the same as any valid cell reference. For example, do not use R88 for the Rome 1988 figures because there is a cell called R88 on row 88 in column R. Using R_88 or 88R would be better. You can use any number of block names and the blocks can overlap. For example, you could separately name each city's four years or each year's five cities.

Edit Fill

The Edit Fill command, described in detail in the next chapter, is a way of producing a column or row of sequential numbers. You can use it to number lists, create a range of values, and so on.

Edit Values

The Block Values command turns all formulas in the cells you block out into the values produced by the formulas. Edit Values is also used in combination with the Edit Transpose command, which is described in Chapter 3.

Calculating

Quattro PRO is designed to update the answers to all formulas quickly. Whenever you enter new information, the program checks to see whether the new data affects any other cells. Cells containing formulas that depend on the new data are automatically updated. There may be times when you will need to alter the way information is calculated, either for the whole worksheet or for only a few cells.

Replacing a Formula with Its Result

At times you may find it necessary to replace the formula in a cell with the number that is the answer to that formula. This could be necessary when you have used the @RAND function, one of the built-in functions that produces random numbers. Many of the examples in this book were created with @RAND to produce values for hypothetical spreadsheets. After the @RAND function has produced a number, you may want to replace the formula with the value it created. To do this to one cell, highlight that cell, press the Edit key (F2) and then press the Calc key (F9). This will replace the formula in a single cell with a value.

Recalculation

Quattro PRO normally calculates the result of a formula when the formula is entered. The program does this *in the background,* meaning that the calculation proceeds while you are working on the worksheet. The default mode of calculation is Background, which can be changed. Occasionally, you may want the program to make you wait until recalculation is finished before allowing you to continue using the worksheet. When you change an entry in a cell used by a formula, the result is automatically recalculated. You can select Recalculation from the Options menu to change the Mode setting from Background to Automatic. However, you will find that as your worksheet begins to increase in size a noticeable amount of time will pass before the recalculations are completed under Automatic mode.

You can turn off the Background recalculation feature in Quattro PRO and avoid the delays involved in Automatic mode. If you pick Manual from the Mode choices offered by the Options Recalculation command you can stop Quattro PRO from doing any calculation until you have finished a series of entries. If you change to Manual mode and make a change to the worksheet you will see the message CALC on the status line. This reminds you that the worksheet is not up to date. You can then press the Calc key (F9), to recalculate formulas all at once. Alternatively, you can return to either Background or Automatic recalculation, which causes Quattro PRO to update the worksheet as soon as you select another cell or make another entry.

Manual recalculation tells Quattro PRO to recalculate formulas only in the following situations:

- When the formulas are entered or edited
- When you press the Calc key (F9)
- When you turn Automatic or Background recalculation back on

Manual recalculation is sometimes useful when you are entering a lot of data and do not want to see the results until all the data is entered. If enough calculated cells are affected, the data entry will be faster with recalculation set to Manual, so that recalculation occurs only after all the data is entered. However, the Background mode of calculation will generally allow you to keep entering data and get up-to-date results in your spreadsheet, without noticeable performance lags or the risks involved in assuming an uncalculated worksheet to be correct.

Protecting Your Work

After you have expended a lot of time and effort getting information into your worksheet, it is a good idea to take steps to protect it. If you work in an office with several people, possibly sharing a computer with them, someone may retrieve a spreadsheet you have been working on and unwittingly damage it by entering new data over the top of complex formulas. As a precaution against this, you can *protect* all or part of a worksheet to prevent new data from being entered.

Global Protection

To protect the entire worksheet you select Protection from the Option menu, followed by Enable. This is effective immediately and you will see the letters **PR** in the cell status area for each cell to remind you that the cell is protected. While you can still move around the spreadsheet, if you try to change the contents of a protected cell, Quattro PRO responds with a beep and the error message "Protected cell or block." You will need to press ENTER or ESCAPE to remove the message. You will not be allowed to enter data into any cell unless it has been specifically unprotected, as described in a moment. If you save the worksheet with protection enabled, anyone who retrieves it will be prevented from changing any data until protection is turned off through the same menu.

Partial Protection

As you develop spreadsheet models that perform useful functions in your business, you may want to have some data entry work done by people who are inexperienced with Quattro PRO. Suppose you are maintaining inventory records. You want the inventory clerk to update the inventory levels for a hundred items. The clerk is not an experienced Quattro PRO user and you are worried that numbers will be entered over labels and so on. In this case, you can apply protection to the entire worksheet and then remove protection from the column where the numbers will be entered.

You can protect the entire worksheet with the Options Protection command, and then unprotect certain cells. You use the Style Protection command to do this. When you pick Protection from the Style menu you are asked whether you want to Protect or Unprotect. Choose Unprotect and you are prompted for a group of cells to change. When you select the cells and press ENTER to confirm the command those cells will be marked **U** in the cell status area. You are free to change these cells. If you later decide that you want to protect these unprotected cells you use the Style Protection Protect option.

Note that Quattro PRO allows you to assign different colors to protected and unprotected cells. This is one of the many customizable features of the program that are discussed in Chapter 6. You will find more information on protection in Chapter 5. The development of unprotected input blocks using selective protection is also covered in Chapter 3.

Printing

The basic procedure for printing from the Quattro PRO spreadsheet is to point out the block of cells to be printed and tell the program to print them. To do this you use the Block command from the Print menu, followed by the Spreadsheet Print command. However, the variable factors such as the size of the paper in the printer and the size of the block of cells to be printed will often need to be adjusted to produce the desired results. This process is described in detail in Chapter 5.

3 *Database Commands*

A database is a collection of information arranged in a meaningful way. Whether the information is laid out in a table of columns and rows or consists of a collection of separate forms, almost anything from a phone book to medical records to an inventory list can be considered a database.

Quattro PRO as a Database

Programs designed to handle large amounts of information are called *database-management software*. In this chapter you will read about the database-management capabilities of Quattro PRO: how they enable you to enter, store, and then manipulate collections of data. Quattro PRO has two database functions: sorting and selecting data. These two functions are referred to as a *database sort* and a *database query*. The sort capability lets you reorder your data according to your specifications. The ability to query a collection of data means that you can ask the program to locate selected data. For example, the program can search the inventory database in Figure 3-1 for all inventory items that have the number 2 in the Bin# column. The query function also lets you extract information such as a list of all inventory items priced less than $1000. Many different software packages offer some level of database management. These programs can be divided into two groups: relational and simple.

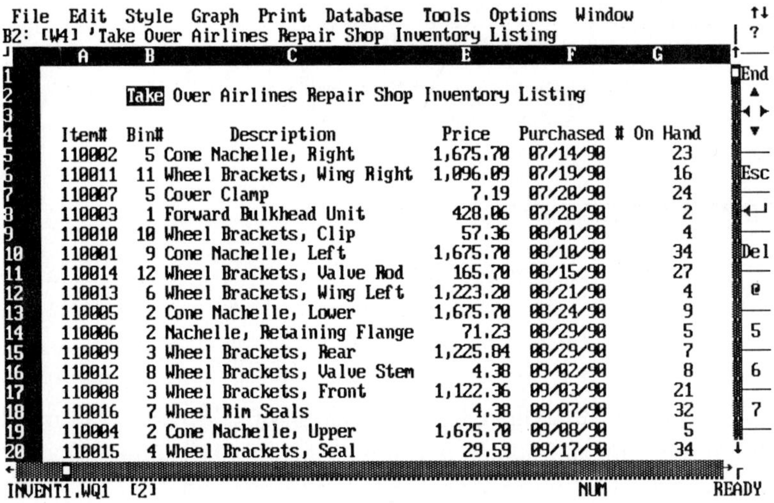

```
     File  Edit  Style  Graph  Print  Database  Tools  Options  Window      ↑↓
  B2: [W4] 'Take Over Airlines Repair Shop Inventory Listing                | ?
  ┘    A    B            C             E          F         G         ├─
  1                                                                      ⬛End
  2            Take Over Airlines Repair Shop Inventory Listing            ▲
  3                                                                       ◀ ▶
  4    Item#  Bin#     Description        Price    Purchased # On Hand      ▼
  5    110002    5 Cone Nachelle, Right   1,675.70  07/14/90      23      ─────
  6    110011   11 Wheel Brackets, Wing Right 1,096.09 07/19/90  16        Esc
  7    110007    5 Cover Clamp               7.19   07/20/90      24      ─────
  8    110003    1 Forward Bulkhead Unit   428.06   07/28/90       2        ↵
  9    110010   10 Wheel Brackets, Clip     57.36   08/01/90       4      ─────
  10   110001    9 Cone Nachelle, Left    1,675.70  08/10/90      34       Del
  11   110014   12 Wheel Brackets, Valve Rod 165.70 08/15/90      27      ─────
  12   110013    6 Wheel Brackets, Wing Left 1,223.20 08/21/90     4        @
  13   110005    2 Cone Nachelle, Lower   1,675.70  08/24/90       9      ─────
  14   110006    2 Nachelle, Retaining Flange 71.23 08/29/90       5        5
  15   110009    3 Wheel Brackets, Rear   1,225.84  08/29/90       7      ─────
  16   110012    8 Wheel Brackets, Valve Stem 4.38  09/02/90       8        6
  17   110008    3 Wheel Brackets, Front  1,122.36  09/03/90      21      ─────
  18   110016    7 Wheel Rim Seals           4.38   09/07/90      32        7
  19   110004    2 Cone Nachelle, Upper   1,675.70  09/08/90       5      ─────
  20   110015    4 Wheel Brackets, Seal     29.59   09/17/90      34        ↓
  ←                                                                      ├─ r
  INVENT1.WQ1  [2]                                          NUM         READY
```

Figure 3-1. *Inventory database*

Relational Databases

A *relational database* is one that can relate the data in several different files based on common elements. These programs can handle large amounts of data. Many of these programs also have a command language that can be used to compose complex sets of instructions in order to present users with complete menu-driven applications. Such programs are referred to as *programmable relational databases*. Examples of these kinds of databases are Ashton-Tate's dBASE series and Paradox from Borland International.

Quattro PRO is not a relational database. However, it can keep a sizable amount of related information in one worksheet: more than 8000 records with as many as 256 fields, each one of which can be over 250 characters in length. Because Quattro PRO is memory-based, it quickly performs database operations like sort and find. Its database commands follow the same pattern as the spreadsheet commands, so you can perform database-management tasks without learning a new program. You have all the power of Quattro PRO's built-in functions and graphics on hand to help analyze your data. Furthermore, Quattro PRO can read data from dBASE, Paradox, and other relational databases and export files to them as well. The adaptable user interface and macro command language of Quattro PRO also make customized menu-driven applications a powerful possibility.

Simple Databases

The personal-computer equivalent of card files, simple databases are designed to make creating, sorting, and searching records as easy as possible. Simple databases, however, usually lack the graphics and math capabilities found in Quattro PRO. For this reason, if you are learning Quattro PRO for spreadsheet work anyway, you will also want to use it for simple database applications. In this way, you can easily add database-management capabilities to your repertoire of computer skills without learning another program, as well as keep all of your data in the same format.

The Quattro PRO Database

Quattro PRO's fast and flexible spreadsheet makes it an excellent place to put together lists of information. There are just a few rules to follow in order for your lists to work with the program's database commands. These rules concern the fields and records by which the database is organized.

Fields

All information in a database is categorized by fields. Fields are the categories into which each set of facts, called a record, is broken down. In Quattro PRO, each field is a separate column, and each field has a name, which is placed at the top of the column. A Quattro PRO database is composed of a series of consecutive columns. Each column typically contains consistent types of data; for example, each column should contain either all values, all labels, or all dates. Each column should have a unique

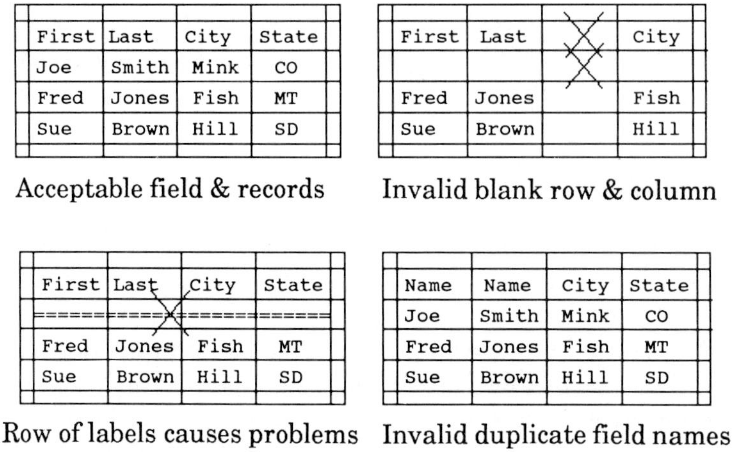

First	Last	City	State
Joe	Smith	Mink	CO
Fred	Jones	Fish	MT
Sue	Brown	Hill	SD

Acceptable field & records

First	Last		City
Fred	Jones		Fish
Sue	Brown		Hill

Invalid blank row & column

First	Last	City	State
======	======	======	======
Fred	Jones	Fish	MT
Sue	Brown	Hill	SD

Row of labels causes problems

Name	Name	City	State
Joe	Smith	Mink	CO
Fred	Jones	Fish	MT
Sue	Brown	Hill	SD

Invalid duplicate field names

Figure 3-2. *Acceptable and unacceptable fields, rows, and columns*

title. Figure 3-2 shows an example of an acceptable field arrangement and some examples of unacceptable ones.

Records

Each set of facts about one item in a database is a record. Records correspond to each line on a list or to each card in a card file. In a Quattro PRO database, each complete set of facts occupies one row. The rows of records are placed one after another with no empty rows between them. There should not be a blank row above the first record. Figure 3-2 shows a model of an acceptable record layout.

Limits

Since a Quattro PRO database consists of a block of consecutive rows and named columns, some limits apply to the database dimensions. The maximum number of fields is 256, the total number of columns. The maximum number of records is the total number of rows minus one row for the field names: 8191. The maximum field size is 253 characters, which is also the maximum column width minus 1 for the label identifier. As you might imagine, you will probably run out of memory before you get to the limits of Quattro PRO's database capacity. For more on memory size and usage, see Chapter 7.

Database Creation

The Quattro PRO database is not a special area of the program. As far as Quattro PRO is concerned, any data entered into a worksheet and falling within the definition of consecutive rows and named columns is a database. You may already have created a database while working on a spreadsheet.

Spreadsheets as Databases

Consider the TOA volume figures used as an example in Chapter 1 and shown here in Figure 3-3. The numbers for each city occupy one row; thus, each row is a record. The columns containing the years plus the city names are the fields. This same data can be rearranged with the Database Sort command, so that the cities are in alphabetical order, as shown in Figure 3-4.

Types of Data

Your entries in a database may be labels or values. The labels can be left-, right-, or center-aligned because their alignment will not affect the operation of the database commands. In the examples in Figures 3-4 and 3-5, the city names are labels. The values can be numbers, or they can be formulas and dates. However, the numbers in columns C through E of Figure 3-5 are formulas for projected revenue, each year being the previous year incremented by a growth formula. In column C, the formulas are shown in Text format. You can see in the upper half of the figure that each row is based on a different growth factor. Cells containing formulas can be sorted based on the results of the formulas. In Figure 3-5 the cities are

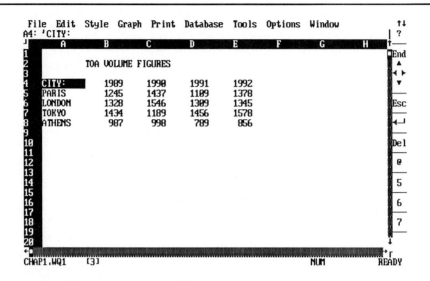

Figure 3-3.   *TOA volume figures*

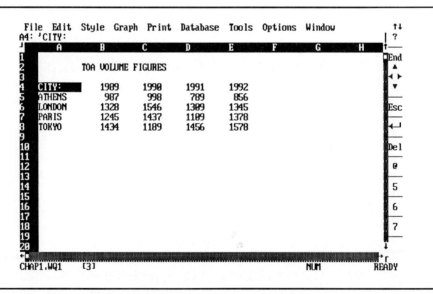

Figure 3-4.   *Cities in alphabetical order*

sorted in descending order according to revenue in the final year of the projection.

If the formulas you use refer only to other cells on the same row within the Sort Block, then sorting cells containing formulas does not pose a problem. However, if you have formulas in a database that refer to cells outside the database, such as a cell containing the rate of growth, you must make those cell references *absolute*. This means that if cell E12 contains the rate of growth by which the volume figures are incremented from year to year, the formula in C15 must be +B15*$E$12, as shown in Figure 3-5. Placing the dollar sign in front of the column and row references prevents the coordinate from changing depending upon its position. Thus, you can safely sort the block of cells A15 through E18 while retaining the rate of growth shown in cell E12. (Absolute referencing of cells is described in detail in Chapter 5.)

Quattro PRO's numeric dates, described in detail in Chapter 9, are particularly important in databases since many collections of information include dates. In many cases, records will need to be sorted or selected according to dates. Consider the inventory listing for the TOA repair shop shown earlier in Figure 3-1. The date that items entered the inventory is

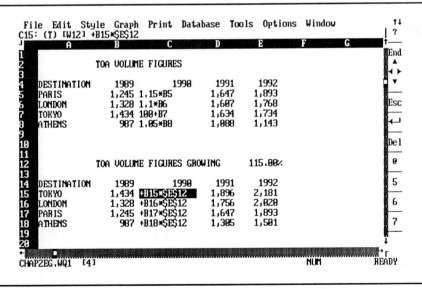

Figure 3-5.   *Projected volume*

an important part of material and asset management. The same information is sorted by date in Figure 3-6 to show the oldest items on hand.

Problem Data

Many databases contain non-numeric numbers, that is, numbers that are
entered as labels. A typical example is ZIP codes in addresses. If you enter
01234 as a number, it will appear as **1234** in the cell because a leading 0
in a number does not register. You get around this problem and the ones
created by 9-digit ZIP codes, telephone numbers, and part numbers that
contain letters as well as digits by entering these figures as numbers
preceded by label prefixes. If you do not do so, the ZIP code **94109-4109**
entered as a number would result in **9000** because Quattro PRO will read
the dash as a minus sign. Note that when you enter telephone numbers
with area codes, beginning the entry with a square bracket will make it a
label, as in **[800] 555-1212**. Quattro PRO can still sort and search for
numbers even if they are entered as labels.

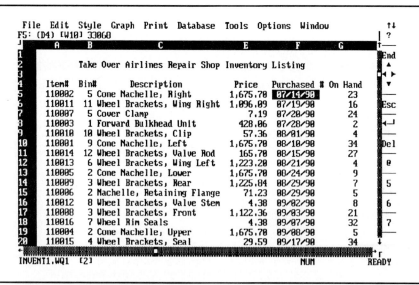

Figure 3-6. *Inventory sorted by date*

The distinction between values and labels gives rise to another data entry problem, one that is immediately apparent when you try to enter a typical street address, such as 10 Downing Street. Quattro PRO takes its cue from the first character of the entry, in this case the number 1. This is a value and it leads Quattro PRO to assume that what follows is also a value, an assumption that proves erroneous when you type the rest of the address and attempt to enter it. You will get the rather ironic error message "Invalid cell or block address." As with numbers such as ZIP codes, the answer is to place a label prefix at the beginning of any alphanumeric entry that is not a formula.

Remembering to type a label prefix in front of a non-numeric number gets very tedious and can give rise to data entry errors. To overcome this problem, Quattro PRO allows you to designate certain cells in a spreadsheet as Labels Only. To do this you use the Data-Entry option on the Database menu. When cells are designated Labels Only, anything you enter into them will be automatically preceded by a label prefix. The Data-Entry option also allows you to restrict entries to Dates Only, a means of avoiding errors in date fields. (Restricting data types is discussed in detail toward the end of this chapter, under the heading "Data Entry Techniques.")

Transpose

You may find that you often need to reorganize information in a spreadsheet so that you can work with it as a database. For example, you might want the TOA volume figures listed with the years as rows and the cities as columns. This can be done with the Edit Transpose command.

After selecting Transpose from the Edit menu, you highlight the cells involved and press ENTER. You can see the result of transposing in Figure 3-7. (Note that the city names were center-aligned in row 10.) The Edit Transpose command is particularly useful when importing data from other programs. It is not effective if your data contains formulas, since the cell references are thrown off by the rearrangement. However, if you convert the formulas to their corresponding values before transposing, the values are not affected by the move. You can use the Edit Values command to highlight a block of cells and convert them from formulas to values.

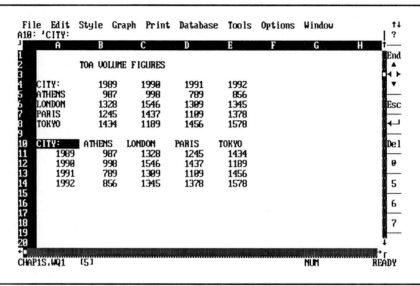

Figure 3-7. *Transposed block*

Column Widths

Since the requirements of a database allow only one row for each record, fields containing lengthy information may require extensive widening of the column. Notice that the Description field in Figure 3-6 had to be made significantly wider than the others. In order to compensate for widening, you can narrow the columns containing short data, such as the Bin# field in Figure 3-6. Keep in mind that you do not have to make each column wide enough to show all the data that it contains in order for Quattro PRO to store long entries. However, if you want all of the data to print, you will need to expand columns prior to printing.

One solution to this dilemma is to use the Auto Width command. This command allows you to set the width of a group of columns all at once, making each column wide enough to display its longest entry, plus a fixed number of blank spaces. A typical use of this command would be after entering data into the database, but prior to printing out reports. Rather than checking each column to make sure it is wide enough, simply select a cell in the leftmost column of the database. Then type / to activate the menu and select Style, followed by Block Widths. You can now pick Auto Width and Quattro PRO will prompt you to enter the extra space between columns, which is measured in characters. In most cases 2 characters is sufficient. When you type **2** and press ENTER you are prompted for the block of columns that you want to adjust. Highlight the columns with the cursor keys or the mouse and press ENTER to confirm. You will immediately see that all of the columns within the block have their column widths set automatically. Note that you need only indicate one row within each column, but the columns must be in a contiguous block. To auto-adjust nonadjacent columns you need to issue the command for each column in turn.

Note that the Style Hide Column command, described in Chapter 5, will let you temporarily remove selected columns from view if necessary. Notice in Figure 3-6 that column D is missing. This is because column D contains original cost information and is currently hidden.

Sort

Sorting is the process of rearranging rows of information according to alphabetical or numerical order. Typically, sorting is used for placing the

Take Over Airline Flights

Flt#	City	Departs		Flt#	City	Departs
101	RIO	10:00		106	LONDON	11:20
102	MADRID	08:15		102	MADRID	08:15
103	PARIS	07:30	SORT	103	PARIS	07:30
104	TOKYO	09:45		101	RIO	10:00
105	VIENNA	12:15		107	ROME	08:45
106	LONDON	11:20		104	TOKYO	09:45
107	ROME	08:45		105	VIENNA	12:15

From Flight # Order Sorted to Alphabetical Order by City

Figure 3-8. *Diagram of Sort*

records in a database into a new order, as diagrammed in Figure 3-8. For example, the airline flights listed in this figure can be sorted numerically according to flight number as shown on the left, or alphabetically according to the city of their destination as shown on the right. However, you do not need field names to sort spreadsheet information with Quattro PRO. For example, you could sort the list of things to do shown in Figure 3-9 according to the priority numbers, without bothering to provide any field names.

Providing Sort Information

To change the order of records in a worksheet, Quattro PRO needs to know two things:

Where the data is located   The Sort Block of cells contains the records but not the field names.

How you want the data sorted   The columns that are the keys on which to sort. You can use up to five keys.

You define the Sort Block and the sort keys by using Database menu items. Quattro PRO will then remember them and allow you to resort the database after editing the records.

The Data Menu

To perform a sort you first type / to activate the menu bar, and then select Database as shown in Figure 3-9. When you pick Sort from the Database menu, you are prompted in logical order for the information that Quattro PRO needs to perform a sort—Block, 1st Key, 2nd Key, and so on—as shown in Figure 3-10. When you have provided this information, you select Go to activate the sort. You can use Reset to move from sorting one area of a worksheet to another. Note the last option, Quit. Selecting Quit returns you to READY mode. This is often a quicker way to move than pressing ESCAPE several times.

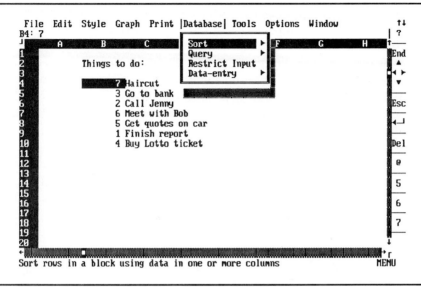

Figure 3-9.   *A simple list*

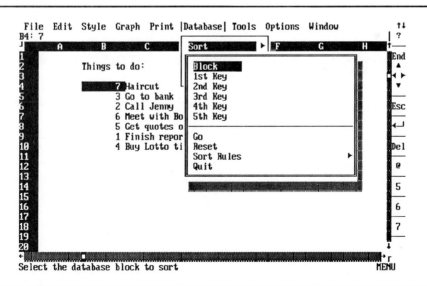

Figure 3-10.   *The Sort menu*

The Sample Database

Figure 3-11 shows a database that will be used to demonstrate the database features of Quattro PRO. This figure is the TOA On-Call Roster, a list of staff members who are on standby to work. Their names and ranks, together with relevant data such as where they are based and how many days notice they must have before working, are recorded. To practice the database commands, enter this database into a blank Quattro PRO worksheet. Enter the names as labels and the numbers as values. Enter dates in *MM/DD/YY* format after first pressing CTRL-D to set the date format. Although this is only a small collection of data, it is a typical Quattro PRO database in form and application and will be an effective model for learning the database commands.

The Sort Block

The first item of information that Quattro PRO needs in order to sort a database is the block of data to be sorted; that is, all of the fields of all of

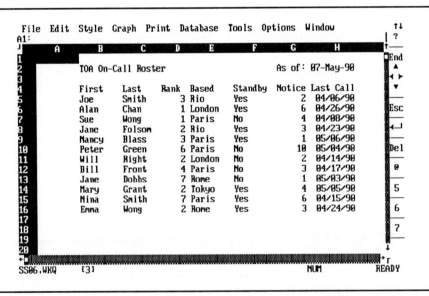

Figure 3-11. *A sample database*

the records. This block consists of the entire database *except* for the field names. In Figure 3-11, the block of data is cells B5 through H16; all of the employee names, their locations, and so on. When you select Block from the Sort menu, you are prompted to point out the cell block containing the records. The easiest way to point out this block is to place the cell selector in the top-left corner of the block (the first record of the first field) before entering the menu system, as shown here:

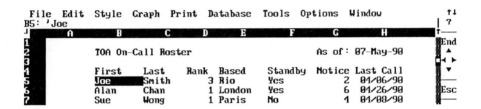

The initial coordinate is always the cell occupied by the cell selector prior to entering the menu system. This coordinate is not locked at this point, as you can see here:

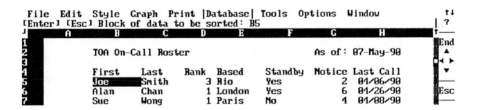

If you are not in the first field of the first record, this is the time to move there. To anchor the block, type a period. Quattro PRO responds by showing you the locked cell coordinates, in this case, B5..B5.

The END Key

To complete the highlighting of the Sort Block, use the END key. Press END once and the word END appears in the lower right of the screen. Now press

RIGHT ARROW. You will see the highlighting move to the last column on the right. The END message will disappear. Next press END again and then DOWN ARROW. Now the highlighting runs through to the last row, completely highlighting, or painting out, the data (cells B5..H16 in this case). Press ENTER to confirm this block, and you will be returned to the Sort menu for the next step. The END key is particularly useful in this instance because it automatically encompasses the entire block of data.

You should avoid defining the data to be sorted as just one or two fields. In other words, do not think "I am going to sort last names," but rather think of the entire database as one entity and decide, "I am going to sort the database according to last names." By defining the Sort Block, you have told Quattro PRO where the data to be sorted is located. You then need to tell Quattro PRO how you want the sort to be ordered.

The Sort Keys

To tell Quattro PRO in what order to put the records, you select *keys*, which are devices for pointing out which column is the key to the sort. For example, to sort the TOA staff alphabetically by last name, you would select the Last Name column as the first key. If you wanted a complete sort by name so that the several Smiths were sorted by first name, you would select a second key, the First Name column. When two or more items have identical entries in the field chosen for the first key, the second key acts as a tie-breaker.

To select keys, simply pick the appropriate number from the Sort menu. As you can see, five keys can be used. This number is sufficient to sort a customer account database by first name, last name, middle initial, ZIP code, and date of last purchase. When you type 1 for the first key, you will be prompted for the column to be used as shown here:

```
 File  Edit  Style  Graph  Print |Database| Tools  Options  Window         ↑·
 [Enter] [Esc] Column to be used as first sort key: B5                      | ?
 ┘        A        B        C      D       E         F        G        H    ↑─
 ▐                                                                           |Enc
 ▐1                                                                          | ▲
 ▐2       TOA On-Call Roster                         As of: 87-May-98        |◄ ›
 ▐3                                                                          | ▼
 ▐4       First    Last    Rank  Based    Standby  Notice Last Call         |─
 ▐5       Joe      Smith      3  Rio      Yes           2  04/06/90          |
 ▐6       Alan     Chan       1  London   Yes           6  04/26/90          |Esc
 ▐7       Sue      Wong       1  Paris    No            4  04/00/90          |
```

The cell location is not anchored; it is the initial cell your selector occupies prior to entering the menu system. Place the cell selector on the first record in that column; that is, highlight the first item in the field. There is no need to anchor the cell with a period. When you press ENTER to confirm the location, you are prompted for either Descending or Ascending order. Descending is, of course, from highest to lowest (3,2,1 or C,B,A); ascending is from lowest to highest (1,2,3 or A,B,C). Thus, to sort from A to Z you select Ascending. Remember that Quattro PRO is thinking numerically, that is, A=1 and Z=26. After picking Descending or Ascending, you are returned to the Sort menu. However, the data has not yet changed. You must select Go to initiate the sort. When you do so, Quattro PRO reorders the database and returns you to the Sort menu.

Successive Sorts

If you are performing a series of sorts—for example, as you edit names and you want to check that the alphabetical order is correct—you do not need to redefine the Sort Block or the sort keys already set. Quattro PRO remembers the locations of these items. For example, if you decide to add a second key column to the sort, such as the First Name column in the TOA staff database, you do not need to redefine the Sort Block. The block is retained in memory. If you pick Block and find the correct block of cells is already defined, simply press ENTER to reconfirm it. Do not press ESCAPE, since this will unlock the block coordinates.

The ability to resort a block of cells without having to redefine the sort parameters is convenient but it can pose a problem when you want to sort several different blocks of cells within the same worksheet. For example, suppose you have sorted cells B2 through E30, based on columns B and C. The 1st Key is cell B3 and the 2nd Key is cell C3. Now you want to sort another set of data, in cells H30 through M50, keyed on cell J30. There can be only one Sort Block defined at once in a Quattro PRO worksheet, so you have to redefine the Sort Block setting from B2..E30 to H30..M50. You also need to redefine the 1st Key from B3 to J30. What is not so obvious is that you should not simply redefine these settings, but you should use the Reset option on the Sort menu before entering the new settings.

The reason for using Reset when changing Sort Blocks comes from the fact that there is no other way to clear a sort-key setting. In the example just given, you were going from a sort where two keys were used, B3 and C3, to a sort where only one is required, 30. The Reset command is the only way to clear C3 from the second key setting and this is something you may overlook if you do not need a second key in this particular sorting operation. If you do not do something about the second key you will get the error message "Key column outside of Sort Block." At this point you will have two choices: to define a second key that is appropriate to the new Sort Block, or to use the Reset option on the Sort menu. The Reset option affects all five keys *and* the Sort Block so using Reset at this stage means that you lose all of your settings. For this reason you will be well advised to use Reset whenever you decide to sort a separate area of a worksheet. A more radical approach to this problem is offered by the multiple-worksheet capability of Quattro PRO. If you have two databases to sort in one worksheet you can always copy one of them to another worksheet and avoid having to change reset sort settings.

Note that when you add data to the bottom of a database Quattro PRO does not automatically include the added data in the Sort Block or place the data in the correct alphabetical order. For example, suppose you are adding new staff names to the bottom of the list in Figure 3-11. After adding the new names, you need to redefine the Sort Block and issue a command to sort the new records into the database.

Sort Block Expansion

Quattro PRO will not automatically extend the Sort Block to cover new additions to a database *unless* you insert a row before the end of the database, as shown in Figure 3-12. Rows inserted into the worksheet within any named or recorded block of cells become part of that block. The coordinates of the block expand to accommodate the new cells. Thus the new employee entered on an inserted row is included in the Sort Block, as shown in the sorted list in Figure 3-13. Inserted rows are added to the Sort Block if you use Edit Insert Rows with your cell selector on any row in the database except the first one. Thus, if you want to add names in their correct alphabetical locations, you can normally do so with Edit Insert Rows. In this way you will be sure that they will be included in the Sort Block.

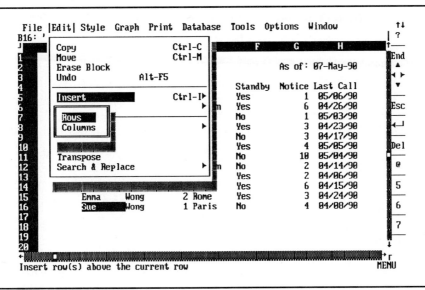

Figure 3-12.   *Adding a row*

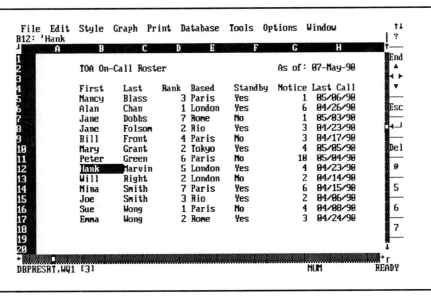

Figure 3-13.   *The new employee in Sort Block*

Rules of Order

You may wonder how Quattro PRO decides exactly in what order to place the rows when the Database Sort Go command is issued. The program looks at the column that is designated as the 1st Key, sorts it, and the rest of the cells are moved according to their entries in the key column. Typically, a column will consist of all labels or all values, in which case the order is fairly easy to predict. If you have picked Ascending, then numbers go from lowest to highest and words go from those beginning with A to those beginning with Z. Dates go from the oldest to the most recent. However, there are some subtleties to alphabetical order, and some rules that Quattro PRO uses to determine sort order when a key column contains a mixture of values and labels. The default sort order used by Quattro PRO is an ascending sort in the order listed in Table 3-1.

There are a couple of situations to watch for where the order may not be what you expect. Accidental spaces at the beginning of a label will cause that label to be placed at the top of a list. You can change the rules slightly using the Sort Rules option on the Database Sort menu. There are two areas that you can affect, as shown in Figure 3-14. The Numbers before Labels option is either Yes or No, with No being the default. When changed to Yes, the effect is to change the order of items in Table 3-1 to 6,1,2,3,4,5.

The Label Order option can either be set to Dictionary, which is the default setting, or to Ascii. The Dictionary setting means that Quattro PRO sorts labels alphabetically, with those that begin with special characters coming after those that begin with ordinary letters. In ascending order the Dictionary sort will place words with uppercase letters before identical words with lowercase letters, as in FRED, FREd, FRed, Fred, fred.

The Ascii order uses the ASCII code of the first character of the label as the basis of the sort. *ASCII* stands for American Standard Code for Information Interchange, a system of codes in which each printer or screen character has a numeric value, from 1 to 250. (You can use the @CODE function described in Chapter 9 to explore ASCII codes.) The effect of selecting Ascii order for sorting a list based on a column of labels is likely to be surprising if you are not familiar with ASCII. For example, all labels beginning with capital letters will come before those beginning with lowercase letters, and some special characters will also come before lowercase letters. In ascending sorts, labels beginning with numbers will precede any labels beginning with letters.

1. Blank cells	These appear at the top of the list, even before cells that contain only blank spaces
2. Labels beginning with spaces	These are arranged according to the number of spaces preceding the first character, with more spaces preceding less; then alphabetically from A to Z, according to characters after an equal number of spaces
3. Labels beginning with numbers	These come before labels that begin with words and are arranged numerically
4. Regular labels	These are arranged according to the alphabet, from A to Z, according to the rules in number 5
5. Labels beginning with special characters	Such characters as @ and $ come after Z. When two labels begin with the same special character they are arranged according to the second character, so that $NEW comes before $OLD. There is a consistent order among special characters that goes, from lowest to highest: ! " # $ % & ( ) * + - . / : ; < = > ? @ [\] ^ ' {	} ~
6. Numbers, from lowest to highest	This applies to the value of the number, not its formatted appearance. Thus 10 and 1.00E+01 are equal, as are 0.1 and 10.00%

Table 3-1. *Ascending Sort Order*

Applying the Sort

Having seen Quattro PRO's ability to sort information, you are ready to consider some applications of this feature. Placing data in order can be especially useful when you are attempting to analyze or report it.

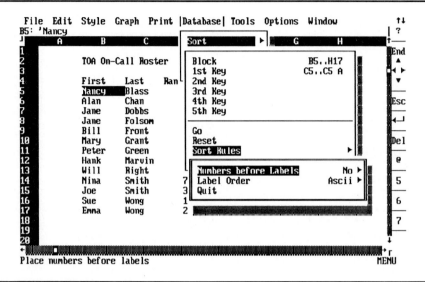

Figure 3-14. *The Sort Rules*

Analytical Sorting

Figure 3-15 shows sales statistics for a company's sales force. Instead of having them arranged alphabetically, as they are now, you may want to sort these numbers according to the Total column to see which people are turning in the best overall performance. To see who is selling more of a particular product you could sort by that product column. Later in this chapter you will learn how to find specific records within a database using the Data Query command, but it is important to bear in mind that simply sorting data makes it easy to find your way around it, and to draw conclusions from it.

Prereport Sorting

In addition to analyzing a database, sorting is useful when you are creating reports from a database. A budget report will look better if the offices are placed in some order rather than arranged haphazardly. If you were a

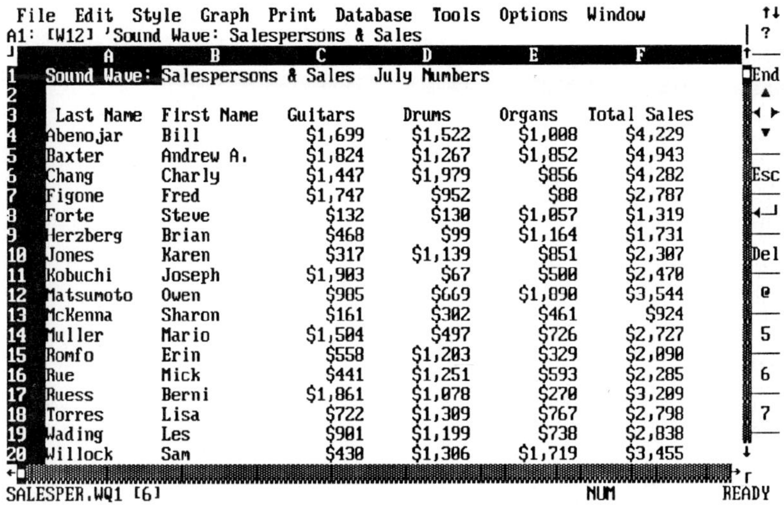

```
      File  Edit  Style  Graph  Print  Database  Tools  Options  Window        ↑↓
   A1: [W12] 'Sound Wave: Salespersons & Sales                            |  ?
   ┘          A        B         C          D        E         F        ┬─────
   1   Sound Wave: Salespersons & Sales  July Numbers                     ▯End
   2                                                                        ▲
   3     Last Name   First Name  Guitars   Drums    Organs  Total Sales    ◄ ►
   4   Abenojar    Bill         $1,699    $1,522    $1,008    $4,229        ▼
   5   Baxter      Andrew A.    $1,824    $1,267    $1,852    $4,943      ─────
   6   Chang       Charly       $1,447    $1,979      $856    $4,282      Esc
   7   Figone      Fred         $1,747      $952       $88    $2,787      ─────
   8   Forte       Steve          $132      $130    $1,057    $1,319      ◄─┘
   9   Herzberg    Brian          $468       $99    $1,164    $1,731      ─────
   10  Jones       Karen          $317    $1,139      $851    $2,307      Del
   11  Kobuchi     Joseph       $1,903       $67      $500    $2,470      ─────
   12  Matsumoto   Owen           $905      $669    $1,090    $3,544      @
   13  McKenna     Sharon         $161      $302      $461      $924      ─────
   14  Muller      Mario        $1,504      $497      $726    $2,727       5
   15  Romfo       Erin           $558    $1,203      $329    $2,090      ─────
   16  Rue         Mick           $441    $1,251      $593    $2,285       6
   17  Ruess       Berni        $1,061    $1,078      $270    $3,209      ─────
   18  Torres      Lisa           $722    $1,309      $767    $2,798       7
   19  Wading      Les            $901    $1,199      $738    $2,838      ─────
   20  Willock     Sam            $430    $1,306    $1,719    $3,455       ↓
   ◄▮▓▓▓▓▓▓▓▓▓▓▓▓▓▓▓▓▓▓▓▓▓▓▓▓▓▓▓▓▓▓▓▓▓▓▓▓▓▓▓▓▓▓▓▓▓▓▓▓▓▓▓▓▓▓▓▓▓▓▓►  r
   SALESPER.WQ1 [6]                                      NUM           READY
```

Figure 3-15. *Database of salespersons*

manager using the database of TOA on-call personnel, you might need to produce lists of TOA staff who are available to work at any given time. Placing the list in alphabetical order makes it easier to read as well as more professional looking.

A related use of the Sort command is to tidy up data entry errors. For example, it is quite possible to enter the same record into a database several times. Duplicate records can be found by sorting the database and then browsing through it.

Nondatabase Sorting

A further application of the Sort command was mentioned earlier: sorting lists that are not databases. This means that you can use the Sort command when building or organizing a spreadsheet project that is not intended to be a database. For example, suppose you are creating a budget and are entering figures for a number of expense categories, as shown in Figure 3-16. You might decide that they will look better in numerical order, from

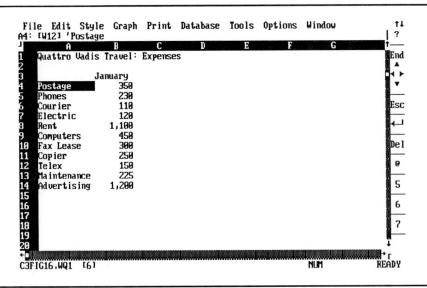

Figure 3-16.   *Expenses before sorting*

largest to smallest, so you use the Sort command to arrange them that way. The quick way to do this is as follows:

1. Select the cells: Using SHIFT-F7 and the cursor keys or the mouse, highlight from cell A4 down through B14. This will probably leave the cell selector in B14, which is fine.

2. Issue the Database Sort Block command: This will pick up A4..B14 as the Sort Block.

3. Pick 1st Key and press ENTER: This will select B14 as the 1st Key, which is what you want. Press ENTER.

4. Now pick Go. This will produce a descending list, as shown in Figure 3-17. Note that you do not have to type **D** as this is the default sort order.

In this example there are two shortcuts: preselecting the Sort Block, and using a cell other than the first cell in the column as the sort key. You can also see that you do not need field names for a sort to work. If you now

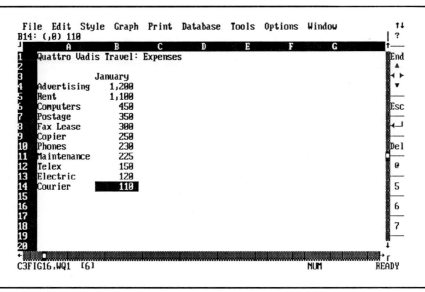

Figure 3-17. *Expenses after sorting*

decide that an alphabetical list might be better, you can change the 1st Key to any cell from A4 through A14 and pick A as the sort order.

Sort Saving

When the sort operation is performed, a large amount of information is moved. Unless you are very sure of the effects of the sort, you should always save a worksheet before sorting. Another safeguard is to make sure that the Undo feature is enabled. (Select Options, Other, Undo, and Enable.) This will allow you to reverse the effect of a sort just by pressing the Undo key (ALT-F5).

Sort Precautions

As mentioned earlier, do *not* think of sorting one column in a database, because information will become detached from its records and cannot be put back together. To guard against unwanted changes to data, always save the file before a sort. That way, if the sort produces an effect you do not want, you can retrieve the presort file. You might also want to check the Sort Block setting on the Sort menu before issuing the Go command. If you cannot see the Sort Block coordinates on your menu, press the Expand key (+) on the numeric pad. This will give you a wide version of the menu, showing the settings.

Reordering with Edit Fill

Although records in a database may not be in numeric or alphabetic order, the order in which they are entered may be significant. If this is the case, you can insert a column to the left of the database and fill it with a series of numbers that correspond to each of the records. You can do this easily with the Edit Fill command.

After you have inserted a new column, you can type a field name such as Record# on the same row as the other database field names. Then you can place the cell selector below the field name on the same row as the first piece of data in the database. If you select Edit Fill, you will be asked to define a block of cells to fill. Anchor this block in the current cell by typing a period and extend the highlighting down the worksheet. You must highlight down to and including the row of the last record. To do this quickly, press RIGHT ARROW, then END and DOWN ARROW, and then LEFT ARROW. This action takes the highlighting into the first column currently occupied by data, down to the last row of data, and then back into the original column you want to fill. Using the END key on completed columns and rows is a quick way of getting around.

When you press ENTER to confirm the fill block, Quattro PRO prompts you for a start number. You can use the suggested default of 0 or any other number, such as 1001. Then press ENTER and you will be prompted for the increment. You will usually select 1, although you can use decimals or units larger than 1. After entering the increment, you must specify the ending number. Simply type a number that is larger than the largest number you want in the block you are filling, and Quattro PRO will stop at the end of the block. Alternatively, if you know the ending number you need, you can type that number. (The default ending number of 8191 comes from numbering all the rows from 0 to 8191.)

If you include this column of numbers (corresponding to the original entry order in the Sort Block), you can always resort the database on this column, which will restore the original order of records. Note that Edit Fill can also produce a horizontal series of numbers if you define a row as the fill block. You can even fill a rectangle with a series of values if you pick a rectangular fill block.

Database Printing

As introduced in Chapter 2, printing information from Quattro PRO involves defining the block of cells to be printed. To print a database, you simply need to define the database as the block of cells to be printed. Quattro PRO arranges the data on pages according to the quantity of information and the size of the page. To print the data in sorted order, be sure to use the Sort Go command before you issue the Print Spreadsheet command.

Quattro PRO's print commands are covered in detail in Chapter 5. Several commands are pertinent to printing databases. Using field names as a heading that will appear across the top of each page is very useful when the list runs onto several pages. Multiple-page listings will also benefit from headers that number the pages.

Once you have defined a print block, Quattro PRO continues to print from those same cells without your having to redefine them. Thus you can sort, print, and then resort and print without having to redefine the print block.

You may want to add a separator line printed at the top of your database below the field names, like this:

First Last Rank Based Standby Notice Last Call
_____

You can use the Line Drawing option on the Style menu to create a line like this, placing the line on the bottom of the field name cells. This avoids having to add an extra line to the database, which could get sorted into the rest of the data.

Making Inquiries

Quattro PRO can not only sort a collection of data in a worksheet, but it can also locate specific records or groups of records. Having located records, you can browse through and edit them. You can even copy matching records to a separate list. The Database Query feature is not the same as the Edit Search & Replace feature described in the last chapter.

Lines of Questioning

As an example of the Database Query feature, imagine you are the personnel manager at TOA. You need to find employees at a specific location and then you want to know which employees are available. You can phrase this need as a question or query. A typical query would be "Find employees based in Rome who are available." Using the TOA on-call database for this management function, you can address this query to the program. The conditions you place on requests to find specific data in Quattro PRO are called *criteria*. In this example, the criteria can be expressed as "Find all employees whose records have Rome in the Based column and Yes in the Standby column." When given this command in the appropriate manner, Quattro PRO will respond either by highlighting records that match the criteria, or by placing a list of matching records in a separate area of the worksheet.

In order to find data that matches certain conditions or criteria, Quattro PRO needs to know two things:

Where the data is located	The Query Block contains the entire database including the field names
Which data to find	The Criteria Table is used to specify the criteria of your search, that is, what data to match

After you have given Quattro PRO these two pieces of information, the program locates matching records by highlighting them. If you provide a third piece of information, called an *Output Block,* Quattro PRO extracts a list of items and places the list in that area of the worksheet.

Where Data Is Located

To undertake any query operation, you first need to tell Quattro PRO about the Query Block, that is, which block of cells contains the data you want to search. If you have just sorted the database, you might think that you have already answered the question "Where is the data?" After all, the Sort menu asked you to define a block of data. However, while the procedure used in a query is similar to that used in a sort, there is an important difference: The Query Block includes the field names; the Sort Block does not.

To define the Query Block, select Database from the menu bar and then Query and you will see the menu shown in Figure 3-18. When you select Block, Quattro PRO prompts you to point out the cells containing the database records. This is the entire database, including the field names. When you first pick Block, the prompt for the cells containing the database records is not anchored and you should move the cell selector to the top-left corner of the database if it is not already there. Anchor the cell by typing a period. Just as in sorting operations, you can use the END key very effectively to highlight the Query Block. Press END and then RIGHT ARROW. Press END again and then DOWN ARROW. This will highlight the entire database. Press ENTER to confirm this block. Now you are ready to tell Quattro PRO what records you want to find.

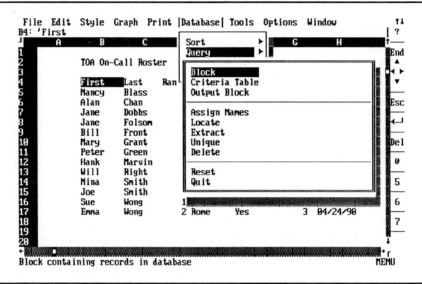

Figure 3-18.   *The Query menu*

Note that you do not have to include the entire database in the block to be searched. You can leave off some records from the bottom of the block. However, you must include field names for the columns you are searching.

Which Data to Find

To tell Quattro PRO which data you are looking for you establish a *Criteria Table.* In its simplest form a Criteria Table consists of a field name above a piece of data. For example, suppose you want to find all personnel in the sample database who are based in London. The Criteria Table would be as follows:

Based   (this is the field name)
London   (this is the data to match)

You enter this information into cells of your worksheet. You then tell the program the location of that criteria and ask it to locate the records.

Quattro PRO does this by trying to match what you have specified in the criteria to each row of the appropriate column in the Query Block. In this example, the program looks in the field or column that is called or headed by the word *Based*. The program checks for the text *London*. When a match for such text is found, the entire record that contains the matching text is highlighted.

The data that you ask Quattro PRO to match can consist of formulas as well as simple text or value entries. You can also use multiple criteria, checking up to 256 fields at once.

Creating a Criteria Table

A typical Criteria Table is shown in Figure 3-19. As you can see, it consists of several field names, with values from those fields entered beneath them. This particular table is being set up to locate anyone based in Rome who is on standby. This means that Quattro PRO will look in two fields, Based and Standby. The program will look for *Rome* in the first field and *Yes* in

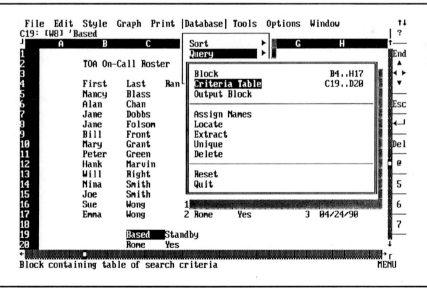

Figure 3-19. *Criteria Table in Query settings menu*

the second. Only when it encounters a record that meets both of these criteria will it accept the record as a match.

To build a Criteria Table, you type the field names of the columns in which you want to match data, followed by the data you want to match, in a separate area of the worksheet. The actual positioning of the Criteria Table on the spreadsheet is not critical to performance of the Locate operation, but the Criteria Table should be set apart from the database in an unused portion of the worksheet. However, there are some practical factors regarding location that you should consider. Do not place the Criteria Table directly to the right or left of the database if you expect to be deleting records or rows from the database with the Edit Delete Row command. Do not remove the Criteria Table too far from the database as you will be needlessly consuming memory.

You define the Criteria Table to Quattro PRO by selecting Criteria Table from the Query menu. You highlight the appropriate block of cells and press ENTER, as shown in Figure 3-20. Be careful not to include any blank lines in the Criteria Table, since this will cause Quattro PRO to find everything in the database. If the entries beneath the field names in a

Figure 3-20. *Setting the Criteria Block*

Criteria Table are all on the same line, as they are in Figure 3-20, then the relationship between them is AND. This means that a record must meet both criteria to be included in the Locate operation. If the entries are on separate lines, the relationship is OR, and the program locates records that match any one of the criteria. For example, the following arrangement selects everyone who is based in Rome, plus everyone who is on standby:

Based	Standby
Rome	Yes

Locating Data

When you have defined the Query Block and the Criteria Table, you are returned to the Query menu. To find the records meeting your criteria, select the Locate command. Locate causes Quattro PRO to highlight the first item meeting your criteria. As you can see from Figure 3-21, this highlighting bar runs the full length of the record. You can then move to

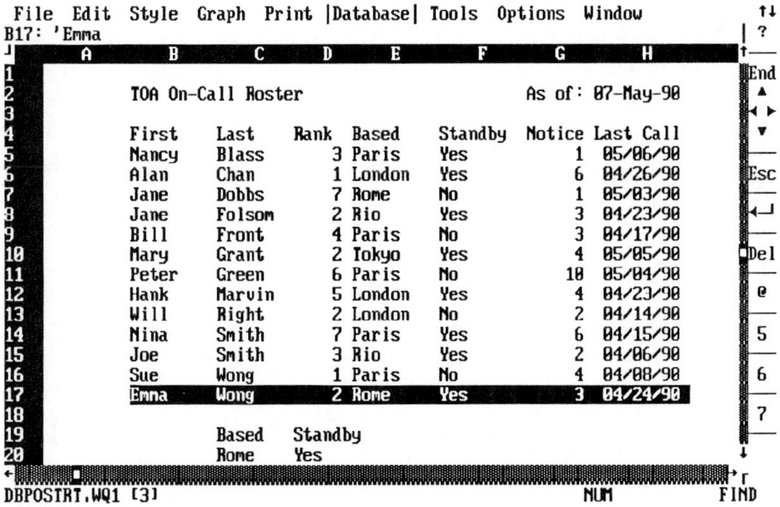

Figure 3-21. *Results of Locate*

the next record that meets the criteria by pressing the DOWN ARROW key. When you get to the last matching record and try to go further, Quattro PRO will beep. You can move back up through the records with the UP ARROW key and continue to browse through the matching items by using the UP and DOWN ARROW keys. The END key takes you to the last record, while HOME takes you to the first. If there are no records meeting your criteria, Quattro PRO will beep in response to the Locate command and return to the Query menu. This is an opportunity to check that you have specified the criteria correctly.

Notice that the cursor flashes within the Locate highlight bar and that you can move it across the bar with the RIGHT and LEFT ARROW keys. The cursor moves from column center to column center. To completely change any cell on the Locate bar, place your cursor in the appropriate column, type the new entry, and press ENTER. Alternatively, you can press F2 and edit the cell contents, returning them to the cell with the ENTER key.

After you have used Locate, you return to the other areas of Quattro PRO by pressing ESCAPE. If you entered from the Query menu, ESCAPE takes you back to the Query menu, where you can make changes. If you entered the query by pressing F7—described in a moment—ESCAPE takes you directly to READY mode. One handy key that takes you from any mode or menu back to the READY mode, regardless of how you got there, is CTRL-BREAK.

The Locate feature is very useful for quick searches when you do not want to print out a separate list, for example, to perform a quick check of a specific item in stock or an employee record. If you want to copy the records that have been located to another part of the worksheet, or to another worksheet, then you need the Extract command, which is described later in this chapter.

Advanced Criteria

So far you have seen that a Criteria Table offers a simple but effective way of indicating the parameters of your search for data. You can take the Criteria Table even further by using formulas and block names to create detailed search specifications.

Assigning Names

You may have noticed an option on the Database Query menu called Assign Names. This allows you to give block names to each cell in the second row of your database, using the field names in the first row. Why would you want to do this? You have already seen that you can query your database without carrying out this operation. The value of the Assign Names command appears when you start to develop more sophisticated search criteria. So far, you have seen how to search for something that is an exact match, telling Quattro PRO to match *Rome* and *Yes*. When you come to search for a range of values, such as *Rank greater than 5,* then block names come in very handy.

The Assign Names command is very easy to use. After you have defined the Query Block, just select Assign Names. You will not see anything happen. However, if you quit from the Query menu and use the Edit Names Create command you will see a list of the block names you have just created. If you press the Expand key (+) you will see the cell coordinates listed next to the names, as shown in Figure 3-22. You can then use these

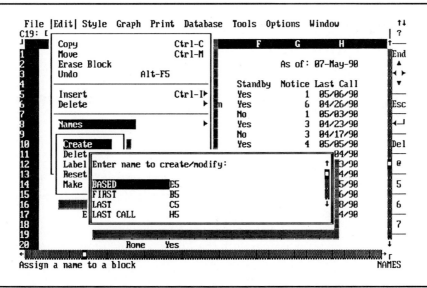

Figure 3-22. *Names Create list after Assign Names*

names in search formulas. Note that block names are stored in capital letters. In fact, Quattro PRO is not at all case-sensitive when it comes to the Query command. A query based on *YES* also finds *yes* and *Yes*. When you put together Criteria Tables and formulated criteria it will not matter if you refer to field names in upper- or lowercase.

Formulated Criteria

You can enter numbers and labels into a Criteria Table and you can also use formulas. These formulas use *logical operators*. They also use the block name associated with each column by the Assign Names command. Thus, you could enter **+RANK>5** in the Rank column of a Criteria Table to find all persons with a rank greater than 5.

Each Criteria Table formula includes three elements: Field, Comparison Operator, and Value. These tell Quattro PRO which field contains the value you are attempting to match, whether you want to match an exact value or a range of values, and the value itself. For example, suppose you need to find all staff with a Rank above 5. This can be expressed as +Rank>5. Note that the plus sign is used here because this is a formula. Rank is the field name, > is the comparison operator (meaning greater than), and 5 is the value. The comparison operators you can use are as follows:

>	Greater than (+Rank>5 means 6,7,8, and so on)
<	Less than (+Rank<5 means 4,3,2, and so on)
>=	Greater than or equal to (+Rank>=5 means 5,6, and so on)
<=	Less than or equal to (+Rank<=5 means 5,4,3, and so on)
<>	Not equal to (+Rank<>5 means anything other than 5)
=	Equal to (+Rank=5 means only 5)

Note that you generally will not use +Rank=5 unless it is part of a larger formula since there is no need to use a formula if the criterion is a single case. Simply use 5 as the criterion.

Since Quattro PRO lists all named blocks for you, you can create formulas using block names with the List key (F3). For example, to create the formula +RANK>5 you first type **+** and press F3. Select RANK from the list by highlighting it and pressing ENTER. Now you can type **>5** and press ENTER to complete the formula. This avoids typing errors such as incorrect spelling of block names.

Complex Formulated Criteria

To place additional qualifications on the criteria you use for querying items, you can add logical operators, which set up more categories to match. The logical operators shown here set up two or three criteria for the personnel list:

AND   as in Based="Rome"#AND#Rank>5
OR   as in Based="Rome"#OR#"Paris"
NOT   as in Based="Rome"#AND#Rank>5#NOT#First="Joe"

The logical operator must be placed in the formula within # signs as shown in the examples. You create multiple conditions with logical operators to make your search more specific. For example, if you wanted to locate all staff based in Paris with a rank greater than 5, you would type **+BASED="paris"#AND#RANK>5** as shown here:

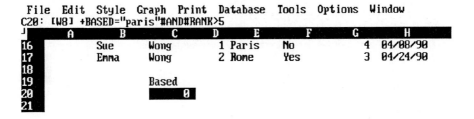

Notice that the field name in the Criteria Table is Based but the Based field is not the only one referred to in the formula. In fact, you can use any field name from your database when you are using formula criteria that reference named cells in the database. For example, in the next illustration you can see a formula referencing Rank and Notice that has been entered under the field name Last.

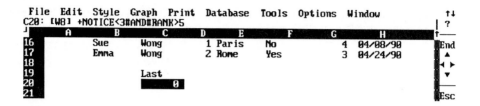

```
 File  Edit  Style  Graph  Print  Database  Tools  Options  Window        ↑↓
C20: [W8] +NOTICE<3#AND#RANK>5                                            | ?
┘     A        B        C        D      E        F       G        H      ├─
16             Sue      Wong     1 Paris       No              4  04/08/90  End
17             Emma     Wong     2 Rome        Yes             3  04/24/90  ▲
18                                                                         ◄ ►
19                      Last                                               ▼
20                        ████0                                            
21                                                                         Esc
```

Criteria Techniques

A quick way to create and use a Criteria Table is to copy the entire set of field names to a new location and then define those names and the row beneath them as the Criteria Table. Enter the data you want to match under the appropriate field name prior to a search and then delete it when the search is completed. You do not have to have an entry in every column of the Criteria Table for it to work.

You can also set up more than one set of cells to be used as criteria in a worksheet. Although only one block at a time can be specified as the Criteria Table, you can quickly switch settings by using block names. For example, in Figure 3-23 you can see three different sets of criteria located

```
 File  Edit  Style  Graph  Print  Database  Tools  Options  Window        ↑↓
B31: (T) +RANK>5                                                         | ?
┘     A        B        C        D      E        F       G        H      ├─
13             Nina     Smith    7 Paris       Yes             6  08/03/87  End
14             Peter    Green    6 Paris       No             10  08/22/87  ▲
15             Sue      Wong     1 Paris       No              4  07/27/87  ◄ ►
16             Will     Right    2 London      No              2  08/02/87  ▼
17
18                                                                         Esc
19
20                                                                         ←┘
21
22             Based                                                       Del
23             London
24                                                                         @
25
26             Standby                                                     5
27             Yes
28                                                                         6
29
30             Rank                                                        7
31             █+RANK>5█
32                                                                         ↓
←▓▓▓▓▓▓▓░░░░░░░░░░░░░░░░░░░░░░░░░░░░░░░░░░░░░░░░░░░░░░░░░░░░░░░░░░░░░░→ ┌
PQFIG323.WQ1 [?]                                                     READY
```

Figure 3-23.   *Three separate Criteria Tables*

in blocks B22..B23, B26..B27, and B30..B31. These blocks have been called CRIT1, CRIT2, and CRIT3 respectively. Suppose you have just performed a Locate operation with B22..B23, otherwise known as CRIT1, as the Criteria Table and now you want to use CRIT2. You simply type / to activate the menu, select Database, Query, and then Criteria Table. When prompted for the Criteria Table coordinates you press F3 for a list of block names. Highlight CRIT2, as shown in Figure 3-24, and press ENTER to confirm. You can now select Locate to perform the search on CRIT2. Note that when you use a named block for your Criteria Table, the name of the block (rather than the coordinates) appears in the menu settings, as shown in Figure 3-25.

Matching Text

If what you are looking to match in a criterion is a piece of text—that is, something that has been entered as a label—and you want to incorporate

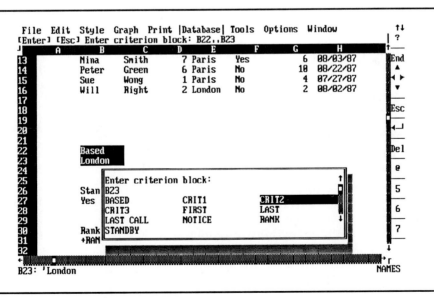

Figure 3-24.   *Selecting named Criteria Block*

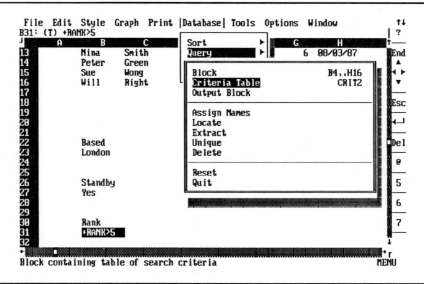

Figure 3-25. *Named Criteria Table setting*

it in a formula, you must place it in double quotes. For example, "paris" will find *PARIS, Paris,* and *paris.* When you use the comparison operators with labels, Quattro PRO interprets > as meaning higher in the alphabet. This means that you can use these operators with non-numeric fields like ZIP codes to specify codes equal to or greater than, say, 94100, which would be written +ZIP"94100".

To add scope to your searches for a text match, you can use *wildcards.* These are the question mark (?), the asterisk (*), and the tilde (~). The question mark stands for any character in that position in a string, as in *V?LE,* which would find *VALE, VOLE, VILE,* and so on. The asterisk means anything from this character to the end of the label, as in *VERN*,* which would find anything beginning with *VERN,* like *VERNAL, VER-NON,* and so on. Tilde means "not", as in *~Paris* meaning anywhere but Paris.

Repeating a Query

The F7 key will repeat the last query you performed. Suppose you have to look up different employee records on a regular basis, and you have a Criteria Table with Last and First as headings. You would type the name of the employee you were looking for under the Last Name and First Name headings in the Criteria Table and select Locate. The next time you needed to look up an employee's record, you would type the name of the employee in the Criteria Table and press F7. The same Criteria Table and Query Locate are used, but with the new entry in the Criteria Table. In this way you can find a succession of employees from a long list with relative ease.

After performing a Query Locate, you will get the same results again when you press F7 if you are working in the same spreadsheet during the same session. If you last performed a Query Extract, which will be discussed next, then Extract is performed the next time you press F7.

Query Extract

So far you have seen that Quattro PRO is adept at locating records in a database. At some point you will probably want a list of items matching your criteria. You do this once you have established the database and the criteria. You can then place the list anywhere in the worksheet.

Providing the Data

You create a list of data selected from a Quattro PRO database by using the Extract command, which copies data meeting your criteria into a separate area of the spreadsheet. The Extract command needs the following four pieces of information.

Where the data is located	The Query Block
What to extract	The Criteria Table
Where to output	The cells in which to place the extracted data
What data to output	The field names of the desired columns

If you have already used the Locate feature, you will have used the first two items. The last two involve moving to an empty part of the worksheet and typing in the names of the fields you want reported.

The Output Block

You have now decided which pieces of information you want and where to have Quattro PRO output the matching records. Next you can extract the information. For example, in Figure 3-26 you can see the results of the

File Edit Style Graph Print Database Tools Options Window								↑↓
C21: [W8] 'Last								?
A	B	C	D	E	F	G	H	
13	Nina	Smith	7	Paris	Yes	6	08/03/87	End
14	Peter	Green	6	Paris	No	18	08/22/87	▲
15	Sue	Wong	1	Paris	No	4	07/27/87	◄ ►
16	Will	Right	2	London	No	2	08/02/87	▼
17								
18		Based	Rank					Esc
19		Paris	+RANK>5					
20								◄┘
21		Last	Last Call					
22		Smith	08/03/87					Del
23		Green	08/22/87					
24								e
25								
26								5
27								
28								6
29								
30								7
31								
32	Based							↓
PQFIG323.WQ1 [7]								READY

Figure 3-26.   *Extract results*

Extract function, using the fields Last and Last Call. This figure shows the names of the staff that meet the criteria plus the date they were last called.

There is no limit to the number of fields you can include in the Output Block, and you do not need to include fields that were part of the criteria. You can extract names for persons meeting the RANK>5 criteria. Of course, as you can see from Figure 3-27, you can include all fields in the output if you want to.

When you have entered the names of the fields you want reported, you must next record the Output Block. Place your cursor on the leftmost field name and select Output from the Query menu. Anchor the cell you are in and press END and RIGHT ARROW to include all of the field names. Now you must extend the Output Block of cells. If you do not move down from the field names, you will be telling Quattro PRO that it can use any number of rows below the field names for the output. If you press PAGE DOWN once, you will be saying that there are 20 lines available, and Quattro PRO will highlight this area. As your worksheets get crowded, it is a good idea to

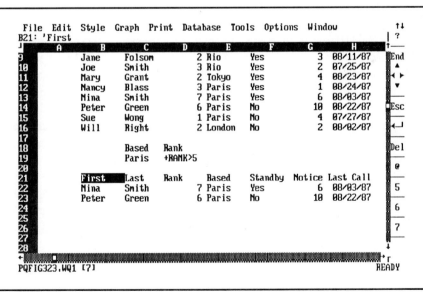

Figure 3-27. *Extracting full record*

limit the Output Block like this so that the program is prevented from outputting over occupied cells.

The Extract

With the Output Block defined, select Extract to tell Quattro PRO to place the items identified by your criteria into the output cells. Quattro PRO uses the last criteria you defined; either the Formula Criteria or the Criteria Table from which to select the items. When you have performed the extract, the data can be printed, copied, or further manipulated. As with the Locate command, you can repeat the last query with F7. Thus, you can change the name of the city you are looking for and press F7 to get a new list.

Note that when Quattro PRO extracts numbers from the database to an output range, they are only numbers. Formulas in the database are converted to their numeric value upon extraction.

Unique Records

When the Extract function is performed, Quattro PRO copies every matching record to the Output Block. If some records are duplicates of each other, the program copies both. You can prevent this by using Unique rather than Extract from the Query menu, so that Quattro PRO will only copy one of the duplicate records to the output. This helps to avoid reporting errors. However, you need to bear in mind that Unique excludes only those records that are exact duplicates, not just those that have identical entries in the fields specified in the Criteria Table or Output Block.

When creating large databases it is not unusual for duplicate records to occur, particularly if more than one person is using the database. However, any sort of the database should reveal duplicates, which can then be deleted.

Deleting Records

When you are cleaning up or maintaining a database, you may need to get rid of records. One way of doing this is to find the record and then delete it with the Edit Delete Row command. However, this has the possibly negative side effect of removing any data that is on the same row as the deleted record, all the way across the worksheet. Quattro PRO has an automated alternative, called Query Delete, that does not interfere with cells outside the database. To use this command you set the criteria for the records you want deleted and then select Delete instead of Locate or Extract. You will be prompted to confirm this action as the program removes cells from the worksheet. Query Delete can be dangerous; be careful that your criteria are correct before using this command and perform a File Save beforehand. You can always perform a Query Locate before a Query Delete, just to make sure that your criteria are working as intended. Another safeguard is to make sure that the Undo feature is enabled (by selecting Options, Other, Undo, and Enable). This will allow you to reverse the effect of Query Delete just by pressing the Undo key (ALT-F5).

Databases and Multiple Worksheets

You can see that managing a database requires several elements in addition to the data itself. Querying the database requires a Criteria Table. An Output Block is required for an Extract to be performed. One way to manage these elements is to divide them between worksheets. For example, you can keep the database in one worksheet and the Criteria Table and Output Block in a separate worksheet. You can see this arrangement in Figure 3-28 where two worksheets, DATABASE and REPORT, are tiled side by side. The REPORT worksheet is where the user is specifying the criteria and extracting the data.

With the REPORT worksheet active you set the Query Block by defining the cells occupied by data in the DATABASE worksheet. When you get the prompt "Enter database block," you use SHIFT-F6, the Next Window key, to make DATABASE the active worksheet; then highlight the database cells. When you confirm this, the setting in the Query menu will look something like: [DATABASE]B4..H16. Keeping the REPORT worksheet active, you proceed to define the Criteria Table and Output Block using cells within the REPORT worksheet. You can see that this has been done in Figure 3-29.

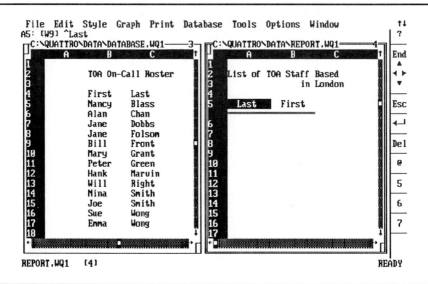

Figure 3-28. *Extracting from a separate file*

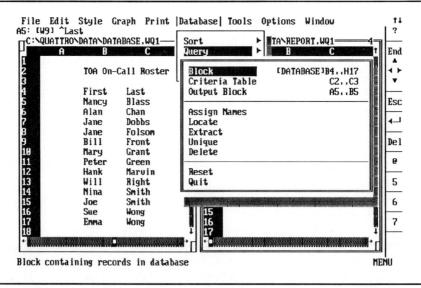

Figure 3-29. *Settings for extract from separate file*

To extract data from the DATABASE worksheet into REPORT you make REPORT the active worksheet and then issue the Extract command. Records from DATABASE that meet the criteria in REPORT will be copied into REPORT. You can also use the Locate command from REPORT. In this case, Quattro PRO takes you to the DATABASE worksheet and shows you the selected records there. When you leave the FIND mode you are returned to the REPORT worksheet.

An extension of the multiple-worksheet approach would be to have several different worksheets for reporting on the same database. This would allow you to switch criteria simply by making a different worksheet window active before executing the query.

Working with Foreign Databases

While many users find that a Quattro PRO worksheet is the ideal place to keep track of their data, no one expects all of the world's databases to be available in Quattro PRO format. Because there is so much useful data stored in databases created by other programs, Borland gave Quattro PRO the ability to read files created by popular database programs. This means that you can use the Data Query command to inspect data in a database file created by another program such as dBASE or Paradox. You can establish criteria in your worksheet that refer to fields in the foreign file. Using the Extract command you can read a selection of data from the foreign file into a Quattro PRO worksheet.

You can also use Quattro PRO to update a foreign database. For example, suppose that your company uses Paradox to maintain a central database of expenses, and that you keep track of your expenses in a Quattro PRO worksheet. You can add your expense records to the Paradox database. The command that does this is Data Append. You can read about Data Append as well as querying of foreign databases in Chapter 13, which covers importing and exporting Quattro PRO data.

Database Reporting

Once you have extracted data, you may well want to print it. Printing a database is much like printing any other part of the worksheet. You may, perhaps, want to format a report from a database.

Sorting Extracted Data

Extracted data is a series of consecutive columns and rows; in fact, by extracting data you have created a new database. This database can now be sorted. If you were asked to provide a list of all the staff, you would want the list alphabetized or put in some other order. You can do this by defining the Sort Block as the output data minus the field names. Remember that Quattro PRO remembers the last Sort Block and keys you used, so it is wise to select the Reset command from the Sort menu before performing a sort on a new block.

Block Search and Replace

In the last chapter you saw that Quattro PRO has a search and replace feature on the Edit menu. This is very useful when you are updating a number of records with the same information. For example, you can use it to change all Rank 3 employees to Rank 4. You can select Search to enter the data you want to match and Replace to enter what it is to be changed to. This will work on databases and on the entire spreadsheet. The Edit menu search and replace feature operates independently of the database query commands.

Data Entry Techniques

Spreadsheets used as databases take far more keystrokes than regular spreadsheets, where the bulk of the entries are created by formulas that are copied. In addition, databases often need extensive editing to be kept current. If you are maintaining a sizable database, you may wish to employ a typist to edit or input the data. There are some steps you can take to make the work easier for someone unfamiliar with Quattro PRO.

Input Form

If you are having someone who is not well versed in spreadsheets perform data-entry for you, you can make an input form to assist them. The first step is to protect the entire spreadsheet. To do this you issue the Options Protection command and select Enable. This prevents any data from being altered. Then you can use the Style Protection command to Unprotect those cells where the data will be entered or edited. When you are ready to have someone work on the database you can issue the Restrict Input command from the Database menu. You highlight a block of the worksheet that includes the unprotected cells. When you press ENTER this area becomes the *Input Block.* User access is now limited to any unprotected cells in the Input Block. The diagram in Figure 3-30 shows how the Input Block and unprotected cells work together to create a *mask* over the worksheet.

The effect of the Restrict Input command is considerable. The message INPUT appears in the mode indicator. The cursor keys will not take you outside of the defined Input Block of cells and will only move to those cells within the Input Block that are unprotected. You can type data and press ENTER, or edit data with F2 and re-enter it. The program menu is not available, and so typing / begins a new label instead of activating the menu.

To break out of the INPUT mode you press ESCAPE or ENTER while the INPUT message is displayed. This means that it is very easy to override the Restrict Input command. In fact, the command is most effective when used in macros that further control the user's access to commands, as described in Chapter 12.

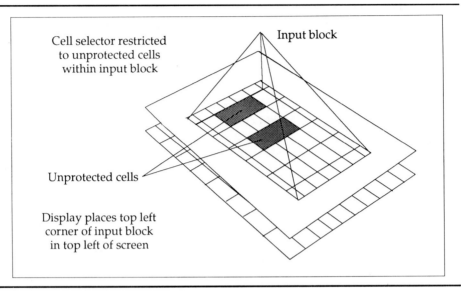

Figure 3-30.   *Diagram of input range*

Data Control

Earlier in this chapter, mention was made of the need to type a label prefix when entering non-numeric numbers such as ZIP codes. Another chore for data-entry workers is making sure that dates are entered as dates. To overcome this problem, Quattro PRO allows you to designate certain cells in a spreadsheet as Labels Only. To do this you use the Data-entry option on the Database menu. When you select the Labels Only command, you highlight an area—usually a field or column—to be affected by the command. From then on, anything entered into those cells will be automatically preceded by a label prefix. You will see the word *Label* in front of the cell address on the input or status line, as shown in Figure 3-31, to remind you that the cell has a forced data type.

The default label prefix, usually the apostrophe for left-alignment, is now added to what you type into a label cell. If the cells you selected with

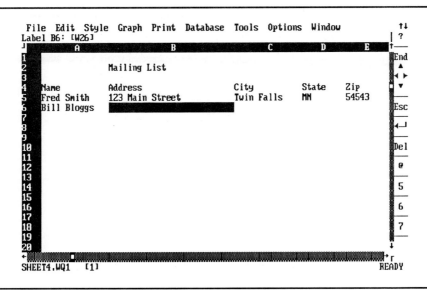

Figure 3-31. *Forced data type: Label*

the Labels Only command already contain numbers or formulas entered as values, then these retain their status. However, if you edit and then re-enter one of these cells it will be converted to a label.

The Database Data-entry command also allows you to restrict entries to Dates Only, a means of avoiding errors in date fields. You will see the word **Date** in front of the cell address in the input and status lines to remind you that what you enter must be a date. Cells selected by the Dates Only command will accept dates typed in any of the standard date formats, which are described in detail in Chapter 9.

4 Formulas and Functions in Depth

In previous chapters you have seen that Quattro PRO understands several formulas of varying complexity, from a simple formula that adds cells to a complex one that calculates a loan payment. In this chapter you will see the ways in which formulas can be applied to typical spreadsheet operations and the many built-in formulas, or functions, that Quattro PRO provides to enhance your formulas.

Formulas Are Instructions

While the word *formula* may remind many people of algebra and science classes, in the context of Quattro PRO the term simply means an *instruction* written in a form that the program can understand. As you have seen, the way you give Quattro PRO instructions can be as straightforward as "add cell A1 and cell A2." In fact, even complex instructions follow a consistent arrangement, or *syntax*. As you learn to manipulate formulas, you will want to use the program's built-in functions for more complex calculations. Quattro PRO offers nearly a hundred functions. Most of these functions follow the same format as the functions in 1-2-3, although Quattro PRO provides some functions that are not available in 1-2-3 Release 2, or even in Release 3.

Formula Formats

Simple Quattro PRO formulas combine values—like numbers or cells containing numbers—with operators, such as the division sign or the plus sign. The formula in cell H7 of Figure 4-1 can be diagrammed like this:

H7 =	H5	*	H6
	Value	Operator	Value

If cells H5 and H6 were named as blocks, the formula could be diagrammed like this:

H7 =	Width	*	Length
	Value	Operator	Value

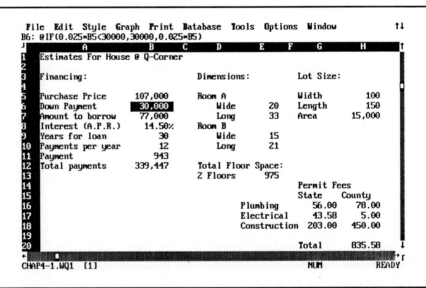

Figure 4-1. *Example of formulas*

Quattro PRO formulas are algebraic in format. Thus, within a formula you can use other formulas separated, or *delimited,* by pairs of parentheses, as in the following:

E13 = ((E6*E7)+(E9*E10))*2

This formula in E13 means "multiply E6 by E7, add that to the product of E9 multiplied by E10, and then double the answer." The formula could calculate the total floor area of a two-story house with two rooms on each floor whose width and length were in cells E6 through E10.

When you ask Quattro PRO to make decisions about the data to be calculated, several elements are required, as in this formula:

B6 = @IF(0.25*B5<30000,30000,0.25*B5)

This formula tells Quattro PRO that the down payment in B6 should be 25% of the purchase price in B5, unless the product of those two values comes to less than 30,000, in which case B6 should be 30,000. This formula is used in Figure 4-1 to calculate the down payment. The buyer must pay at least 25% of the purchase price and no less than $30,000.

An expense report that breaks down expenses for each week by type might contain the formula

G13=@IF(@SUM(WEEK)=@SUM(TYPE),@SUM(TYPE),@ERR)

This formula says that G13 will have one of two possible answers, depending on a decision made by the @IF function. If the sum of the block of cells called WEEK is equal to the sum of the block of cells called TYPE, the program should insert that sum; otherwise, it should give an error message (@ERR). By the end of this chapter you will be able to read such formulas and compose them with Quattro PRO's formula syntax and functions.

Notice that none of the previous formulas have spaces entered in them. No spaces is a general rule in all Quattro PRO formulas. Also note that the program capitalizes cell references, block names, and function names. It does not matter if you enter these as upper- or lowercase letters; Quattro PRO will store and display them in uppercase.

Acceptable Values

The values in a Quattro PRO formula can be cells containing values, as in +H5*H6. They can be a block of cells containing values, either stated as coordinates as in +G16..G18+H16..H18, or described by block names, as in STATE+COUNTY. They can also be functions like @PMT, which was used in Chapter 1 to calculate a car loan payment. The same function is used in Figure 4-2 to calculate a mortgage payment in cell B11. Note the use of a separate cell for number of payments per year. As shown below, you can calculate the total payments to be made on a 30-year loan if you multiply the number of payments (B9*B10) by the calculated payment amount.

```
 File  Edit  Style  Graph  Print  Database  Tools  Options  Window
B12: +B9*B10*B11
⌐               A              B      C      D        E     F    G        H
 7  Amount to borrow         77,000         Long      33    Area     15,000
 8  Interest (A.P.R.)        14.50%   Room B
 9  Years for loan              30         Wide       15
10  Payments per year           12         Long       21
11  Payment                    943
12  Total payments         339,447         Total Floor Space:
13                                         2 Floors       975
```

The many Quattro PRO @functions that can be used in formulas are described later in this chapter.

Values in Quattro PRO formulas can also be constants. A *constant* is a number, date, or piece of text that you enter directly, such as the 1 in 1+B3. Constants are used in formulas for projections; for example, a formula to figure projected sales might be Sales*1.1. A constant is also used in calculations like finding the circumference of a circle (2*@PI*Radius).

Operators and Priorities

There are many different operators that you can use in Quattro PRO formulas. First, there are the standard arithmetic operators: add (+), subtract (−), multiply (*), and divide (/). Another operator, the exponent (^), produces powers of a number. In Chapter 3 you saw how you can set search conditions using logical operators, such as the greater-than sign in Rank > 5. All of the operators recognized by Quattro PRO are listed in Table 4-1, where the order of operations in a formula is also shown. If all

```
 File  Edit  Style  Graph  Print  Database  Tools  Options  Window          ↑↓
B11: @PMT(B7,B8/B10,B9*B10)
┌─────────────A──────────────B────C────D───────E─────F──────G──────────H────────┐
1 Estimates For House @ Q-Corner
2
3 Financing:                      Dimensions:        Lot Size:
4
5 Purchase Price      107,000     Room A             Width          100
6 Down Payment         30,000       Wide       20    Length         150
7 Amount to borrow     77,000       Long       33    Area        15,000
8 Interest (A.P.R.)    14.50%     Room B
9 Years for loan           30       Wide       15
10 Payments per year       12       Long       21
11 Payment                 943
12 Total payments      339,447     Total Floor Space:
13                                 2 Floors      975
14                                                   Permit Fees
15                                                   State    County
16                                 Plumbing          56.00     78.00
17                                 Electrical        43.58      5.00
18                                 Construction     203.00    450.00
19
20                                                   Total     835.58    ↓
└──────────────────────────────────────────────────────────────────────────────┘
CHAP4-1.WQ1  [1]                                       NUM         READY
```

Figure 4-2. *Payment calculation*

the operators are the same, as in 2*3*4 (=24), the calculation is performed from left to right. You can affect the order of calculation by using parentheses, as in these two calculations:

2*3+4=10
2*(4+3)=14

When you nest calculations within several parentheses, the innermost calculations are performed first. Earlier you saw the formula ((E6*E7)+(E9*E10))*2. This arrangement of parentheses means that the E6*E7 and E9*E10 calculations will occur first, then the two products will be added together, and finally that sum will be multiplied by the 2 that stands outside the parentheses. Actually, the two inner sets of parentheses are not necessary because, as is shown in Table 4-1, * will occur before +.

Operator	Used for	Priority
&	Placing text in string formulas	1
#AND#	Logical AND formulas	1
#OR#	Logical OR formulas	1
#NOT#	Logical NOT formulas	2
=	Equal in conditional statements	3
<>	Not equal in conditional statements	3
<=	Less than or equal to	3
>=	Greater than or equal to	3
-	Subtraction	4
+	Addition	4
*	Multiplication	5
/	Division	5
-	Negation (preceding a formula)	6
+	Positive (preceding a formula)	6
^	Exponentiation (to the power of)	7

Table 4-1. *Operators and Order of Precedence, 7 Being Highest*

Using Formulas

Much of a spreadsheet's power clearly lies in formulas. Whether you are simply adding two cells together or calculating the sum of the year's depreciation of an asset, the ability to establish a relationship between cells gives you tremendous number-crunching ability.

Methods for Creating and Entering Formulas

You can create formulas in several ways. First, there is the literal method: you look at the worksheet and decide which cells are involved; then you type their addresses into the formula. For example, you can see that the total of the state permit fees in Figure 4-2 is going to be +G16+G17+G18. You can type this formula directly and Quattro PRO will accept it, unless you type an invalid coordinate. The formula will be correct if the cells you have described are the correct cells for the formula.

For the more cautious spreadsheet user and the less adept typist, there is the pointing method of entering formulas. This method begins with the + sign or other value indicator, which places Quattro PRO in VALUE mode. You then use the arrow keys to highlight the first cell you want in the formula. You have seen that, when you do this, Quattro PRO types the cell address for you. You can then type the next math sign or value indicator, and the cell selector will move back down to the cell in which you are building the formula. The basic sequence is math sign, point, math sign, point. You can point to each cell that needs to go into the formula, and it is added on the edit line at the top of the screen as you build the formula. Place the completed formula into the original cell with the ENTER key. This method is very useful when you have lots of cells scattered throughout the spreadsheet and cannot remember the location of a particular number.

You can use the pointing method effectively with formulas that involve functions, as in the case of the loan payment. Separate each argument of the @PMT function by a comma, so that after you initiate the formula with @PMT (you can move the cell selector to the cell containing the first argument. At that point, enter a comma to add that location to the formula and return the cell selector to the cell in which the formula is originating. When you then point out the cell for the second argument and type another comma, that location is pulled into the formula, and the cell selector is returned to the original cell. Lastly, point out the third and final argument, and with the cell selector on the third cell, type the closing parenthesis, which completes the formula. The cell selector is now back at the original cell. You can incorporate additional values into the formula by pressing the desired math sign (as in * to multiply this payment by a cell or number). Otherwise, press the ENTER key can be pressed to place the completed formula in the cell.

Formulas and Blocks

Some formulas and functions use blocks of cells. You can enter blocks by typing the diagonal coordinates of the block directly as you create the formula. Alternatively, you can use the pointing method to block out the cells to be included, anchoring the upper-left corner by typing a period and then using the DOWN and/or RIGHT ARROW as necessary to complete the highlighting of the block.

Results of Entering a Formula

After you have entered a formula, the cell displays the *result* of the formula, not the formula itself. However, the cell identifier still displays the formula, not the value, whenever you highlight a cell that contains a formula. You may not want the value generated by the formula to be *dynamic* and therefore change when the worksheet is recalculated. To *fix* a value, you can convert the formula to the value it produces. This can be done in two ways. If you press F2 while highlighting the cell containing the formula, the formula is placed on the edit line at the top of the screen. If you press the Calc key (F9), then the formula is turned into its result and you can then place this result into the cell with the ENTER key. Alternatively, you can use the Edit Values command, described in Chapter 2, to convert a block of cells from formulas to values.

Named Blocks

Naming blocks with the Edit Name command is very useful when you are developing formulas, because you can use block names instead of cell coordinates. Even attaching a name to a single cell is productive. It is often easier to type LENGTH * WIDTH than H5*H6, particularly if you are composing the formula in Q33. You do not need to check where these elements are and do not need to take the time to point them out. Furthermore, if you type H555*H6 by mistake, Quattro PRO will not tell you that this is an error. But if you try to enter an invalid block name, the program will beep and place you in EDIT mode so that you can correct the mistake. Many people find that block names are easier to use than cell coordinates for groups of cells. Consider the columns of permit fees in Figure 4-3. It is much easier to type @SUM(STATE) than @SUM(G16..G18). The benefits of block names rapidly increase as you create more formulas. Thus, @SUM(STATE,COUNTY) is a lot easier to type than @SUM(G16..G18,H16..H18), particularly because you can press the Choices key (F3), to pop up a list of block names from which to choose.

Formulas and Mice

Instead of pointing and highlighting with the arrow keys, you can use the mouse to indicate cell addresses when building formulas. You can type a

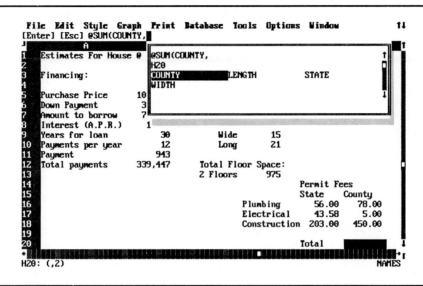

Figure 4-3. *Block choices*

math sign and then click on a single cell to pull it into a formula, or you can click and drag to define a group of cells. If you use the F3 key to list block names you can scroll or expand the list by clicking anywhere on the top row of the box, as shown here:

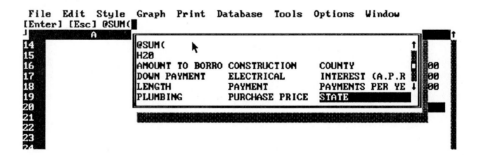

Click on the up and down arrows to page sections of the list into view. The expanded list shows the actual coordinates of the blocks:

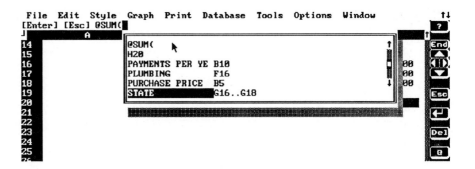

You can click on any name in the list to paste it into the formula you are building on the edit line.

If you use the ALT-F3 key combination to list functions, as described later in this chapter, you can use the mouse pointer to scroll the list of functions. You can click on any function in the list to paste it into the formula you are creating on the edit line. You can simulate ALT-F3 by clicking on the @ sign in the mouse palette.

Editing Formulas

If there is a mistake in a formula that you are creating, such as a misspelled block or function name or an invalid cell reference or unrecognized symbol, Quattro PRO will not accept the formula when you press ENTER. Instead, it will beep and display a message. When you press ENTER or ESCAPE to acknowledge the message, the program changes to EDIT mode and attempts to position the edit cursor near the error you have made. Formulas are always edited on the input line and are placed there either by Quattro PRO when it rejects a formula, or by you when you need to change a previously entered formula. To initiate editing a formula, you highlight the cell and press F2 to enter EDIT mode. The formula will be displayed on the edit line.

Common Formula Errors

If you spell a formula correctly but used improper elements within it, Quattro PRO displays an error message. The exact message will depend upon the error. For example, entering @SUM(B2..TC12) earns the response "Invalid Character" since there cannot be a cell TC12. When you see a message of this type, check the formula to find the error. The program attempts to put the cursor near the error, so look there first. You may have neglected to close a pair of parentheses or quotations, or omitted the @ sign before a function name. A list of error messages is provided in Table 4-2.

A common mistake is to enter spaces between the elements of a formula. Although the documentation occasionally appears to show spaces, they are generally not allowed in formulas. Unlike 1-2-3, Quattro PRO does sometimes allow spaces in formulas, although you do not need to type any. To be on the safe side, however, you would do best to avoid spaces completely.

Named blocks must be spelled correctly. You can press the Choices key (F3) to select from a list of block names when writing formulas. As you can see from the box in the upper-right corner of Figure 4-3, the list makes block names very easy to use. The main advantage of using the F3 key for placing block names in formulas is to avoid typographical errors.

You may succeed in entering a formula only to see the message CIRC appear among the status indicators. This message tells you there is a circular reference in your formula, meaning that the formula refers to itself. You cannot ask Quattro PRO to multiply the current cell by 1.1 and to put the answer in the current cell. This kind of problem, which usually becomes apparent as soon as you see what you have attempted to do, is solved by retyping the formula. If you see the CIRC message and cannot determine which cell is producing it, then you can use the Options Recalculation command to find out. The menu that the Options Recalculation command gives you shows the location of the circular reference. You can then pick Quit to leave the menu and edit the cell in question.

A somewhat similar problem is to refer to a block in your formula that is as yet unnamed. When this happens, you must stop typing the formula to name the block. This is especially annoying when the formula is complex and lengthy. You can avoid the problem by defining a named block as soon as you create it and by using the Choices key (F3) to select block names.

One trick to save the typing you have already done on a rejected formula is to press HOME when Quattro PRO places you in EDIT mode and then type an apostrophe. This will allow you to enter the formula as a label and then review it. When you edit the formula and are ready to re-enter it as a value, press HOME and then DELETE to remove the apostrophe before pressing ENTER.

Message	Problem/Solution
Formula too long	You exceeded the limit of 254 characters in a formula; break formula into several subformulas
Incomplete formula	You left something out; check for operators not followed by arguments
Invalid argument type	You have tried to use an argument that does not fit the @function you are using; check the syntax of the argument
Invalid cell or block address	You entered something that is being read as a nonexistent cell reference or block name; check that you have typed formula correctly and defined all block names used in the formula
Invalid character	You used a character that does not fit the syntax; check for trailing commas, other punctuation that is out of place
Missing arguments	You forgot to supply an argument where one is expected; check your entry
Missing operator	You forgot to separate values or functions with an operator; check your entry
Missing right parenthesis	You opened one more set of parentheses than you closed; check for missing right parenthesis or extra left parenthesis
Syntax error	You have made an error that does not fall into the other categories; check spelling of your entry and syntax requirements of the functions you are using
Too many arguments	You have supplied more arguments than the function can accept; check syntax and punctuation of what you entered
Unknown @ function	You used a function name that is not recognized; check spelling and try using Choice list

Table 4-2. *Common Entry Error Messages*

Functions Are Built-in Formulas

Quattro PRO provides you with the basic building blocks of complex formulas in the form of functions. These built-in formulas are specially coded commands that facilitate typical calculations. Using functions, you do not have to enter lengthy instructions.

Function Arguments

Some functions simply generate values by themselves. For example, @PI gives the value of PI. The date function @NOW tells you what your PC thinks the current date and time is. However, most functions require additional information, called arguments. For example, the principal, interest, and term required by the @PMT function are said to be the arguments of @PMT. Some functions require just one argument, like @SUM, which only needs to know what block of cells you want to sum. Others, such as @PMT, require several arguments.

The arguments required by functions can be broken down into three types: *numeric,* such as cells containing numbers, as in @PMT(E1,E2,E3); *block,* such as a block of cells being summed with @SUM(B1..B3), or a named block, such as @SUM(TOTAL SALES); and *string,* a label or piece of text entered into a cell, entered into a function in quotes, or produced by another function.

Some functions can accept more than one argument, in which case the arguments are separated by commas, as in @SUM(B1..B3,C1..C3,E1..E3). This function totals the first three rows of columns B, C, and E. Numeric functions can reference a mixture of cell coordinates and block names, as in @PMT(E1, INTEREST, TERM). Functions are often combined with operators and values in formulas, just like any other formula element.

Function Syntax

There are about a hundred functions and several ways of classifying them. In addition to the distinction between numeric and string functions, which closely follows that between values and labels, functions can be grouped by the type of work they apply to: financial, date, logical, and so on.

However, all Quattro PRO functions are always entered in the same basic format, using a standard arrangement of parts, or *syntax:*

■ Functions begin with the leading @ sign.

■ Next is the name of the function, typed in upper- or lowercase or a combination and spelled accurately.

■ The arguments, when required, follow the function name enclosed in parentheses.

■ With more than one argument, you must separate the arguments by commas; the arguments must be in proper order.

■ There should be no spaces between the @ and the function name. (There may be spaces between the components, the left parenthesis, the arguments, and the commas, but they are not required.)

A function combined with any arguments is a *function statement.* If you try to enter a function statement that contains an error—for example, an incorrectly spelled function name—Quattro PRO will beep and place the entry on the edit line. It will attempt to place the edit line cursor in the area of the mistake. This can be very helpful if you have omitted a comma between arguments or left a pair of parentheses unclosed. See Table 4-2 for a list of error messages.

The Functions Key

One way to prevent errors like misspelled function names is to use the Functions key (ALT-F3). Pressing ALT-F3 when you are in either VALUE mode or EDIT mode pops up a list of the functions, as shown in Figure 4-4. You can then browse through this list with the arrow keys, moving a page a time with PGUP or PGDN. When you see the function that you need, highlight it and press ENTER to place it onto the edit line. This avoids mistyping the name. Mouse users can use the scroll bar on the right side of the list to view the functions.

You can also look up a function by spelling part of the name. When the function list appears, press the Edit key (F2), and you will see the message

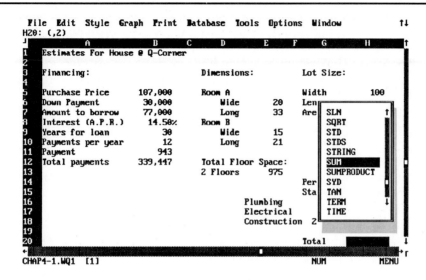

Figure 4-4.   *The function choices*

"Search for: *" appear in the status line at the bottom of the screen. Just start typing what you can remember of the name and the list box will move to the closest match. For example, if you type **P**, then you will be taken to the first function beginning with *P,* which is PAYMT. Type **M** and you will get to PMT. To back up a step press BACKSPACE and you will move back to PAYMT. Press ENTER to confirm you selection.

Mastering Functions

It would be hard to memorize Quattro PRO's more than 90 functions. By using a few simple techniques, however, you can make full use of them.

First, you should *always assume there is an appropriate function.* Chances are that the calculation you want to perform is one that many other spreadsheet users need to perform, so it is probably provided by Quattro PRO.

Sometimes you may need to combine several functions in one formula to do the job. Occasionally, you will need to use an intermediate cell to produce part of the answer before completing the calculation in another cell. Remember that columns can be hidden from the display and printed reports so that extra columns for calculations need not affect the way the worksheet looks.

It is a good idea to use the Functions key (ALT-F3) to look up and enter functions. The Functions key not only prevents typos but also reminds you of the wide range of functions that can be used. You may realize that there is a quicker way to solve your formula. When you are constructing formulas containing block names, use the Choices list (F3) to make sure you use correctly defined block names.

You will also want to save particularly useful function statements. When you come up with a good formula that you are likely to use often, you might consider saving the worksheet under a different name to keep a copy of the formula for reference. Chapter 13 discusses how to save portions of a spreadsheet to separate files and how to combine several files into one. This technique allows you to build a library of useful functions. You can also print useful formulas by highlighting the appropriate cell and pressing the PRTSC key. This will print the information from the whole screen, including the cell identifier.

If you follow these guidelines and are prepared to spend some time experimenting with and reading about functions, you will find that they offer tremendous power. A complete examination of each function is beyond the scope of this book. With three pages per function, this chapter alone would grow to 300 pages. What you will find in the rest of this chapter is a series of discussions on different sets of functions grouped according to their practical roles. Examples are given in most cases together with references to other parts of the book where the functions are used. You will find the functions indexed at the back of the book and listed on the Quattro PRO command card.

Aggregate Functions

Aggregate functions perform some of the most commonly used calculations in spreadsheet work. In addition to @SUM, which was used in Chapter 2, this group includes functions that aggregate a block of cells, count the contents and average the block, find the largest and smallest numbers in the block, and determine degree of variance. These functions also work with several different blocks at once or with numerous individual cells.

Sum

The @SUM function is one of the most frequently used functions. In Figure 4-5, @SUM is used to add the values in a block of cells—the earnings of a group of commodity brokers. You can use @SUM to total columns, rows, and blocks including columns and rows. All that @SUM needs to know is the coordinates of the block to be summed. Its syntax is

@SUM(Block)

The block does not need to have values in every cell; the empty cells will be ignored. The @SUM function works well with block names. For example,

```
  File  Edit  Style  Graph  Print  Database  Tools  Options  Window          ↑↓
[Enter] [Esc] @SUM(G4..G14)
J      A         B          C       D      E       F      G        H        ↑
1          Broker Performance
2
3                  First Last     Base    Fees   Deals Earnings  Region
4                  Harry Smith    20.00   34.00   61    54.00 South
5                   Ben Gore      25.00   45.00   81    70.00 East
6                 Roger Sloan     25.00   54.00   97    79.00 North
7                  Earl James     20.00   23.00   41    43.00 West
8                  Joan Quest     25.00   46.00   83    71.00 South
9                  Bill Noles     25.00   54.00   97    79.00 South
10                 Pete Reese     25.00   43.00   77    68.00 West     □
11                 Tracy Wentz    25.00   45.00   81    70.00 South
12                 Karin Weir     25.00   46.00   83    71.00 South
13                 Hilda Rolf     25.00   75.00  135   100.00 West
14                 Quincy Erie    20.00   35.00   63    55.00 South
15
16          Total Earnings @SUM(EARNINGS)
17             Most Deals @MAX(DEALS)
18           Average Fees @AVG(FEES)
19         Lowest Earnings @MIN(EARNINGS)
20                                                                       ↓
C16: (T) [W15] @SUM(EARNINGS)                                         EDIT
```

Figure 4-5. *@SUM function*

@SUM(TOTAL) will give the total of values in the block of cells named TOTAL. In Figure 4-6 you can see an expense report where this feature is used to arrive at the total expenses for one week. The block named TOTAL is cells B5 through F15. You can sum several different blocks at once if you separate them by a comma, as in @SUM(TA,TD), which would sum two blocks, one named TA, the other TD.

There are several advantage to using @SUM to add up cells, rather than a "cell+cell+cell" formula. Rows or columns entered within a summed block are automatically included in the block. For example, consider these two approaches to adding up values.

B2:	100		B2:	100
B3:	200	or	B3:	200
B4:	300		B4:	300
B5:	============		B5:	==========
B6:	@SUM(B2..B4)		B6:	+B2+B3+B4

File Edit Style Graph Print Database Tools Options Window   ↑↓
D19: @SUM(TOTAL)

	A	B	C	D	E	F	G
1							
2		Monday	Tuesday	Wednesday	Thursday	Friday	Totals
3							
4	Meals						
5	B'fast	3.45	0.00	3.89	4.76	5.98	18.08
6	Lunch	5.00	8.95	6.74	5.78	18.96	45.43
7	Dinner	0.00	23.87	5.89	13.45	0.00	43.21
8	Travel						
9	Air	0.00	143.89	0.00	0.00	148.00	291.89
10	Mileage	0.00	0.00	0.00	0.00	3.50	3.50
11	Parking	0.00	0.00	12.00	12.00	12.00	36.00
12	Taxi	8.00	0.00	0.00	0.00	0.00	8.00
13	Miscellaneous						
14	Supplies	34.00	0.00	6.00	0.00	3.00	43.00
15	Other	0.00	0.00	0.00	23.87	0.00	23.87
16	===						
17		50.45	176.71	34.52	59.86	191.44	512.98
18							
19			Total =	512.98			
20							

SS09.WK2   [3]   NUM   READY

Figure 4-6. *The sum in the expense report*

In the example on the left it will not matter if you need to insert an extra row into the spreadsheet to include another value in the calculation. For example, if you place the cell selector on row 4 and issue the Edit Insert Row command to include one more row, cells B4, B5, and B6 become cells B5, B6, and B7. The formula that was in B6 but is now in B7, becomes @SUM(B2..B5). If you enter a new value in B4 it will be included in the @SUM calculation.

The same is not true if you have used the cell+cell method of adding. Here you can see the results for both of the examples above, after a row and a new value of 250 was inserted at B4:

B2:	100		B2:	100	
B3:	200		B3:	200	
B4:	250	or	B4:	250	
B5:	300		B5:	300	
B6:	===========		B6:	=========	
B7:	@SUM(B2..B5)		B7:	+B2+B3+B5	

Inserting new rows within the summed range increases the range to include the new cells. Individually referenced cells are not automatically added to + formulas.

The integrity of the @SUM formula is preserved if you insert a row at B2, because the whole set of numbers is moved down. However, because Quattro PRO inserts new rows above the current cell, the new B2 would not be included in the @SUM formula. If you were to enter a value into B2 at that point it would not be included in the sum. If you insert a row into the original example at B5, then the accuracy of the formula is preserved, but again, the new cell is not included. As a rule then, you add a cell to a summed column if you insert the row while selecting the second cell of the block, or the last cell, or any cell in between.

Since it is quite natural to add numbers to the bottom of a list, you might want to include the row below the last number when you create an @SUM formula. For instance, you could include cell B6 in the @SUM argument in the last example. Then you could place the cell selector on row 6 below the last number, insert a new row, and have that row be included in the summed block. When Quattro PRO finished calculating, the labels in the block would have a value of 0, and thus would not affect the answer.

Sum Product

A function that is new with Quattro PRO is @SUMPRODUCT. This function is used to sum up the results of multiplication between blocks of cells. For example, here you have two sets of numbers in two columns and you want to know what you get if the pairs of numbers that are on the same row are multiplied together, and the results added up:

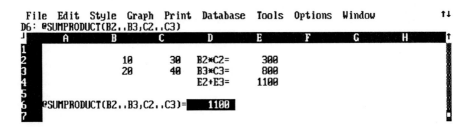

When you multiply 10 by 30 you get 300. When you multiply 20 by 40 you get 800. Add together 300 and 800 and you get 1100, which is the answer returned by @SUMPRODUCT. For its arguments the @SUMPRODUCT function requires two blocks of equal size, separated by a comma. This function does not work if any of the cells in the blocks are empty. As you can see from Figure 4-7, the blocks can be either columns or rows, as long as their dimensions are equal.

Count

The @COUNT function counts the number of items or nonempty cells in a block of cells. This function is useful for such projects as inventory tracking, since @COUNT can tell you how many entries there are in a column, and thus how many inventory items there are in a list. You simply need to tell the function the location of the cells to be counted. The syntax is

@COUNT*(Block)*

Note that Quattro PRO includes labels when calculating @COUNT. Thus the count for a summed range that includes a line of labels might be greater

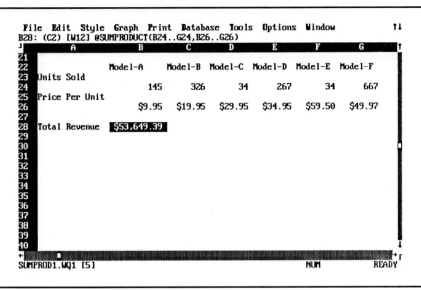

Figure 4-7. *@SUMPRODUCT function*

than you expect. For example, the following arrangement results in an answer of 6 when summed, an answer of 4 when counted.

B1:	2	B1:	2
B2:	2	B2:	2
B3:	2	B3:	2
B4:	===========	B4:	==============
B5:	@SUM(B1..B4)	B5:	@COUNT(B1..B4)

Only if cell B4 was empty would the count be 3.

Average

@AVG is used to give the average of values in a block of cells. You can see the usefulness of this function in Figure 4-5, where it was used to calculate the average of fees earned by brokers. The function is simply

@AVG(Block)

Like @SUM, the @AVG function works well with columns, rows, and larger blocks, particularly if you use a block name. However, label cells are used in calculating the average. Essentially, the @AVG function combines @SUM with @COUNT. you could say that @AVG=@SUM /@COUNT. Since @COUNT gives a value of 1 to a label, the arrangement seen here would produce 6 when summed, but 1.5 when averaged.

B1:	2		B1:	2
B2:	2		B2:	2
B3:	2		B3:	2
B4:	======		B4:	======
B5:	@SUM(B1..B4)		B5:	@AVG(B1..B4)

Only if cell B4 were empty would the average of the values, 2, be correctly determined by @AVG.

Maximum

Shown earlier in Figure 4-5, this function will find the largest value in a specified block:

@MAX(Block)

Like the @SUM function, @MAX works well with block names. In Figure 4-5, for example, the block name DEALS was used for the cells in column F. The @MAX function is useful when evaluating projections, since it can tell you the largest number that results from a change in assumptions.

You can also use @MAX with single cells if you separate them with commas. Thus @MAX(B5,G3,K7) will tell you the largest amount in those three cells. This is handy when you want to perform a tax-form calculation and need to enter the larger of the numbers on two rows. You can also use @MAX to compare a cell to a number. Thus @MAX(G5,10) will return the value in G5 if it is greater than 10; otherwise, you will get the value 10. This is also useful for tax calculations, when a subtraction results in a negative number but you must enter 0 instead of the negative number. The formula @MAX(G5,0) will return either the value in G5 or 0, whichever is greater. If G5 is negative the result is 0.

Minimum

Corollary to the @MAX function, the @MIN function returns the smallest value in a block of cells:

@MIN(Block)

This function can be used to identify low levels in projections and inventory lists. You can also use @MIN and @MAX to determine the highest and lowest balances for a customer's credit or checking account.

Standard Deviation

This function returns the standard deviation for a given block of cells that represent a population of data.

@STD(Block)

The standard deviation of a set of values is a measure of how much variation there is from the average of the values. The standard deviation is the square root of the variance. If you want to compute sample standard deviation, use the @STDS function, but be aware that this function is unique to Quattro PRO and is not compatible with earlier programs. For a description of how this function is handled when it is saved in formats other than WQ1, see Appendix B.

Variance

The @VAR function returns a measure of variance for a block of cells, that is, the amount of variation between individual values and the mean of the population.

@VAR(Block)

The result of the @VAR function is the square of the standard deviation of the same set of values. To calculate variance for a sample rather than a population, use @VARS, but bear in mind that this function is unique to

Quattro PRO and is not compatible with earlier programs. For a description of how functions like this are handled during a file save, see Appendix B.

Arithmetic Functions

These functions affect the way numbers are calculated. They are often used when the outcome of a formula needs to be modified; for example, the outcome should be rounded, or a negative number should be turned into a positive number.

Absolute

To arrive at the absolute value of a number, you use the @ABS function. The syntax is

@ABS(Value)

For example, the formula @ABS(B5) returns the absolute value of the contents of B5. The absolute value of a number is its positive equivalent, so if B5 is −1.5, @ABS(B5) equals 1.5.

Integer

At times you need to drop the decimal places from a number, rather than round them up or down. This can be done with the integer function.

@INT(Value)

Thus, the formula @INT(B5) equals 2, when B5 contains 2.75. The value is stripped of digits following the decimal place, rather than rounded up to 3.

Modulus

You use the modulus function when you need the number that is left after two other numbers are divided. This returns the remainder of X divided by Y, as in

@MOD(X,Y)

Thus, the formula @MOD(B5,5) equals 1 when B5 contains the value 36. This function is very useful when you need to figure shipping factors. You could use, for example,

@MOD(Cases In Order,Cases Per Truck)

to determine how many cases will be left after a large order has been put on the trucks. Note that using zero as the value for Y is not valid since you cannot divide by zero. Doing so produces an ERR message in the formula cell.

Random

When you need a random number in a cell you can use @RAND. This function takes no argument:

@RAND

@RAND produces a uniformly distributed random number greater than or equal to 0 and less than 1. You normally want to combine it with a formula to produce a random number within a certain range. You do this by putting the high end of the range and the low end, separated by a minus sign, in a pair of parentheses and then multiplying that by the @RAND function added to the low-end number. Thus, a random number from 3 to 12 would be produced by

(12-3)*@RAND+3

If you need to get a whole number from the @RAND function, you will need to use @INT or @ROUND.

Although random numbers might not seem to be very useful in a program that is designed to help you organize and accurately analyze information, they can be useful when you want to fill cells with numbers to test a spreadsheet design. Several of the models in this book were created from random numbers.

The @RAND function returns a new random number every time the worksheet recalculates. This can cause problems if you are trying to use the function to create values used elsewhere in the worksheet. Data generated by @RAND can be fixed by using the Edit Values command to change the formula to a value. This allows you to hide the fact that the numbers you have created with @RAND are just random numbers.

Round

For some records, you may need to have the numbers displayed and printed to be rounded. Quattro PRO retains up to 15 decimal places in calculations that result in fractions. When you use a display format that sets the number of decimal places to less than 1, these fractions are not displayed but are still active. This produces a visual problem when numbers containing fractions are summed but formatted for a small fixed number of decimal places. As the fractions accumulate, the total appears incorrect. Thus, if the numbers here in column B were the result of calculations, and they were shown in Fixed format with 0 decimal places in column C, the total would look wrong:

B		C	
B1	3.33	C1	3
B2	3.33	C2	3
B3	3.33	C3	3
Total	10	Total	10

To solve this problem, the numbers being totaled need to be rounded with @ROUND. The format of the function is as follows:

@ROUND(X,Y)

The function rounds off the value of X using Y as the number of digits to round to. The value of Y should be between −15 and +15 and should be an integer (whole number). Quattro PRO will round X to an integer. The effect on the preceding example is shown here:

```
B1 @ROUND(3.33,0) =        3
B2 @ROUND(3.33,0) =        3
B3 @ROUND(3.33,0) =        3
Total                      9
```

You can combine @ROUND with @RAND to produce a whole number within a specified range, as in the following formula:

@ROUND(((48-18)*@RAND+18),0)

This produces a number from 18 to 48 with no decimal places.

Exponent

The exponent function returns the value of *e* (a constant, approximately 2.7182818) raised to the power of X, as in

@EXP(X)

where X is a numeric value less than or equal to 709. Thus, if X is 2, then *e* will be squared. This function is the inverse of a natural logarithm, @LN. If the value of X is greater than 709.85, then the @EXP function returns ERR.

Square Root

You can find the square root of a number or formula in Quattro PRO with the @SQRT function. This function uses the syntax

@SQRT(Value)

For example, @SQRT(B5) returns the square root of the value in B5. Square roots of negative numbers produce the response ERR. Use the negation operator or the @ABS function to make the value a positive number.

One typical application of @SQRT is in the calculation of the hypotenuse, or slope, of a triangle. For example:

@SQRT(Base*Base+Height*Height)

Log and Log Base

The @LN(X) and @LOG(X) functions return the log base *e* of X and the log base 10 of X, respectively. Thus, @LN(100) equals 4.60517 and @LOG(100) equals 2. If the value of X is less than or equal to 0, these functions return the ERR message in the cell in which they were applied.

Database Functions

When you want to find the total of a column, you normally use the aggregate function @SUM. Likewise, to calculate the average of a column of numbers, you use the @AVG function. If you want to sum selected records, however, such as the fees for all brokers in the south, you would turn to the database functions shown in Figure 4-8. In the lower half of the figure you can see the seven database functions typed out in formulas. To the right are the answers that those formulas produce. In the upper half of the screen are some of the records referred to in the formulas as well as a small Criteria Table. The database functions use several of the concepts discussed in Chapter 3 such as Query Block and Criteria.

The basic operation of a database function is to tell Quattro PRO which block of cells are involved, which column of the block you want the function applied to, and which records to include based on the Criteria Table. For example, in Figure 4-8 @DAVG averages only the records for column 4 (Earnings) specified by the Criteria Table, in this case where Region = South. All database functions have the same syntax. In the case of @DAVG it is

@DAVG(Block,Column,Criteria)

The Block is the cell block containing the database, the rectangular group of consecutive rows and named columns that constitute a database, including the field names at the top. The Column is the number of the column containing the field you want to average, with the first column as 0, the second as 1, and so on. Criteria is a cell block containing search criteria.

The @DAVG function averages selected field entries in a database. It includes only those entries in the column number specified whose records

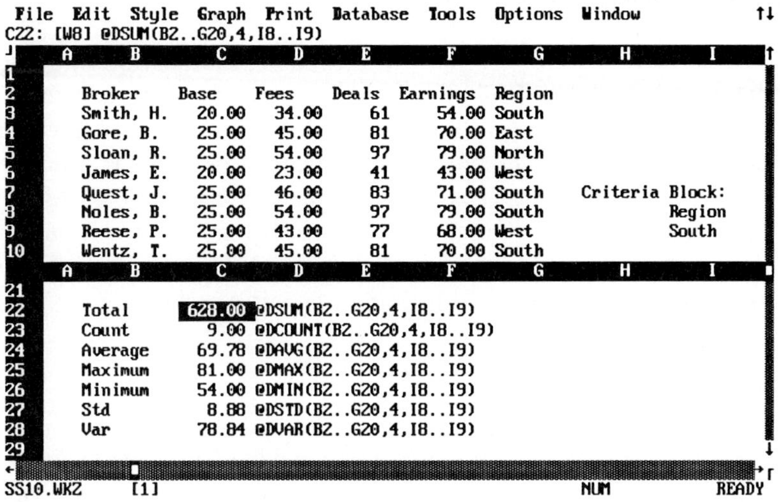

File Edit Style Graph Print Database Tools Options Window   ↑↓
C22: [W8] @DSUM(B2..G20,4,I8..I9)

	A	B	C	D	E	F	G	H	I
1									
2		Broker	Base	Fees	Deals	Earnings	Region		
3		Smith, H.	20.00	34.00	61	54.00	South		
4		Gore, B.	25.00	45.00	81	70.00	East		
5		Sloan, R.	25.00	54.00	97	79.00	North		
6		James, E.	20.00	23.00	41	43.00	West		
7		Quest, J.	25.00	46.00	83	71.00	South	Criteria Block:	
8		Noles, B.	25.00	54.00	97	79.00	South		Region
9		Reese, P.	25.00	43.00	77	68.00	West		South
10		Wentz, T.	25.00	45.00	81	70.00	South		

	A	B	C	D	E	F	G	H	I
21									
22		Total	628.00	@DSUM(B2..G20,4,I8..I9)					
23		Count	9.00	@DCOUNT(B2..G20,4,I8..I9)					
24		Average	69.78	@DAVG(B2..G20,4,I8..I9)					
25		Maximum	81.00	@DMAX(B2..G20,4,I8..I9)					
26		Minimum	54.00	@DMIN(B2..G20,4,I8..I9)					
27		Std	8.88	@DSTD(B2..G20,4,I8..I9)					
28		Var	78.84	@DVAR(B2..G20,4,I8..I9)					
29									

SS10.WK2   [1]   NUM   READY

Figure 4-8. *Database formula example*

meet the chosen criteria. Criteria refers to the coordinates of a block containing a Criteria Table that specifies search information, as in I8..I9. This is the Criteria Table for all the formulas in the lower half of Figure 4-8, which analyze the earnings for all brokers in the South region. (Criteria Tables were described in detail in Chapter 3.) The field specified in the criteria and the field being averaged need not be the same; you can average earnings for all brokers in the South Region, or average fees for all brokers earning over 45. The field averaged is that contained within the column you specify with the column number. You can specify all or part of a database as the block, but field names must be included for each field you include in the block. All of the other database functions use the same three arguments: Block, Column, and Criteria.

Maximum Value

The @DMAX function finds the maximum value of selected field entries in a database. It includes only those entries in the specified column whose records meet the criteria in the Criteria Table.

@DMAX(Block,Column,Criteria)

@DMAX is a very useful function when you are analyzing a large group of numbers, such as the broker earnings reports for each of four regions. Instead of sorting through the records and manually choosing which ones to compare to find the largest earnings number for brokers in one region, the @DMAX function does that for you. You might also find @DMAX useful for determining the largest figure in the earnings column for all brokers who had earnings greater than a certain level. This would give you some basis with which to compare the higher-earning brokers.

Minimum Value

@DMIN finds the minimum value of selected field entries in a database. It includes only those entries in the specified column whose records meet the criteria in a Criteria Table. Its syntax is

@DMIN(Block,Column,Criteria)

You can use this function for such applications as inventory tracking. If one column in your inventory database is called Quantity On Hand and another is called Required Delivery Time, you can have @DMIN show the smallest current quantity on hand for all inventory items that need less than ten days' delivery time. By watching this number as inventory is added or deleted from the database, you will know when ordering is required.

Standard Deviation Measure

The @DSTD function finds the standard deviation value of selected field entries in a database. It includes only those entries in the specified column whose records meet the criteria in a Criteria Table. Its syntax is

@DSTD(Block,Column,Criteria)

If you want to compute sample standard deviation, use the @DSTDS function, but be aware that this function is unique to Quattro PRO and is not compatible with earlier programs. For a description of how this function is handled during a file save, see Chapter 7.

Sum Value

The @DSUM function totals selected field entries in a database. It includes only those entries in the specified column whose records meet the criteria in the Criteria Table. Its syntax is

@DSUM(Block,Column,Criteria)

This function will quickly return you such useful answers as the total earnings paid to brokers in one region.

Variance Measure

The @DVAR function calculates variance for selected field entries in a database. It includes only those entries in the column specified whose records meet the criteria in the Criteria Table. Its syntax is

@DVAR(Block,Column,Criteria)

To calculate variance for a sample rather than a population, use @DVARS, but bear in mind that this function is unique to Quattro PRO and is not compatible with earlier programs. For a description of how this function is handled during a file save, see Chapter 7.

Financial Functions

The functions provided for financial calculations in Quattro PRO are extensive. You can calculate annuities, mortgage payments, present values, and numerous other figures that would otherwise require a lengthy formula to be composed. There are some basic terms and conditions common to all Quattro PRO financial functions. Table 4-3 lists the argu-

Argument	Definition
Rate	Interest rate, per period as defined in Nper, should be greater than −1
Nper	Number of periods—for example, 12 months or 1 year; an integer greater than 0
Pv	Present value; an amount valued today
Pmt	A payment; a negative cash flow amount
Fv	Future value; an amount to be accumulated
Type	Either 0 or 1. Type indicates the difference between ordinary annuity (0) and annuity due (1). Argument of 0 means payments made are at the end of each period; 1 means they are made at the beginning. The default assumption is that type = 0

Table 4-3. *Financial Function Arguments*

ments that Quattro PRO financial functions require and the abbreviations used for them. These abbreviations are used in the following descriptions.

Quattro PRO stipulates that when interest rates are required in financial function arguments, they must be stated as a percentage per period. For example, when figuring monthly loan payments with the @PMT or @PAYMT functions, the interest argument must be stated as percentage per month.

A connoisseur of spreadsheet programs might describe the financial functions in Quattro PRO as a subtle blend of the best from 1-2-3 and Excel. While retaining "backward" compatibility with 1-2-3 Release 2 and Quattro 1.0, Quattro PRO allows more sophisticated financial calculations, using optional arguments for the timing of payments. In Table 4-4 you can see the older functions and the improved alternatives. Unless you are creating worksheets that need to be compatible with older programs you will probably want to employ the new Quattro PRO functions.

Old Style Functions	New Style Functions
@CTERM(Rate,Fv,Pv)	@NPER(Rate,0,-Pv,Fv,0)
@FV(Pmt,Rate,Nper)	@FVAL(Rate,Nper,-Pmt,0,0)
@PMT(Pv,Rate,Nper)	@PAYMT(Rate,Nper,-Pv,0,0)
@PV(Pv,Rate,Nper)	@PVAL(Rate,Nper,-Pmt,0,0)
@RATE(Fv,Pv,Nper)	@IRATE(Nper,0,-Pv,Fv,0)
@TERM(Pv,Rate,Fv)	@NPER(Rate,-Pmt,0,Fv,0)

*Note that negative arguments indicate cash flows assumed to be negative.

Table 4-4. *Older Functions and New Alternatives**

Payment Functions

There are several financial functions that relate to loan payments. They are @PMT, @PAYMT, @IPAYMT, and @PPAYMT. They will be considered as a group since they serve as a good example of the power and flexibility provided by Quattro PRO's financial functions. For example, the @PAYMT function can be used to perform several different calculations, depending upon the number of arguments provided.

@PMT   As you saw in Chapter 1, the @PMT function calculates the amount required to pay back a loan in equal payments based on a given principal or amount borrowed, a rate of interest, and a loan term. The format of the function is

@PMT(Pv,Rate,Nper)

Present value (Pv) is the principal, the amount being borrowed. The Rate is the interest being charged and number of payments (Nper) is the life of the loan. The values for Pv, Rate, and Nper can be numeric constants, numeric fields, or formulas that result in a number. Note that Rate must be greater than −1 and Nper cannot be zero.

Figure 4-9 shows a loan calculation worksheet, which demonstrates the argument requirements of the @PMT function. Since the rate is requested in percentage per period but is normally quoted as an annual percentage rate, the loan payment formula divides the contents of cell M4 by 12. Likewise, the term of the loan (Nper) is stated in years in M3 for convenience and then multiplied by the payments per year (12) in the formula. This value could be adjusted for quarterly (4), semiannual (2), or annual (1) payments.

@PAYMT   A more sophisticated function for calculating loan payments and other values is @PAYMT. In its simplest form, the @PAYMT function works like @PMT to return the size of payment required to amortize a loan across a given number of periods, assuming equal payments at a constant rate of interest. However, the first difference between the two functions is apparent in the order and number of arguments they use. The format of the @PAYMT function is

@PAYMT(Rate,Nper,Pv,Fv,Type)

```
 File  Edit  Style  Graph  Print  Database  Tools  Options  Window          ↑↓
 M5: (,2) @ROUND(@PMT(M2,M4/12,M3*12),2)
J    I        J          K          L          M           N              ↑
1
2           Principal                         15,000.00                  ■
3           Term, in years                         5.00
4           Interest rate (%A.P.R)               8.80%
5           Monthly payment                      309.92
6           Total of payments                 18,595.20
7           Total interest paid                3,595.20
8
9
10   PMT    Paid in      Paid in    Cumulative  Remaining
11    #     Interest     Prinicipal  Interest   Balance
12
13     1  +M2*$M$4/12  +$M$5-J13   +J13        +M2-K13
14     2  +M13*$M$4/12 +$M$5-J14   +L13+J14    +M13-K14
15     3  +M14*$M$4/12 +$M$5-J15   +L14+J15    +M14-K15
16     4  +M15*$M$4/12 +$M$5-J16   +L15+J16    +M15-K16
17     5      104.07      205.85     535.23    13,985.63
18     6      102.56      207.36     637.79    13,778.27
19     7      101.04      208.88     738.83    13,569.39
20     8       99.51      210.41     838.34    13,358.98            ↓
 CHAP4PMT.WQ1 [5]                                     NUM        READY
```

Figure 4-9.   *Loan calculation worksheet*

The function's purpose can be defined as determination of the fully amortized mortgage payment for borrowing present value amount at rate percent of interest per period over a specified number of periods.

You can use a numeric constant, a numeric field, or a formula that results in a number for the principal (Pv), Rate, and term (Nper) arguments. Note that the interest rate must be greater than –1 and that the term cannot equal 0. The last two arguments, future value (Fv) and Type, are optional and are discussed in a moment. Figure 4-10 shows an example of the @PAYMT function being used to calculate the payment required to repay $26,000 over 36 months when borrowed at 12.00% A.P.R. Here you can see the second major difference between @PMT and @PAYMT; the latter produces a negative value. The reason for this is the financial assumption that a payment is a negative item from a cash flow point of view.

In the example in Figure 4-10 column B is used to identify the figures in column C. Note that the interest rate is stated as 12% in cell C11, meaning 12.00% per year. It is then divided by 12 when used as the rate argument in the @PAYMT function statement in cell C14. This is to comply with the Quattro PRO requirement that the rate argument be stated as

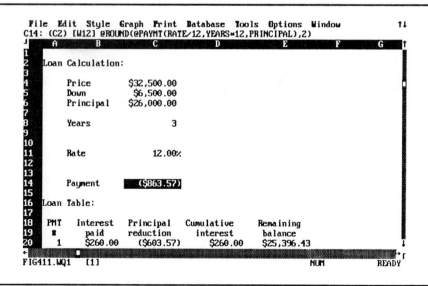

Figure 4-10.   *@PAYMT for loan calculation*

interest per period. You could use an expanded model like the one in Figure 4-11 to make this calculation even more explicit.

Future Value and @PAYMT   The optional future value argument in a @PAYMT function statement is used when you apply the @PAYMT function to the task of calculating the size of payments you need to make each month to accumulate a specific sum of money in the future. For example, suppose you want to accumulate $26,000 to purchase a new car. You are going to put away an amount of money every month for two years. That money will earn 8.00% interest. How large does the monthly payment have to be? You can see the answer calculated in Figure 4-12.

In this example, the argument cells in column C have been named according to the labels in column B, using the Edit Names Create Labels command (described in Chapter 11). Note that when you use the future value argument you cannot just omit the present value argument. A zero is commonly used as a place-holder for the present value argument, as in

@PAYMT(Rate/12,Nper,0,Fv,Type)

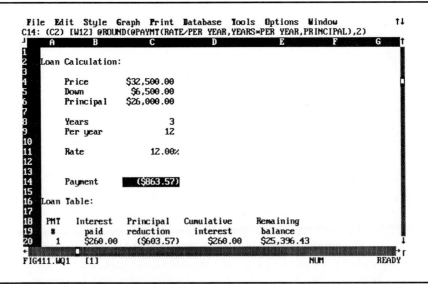

Figure 4-11.   *Expanded loan model*

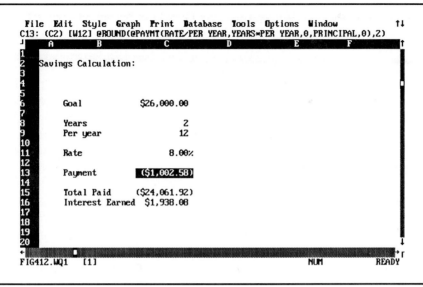

Figure 4-12. *Savings plan with type argument of 0*

You might also note in Figure 4-12 the calculation of principal paid into the account and the amount of interest earned. These calculations are not automatically carried out by Quattro PRO but provide a useful perspective on the @PAYMT function. Economists might note that a $26,000 car loan at 12.00% for two years costs approximately $1224 per month while a two-year savings plan at 8.00% to obtain the same amount costs $996. However, the borrower gets the use of the car for two years and possibly a tax deduction as well, while the saver gets a tax bill and will probably need more than $26,000 to buy the same car at the end of the plan.

The Type Argument   In Figure 4-12 you can see the other optional argument for the @PAYMT function: Type. Quattro PRO can calculate interest based on two types of repayment arrangement. The program assumes, as do many consumer loans, that the payment is due at the end of the loan period. In other words, the first payment is due one month from when you receive the principal of the loan, and at the end of each one-month period after that. This assumption is type 0. If you omit a type argument, Quattro PRO will assume type 0. The alternative type, based on having the payment due at the beginning of each loan period, is type 1. You can force this assumption by including 1 as the type argument, as shown in the revised loan payment plan in Figure 4-13. You can see that the amount of each payment is less under a type 1 loan. Of course, the practical effect of going to a type 1 loan is to reduce the term of the loan by one period and pay the first payment from the proceeds of the loan, a practice once followed by some banks.

In Figure 4-14 you can see the effect of going to type 1 on a future value savings plan calculation. Here the effect is positive since it assumes that you begin the savings plan by making the first deposit. In Figure 4-12 the assumption was that the payment on the plan was at the end of the period, thus requiring larger payments to achieve the same goal. You can see that the type argument is likely to be 0 for such calculations as loans, but 1 for such items as annuities and savings plans.

Loan Tables You may want to see a table of payments for a mortage loan, showing the split between interest and principal and the amount of principal left unpaid. A table of payments can be laid out below the mortgage calculations, as shown in Figure 4-15. Notice the formula for the

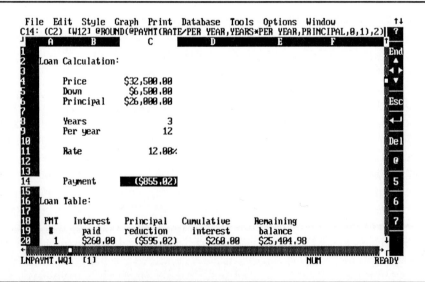

Figure 4-13. *Loan plan with type argument of 1*

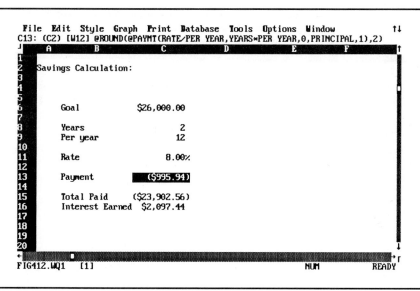

Figure 4-14. *Savings plan with type argument of 1*

payment in E7. The term of the loan is stated in years in cell E5 and then multiplied by 12 to produce monthly payments in E7. Also note that the @ROUND function is used to round the payment to the nearest cent (two decimal places). This is necessary when you are performing real-world loan calculations rather than just estimates.

The loan payment table consists of five columns, starting with the payment number, which runs from 1 to 300. The Window Options Locked Titles command has been used to show the bottom of the table as well as the top. (This command is described in the next chapter.) Column B calculates the amount of each payment that is interest, while column C shows the amount paid to reduce the principal. In column C a running total of interest is maintained while the declining principal is tracked in column E. You can see the formulas that make up this table in Figure 4-16. Notice the use of the @IF function in columns B, C, and D. (The @IF function is discussed in detail in the next chapter.) The @MAX function is used in column E to produce a zero value when the loan is completely amortized.

The total figures in E8 and E9 show the total interest and principal payments respectively. You might notice that the total principal reduction

File Edit Style Graph Print Database Tools Options Window   ↑↓
E7: (,2) [W12] @ROUND(@PMT(E4,E6/12,E5*12),2)

	A	B	C	D	E	F
1						
2		Mortgage Table				
3						
4		Principal.........................			80,000.00	
5		Term, in years....................			25	
6		Interest rate (%A.P.R)............			11.50%	
7		Monthly payment...................			**813.18**	
8		Total of payments.................			243,954.00	
9		Total interest paid...............			163,954.00	
10						
11		PMT	Paid in	Paid in	Cumulative	Remaining
12		#	Interest	Prinicipal	Interest	Balance
13		1	766.67	46.51	766.67	79,953.49
14		2	766.22	46.96	1,532.89	79,906.53
15		3	765.77	47.41	2,298.66	79,859.12

	A	B	C	D	E	F
309	297	30.36	782.82	163,899.91	2,385.45	
310	298	22.86	790.32	163,922.77	1,595.13	
311	299	15.29	797.89	163,938.06	797.24	
312	300	7.64	805.54	163,945.70	0.00	

CHAP417.WQ1 [6]   NUM   READY

Figure 4-15.   *Mortgage table*

File Edit Style Graph Print Database Tools Options Window   ↑↓
E7: (,2) [W16] @ROUND(@PMT(E4,E6/12,E5*12),2)

	A	B	C	D	E
1					
2	Mortgage Table				
3					
4	Principal............................				80,000.00
5	Term, in years.......................				25
6	Interest rate (%A.P.R)...............				11.50%
7	Monthly payment......................				**813.18**
8	Total of payments....................				243,954.00
9	Total interest paid..................				163,954.00
10					
11	PMT	Paid in	Paid in	Cumulative	Remaining
12	#	Interest	Prinicipal	Interest	Balance
13	1	@IF(A13>$E$5*12,0,E4*$E$6/12)	+$E$7-B13	+B13	+E4-C13
14	2	@IF(A14>$E$5*12,0,E13*$E$6/12)	+$E$7-B14	+D13+B14	@MAX(E13-C14,0)

	A	B	C	D	E
16	4	@IF(A16>$E$5*12,0,E15*$E$6/12)	+$E$7-B16	+D15+B16	@MAX(E15-C16,0)
17	5	@IF(A17>$E$5*12,0,E16*$E$6/12)	+$E$7-B17	+D16+B17	@MAX(E16-C17,0)
18	6	@IF(A18>$E$5*12,0,E17*$E$6/12)	+$E$7-B18	+D17+B18	@MAX(E17-C18,0)
19	7	@IF(A19>$E$5*12,0,E18*$E$6/12)	+$E$7-B19	+D18+B19	@MAX(E18-C19,0)
20	8	@IF(A20>$E$5*12,0,E19*$E$6/12)	+$E$7-B20	+D19+B20	@MAX(E19-C20,0) ↓

CHAP417.WQ1 [6]   NUM   READY

Figure 4-16.   *Mortgage table formulas*

is actually $5.17 more than the amount of the loan. This is a result of the need to accept payments in dollars and whole cents. As any banker knows, there are several ways of dealing with this kind of minor imbalance in a loan amortization. (You might want to experiment with these using Quattro PRO; for example, the actual payment required to retire the sample loan in exactly 300 payments is 1560.905236.)

The formulas used in the model in Figure 4-16 are not the only way to generate a loan table. One unusual feature of the model shown in Figures 4-15 and 4-16 is the use of string formulas to create the ellipses in the labels in the top part of the model. String formulas like this are discussed in Chapter 8.

Finally, it should be noted that the method of calculating the remaining balance on the loan shown in Figure 4-15 is simple interest, the method commonly used by banks for mortgages and personal loans. Some lending institutions use the rule of 78 to determine the amount left unpaid. This method uses a system like sum-of-the-years, shown later in the discussion of the @SYD function, to determine interest.

@IPAYMT and @PPAYMT   There may be times when you want to figure out how much of a loan payment is going toward interest and how much toward principal. Quattro PRO has functions for both of these calculations. The interest portion of a payment is calculated with @IPAYMT while the principal portion is calculated with @PPAYMT. Of course, if you already know the size of the payment already you can easily calculate these amounts from a loan table, or you can take the result of @IPAYMT away from the amount of the payment to get the result of @PPAYMT. However, both @IPAYMT and @PPAYMT can be used without first figuring the payment amount. They return the portion of the total payment for a specific payment, for example, for the thirtieth payment of thirty-six. The form of both functions is the same:

@IPAYMT(Rate,Period,Nper,Pv,Fv,Type)

and

@PPAYMT(Rate,Period,Nper,Pv,Fv,Type)

where Rate is the interest rate, Period is the period of the loan you are calculating interest for, Nper is the total number of periods in the loan, and Pv is the principal of the loan. Quattro PRO will assume the Fv argument to be zero if not supplied, and that the Type is zero unless otherwise specified. The Fv argument is used when calculating an accumulated future amount.

To apply the @IPAYMT argument to the loan in Figure 4-16 and get the interest portion of the 297th payment you would use the formula:

@IPAYMT(E6/12,297,E5*12,E4)

The result would be −45.9621, which is a few cents different from the result in the loan table, due to the rounding of the payment in the table. Despite this minor discrepancy, the @PPAYMT and @IPAYMT functions are handy for a number of lending related calculations.

@NPER A great function for window shoppers is the @NPER function, which calculates the number of payments required to pay off a loan at a given payment amount. Suppose you want to buy a $10,000 car and can afford $200.00 per month. If the going rate of interest on car loans is 13% you would use the formula

@NPER(0.13/12,-200,10000)

to calculate that just over 72 payments are required to pay off the loan. Note that the payment argument is entered as a negative value since it is a negative cash flow item. The @NPER function uses the form

@NPER(Rate,Payment,Pv,Fv,Type)

and returns ERR if the Payment amount is not enough to amortize the loan. (As you might expect, the Payment amount must at least equal the interest rate per period times the principal.) The Type argument is used to indicate whether the payments are being made at the beginning or end of the period. The default, assumed if you omit the final argument, is 0, meaning at the end of the period.

The optional Fv argument is used when you want to calculate the payments required to create a future sum of money. For example, to calculate how many payments of $200 per month are required to reach a lump sum of 50,000 when you are earning 10% interest per year and have $2,000 already invested, you would use the following:

@NPER(0.1/12,-200,-2000,50000,0)

The answer is roughly 132 payments. Note that this changes to 131 if you change the final argument from 0 to 1 to indicate that the payments are made at the beginning of the period. Also note that the current balance is a negative amount, as are the payments.

@TERM   An alternative function to use if you have a target figure or goal in mind for your investments, is @TERM. Like @NPER, this function calculates how long it will take a series of equal, evenly spaced investments to accumulate to a target amount based on a steady rate of interest. The syntax of the @TERM function is

@TERM(Payment,Rate,Fv)

This function does not offer a present value or type argument and is provided in Quattro PRO essentially for backward compatibility.

@CTERM   The @CTERM function calculates the number of periods it takes for a single investment to grow to some future amount. The @CTERM function has the following format:

@CTERM(Rate,Fv,Pv)

The Rate is a numeric value representing the fixed interest rate per compounding period. The Fv argument is a numeric value representing the future value that an investment will reach at some point. The Pv argument is a numeric value representing the present value of the investment.

   In Figure 4-17 you can see that the goal of reaching $1 million from an initial investment of $10,000 earning 12% per year will take 41 years to achieve.

Investment Functions

Quattro PRO offers several financial functions that assist in the task of evaluating investments. These are @PV, @PVAL, @NPV, @FV, @FVAL,

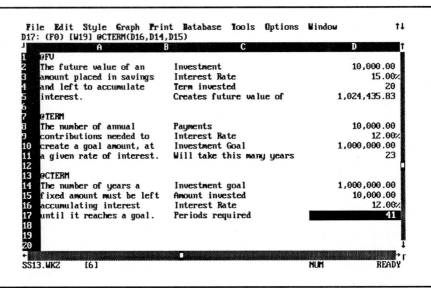

File Edit Style Graph Print Database Tools Options Window   ↑↓
D17: (F0) [W19] @CTERM(D16,D14,D15)

```
     A                      B                    C                    D
1  @FU
2  The future value of an   Investment                            10,000.00
3  amount placed in savings Interest Rate                            15.00%
4  and left to accumulate   Term invested                               20
5  interest.                Creates future value of            1,024,435.83
6
7  @TERM
8  The number of annual     Payments                              10,000.00
9  contributions needed to  Interest Rate                            12.00%
10 create a goal amount, at Investment Goal                    1,000,000.00
11 a given rate of interest. Will take this many years                  23
12
13 @CTERM
14 The number of years a    Investment goal                    1,000,000.00
15 fixed amount must be left Amount invested                      10,000.00
16 accumulating interest    Interest Rate                            12.00%
17 until it reaches a goal.  Periods required                            41
18
19
20
```

SS13.WKZ   [6]   NUM   READY

Figure 4-17. *The @CTERM function*

@RATE, @IRATE, and @IRR, and they are discussed in the following sections.

The Importance of Present Value   When you are evaluating a potential investment it helps to know the present value of the investment. Suppose you have been offered an investment opportunity that promises to pay you $1050 after one year if you invest $1000 now. You know that simply putting the $1000 in a good savings account will turn that $1000 into $1060 so the investment does not seem worthwhile. To put it another way, the investment promises a 5% yield whereas you can get 6% elsewhere. Another way of comparing the promised yield of an investment with your estimate of realistic alternative yields is to *discount* the payment from the investment. If the discounted value is greater than the amount you are considering investing, then the investment is a good one. Another term for the discounted value is *present value.*

Consider the present or discounted value of a venture offering a 12-month return of $1050 on an initial investment of $1000. You would take the $1050 and divide it by the number of payments plus the rate of return on the alternative investment, in this case 6%. The formula is thus 1050/(1+.06) and the answer, the present value of $1050 received a year from now discounted at a rate of 6%, is $991. Since the present value of the promised return is less than the price of the investment, $1000, the investment is not a good one. To use Quattro PRO for this kind of analysis, you use the @PV and @PVAL functions, which can handle investments promising more than one annual payback amount.

@PVAL   The full definition of @PVAL is that it returns the present value of an investment based on periodic and constant payments and a constant interest rate. The function has the following format:

@PVAL(Rate,Nper,Pmt,Fv,Type)

Payments (Pmt), interest Rate, and term (Nper) can be numeric constants, numeric fields, or formulas that result in a number. Interest must be greater than or equal to –1. The future value (Fv) and Type arguments are optional.

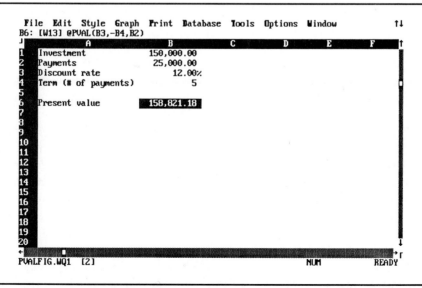

Figure 4-18.   *The @PVAL function*

An example of a @PVAL calculation is shown in Figure 4-18. The promised return on an investment of $150,000 is five annual payments of $25,000. Entering the payments, the discount rate, and the term into the @PVAL function in B6 you get the result $158,821.18, the most you should consider investing to get the promised return. Note that Quattro PRO treats payments as negative values. The entry of -B4 in the @PVAL statement causes the function to return a positive value for the present value rather than a negative value.

Since the present value of the promised return is shown to be greater than the proposed investment amount, you might want to approve the investment. However, while the @PVAL function allows you to take the time value of money into account when comparing investment opportunities, you must still bear in mind less readily quantifiable factors such as risk. Typically the discount rate represents a zero risk alternative such as CDs or Treasury notes.

Suppose that an investment of $100,000 was going to pay a lump some of $150,000 at the end of the five years, rather than installments of $30,000. This can be calculated using the optional future value argument of the @PVAL function, as in

@PVAL(0.12,5,0,-150000)

The result is $85,114.03, considerably less than the amount of the proposed investment, indicating that the investment is not a good one. This makes sense since you are deprived of the use of the money until the end of the investment period. You would have to get over $190,000 at the end of five years for the use of your $100,000 to exceed the return from the 12% discount rate. Note that the 0 in the above @PVAL statement represents the missing present value argument.

While the future value option makes the @PVAL function more versatile, most @PVAL calculations do not use the other optional argument, type. Quattro PRO assumes that the payments from the investment will be made at the end of the periods, not at the beginning. To change the assumption to the beginning, include the argument 1 for type, as in

@PVAL(0.12,5,-30000,0,1)

The result of this formula is @121,120.48, indicating that the investment is more attractive if the return is paid at the beginning of the periods.

@PV   Another way to calculate the present value of a simple annuity—that is, a regular series of equal payments—is to use the @PV function, which takes the form

@PV(Payment,Rate,Nper)

Payment, Rate of interest, and number of payments (Nper) can be numeric constants, numeric cells, or a formula that results in a number. Interest must be greater than –1.

An example of this calculation is shown in Figure 4-19. The promised return is five annual payments of $30,000, or $150,000. Entering the payments, the discount rate, and the term into the @PV function gives you the result of $108,143.29, the most you should consider investing to get the promised return. The @PV function allows you to take the time value of money into account when comparing investment opportunities. However, the @PV function is mainly included for backward compatibility with programs like 1-2-3.

Net Present Value   A function closely related to @PVAL is @NPV which calculates the *net present value* of returns on an investment, based on a discount rate. The net present value of an investment should be greater than zero, otherwise it offers no better return than investing at the discount rate. Whereas @PVAL assumes equal amounts of cash flow from the investment or a single lump sum, the @NPV function handles unequal amounts returned from the investment, using the format

@NPV(Rate,Block,Type)

where Rate is the discount rate of interest and Block is cells containing the cash outlay and flows from the investment. Typically, the first value in the Block is the amount invested, and further amounts are returns on the investment. The stream of cash is assumed to be constant, that is, at regular intervals, but the amounts can vary. For example, suppose you are promised three annual payments of $30,000, $40,000, and $50,000, in return for your investment of $100,000. The net present value of this proposition is calculated with the formula

@NPV(0.12,B1..B4)

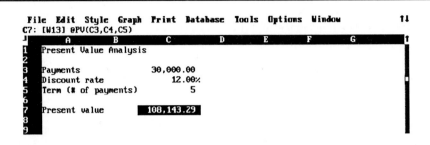

Figure 4-19.   *Present value*

The first argument is the discount rate of 12%. The second argument is the block of cells containing the values 100,000, 30,000, 40,000, and 50,000. The result is less than zero (–5,122.78 in fact), which suggests that this is not a good investment.

Suppose you are still interested in the investment and counter with a demand for returns of $35,000, $45,000, and $50,000. When you enter these in cells B2..B4, the result is positive (2,422.09) suggesting that the investment is now much more profitable. In Figure 4-20 you can see a worksheet used to evaluate a further proposal that offers payments over four years in return for an initial investment of $110,000. Note that you can state the @NPV value arguments as a range, rather than as separate cells.

With all financial functions, including @NPV, you need to pay attention to Quattro PRO's assumptions about timing. In 1-2-3 Release 2.0, the @NPV function has no type argument to alter the timing assumption. Quattro PRO allows you to specify a type argument, which can be either 0 or 1, depending on whether the cash flows are at the beginning or end of the period. If you do not specify a type argument, Quattro PRO assumes payment at the end of the period in @NPV calculations. This means that the model shown in Figure 4-20 actually represents putting out $110,000 one year from the beginning of the project and receiving the first payment of $27,500 at the end of the second year. It is more likely that you will want to base calculations upon paying out the funds for the investment at the beginning of the first period and receiving the first payment in return at

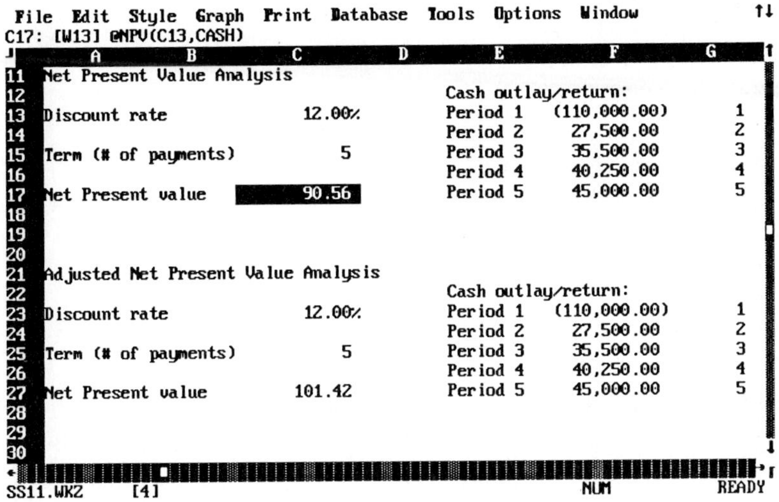

```
    File  Edit  Style  Graph  Print  Database  Tools  Options  Window           ↑↓
    C17: [W13] @NPV(C13,CASH)
    J     A         B         C        D       E        F           G        1
    11  Net Present Value Analysis
    12                                              Cash outlay/return:
    13  Discount rate              12.00%           Period 1    (110,000.00)      1
    14                                              Period 2      27,500.00       2
    15  Term (# of payments)         5              Period 3      35,500.00       3
    16                                              Period 4      40,250.00       4
    17  Net Present value       [  90.56  ]         Period 5      45,000.00       5
    18
    19
    20
    21  Adjusted Net Present Value Analysis
    22                                              Cash outlay/return:
    23  Discount rate              12.00%           Period 1    (110,000.00)      1
    24                                              Period 2      27,500.00       2
    25  Term (# of payments)         5              Period 3      35,500.00       3
    26                                              Period 4      40,250.00       4
    27  Net Present value         101.42            Period 5      45,000.00       5
    28
    29
    30
    SS11.WK2     [4]                                            NUM       READY
```

Figure 4-20.   *@NPV calculations*

the beginning of the second period. To accommodate this assumption you can either specify a type argument of 1 or take the initial investment out of the @NPV argument and place it at the end of the formula, as in Figure 4-20 where the range of returns is F24..F27. The initial outlay is placed in cell F23 and subtracted from the result of the @NPV function. The result shows that the investment is slightly better under the new assumptions.

@IRATE   Suppose you are considering two investments. One offers to pay you four annual payments of $1,000 in return for your investment of $3,000. The other offers 48 monthly payments of $80 for the same $3,000. You might want to calculate a rate of return for both of these investments in order to see which is the better deal. The rate at which your $1,000 is expected to grow is the compound growth rate, calculated by the @IRATE function, using this format:

@IRATE(Nper,Pmt,Pv,Fv,Type).

The last two arguments are optional. In the case of the first investment the formula would be

@IRATE(4,1000,-3000)

The result is an annual rate of return percentage, since the Nper argument is entered as years. In this case the result is .125898325, or 12.59% when expressed with just two decimal places. The rate of return of the second investment is expressed as

@IRATE(48,80,-3000)

The result is .010562829, or 1.06%, which is a monthly rate of interest since the Nper argument is expressed in months. To calculate an annual rate of return for the second investment you would use

@IRATE(48,80,-3000)*12

The result is 12.68%, which is marginally better than the first investment despite the fact that it pays less cash (48*$80=$3,840 as opposed to $4,000).

The @IRATE function arrives at its answer by performing a net present value calculation. Quattro PRO guesses at the rate of return on the investment and figures the net present value of the investment at the guess rate. If the resulting net present value is greater than zero, the program guesses a higher rate and recomputes the net present value. If the guess rate results in a net present value lower than zero, a lower rate is used. In fact, the rate of return on an investment is the percentage that most closely results in a net present value of zero. Quattro PRO repeats, or iterates, the calculation until it arrives at the correct rate or has completed 20 iterations. If it does the 20 iterations without getting the right rate you will get an error message.

@RATE   An alternative to the @IRATE function is the @RATE function, which takes the following form:

@RATE(Fv,Pv,Nper)

The @RATE function returns the rate of interest required to grow a present value sum into a specified target value over a stated term. This function is mainly provided for backward compatibility with earlier programs.

Internal Rate of Return   When you want to compare the pay back you will receive from different investments, you can use the @IRR function to calculate the internal rate of return. This function uses the format

@IRR(Guess,Block)

where Guess is your estimate of what the answer will be and Block is a reference to a range of cells containing amounts of cash flow. Typically, the first number in the range will be a negative one, indicating the initial payment or investment. The @IRR function assumes that the payments occur at the end of the period. This function works much like the @IRATE function except that, like the @NPV function, it can handle a range of unequal cash flows.

Generally, an investment is attractive if it shows an internal rate of return greater than the rate you can obtain elsewhere, the rate known as comparison or hurdle rate. The @IRR function can be seen at work in Figure 4-21, where three different investments are compared. The third one offers the best return as it results in the highest @IRR. Notice that the formula in I12 does not include a guess argument. This is because the guess argument is optional and only required if Quattro PRO has difficulty reaching an @IRR result. If you enter an @IRR formula and get an error in return, try altering or adding the guess argument, using a percentage close to what you would estimate the return to be.

@FVAL   To see what a series of payments will be worth over time, given that they earn interest, you use the @FVAL function. This is shown in Figure 4-22, where the @FVAL function returns the future value of the annual retirement fund contribution of $10,000, which earns 15% per year. The @FVAL function has the following format:

@FVAL(Rate,Nper,Payment,Pv,Type)

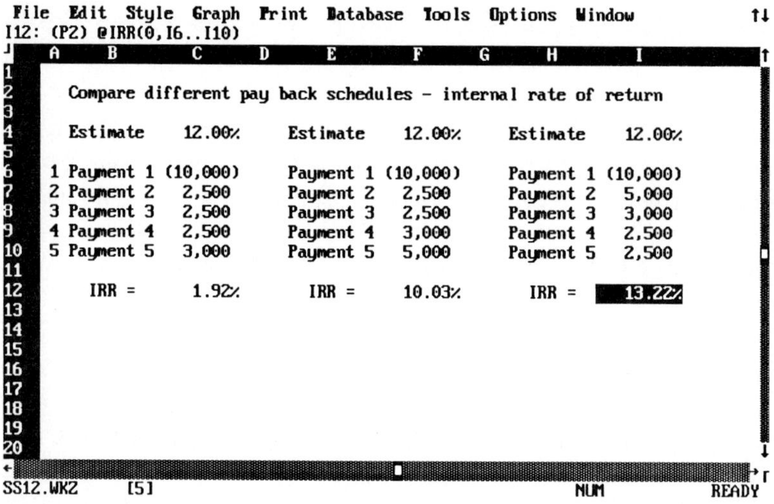

```
 File  Edit  Style  Graph  Print  Database  Tools  Options  Window          ↑↓
I12: (P2) @IRR(0,I6..I10)
⌐   A     B      C      D     E      F      G     H        I              ↑
1
2        Compare different pay back schedules - internal rate of return
3
4        Estimate   12.00%      Estimate   12.00%      Estimate   12.00%
5
6      1 Payment 1 (10,000)     Payment 1 (10,000)     Payment 1 (10,000)
7      2 Payment 2  2,500       Payment 2  2,500       Payment 2  5,000
8      3 Payment 3  2,500       Payment 3  2,500       Payment 3  3,000
9      4 Payment 4  2,500       Payment 4  3,000       Payment 4  2,500
10     5 Payment 5  3,000       Payment 5  5,000       Payment 5  2,500
11
12        IRR =     1.92%        IRR =    10.03%        IRR =    13.22%
13
14
15
16
17
18
19
20
SS12.WK2    [5]                                           NUM        READY
```

Figure 4-21. *@IRR calculations*

Rate is a numeric value greater than 0, representing periodic interest rate. Nper is a numeric value, representing the number of periods of the investment. Payment is a numeric value, representing the amount of equal payments to be made. The @FVAL function calculates the future value of

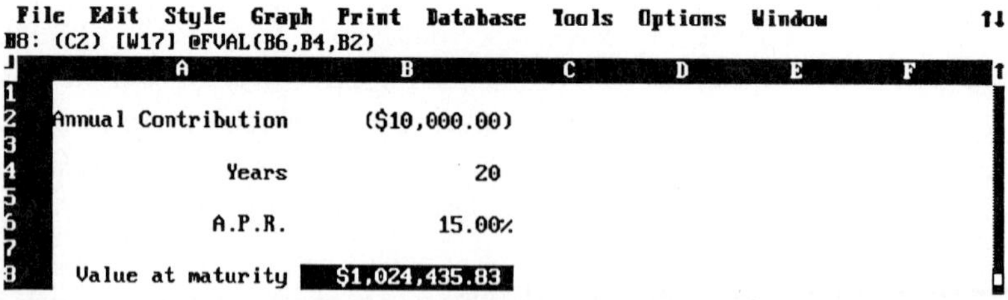

```
 File  Edit  Style  Graph  Print  Database  Tools  Options  Window          ↑↓
B8: (C2) [W17] @FVAL(B6,B4,B2)
⌐            A                 B            C        D        E        F    ↑
1
2  Annual Contribution     ($10,000.00)
3
4           Years              20
5
6           A.P.R.           15.00%
7
8  Value at maturity      $1,024,435.83
```

Figure 4-22. *The @FVAL function*

an investment where the payment is invested for a number of periods at the specified rate of interest per period. You can use @FVAL to see the effects of regular savings plans and evaluate such investments against alternative uses of funds. You can use the Pv argument to indicate an existing value in the program and the type argument to indicate whether the payment is made at the beginning or end of the period. For example, you might want to put $1,000 into a savings account at the beginning of each of seven years, and you would like to know what the account would be worth at the end of the seven years. The account earns 8.5% per year and therefore the formula would be

@FVAL(.085,7,-1000,0,1)

which returns the answer of $9,830.64. Now, if the account already had $2,500 in it when the plan began, the formula would be

@FVAL(.085,7,-1000,-2500,1)

which returns the answer of $14,255.99. Now, if you decided to make the payments at the end of each period the formula would be

@FVAL(.085,7,-1000,-2500,0)

which yields $13,485.85.

@FV   Another function for calculating future value is @FV. This function is shown in Figure 4-23, where it returns the future value of an annual retirement fund investment of $2,500, earning 12.5% per year over a 10-year term. The @FV function has the following format:

@FV(Payment,Rate,Nper)

Payment is a numeric value representing the amount of equal payments to be made. Rate is a numeric value greater than 0 representing periodic interest rate. Nper is a numeric value representing the number of periods of the investment. While you can use @FV to see the effects of regular

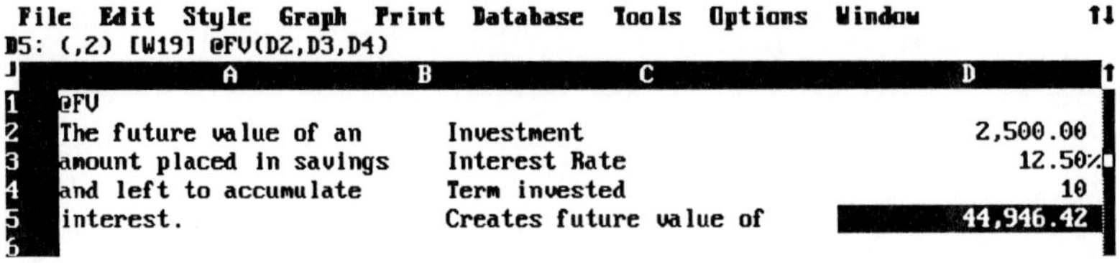

```
 File  Edit  Style  Graph  Print  Database  Tools  Options  Window          ↑↓
D5: (,2) [W19] @FV(D2,D3,D4)
J            A              B              C              D                ↑
 1  @FV
 2  The future value of an     Investment               2,500.00
 3  amount placed in savings   Interest Rate              12.50%
 4  and left to accumulate     Term invested                  10
 5  interest.                  Creates future value of  44,946.42
 6
```

Figure 4-23. *The @FV function*

savings plans and evaluate such investments against alternative uses of funds, it is mainly provided in Quattro PRO for backward compatibility. The assumption in @FV is that the payments are made at the beginning of the period.

Depreciation Functions

Quattro PRO offers three different methods for calculating depreciation, all of which are shown in Figure 4-24. These methods are used because most goods lose value over time, and most state and federal tax laws allow businesses to deduct some of this lost revenue from taxable income.

Straight-Line Depreciation   The straight-line method results in an equal amount of depreciation per period:

@SLN(Cost,Salvage,Life)

This is the simplest form of depreciation.

Sum-of-Years Depreciation   The @SYD function uses a method called the Sum-of-Years-Digits to vary the rate at which depreciation is taken. This function needs to know the year for each calculation.

@SYD(Cost,Salvage,Life,Period)

An interesting application of the @SYD function is in the computation of a loan payout based on the "rule of 78," which results in a larger payoff for

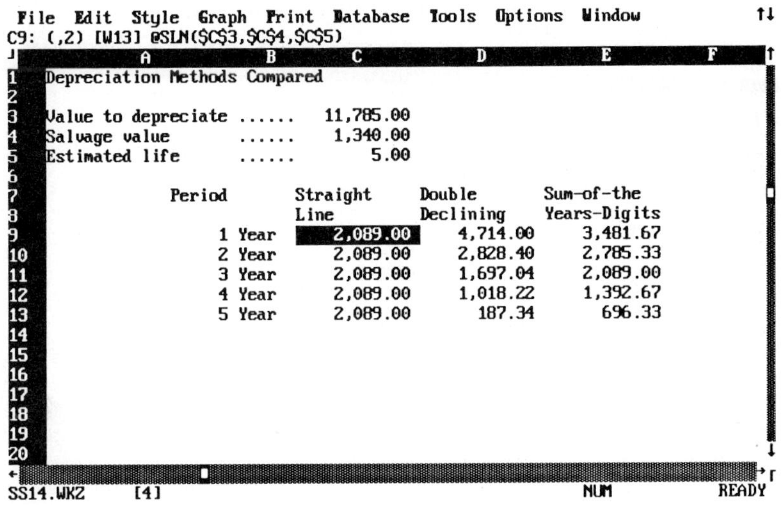

```
 File  Edit  Style  Graph  Print  Database  Tools  Options  Window        ↑↓
C9: (,2) [W13] @SLN($C$3,$C$4,$C$5)
 ⌐      A        B         C         D            E          F      ┐↑
1  Depreciation Methods Compared
2
3  Value to depreciate ......   11,785.00
4  Salvage value       ......    1,340.00
5  Estimated life      ......        5.00
6
7             Period       Straight   Double     Sum-of-the
8                          Line       Declining  Years-Digits
9             1 Year       2,089.00    4,714.00   3,481.67
10            2 Year       2,089.00    2,828.40   2,785.33
11            3 Year       2,089.00    1,697.04   2,089.00
12            4 Year       2,089.00    1,018.22   1,392.67
13            5 Year       2,089.00      187.34     696.33
14
15
16
17
18
19
20
←
 SS14.WKZ    [4]                                      NUM        READY
```

Figure 4-24. *Depreciation*

loans than the simple interest calculation shown earlier in Figure 4-15. The rule of 78 payout table is shown in Figure 4-25.

Double-Declining-Balance Depreciation   The @DDB function calculates depreciation based on the double-declining method, using the following elements:

@DDB(Cost,Salvage,Life,Period)

As in all of the depreciation functions, Cost is a numeric value representing the amount paid for an asset. Salvage is a numeric value representing the worth of an asset at the end of its useful life. Life is a numeric value representing the expected useful life of an asset. Period is a numeric value representing the time period for which you want to determine the depreciation expense. The @DDB function determines accelerated depreciation values for an asset, given the initial cost, life expectancy, end value, and depreciation period.

```
 File  Edit  Style  Graph  Print  Database  Tools  Options  Window        ↑↓
B13: (,2) @IF(A13>E$3,0,@ROUND(@SYD($E$7,0,$E$3,A13),2))
┌    A        B          C          D          E         F      G        ↑
│1
│2            Principal                       25,000.00
│3            Term, in months                    48.00
│4            Interest rate (%A.P.R)              8.80%
│5            Monthly payment                   619.75
│6            Total of payments              29,748.00
│7            Total interest paid             4,748.00
│8
│9            Payout based on rule of 78
│10   PMT    Interest    Principal    Cumulative    Remaining
│11    #     paid        reduction    interest      balance
│12
│13    1      193.80       425.95        193.80   24,574.05
│14    2      189.76       429.99        383.56   24,144.06
│15    3      185.72       434.03        569.28   23,710.03
│16    4      181.68       438.07        750.96   23,271.96
│17    5      177.65       442.10        928.61   22,829.86
│18    6      173.61       446.14      1,102.22   22,383.72
│19    7      169.57       450.18      1,271.79   21,933.54
│20    8      165.53       454.22      1,437.32   21,479.32   ↓
←▓▓▓▓▓░░░░░░░░░░░░░░░░░░░░░░░░░░░░░░░░░░░░░░░░░░░░░░░░░░░░░▓▓▓→ ┌
CHAP4PMT.WQ1 [4]                                  NUM        READY
```

Figure 4-25.   *Loan payout based on rule of 78*

Accelerated Cost Recovery   Most tax calculations no longer use the three methods of depreciation described above, but rather a method known as the Accelerated Cost Recovery System (ACRS). The rate of depreciation allowed by ACRS varies each year of the asset's life and depends on when the asset was placed in service. There is no ACRS function in Quattro PRO, but you can use the @INDEX function to create IRS tables of depreciation rates, based on the month placed in service and the year of the asset's life. @INDEX is a logical function, described in the next section.

Logical Functions

Quattro PRO provides a variety of functions that can be very useful in situations where logical arguments need to be entered into fields.

@If

The @IF function instructs Quattro PRO to choose between two actions based on a condition being either true or false. Suppose that you are budgeting quarterly revenue and expenditures for a computer store, using a spreadsheet like that shown in Figure 4-26. You have gotten good results from spending 5% of all sales revenue on advertising. Thus, advertising is normally Sales*0.05. However, you know that money spent on advertising beyond a certain dollar amount is not effective (say, $110,000, expressed as 110.00 in the model).

What you want to do is to budget your advertising expenditures with a ceiling of 110. You can do this by adding the @IF function to the advertising expense formula to tell Quattro PRO that if Sales*0.05 is less than 110, Advertising=Sales*0.05; otherwise, Advertising=110. In the spreadsheet this is written as

@IF(0.05*B10<110,0.05*B10,110)

```
      File  Edit  Style  Graph  Print  Database  Tools  Options  Window         ↑↓
B17: (,2) @IF(0.05*B10<110,0.05*B10,110)                                         ?
           A          B          C          D          E          F
                                                                              End
1
2                 Quarter 1  Quarter 2  Quarter 3  Quarter 4                   ▲
3          ----------------------------------------------------                ◀ ▶
4   SALES (000s)                                                                ▼
5
6   PC Systems  1,205.00   1,325.50   1,458.05   1,603.86                      Esc
7   Monitors      210.00     231.00     254.10     279.51
8   Printers      532.00     585.20     643.72     708.09                       ↵
9          ====================================================
10  TOTAL       1,947.00   2,141.70   2,355.87   2,591.46                      •Del
11         ----------------------------------------------------
12                                                                              @
13  EXPENSES (000s)
14                                                                              5
15  Salaries      194.70     214.17     235.59     259.15
16  Bonuses        48.68      53.54      58.90      64.79                       6
17  Advertising    97.35     107.09     110.00     110.00
18  Other          50.41      64.25      70.68      77.74                       7
19         ====================================================
20  TOTAL         399.14     439.05     475.16     511.68
C4IFADV.WQ1  [1]                                          NUM         READY
```

Figure 4-26. *Store budget*

The format of the @IF function is as follows:

@IF(Condition,True,False)

This syntax means that if the condition is true, then the response is that stated in the True part of the argument. Otherwise, the result is that in the False part. True and false results can be constants, value or label cells, or other formulas. The true result and the false result can be any type of data.

The @IF function is extremely versatile because it allows the spreadsheet to become intelligent, that is, to do one of two things based on a condition that you establish. This can be used in numerous situations in a typical worksheet. For example, you can use @IF to test the integrity of a spreadsheet, as in the expense report worksheet shown in Figure 4-27. Anyone who has filled out expense reports knows that the sum of the rows should equal the sum of the columns. When you lay out this kind of report in Quattro PRO, the calculation is done for you. However, you should never

```
 File  Edit  Style  Graph  Print  Database  Tools  Options  Window          ↑↓
G17: (,2) @IF(@SUM(TD)=@SUM(TA),@SUM(TD),@ERR)
        A          B        C        D        E        F        G          ↑
1
2              Monday   Tuesday  Wednesday Thursday  Friday   Totals
3        ─────────────────────────────────────────────────────────────
4   Meals
5       B'fast      3.45     0.00     3.89     4.76     5.98    18.08
6       Lunch       5.00     8.95     6.74     5.78    18.96    45.43
7       Dinner      0.00    23.87     5.89    13.45     0.00    43.21
8   Travel
9         Air       0.00   143.89     0.00     0.00   148.00   291.89
10    Mileage       0.00     0.00     0.00     0.00     3.50     3.50
11    Parking       0.00     0.00    12.00    12.00    12.00    36.00
12       Taxi       8.00     0.00     0.00     0.00     0.00     8.00
13  Miscellaneous
14    Supplies     34.00     0.00     6.00     0.00     3.00    43.00
15       Other      0.00     0.00     0.00    23.87     0.00    23.87
16  ═════════════════════════════════════════════════════════════════
17               50.45   176.71    34.52    59.86   191.44  ▐512.98▌
18
19                        Total =   512.98
20                                                                          ↓
SS09.WKZ     [3]                                        NUM         READY
```

Figure 4-27.   *The expense report*

assume that just because the work is done electronically it is always done correctly. The @IF formula in cell G17 says that if the sum of the columns (TD) equals the sum of the rows (TA), the cell should contain the sum of the rows; otherwise, it should contain an error message (produced by the @ERR function) to show that a mistake has been made. When a mistake has been detected, the ERR message appears as a label in cell G17.

Suppose Quattro PRO detects an error. You review the spreadsheet. Close examination reveals that someone typed a number over the top of a formula in column G. This caused the sum of the columns to be incorrect. When the erroneous value is replaced by the correct formula, the ERR message will disappear and the expense report will be correct.

When you want to apply several conditions to a calculation, you can *nest* @IF statements. For example, in a large report you may want to allow a small margin of error in the figures. In the case of Figure 4-27 this would not exactly be appropriate, but you could amend the statement in G17 to read as follows:

@IF(@SUM(TD)>@SUM(TA)*1.01,@ERR,

@IF(@SUM(TA)>@SUM(TD)*1.01,@ERR,

@SUM(TD,TA)/2))

This tells Quattro PRO that if the total down exceeds 101% of the total across, there is an error. Likewise, if the total across exceeds 101% of the total down, there is an error. Otherwise, the answer should be the average of the total down and the total across. If the figures are entirely accurate, the answer will be accurate. Otherwise, the answer will be within 1% of the correct total.

Another example of nesting @IF statements is shown in the formula used in Figure 4-28 to calculate commissions based on a percentage (4% to 6%) of sales. The statement in D5 reads

@IF(C5<40000,0.04*C5,@IF(C5<50000,0.05*C5,C5*0.06))

This formula says that if the sales in C5 are less than $40,000, the commission will be 4% (0.04) of sales; otherwise, if sales are greater than or equal to $40,000 but less than $50,000, the commission will be 5%. If

```
 File  Edit  Style  Graph  Print  Database  Tools  Options  Window          ↑↓
D5: (C2) [W13] @IF(C5<40000,0.04*C5,@IF(C5<50000,0.05*C5,C5*0.06))
╛     A        B        C            D             E           F         ↑
1  July Sales Report
2
3          Broker    Sales    Commission
4          ─────────────────────────────
5          Smith, H.  $50,005    $3,000.30
6          Gore, B.   $49,950    $2,497.50
7          Sloan, R.  $39,950    $1,598.00
8          James, E.  $40,050    $2,002.50
9          Quest, J.  $35,070    $1,402.80
10         Noles, B.  $51,009    $3,060.54
11         Reese, P.  $40,000    $2,000.00
12         Wentz, T.  $31,454    $1,258.16
13
14
15
16
17
18
19
20
←                                                                         →
SS16.WKZ       [1]                                     NUM         READY
```

Figure 4-28.   *Nested @IF statement*

sales are greater than or equal to $50,000, the commission will be 6%. The nesting of @IF statements takes a little planning, but if you write out the statement first, you can usually frame the actual formula to fit most conditional situations. The @IF function can return labels as well as values. For example, in the broker transaction record shown here, the word *Yes* in cell K9 is the result of an @IF formula:

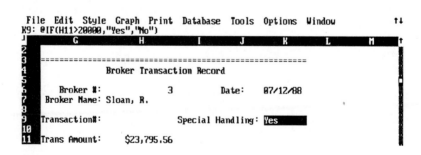

```
 File  Edit  Style  Graph  Print  Database  Tools  Options  Window          ↑↓
K9: @IF(H11>20000,"Yes","No")
╛       G           H          I         J        K        L        M     ↑
2
3  ==================================================================
4              Broker Transaction Record
5
6      Broker #:              3        Date:     07/12/88
7    Broker Name: Sloan, R.
8
9  Transaction#:              Special Handling:  Yes
10
11 Trans Amount:    $23,795.56
```

The record needs to show if special handling is required. This is based on the amount of the transaction, shown in H11. The formula in K9 states @IF(H11>20000,"Yes","No"). Thus the word *Yes* is returned in this case because the amount in H11 is greater than 20,000.

The name of the broker could also be entered with an @IF formula that looks for the broker number entered in H6 and responds with one of three names, like this:

@IF(H6=3,"Sloan, R.",@IF(H6=2,"Doe, J.",
@IF(H6=1,"James, E.",@ERR)))

This formula will result in the ERR message if the broker number is not 1, 2, or 3.

Lookup Tables

When you want to make a formula dependent on a range of conditions, you have an alternative to nesting @IF functions. You can have Quattro PRO refer to a table of conditions, called a *lookup table*. This is a vertical or horizontal list of numbers or labels that you can use to look up related numbers or labels. Figure 4-29 shows a commission table that offers a simple way to determine the rate based on a broader range of sales levels. The vertical list of sales levels in column E and related commission rates in column F show the rate applicable to any given level of sales. Any sales amount below $35,000 earns a commission of 3.50%. Sales from $35,000 to $35,999 earn 3.75%, and so on. The bottom of the table shows that sales of $50,000 and up earn 8.00%. This table of numbers, consisting of cells E3 through F19, have been named TABLE with the Block Advanced Create command. In cell D3 the formula reads

@VLOOKUP(C3,$TABLE,1)*C3

This means that the vertical lookup function is invoked to look up the value of cell C3 in the block of cells named TABLE in column 1. The value that is found in the table, in this case the commission rate of 8%, is then multiplied by cell C3 to calculate the commission amount.

```
 File  Edit  Style  Graph  Print  Database  Tools  Options  Window        ↑↓
D3: (C2) [W13] @VLOOKUP(C3,$TABLE,1)*C3
```

	Broker	Sales	Commission		Sales Level	Commission
1						
2						
3	Smith, H.	$50,005	$4,000.40		$0	3.50%
4	Gore, B.	$49,950	$3,621.38		$35,000	3.75%
5	Sloan, R.	$39,950	$1,897.63		$36,000	4.00%
6	James, E.	$40,050	$2,002.50		$37,000	4.25%
7	Quest, J.	$35,070	$1,315.13		$38,000	4.50%
8	Noles, B.	$51,009	$4,000.72		$39,000	4.75%
9	Reese, P.	$40,000	$2,000.00		$40,000	5.00%
10	Wentz, T.	$31,454	$1,100.89		$41,000	5.25%
11					$42,000	5.50%
12					$43,000	5.75%
13					$44,000	6.00%
14					$45,000	6.25%
15					$46,000	6.50%
16					$47,000	6.75%
17					$48,000	7.00%
18					$49,000	7.25%
19					$50,000	8.00%
20						

```
C4LOOKIF.WQ1 [1]                                          NUM        READY
```

Figure 4-29.   *Lookup table*

The syntax of the vertical lookup function is thus

@VLOOKUP(Index,Table,Column)

The Index is the cell containing the value you are looking up in the table. The Table should be consecutive columns of values. The Column is the column in the table that the formula should look to for its result. The column numbering is 0 for the first column, 1 for the next column to the right, and so on. In the example, the contents of C3 and column 0 of the lookup table must be values. The column 0 values must be a consecutive range. However, the contents of column 1 and any additional columns in the table can be labels.

The lookup table can be laid out horizontally, as shown in Figure 4-30. The formula in H25 uses the @HLOOKUP function. This example supposes that each broker has a number and writes that number on sales transaction slips. A clerk then records the slips in the format shown in Figure 4-30. As

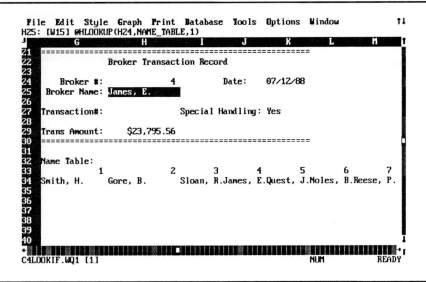

Figure 4-30. *Horizontal lookup table*

the clerk enters the broker number, Quattro PRO looks up that number in the horizontal table of names. (The table is shown on screen in Figure 4-30 for the purposes of illustration.) The first row of a horizontal table is row 0; successive rows are numbered 1, 2, 3, and so on. The syntax of the @HLOOKUP function is

@HLOOKUP(Index,Table,Row Number)

Row 0 must be a series of values or an alphabetical list of labels. Successive rows can be values or labels. Row 1, which the formula references in this case, is a set of labels.

Note that you do not have to use a block name for the lookup table reference in the formula. None was used in Figure 4-30. However, a block name makes it easier to refer to the cells of the table than typing G33..M34, particularly if you want to copy the formula containing the reference to the table and thus need to make the cell references absolute, as in

$G$33.$M$34. A reference to a block named TABLE can be made absolute by preceding it with a dollar sign.

Choose

A function directly comparable to a lookup table is @CHOOSE, which selects its responses based on a number. For example, if there were just a few brokers, you could use the @CHOOSE function in place of @HLOOKUP in cell H25 of Figure 4-30. If there were just four brokers, the formula in H25 could read

@CHOOSE(H6,"Smith, H.","Gore, B.","Sloan, R.","James, E.")

The number entered in cell H6 would thus determine the name placed into H7. The syntax of the @CHOOSE function is

@CHOOSE(X, Case0, Case1,...,Casen)

If X equals 1, Case0 is used. If X equals 2, Case1 is used, and so on. The value of X must be a number between 1 and the total number of results in the argument. Values of X outside that range will cause an error. If X includes a decimal, Quattro PRO rounds off the value. The X value can be a numeric constant, a cell, or a formula, as in the previous example, where this function is a compact way of handling small lists of results. The results can be constants or formulas of any data type. However, all results must have the same data type.

Error

When you want a cell to reflect an error you can use the @ERR function. This function takes no arguments; it is simply entered as

@ERR

@ERR returns the value ERR in the current cell and, in most cases, also creates the ERR message in any other cells that reference the cell in which you created the ERR condition. The exceptions to this are @COUNT, @ISERR, @ISNA, @ISNUMBER, @ISSTRING, @CELL, and @CELL-POINTER formulas. These formulas do not result in ERR if they reference a cell that contains ERR. The ERR value resulting from this function is the same as the ERR value produced by Quattro PRO when it encounters an error.

@NA

The @NA function works the same as @ERR except that it returns the value NA, which distinguishes it from the ERR message that Quattro PRO uses when a formula is typed incorrectly.

Index

The @INDEX function is a hybrid of the vertical and horizontal lookup tables. For this function you state the column number and row number for a value set in a table of values. The function has the syntax

@INDEX(Range,Column,Row)

There are a number of interesting applications for this function, including the accelerated depreciation schedule shown in Figure 4-31. This is a table of the allowed rates of depreciation for real property placed in service before March 15, 1984. The months are numbered across the top and the years of asset life are listed down the side. By answering the questions in rows 2 through 5 in column E, you provide the index data needed for the formula used in J5: @INDEX(A9..M17,E4,E5). The number 7 in E4 is the column coordinate; the number 4 in E5 is the row coordinate. The cell at which they intersect, H13, contains the value 9% returned by the @INDEX formula. Note that the number of the indexed block corresponds to the

```
 File  Edit  Style  Graph  Print  Database  Tools  Options  Window        ↑↓
J5: (P0) [W5] @INDEX(A9..M17,E4,E5)
J          A     B     C     D     E     F     G     H     I     J     K     L     M   ↑
1
2    When placed in service:      1983
3    Tax year being calculated: 1987
4    Month placed in service:      7        Percentage to be used:
5    Year to be used:              4                         9%
6
7    15 year real property - Property placed in service 1/1/80-3/15/84
8    Use the column for the month of taxable year placed in service.
9    Year       1     2     3     4     5     6     7     8     9    10    11    12
10          1  12%   11%   10%    9%    8%    7%    6%    5%    4%    3%    2%    1%
11          2  10%   10%   11%   11%   11%   11%   11%   11%   11%   11%   11%   12%
12          3   9%    9%    9%    9%   10%   10%   10%   10%   10%   10%   10%   10%
13          4   8%    8%    8%    8%    8%    8%    9%    9%    9%    9%    9%    9%
14          5   7%    7%    7%    7%    7%    7%    8%    8%    8%    8%    8%    8%
15          6   6%    6%    6%    6%    7%    7%    7%    7%    7%    7%    7%    7%
16          7   6%    6%    6%    6%    6%    6%    6%    6%    6%    6%    6%    6%
17          8   6%    6%    6%    6%    6%    6%    6%    6%    6%    6%    6%    6%
18
19
20                                            ■                          ↓
←                                                                        →
INDEXIRS.WQ1 [2]                                             NUM      READY
```

Figure 4-31.   *ACRS with @INDEX*

numbers you assign to the header column and row; not the 0, 1, 2, 3 numbering used in the @VLOOKUP function.

True and False

If you want to give a value to a conditional statement, you can use the @TRUE and @FALSE functions to provide a 1 and a 0, respectively. These functions require no arguments and are discussed in depth in Chapter 9.

The @IS Functions

You will notice a series of functions in the Functions list (SHIFT-F3) beginning with @IS. They are @ISERR, @ISNA, @ISNUMBER, and @ISSTRING. Used in a variety of situations, these functions relate to errors and nonvalues for numbers and dates. They are described in detail in Chapter 13.

String Functions

A particularly powerful group of Quattro PRO functions are those that help you manipulate strings. This is not an electronic version of marionettes, but rather a sophisticated way of handling sequences of characters or text. To Quattro PRO, a *string* is a sequence of characters with no numerical value. This can be a word, like *Quattro PRO,* or a group of characters, like *'123,* since they are preceded by a label prefix. The words *John* and *Doe* entered into separate cells can be pulled together, or *concatenated,* by string formulas. As you can see in Figure 4-32, you can use string functions to create text from spreadsheet entries. The string functions can convert numbers to strings and vice versa. Because string functions relate directly to the way in which Quattro PRO handles text, they are included in Chapter 10, "Handling Text."

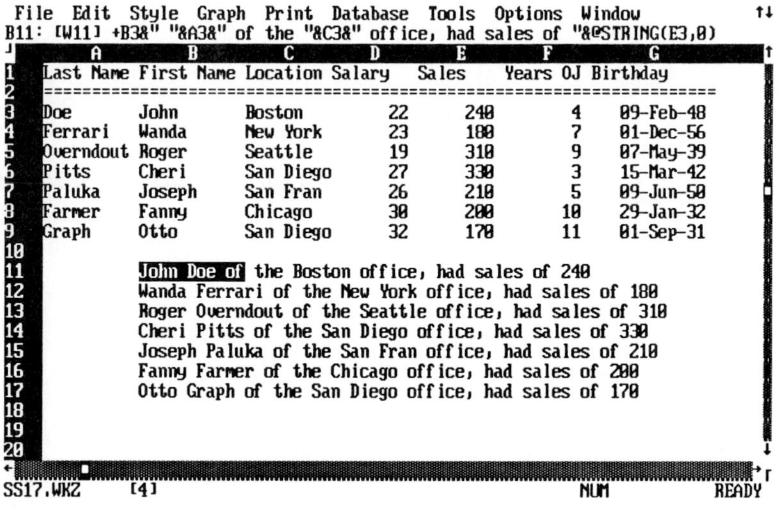

```
   File  Edit  Style  Graph  Print  Database  Tools  Options  Window        ↑↓
B11: [W11] +B3&" "&A3&" of the "&C3&" office, had sales of "&@STRING(E3,0)
┘     A          B         C          D       E      F      G               ↑
1  Last Name First Name Location  Salary   Sales   Years OJ Birthday
2  =================================================================
3  Doe       John       Boston      22      240        4    09-Feb-48
4  Ferrari   Wanda      New York    23      180        7    01-Dec-56
5  Overndout Roger      Seattle     19      310        9    07-May-39
6  Pitts     Cheri      San Diego   27      330        3    15-Mar-42
7  Paluka    Joseph     San Fran    26      210        5    09-Jun-50
8  Farmer    Fanny      Chicago     30      200       10    29-Jan-32
9  Graph     Otto       San Diego   32      170       11    01-Sep-31
10
11         John Doe of the Boston office, had sales of 240
12         Wanda Ferrari of the New York office, had sales of 180
13         Roger Overndout of the Seattle office, had sales of 310
14         Cheri Pitts of the San Diego office, had sales of 330
15         Joseph Paluka of the San Fran office, had sales of 210
16         Fanny Farmer of the Chicago office, had sales of 200
17         Otto Graph of the San Diego office, had sales of 170
18
19
20
←                                                                           ↓
SS17.WK2    [4]                                            NUM        READY
```

Figure 4-32. *String example*

Special Functions

The complex set of functions referred to as miscellaneous or special functions are used in advanced worksheets and are explained in Chapter 12, where they are shown applied to practical situations. These functions are @@, @CELL, @CELLINDEX, @CELLPOINTER, @COLS, @ROWS, @CURVALUE, @FILEXISTS, @MEMAVAIL, @MEMSAVAIL, @NUM-TOHEX, and @HEXTONUM.

Trigonometric Functions

If you work with geometry and trigonometry, Quattro PRO offers many useful functions. While these are mainly used in engineering and scientific applications, they can be very handy in many situations.

Pi

The @PI function provides the value of pi to eleven decimal places. For calculations that require the value of pi, you can type **@PI**. The @PI function takes no argument; it simply returns the value 3.14159265359. The formula to calculate the circumference of a circle is thus 2@PI*Radius. The area of a circle can be calculated by combining @PI and the exponent function; @PI*(Radius^2), which calculates pi times the square of the radius.

Degrees and Radians

Another application of @PI is to convert radians to degrees. In Quattro PRO as well as 1-2-3, the trigonometric functions like @SIN and @COS produce answers in radians. You can use pi to express angles measured in radians as degrees, and to convert degrees to radians, using the following formulas:

1 Radian = $\dfrac{360°}{\text{pi} \times 2}$ or 180/pi

1 Degree = $\dfrac{\text{pi} \times 2 \times \text{radian}}{360}$ or pi/180

For trigonometric functions in 1-2-3, you must use 180/@PI and @PI/180 to make the necessary conversions from radians to degrees and vice versa. However, Quattro PRO has two functions called @DEGREES and @RADIANS that simplify this conversion.

@DEGREES   Used to convert radians to degrees, the @DEGREES function is an alternative to using *180/@PI when you need to calculate an angle measurement. The syntax is @DEGREES(X), where X is a measurement in radians. You can see an example of this in Case 3 of Figure 4-33, where an angle is calculated by the @SIN function from the measurements of two sides of a right-angled triangle.

@RADIANS   Used to convert degrees to radians, this function is an alternative to multiplying by @PI/180. The syntax is @RADIANS(X), where X is a measurement in degrees. You can see an example of this in Case 1 of Figure 4-33, where the @TAN function is being used to calculate the length of one side of a triangle.

Sine, Cosine, and Tangent

These three functions—expressed as @SIN(X), @COS(X), and @TAN(X) — return the trigonometric sine, cosine, and tangent of X, an angle measured in radians. You can convert an angle measured in degrees to one expressed in radians by using the @RADIANS function. Thus, @SIN(@RADIANS(60)) returns the sine of a 60-degree angle. A result in radians can be converted to degrees with the @DEGREES function, so that @DEGREES(@ACOS(a/b)) returns the angle between a and b expressed in degrees. These functions are shown in the problems in Figure 4-33.

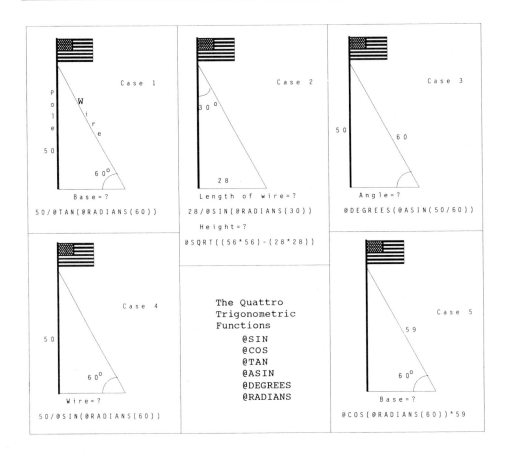

Figure 4-33.   *Flagpole example*

Inverse

The inverse trigonometric functions— expressed as @ASIN(X), @ACOS(X), @ATAN(X) —save you from having to create them from the @COS, @SIN, and @TAN functions. They return an angle measured in radians, given its sine, cosine, or tangent. The @ATAN2(X,Y) function calculates a 4-quadrant arctangent from the X and Y coordinates of a point.

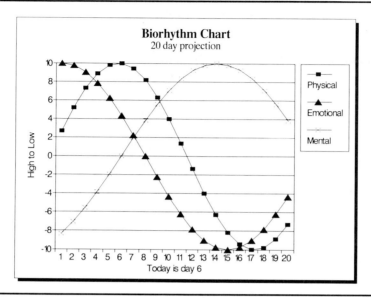

Figure 4-34.   *Sine curves on biorhythm chart*

```
 File  Edit  Style  Graph  Print  Database  Tools  Options  Window          ↑↓
F6: 10*@SIN(E6*@PI/11.5)
```

	A	B	C	D	E	F	G	H
1	Birthday	10/17/52						
2	Today	06/06/90				BIORYTHM CHARTING		
3	Days Projected	20						
4								
5				Today >	Birth-Day	Physical	Emotional	Mental
6			1	33,025	13,741	**3.98**	(10.00)	5.56
7			2	33,026	13,742	1.36	(9.75)	3.83
8			3	33,027	13,743	(1.36)	(9.01)	1.95
9			4	33,028	13,744	(3.98)	(7.82)	0.00
10			5	33,029	13,745	(6.31)	(6.23)	(1.95)
11			6	33,030	13,746	(8.17)	(4.34)	(3.83)
12			7	33,031	13,747	(9.42)	(2.23)	(5.56)
13			8	33,032	13,748	(9.98)	0.00	(7.07)
14			9	33,033	13,749	(9.79)	2.23	(8.31)
15			10	33,034	13,750	(8.88)	4.34	(9.24)
16			11	33,035	13,751	(7.31)	6.23	(9.81)
17			12	33,036	13,752	(5.20)	7.82	(10.00)
18			13	33,037	13,753	(2.70)	9.01	(9.81)
19			14	33,038	13,754	(0.00)	9.75	(9.24)
20			15	33,039	13,755	2.70	10.00	(8.31)

```
BIOSOFT.WQ1  [1]                                    NUM           READY
```

Figure 4-35.   *The biorhythm worksheet*

Trigonometric Applications

Of course, there are a wide variety of ways in which the trigonometric functions can be used. You can use them to generate curves that show one set of values plotted against another. An example of this is a biorhythm chart, which is used to plot levels of physical, emotional, and mental energy on a time scale. The @SIN function is used to generate the curve shown in Figure 4-34, a simple biorhythm chart. The worksheet from which this was calculated is shown in Figure 4-35. The current date and the subject's birthdate are recorded and then extrapolated for the three different cycles: 22 days for the physical level, 28 for the emotional level, and 32 for the mental level.

5 Building, Viewing, and Printing

In previous chapters you saw several methods of entering information into Quattro PRO. You have seen how formulas are created and copied to produce extensive spreadsheets from a few simple entries. You have also seen how data is organized in the worksheet so that the worksheet can be treated like a database. This chapter reviews the process of building a spreadsheet model and explains the commands for viewing information on the screen and for printing it on paper.

Building a Typical Worksheet

This chapter provides step-by-step instructions for creating a sample worksheet. You can use the techniques presented here to build a typical spreadsheet model. You will see how to organize and print the worksheet as well as how to dress it up with Style commands. You can perform these steps yourself as a practical exercise, or you can use them as a reference when building your own models.

Suggestions made here offer approaches you can take when using Quattro PRO's features. These are methods that have been effective, but they are not rules. As you become more experienced with Quattro PRO, you may develop other techniques that are more suited to the particular demands of your work.

Basic Design

The first sample worksheet presented in this chapter is a 12-month expense projection for a group of travel agencies. Part of the expense projection is shown in Figure 5-1. Five expense items are calculated for each of several agencies:

Lease   The rent of the office space
Phones   The cost of telephone service
Telex   The cost of Telex services
Electric   The monthly utility bill
Res. Rent   The monthly charge for renting airline reservations terminals

The January figures are multiplied by a growth factor to produce the February figures. In each successive month the expenses increase by the same factor. The growth factor ensures that the company running the agencies budgets sufficient funds to cover rising expenses.

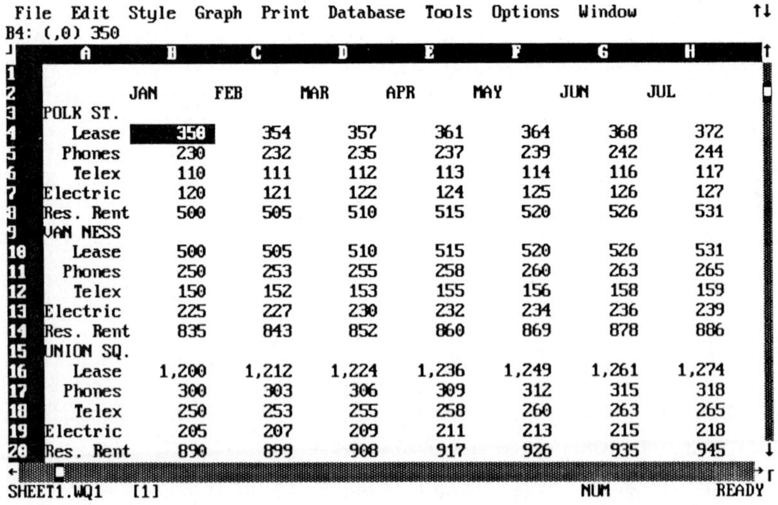

```
 File   Edit  Style  Graph  Print  Database  Tools  Options  Window              ↑↓
 B4: (,0) 350
 ⌐         A        B        C        D        E        F        G        H      ↑
 ⌐
 2              JAN      FEB      MAR      APR      MAY      JUN      JUL         ■
 3  POLK ST.
 4     Lease    350      354      357      361      364      368      372
 5    Phones    230      232      235      237      239      242      244
 6     Telex    110      111      112      113      114      116      117
 7  Electric    120      121      122      124      125      126      127
 8  Res. Rent   500      505      510      515      520      526      531
 9  VAN NESS
 10    Lease    500      505      510      515      520      526      531
 11   Phones    250      253      255      258      260      263      265
 12    Telex    150      152      153      155      156      158      159
 13 Electric    225      227      230      232      234      236      239
 14 Res. Rent   835      843      852      860      869      878      886
 15 UNION SQ.
 16    Lease  1,200    1,212    1,224    1,236    1,249    1,261    1,274
 17   Phones    300      303      306      309      312      315      318
 18    Telex    250      253      255      258      260      263      265
 19 Electric    205      207      209      211      213      215      218
 20 Res. Rent   890      899      908      917      926      935      945      ↓
 ←                                                                          →  ␛
 SHEET1.WQ1   [1]                                               NUM         READY
```

Figure 5-1.   *The basic model*

Building Principles

In general, the best approach to building spreadsheets is to enter data in the following order:

■ *Labels* You use labels to identify the contents and arrangement of the model. Do not worry about the exact titles for columns and rows, since you can change them later. Also, do not worry about the width of columns, since these too can be adjusted after most of the model has been built.

■ *Numbers* Numbers make up the basic data in a worksheet. As you enter the numbers you will get a general idea of the dimensions of the model.

■ *Formulas* Enter the first few formulas and make sure they work before copying them. Do not worry about the format of the results.

■ *Formats* When you know what kind of numbers you are using, make any necessary format changes. Use the Options Formats Numeric Format command for the most common format and Style Numeric Format for exceptions. Add any special alignment to labels with the Style Alignment command.

■ *Widths* Adjust column widths as needed. Use a global setting (Options, Formats, Global Width) for the most common width and adjust other columns individually (Style, Column Width).

You will proceed more quickly working in this order than if you spend a lot of time adjusting formats and column widths before most of the data is entered. You will probably need to readjust some widths and formats after the model is completed. Whether you build the model column by column or row by row depends upon the kind of data with which you are working.

Although this is the general order of building spreadsheets, there are a few exceptions to keep in mind. If you know you will need to copy a label and that the label will eventually have an alignment different from the default, you should align the label before copying. The same is true of cells that contain values with special formats. Set Style Numeric Format before copying, since the Edit Copy command copies a cell's format as well as its contents. The sample model will be built column by column; the column of labels will be followed by the starting values and then the first column of formulas. The first formula column will then be copied to the rest of the columns. This approach follows the natural progression of the data and will require the least number of keystrokes.

Entering and Reusing Labels

Whenever possible you should use the Edit Copy command to reuse labels that you have already entered into the worksheet. Doing so saves time and also avoids inconsistent spellings and typos. Make sure you check your data before copying it. If the labels are specially aligned, apply the alignment command before copying to reduce the need for later adjustments.

For example, to copy the labels for the sample worksheet, follow these steps:

1. Use the DOWN ARROW key to move the cell selector to cell A3. Then type in the labels in column A as they appear in the following illustration. The label in capital letters is the name of the office, which is followed by five categories of expenses incurred by that office. Enter all six lines as left-aligned labels.

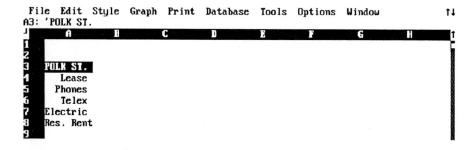

2. To offset the expense categories from the office names, right-align the expenses. With your cell selector in A4, select Style Alignment and choose Right Align.

3. When prompted for the block to be modified, you can use the END and arrow keys shortcut: Press END and then press DOWN ARROW. This will highlight all of the labels in one step as shown here:

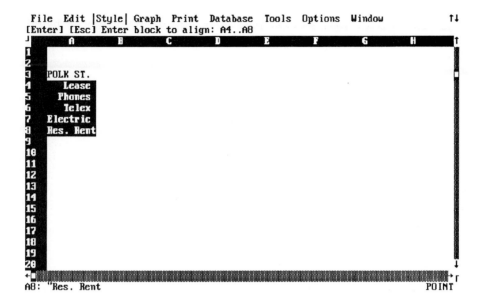

4. Press ENTER to confirm A4..A8 as the block to be right-aligned.

5. From the menu pick Style and then Column Width; type **12** and press ENTER to widen the column to 12 characters and better separate the labels.

The Style Alignment command deletes the current label prefix and replaces it with the one you specify: left ('), right ("), or center (^).

Straight Block Copy

After aligning the labels through row 8 of column A, you need to enter the name of the second office, **VAN NESS**. With this done, you can reuse the expense category labels from cells A4 through A8.

1. Move the cell selector up to A4 and select Edit Copy. Quattro PRO assumes that the Source Block begins at A4, where your cell selector was located when you issued the command. This coordinate is already anchored as the beginning point of the Source Block, as indicated by the double dots in A4..A8.

2. Highlight the other expense labels with the DOWN ARROW key. If you want to use END and DOWN ARROW, be sure to press UP ARROW once to exclude cell A9.

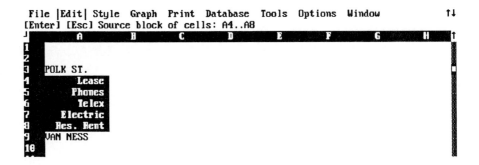

3. Press ENTER to confirm A4..A8 as the Source Block.

4. To indicate the correct destination for this block, press DOWN ARROW to move the cell selector to A10.

5. Press ENTER to confirm the destination. The labels, complete with right-alignment indicators, will be copied into position for the second office. Your cell selector will be left in A4. Use END and then DOWN ARROW to move to the last cell of the model.

Reverse Copy

Now type the name of the third office, **UNION SQ.**, at A15 and press DOWN ARROW to enter it into the cell and move to A16. To copy the expense labels from the second office to the third, you can use a technique known as *reverse copy*. As a spreadsheet grows, you might find it inconvenient that the Copy command leaves the cell selector in the top-left cell of the block you copied from. This can be particularly cumbersome when copying across several screens of the worksheet. Reverse copy overcomes this problem, because it invokes the Copy command from the block's destination, in this case, A16.

1. Select Edit Copy. Initially the suggested Source Block, which will be locked in at A16, is represented by A16..A16. Press ESCAPE to unlock this block. The display at the top of the screen changes to A16 only, as shown here:

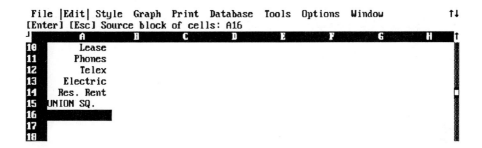

2. Move the cell selector up to the expense label in A10 and type a period to anchor this as the beginning point of the Source Block.

3. Highlight the other expense labels through A14 with the DOWN ARROW and press ENTER.

4. Because you started the copy from A16, Quattro PRO assumes that this is where you want the block of labels copied to.

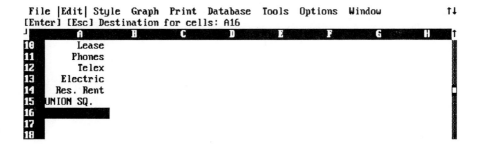

There is no need to lock the destination point; simply press ENTER to confirm it.

Entering the Months

Since this worksheet is a 1-year projection divided into months, you need to enter the names of the months across the worksheet. While these headings do not have to be entered at this point, they do make the model easier to develop. Place the cell selector on row 2 and, starting in column B, type **JAN** and then press RIGHT ARROW. Then type **FEB** and press RIGHT ARROW. Type **MAR** and so on through to **DEC**. After **DEC**, move to cell N2 and enter **YEAR** for the year-end totals that will eventually be created.

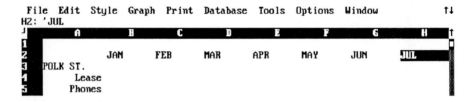

When entering a series of labels like this, you can appreciate the usefulness of the arrow method for entering data.

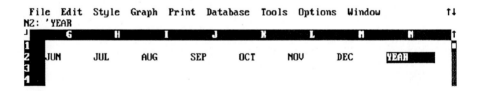

In Chapter 10 you will read how to enter the same month headings with Quattro PRO's date arithmetic feature.

Beginning Values

All projections must have a starting point. In the case of a budget such as the one you are building here, the January figures are based on the actual figures for the last month of the previous year. This data is entered in

File Edit Style Graph Print Database Tools Options Window   ↑↓
B20: 890

	A	B	C	D	E	F	G	H
1								
2		JAN	FEB	MAR	APR	MAY	JUN	JUL
3	POLK ST.							
4	Lease	350						
5	Phones	230						
6	Telex	110						
7	Electric	120						
8	Res. Rent	500						
9	VAN NESS							
10	Lease	500						
11	Phones	250						
12	Telex	150						
13	Electric	225						
14	Res. Rent	835						
15	UNION SQ.							
16	Lease	1200						
17	Phones	300						
18	Telex	250						
19	Electric	205						
20	Res. Rent	890						

SHEET1.WQ1   [1]   NUM   READY

Figure 5-2.   *The January numbers*

column B, as shown in Figure 5-2. Again, you can make use of the arrow method as you enter the list of numbers.

Total Calculation

After you enter the figures for the first three offices, the worksheet should look like the one shown in Figure 5-2. You now need to add a fourth office, **EMBARCADERO,** as shown in the following illustration. Enter the office name and then copy down the expense categories and enter the starting figures. At the bottom of column B you want to enter a formula that will sum the January expenses for all four offices. Enter the label **TOTALS** in A28, and move to B28 to create the formula, which will use the @SUM function.

1. Type **@SUM(** to begin the formula. You are now ready to use the pointing method to indicate which cell block is to be summed.

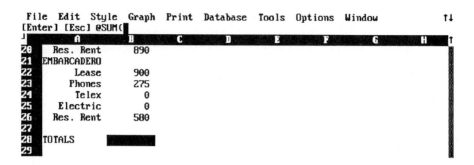

2. Use the UP ARROW key to get to B4, and anchor the beginning point of the block by typing a period. You now need to move the highlighting down the column. There is a quick way to do this. If you use the END and DOWN ARROW keys, your highlighting will go only to the next gap in the rows, in this case, cell B8. This is not the quickest way to move to the bottom of a column that is not made up of solid rows of data. A better method is to move your cell selector to a solid column of data.

3. Press LEFT ARROW, and your cell selector will be in a column (column A) that contains consecutive rows of data.

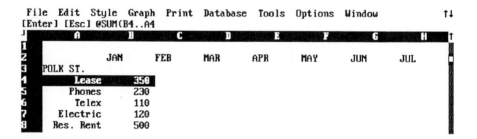

4. Now press END and DOWN ARROW. Doing so takes you directly to row 26. Do not press ENTER yet.

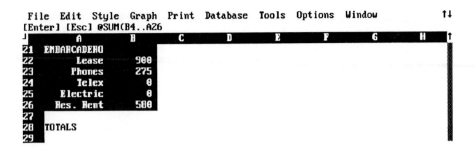

5. In essence you have hitched a ride on a block of occupied cells that is continuous in your desired direction. You now need to press RIGHT ARROW to move back into the original column. The highlighting will appear in B4..B26, as shown in Figure 5-3.

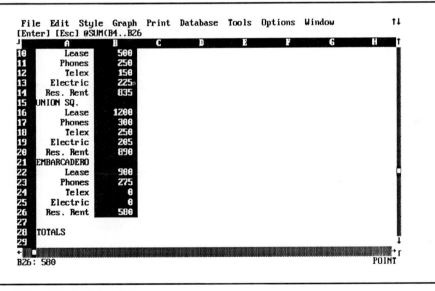

Figure 5-3. *Block highlighting*

6. Complete the formula with the closing parenthesis and then press ENTER. The ride-hitching method is very useful as you are building a model, since often you need to move the cell selector to the end of the model in a row or column that is not yet completely filled. However, you must always remember to come back to the original column or row before completing the maneuver.

7. With the cell selector still in B28, select Edit Copy and press ENTER. Then press RIGHT ARROW and ENTER to complete copying the formula to C28.

Copying Formulas

The figures that occupy column C are actually formulas that multiply the expenses in column B by a factor that increases them. These formulas are repeated across the model so that a steady month-to-month increase in expenses is built into the budget. Although in practice lease payments rarely increase on a gradual monthly basis, the overall effect will be to allocate sufficient funding for probable long-term lease cost increases.

The formula in C4 is 1.01 times the value in the cell one column to the left, or 1.01*B4. You need to enter this formula in C4 now, leaving your cell selector in C4, since the formula will be copied down the column, making each cell in the C column 1.01 times the value in the cell to the left. To perform the copy, follow these steps:

1. Select Edit Copy. The Source Block will be C4..C4, which Quattro PRO is already suggesting. Press ENTER to confirm this.

2. The quickest way to point out the destination for the copy is to press a period while the cell selector is still in C4. This anchors the beginning point of the block in C4, and you can use the DOWN ARROW key to highlight down to C26. This is shown in Figure 5-4.

3. Press ENTER to confirm C4..C26 as the destination cells. This will complete the copy process. Including the source cell C4 in the destination causes that cell to be copied over itself, but this causes no problems.

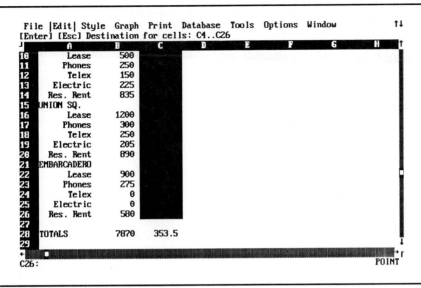

File |Edit| Style Graph Print Database Tools Options Window   ↑↓
[Enter] [Esc] Destination for cells: C4..C26

	A	B	C	D	E	F	G	H
10	Lease	500						
11	Phones	250						
12	Telex	150						
13	Electric	225						
14	Res. Rent	835						
15	UNION SQ.							
16	Lease	1200						
17	Phones	300						
18	Telex	250						
19	Electric	205						
20	Res. Rent	890						
21	EMBARCADERO							
22	Lease	900						
23	Phones	275						
24	Telex	0						
25	Electric	0						
26	Res. Rent	580						
27								
28	TOTALS	7870	353.5					
29								

C26:   POINT

Figure 5-4. *Destination highlighted*

Note that each cell in column C from rows 4 to 26 is 1.01 times the value of the corresponding cell in column B. One small problem is that the rows without expenses in column B are also multiplied in column C. You can easily remove these rows by erasing the contents of cells C9, C15, and C21. Simply highlight each one in turn and press the DELETE key to remove its contents. Do that now.

Copying Columns

Since you have already copied the @SUM formula from the bottom of column B to the bottom of column C (from B28 to C28), you can copy the whole of column C, from rows 4 through 28, to columns D through M to complete the projection for 12 months. C4..C28 is highlighted as the Source Block, the last screen of which is shown in Figure 5-5. The following steps will perform the copy for the column.

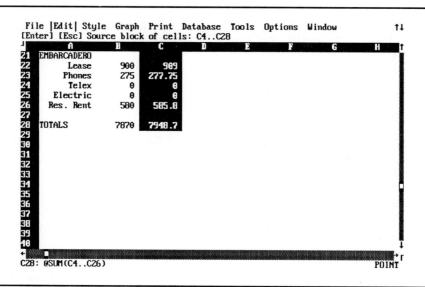

```
File |Edit| Style  Graph  Print  Database  Tools  Options  Window          ↑↓
[Enter] [Esc] Source block of cells: C4..C28
┘          A          B        C          D        E        F        G        H    ↑
21 EMBARCADERO
22       Lease       900       909
23       Phones      275     277.75
24       Telex         0         0
25      Electric       0         0
26     Res. Rent      580     585.8
27
28 TOTALS            7870    7948.7
29
30
31
32
33
34
35
36
37
38
39
40                                                                                ↓
←                                                                             →
C28: @SUM(C4..C26)                                                         POINT
```

Figure 5-5. *Source Block*

1. With your cell selector in C4, select Edit Copy. The Source Block needs to be expanded downward. Press PAGE DOWN and you will move the highlighting to C24. Press the DOWN ARROW key a few more times to include C28. Press ENTER to confirm C4..C28 as the Source Block.

2. Move the cell selector to D4 and anchor it with a period. Press UP ARROW twice, and you will be able to hitch a ride to the end of the model using the line of months in row 2.

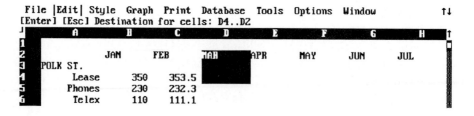

```
File |Edit| Style  Graph  Print  Database  Tools  Options  Window          ↑↓
[Enter] [Esc] Destination for cells: D4..D2
┘          A          B        C          D        E        F        G        H    ↑
1
2             JAN       FEB      MAR     APR      MAY      JUN      JUL
3  POLK ST.
4        Lease       350     353.5
5        Phones      230     232.3
6        Telex       110     111.1
```

3. Press END and then RIGHT ARROW. The highlighting will move to column N, which is labeled YEAR. Then press LEFT ARROW once and DOWN ARROW twice so that the highlighted Destination Block is row 4 of all of the month columns, D4..M4.

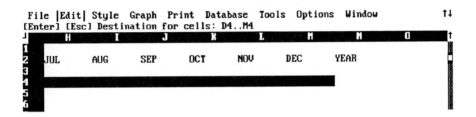

4. Quattro PRO will assume that row 4 and the area below it, down as far as row 28, are available for copying into. If you want to be sure, move the highlighting down to line 28 to correspond with the Source Block and to view the full range of destination cells. However, this is not essential since you are working on a new worksheet and therefore know that nothing has already been entered. Press ENTER to confirm the destination of the copy.

The impressive results of this copy are shown in Figure 5-6. You have seen the speed with which Quattro PRO reproduces a set of formulas. Since much of the work you do with numbers requires repetition of the same calculations, you will probably use the Copy command a great deal in your own spreadsheets.

Saving Your Work

At this point you can issue the File Save As command to give the worksheet a name and store the work you have done so far. When you issue the File Save As command for a worksheet that has not yet been saved, you are provided with a list of files in the current directory, as shown here.

```
5   Phones      230      232.3  234.623 236.9692 239.3389 241.7323 244.1496
6  ┌─────────────────────────────────────────────────────┐ 664  115.6111 116.7672
7  │ Enter save file name:                            ↑ │ 25   126.1212 127.3824
8  │ C:\QUATTRO\DATA\*.WQ1                               ▢ │ 02   525.505  530.7601
9 VA│ AB1.WQ1        ABC.WQ1        ADDLIST.WQ1           │
10  │ ARROWS.WQ1     BIOSOFT.WQ1    C3FIG16.WQ1           │ 02   525.505  530.7601
11  │ C4CTERM.WQ1    C4FVAL.WQ1     C4IFADV.WQ1         ↓ │ 51   262.7525   265.38
12  │ C4LOOKIF.WQ1   CHAP1.WQ1      CHAP1MOD.WQ1           │ 06   157.6515  159.228
13  │                                                      │ 59   236.4773  238.842
14  R│▐│││││││││││││││││││││││││││││││││││││││││││││││││││││▌│ 43   877.5934 886.3693
15 UNION SQ.
16   Lease      1200     1212  1224.12 1236.361 1248.725 1261.212 1273.824
```

Enter an appropriate name, such as QVBUDG01, simply by typing at the
prompt. There is no need to type the extensions as the WQ1 is automatically added at the end of the file name. Press ENTER to confirm the name,
and your work so far will be stored in a file called QVBUDG01.WQ1. You
can see this name on the left of the status line at the bottom of the screen.
As you continue to build the worksheet and improve it, you can quickly
save further changes to the same file with the File Save command.

```
  File  Edit  Style  Graph  Print  Database  Tools  Options  Window          ↑↓
  C4: 1.01*B4
  ┘    A         B         C         D         E         F         G         H      ↑
  1
  2         JAN       FEB       MAR       APR       MAY       JUN       JUL
  3 POLK ST.
  4   Lease   350     353.5   357.035 360.6054 364.2114 367.8535 371.5321
  5   Phones  230     232.3   234.623 236.9692 239.3389 241.7323 244.1496
  6   Telex   110     111.1   112.211 113.3331 114.4664 115.6111 116.7672
  7  Electric 120     121.2   122.412 123.6361 124.8725 126.1212 127.3824
  8  Res. Rent 500    505     510.05  515.1505 520.302  525.505  530.7601
  9 VAN NESS
 10   Lease   500     505     510.05  515.1505 520.302  525.505  530.7601
 11   Phones  250     252.5   255.025 257.5753 260.151  262.7525  265.38
 12   Telex   150     151.5   153.015 154.5452 156.0906 157.6515 159.228
 13  Electric 225    227.25  229.5225 231.8177 234.1359 236.4773 238.842
 14  Res. Rent 835   843.35  851.7835 860.3013 868.9043 877.5934 886.3693
 15 UNION SQ.
 16   Lease  1200    1212   1224.12 1236.361 1248.725 1261.212 1273.824
 17   Phones  300     303    306.03  309.0903 312.1812 315.303  318.456
 18   Telex   250     252.5   255.025 257.5753 260.151  262.7525  265.38
 19  Electric 205    207.05 209.1205 211.2117 213.3238 215.4571 217.6116
 20  Res. Rent 890    898.9  907.889 916.9679 926.1376 935.3989 944.7529  ↓
  ←                                                                    → ┌
  SHEET1.WQ1  [1]                                         NUM         READY
```

Figure 5-6.   *The completed copy*

Display Format

After a large copy operation, you will probably want to fine-tune some of the results. As you can see in the example, the appearance of many of the numbers leaves something to be desired. This is because they are displayed in the General format, which shows as many decimal places as it takes to complete the calculation or fill the cell. When the growth factor produces lengthy fractions, the cell fills with many decimal figures. To correct this and format the numbers consistently, you can use the Style Numeric Format command, and select the Comma format for the value cells of the model. This format places a comma in the thousands and lets you limit the number of decimal places displayed, in this case to zero places.

1. Place your cell selector in B4, the top left of the range of cells that need to be reformatted. Select Style Numeric Format. You will see the menu shown in Figure 5-7.

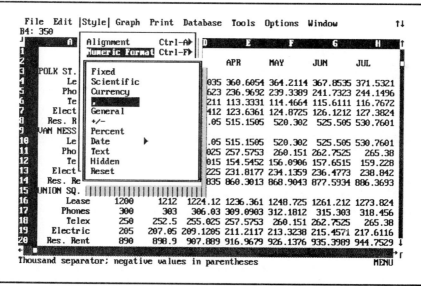

Figure 5-7. *Setting a format*

2. Pick the Comma format by typing a comma (,).

3. This format assumes that you want two decimal places, but you can easily change that to zero by typing **0** and pressing ENTER.

4. You will then be prompted for the block of cells to be formatted. Press PAGE DOWN and then DOWN ARROW several times to include the last line of the model. Press END and then RIGHT ARROW to include a range of cells that extends all the way to the last column of the model. Press ENTER to confirm this block.

The results are very tidy and can be seen back in Figure 5-1. Notice that the decimal places are rounded by the Display format, rather than truncated. If you later change the format to display several decimal places, Quattro PRO will reveal the decimal digits that the zero decimal format removed from view. Now try placing your cell selector in one of the cells that has a lot of decimal places, such as E4. You will see from the cell identifier in the bottom status area that the real content of the cell is the formula 1.01*D4, together with the format notation (,0) for Comma format, zero decimal places. A cell will still produce decimal places, however, if you change the format to display them.

Summing the Rows

Now you are ready to perform the last calculation needed to complete the model in column N, which will hold the totals for each expense category over the 12-month period. These totals will be a series of @SUM formulas, the first of which you enter in N4.

1. In cell N4 type **@SUM(**. Press END and LEFT ARROW, and then END and LEFT ARROW again to move to the extreme left of the model. Now press RIGHT ARROW once so that you are in cell B4. Type a period to anchor the beginning point of the block in this cell.

2. Press END and then RIGHT ARROW to include all the cells in the range B4..M4. Type the closing parenthesis to complete the formula and press ENTER to place the formula in N4.

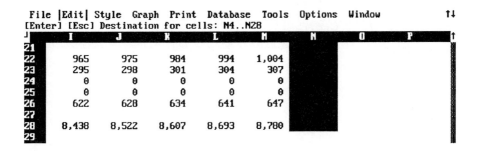

3. To sum all the rows in the model, select Edit Copy with the cell selector still in N4. Press ENTER to accept N4..N4 as the Source Block.

4. Type a period to anchor N4 as the start of the Destination Block and press PAGE DOWN. Press the DOWN ARROW key several more times to include the last row of the model, 28, the one that sums all the columns. Press ENTER to confirm the copy.

5. The formula in cell N28 is actually the grand total of all the expenses, since it sums the row of column totals. You will find several cells in column N containing zeros, because the formula copied into them is inappropriate. Simply delete these with the DELETE key.

You may have noticed that the Comma format has not yet been applied to the figures in column N. You will probably want to do so to make them consistent with the rest of the model. With your cell selector on N4, select Style Numeric Format and select comma (,). Type **0** to indicate the number of decimal places. Use PAGE DOWN and DOWN ARROW to extend the highlighting through N28 before pressing ENTER to complete the operation.

Using and Viewing the Model

Having built the model, you are almost ready to use it. However, before going any further you should make sure that the latest changes are stored. Assuming that you have used the File Save As command to give the worksheet an appropriate file name, issue the File Save command to update the file. If you have not yet used the File Save As command see the earlier section, "Saving Your Work."

From a practical point of view the model has several uses. The basic use is to determine the total expenses for the year based on the assumed beginning values and growth factor. In Figure 5-8 the **Res. Rent** is updated to reflect a new minimum rental amount of $1,000 per month. As soon as the new amount is entered, the change affects the totals across the model.

File Edit Style Graph Print Database Tools Options Window							↑↓
B26: (,0) 1000							
A	**B**	**C**	**D**	**E**	**F**	**G**	**H**
9 VAN NESS							
10 Lease	500	505	510	515	520	526	531
11 Phones	250	253	255	258	260	263	265
12 Telex	150	152	153	155	156	158	159
13 Electric	225	227	230	232	234	236	239
14 Res. Rent	835	843	852	860	869	878	886
15 UNION SQ.							
16 Lease	1,200	1,212	1,224	1,236	1,249	1,261	1,274
17 Phones	300	303	306	309	312	315	318
18 Telex	250	253	255	258	260	263	265
19 Electric	205	207	209	211	213	215	218
20 Res. Rent	890	899	908	917	926	935	945
21 EMBARCADERO							
22 Lease	900	909	918	927	937	946	955
23 Phones	275	278	281	283	286	289	292
24 Telex	0	0	0	0	0	0	0
25 Electric	0	0	0	0	0	0	0
26 Res. Rent	**1,000**	1,010	1,020	1,030	1,041	1,051	1,062
27							
28 TOTALS	8,290	8,373	8,457	8,541	8,627	8,713	8,800
QUBUDG01.WQ1 [1]					NUM		READY

Figure 5-8.   Updating the completed model

Advanced Maneuvers

Quattro PRO has a number of commands that enable you to move around the spreadsheet and change its appearance. When the spreadsheet begins to grow and becomes complex, you will want to exercise greater control over its appearance and also use some shortcuts to maneuver about in it.

END Keys   You have already seen that the END keys can be a great help during copy operations. Now that the model is built, END and RIGHT ARROW move you to the right side of the model. Be sure to have your cell selector on a completed row of data before using this combination. Asking Quattro PRO to go to the end of the right side of a blank line means you end up in column IV. Simply press HOME, or END and LEFT ARROW to return to the worksheet area.

Goto   You may have noticed that the arrow keys are not always the most efficient way to move to a specific location, particularly if that location is some distance from your current position. For this reason, you will often want to use the Goto key (F5). When you press F5, you are prompted for the location you want the cell selector moved to. Quattro PRO will show the destination cell as a default in the top left of the screen. Simply type in the coordinates of your destination and press ENTER. The cell selector will be placed in the new cell. Unless the destination cell is very close to A1, this move may disorient you at first; for example, when you are using Goto to move to the bottom-right corner of the model. If you use Goto to get to N28, Quattro PRO shows just one cell, N28, on the screen. To get around this and to avoid having to remember cell coordinates, you can use block names.

Block Names   Obviously, remembering cell coordinates in large models becomes increasingly difficult. Here, Edit Names can be a great help. You can attach a name to a single cell or group of cells just for the purpose of moving it around. After you have attached a name to the group of cells with

Edit Names Create, you can type the block name at the Goto prompt. Or, you can use the F3 key to list the block names, highlight the destination, and press ENTER to insert it on the Goto prompt line.

If the block name refers to a group of cells, your cell selector will be placed in the cell that is at the top-left corner of the block. That cell will be placed in the top left of your screen. For example, one way of quickly moving to a view of the lower-right section of the example spreadsheet would be to name cells K20..N28 as the block TOTAL. You could then press F5 and type **TOTAL** as the address you want to go to. Press ENTER, and you would be placed in the position shown in Figure 5-9, where cell K20 is in the top-left corner of the screen.

You will also find this technique useful if you are constantly working between the home position at A1 and another location. You can label the second location HOME and move there by pressing F5, typing **HOME**, and pressing ENTER. Here you see the F3 key being used with the F5 key. Note

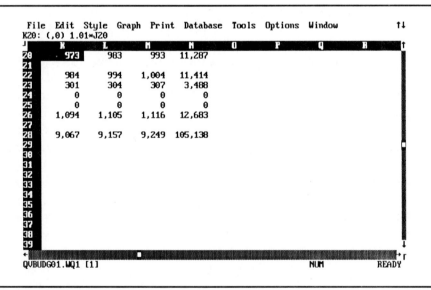

Figure 5-9.   *Using block name Goto*

that the list of cell names is alphabetical. For this reason, cells that are frequently referenced should be labeled with names that will appear at the top of the alphabetized list.

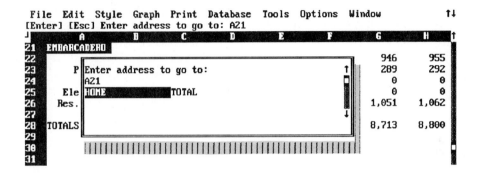

Windows Within a Worksheet

In the course of using the model, you will encounter several situations that call for further Quattro PRO commands. For example, you have already found that you cannot see the YEAR total column when you are viewing the JAN column. Quattro PRO provides a simple method for letting you see two parts of the same spreadsheet at the same time. You split the screen either horizontally or vertically into two parts, called windows.

Quattro PRO uses the term *window* for two different features. *Worksheet window* refers to the space within which each spreadsheet is displayed when more than one is open. You can also have a *split window* within a worksheet window. In each split window you can view a different part of the worksheet. As you move the cell selector in one window you can scroll the view in the other, or you can remove the synchronization from the windows to view each window independently.

To try using windows with the example, first position the cell selector in column E and select Window, followed by Options. The first two options shown here are Horizontal and Vertical splitting.

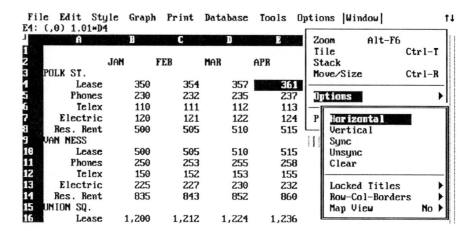

```
File  Edit  Style  Graph  Print  Database  Tools  Options |Window|          ↑↓
E4: (,0) 1.01*D4
┘         A        B        C        D        E      ┌─────────────────────────┐
1                                                    │ Zoom        Alt-F6       │
2                  JAN      FEB      MAR      APR     │ Tile        Ctrl-T       │
3        POLK ST.                                     │ Stack                    │
4            Lease      350      354      357   361   │ Move/Size   Ctrl-R       │
5            Phones     230      232      235   237   ├─────────────────────────┤
6            Telex      110      111      112   113   │ Options                ▶ │
7          Electric     120      121      122   124  P├──────────────┬──────────┤
8          Res. Rent    500      505      510   515   │ Horizontal   │          │
9        VAN NESS                                     │ Vertical     │          │
10           Lease      500      505      510   515 ││ Sync        │          │
11           Phones     250      253      255   258   │ Unsync       │          │
12           Telex      150      152      153   155   │ Clear        │          │
13         Electric     225      227      230   232   ├──────────────┘          │
14         Res. Rent    835      843      852   860   │ Locked Titles          ▶ │
15       UNION SQ.                                    │ Row-Col-Borders        ▶ │
16           Lease    1,200    1,212    1,224  1,236  │ Map View            No ▶ │
                                                      └─────────────────────────┘
```

The Sync and Unsync options allow you to switch between the default mode of synchronized split windows and the alternative, unsynchronized mode. The split occurs at the current position of the cell selector, which is why you moved to column E before issuing the command. The Clear option closes the second window. Select Vertical, and the screen will appear divided.

```
File  Edit  Style  Graph  Print  Database  Tools  Options  Window           ↑↓
N8: (,0) @SUM(B8..M8)
┘       A        B        C        D    │      L       M       N           ↑
1                                       │1
2                JAN      FEB      MAR   │2 NOV      DEC     YEAR
3      POLK ST.                         │3
4          Lease     350      354    357│4    387     390    4,439
5          Phones    230      232    235│5    254     257    2,917
6          Telex     110      111    112│6    122     123    1,395
7        Electric    120      121    122│7    133     134    1,522
8        Res. Rent   500      505    510│8    552     558    6,341
9      VAN NESS                         │9
```

You can move between split windows by pressing the Windows key (F6). Press it several times, and you will see that it toggles between windows. This illustration shows the result of first toggling the cell selector to the left window and placing it on cell B8, where the Res. Rent needs to be updated. The F6 key was then pressed to move to the right window, and the RIGHT ARROW key was pressed until the end of the model was placed in view as shown. Pressing F6 again returns you to the cell you left from. Entering a new amount for Res. Rent will produce a result immediately visible on the other side of the screen.

Initially, the split windows are synchronized. With a vertical split this means that pressing UP or DOWN ARROW will scroll the worksheet on both sides of the split. You can see that the row numbers in the dividing line match those in the left border. With a horizontal window, this means that RIGHT or LEFT ARROW will move the worksheet on the top and bottom halves of the screen, and the column letters in the dividing line will match those in the top border. Figure 5-10 shows the effect of unsynchronizing the windows. To unsynchronize windows, select Window Options Unsync. Place the cell selector on the right of the screen and move down to the bottom line of the budget. The budget is unmoved on the other side. You can see that the row numbers in the dividing line no longer match those in the left border. To clear windows, select Window Option Clear.

| File | Edit | Style | Graph | Print | Database | Tools | Options | Window | | ↑↓ |

B8: (,0) 500

	A	B	C	D		L	M	N	
1					15				
2		JAN	FEB	MAR	16	1,326	1,339	15,219	
3	POLK ST.				17	331	335	3,805	
4	Lease	350	354	357	18	276	279	3,171	
5	Phones	230	232	235	19	226	229	2,600	
6	Telex	110	111	112	20	983	993	11,287	
7	Electric	120	121	122	21				
8	Res. Rent	500	505	510	22	994	1,004	11,414	
9	VAN NESS				23	304	307	3,488	
10	Lease	500	505	510	24	0	0	0	
11	Phones	250	253	255	25	0	0	0	
12	Telex	150	152	153	26	1,105	1,116	12,683	
13	Electric	225	227	230	27				
14	Res. Rent	835	843	852	28	9,157	9,249	105,138	
15	UNION SQ.				29				
16	Lease	1,200	1,212	1,224	30				
17	Phones	300	303	306	31				
18	Telex	250	253	255	32				
19	Electric	205	207	209	33				
20	Res. Rent	890	899	908	34				

QVBUDG01.WQ1 [1]   NUM   READY

Figure 5-10. *Unsynchronized windows*

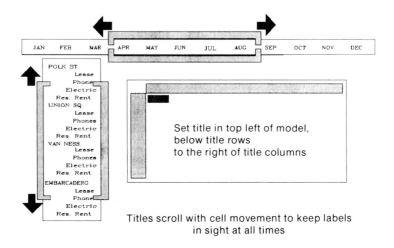

Set title in top left of model,
below title rows
to the right of title columns

Titles scroll with cell movement to keep labels
in sight at all times

Figure 5-11.   *Diagram of titles*

Titles

You can see from Figure 5-10 that when you are using windows the column headings disappear if the right side of the worksheet is moved down. In fact, you may have found this to be a problem when working without windows, as in Figures 5-8 and 5-9. As you move to the lower areas of the worksheet and the month labels disappear, it becomes difficult to know which months you are viewing. Knowing where you are is particularly important when you have to update cells in the middle of a large spreadsheet.

The solution is to *freeze* certain rows and columns so that titles do not disappear. To freeze titles, place the cell selector in the top left of the area you want to move, as diagrammed in Figure 5-11. When you use the Window Options Locked Titles command, you can choose Horizontal, which freezes the area above the cell selector; Vertical, which freezes the area to the left of the cell selector; or Both, which locks areas above and to the left of the cell selector. You can see this in the sample spreadsheet if you place the cell selector in B3 and select Window Options Locked Titles. The following Locked Titles menu appears:

13	Electric	225	227	230	232	**Locked Titles**	▶
14	Res. Rent	835	843	852	860	Row—	▶
15	UNION SQ.					Map	Horizontal
16	Lease	1,200	1,212	1,224	1,236		Vertical
17	Phones	300	303	306	309		**Both**
18	Telex	250	253	255	258	260	Clear
19	Electric	205	207	209	211	213	
20	Res. Rent	890	899	908	917	926	

Lock columns to left and rows above current cell   MENU

You can use only the rows above the cell selector as titles or only the columns to the left of the cell selector. In this case, you want to pick Both, so that both the months and the expense categories stay on the screen while you scan the model. When you pick your Titles choice, you are returned to the spreadsheet. Now press TAB and PAGE DOWN. Notice that the column and row headings remain on the screen.

The effect of moving the cell selector after fixing titles is shown in Figure 5-12, where cell I24 is being updated to reflect the anticipated August installation of Telex in the EMBARCADERO office. You can see how much easier this is with titles visible than without them. After making the

File   Edit   Style   Graph   Print   Database   Tools   Options   Window   ↑↓
I24: (,0) 150

	A	H	I	J	K	L	M	N
1								
2		JUL	AUG	SEP	OCT	NOV	DEC	YEAR
10	Lease	531	536	541	547	552	558	6,341
11	Phones	265	268	271	273	276	279	3,171
12	Telex	159	161	162	164	166	167	1,902
13	Electric	239	241	244	246	249	251	2,854
14	Res. Rent	886	895	904	913	922	932	10,590
15	UNION SQ.							
16	Lease	1,274	1,287	1,299	1,312	1,326	1,339	15,219
17	Phones	318	322	325	328	331	335	3,805
18	Telex	265	268	271	273	276	279	3,171
19	Electric	218	220	222	224	226	229	2,600
20	Res. Rent	945	954	964	973	983	993	11,287
21	EMBARCADERO							
22	Lease	955	965	975	984	994	1,004	11,414
23	Phones	292	295	298	301	304	307	3,488
24	Telex	0	**150**	152	153	155	156	765
25	Electric	0	0	0	0	0	0	0
26	Res. Rent	1,062	1,072	1,083	1,094	1,105	1,116	12,683
27								

QUBUDG01.WQ1 [1]   NUM   READY

Figure 5-12.   *Effect of fixing titles*

change to this cell, press HOME and you will see that this is now B3, the cell in which you performed the title lock. You may wonder how you can change headings if you are locked out of those cells. For example, you may want to change the entry in cell A24 to show the addition of Telex in August. You can do this with the Goto key (F5). Press F5 and type the address of the title cell you want to edit, in this case **A24**; then press ENTER.

```
 File  Edit  Style  Graph  Print  Database  Tools  Options  Window            ↑↓
A24: [W12] "Telex
J         A            A         B        C        D        E        F      ↑
1
2                             JAN      FEB      MAR      APR      MAY
24        Telex        Telex       0        0        0        0        0
25        Electric     Electric    0        0        0        0        0
26        Res. Rent    Res. Rent 1,000    1,010    1,020    1,030    1,041
27
28 TOTALS        TOTALS         8,290    8,373    8,457    8,541    8,627
```

The cell is placed on the edit line for you to change. Press F2 to edit the cell, and then press ENTER to place the cell contents back in the cell. To put the updated title back into place, press PAGE DOWN, TAB, and then HOME.

Locking titles works well when a model has been built and only the data is being updated. However, you may need to unlock the titles when making major changes to the spreadsheet. To clear the titles, select Window Options Locked Titles Clear.

Hiding Columns

At times the data you see on the screen is not the data you need. You may even rearrange titles and windows and the spreadsheet will still not be to your liking. In such cases, you might want to try hiding certain columns with the Style Hide Column command. Quattro PRO lets you place selected columns in the background and closes up the ones in the foreground. This is diagrammed in Figure 5-13. Thus, you can pick and choose which columns to view. The Style Hide Column command is also useful when you are dealing with confidential data or arranging a worksheet prior to printing. The hidden data is not lost, and hidden formulas continue to be active.

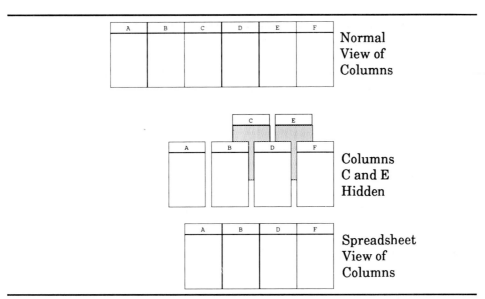

Figure 5-13. *The Hide Column command*

To hide the first six months of the sample model, place the cell selector on any row in column B and select Style Hide Column. Your choices are Hide or Expose. Choose Hide and then anchor the beginning column by typing a period; press RIGHT ARROW to move the highlighting through to column G. Here you can see the range of columns from B through G being hidden.

```
 File   Edit  |Style|  Graph   Print   Database   Tools   Options   Window              ↑↓
[Enter] [Esc] Hide columns from view: B3..G3
         A          B          C          D          E          F          G          H    ↑
 1
 2                 JAN        FEB        MAR        APR        MAY        JUN        JUL
 3  POLK ST.
 4        Lease     350        354        357        361        364        368        372
 5        Phones    230        232        235        237        239        242        244
```

When you press ENTER, the columns disappear from view and cannot be accessed. To return the columns to view, simply select Style Hide Column

Expose. Asterisks next to the column letters indicate the columns that are currently hidden.

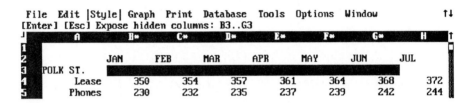

To return columns to the display, simply highlight them and press ENTER. If you press ESCAPE and do not select any columns, the marked columns remain hidden.

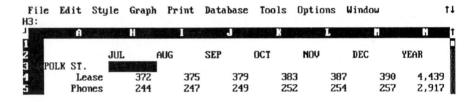

The column width and format remain unaffected by the hide-and-expose process. When you carry out any command using the POINT mode to indicate cell references, Quattro PRO temporarily reveals hidden columns, marked by asterisks, so that they can be considered in the command. For example, if you use the Edit Move or Edit Copy command or formulas built with the point method, the columns will be temporarily revealed so you can correctly complete the operation.

Adding Rows

Occasionally you will need to add more rows to your model. In the sample model you need room for a title across the top. You do so by inserting several rows at the top of the spreadsheet. This will not affect any of the calculations in the model. With the cell selector in row 1, select Edit Insert Row to insert just one row. You would normally press ENTER, but to add four rows you press the DOWN ARROW key three times. When you press ENTER you will insert a total of four rows.

```
 File |Edit| Style  Graph  Print  Database  Tools  Options  Window          ↑↓
[Enter] [Esc] Enter row insert block: D1..D4
┘       A        B        C        D        E        F        G        H      ↑
1
2              JAN      FEB      MAR      APR      MAY      JUN      JUL
3  POLK ST.
4      Lease    350      354      357      361      364      368      372
5      Phones   230      232      235      237      239      242      244
6      Telex    110      111      112      113      114      116      117
```

Adding Titles

There is no Quattro PRO command for centering a title over a model. You have to center titles yourself. To begin, try typing the name of the travel company, **Quattro Vadis Travel,** in cell D2. This can be moved later. Below this, in C4, type **'90 Budget—Based On Monthly Growth Factor of** and press ENTER. Notice that the leading apostrophe is the left label indicator and allows Quattro PRO to accept what would otherwise be an unacceptable mix of numbers and letters. In cell H4 the actual figure for the growth factor, 1.01, has been entered as a number.

```
 File  Edit  Style  Graph  Print  Database  Tools  Options  Window          ↑↓
H4: 1.01
┘       A        B        C        D        E        F        G        H      ↑
1
2                          Quattro Vadis Travel
3
4              90 Budget - Based On Monthly Growth Factor of    1.01
5
6              JAN      FEB      MAR      APR      MAY      JUN      JUL
7  POLK ST.
8      Lease    350      354      357      361      364      368      372
9      Phones   230      232      235      237      239      242      244
```

Updating the Model

Having built the model and explored several ways of making it easier to view, you may want to update it to reflect a revised estimate of how much costs will rise. Recall that all of the expenses in columns C through M are based on a factor of 1.01. This was done by copying the formula 1.01*B4 from C4 to all the other cells. To change the growth basis of the spreadsheet to 1.005, you could write a new formula. The new starting location is C8, and you could enter 1.005*B8 in C8 and then copy it to all the other cells. That would involve several steps, however, and you would have to repeat all those steps every time you wanted to see the effect of a different factor. As you will see, this is not necessary with Quattro PRO.

Problems with Relatives

Since the growth rate is stated in H4, you might be tempted to write a new formula (+H4*B8) in C8 and copy it to all the other cells. That way you could simply change the factor in H4 and it would be reflected throughout the budget. This approach can run into problems, however. Remember that entering a formula like 1.01*B8 in C8 means that B8, the cell to the left of C8, is multiplied by 1.01. When you copy this formula to D8, D8 becomes 1.01*C8, 1.01 times the cell to the left of D8. The formula +H4*B8 means the cell that is up four rows and over five, times the cell to the left. If you copy this formula from C8 to D8, you get +I8*C8, the cell that is up four rows and over five times the cell to the left. Since I4 is empty, the answer is 0. The same would apply to all other cells in the row if you copied the formula across the row, as you can see here:

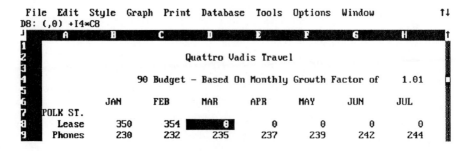

If you copy a formula and the answer is an unexpected zero, move the cell selector to the first offending cell and check the contents in the cell identifier. In the case of D8, it is **+I8*C8** as predicted.

Absolute Solutions

The solution to the relative problem is to make any references to fixed cells absolute. Thus, you can say that C8 is absolutely H4 times B8. You indicate this in the formula by placing a dollar sign in front of the coordinates. Thus, $H$4*B8 can be copied anywhere, and the result will always be H4 times the cell to the left, since the formula was created to the right of B8.

There are two ways to make a cell reference absolute: You can type the dollar signs yourself, or—with the cursor next to the cell reference on the edit line—press the Absolute, or Abs key (F4). Quattro PRO will add dollar signs for you. In fact, if you keep pressing F4, the program will show you the four possible cell references:

$H$4	Absolutely column H row 4
$H4	Absolutely column H, but any row
H$4	Any column, but absolutely row 4
H4	Completely relative

In the case of the sample model, type the formula **$H$4*B8** into C8. Then copy the formula across the columns to M8, taking care not to copy over the very last cell on row 8, since that holds the @SUM formula. Then copy C8..M8 down to C9..M30. (You will create several extra rows of zeros that you can remove with Edit Erase.) You will find that the formula works correctly now, and you can update the rate in H4, perhaps to 1.015, and see all of the affected cells change.

You can use the Abs key (F4) in either the pointing method of building formulas or while editing a formula. The absolute reference is necessary whenever you are writing formulas that are going to be copied but need to be referred to as a specific cell or block of cells in their new locations. A typical example of this is a rate, growth factor, or other spreadsheet assumption referenced to a cell outside the model.

Referencing the Total

Perhaps you would like the title of the model to reflect the total expenses for the year. This is easily done by adding a formula to cell H2. Simply type **+N32** and enter it into H2. This will pull the grand total from N32 into H2.

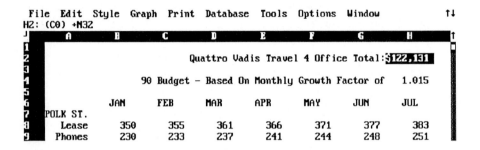

You can edit the label in D1 to match the illustration. To produce the dollar sign on the figure in H2, you would format that cell in Currency format with zero decimal places using the Style Numeric Format command.

Having improved and expanded the model, you are almost ready to print it. However, before going any further you should make sure that the latest changes are stored. Assuming that you have used the File Save As command to give the worksheet an appropriate filename, you can issue the File Save command to update the file. However, at this point you might want to keep the earlier version, in which case you can use File Save As and give the improved worksheet a new name such as QVBUDG02.WQ1. If you have not yet used the File Save As command to store the worksheet you have been building, see the earlier section, "Saving Your Work."

Printing

Now that you have explored various methods for viewing and updating the spreadsheet, it is time to look at how you produce a printed copy. Quattro PRO can produce anything from a simple, one-page printout to a carefully formatted multipage report with headers, footers, and other enhancements.

You begin all printing, simple or complex, by selecting the Print menu from the main menu, as shown in Figure 5-14.

Basic Block Printing

While there are numerous options available for print operations in Quattro PRO, you can get results with just two commands, Block and Spreadsheet Print. Block is used to tell Quattro PRO which cells are to be printed. As you might expect, Block on the Print menu works like any other Quattro PRO Block command. You specify the desired coordinates, either by typing them or by pointing out the cells. Use Spreadsheet Print to initiate printing once you have specified a block.

CAUTION   Do not pick Spreadsheet Print unless you have followed the golden rule of PC printing: plug in, turn on, load up. You must have a printer connected to your PC. That printer must be powered up and loaded with paper before printing. Otherwise, the program may delay and lock you out of the keyboard.

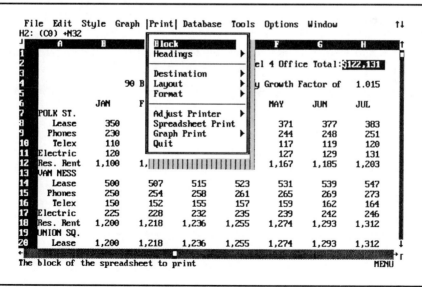

Figure 5-14.   *The Print menu*

Print Block

You can define a Print Block from any point in the spreadsheet. To see the basics of printing, try printing part of the sample worksheet. The basic operation is as follows:

1. Select Print and then Block. The initial coordinate is not locked, so you can move it freely to identify the top-left corner of the range of cells to be printed.

2. Press HOME, and unless your titles are frozen, you will be moved to A1, which is an appropriate point at which to begin printing this spreadsheet. If your titles are frozen, use the arrow keys to move to A1.

3. Anchor the block coordinates at A1 by typing a period, and then press TAB to move over to column H. Now press PAGE DOWN and move down to include all the cells through H32. Press ENTER to confirm this block.

4. Select Adjust Printer, and then pick Align to make sure that Quattro PRO knows that your paper is positioned correctly in the printer.

5. Quattro PRO returns you to the Print menu, from which (if your printer is hooked up, powered up, and has paper in it) you can now select Spreadsheet Print.

The mode indicator will flash the word WAIT for a moment and the completed print job will emerge from the printer, looking like the printout shown in Figure 5-15.

Large Blocks

You often do not need to print all of a spreadsheet at once. Sometimes, the area you need is just a summary of a large area of calculations. However, there will be times when you want to print more worksheet than will fit neatly onto a regular page. In this case, you need something more complex than simple Block and Spreadsheet Print printing.

```
                           Quattro Vadis Travel 4 Office Total:$122,131

                    90 Budget - Based On Monthly Growth Factor of    1.015

                    JAN      FEB      MAR      APR      MAY      JUN      JUL
        POLK ST.
           Lease    350      355      361      366      371      377      383
          Phones    230      233      237      241      244      248      251
           Telex    110      112      113      115      117      119      120
        Electric    120      122      124      125      127      129      131
        Res. Rent 1,100    1,117    1,133    1,150    1,167    1,185    1,203
        VAN NESS
           Lease    500      507      515      523      531      539      547
          Phones    250      254      258      261      265      269      273
           Telex    150      152      155      157      159      162      164
        Electric    225      228      232      235      239      242      246
        Res. Rent 1,200    1,218    1,236    1,255    1,274    1,293    1,312
        UNION SQ.
           Lease  1,200    1,218    1,236    1,255    1,274    1,293    1,312
          Phones    300      304      309      314      318      323      328
           Telex    250      254      258      261      265      269      273
        Electric    205      208      211      214      218      221      224
        Res. Rent 1,000    1,015    1,030    1,046    1,061    1,077    1,093
        EMBARCADERO
           Lease    900      913      927      941      955      970      984
          Phones    275      279      283      288      292      296      301
        Telex (AU     0        0        0        0        0        0        0
        Electric      0        0        0        0        0        0        0
        Res. Rent 1,000    1,015    1,030    1,046    1,061    1,077    1,093

        TOTALS    9,365    9,505    9,648    9,793    9,940   10,089   10,240
```

Figure 5-15. *The first report*

Defaults

When you use the basic Block and Print method, your printed output is based on the size of the Print Block you define and the current menu settings. These settings include the size of the paper and the margins that define the printing area. In other words, they are the parameters by which Quattro PRO relates to a piece of paper. The defaults for these settings are shown in Figure 5-16. You can change margins and page length to accommodate different sizes of paper and type styles.

If you define the entire sample spreadsheet as the Print Block, from A1..N32, Quattro PRO's defaults produce the results shown in Figure 5-17. However, the defaults have several problems. The information flows over two pages and the second page lacks headings to explain the data. The solutions to these problems are numerous. You can increase the size of the paper, reduce the size of the type, repeat some information on successive pages, and add headers and footers.

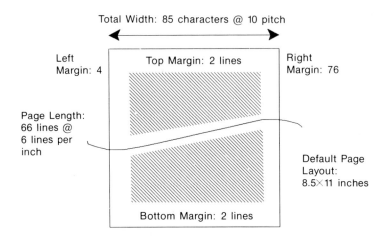

Figure 5-16. *Page layout*

Setting Headings

You can add missing column and row headings in a printout in much the same way as you can with the Locked Titles command when viewing a spreadsheet. You use the Print Heading command to identify columns and rows containing headings as print borders that are then repeated on each page. This procedure is shown in Figure 5-18. You must then redefine the Print Block to exclude areas included in the borders.

Figure 5-19 shows the right side of the top area of the sample spreadsheet, where cells B2..N6 are defined as the Top Heading in preparation for printing the entire spreadsheet. This area will repeat if any part of the printout does not fit on a single page. The Left Heading is defined here as A7..A32.

```
                          Quattro Vadis Travel 4 Office Total:$122,131

              90 Budget - Based On Monthly Growth Factor of    1.015

            JAN       FEB       MAR       APR       MAY       JUN       JUL
POLK ST.
  Lease     350       355       361       366       371       377       383
  Phones    230       233       237       241       244       248       251
  Telex     110       112       113       115       117       119       120
Electric    120       122       124       125       127       129       131
Res. Rent   1,100     1,117     1,133     1,150     1,167     1,185     1,203
VAN NESS
  Lease     500       507       515       523       531       539       547
  Phones    250       254       258       261       265       269       273
  Telex     150       152       155       157       159       162       164
Electric    225       228       232       235       239       242       246
Res. Rent   1,200     1,218     1,236     1,255     1,274     1,293     1,312
UNION SQ.
  Lease     1,200     1,218     1,236     1,255     1,274     1,293     1,312
  Phones    300       304       309       314       318        323      328
  Telex     250       254       258       261       265       269       273
Electric    205       208       211       214       218       221       224
Res. Rent   1,000     1,015     1,030     1,046     1,061     1,077     1,093
EMBARCADERO
  Lease     900       913       927       941       955       970       984
  Phones    275       279       283       288       292       296       301
Telex (AU   0         0         0         0         0         0         0
Electric    0         0         0         0         0         0         0
Res. Rent   1,000     1,015     1,030     1,046     1,061     1,077     1,093

TOTALS      9,365     9,505     9,648     9,793     9,940     10,089    10,240

            AUG       SEP       OCT       NOV       DEC       YEAR

            388       394       400       406       412       4,564
            255       259       263       267       271       2,999
            122       124       126       128       130       1,435
            133       135       137       139       141       1,565
            1,221     1,239     1,258     1,277     1,296     14,345

            555       563       572       580       589       6,521
            277       282       286       290       294       3,260
            166       169       172       174       177       1,956
            250       253       257       261       265       2,934
            1,332     1,352     1,372     1,393     1,414     15,649

            1,332     1,352     1,372     1,393     1,414     15,649
            333       338       343       348       353       3,912
            277       282       286       290       294       3,260
            228       231       234       238       241       2,673
            1,110     1,126     1,143     1,161     1,178     13,041

            999       1,014     1,029     1,044     1,060     11,737
            305       310       314       319       324       3,586
            0         0         0         0         0         0
            0         0         0         0         0         0
            1,110     1,126     1,143     1,161     1,178     13,041

            10,394    10,550    10,708    10,868    11,031    122,131
```

Figure 5-17. *The way Quattro PRO divides blocks*

```
 File  Edit  Style  Graph |Print| Database  Tools  Options  Window          ↑↓
[Enter] [Esc] Row headings to print on the left of each page: A7..A32
J        A          B        C        D        E        F        G        H     ↑
25  EMBARCADERO
26      Lease      900      913      927      941      955      970      984
27      Phones     275      279      283      288      292      296      301
28  Telex (AUG)      0        0        0        0        0        0        0
29     Electric      0        0        0        0        0        0        0
30    Res. Rent  1,000    1,015    1,030    1,046    1,061    1,077    1,093
31
32  TOTALS       9,365    9,505    9,648    9,793    9,940   10,089   10,240
33
```

This heading will repeat if the printout has to divide the data. The Print Block was redefined as B7..N32, and the results of printing with those headings are shown in Figure 5-20.

Changing Margins

As you saw in Figure 5-15, the margins are a critical factor when you are adjusting print settings. If you use wider paper, you must use the Print Layout Margins command to increase the right margin. The 15-inch-wide

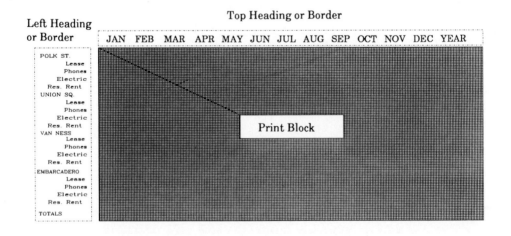

Figure 5-18. *Diagram of headings*

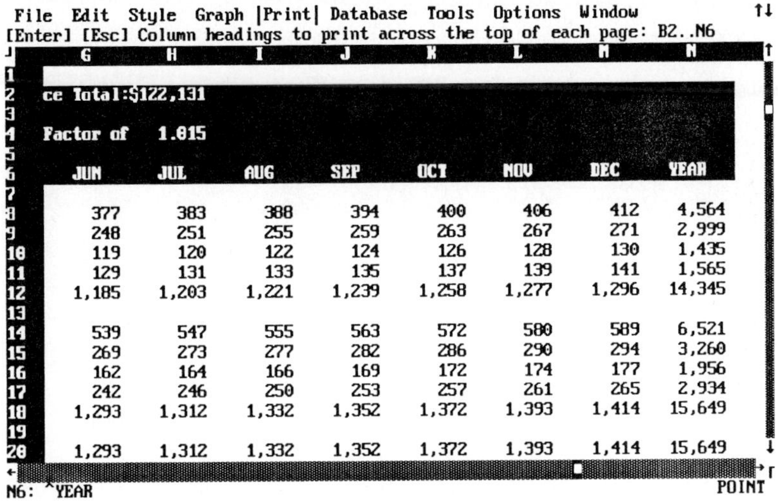

```
    File   Edit   Style   Graph  |Print|  Database   Tools   Options   Window       ↑↓
    [Enter] [Esc] Column headings to print across the top of each page: B2..N6
  ┘       G      H       I       J       K       L       M       N                  ↑
  1
  2  ce Total:$122,131
  3
  4  Factor of    1.015
  5
  6     JUN      JUL     AUG      SEP     OCT     NOV     DEC     YEAR
  7
  8     377      383     388      394     400     406     412    4,564
  9     248      251     255      259     263     267     271    2,999
 10     119      120     122      124     126     128     130    1,435
 11     129      131     133      135     137     139     141    1,565
 12   1,185    1,203   1,221    1,239   1,258   1,277   1,296   14,345
 13
 14     539      547     555      563     572     580     589    6,521
 15     269      273     277      282     286     290     294    3,260
 16     162      164     166      169     172     174     177    1,956
 17     242      246     250      253     257     261     265    2,934
 18   1,293    1,312   1,332    1,352   1,372   1,393   1,414   15,649
 19
 20   1,293    1,312   1,332    1,352   1,372   1,393   1,414   15,649          ↓
  ←                                                                          →  r
 N6:  ^YEAR                                                                    POINT
```

Figure 5-19. *The top headings*

paper used in many wide-carriage printers calls for a right margin of 140. A sheet of 8 1/2-by-14-inch legal paper turned on its side so the width is 14 inches can use a 132-character right margin. If you reduce printer pitch you must increase margins. The condensed pitch of 17 characters per inch used on many dot matrix and laser printers allows a right margin of 140 on 8 1/2-inch-wide paper and 250 on 15-inch-wide paper. You must set the margin yourself when you change paper size or print pitch.

Altering Page Size

In the rapidly changing field of personal computers, one is grateful for any standards that can be relied upon. Such a standard is the six lines per inch used by every popular printer. This makes an 11-inch page 66 lines long. As you can see in Figure 5-15, Quattro PRO leaves a top and bottom margin. If you are working with paper longer or shorter than 11 inches, you must tell Quattro PRO the length measured in lines. Thus an 8 1/2-by-11-inch piece of paper printed on its side is 53 lines long. You can

Quattro Vadis Travel 4 Office Total:$122,131

90 Budget - Based On Monthly Growth Factor of   1.015

	JAN	FEB	MAR	APR	MAY	JUN	JUL
POLK ST.							
Lease	350	355	361	366	371	377	383
Phones	230	233	237	241	244	248	251
Telex	110	112	113	115	117	119	120
Electric	120	122	124	125	127	129	131
Res. Rent	1,100	1,117	1,133	1,150	1,167	1,185	1,203
VAN NESS							
Lease	500	507	515	523	531	539	547
Phones	250	254	258	261	265	269	273
Telex	150	152	155	157	159	162	164
Electric	225	228	232	235	239	242	246
Res. Rent	1,200	1,218	1,236	1,255	1,274	1,293	1,312
UNION SQ.							
Lease	1,200	1,218	1,236	1,255	1,274	1,293	1,312
Phones	300	304	309	314	318	323	328
Telex	250	254	258	261	265	269	273
Electric	205	208	211	214	218	221	224
Res. Rent	1,000	1,015	1,030	1,046	1,061	1,077	1,093
EMBARCADERO							
Lease	900	913	927	941	955	970	984
Phones	275	279	283	288	292	296	301
Telex (AU	0	0	0	0	0	0	0
Electric	0	0	0	0	0	0	0
Res. Rent	1,000	1,015	1,030	1,046	1,061	1,077	1,093
TOTALS	9,365	9,505	9,648	9,793	9,940	10,089	10,240

	AUG	SEP	OCT	NOV	DEC	YEAR
POLK ST.						
Lease	388	394	400	406	412	4,564
Phones	255	259	263	267	271	2,999
Telex	122	124	126	128	130	1,435
Electric	133	135	137	139	141	1,565
Res. Rent	1,221	1,239	1,258	1,277	1,296	14,345
VAN NESS						
Lease	555	563	572	580	589	6,521
Phones	277	282	286	290	294	3,260
Telex	166	169	172	174	177	1,956
Electric	250	253	257	261	265	2,934
Res. Rent	1,332	1,352	1,372	1,393	1,414	15,649
UNION SQ.						
Lease	1,332	1,352	1,372	1,393	1,414	15,649
Phones	333	338	343	348	353	3,912
Telex	277	282	286	290	294	3,260
Electric	228	231	234	238	241	2,673
Res. Rent	1,110	1,126	1,143	1,161	1,178	13,041
EMBARCADE						
Lease	999	1,014	1,029	1,044	1,060	11,737
Phones	305	310	314	319	324	3,586
Telex (AU	0	0	0	0	0	0
Electric	0	0	0	0	0	0
Res. Rent	1,110	1,126	1,143	1,161	1,178	13,041
TOTALS	10,394	10,550	10,708	10,868	11,031	122,131

Figure 5-20.   *Actual headings*

actually tell Quattro PRO you have a 33-line sheet of paper and it will treat a regular sheet of paper as though it were two sheets. This can be useful if you print a model that is less than 18 rows long.

Printer Setups

Many printers can be told to change their print style, print pitch, and other aspects by codes transmitted as part of the print data sent from the program. Quattro PRO accommodates these codes as printer setup strings, which are sent ahead of the data to set the printer. The codes for several popular printer models are provided in Appendix B. For example, most IBM and EPSON dot matrix printers respond to the characters \015 as meaning condensed print.

Writing Headers and Footers

In addition to setting parts of the spreadsheet as border headings, you can have other information repeat from page to page in a multipage Quattro PRO printout by using the header and footer commands. These commands provide areas into which you type the text to be printed, along with formatting instructions that tell the program how to align the text. You can use special codes in headers and footers to print such information as the correct page number. The # sign enters the page number in a header or footer. The @ sign causes the current date, according to your PC's clock, to be printed. The straight line symbol | is used like a tab stop to position header and footer text across the line. Typing the header text with no | symbol causes Quattro PRO to left-align everything. Preceding text with one | results in centering. Using two | | places the subsequent text on the right.

Making Page Breaks

Quattro PRO automatically inserts page breaks according to the page length setting. These settings are referred to as *soft page breaks*, since they change position according to the size of the Print Block. However, you can specify *hard page breaks* to force breaks at chosen points in the printout. Hard page breaks are indicated by the | character and two colons inserted manually into the spreadsheet on a blank row. These characters are stored as part of the spreadsheet and are not removed until you delete them individually.

To create hard page breaks, either type them in or select Insert Break from the Style menu. When you use the Insert Break command, Quattro PRO automatically inserts a blank nonprinting row that contains the page break command. If you are creating a page break manually, then create a blank row first, because any other data on a page-break row will not be printed. You should not insert page breaks in top heading cells.

Resetting Options and Storing Defaults

When you save a spreadsheet, the print settings in effect at the time you perform the save are stored together with the worksheet data. If you need to change the print settings completely, perhaps to print out a different section of the same worksheet, you can use Reset to clear the Print Block, the borders, the margin settings, and so on.

If you will be using the same settings on a regular basis, you can incorporate them into the system defaults by selecting Update from the Layout menu. (Defaults are described in the next chapter.)

Adjusting the Printer

You may want to advance the paper in the printer by line or by page. You use the Adjust Printer menu to move the paper forward a line at a time (Skip Line). You can use the Align Paper option to let Quattro PRO know that the current position of the paper in the printer is correct; that is, the print head is at the top of the form. You can use the Form Feed command to eject the current sheet of paper. This is particularly useful if you have a Hewlett-Packard LaserJet and find that the last page of the printout is not automatically ejected.

Unformatted Printing

Quattro PRO recognizes hard page breaks and inserts others as needed, making room for headers and footers. If you need a continuous stream of print, for example, to print mailing labels, then use the Print Page Layout command and set Break Pages to No. Quattro PRO will still respond to hard page breaks you have placed in the worksheet but will not print headers and footers or insert soft page breaks.

Cell Listings

What you want to print from Quattro PRO is not always a neatly arranged set of numbers, but may sometimes be a quick snapshot of what is on the screen. Perhaps you also wish to include a complex formula in the cell identifier to show someone how an aspect of a model works. You can do this easily with the PRTSC key. Combined with SHIFT on some keyboards, the PRTSC key sends a literal picture of the cell and row numbers on the screen to your printer. This does not work when you are using graphics display mode.

If you want a list of what is in every cell in a worksheet, including the cell format and width if they differ from the global setting, select the Cell-formula option from the Print Format menu. The resulting printout will include the cells that are in the Print Block down the side of the page. This is useful for reference or for communicating with other users. An example is shown in Figure 5-21, where the cell contents are printed as they appear in the cell identifier when it is highlighted. Another user could recreate a spreadsheet design from a listing such as this.

Print Destinations

When you select the Destination option on the Print menu you can see that there are several different places to which Quattro PRO can send what you print.

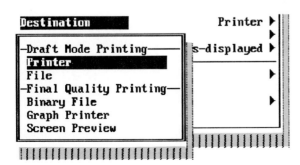

The default destination is Printer for Draft Mode Printing. This is the destination that you would normally use for quick spreadsheet output. Quattro PRO can perform a print to disk, represented by the File option. This operation exports data to other programs such as word processors and is discussed in Chapter 10. The Graph Printer option is used when you are

```
D2:  'Quattro Vadis Travel 4 Office Total:
H2:  (C0) +N32
C4:  '90 Budget - Based On Monthly Growth Factor of
H4:  1.015
B6:  ^JAN
C6:  ^FEB
D6:  ^MAR
E6:  ^APR
F6:  ^MAY
G6:  ^JUN
H6:  ^JUL
I6:  ^AUG
J6:  ^SEP
K6:  ^OCT
L6:  ^NOV
M6:  ^DEC
N6:  ^YEAR
A7:  'POLK ST.
A8:  "Lease
B8:  (,0) 350
C8:  (,0) +$H$4*B8
D8:  (,0) +$H$4*C8
E8:  (,0) +$H$4*D8
F8:  (,0) +$H$4*E8
G8:  (,0) +$H$4*F8
H8:  (,0) +$H$4*G8
I8:  (,0) +$H$4*H8
J8:  (,0) +$H$4*I8
K8:  (,0) +$H$4*J8
L8:  (,0) +$H$4*K8
M8:  (,0) +$H$4*L8
N8:  (,0) @SUM(B8..M8)
A9:  "Phones
B9:  (,0) 230
C9:  (,0) +$H$4*B9
D9:  (,0) +$H$4*C9
E9:  (,0) +$H$4*D9
F9:  (,0) +$H$4*E9
G9:  (,0) +$H$4*F9
H9:  (,0) +$H$4*G9
I9:  (,0) +$H$4*H9
J9:  (,0) +$H$4*I9
K9:  (,0) +$H$4*J9
L9:  (,0) +$H$4*K9
M9:  (,0) +$H$4*L9
N9:  (,0) @SUM(B9..M9)
A10: "Telex
B10: (,0) 110
C10: (,0) +$H$4*B10
D10: (,0) +$H$4*C10
```

Figure 5-21.   *Listing cells*

sending spreadsheet output to a graphics device. The final option is Screen Preview, which allows you to see what printed output will look like without having to put it on paper. This option is discussed later in this chapter.

Printing a Column-and-Row Form

Quattro PRO can print many different items that simply require a column-and-row format. If you have ever tried to type a lot of columns and rows on a typewriter or word processor, you know how difficult this can be. A form like the one shown in Figure 5-22 is very simple to arrange in Quattro PRO. You can make lines in a spreadsheet by using the cell fill character (\) to fill cells with hyphens and equal signs. Alternatively, you can use the drawing commands from the Style menu, as described later in this chapter. The Edit commands allow you to quickly replicate patterns is the spreadsheet to create elaborate forms for many office applications. Notice that the form in Figure 5-22 uses a string formula to become an interactive form that changes with user input. (For more on string formulas, see Chapter 10.)

Dressing Up Worksheets

Up to this point the appearance of the model has depended mainly on the location of the columns and rows, the alignment of the labels, and the formatting of the numbers. There are several other ways of affecting the appearance of your spreadsheets, both on the screen and on paper. Using the Style commands you can add lines and shading to your spreadsheets. You can also employ a variety of fonts to add visual appeal to your work.

Working in Graphics Mode

You can use the Line Drawing and Shading Style commands regardless of whether you have a graphics display. However, you may find it easier to work with these commands if you use one of the graphics display modes. Use the Options Display Mode to pick from one of the graphics choices, as

```
                    Art List for Manuscript Submission
Date:_____      Title:_____      Author:_____
CHAPTER #:   5        FIGURES       ILLUSTRATIONS       TABLES
=================================================================
Number    5-1 |           |               |             | 1
-----------------------------------------------------------------
Number    5-2 |           |               |             | 2
-----------------------------------------------------------------
Number    5-3 |           |               |             | 3
-----------------------------------------------------------------
Number    5-4 |           |               |             | 4
-----------------------------------------------------------------
Number    5-5 |           |               |             | 5
-----------------------------------------------------------------
Number    5-6 |           |               |             | 6
-----------------------------------------------------------------
Number    5-7 |           |               |             | 7
-----------------------------------------------------------------
Number    5-8 |           |               |             | 8
-----------------------------------------------------------------
Number    5-9 |           |               |             | 9
-----------------------------------------------------------------
Number    5-10|           |               |             |10
-----------------------------------------------------------------
Number    5-11|           |               |             |11
-----------------------------------------------------------------
Number    5-12|           |               |             |12
-----------------------------------------------------------------
Number    5-13|           |               |             |13
-----------------------------------------------------------------
Number    5-14|           |               |             |14
-----------------------------------------------------------------
Number    5-15|           |               |             |15
-----------------------------------------------------------------
Number    5-16|           |               |             |16
-----------------------------------------------------------------
Number    5-17|           |               |             |17
-----------------------------------------------------------------
Number    5-18|           |               |             |18
-----------------------------------------------------------------
Number    5-19|           |               |             |19
-----------------------------------------------------------------
Number    5-20|           |               |             |20
-----------------------------------------------------------------
Note:  To link Numbers to Chapter # use the following formula
       in column B:
              @STRING($B$5,0)&"-"&@STRING(J45,0)
       where J contains the series of numbers on the right.
       Changing the Chapter # will then change the Numbers.
```

Figure 5-22.   *Form design*

shown in Figure 5-23. To do this you will need a system that supports very high-resolution graphics, such as an EGA or VGA display. If you have a system that is specifically listed you will select it; otherwise, you can try the generic Graphics Mode. (For more on graphics modes see Chapter 8.) The display that you will get when you choose Graphics Mode will look something like Figure 5-24, where the mouse palette is displayed.

Line Drawing

Quattro PRO's line drawing commands work by placing lines in locations that you specify, relative to cells that you select. The lines can be single, double, or thick. They can be placed all around a cell or block of cells, or just on the top or bottom. Lines can be draw between columns or rows, or an entire grid can be drawn. For an example of line drawing you can use the budget worksheet that has been the main subject of this chapter, and which appears in Figure 5-24. The first lines will be drawn to set apart the month headings.

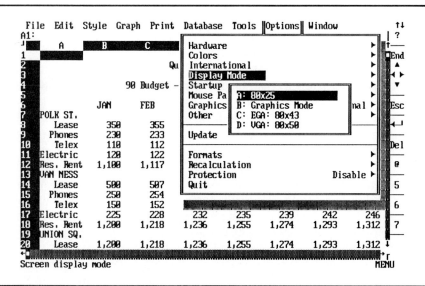

Figure 5-23. *Display mode options*

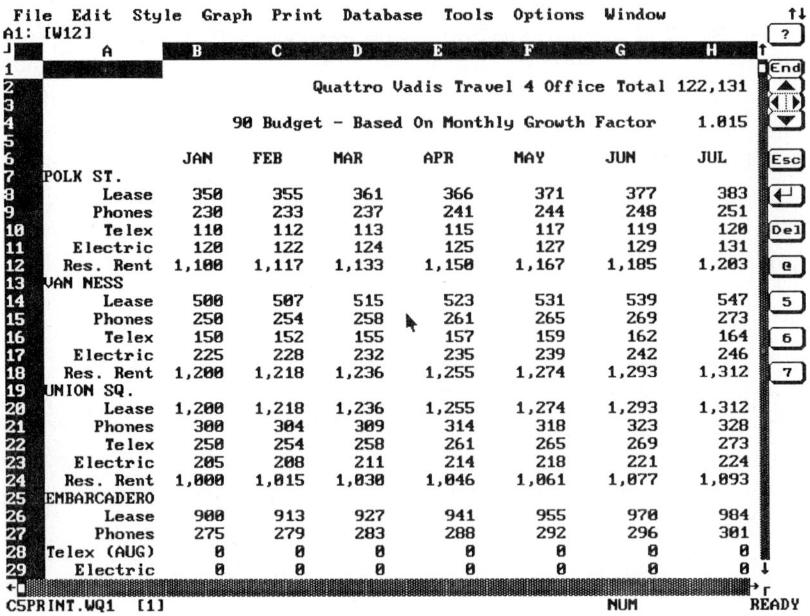

File Edit Style Graph Print Database Tools Options Window   ↑↓

A1: [W12]   ?

```
      A          B        C        D        E        F        G        H
 1                                                                              End
 2                                 Quattro Vadis Travel 4 Office Total 122,131   ▲
 3                                                                              ◄│▶
 4                      90 Budget - Based On Monthly Growth Factor       1.015   ▼
 5
 6                   JAN      FEB      MAR      APR      MAY      JUN      JUL    Esc
 7  POLK ST.
 8       Lease      350      355      361      366      371      377      383    ↵
 9      Phones      230      233      237      241      244      248      251
10       Telex      110      112      113      115      117      119      120    Del
11    Electric      120      122      124      125      127      129      131
12    Res. Rent  1,100    1,117    1,133    1,150    1,167    1,185    1,203     @
13  VAN NESS
14       Lease      500      507      515      523      531      539      547     5
15      Phones      250      254      258    ▶ 261      265      269      273
16       Telex      150      152      155      157      159      162      164     6
17    Electric      225      228      232      235      239      242      246
18    Res. Rent  1,200    1,218    1,236    1,255    1,274    1,293    1,312     7
19  UNION SQ.
20       Lease    1,200    1,218    1,236    1,255    1,274    1,293    1,312
21      Phones      300      304      309      314      318      323      328
22       Telex      250      254      258      261      265      269      273
23    Electric      205      208      211      214      218      221      224
24    Res. Rent  1,000    1,015    1,030    1,046    1,061    1,077    1,093
25  EMBARCADERO
26       Lease      900      913      927      941      955      970      984
27      Phones      275      279      283      288      292      296      301
28  Telex (AUG)      0        0        0        0        0        0        0     ↓
29    Electric       0        0        0        0        0        0        0
```

C5PRINT.WQ1 [1]   NUM   READY

Figure 5-24.   *Example of graphics mode*

The Style commands are a typical situation where the preselection feature in Quattro PRO can be put to good use. You want to add a line or lines to cells A6 through N6. Keyboard users can select cell A6, press SHIFT-F7, and then press END and then the RIGHT ARROW key to select all the way through N6. Mouse users can click on A6 and then drag the highlighting through N6. Once you have selected this block of cells you can use the Style command and pick Line Drawing. The command you issue now will apply to the cells that you have preselected. You do not have to use preselection with the Style commands. If you do not, you will be prompted for the block of cells after you have issued the command, but preselection allows you to identify the cells you want to affect before having to think about the commands that you will use.

When you pick Line Drawing you will see the Placement options listed, as shown in Figure 5-25. This menu allows you to specify where the lines will be placed in relation to the cells you have selected. You can browse

```
 File  Edit ║Style║ Graph  Print  Database  Tools  Options  Window        ↑↓
Enter block to draw lines: B6..N6                                        [ ? ]
┌─────────┬───────┬───────┬───────┬───────┬───────┬───────┬───────────────┐
J          H       I       J       K       L       M       N        [End]
1
2  $122,131                                                          ▲
3                                                                   ◄║▶
4      1.015                                                         ▼
5
6     JUL     AUG     SEP     OCT     NOV     DEC     YEAR          [Esc]
7
8        383     388     394     400     406     412     4,564      [↵]
9        251     255     259     263     267     271     2,999
10       120                     126     128     130     1,435      [Del]
11       131   ┌Placement:─┐     137     139     141     1,565
12     1,203   │All        │   1,258   1,277   1,296    14,345       [ e ]
13             │Outside    │
14       547   │Top        │     572     580     589     6,521       [ 5 ]
15       273   │■Bottom■■■■│     286     290     294     3,260
16       164   │Left       │     172     174     177     1,956       [ 6 ]
17       246   │Right      │     257     261     265     2,934
18     1,312   │Inside     │   1,372   1,393   1,414    15,649       [ 7 ]
19             │Horizontal │
20     1,312   │Vertical   │   1,372   1,393   1,414    15,649
21       328   │Quit       │     343     348     353     3,912
22       273   └───────────┘     286     290     294     3,260
23       224             ■■■■■   234     238     241     2,673
24     1,093   1,110   1,126   1,143   1,161   1,178    13,041
25
26       984     999   1,014   1,029   1,044   1,060    11,737
27       301     305     310     314     319     324     3,586
28         0       0       0       0       0       0         0
29         0       0       0       0       0       0         0      ↓
                                                                    ►r
Draw a line on the bottom of block                                 MENU
```

Figure 5-25. *Line drawing placement options*

through the options on this list with the UP and DOWN ARROW keys, noting the explanations that appear in the status line as you do this. The results of picking any one of these choices will appear on the screen right away and you can make several choices from this menu before you pick Quit. For example, select Bottom and you will see a selection of line types: None, Single, Double, and Thick. Select Single for now and you will see the line drawn underneath the months, as shown in Figure 5-26. Note that the Placement menu reappears. (If you had not preselected the block to be affected you would be prompted to do so before the Placement menu returned.)

Suppose that you would like to place a line above the month labels as well. From the Placement menu select Top. Now select Single again, and the screen will look like Figure 5-27. You will keep coming back to the Placement menu until you select Quit. Try selecting Bottom and then Double. This will put a double line below the months.

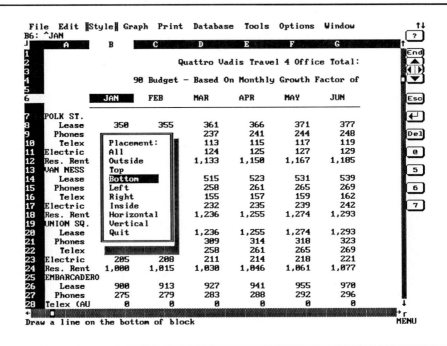

Figure 5-26.   *Line drawn below months*

Removing Lines

If you decide that these lines are not what you want, you can pick All from the Placement menu and then pick None from the line type choices. This is the way that you erase lines: Select the cells with lines attached to them and then use All followed by None. You can also selectively remove certain lines. For example, in Figure 5-27 you could pick Top and then None to remove just the line at the top of the cells.

More Line Styles

Suppose that you decide the top and bottom lines look good for the months. You pick Quit from the Placement menu to leave the Line Drawing command. Now you want to put lines between the offices. In Figure 5-28

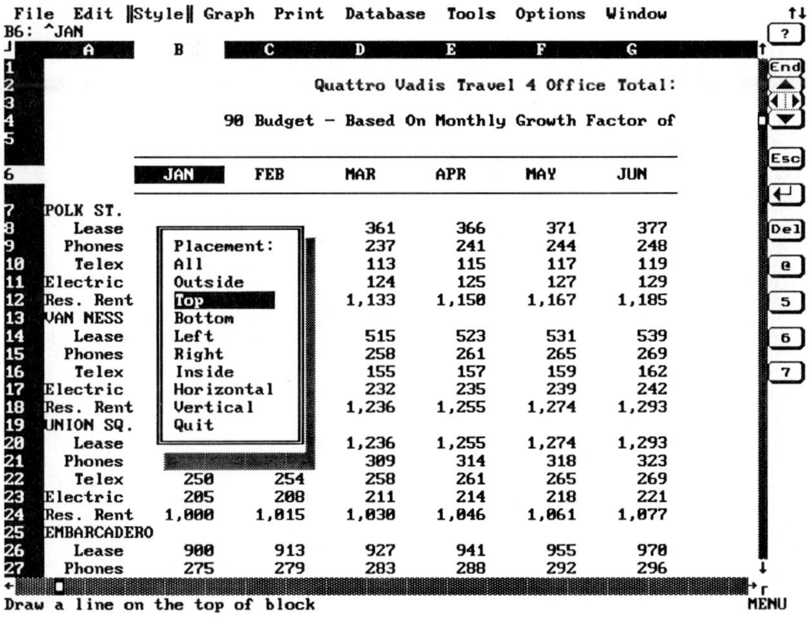

```
  File  Edit ‖Style‖ Graph  Print  Database  Tools  Options  Window        ↑↓
B6: ^JAN                                                                    ?
┘      A        B      C        D       E       F       G       ↑          End
1                                                                          ▲
2                             Quattro Vadis Travel 4 Office Total:         ◄│►
3                                                                          ▼
4                     90 Budget — Based On Monthly Growth Factor of
5                                                                          Esc
6                 JAN     FEB      MAR     APR     MAY     JUN              ↵
7    POLK ST.                                                              Del
8       Lease                     361     366     371     377
9       Phones    Placement:      237     241     244     248              @
10      Telex     All             113     115     117     119
11   Electric     Outside         124     125     127     129              5
12   Res. Rent    Top           1,133   1,150   1,167   1,185
13   VAN NESS      Bottom                                                  6
14      Lease     Left            515     523     531     539
15      Phones    Right           258     261     265     269              7
16      Telex     Inside          155     157     159     162
17   Electric     Horizontal      232     235     239     242
18   Res. Rent    Vertical      1,236   1,255   1,274   1,293
19   UNION SQ.    Quit
20      Lease                   1,236   1,255   1,274   1,293
21      Phones                    309     314     318     323
22      Telex     250     254     258     261     265     269
23   Electric     205     208     211     214     218     221
24   Res. Rent  1,000   1,015   1,030   1,046   1,061   1,077
25   EMBARCADERO
26      Lease     900     913     927     941     955     970
27      Phones    275     279     283     288     292     296              ↓
← ▓▓▓▓▓ ░ ▓▓▓▓▓▓▓▓▓▓▓▓▓▓▓▓▓▓▓▓▓▓▓▓▓▓▓▓▓▓▓▓▓▓▓▓▓▓▓▓▓▓▓▓▓▓▓▓▓▓▓▓▓▓ ► ⌐
Draw a line on the top of block                                    MENU
```

Figure 5-27. *Line drawn above months*

you can see the far right side of the worksheet after selecting cells A13 through N13 At this point you can put in a line that separates the two offices by using Style, Line Drawing, Top, Single, then Quit. If you repeat this command for rows 19 and 25 you will get the results shown in Figure 5-29.

You might have noticed that the addition of lines also adds space to the model. These unnumbered rows that are added do not affect any formulas or block commands. You cannot select lines themselves, only the cells to which they are attached. When you use the mouse or the SHIFT-F7 key to select cells, the cell selector increase in size when it encounters a cell with a line attached so that the line is included. When you copy or move cells that have lines attached, the lines travel with the cells. In some situations it makes sense to add lines to cells early in the creation of a model, as with other Style commands, thus avoiding repetition of the Line Drawing command.

File	Edit	‖Style‖	Graph	Print	Database	Tools	Options	Window	↑↓

N13:

J	H	I	J	K	L	M	N
1							
2	$122,131						
3							
4	1.015						
5							
6	JUL	AUG	SEP	OCT	NOV	DEC	YEAR
7							
8	383			400	406	412	4,564
9	251	Placement:		263	267	271	2,999
10	120	All		126	128	130	1,435
11	131	Outside		137	139	141	1,565
12	1,203	Top		1,258	1,277	1,296	14,345
13		Bottom					
14	547	Left		572	580	589	6,521
15	273	Right		286	290	294	3,260
16	164	Inside		172	174	177	1,956
17	246	Horizontal		257	261	265	2,934
18	1,312	Vertical		1,372	1,393	1,414	15,649
19		Quit					
20	1,312			1,372	1,393	1,414	15,649
21	328			343	348	353	3,912
22	273	277	282	286	290	294	3,260
23	224	228	231	234	238	241	2,673
24	1,093	1,110	1,126	1,143	1,161	1,178	13,041
25							
26	984	999	1,014	1,029	1,044	1,060	11,737
27	301	305	310	314	319	324	3,586

Draw a line on the top of block   MENU

Figure 5-28. *Drawing a line between offices*

The next step in dressing up this model is to add a vertical line that will appear between columns A and B, separating the category labels from the values. First select cells A6 through A32. Then use Style, Line Drawing, Right, Single, and then Quit. The resulting vertical line is shown in Figure 5-30.

Shading

A further style improvement is to add some shading to the bottom of the model, just above the totals. Shading is inserted into cells, in this case cells A31 through N31. Select this block and then use Style, Shading, Grey. The command will insert the grey characters into the cells and quit back to the READY mode. The results are shown on a partial printout of this model in Figure 5-31. Note that Quattro PRO keeps track of line locations and shading in headings so that they are aligned properly with the Print Block.

```
    File   Edit   Style   Graph   Print   Database   Tools   Options   Window      ↑↓
A1:                                                                                [ ? ]
      A        B        C        D        E        F        G                      ↑
1                                                                                  [■End]
2                         Quattro Vadis Travel 4 Office Total:                     ▲
3                                                                                  ◄■►
4             90 Budget - Based On Monthly Growth Factor of                        ▼
5
6             JAN      FEB      MAR      APR      MAY      JUN                      [Esc]
                                                                                   [ ↵ ]
7  POLK ST.
8    Lease    350      355      361      366      371      377                     [Del]
9    Phones   230      233      237      241      244      248
10   Telex    110      112      113      115      117      119                     [ @ ]
11 Electric   120      122      124      125      127      129
12 Res. Rent 1,100    1,117    1,133    1,150    1,167    1,185                    [ 5 ]

13 VAN NESS                                                                        [ 6 ]
14   Lease    500      507      515      523      531      539
15   Phones   250      254      258      261      265      269                     [ 7 ]
16   Telex    150      152      155      157      159      162
17 Electric   225      228      232      235      239      242
18 Res. Rent 1,200    1,218    1,236    1,255    1,274    1,293

19 UNION SQ.
20   Lease   1,200    1,218    1,236    1,255    1,274    1,293
21   Phones   300      304      309      314      318      323
22   Telex    250      254      258      261      265      269
23 Electric   205      208      211      214      218      221
24 Res. Rent 1,000    1,015    1,030    1,046    1,061    1,077
←■                                                                            → r
QVBUDG02.WQ1 [1]                                                             READY
```

Figure 5-29. *Lines between offices*

The Shading command does not overwrite values and labels in a cell. You can therefore select a large area and have all nonempty cells shaded at once. The Black option on the shading menu creates a much darker shading. Between the Grey and Black options you have useful tools for adding visual appeal to your documents.

Combining Styles

You can attach lines to blocks as well as shade them. You can also put lines all the way around a large section of the worksheet. For example, you could select the entire model and then use the Outside command from the Line Drawing Placement menu to draw a line all the way around the outside of the model. If you want to create a gridwork of lines within an area of the spreadsheet you select the block and then use the Inside option from the

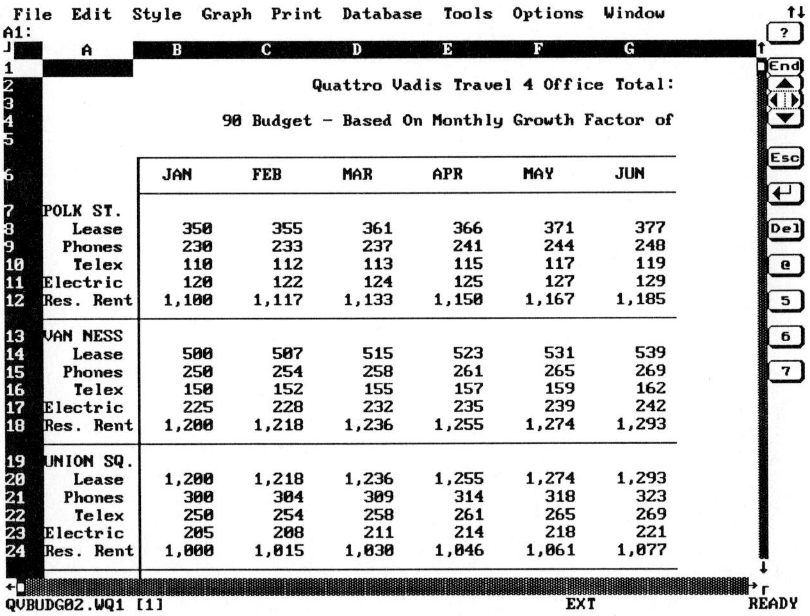

File	Edit	Style	Graph	Print	Database	Tools	Options	Window	↑↓

A1:

J	A	B	C	D	E	F	G	↑
1								
2				Quattro Vadis Travel 4 Office Total:				
3								
4			90 Budget – Based On Monthly Growth Factor of					
5								
6		JAN	FEB	MAR	APR	MAY	JUN	
7	POLK ST.							
8	Lease	350	355	361	366	371	377	
9	Phones	230	233	237	241	244	248	
10	Telex	110	112	113	115	117	119	
11	Electric	120	122	124	125	127	129	
12	Res. Rent	1,100	1,117	1,133	1,150	1,167	1,185	
13	VAN NESS							
14	Lease	500	507	515	523	531	539	
15	Phones	250	254	258	261	265	269	
16	Telex	150	152	155	157	159	162	
17	Electric	225	228	232	235	239	242	
18	Res. Rent	1,200	1,218	1,236	1,255	1,274	1,293	
19	UNION SQ.							
20	Lease	1,200	1,218	1,236	1,255	1,274	1,293	
21	Phones	300	304	309	314	318	323	
22	Telex	250	254	258	261	265	269	
23	Electric	205	208	211	214	218	221	
24	Res. Rent	1,000	1,015	1,030	1,046	1,061	1,077	

QVBUDG02.WQ1 [1]   EXT   READY

Figure 5-30.   *Vertical line*

Placement menu. This draws lines around all of the cells. A version of the form shown earlier in Figure 5-22 was created with this option. You can see it in Figure 5-32.

Spreadsheet Graphics and Previews

You might think that the printed output in Figures 5-31 and 5-32 lacks some of the sophistication of which today's printers are capable. You might also object to having to print spreadsheets just to see if the print settings you have chosen work the way you expect. Quattro PRO responds to both

		Quattro Vadis Travel 4 Office Total:				
	90 Budget	- Based	On Monthly	Growth	Factor of	
Lease	350	355	361	366	371	377
Phones	230	233	237	241	244	248
Telex	110	112	113	115	117	119
Electric	120	122	124	125	127	129
Res. Rent	1,100	1,117	1,133	1,150	1,167	1,185
VAN NESS						
Lease	500	507	515	523	531	539
Phones	250	254	258	261	265	269
Telex	150	152	155	157	159	162
Electric	225	228	232	235	239	242
Res. Rent	1,200	1,218	1,236	1,255	1,274	1,293
UNION SQ.						
Lease	1,200	1,218	1,236	1,255	1,274	1,293
Phones	300	304	309	314	318	323
Telex	250	254	258	261	265	269
Electric	205	208	211	214	218	221
Res. Rent	1,000	1,015	1,030	1,046	1,061	1,077
EMBARCADERO						
Lease	900	913	927	941	955	970
Phones	275	279	283	288	292	296
Telex (AUG)	0	0	0	0	0	0
Electric	0	0	0	0	0	0
Res. Rent	1,000	1,015	1,030	1,046	1,061	1,077
TOTALS	9,365	9,505	9,648	9,793	9,940	10,089

Figure 5-31. *Shading above totals*

of these concerns. You can use all of your printer's graphics capability to print presentation-quality spreadsheets, and preview print jobs on your screen before ever putting ink on paper.

Higher Destinations

Earlier you saw that Quattro PRO offers several different destinations for your print activity. When you select Destination from the print menu you see five options split into two sections, Draft Mode Printing and Final Quality Printing.

```
                    Art List for Manuscript Submission
Date:_____Title:_____ Author:_____

+---------------+---------------+---------------+---------------+---
|CHAPTER #  5 | FIGURES       |ILLUSTRATIONS  |   TABLES      |
+---------------+---------------+---------------+---------------+---
|Number   5-1 |               |               |               | 1
+---------------+---------------+---------------+---------------+---
|Number   5-2 |               |               |               | 2
+---------------+---------------+---------------+---------------+---
|Number   5-3 |               |               |               | 3
+---------------+---------------+---------------+---------------+---
|Number   5-4 |               |               |               | 4
+---------------+---------------+---------------+---------------+---
|Number   5-5 |               |               |               | 5
+---------------+---------------+---------------+---------------+---
|Number   5-6 |               |               |               | 6
+---------------+---------------+---------------+---------------+---
|Number   5-7 |               |               |               | 7
+---------------+---------------+---------------+---------------+---
|Number   5-8 |               |               |               | 8
+---------------+---------------+---------------+---------------+---
|Number   5-9 |               |               |               | 9
+---------------+---------------+---------------+---------------+---
|Number   5-10|               |               |               |10
+---------------+---------------+---------------+---------------+---
|Number   5-11|               |               |               |11
+---------------+---------------+---------------+---------------+---
|Number   5-12|               |               |               |12
+---------------+---------------+---------------+---------------+---
|Number   5-13|               |               |               |13
+---------------+---------------+---------------+---------------+---
|Number   5-14|               |               |               |14
+---------------+---------------+---------------+---------------+---
|Number   5-15|               |               |               |15
+---------------+---------------+---------------+---------------+---
|Number   5-16|               |               |               |16
+---------------+---------------+---------------+---------------+---
|Number   5-17|               |               |               |17
+---------------+---------------+---------------+---------------+---
|Number   5-18|               |               |               |18
+---------------+---------------+---------------+---------------+---
|Number   5-19|               |               |               |19
+---------------+---------------+---------------+---------------+---
|Number   5-20|               |               |               |20
+---------------+---------------+---------------+---------------+---
```

Figure 5-32. *Form with line drawing*

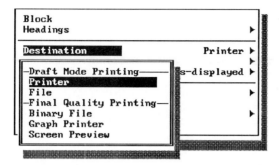

The first and default option, Printer, was used for all of the printouts shown so far in this chapter. The Printer option gives you traditional spreadsheet output, plain-vanilla character text that is good for drafts of documents. The standard text characters of your printer are used. Draft Mode Printing is the quickest way to print, but it ignores the presentation- or graphics-quality printing features possessed by many of today's printers. While you can use the line-drawing and shadow features with the Printer option, they are more effective when you use the Graph Printer option. Figure 5-33 shows a graphics print version of the sample spreadsheet shown in Figure 5-31. As the menu suggests, the Graph Printer option is used for final quality printing when you are concerned about the appearance of your reports.

Do not be confused by the term *Graph Printer*. Selecting this option from the Destination choices does not mean that you have a graph or chart in your worksheet. When you choose Graph Printer as the destination for your spreadsheet printing, Quattro PRO applies graphics features to the output. On some printers, such as dot matrix models, this can cause printing to take quite a while. However, the results will be well worth it in terms of quality appearance.

About Fonts

What exactly are the graphics features supported by Graph Printer? They include line drawing and shading, which have been discussed already, but also fonts. A *font* is a style of writing a set of characters. Figure 5-34 shows words printed in a number of different fonts. Most of the print examples shown so far in this chapter, including that in Figure 5-31, have used the Courier font. This is the default font of the LaserJet printer. The Printer option on the Destination menu uses whatever font

Quattro Vadis Travel 4 Office Total: $122,131

90 Budget - Based On Monthly Growth Factor of   1.015

		JAN	FEB	MAR	APR	MAY	JUN	JUL	AUG	SEP	OCT
	Lease	350	355	361	366	371	377	383	388	394	400
	Phones	230	233	237	241	244	248	251	255	259	263
	Telex	110	112	113	115	117	119	120	122	124	126
	Electric	120	122	124	125	127	129	131	133	135	137
	Res. Rent	1,100	1,117	1,133	1,150	1,167	1,185	1,203	1,221	1,239	1,258
VAN NESS											
	Lease	500	507	515	523	531	539	547	555	563	572
	Phones	250	254	258	261	265	269	273	277	282	286
	Telex	150	152	155	157	159	162	164	166	169	172
	Electric	225	228	232	235	239	242	246	250	253	257
	Res. Rent	1,200	1,218	1,236	1,255	1,274	1,293	1,312	1,332	1,352	1,372
UNION SQ.											
	Lease	1,200	1,218	1,236	1,255	1,274	1,293	1,312	1,332	1,352	1,372
	Phones	300	304	309	314	318	323	328	333	338	343
	Telex	250	254	258	261	265	269	273	277	282	286
	Electric	205	208	211	214	218	221	224	228	231	234
	Res. Rent	1,000	1,015	1,030	1,046	1,061	1,077	1,093	1,110	1,126	1,143
EMBARCADERO											
	Lease	900	913	927	941	955	970	984	999	1,014	1,029
	Phones	275	279	283	288	292	296	301	305	310	314
	Telex	0	0	0	0	0	0	0	0	0	0
	Electric	0	0	0	0	0	0	0	0	0	0
	Res. Rent	1.000	1.015	1.030	1.046	1.061	1.077	1.093	1.110	1.126	1.143
TOTALS		9,365	9,505	9,648	9,793	9,940	10,089	10,240	10,394	10,550	10,708

Figure 5-33.   *Report printed on Graph Printer*

Courier 12 point (about 10 pitch)
Times or Dutch in 10 point
Times or Dutch in 12 point
Times or Dutch in 14 point italic
Helvetica or Swiss in 10 point
Helvetica or Swiss in 12 point
Helvetica or Swiss in 14 point
Helvetica or Swiss in 18 point bold

Figure 5-34.   *Sample fonts*

is your printer's default; that is, it does not send any font information to the printer. The printer is just told what characters to print and where to place them. The exact shape of the characters is left up to the printer.

Courier is a general-purpose font that is *monospaced*, meaning that each character occupies the same width on a line. Unlike *proportional* text such as that you are reading now, monospaced text gives as much space to the word *fill* as it does to the word *wine*. Using proportional fonts tends to give documents a more finished and professional appearance. Some fonts have names that are proprietary because they were designed by a particular person or company. Among the better known proportional fonts are Helvetica (sometimes called Swiss) and Times (sometimes referred to as Dutch or Roman). Fonts often come in different sizes, measured in *points*. A 10-point font is about the same as elite on a typewriter. Fonts can also come in different styles: bold, italic, and underlined.

Font Choices

Quattro PRO supports a wide range of fonts in different sizes and styles that you can use to print out your spreadsheet. You access these fonts through the Style menu. When you select Font from the Style menu you see a list of eight fonts, as shown in Figure 5-35. At first, all eight will be the same font. But if you select Edit Fonts you can change each of the font to your choice. For example, suppose that you want to change Font 2. You select Edit Fonts and pick Font 2, as shown in Figure 5-36, where the submenu of variables is displayed. These include Typeface, Point Size, Style, and Color. If you select Typeface, you will get a list of possibilities like the one in Figure 5-37, which is for a LaserJet printer.

The choices on the Typeface list fall into several groups. There are Hershey fonts—such as Roman, Script, and Sans Serif—that are fairly simple in appearance and do not occupy much space in memory. There are also Bitstream fonts, such as Dutch and Swiss, that take up quite a bit of space but look very professional. (The report in Figure 5-33 uses the Bitstream Dutch font.) Quattro PRO allows most printers to print both of these types of fonts. There may also be fonts available for specific printers, such as the LaserJet fonts shown in Figure 5-37. Many printers like the LaserJet support print cartridges that store fonts, and Quattro PRO knows about these. For more information on font selection for your printer see the "Hardware Options" section in the next chapter.

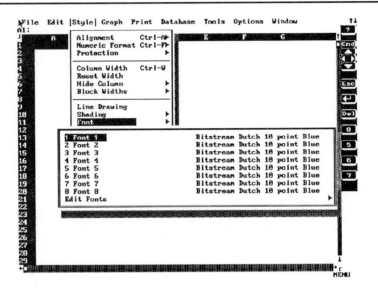

Figure 5-35.   *Font selection menu*

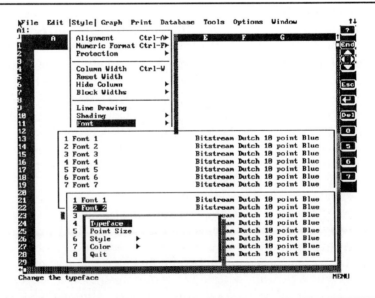

Figure 5-36.   *Editing Font 2*

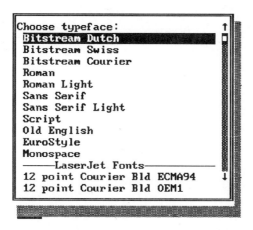

Figure 5-37. *Typeface selection*

Setting a Font

Suppose that you select Bitstream Swiss from the menu in Figure 5-37 and then select Point Size. Your choices are from 8 to 72, as shown in Figure 5-38. You pick 14 and are returned to the Font 2 menu. You decide to make this font bold, so you select Style from the list that includes Bold, Italic, and Underlined. Selecting Bold turns on this feature.

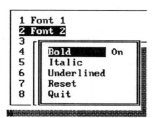

You can also turn on Italic to produce bold italic. When you have selected the style combination you want, you pick Quit. You can then select a color

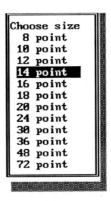

Figure 5-38.   *Point size selection*

if you like, but remember that black and white printers cannot print color. Blue will print as black and so you do not need to change it to black if you have a black and white printer. You can now select Quit to move back in the menu tree and you will see that your choices are reflected on the Font menu under Font 2, as shown in Figure 5-39.

You are now ready to assign this font to a section of your spreadsheet. When you select Style Font and then a number, such as 2, you are prompted for a block as shown in Figure 5-40. The two labels at the top of the model spreadsheet have been included in the block. The special font will emphasize them in the printed version. When you have selected the block to be affected by the new font, press ENTER. You will see a notation of [F2] in the cell description of the affected cells. This stands for Font 2. This cell will be printed in Font 2 whenever you select Spreadsheet Print with Graph Printer as the Destination choice. Font 2 will appear with whatever font you have selected for the second font on the font list. If you want to return a cell's font setting to Font 1, you simply select Style, Font 1, and then highlight the cell. Note that all cells of every Quattro PRO worksheet are Font 1 by default. For this reason you will not see [F1] in any cells. (The example in Figure 5-33 was printed entirely in Font 1.)

Even if you are using the graphics mode for your Quattro PRO display you will not see the font changes on screen while you are working on your

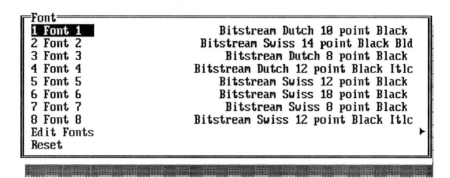

```
┌─Font────────────────────────────────────────────────────────┐
│ 1 Font 1                      Bitstream Dutch 10 point Black │
│ 2 Font 2               Bitstream Swiss 14 point Black Bld    │
│ 3 Font 3                   Bitstream Dutch 8 point Black     │
│ 4 Font 4             Bitstream Dutch 12 point Black Itlc     │
│ 5 Font 5                  Bitstream Swiss 12 point Black     │
│ 6 Font 6                  Bitstream Swiss 18 point Black     │
│ 7 Font 7                   Bitstream Swiss 8 point Black     │
│ 8 Font 8             Bitstream Swiss 12 point Black Itlc     │
│ Edit Fonts                                                 ▶ │
│ Reset                                                        │
└──────────────────────────────────────────────────────────────┘
```

Figure 5-39.   *Update font menu*

```
 File  Edit |Style| Graph  Print  Database  Tools  Options  Window        ↑↓
[Enter] [Esc] Enter block to set font: C2..H4                             ?
         B        C        D        E        F        G        H
  1                                                                      End
  2              Quattro Vadis Travel 4 Office Total:$122,131             ◀▮▶
  3                                                                       ▼
  4        90 Budget - Based On Monthly Growth Factor of   1.015
  5                                                                      Esc
  6    JAN      FEB      MAR      APR      MAY      JUN      JUL
  7                                                                       ←┘
  8    350      355      361      366      371      377      383         Del
  9    230      233      237      241      244      248      251
 10    110      112      113      115      117      119      120          e
 11    120      122      124      125      127      129      131
 12  1,100    1,117    1,133    1,150    1,167    1,185    1,203          5

 13                                                                       6
 14    500      507      515      523      531      539      547
 15    250      254      258      261      265      269      273          7
 16    150      152      155      157      159      162      164
 17    225      228      232      235      239      242      246
 18  1,200    1,218    1,236    1,255    1,274    1,293    1,312

 19
 20  1,200    1,218    1,236    1,255    1,274    1,293    1,312
 21    300      304      309      314      318      323      328
 22    250      254      258      261      265      269      273
 23    205      208      211      214      218      221      224
 24  1,000    1,015    1,030    1,046    1,061    1,077    1,093

 H4: 1.015                                                          POINT
```

Figure 5-40.   *Assigning a font to cells*

spreadsheet. The reason for this is the tremendous strain on your computer's resources that fonts represent. If you have used Microsoft Excel you will know that as you start to mix fonts within a worksheet, your ability to quickly move around the worksheet deteriorates. While Quattro PRO has the ability to print twice as many different fonts per worksheet as Microsoft Excel, fonts are not included in the regular display in order to keep performance levels acceptable. This means that you can have a spreadsheet that prints impressively and also calculates quickly.

To print the results of font changes in your spreadsheet you select Print, Destination, and Graph Printer; then select Spreadsheet Print. You can see a sample of the very impressive results in Figure 5-41. Do not use Graph Print from the Print menu because Quattro PRO will try to print a graph you have defined for the spreadsheet.

Remember that you can still get a quick printout from your worksheet by selecting plain Printer from the Print Destination menu. Also remember to save your worksheet after making font changes; otherwise, they may be lost. The selections you make for Fonts 1 through 8 are specific to the worksheet in which you make them. This means that if you want to use

Quattro Vadis Travel 4 Office Total: $122,131

90 Budget - Based On Monthly Growth Factor of   1.015

POLK ST.	JAN	FEB	MAR	APR	MAY	JUN	JUL	AUG	SEP	OCT	NOV
Lease	350	355	361	366	371	377	383	388	394	400	406
Phones	230	233	237	241	244	248	251	255	259	263	267
Telex	110	112	113	115	117	119	120	122	124	126	128
Electric	120	122	124	125	127	129	131	133	135	137	139
Res. Rent	1,100	1,117	1,133	1,150	1,167	1,185	1,203	1,221	1,239	1,258	1,277

Figure 5-41.   *Graph Printer sample*

Bitstream Swiss 14 point Bold as Font 2 in another worksheet you will have to repeat the selection process. An alternative is to establish a blank worksheet as a style sheet and use it as the starting point for a new spreadsheet whenever you want to use a particular selection of fonts. (Style sheets are discussed in detail in Chapter 7.)

Font Sizing

The default font for high-quality graphics printing of your Quattro PRO worksheets is Bitstream Dutch 10-point. This is considerably smaller in height than the normal text output of most printers, which is 10 pitch (10 characters to the inch), not 10 points. For example, Figure 5-31 is printed in 10-pitch Courier, whereas Figure 5-33 is in the default Dutch 10-point. You will find that you can get more lines to the inch with a 10-point font. Quattro PRO will automatically adjust the printed row height for you. In some cases you will get more characters to the inch with 10-point text, but sometimes you will require wider column settings to accommodate a proportionally spaced font like Dutch 10-point.

The need for wider columns when using fonts in Quattro PRO arises from the way in which the program determines width spacing when printing in graphics mode. There is no such measurement as "one character wide" when using a proportional font since all characters have their own width. Therefore, Quattro PRO uses an average measurement for the font and allows for that width times the character setting of the column to determine the printed column width. Occasionally, this will not be enough. For example, the 12-character-wide column A of the sample model was increased to 22 characters to accommodate the word *EMBARCADERO*, which takes up a lot of space in 10-point Dutch. You will need to check your column widths after setting fonts, either by a test print or by using the screen preview feature described later in this chapter.

Font Building

If you have a graphics display you can also view fonts when displaying graphs or when using the print preview feature. With so many choices of fonts available and the need for screen and printer versions of each font there is considerable potential for confusion, and for overloading your computer system. To print and display an attractive font, your computer requires a lot of information. To store every point size and style for every font would require many megabytes of disk space. For this reason Quattro PRO provides some fonts in a special format that stores the essence of a font in a condensed format.

When you ask Quattro PRO to use a particular size and style of the font, the program extracts the font from the condensed file in a process known as *font building.* When you install Quattro PRO you can select groups of fonts (as discussed in Appendix A) or you can decline font installation and perform font building only on demand. This latter approach saves a lot of disk space. What happens is that when you use a particular font and font size that has not yet been built, Quattro PRO will build it, resulting in a slight delay and a message box that says "Building font." Thereafter, you have access to that font and font size without the program having to repeat the building operation. However, each font is built for a particular printer, and changing printers may require Quattro PRO to repeat some font building, which is done automatically.

Fonts are built on several occasions: when you select Spreadsheet Print or Graph Print, and when you view a print job with either View from the Graph menu or Screen Preview (described later in this chapter). An exception to this font-building process is the set of Hershey fonts. These are always available without building, and they work the same on all graphics printers. The Hershey fonts are Roman, Roman Light, Sans Serif, Sans Serif Light, Script, Old English, EuroStyle, and Monospace. Hershey fonts require very little memory, but Bitstream fonts are quite large.

Fonts and Memory

You may find that you get a memory full message when you attempt an action that requires Quattro PRO to build a font. If this happens you may want to reduce the number of fonts that you are using, reduce the size of your worksheet, or otherwise conserve on memory. While a variety of fonts allows very professional-looking printouts, the cost in memory is high. Only by beefing up your system's memory can you make full use of fonts. One way to mix fonts within tight memory constraints is to use the Hershey fonts just described. These use far less memory but provide acceptable appearance for many types of printout.

Another course of action can assist you in getting good printouts without giving up fonts. Select the Graphics Quality option on the Options menu, as shown in Figure 5-42. This allows you to control the building of fonts for screen display and printing. The choices are Draft and Final. When you choose Draft, Quattro PRO will only use Bitstream fonts that have already been created. A Hershey font will be substituted if the requested Bitstream font is not available. When you select Final, Bitstream fonts will be used whenever requested. New font sizes will be created whenever required.

Screen Previews

Introducing graphic elements such as lines and fonts into your worksheets makes it difficult to tell exactly what the printed results will look like. For example, when you use a larger font for part of the spreadsheet, you need

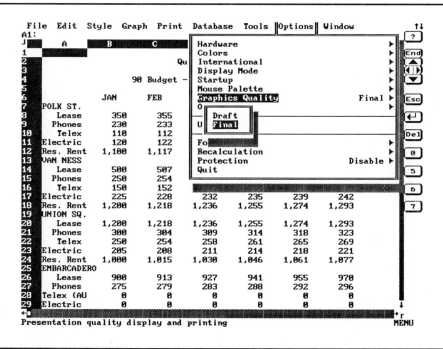

Figure 5-42. *Graphics Quality option*

to know what effect this will have on text spacing. Quattro PRO provides a screen preview feature that lets you examine very closely what your text will look like when printed. You can see fonts, lines, headers, and footers. Page breaks are revealed as well as headings. You can zoom the view to a high level of detail. You can check that your column settings are wide enough for the fonts you have chosen.

Choosing Screen Preview

Before you can use screen preview you must be in graphics mode, which you select from the Options Display mode menu. When you want to see what your spreadsheet will look like when printed with the Graph Printer option, select Destination from the Print menu and select Screen Preview. Now choose Spreadsheet Print and you will see a preview screen like the one shown in Figure 5-43. This is a representation of an 8 1/2-×-11 piece

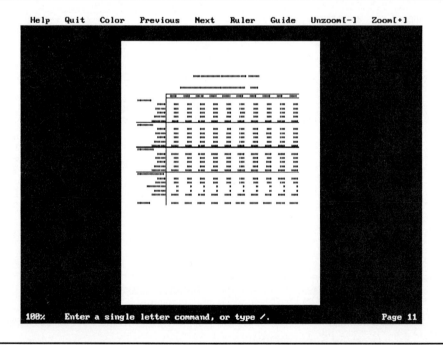

Figure 5-43.   *Preview screen*

paper with the information to be printed displayed to scale. Because the text that the program is trying to show is quite small it is "greeked" or made into symbolic characters.

A special menu across the top of the preview screen provides options to assist you in viewing your work. You can select items from the menu by their first letter, or type / and choose them by pointing and pressing ENTER. When you activate the menu with / you get explanations of the items as you highlight them.

In addition to Help and Quit, which returns you to the regular worksheet, there is a Color option to show the colors that will be printed if you have a color printer. The Previous and Next options show additional pages. By picking Ruler you can add a 1-inch grid to the display. This helps you judge the placement of text on the page.

The Preview Zoom

You can use the Guide option on the preview screen menu only when you are in ZOOM mode. To zoom you use either the plus (+) or the minus (−) key to enlarge or reduce the display. You can see the first level of zoom in Figure 5-44. Notice that a problem has been revealed: the use of a large

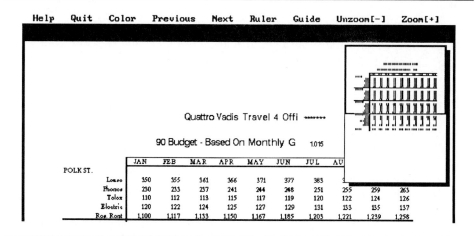

Figure 5-44.   *Zoomed preview screen*

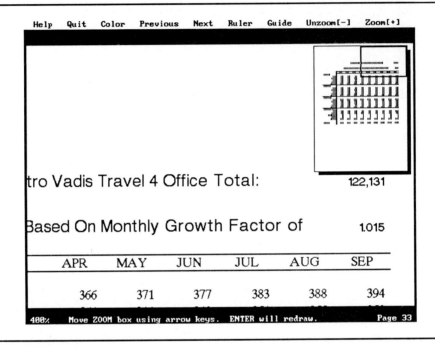

| Help | Quit | Color | Previous | Next | Ruler | Guide | Unzoom[-] | Zoom[+] |

tro Vadis Travel 4 Office Total: 122,131

Based On Monthly Growth Factor of 1.015

APR	MAY	JUN	JUL	AUG	SEP
366	371	377	383	388	394

400% Move ZOOM box using arrow keys. ENTER will redraw. Page 33

Figure 5-45. *Further zoom*

font for the titles has meant that the figures in cells H2 and H4 are overlapped. In Figure 5-45 you can see a further level of zoom used after this problem has been corrected.

There are two approaches to the problem of overlapping labels when using larger fonts: you can move one set of labels or you can join the labels together with string formulas. You can learn more about string formulas in Chapter 9.

Note that when you are in ZOOM mode you have a small picture of the page on the right of the screen. On this page is a box that shows you which section of the total page you are viewing. This is the guide. You can use the arrow keys to move the guide box around on the page and then press ENTER to redraw the screen with the new area enlarged. If you find the guide box obscuring your view you can select Guide from the menu to turn it off. Select Guide again and you will turn it back on.

When you have examined the preview you can pick Quit to get back to the Print menu. Select Destination and change it to Graph Printer when you are ready to print out a final quality version of your worksheet. Select Spreadsheet Print from the Print menu to send the report to the printer. If you find this procedure tedious you can set up a macro to automate some of the steps, as described in Chapter 12.

6 *Working with Defaults*

This chapter shows you how to customize many aspects of Quattro PRO. In Chapter 1 you learned that the program automatically detects several aspects of your computer system and provides default settings for many commands. Quattro PRO's installation procedure gives you an opportunity to select some hardware defaults such as the make and model of the printer. Using the Options menu after installation, you can change the ways the program runs on your system. You can also adjust default settings of individual worksheets to fit your needs and preferences. In fact, the extent to which the details of Quattro PRO can be tailored is quite exceptional. You can create customized menus and even add macros to menus. Some of these advanced features are covered in Chapter 12. However, you can begin with a number of simple changes that can make your work more efficient and more effective.

The Menu of Options

The changes to Quattro PRO discussed in this chapter are made from the Options menu shown in Figure 6-1. You can see that this menu is made up of three parts. The first section consists of eight commands that deal with such basics as coloring the screen and the display mode used. The Update command stores the current settings from the first eight commands into a

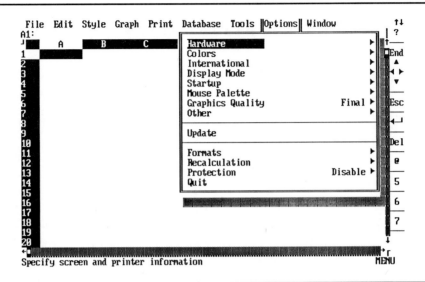

Figure 6-1.   *Options menu*

special file so that they can be used in the next session. The third section covers three areas of default settings that apply to the current worksheet.

About Defaults

A computer program's defaults are what the program does unless you tell it to do something differently. Most programs have defaults of one kind or another because the program has to make some basic assumptions about how you will be using it. For example, most word processing programs arrange text between margins and tabs, and so they begin with default margin and tab settings. In the same way, Quattro PRO has default column and format settings that determine how wide the columns will be and how numbers will be displayed. The starting defaults—the ones that the program uses when you first install it on your computer—are listed in Table 6-1.

Worksheet Settings

Column Width	9 characters
Format	General
Label Alignment	Left
Hide Zeroes	No
Recalculation	Background
Currency	$ prefix
Protection	Off
Font	Dutch 10-point (with graphics printer)

Program Settings

Wide Menus	Yes
Remember Menu Choices	Yes
Shortcuts Active	Yes
Mouse Palette	Displayed (if mouse installed)
Display Mode	Character 80×25
Undo	Disabled
Transcript Recording	Active
Failure Protection	100 keystrokes between saves
Expanded Memory	Formulas & Labels
Clock	None

Table 6-1. *Starting Defaults*

Worksheet Defaults

As you can see from Table 6-1, the defaults for Quattro PRO can be divided into two categories: program and worksheet. The program defaults affect all program activity. If you use the Update command, then the changes carry over to the next session when you reload Quattro PRO.

The worksheet defaults are set for a specific worksheet. They do not affect new worksheets created in the same session, or in any following sessions. Thus you can display a spreadsheet called SALES.WQ1, change the default label alignment to Right, and all new labels that you enter will be automatically right-aligned. However, the next worksheet you open with File Open or create with File New will revert to left-alignment of labels. This allows you maximum control over the formatting of your worksheets without unpredictable results. Altering worksheets defaults with Quattro PRO will not change formats that you have already established for specific cells. In the section on "Format Templates" in Chapter 7 you will learn how to set up blank worksheets to store customized format settings.

Configuration File

The program defaults for Quattro PRO are stored in the configuration file called RSC.RF. When you start the program, it reads the default settings from this file. You can update the configuration file to reflect your preferences. Suppose that you want on-screen display of the current date and time while you are working with Quattro PRO. You activate the menu and select Options followed by Other and then Clock. Your choices are Standard, International, or None. You pick Standard. Quattro PRO returns to the READY mode, and the date and time are displayed on the status line. They remain there whatever worksheets you open or close. However, when you exit from Quattro PRO and reload the program, then the clock will not be displayed, *unless* you use the Options Update command.

To make your default selections permanent, you select the Update option from the Options menu. Selecting Update writes the current settings into the configuration file, so Quattro PRO can reload them the next time you start the program. The work that you do may fall into two or more different categories and thus may require that you have several different sets of default choices. If you want to preserve a set of default choices, you can copy the RSC.RF file to another file, such as MY-RSC.RF, before you select Update. When the RSC.RF file is updated, the MY-RSC.RF copy will not be. This allows you to keep two different sets of defaults. You can keep many different sets of defaults in separate files and select the one you want for a particular session just prior to loading Quattro PRO. This process is described in Appendix A, "Enhanced Installation."

Format Options

The first default options discussed here are those that determine how your data appears on the worksheet. Careful manipulation of the format defaults can save a lot of time when you are applying formats to individual cells. The Formats menu contains the following options:

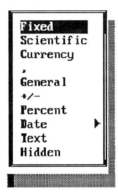

Numeric Format

You can select any of the format choices from the Style Numeric Format menu described in Chapter 2 as the default format for the display of values. These choices are listed with examples in Table 6-2. Many of the formats allow you to specify the number of decimal places (from 1 to 15). While the Numeric Formats option can be very convenient, saving you the trouble of formatting blocks of cells separately, you should exercise some care. For example, if you select a format with zero decimal places, and then you have to work with percentages, you might find it confusing to enter a percentage only to see Quattro PRO respond by displaying 0. A percentage will appear as 0 until the cell it occupies has a format of at least one decimal place. As a rule you will not want to use a default format that has no decimal places.

Format Name	Description of Format
Fixed	No commas in 1,000s, negatives in parentheses, user-defined decimal places: 2,000.99 (2,000.99)
Scientific	Exponential notation, negatives in parentheses, user-defined decimal places: 2.00E + 03 (2.00E + 03)
Currency	Commas placed in 1,000s, negatives in parentheses, user-defined decimal places, user-defined currency symbol; default is $: $2,000.99
,(Financial)	Commas placed in 1,000s, negatives in parentheses, user-defined decimal places: 2,000.99
General	Varies decimal places; uses exponential notation for large numbers
+/–	Represents positive numbers as plus signs (+), negatives as minus signs (–) for simple bar charts
Percent	Divides contents by 100; uses % sign as suffix
Date	Various options, described in Chapter 9, including formats for time values
Text (Show Formulas)	Displays formulas in cells rather than their values
Hidden	Hides cell contents from view; shows contents only on the descriptor line

Table 6-2. *Format Choices*

Align Labels

You have seen that you can align labels and values to the left, to the right, or in the center of columns by using the Style Alignment command. The alignment of labels is determined by the leading character: ' for left, " for right, or ^ for center. To avoid starting every label with one of these signs,

Quattro PRO lets you select one of them as the default. Normally, this is left-aligned, but you can change it to right or center.

Making a change to Align Labels under the Options menu can save time if you think you will be using the Style Alignment command to realign most of your labels after they are entered. However, changing the default alignment does not affect labels that are already entered. Typically, you will use the Options Formats Align Labels command before you build your worksheet. If your worksheet is already built you can use the Style Alignment command to change the alignment of a whole group of labels at once. Alignment set with Style Alignment is not affected by the Options Formats Align Labels command.

Note that if you are working with long labels, these are generally easier to use if they are left-aligned. Also, the alignment of values cannot be altered with the Options Formats Align Labels command. Values in your worksheet are usually right-aligned by default but you can use Style Alignment to center- or left-align them on a cell-by-cell or block basis. String functions that create labels from values create left-aligned labels by default. You can individually center or right-align them with the Style Alignment command.

Hide Zeroes

You may have noticed that a formula resulting in zero is displayed as **0** in the worksheet. Some worksheets have a lot of zeroes in them to show that no values have yet been entered in those cells, for example, in Figure 6-2 where part of a travel agency pricing worksheet is displayed. When you are preparing a worksheet containing many zero entries, you may want to hide or suppress them. The effect of this is shown in Figure 6-3.

Bear in mind that Quattro PRO will hide only true zeroes, not numbers like 0.01 that a display format of one decimal place has rounded to 0. It also does not erase the contents of cells containing zero that are hidden. The zeroes return when you change the Hide Zeroes option to No. Since many of the cells producing zeroes may actually be formulas that need to become active if certain other cells receive values, be careful not to accidentally overwrite these apparently empty cells. For example, in Figure 6-3 you may need to enter a code in cell C12, which would then activate the formula in cell C3 that calculates airfare.

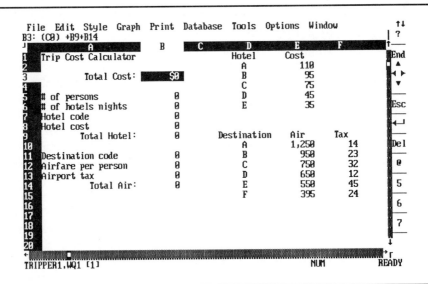

Figure 6-2. *Numerous zeroes*

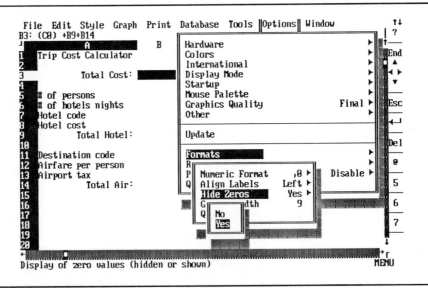

Figure 6-3. *Zeroes hidden*

To prevent accidental overwriting of cells, you can use the protection commands described later in this chapter.

Global Column Width

You have already seen that column width can be changed for a single column with the Style Column Width command, or for all columns in a block with the Block Widths command. To change the global width of the columns in the current and successive worksheets, use Options Formats Global Width.

Recalculation Options

One of the great features of a spreadsheet is that you can enter numbers and formulas and immediately see the effect of changes. This feature is known as *automatic recalculation,* the constant rechecking of all cells affected by each new entry into the worksheet. However, such a powerful feature has its drawbacks: As your worksheet grows, the time taken for each new item to be checked against the other cells increases. This recalculation time can take so long that it slows down the entry of new data. To avoid this problem Quattro PRO has an added feature called *background recalculation.* This allows you to carry on working while the program is recalculating in the background. You have three options for the mode of recalculation in Quattro PRO: Automatic, Manual, and Background. You are presented with these options when you select Mode from the Options Recalculation menu, as shown in Figure 6-4.

Since background recalculation does your math automatically while you work on other things, you may wonder what is the point of the other two choices. You use the Manual option when you do not want new worksheet entries or changes to old ones to affect other cells. This is valuable when you have a lot of data to enter into a large worksheet that is beginning to slow down Quattro PRO's normally fast response time. Time is saved because in manual mode, the program does not check whether a newly entered formula affects other results on the worksheet.

Although manual mode means that your spreadsheet is not always up to date, Quattro PRO has safeguards to prevent errors. Even when you are

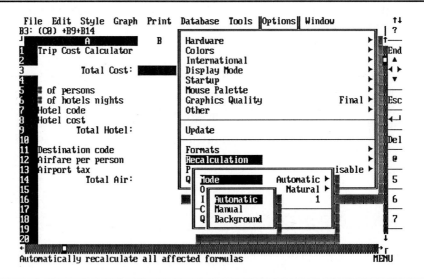

Figure 6-4. *The Recalculation options*

in manual mode, however, the program will calculate a formula as it is entered. It will also recalculate formulas that are edited or copied to other cells. Although Quattro PRO will not update other cells when in manual mode, it does know when you make changes to the worksheet. It reminds you that you have made changes that may affect the contents of other cells by displaying the CALC message in the status area. Whenever it is convenient, for example, after entering a new set of data, you can press the Calc key (F9), and Quattro PRO will perform a complete recalculation of the worksheet. The CALC message is removed to let you know all changes have been accounted for.

If you use manual mode you should make sure that before you print, save, or make decisions based on the worksheet figures, you press the Calc key (F9). Otherwise, you may be working with inaccurate data.

The automatic mode of recalculation is primarily used as an alternative to background, the difference being that automatic mode will not let you proceed with further data entry until recalculation is complete. This can be annoying when your spreadsheet begins to grow and yet you do not want to switch to manual mode.

Order of Recalculation

The way in which Quattro PRO calculates your spreadsheet is based on the natural mathematical relationship between cells in formulas. This is referred to as *natural recalculation*. The least dependent cells are calculated first, on through to the most dependent. Earlier spreadsheet programs could only calculate row by row down the spreadsheet or column by column across. These methods were called row-wise and column-wise respectively, but they were not always that wise. For example, row-wise calculations can produce errors if row 5 is based on the outcome of a calculation in row 10. Users of these programs usually worked around this problem and produced spreadsheet models that worked correctly if they were calculated in the correct order, either by column or by row. As you can see when you select Order from the Recalculation menu, Quattro PRO allows you to emulate these earlier programs and so can accommodate spreadsheets designed to use these methods of calculation.

Unless you know a specific reason why the worksheets you are working on will not be accurate unless calculated in a specific order, you will not need this option. Most Quattro PRO users can enjoy the benefits of natural recalculation.

Iteration

Many of the problems of row-wise and column-wise calculations can be solved by repeating the calculation process a number of times to take care of such dependencies. The repetition of calculation is called *iteration*. You can use the Iteration option to repeat the recalculation process as many as 255 times each time you press F9. If you have selected row-wise or column-wise as the method of calculation, you should set iteration to at least 2 to avoid errors. If you are constructing complex financial formulas containing circular cell references that require a specific number of iterations to produce a correct answer, you can enter this number on the Iteration menu.

If you are using natural recalculation, Quattro PRO refers to the iteration number only if you have circular references in the worksheet. The last item on the Recalculation menu is Circular Cell. This will show you the location of a circular cell reference in the worksheet if you have the CIRC message in the bottom status area of your screen. The CIRC message means you have entered a formula into a cell that uses the result of the cell to solve the formula. For example, @SUM(A1..A5) entered into any cell from A1 through A5 would create a circular reference. Sometimes it is difficult to see what is causing a CIRC message from just viewing the spreadsheet. Use Options Recalculation to see which cell contains the circular reference.

Note that the calculation preferences you select are specific to the worksheet, and the setting is stored with the worksheet. This helps to prevent errors and inconvenience. Whenever you retrieve that large spreadsheet in which you set recalculation to Manual, the mode is already set. But when you switch to a small worksheet where you have set Background or Automatic, the correct mode is still in operation.

Protection

To preserve the hours of work that go into making a good worksheet and to allow less proficient users to enter data into a spreadsheet without undue risk of damaging its underlying formulas, Quattro PRO provides several methods of cell and worksheet protection. You saw earlier that the Style menu has a protection option that allows you to specify the protected status of specific cells and groups of cells.

When you select Protection from the Options menu you have two choices: Enable and Disable. Selecting Enable is like placing a sheet of glass over the current worksheet. You will be able to see the data but you will not be able to change it. New data cannot be placed into the worksheet, and none of the cells can be edited. Selecting Disable turns off this protection. Saving a file with protection enabled means that anyone who retrieves the worksheet will have to turn off the protection before changing the data.

If you want to allow limited changes to cells on the worksheet, for example, for data entry work, you can turn on protection with Enable and then unprotect specific cells with the Style Protection Unprotect command. In this mode you can move around in the spreadsheet but only change those cells formatted with the Style Protection Unprotect command. These cells will appear highlighted, or in a different color, making it easy for data entry personnel to locate them. You can adjust the shading of unprotected cells with the Options Colors command described later in this chapter.

Going International

Having looked at the defaults that can be established for a particular worksheet, it is time to examine those aspects of Quattro PRO that can be altered for an entire session or permanently. This section begins with the International options.

Quattro PRO is used in many different countries that use various notations for numbers and dates. When you select International from the Options menu, as shown in Figure 6-5, you can see that there are several areas of the program that can be changed to accommodate the needs of users in other countries. In fact, you may want to use some of the options even if you are working in the United States. For example, when you are using Quattro PRO for calculations in currencies other than U.S. dollars, you may want to change the way the Currency format displays your values. Note that the menu shown in Figure 6-5 is the expanded version, which is

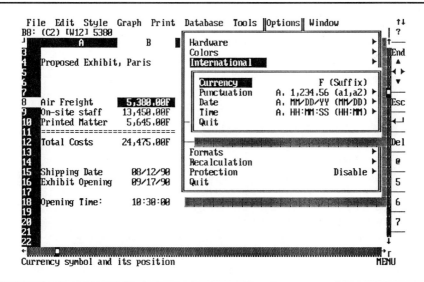

Figure 6-5. *International currency*

produced by pressing the plus key on the numeric key pad. This is helpful because it shows you the current default settings as well as the menu options.

Currency

You have seen that when you first install and use Quattro PRO and select the Currency format, the program displays numbers in the form of U.S. currency. The dollar sign precedes the number, as in $50. When you select Currency from the International menu, you type the character you want for the monetary symbol. You can change the symbol for currency from the dollar sign to any other character. For example, the French use F for francs and the British use £ for pounds, as shown in Figure 6-6.

To change the symbol for the currency, simply type the character you want in the dialog box that appears, and press ENTER. You will then be asked if this is to be a prefix preceding the value or a suffix following the value, as shown in Figure 6-7. When you select one of these two options, you are returned to the International menu.

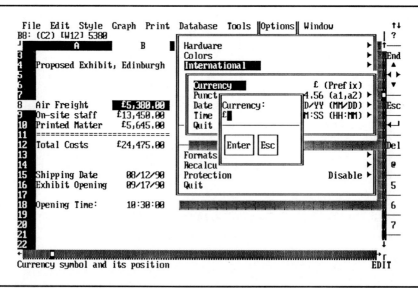

Figure 6-6. *Entering a symbol*

To convert to the francs shown in Figure 6-5, you type **F** as the currency character and select Suffix for the location of the string. If the foreign character you want to use is not on your keyboard—such as the pound sign (£), which is not on American keyboards—you can choose the appropriate ASCII character from those shown in Figure 6-8. When prompted for the currency symbol, hold down the ALT key and type the number corresponding to the character you want from the numeric keypad (not the numbers across the top of the keyboard). Note that £ is 156, and 159 is the *f*. sometimes used for francs.

Punctuation

If you are preparing a French spreadsheet, you may want to make changes to the numbers in addition to those shown in Figure 6-7, where the franc symbol is used. The French and other Europeans use different notations for thousands and decimals. Selecting the Punctuation option from the International menu reveals an extensive list of options, as shown in Figure 6-9. You can see that option D, which uses dots for thousands and commas for decimals, was used in the underlying worksheet.

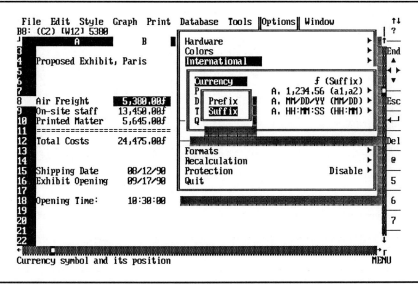

Figure 6-7. *Specifying a suffix*

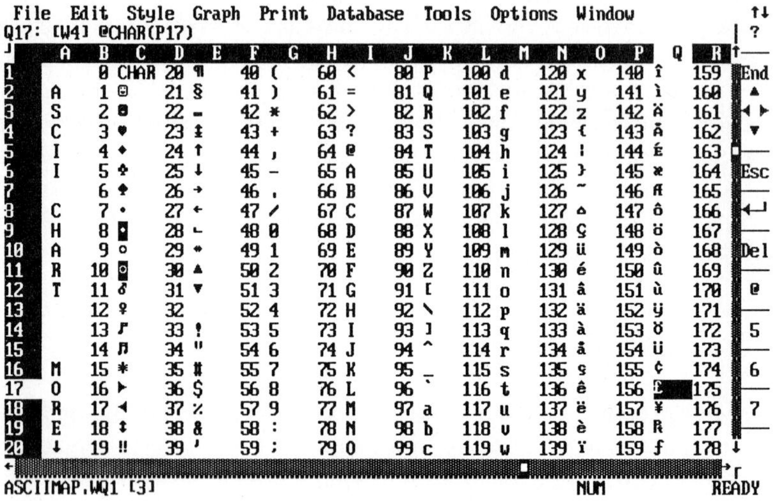

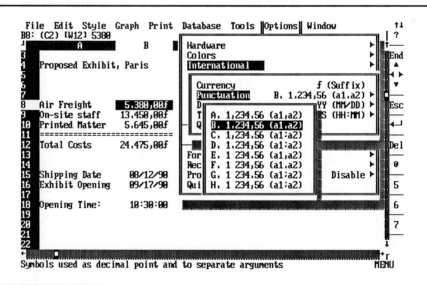

Figure 6-8. *An ASCII table*

Figure 6-9. *Punctuation options*

The second column of the list of punctuation options refers to the character used when separating arguments in functions. Instead of commas between arguments, you can use periods, as in option F. Thus you would type **@PMT(PRINCIPAL.INTEREST.TERM)** instead of **@PMT(PRINCIPAL,INTEREST,TERM)**. You can also use semicolons, as in options C,D,G, and H.

Date

The way that dates are written varies greatly throughout the world. You can change the way Quattro PRO displays dates in your worksheet. When you use the Style Numeric Format menu and select Date to assign a date format to a cell or group of cells, you have the following date style options:

1. DD-MMM-YY

2. DD-MMM

3. MMM-YY

4. Long International (day, month, and year)

5. Short International (day and month, or month and year)

The actual format used by items 4 and 5 will depend on the selection you make from the International menu. Normally, the Date option in the International menu is set to MM/DD/YY, which is how dates formatted with style number 4 appear. However, if you change the International Date setting to one of the other three possibilities, all dates in the current worksheet formatted with the D4 format will change to reflect the new format. These are the International date options:

1. MM/DD/YY (MM/DD)

2. DD/MM/YY (DD/MM)

3. DD.MM.YY (DD.MM)

4. YY-MM-DD (MM-DD)

You can see that each one has a long and short version. Dates formatted with the Short International format from the Style Numeric Format menu (D5) will appear in the short format shown in parentheses.

Remember that the format you select from the International Date menu is the one used by the on-screen calendar and clock display when you select International from the Clock option on the Options Other menu. This format is also used by the CTRL-D date entry command. For more discussion of dates, see Chapter 9.

Time

Just like dates, the way that times are written also varies considerably from country to country. When you are working with time values in a worksheet and want to format a value as a time, you select Time from the Style Numeric Format Date menu. These are the options:

1. HH:MM:SS (D6)

2. HH:MM (D7)

3. Long International (24-hour clock—hours, minutes, and seconds) (D8)

4. Short International (24-hour clock—hours and minutes) (D9)

These options, when applied to cells, are shown in the status line as D6 through D9. The choice you make in the Time option of the International defaults is reflected in the D8 and D9 time formats used in the worksheet, as well as in the on-screen calendar and clock display. Thus, the format you get when selecting items 3 and 4 will depend on the choice you make with the Options International Time command. Selecting Time from the International menu reveals the options shown in Figure 6-10. All of the international options for time use 24-hour notation, and each has both a long (D8) and a short (D9) form.

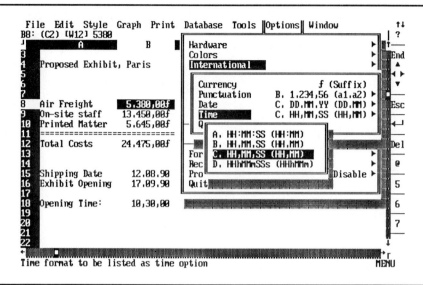

Figure 6-10. *Time format options*

Start-up Options

The Options Start-up menu shown in Figure 6-11 covers several areas of Quattro PRO's operation that are effective when the program is first loaded. You can also use this menu to change some aspects of the way in which the menu system works.

Directory Options

In Chapter 1 you saw that the first time you use the File Save command, Quattro PRO assumes you want to store your worksheet in the same area as the program files. You can use the File Directory command to change

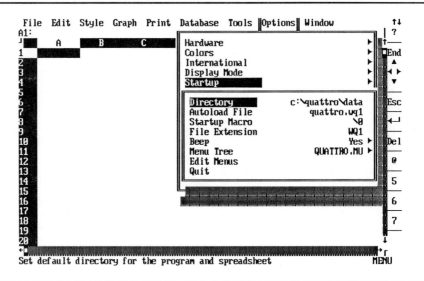

Figure 6-11.   *The Startup menu*

this choice for the current session. To use a new default area for storage at all times, you use the Directory option on the Startup menu. When you pick this option you get a dialog box like the one shown in Figure 6-12. The directory you set in this dialog box is the area in which you want the program to store your worksheets. It can be the name of any drive that you have available on your system, such as A:, B:, C:, D:, E:, and so on. You can follow the drive name with the name of the subdirectory that has been set up on that drive, such as \DATA or \QUATTRO\DATA.

If you want to use a directory that has not yet been created, use the File Utilities DOS Shell command to leave Quattro PRO temporarily. This command returns you to the disk operating system, which you can use to create a directory. You can also create directories with Quattro PRO's File Manager, which you access from the File Utilities menu. Operating system commands are discussed in Chapter 7.

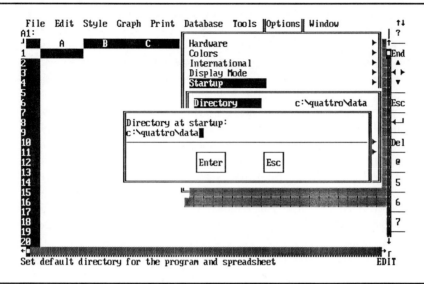

Figure 6-12. *Changing default directory*

Automatic File Loading

You may find that your work with Quattro PRO involves extensive use of one particular worksheet. For example, if you are almost exclusively pricing contracts, you may start with the same pricing spreadsheet every time you work with the program. To simplify your work, you can have Quattro PRO retrieve a file automatically whenever the program is loaded. When you pick Autoload File from the Start-up menu, you are asked to enter the name of the worksheet you want loaded whenever the program is started.

Suppose the file is a pricing spreadsheet called PRICING.WQ1. You simply type this name and press ENTER. You will immediately see the file listed on the menu. However, you must use the Update command on the Options menu to record this change and to make the autoload feature effective the next time the program is loaded. After you pick Update and reload Quattro PRO, the PRICING.WQ1 file will be retrieved. You can then enter the necessary data and save the new file under a different name, leaving the standard pricing worksheet unchanged on disk.

The autoload feature is always active. Whenever you load Quattro PRO it looks for the file name that is recorded in the Startup menu. As you can see from Figure 6-11, the default name is QUATTRO.WQ1. If Quattro PRO finds that file in the default directory when the program is loading, it retrieves the file. You can use the autoload feature either by changing the file name as just discussed, or you can save the file you want to autoload as QUATTRO.WQ1. This file can contain not only commonly used data, but it can also be a file of instructions. You could even produce a setup file for a novice Quattro PRO user. You can also place macros, stored keystrokes, commands, and even custom menus in the autoload file to further assist the spreadsheet user. (If you also use 1-2-3, you can make AUTO123.WK1 the autoload file name in order to use existing spreadsheets designed around this feature.)

Automatic Macro

You can designate a specific set of stored keystrokes (a macro) to be played back as soon as Quattro PRO loads any spreadsheet containing the macro named in this section of the Start-up menu. This autoload macro is initially called \0 (backslash zero). You can change the name to any valid macro name. (See Chapter 11 for more details on naming macros.) To supply a macro name, pick Start-up Macro from the Start-up menu. You can then type the name of the macro and press ENTER. Remember that to record this change to the automatic macro, you must use Update.

Each worksheet can have a macro with the designated autoload name. If you create an autorun macro in the autoload worksheet, you can have Quattro PRO carry out a whole series of commands every time the program starts. This process enables you to provide automated applications for other users and is described in Chapter 12.

File Extensions

The file name used by Quattro PRO when it stores your worksheets on disk consists of two parts. The first part of the name can be as many as eight characters long. The second part, separated from the first part by a period, can be three letters long and is called the *extension*. Initially, the program assigns the extension WQ1 to your worksheets. However, if you are sharing worksheets with a 1-2-3 user, you will want to save files with the WK1 extension so that 1-2-3 can read the files. You can make WK1 the default extension by selecting Extension from the Startup menu, typing **WK1**, and pressing ENTER. Note that you can always see both WQ1 and WK1 files on the file lists used by the File commands since Quattro PRO looks for ∗.W??, which means any file name with *W* as the first letter of the extension and any other characters as the second and third. This wildcard pattern also lists files from earlier versions of Quattro, which have the extension WKQ.

To Beep or Not to Beep

If you press HOME and then press UP ARROW, Quattro PRO will beep to let you know that the key you pressed was not appropriate, because you cannot go up from the home position. The beep is designed to be helpful, and many users appreciate knowing they have pressed the wrong key when entering data and formulas. However, if you find this beep annoying, or if those around you object to it, you can turn it off by selecting Beep from the Startup menu. A small No/Yes box pops up.

You choose Yes to turn on the beep and No to turn it off. Turning off the beep can be helpful as a temporary measure when you are working on an airplane or in other close quarters, where the noise of the beep would be distracting to others. If you want to keep the beep turned off in future work sessions, remember to use the Update option from the Start-up menu to record your preference.

Menu Trees

As mentioned in Chapter 1, Quattro PRO allows you to customize your menus. The feature of the program that does this is called the Menu Builder. A set of menus is called a *menu tree* and is stored in a file with the extension MU. You can create your own personalized menu tree and store it in an MU file. For example, if Debbie redefined her menu system, she could call it DEBBIE.MU. The Quattro PRO program comes with three menu trees: QUATTRO.MU, the one that the program uses to begin with and which is pictured in most of the illustrations in this book; Q1.MU, which mimics the menus of the first version of Quattro; and 123.MU, which is designed for those who are familiar with 1-2-3 and want to operate Quattro PRO with similar groupings of menu choices. You can see from the Start-up menu that the current selection is QUATTRO.MU.

To activate a user menu tree other than the default QUATTRO.MU, you select Menu Tree from the Start-up menu. You are presented with the choices shown in Figure 6-13. The choices are the 1-2-3 menu tree, the original Quattro menu tree, and the standard Quattro PRO menu tree. To change to the 1-2-3 menu tree, highlight the filename 123.MU and press ENTER. You will be returned to the READY mode and the 1-2-3 menu will be in effect. Just type / and you will see it displayed, as shown in Figure 6-14. To return to the Quattro PRO menu, you pick Worksheet, Global, Default, Files, and Menu Tree. Then you can select the QUATTRO.MU file from the list. You are returned immediately to the normal arrangement of menus. A change to the menu tree will remain in place after the current session only if you select Update to write the change to the RSC.RF file. To do this from the 1-2-3 menu system you select Worksheet, Global,

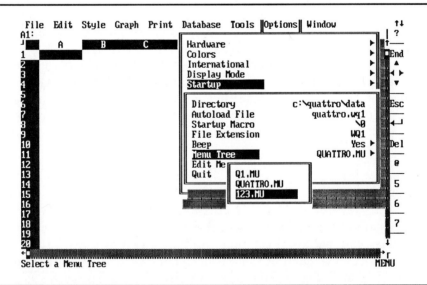

Figure 6-13.   *Menu Tree choices*

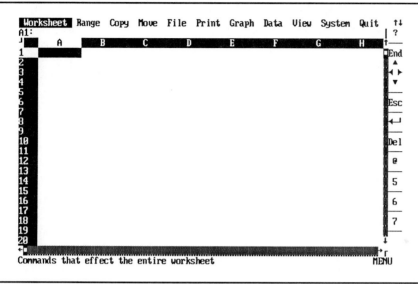

Figure 6-14. *The 1-2-3 menu tree*

Default, and Update. If you want to stick with the old Quattro menus, use the Default Update command. To change from the old Quattro menus to either the 1-2-3 or Quattro PRO menus, use the Default Menu Tree command.

Edit Menus

Not only does Quattro PRO allow you to choose from a range of alternative menu trees, but with the Menu Builder feature you can create your own. You access the Menu Builder by using the Edit Menus command on the Options Start-up menu. Suppose that you want to be able to select the Spreadsheet Print command from the File menu rather than from the Print menu. Using procedures that are described later in Chapter 12, you can use the Menu Builder to redefine the File menu and change Spreadsheet Print on the Print menu to Print on the File menu.

About Your Hardware

The Hardware option on the Options menu is where you tell Quattro PRO about your screen and printer. You can also use this menu to check the status of various aspects of your system, as you can see from Figure 6-15.

Screen Questions

When you installed Quattro PRO on your PC you may have noticed that, unlike many other programs, you did not have to specify what kind of display you were using. Many programs require you to select a set of program instructions, or *driver,* specific to your display before the program will run properly. This driver then has to be changed if you want to work with a different type of display. Quattro PRO automatically detects the

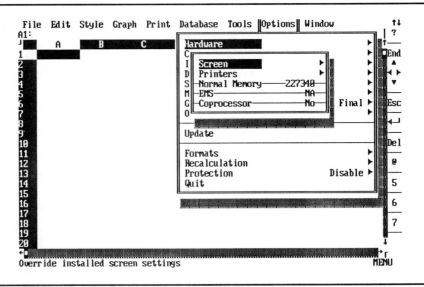

Figure 6-15. *The Hardware menu*

kind of display you have and operates most standard displays from a single driver file. In fact, if you are running Quattro PRO on a system that has a color display and you need to move to a computer that has a monochrome display, you do not need to make any changes to the program disks.

When you pick Screen from the Hardware menu, you are presented with the menu shown in Figure 6-16. The menu has four commands besides Quit. The only time you will need to select the Screen option from the Hardware menu is if you are using a display system that Quattro PRO does not know about or if you want to override the autodetect feature. If you want to change the color or shading of your display, you use the Colors command from the Options menu, rather than the Hardware command. If you want to change from character display to graphics display you use the Display Mode command described later in this chapter in the section of the same name.

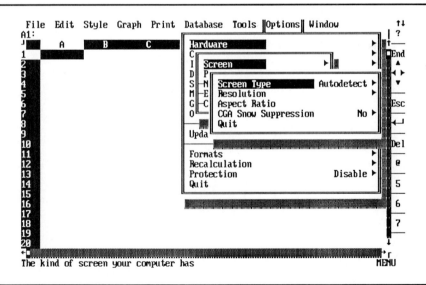

Figure 6-16.   *Screen options*

Screen Type

The first Screen setting is Screen Type, and this is normally Autodetect.
This is because Quattro PRO can detect most common display systems and
drive them from the standard SCREENS.BGI file. If your PC is displaying
spreadsheets clearly, you do not need to change the screen type. If you want
to force Quattro PRO to consider your display system to be a particular
type, you can change to one of the listed alternatives shown in Figure 6-17.

Resolution

Graphic display systems create images from a collection of dots. The
number of dots on a screen is referred to as the display's *resolution*. The
resolution determines the sharpness of the displayed image. Resolution is
measured by the number of dots across the screen and the number of lines
of dots going down it, as in 640 × 200. Since some displays can operate at
different resolutions, Quattro PRO provides the Resolution option, which

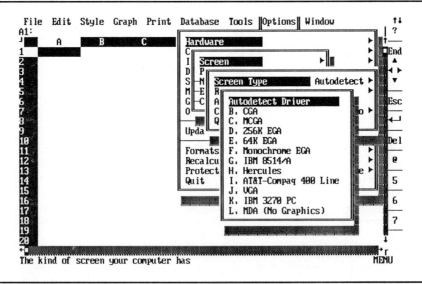

Figure 6-17.   *Screen type options*

lets you choose between them. Figure 6-18 was produced by a PC using a Hercules display card, and so the standard Hercules resolution was automatically selected by Quattro PRO. In Figure 6-19 you can see the options offered by a VGA card.

Aspect Ratio

The ratio of the width of your monitor to its height is called the *aspect ratio*. This ratio affects the monitor's ability to show circles as truly round. Although Quattro PRO can detect the display method used by your screen, it has no way of knowing the physical dimensions of the display. Dimensions vary from model to model. In fact, many models actually allow you to change the height of the screen display area, so different users of the same model can have different screen dimensions. For Quattro PRO to display circles, such as those used in pie graphs, as circles and not as an ellipse, you need to tell Quattro PRO the aspect ratio of your screen. In some ways this is merely a cosmetic concern, since Quattro PRO will print round pie graphs regardless of this setting. However, if you are using a screen capture system to make Quattro PRO graphs part of a presentation,

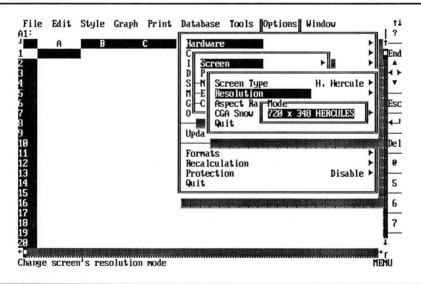

Figure 6-18. *Resolution option - Hercules*

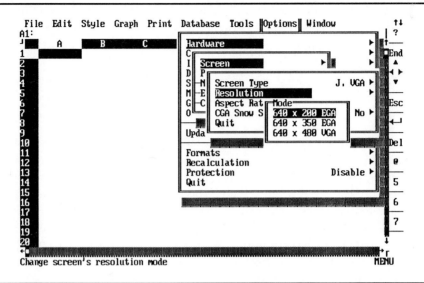

Figure 6-19.   *Resolution options - VGA*

then entering the ratio can be important. The screen used to set the ratio is shown in Figure 6-20.

Suppressing Snow

If you are using a CGA display system, that is, one based on the old IBM Color Graphics Adaptor, you may find that certain actions in Quattro PRO produce a fuzzy effect on the screen. This is referred to as "snow" and can usually be eliminated by setting CGA Snow Suppression to Yes.

About Printers

At the Hardware menu you can select Printers to let Quattro PRO know about the equipment you will be using for hard copy. As you can see from Figure 6-21, you can define two printers and select one of them as the default.

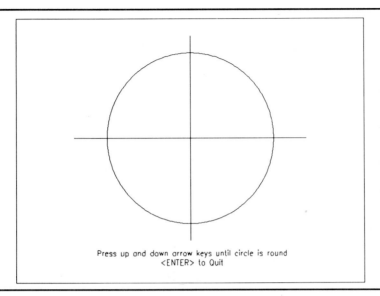

Figure 6-20. *Setting aspect ratio*

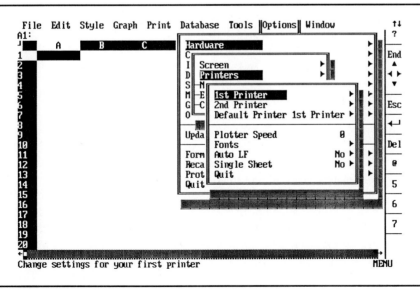

Figure 6-21. *Printer options*

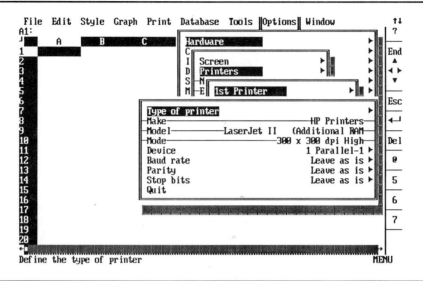

Figure 6-22. *Selecting printer type*

When you pick 1st Printer you see the menu shown in Figure 6-22. This lists the current settings, including Make and Model. If you selected a printer during installation, it will be listed here. If you did not select a printer during installation, you can do so now by selecting the first menu item, Type of printer. If you want to define a second printer, use the 2nd Printer option on the Printers menu and select Type of printer.

When you select Type of printer, you will see a list of brand names, such as Apple, EPSON, and HP. After picking the correct brand name for the printer you want to use, pick the exact model name. In some cases, such as the HP LaserJet II, you will also need to pick the print resolution that you want to use. When you have selected the type of printer, you are returned to the menu shown in Figure 6-22.

For most printers and computers you will not need to change the options on this menu, but these options allow you to modify Quattro PRO so that it can work with a wide range of printing devices. When you select Device you can see that your printer is either parallel or serial. Most printers are parallel printers on port number 1, which is the first item on the list.

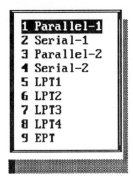

If you pick Serial-1, you must select various parameters to match your printer input requirements.

Baud, Stop Bits, and Parity   If you have a serial printer, you may need to match it to Quattro PRO by using settings such as Baud shown here:

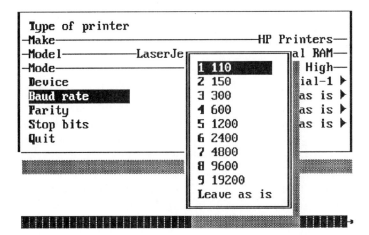

Consult your printer manual for the correct baud rate, stop bits, and parity setting. You may need to use the DOS command MODE to prepare your serial printer for use with Quattro PRO.

Plotter Speed This setting allows you to slow down the speed at which the plotter pen moves if you are using a plotter. This can be helpful when you are plotting onto some materials that are apt to smudge when written on at high speed. The default setting of 0 is the fastest plotter speed. Using a higher number will slow the plotter down.

Fonts As you saw in Chapter 5, Quattro PRO provides extensive support for fonts, allowing you to print and display text in a variety of typefaces, sizes, and styles. You can print out a mixture of fonts in a worksheet report when you use Spreadsheet Print after setting the print destination to Graph Printer. You can see a worksheet report formatted with fonts if you set the print destination to Screen Preview. You can view fonts in a graph if you use the Graph View command (F10). Graphs always print with their assigned fonts. You assign fonts to graphs with the Graph Text command, described in Chapter 8. Fonts for worksheets are assigned under the Style Font menu, discussed in Chapter 5. The Fonts command under the Options menu is seen in Figure 6-23.

Your font-printing capability depends to a certain extent on your printer. If you have installed a printer that uses font cartridges, such as the HP LaserJet, then Quattro PRO allows you use the Fonts option to specify which cartridges are installed. For example, the HP LaserJet II has a left and right cartridge. In Figure 6-24 you can see the submenu that lets you choose which one to specify. In Figure 6-25 you can see that the user has selected the Left Cartridge. This produces a list of possible cartridges from which to select, a list that will be familiar to users of the LaserJet. You can use the cursor movement keys to scroll down the list. To tell Quattro PRO about your printer, simply highlight the name/letter of the cartridge that you have in the left cartridge slot of your printer and press ENTER. Quattro PRO returns you to the Printers menu. You can repeat the process for the right cartridge if you have a set of fonts installed there.

The other option on the Fonts menu is Autoscale Fonts. This controls Quattro PRO's automatic font scaling option for graphs. The default setting is Yes, which means Quattro PRO adjusts font point size to fit the dimensions of a graph. If you set this option to No, Quattro PRO prints graph fonts in exact point size regardless of graph dimensions.

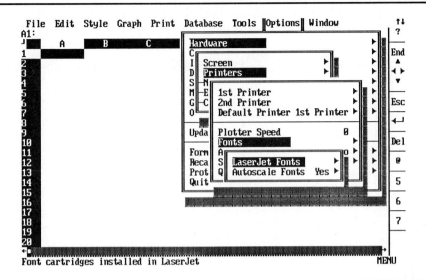

Figure 6-23. *Font options*

Auto LF Most printers today do not have an automatic line feed. Instead, the software tells the printer to advance the paper after each line of text. However, if you have a printer that adds a line feed after a line of text, you may find your output is unintentionally double spaced. If this is the case, change the Auto LF setting to Yes to solve this problem.

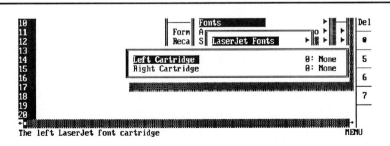

Figure 6-24. *LaserJet Fonts submenu*

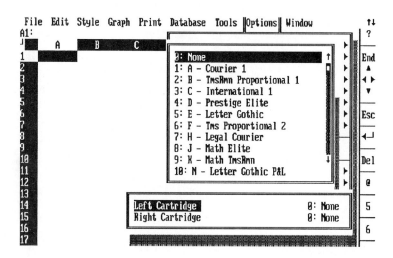

Figure 6-25.   *LaserJet Left Cartridge sub-submenu*

Single Sheet   You activate this option by picking Yes from the Yes/No choice box. Picking Yes will make Quattro PRO pause and prompt you to insert paper in a single-sheet printer. Note that this is only required for manual feed printers; do not pick Yes for this option if you are using an HP LaserJet or other printer that continually feeds sheets from a paper tray.

Other Hardware

At the Hardware menu you can see three items with a line across that cannot be selected. These items are simply status reports. Several Quattro PRO menus use this display style to show that the items are not active choices.

Normal Memory   The random-access memory, or *RAM,* in your computer is the area in which most of your work with Quattro PRO takes place. The size of this area is measured in bytes, and the normal memory indicator on the status line tells you how much RAM is still available. When you turn on your PC, the RAM area is empty, but shortly after the system starts up, the core of the disk operating system (DOS) is loaded into RAM. The amount of memory DOS takes depends on the version of DOS you are using. Version 3.3 uses about 60,000 bytes or 60K (there are 1024 bytes in 1 kilobyte). When you load Quattro PRO it takes up space in RAM. As you enter data into a worksheet, the amount of available RAM decreases. For example, the travel agency budget shown in Chapter 5 occupies 3K of RAM. You can monitor your use of RAM by periodically using the Options Hardware command or the @MEMAVAIL function.

Expanded Memory   A lot of computers have 640K of RAM because that amount is the most that can be recognized by versions of DOS up to version 3.3. However, numerous hardware and software manufacturers have designed ways of adding memory that can be recognized by programs. This is called *expanded memory,* or EMS. If you have such memory installed, Quattro PRO will recognize it and report its status on the EMS section. If you have expanded memory in your PC but it is not shown on this menu, check that you have installed the drivers that came with the board. You can use the @MEMEMSAVAIL function to report available memory in a worksheet. For more on the types of memory and how to utilize memory effectively with Quattro PRO, see Appendix A.

Coprocessor   There is one computer chip inside your PC that does most of the processing of data. This chip is called the *CPU,* or *central processing unit.* Typically these units are called 8088, 80286, or 80386. However, many PCs have room for additional chips that can share the processing load. These are called *coprocessors,* and Quattro PRO will detect and use one if it is installed. The most common type of coprocessor helps the CPU take care of mathematical calculations. Called numeric or math coprocessors, these units are typically named 8087, 80287, or 80387. You can see from the Hardware menu whether Quattro PRO has found a coprocessor in your system. If you have a coprocessor physically installed in your system but it is not listed on the Hardware menu, recheck the installation instructions for the chip.

Display Mode

On today's PCs there are two basic technologies for displaying information on the screen: character mode and graphics mode. In character mode the display is made up of 2000 characters arranged in 25 lines of 80 characters each. This is the default mode used by Quattro PRO and the one seen in most of the screens in this book. The alternative is a graphics mode in which the screen is composed of a series of dots that draw shapes, including numbers, text, and circles. The graphics mode offers advantages when it comes to drawing pictures such as charts. The disadvantage is that graphics mode requires a lot of memory and responds more slowly than character mode.

Quattro PRO has the unique ability to switch between different modes of display. This means that typical spreadsheet operations such as data entry and calculation can take place in the faster environment of character mode. However, when you want to design a high-quality report or a graph, you can switch to graphics mode. The mode you use is set through the Display Mode command on the Options menu. In Figure 6-26 you can see the menu of choices you get when you issue this command. The first option is character mode in the standard 80 characters by 25 lines. The second option is graphics mode.

When you use the graphics mode, some display systems such as EGA and VGA allow you to adjust the display resolution; that is, how sharply the graphics images are formed. You do this in Quattro PRO with the Hardware Screen Resolution command. However, you must set resolution

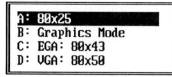

Figure 6-26.   *Display mode options*

before switching to graphics mode. Quattro PRO cannot change resolution while you are in graphics mode. You can record your desired resolution and mode as the new defaults for Quattro PRO by selecting the Update command on the Options menu.

Note the options C and D on the Display Mode list in Figure 6-26. These offer more lines and characters than the regular character mode, using special abilities of the different display cards. These options can give you more columns and rows of worksheet on screen, which is helpful for designing large worksheets.

Changing Attributes and Colors

Quattro PRO provides tremendous flexibility in the way the various elements of the program are displayed on your monitor. As you can see from Figure 6-27, a system of menus allows you to choose how each part of the screen is displayed. If your screen can display colors, Quattro PRO

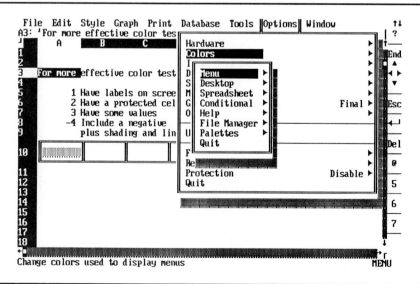

Figure 6-27. *Setting colors*

lets you customize the colors used by the different parts of the spreadsheet. For example, you can have a brown background with the cell selector in blue with white letters, or a white background with blue letters. The number of possible combinations are far too numerous to describe. If you have a monochrome display, you can control the video attributes of the screen, choosing between Normal, Bold, Inverse, Underlined, and Empty attributes. In Figure 6-28, the first choice on the Colors menu, which is Menu, has been selected.

At first the ability to change shades and colors may seem somewhat frivolous. However, such changes can improve efficiency. For example, special shading can be assigned to negative numbers, thus making them easier to locate. Labels can be displayed differently than values and make the spreadsheet easier to read. You can even tell Quattro PRO to highlight values outside of specified ranges, thus alerting users to incorrect answers.

If you have a color display system or one that emulates a color system and a black-and-white or LCD screen, changing the shading can be very useful. For example, if you are using a laptop computer with an LCD screen, you will probably find the standard Quattro PRO colors hard to

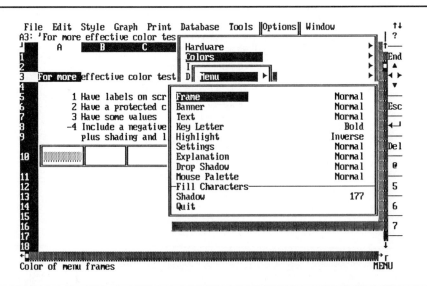

Figure 6-28. *The Menu settings*

read when they are interpreted by your system. Changing them can enhance their legibility. Even if you have a full-size color display and see Quattro PRO in vibrant colors, you may not like the the default program colors.

Changing Colors

When you pick Colors from the Options menu the first item is Menu. When you choose this option you can see how Quattro PRO breaks down the parts of the menu and—if you have a color monitor—the current color settings. These are shown in Figure 6-29. Suppose you want to alter the color of the menu frame. You select Frame and immediately a small paint box of colors appears with the current setting marked by a rotating cursor. By using the cursor-movement keys you can move around the paint box. Each band of color is a different background hue and each dot is a foreground shade. When you have placed the cursor on the choice you want you press ENTER. The choice is immediately reflected in the text of the menu setting, but may not be displayed until you use the Quit command to leave the menu system. Quit takes you back to the READY mode. If you want to make a further change you can use the Remember feature of the Quattro PRO menus to get straight back to the area you were in before. You can adjust all of the areas of the menu listed in Table 6-3. You can alter all of the areas of the program shown in Figure 6-27.

Frame
Banner
Text
Key Letter
Highlight
Settings
Explanation
Drop Shadow
Mouse Palette

Table 6-3. *Menu Display Areas*

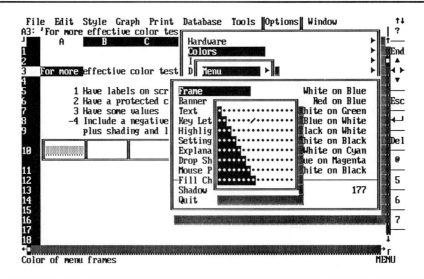

Figure 6-29. *The color choices*

Desktop Appearance

Table 6-4 describes the parts of the Desktop that you can adjust. The *Desktop* is the area of the screen that is behind your worksheets. In Figure 6-30 you can see the status line being changed on a monochrome system. Notice that instead of the paint box of colors, a list of attributes is provided. The Fill Characters portion of the Desktop menu refers to the way Quattro PRO makes up the pattern behind your worksheet windows when you are in character mode. You can see the default character, 178, at work in Figure 6-30. The pattern is simply a repetition of the shading character. You can use the ASCII chart in Figure 6-8 to choose an alternative character, and enter the number in the Desktop option under Fill Characters.

Spreadsheet

The parts of the spreadsheet that you can color are listed in Table 6-5. Two areas that deserve special attention are Unprotected and Labels. The Unprotected option lets you choose a special color or shading scheme for

Status
Highlight-status
Errors
Background
Desktop Fill Character (default ASCII 178)

Table 6-4. *Desktop Display Areas*

cells that are specifically protected or unprotected. This coloring helps you distinguish these cells more clearly. Note that Quattro PRO's initial color and shading settings already distinguish these cells. You may also find it helpful and attractive to see cells that contain labels displayed with a different color or attribute. The Labels option allows you to do this. You can make column and row headings form a contrasting frame around the calculation areas.

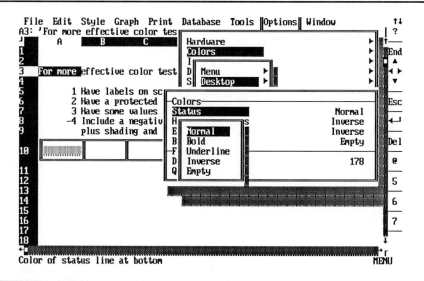

Figure 6-30. *Desktop settings*

Frame
Banner
Cells
Borders
Titles
Highlight
Graph Frames
Input Line
Unprotected
Labels
Shading
Drawn Lines

Table 6-5. *Spreadsheet Display Areas*

Conditional

Possibly the most exciting of Quattro PRO's colorization options is Conditional. When you select this item from the Color menu, you see the menu shown in Figure 6-31. (Note that the settings on this menu have been changed from the defaults for purposes of illustration.) The Conditional menu allows you to change the color or attributes of cells based on the value of their contents. Thus, negative numbers could be shown in bold, ERR cells in an eye-catching inverse, and so on. You can even set value parameters so that Quattro PRO will highlight excessively high or low numbers.

On/Off Since the use of different colors or shadings for cells based on the value of their contents can be disconcerting to those not used to this feature, it can be turned off. When you select On/Off from the Conditional menu, you can select either Enable or Disable to activate or deactivate the conditional coloring of cells.

ERR You can bring errors to people's attention more dramatically by setting a special coloring for any cell that has the contents ERR. When the

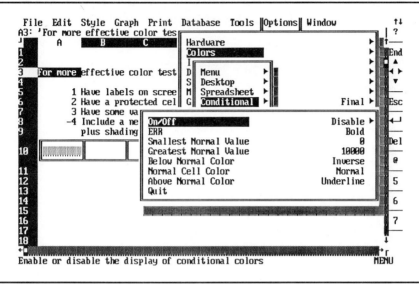

Figure 6-31. *Conditional settings*

error is resolved and the ERR content is changed to a correct result, the cell color will return to normal.

Value Colors   If you select Smallest Normal Value or Greatest Normal Value from the Conditional menu, you can set value limits beyond which Quattro PRO alters the color of cells selected with the Normal Cell Color and Above Normal Color options. This feature is particularly helpful for data-entry personnel because it can visually alert them to data-entry mistakes that result in numbers that are outside of expected ranges.

An example of this is shown in Figure 6-32, where the conditional display attributes have been set up to help users of the Trip Cost Calculator worksheet. The premise of this worksheet is that it will calculate the total cost of a vacation trip. That cost will normally be less than $10,000. Any number higher than 10,000 will be underlined to alert the user to possible miscalculations. Thus, the total cost cell is underlined in the figure because it exceeds the Greatest Normal Value setting.

Since a set of conditional parameters can be disabled with the On/Off option, you can easily activate it temporarily to help inexperienced users.

```
File  Edit  Style  Graph  Print  Database  Tools  Options  Window        ↑↓
B8: @VLOOKUP(B7,HOTEL,1)                                                  | ?
┌         A              B    C       D        E        F        ┬───
1 │Trip Cost Calculator              Hotel    Cost                   End
2 │                                    A       110                    ▲
3 │         Total Cost: $10,398        B        95                  ◄ ►
4 │                      ─────         C        75                    ▼
5 │# of persons             6          D        45
6 │# of hotels nights       8          E        35                  ┤Esc
7 │Hotel code           B
8 │Hotel cost              95                                        ↵
9 │       Total Hotel:  4,560      Destination  Air      Tax
10│                                    A        1,250     14        Del
11│Destination code     B              B          950     23
12│Airfare per person     950          C          750     32         @
13│Airport tax             23          D          650     12
14│      Total Air:     5,830          E          550     45         5
15│                                    F          395     24
16│                                                                   6
17│
18│                                                                   7
19│
20│
←├▓▓▓▓▓▓□▓▓▓▓▓▓▓▓▓▓▓▓▓▓▓▓▓▓▓▓▓▓▓▓▓▓▓▓▓▓▓▓▓▓▓▓▓▓▓▓▓▓▓▓▓▓▓▓├►┌
TRIPPER1.WQ1 [1]                                                READY
```

Figure 6-32. *Conditional example*

For example, highlighting of error cells and abnormally low or high entries
can be turned on to help data-entry personnel, possibly by using a macro,
as will be described in Chapter 11. The conditional coloring can be turned
off for more experienced users. Remember that conditional color settings,
like all the other customized color settings, are not permanently stored
until you use the Update option on the Default menu to write the current
settings to the configuration file.

Help

You can customize the appearance of the help screens with the Help option
on the Colors menu. This option divides the help screen into five areas. The
Frame is the edge of the help screen; Banner is the heading for the screen;
and Text is the actual wording of the help information. The Keywords are
words that are used to select further help screens, and the Highlight is the
shading you move around the help screen to pick keywords.

Color Palettes

The Palettes option on the Colors menu lets you select the standard color or monochrome settings. This option is useful when you want to restore the original settings. When you select Palettes from the Colors menu, the choices are simply Color, Monochrome, and Quit. You could use this menu, for example, to temporarily switch between a customized set of colors that were stored in your RSC.RF file and the standard palette.

The Mouse Palette

If you are using a mouse you can alter the selections available to you in the mouse palette at the right of the screen. There are a total of seven buttons to which you can assign keystrokes. Note that these are the target areas of the palette on the right, not the actual buttons you press on your mouse.

The first four buttons are already assigned as Escape, Enter, Delete, and @. You can attach whatever you want to buttons 5, 6, 7, and 8. You can even alter buttons 1, 2, 3, and 4, but this is not recommended unless you are sure you know what you are doing. As you can see from Figure 6-33, the definition box for each mouse button consists of two fields: Text and Macro. The Text is a selection of three letters, such as *Esc*, or three ASCII characters that represent ENTER. You can see from Figure 6-33 that button 7 is marked by a **7**. The Macro field is where you tell Quattro PRO what keys you want the button to type. You enter a macro code for the keystrokes, such as {ESC} for Escape, ~ for ENTER, or {BEEP} to cause a beep when you pick the inactive button 7. See Chapter 11 for more on macro codes.

As an example of expanding the mouse palette, suppose that you want clicking button 5 to be the same as pressing the HOME key. You select 5th Button and then Text. You type **Top**, or **Hom**, or any other three characters to represent *Home*. Then you press ENTER and select Macro, type {HOME}, and press ENTER. When you quit back to the READY mode you can then use button 5 to take you to the top of your worksheet.

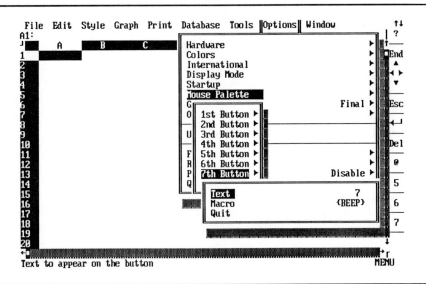

Figure 6-33.   *Mouse palette settings*

Graphics Quality Control

The Options Graphics Quality command allows you to control when Quattro PRO creates or renders Bitstream high quality fonts. Select the default setting of Final and Quattro PRO will always use the Bitstream fonts you request for screen display and printing. Select Draft and Quattro PRO will only use the Bitstream fonts you request if they have already been rendered. Otherwise, Quattro PRO uses Hershey fonts to simulate the approximate appearance of the Bitstream fonts.

Other Options

There are several useful options grouped under the heading "Other." This is where you enable the Undo command that reverses many of the commands and actions that you perform with Quattro PRO. The Macro command allows you to adjust screen updating during macros for faster execution. The Expanded Memory command determines what information can be placed in extra memory if you have such memory installed. See Appendix A for more on the types of memory and what you can store there.

The Clock command allows you to turn on and off the display of the date and time in the lower left corner of the screen. You can either display the date and time in Standard format or in International format, which will be the format currently in effect from the International Date and Time options. The Paradox command allows you to fine tune the use of Paradox data files over a network. You can tell Quattro PRO where to look for data and for the PARADOX.NET file.

Conclusions

The Quattro PRO Default menu is a powerful tool for extensive personalizing of the program. You can save a lot of time by making your preferred choices permanent program choices with the Update option.

How to use the Menu Builder feature, invoked by the Edit Menus option or the Start-up menu, will be covered in Chapter 12. That chapter also covers how to use Transcript for making macros. The use of Transcript for restoring data is discussed in the next chapter.

7 *Handling Files*

In this chapter you will learn how to work with multiple windows and linked files and how to bring data into a Quattro PRO spreadsheet from other programs such as dBASE and 1-2-3. Doing so enables you to share and exchange data with other users. To simplify file-management tasks Quattro PRO provides a feature called the File Manager. Using the File Manager you can manipulate files and organize your hard disk without leaving Quattro PRO. The chapter begins with a review of the basic procedures for saving and retrieving worksheets.

The Filing Process

The File menu shown in Figure 7-1 is one of the most important menus in Quattro PRO. You use this menu to store and retrieve your worksheet files. You have seen that the data you enter into a worksheet window is not immediately stored in a worksheet file on disk. Instead, it is temporarily retained in the computer's memory. The memory area, the random access memory (RAM), is like an electronic desktop. Because it is electronic, the work that you do there, such as entering and calculating, is performed very quickly. By retaining most of your worksheet in memory while you manipulate it, Quattro PRO can provide fast responses and rapid calculations. However, even an electronic desktop has its disadvantages. The problem with RAM is that everything you have entered into it is erased when the power to your PC is turned off or interrupted. Although Quattro PRO

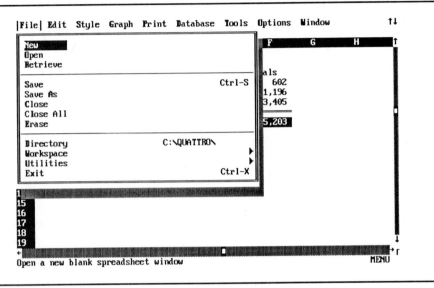

Figure 7-1.   *The File menu*

records all of your keystrokes as you work, just in case you need to recover from a disaster like a power loss, it is important to use the File menu on a regular basis to transfer a copy of the worksheet from memory to disk.

Operating System Basics

For those who do not completely understand how a computer manipulates disk storage and memory operations, this section describes what happens when you turn on your PC. The first thing a computer does when you flip on the switch is to look to the disk drives to find information stored on disks. Disks are made of the same material as cassette tapes and video cassettes. On a disk, this magnetic storage medium is laid out flat and divided into a series of concentric circles. Information is both read from and written to a disk by a moving head. This head is essentially the same as a head in a cassette tape player.

The first piece of information that the computer looks for is the operating system. On an IBM PC or PC-compatible, the operating system is called the *disk operating system,* or DOS. This system can be either PC-DOS (distributed by IBM) or MS-DOS, which is the version licensed by Microsoft to many other computer manufacturers. When the computer finds DOS, it reads the essential parts from the disk and loads them into memory. While the disk and disk drive use a combination of electronic and mechanical components, the computer's memory is purely electronic. It is a place where information can be changed much faster than on a disk. Quattro PRO takes good advantage of this speed: as much of the program is loaded into memory as will fit. The amount of program in memory is adjusted to make room for data as your worksheets expand and you open more worksheet windows. This is done automatically by Quattro PRO—you do not have to worry about it.

The role of DOS is twofold. First, it is a flow manager, managing the flow of information in and out of the computer. When you type the letter *q*, DOS makes sure that a *q* appears on the screen and that the character is stored and printed as a *q*. When you give a command to print out data, Quattro PRO passes that request on to DOS for execution. The second role for DOS is as a file manager. The information your computer uses is stored in either program files or data files. The arrangement of these files on the disk is managed by DOS. Thus, DOS actually executes your request to Quattro PRO to store data on disk.

Once the computer has loaded DOS, it can start handling your information. Two important pieces of information that are usually supplied to the disk operating system at this point are the date and the time. You can type these manually or they may be read from a clock within the computer. Quattro PRO uses the date and time for the optional on-screen clock display. DOS stores a record of when a file is written to the disk and displays this date and time when files are listed. This information can help you manage files.

Loading Programs

After the date and time have been entered into memory, the computer wants to know what programs you wish to execute. The way it asks you this is to display the *system prompt*. The prompt can consist of several pieces of information. The first is usually the name of the drive that the computer is using (normally C for a hard drive). The second is the *cursor.* The cursor points out where you are and where the next character you type will appear.

To start running a program, you normally type the name of the program at the system prompt and press ENTER to send the request to the disk operating system. DOS will then look on the disk for the program and begin to load it into memory. In the case of Quattro PRO, this means you type **Q** and press ENTER. You do not have to worry about upper- or lowercase letters when sending information to DOS, which does not distinguish between the two. When you ask Quattro PRO to store information on disk and Quattro PRO passes this request on to DOS, you can type the name of the file in either upper- or lowercase. However, DOS will store the name in all capital letters.

Data Entry

When you have loaded Quattro PRO you are ready to enter worksheet data. When you first type labels, values, and formulas, the data is held in RAM. The program does not store the worksheet on disk as you build it. Later, you must issue a command to tell Quattro PRO to store the worksheet. However, the program has a special file that contains a log of your keystrokes, and this information is recorded on disk as you type. If you suddenly lose power and RAM is erased, Quattro PRO can recover your work from the keystroke log. Of course, you should save your worksheet file in the normal manner, rather than relying on rebuilding the file from the keystroke log.

Naming Files

Every file in the same directory of a disk must have a unique name. This name is composed of three parts: a file name, a period, and an optional extension. The file name consists of one to eight letters or numbers without spaces. You can use some punctuation marks in a file name, but it is usually easier to use numbers and letters rather than to try to remember which punctuation marks are acceptable. Valid punctuation characters in a file name are

( ) ! @ # $ % & - _ ' { } ~ ' ^

If you use invalid characters, DOS responds with "Invalid File Name" and so does Quattro PRO.

One piece of punctuation has a special role in file names: the period. It connects the file name with its extension. The extension is usually three characters long and follows the same rules as those for file names. When they are used, extensions are often chosen to distinguish between types of files. For example, Quattro PRO worksheets have the extension WQ1. Earlier versions of Quattro used the extension WKQ. 1-2-3 files use WKS or WK1, depending on the version of the program (version 1 uses WKS; version 2 uses WK1). Quattro PRO normally assigns an extension to the file name you create depending upon what kind of data you are saving in the file. Table 7-1 lists several Quattro PRO files, showing their extensions and their use. If you want Quattro PRO to save to a format that can be read by another program—for example, 1-2-3—simply enter the file name and the appropriate extension. For example, Quattro PRO would save BUDGET.WK1 as a 1-2-3 file. If you want Quattro PRO to use a particular extension all the time, you can enter that extension as part of the program defaults using the Options Startup File Extension command described in the previous chapter.

File Name	Ext.	Size	Date/Timestamp		Use
Q	EXE	219958	8-01-89	12:39p	Program file
RSC	RF	827	5-30-90	12:34p	Definition file
FRWK!	TRN	21719	8-01-89	12:04a	File retrieve translator
FSWK!	TRN	21719	8-01-89	12:04a	File save translator
BUDGET	WQ1	34432	6-13-90	2:00p	Quattro PRO worksheet
BUDGET09	WKQ	34432	6-13-90	2:00p	Quattro 1.0 worksheet
BUDGET	WK1	45567	6-12-90	11:00a	1-2-3 2.0 worksheet
BUDGET	PRN	18000	6-14-90	11:00p	Print file
BUDGET09	PRN	12000	6-14-90	9:00a	Print file
BUDGET	PIC	11111	6-13-90	9:15a	Graph file
BUDGET09	PIC	12121	6-13-90	10:01a	Graph file

Note: The first five columns are displayed by DOS with the DIR command. The last column, Use, was added for this table and is not shown by DOS.

Table 7-1. *Quattro PRO Files*

Copying Files

At the DOS prompt you can copy files from one disk to another, from one subdirectory of a disk to another, and from one file name to another. If you want to copy a group of files, you use special characters called wildcards to denote more than one file, as in

COPY *.WQ1 A:

This command tells the system to copy all Quattro PRO spreadsheet files in the current directory of the current disk to the disk in drive A. The command

COPY SALES.W?? A:

tells the system to copy all of the worksheet files related to the SALES database (including WKS, WK1, WKQ, as well as WQ1 files) to drive A. The asterisk is used to represent a number of characters, whereas the question mark is used to represent a single character. Thus, SALES?A.* includes SALES1A.WQ1 and SALES2A.WK1 but not SALES3.WQ1.

As shown in Table 7-1, the size of files is measured in *bytes*. This is a relative measure of electronic space. One byte is the amount of space it takes to store one character, number, space, or piece of punctuation. However, you cannot directly relate the size of a data file to the number of characters you type into it. For example, files may contain information about how the data is arranged. Quattro PRO stores a typical worksheet of 1800 active cells containing over 30,000 characters in 80,000 bytes of disk space. If you use the !SQZ! option described later, you can store the same worksheet in 24,000 bytes.

Since one byte is a minute unit of measurement, you will often see bytes measured in units of *kilobytes,* abbreviated as *K.* Each kilobyte is 1024 bytes. Do not worry about the extra 24; just use 1000 when converting from bytes to kilobytes. Thus, a worksheet that contains 82,944 bytes can be described as 83K in size. When files get really big they occupy megabytes. One *megabyte,* or *MB,* is 1000K, or a million bytes. The capacity of your disks is usually measured in kilobytes and megabytes. The standard 5 1/4-inch floppy disk stores 360K. The special 5 1/4-inch disks used in the

IBM PC AT can store 1.2 megabytes. The hard-jacketed 3 1/2-inch disks used in many laptop PCs and the new PS/2 series from IBM can store 720K, or 1.4 megabytes, depending on how they are formatted. Most hard disks hold at least 10 megabytes and can exceed 100 megabytes in capacity.

Disks and Directories

Just as Quattro PRO comes to you on disks, data created with the help of programs is also stored on disks. Information is stored on disks in files. As you work with your computer you quickly create many files. To keep these files manageable, there is a practical limit to how many files you should store on a disk. (An actual limit of 512 files per directory exists in some versions of DOS.) Large-capacity disks, particularly hard disks, are often divided into small, manageable parts called *subdirectories*. This division is much like that used in the telephone directory of a large company. The directory may list departments in its main section but not every single person in the company; each department might have its own subdirectory listing each staff member. Subdirectories are an important part of organizing your Quattro PRO work on your hard disk.

Handling Hard Disks

A hard disk directory system for a computer running Quattro PRO and WordPerfect might look like the one shown in Figure 7-2. For your computer to find either a program file or a data file, you must specify a path for it to follow. For example, the path to the file EDITOR.DOC is \WP\LETTERS\. The path to the purchase-order entry worksheet in the SALES subdirectory of the QUATTRO directory is \QUATTRO\SALES\. You can have more than one file with the same name on the same hard disk if you keep them in separate directories. It is generally safer, however, to give each file a unique name. To identify files on a hard disk accurately, include the path to the file as part of the file name. Thus, the full name of the EDITOR.DOC file is

C:\WP\LETTERS\EDITOR.DOC.

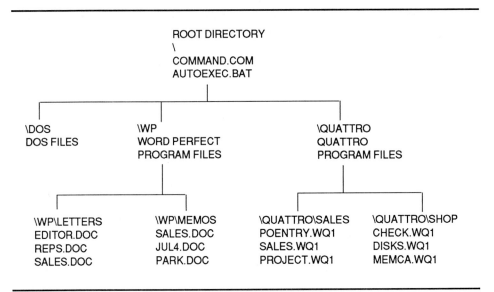

Figure 7-2. *Hard drive directory system*

When using a hard disk you cannot, of course, be in two places at once. Normally, you begin working with a hard disk in the *root directory*. You are said to be in the root directory of a drive when you are at the uppermost level, which is signified by A:\, B:\, C:\, and so on. The directory you are in at any particular time is called the *current* or *default directory,* which simply means the one you are using. To experiment with this, you can enter the following commands from the DOS prompt. Try these commands from the DOS prompt, either before or after using Quattro PRO. (You can temporarily exit Quattro PRO to use DOS commands by using the File Utilities DOS Shell command described later in this chapter.)

Determining the Root   You can ensure that you are in the root directory by typing **CD ** and pressing ENTER. This command tells DOS to change to the root directory. You can quickly tell which directory is the current directory by typing **CD** without the backslash at the C> prompt. DOS responds by telling you the name of the current directory.

A Better Prompt   In order to navigate a hard disk with one or more subdirectories, it is useful to change the uninformative C> prompt, which just tells you that you are using drive C, to the C:\> prompt, which tells you that you are using drive C and are in the root, or main, directory. This more informative prompt will always tell you what subdirectory you are in. For example, if you moved into a subdirectory of the root directory called DOS, the prompt would read C:\DOS>. (If your hard disk is not drive C but drive D or E or any other valid letter, just substitute that letter for C in the instructions that follow.)

To change the prompt to a more informative version, type **PROMPT PG** at the C> prompt. When you press ENTER you will see the drive letter and the path ($P) to whatever subdirectory you are in, and the greater-than sign (represented by $G). Once you enter the Prompt command, the new prompt remains in effect until you turn off or reset your computer. To get around having to re-enter the command each time you turn on your computer, you might want to add the Prompt command to your AUTOEXEC.BAT file, as described in Appendix A, "Advanced Setups."

Working with Directories   To see the path prompt in action and to explore the directory commands, change your location to a subdirectory such as the one for Quattro PRO. Type **CD \ QUATTRO** and press ENTER. You will see your prompt change. To change your current location back to the root directory, type **CD ** and press ENTER. To make a subdirectory directly below the root directory, type **MD \TEMP** and press ENTER. To make a subdirectory of the TEMP directory, type **MD \TEMP\MINE** and press ENTER. If you wanted to copy all the files from a disk in drive A into this new directory, you could move into the subdirectory by typing **CD \TEMP\MINE** and pressing ENTER, followed by **COPY A:*.*.** Or you could type **COPY A:*.* C:\TEMP\MINE** from the root directory.

To remove a subdirectory you must first remove all data and program files from it. If you are in a subdirectory and use the command DEL *.*, you will only delete files in that subdirectory, not across the whole disk. You can delete files from a subdirectory from anywhere. For example, if you were in the root directory, you could type **DEL \TEMP\MINE*.WQ1** to delete all files with the WQ1 extension in the MINE subdirectory of the TEMP subdirectory. To remove an empty subdirectory you would remove the

lowest levels first. For example, type **RD \TEMP\MINE** and press
ENTER, and then type **RD \TEMP** and press ENTER.

Help with DOS

Since DOS commands are not the easiest to learn and apply accurately,
you may sometimes make mistakes. One of the worst is to delete the wrong
file. Fortunately there is a cure. If you realize you have erased a file that
you wanted to keep, do not continue to move or store additional files. Reach
for a program called The Norton Utilities or another called Mace Utilities.
These programs will, among other things, enable you to restore the file in
most cases.

If you find the DOS directory commands difficult to use, you may want
to purchase a hard disk organizing program such as QuickDOS II from
Gazelle Systems of Provo, Utah. This program draws a picture of your
directory system and provides alphabetical lists of files. QuickDOS II uses
menus similar to those in Quattro PRO for all of the DOS commands, such
as COPY and DEL. Of course, you may find it easier to use the File
Manager that is a part of Quattro PRO itself. This feature is described later
in this chapter.

Saving Worksheets

Having seen how your PC handles different storage areas and stores data,
you can experiment with Quattro PRO's file-related commands. The most
important of these are the ones used to save worksheets.

File Save Options

When you want to save a worksheet you can either use the File Save
command or the File Save As command. The File Save command saves the
current worksheet using the current name displayed in the lower-left
status area of the current worksheet window. The File Save command does

not give you a chance to alter the name of the file, but you are asked whether you want to overwrite the existing file with the current version. If you select Replace, the File Save command writes the current worksheet to disk. If you want to save a worksheet, plus you want the opportunity to alter the current name, then you should use the File Save As command. For Quattro PRO to carry out the File Save As command and safely store a copy of your worksheet file on disk, it needs two pieces of information: where to store the data and what file name to use.

Where to Store Data

Quattro PRO needs to know in which directory of which drive you want the worksheet stored. In Chapter 1 you saw that Quattro PRO initially assumes that you want to save the data to the drive and directory from which you started the program. You can change this temporarily by using the File Directory command.

Suppose you have Quattro PRO installed on drive C in a directory called QUATTRO. The full name of this storage area, its path, is C:\QUATTRO. However, you would like Quattro PRO to store a series of worksheets on drive A. You select the Directory command from the File menu and are prompted with "Enter name of directory:" as shown in Figure 7-3. The currently selected directory is shown, in this case, C:\QUATTRO. The cursor is flashing under the first letter of this path name. Simply type the path name of the new storage area, in this case **A:**, and it will replace the current one. If you wanted to specify a particular directory you have created on A, you would add a backslash (\) and the name of the directory, as in **A:\WORK**. When you have typed the new directory, press ENTER. From now until you end the current session with Quattro PRO (or until you use the File Directory command again to select a different area) Quattro PRO will store files to and retrieve files from the new directory.

To make a more permanent change to the data directory setting, use the Options Startup Directory command (described in Chapter 6) and specify the directory you want Quattro PRO to use. You must then use the Options Update command to add this preference to the program's configuration file, which is read each time you load Quattro PRO. To store just one file to an area other than the default directory, use the File Save As command and edit the path and file name to include the desired path.

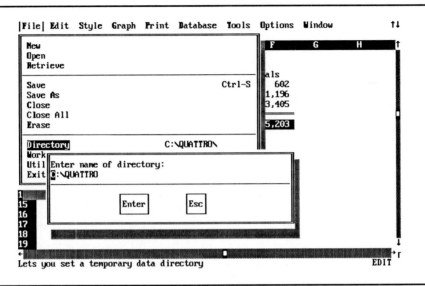

Figure 7-3.   *Setting a temporary directory*

What File Name to Use

When you are ready to save a worksheet that you have built from scratch, you select File Save As. Quattro PRO responds by prompting you to "Enter save file name:" as shown in Figure 7-4. This name will be from one to eight letters or numbers, following the rules described in the previous section, "Naming Files." The extension that Quattro PRO places on the file name will normally be WQ1. You can use a different extension to indicate that Quattro PRO should store the file in a format that can be read by a different program. This is described later in the section entitled "Foreign Files."

The "Enter save file name:" prompt is always followed by the current file path together with one of two additions. If the worksheet you are about to save was originally retrieved from a file on disk, you are prompted with the name of that file, as shown in Figure 7-5. If you retrieve the file QNORTH01.WQ1 from the DATA subdirectory of the QUATTRO directory on drive C and update the figures, you will be prompted with the name

C:\QUATTRO\DATA\QNORTH01.WQ1

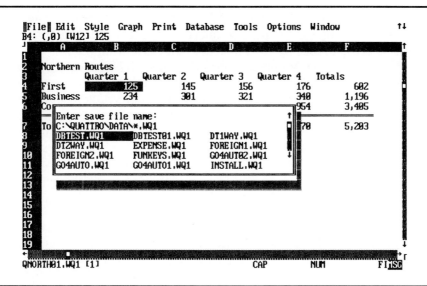

Figure 7-4. *File name list*

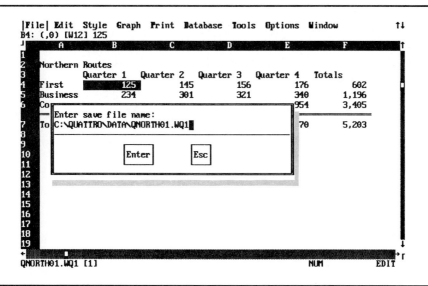

Figure 7-5. *File Save As prompt*

when you go to save the file. If you press ESCAPE at this point the suggested name will disappear and will be replaced with a generic file prompt: *.W??. This is accompanied by a list of files in the current directory.

If the worksheet you are saving has never been saved before, the "Enter save file name:" message is immediately followed by the generic name prompt, which uses a DOS wildcard as in C:\QUATTRO\DATA*.WQ1. This means any file name in C:\QUATTRO\DATA with an extension of WQ1. You also see a list of files already saved in the current directory shown in a box, as seen in Figure 7-4.

File List

The list of file names Quattro PRO shows you when saving a file allows you to see the names already in use. You can pick an existing file from this list and save the current worksheet into it, but bear in mind that doing so will replace the contents of that disk file with the worksheet you are about to store. To pick a name from the list, press RIGHT ARROW and DOWN ARROW to highlight the name. If there are more than 12 files on the list, the list scrolls as you continue to press either RIGHT or DOWN ARROW.

To search for a specific file you can press the Edit key (F2). This will return a prompt on the status line at the bottom of the screen, asking what you are searching for. This search mechanism works the same way as the name search in the function list. Just type the first character of the name you are seeking. You will either be taken to the first file in the list that begins with that character or Quattro PRO will beep to let you know that there are no names that begin with the character you typed. To continue the search type the second character of the name you are looking for, and so on, until it is located. Press ENTER to use the file name you have highlighted. There are several other keys that you can use to manipulate this list, as shown in Table 7-2.

If you are not sure about the name of the file you are looking for, you might find it helpful to see the date and time it was last saved to disk. This data is available by pressing the Expand key (+), using the plus on the numeric keypad. An example of the resulting display is shown in Figure 7-6. Notice that this display also includes the size of the worksheet, which is useful information when you are attempting to recall which file contains what data.

Key	Action
DOWN ARROW	Down one file
TAB	Down one file
RIGHT ARROW	Down one file
UP ARROW	Up one file
SHIFT-TAB	Up one file
LEFT ARROW	Up one file
PAGE DOWN	Down one screen
PAGE UP	Up one screen
HOME	Top of the list

Table 7-2. *Keys Used in File List*

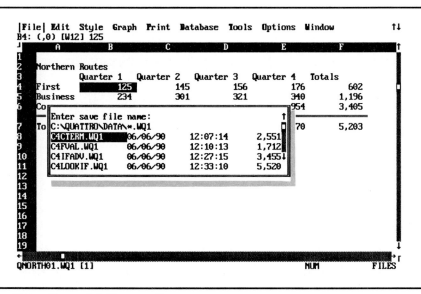

Figure 7-6. *Expanded file name list*

Saving Previously Named Files

If the worksheet you are saving has previously been saved and you want to resave it under the original name, use the File Save command. Alternatively, you can use File Save As command and press ENTER when the file name prompt appears. However, if you want to save the file under a different name, you must use the File Save As command. This gives you the existing file name, as shown in Figure 7-7, which you can then edit. This is very useful when you are creating different versions of the same basic worksheet.

For example, suppose you have stored the sales figures for the first quarter of 1990 in a worksheet called 90SALE01.WQ1. You want to create a worksheet for the second quarter sales figures. You retrieve the file 90SALE01.WQ1, make the changes, and then issue the File Save As command. You want to store the new file as 90SALE01.WQ1, but you do not want to have to retype the entire name to change it from 90SALE01.WQ1 to 90SALE02.WQ1. Instead, you press the Edit key (F2). This allows you to use the edit keys to change the name, just as you edit

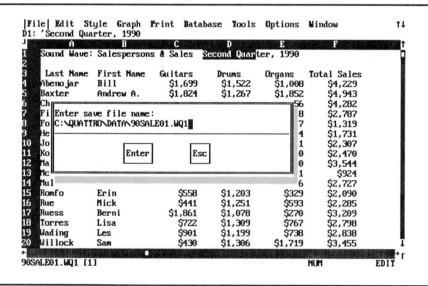

Figure 7-7. *"Enter save file name" prompt*

entries in the worksheet. In this example, you can press SHIFT-TAB to move the cursor left five spaces, under the 1. Then press INSERT to go into OVERSTRIKE mode. This means that when you type **2** it will replace the 1, and you can press ENTER to confirm the new name.

If you use File Save As with a previously saved file and want to see the names already in use, just press ESCAPE at the default name prompt. You will get the generic file name prompt and the file list. This list includes any subdirectories of the current directory. You will find these subdirectories listed at the bottom of the file list. By highlighting a subdirectory name and pressing ENTER you can view a list of existing files in that subdirectory. If you want to save the file to a directory other than the current one, you can press ESCAPE and type the complete path name of the directory and the file name, as in

C:\QUATTRO\SALES\BUDGET.WQ1

To see what files are already in a directory other than the current one, you can press ESCAPE to clear the "Enter save file name" prompt. Then type the path name of the storage area you are interested in *together with* the generic file specification *.WQ1, and press ENTER. Quattro PRO will respond with a list of files in that directory. If you do not use a file specification the program will save your file in the wrong area.

Save Confirmation

When you have the right path and file name entered for the worksheet you are about to save, press ENTER to confirm the name. If you are using either the File Save command or the File Save As command the program will not immediately save the file but will check to see if a file of the same name already exists in the current storage area. If such a file exists, Quattro PRO responds with a three-line menu box offering the choices Cancel, Replace, and Backup as shown in Figure 7-8.

Cancel The Cancel option is your chance to change your mind about the save operation. Selecting Cancel will prevent the existing file from being overwritten and return you to the READY mode.

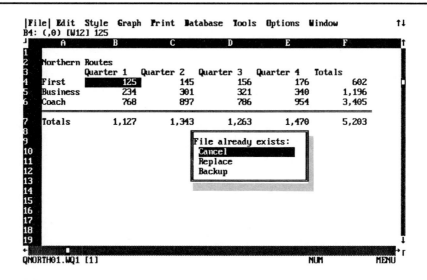

Figure 7-8.   *Cancel, Replace, or Backup option*

Replace   Selecting the Replace option confirms that you want to over-write the old file. You normally use this option when you are updating a file or when you are saving successive unfinished versions of a model you are building.

Backup   The Backup option will preserve the existing file by changing the extension to BAQ and will then save the new file with the name you requested.

Saving Your Workspace

When you are working with more than one worksheet at once and have arranged multiple windows in a particular way, you may want to store this arrangement. Quattro PRO provides the File Workspace command to store an arrangement of windows. When you issue the File Workspace command you are asked if you want to save or restore the workspace, as shown in Figure 7-9. When you select Save you are prompted for a file name. The

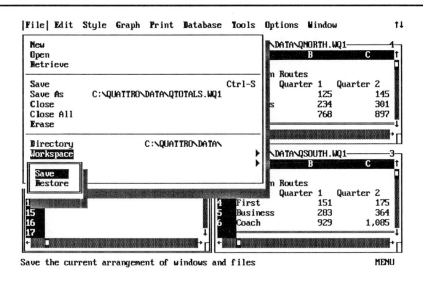

Figure 7-9. *Workspace menu*

default name is RESTART.WSP. Note the WSP extension, which is used for workspace files. The File Workspace command does not save the contents of the worksheets that are displayed in the windows; rather, it saves the size, shape, and placement of the windows, and the names of the files that are displayed in them. The workspace file is thus a collection of settings and is distinct from a regular worksheet. You can use the default name unless you want to store several different workspaces. Bear in mind that the File Workspace command does not list files, so you will need to keep track of the names you use for workspaces.

You can use the File Workspace Restore option when you want to recreate a particular arrangement of windows and worksheets, for example, when you start work the next day. When you select Restore you are prompted for the workspace file name, and the default name is suggested, as shown in Figure 7-10. If you have used a different name, then type that name; otherwise, just press ENTER to accept the default workspace name.

The File Workspace command is very useful when you are working with multiple windows and is discussed again in the section "Working with Multiple Windows" later in this chapter. Bear in mind that if you want to

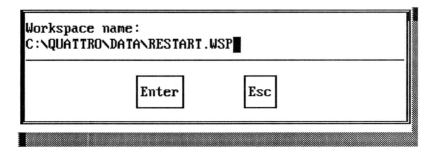

```
Workspace name:
C:\QUATTRO\DATA\RESTART.WSP█

        ┌─────────┐        ┌─────┐
        │ Enter   │        │ Esc │
        └─────────┘        └─────┘
```

Figure 7-10. *Retrieving a workspace file*

save the work you have done in multiple windows you still need to move to each window in turn—using the Next Window key (SHIFT-F6)—and issue a File Save command in each one.

Opening and Retrieving Files

When you want to bring back into memory a copy of a worksheet that you have stored on disk you can use either the Retrieve or the Open command from the File menu. Both commands assume that you want to retrieve a worksheet from the current drive and directory.

File Listing

When you select either File Retrieve or File Open, Quattro PRO helps you to identify the file you want by displaying an alphabetical list of files, showing up to 12 files at once, as seen in Figure 7-11. You can use the movement keys described earlier in Table 7-2 to move down this list and highlight the file you want. If the number of worksheet files in the current storage area is greater than 12, scroll down the list. To see the date and time the files were saved as well as their size, view the expanded version of the menu, which you obtain by pressing the Expand key (+), using the plus on the numeric keypad. When you have highlighted the file you want to retrieve, press ENTER and Quattro PRO will read that file into memory.

If you want to retrieve a file from a storage area other than the current one, you have several options. When you select File Retrieve or File Open and are prompted for a file name, you can press ESCAPE and then edit the path of the area from which you want to retrieve the file. You press ENTER to see a list of the files in that area. For example, suppose you want to see all of the worksheets in the SALES subdirectory of the QUATTRO directory but the DATA subdirectory is current. The initial prompt is

C:\QUATTRO\DATA*.W??

When you press ESCAPE this changes to

C:\QUATTRO\DATA

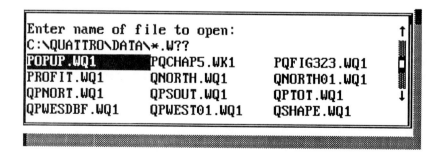

Figure 7-11. *File to open prompt*

You can then press BACKSPACE five times so that you remove the DATA subdirectory. Now you can type in the new directory, as in

C:\QUATTRO\SALES

and press ENTER to see all of the worksheets in this directory. An alternative way of editing the prompt is to press SHIFT-TAB to move the cursor left five characters and then press INSERT to get into OVERSTRIKE mode. Type the new directory over the existing prompt.

Quattro PRO will automatically add the *.W?? specification for you. Notice the backslash at the end of the edited prompt. If you do not include this, Quattro PRO will assume that you are looking for the file SALES.WQ1 in the QUATTRO directory. When you are at a file name prompt and want to change it completely you can press CTRL-BACKSPACE. This removes the text of the prompt and allows you to type something completely different.

If you want Quattro PRO to retrieve a foreign file (one that does not have the WQ1 extension) you can type a specific extension in the edited file name prompt, such as DBF for dBASE files. If you know the exact path and file name of the worksheet you want to recover, you can type that information and press ENTER.

File Retrieve

There is an important difference between the effects of the File Open and File Retrieve commands. When you read a file from disk with the File Retrieve command the data from the file is placed in the current worksheet window. If you have just started Quattro PRO you have one worksheet window open, window [1], named with the default name of SHEET.WQ1. Using File Retrieve places the data from the specified file on disk into that window. If you already have data in the current window and use the File Retrieve command, Quattro PRO assumes that you want to replace the current contents of the window with the data you are going to read from disk. The data read from the file will replace all that was there before it, from cell A1 through cell IV8192.

There is the potential to lose some of your work when issuing the File Retrieve command. To prevent accidental loss of data Quattro PRO checks to make sure that your work in the current window is saved. If some of your work is not saved, the program will ask whether you want to lose your changes. You will have to reply Yes or No before the File Retrieve command erases the current window contents and reads a data file from the disk. If you pick Yes, Quattro PRO proceeds with the File Retrieve command, presenting a list of files from which to choose. If you pick No you are returned to the File menu where you can issue one of the Save commands to store the current worksheet before reissuing the Retrieve command.

File Open

When you issue the File Open command and select a file name Quattro PRO performs two operations, the first of which is to create a new worksheet window. The second operation is to read the requested file into the new window. For example, in Figure 7-12 the current worksheet is QNORTH.WQ1, which is a list of passenger volumes on northern routes. This worksheet is displayed in window [1]. The user wants to work on a

```
File  Edit  Style  Graph  Print  Database  Tools  Options  Window          ↑↓
B4: (,0) [W12] 125
      A           B           C           D           E           F
1
2  Northern Routes
3           Quarter 1   Quarter 2   Quarter 3   Quarter 4   Totals
4  First            125         145         156         176         602
5  Business         234         301         321         340       1,196
6  Coach            768         897         786         954       3,405

7  Totals         1,127       1,343       1,263       1,470       5,203
8
9
10
11
12
13
14
15
16
17
18
19
QNORTH.WQ1    [1]                                      NUM         READY
```

Figure 7-12. *First worksheet*

second set of figures for southern routes, stored in a file called QSOUTH.WQ1. The File Open command is issued and the QSOUTH.WQ1 file is specified. The immediate result is shown in Figure 7-13. The newly opened file is displayed in window [2], completely obscuring window [1]. At this point you do not know whether window [1] is still open. You can use the Next Window key (SHIFT-F6) and see whether this takes you to the other window. However, if you issue the Windows Stack command you can see from the file names displayed in the window frame that two windows are opened, as shown in Figure 7-14. If you issue the File Open command again, a third window will be opened containing the worksheet you have requested. The more worksheets you work with at once, the more important the Windows commands become.

Multiple Worksheet Windows

When you have several worksheet windows open at once you will want to arrange them so that you can work effectively. For example, in Figure 7-14 two windows are open and they are stacked. You can also tile, resize, and move windows. In this section the commands for organizing multiple windows are discussed. The first commands examined are those that allow you to create multiple windows.

Opening Windows

You have seen that when you issue the File Open command Quattro PRO creates a new window in which to display the requested file. You may want to create a new window without actually opening a file. For example, if you were working on the north and south worksheets shown in Figure 7-14 you might want to create a third worksheet to consolidate the two sets of numbers. To do this you would use the File New command. The result of issuing this command is shown in Figure 7-15. At first the new worksheet obscures the existing windows. The new worksheet window is numbered; in this case it is window [3]. The default file name of SHEET2.WQ1 has been assigned to the new worksheet as it was the second fresh worksheet of the current session. If you issue the Windows Stack command the new

File Edit Style Graph Print Database Tools Options Window   ↑↓
B4: (,0) [W12] 151

	A	B	C	D	E	F	
1							
2	Southern Routes						
3		Quarter 1	Quarter 2	Quarter 3	Quarter 4	Totals	
4	First	151	175	189	213	728	
5	Business	283	364	388	411	1,446	
6	Coach	929	1,085	951	1,154	4,119	
7	Totals	1,363	1,624	1,528	1,778	6,293	
8							
9							
10							
11							
12							
13							
14							
15							
16							
17							
18							
19							

QSOUTH.WQ1   [2]   NUM   READY

Figure 7-13.   *Second worksheet*

File Edit Style Graph Print Database Tools Options Window   ↑↓
B4: (,0) [W12] 151

C:\QUATTRO\DATA\QNORTH.WQ1————————————————————————————————————1
C:\QUATTRO\DATA\QSOUTH.WQ1———————————————————————————————————2

	A	B	C	D	E	F	
1							
2	Southern Routes						
3		Quarter 1	Quarter 2	Quarter 3	Quarter 4	Totals	
4	First	151	175	189	213	728	
5	Business	283	364	388	411	1,446	
6	Coach	929	1,085	951	1,154	4,119	
7	Totals	1,363	1,624	1,528	1,778	6,293	
8							
9							
10							
11							
12							
13							
14							
15							
16							

QSOUTH.WQ1   [2]   NUM   READY

Figure 7-14.   *Stacked worksheets*

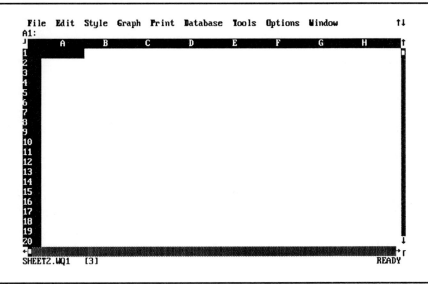

Figure 7-15. *Fresh worksheet*

window is placed above the existing windows, as shown in Figure 7-16. Notice that the Windows menu is displayed in Figure 7-16 although this menu actually disappears as soon as you issue the Stack command.

Closing Windows

If you keep using the File Open and File New commands, you will eventually hit Quattro PRO's limit of 32 windows, although you may well run out of memory in your system before reaching that limit. Issuing the Save or Save As commands does not alter this situation. This is because neither File Save nor File Save As put away your work. The Save commands store the contents of windows onto disk—they do not close the windows themselves. To close a window you need to use the File Close command, which affects the current worksheet. When you request a File Close, Quattro PRO checks for unsaved changes in the worksheet, and removes the window from display if none are encountered. If unsaved changes are encountered you are prompted to save them first.

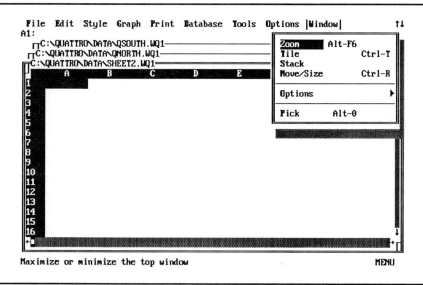

File   Edit   Style   Graph   Print   Database   Tools   Options |Window| ↑↓

A1:

┌C:\QUATTRO\DATA\QSOUTH.WQ1─────────────────
┌C:\QUATTRO\DATA\QNORTH.WQ1─────────────────
┌C:\QUATTRO\DATA\SHEET2.WQ1═════════════════

	Zoom	Alt-F6
	Tile	Ctrl-T
	Stack	
	Move/Size	Ctrl-R
	Options	►
	Pick	Alt-0

Maximize or minimize the top window   MENU

Figure 7-16.   *Window menu and stacked worksheets*

Mouse users have a quick way to close a window: click on the square on the top-left corner of the active window border. This will close the window immediately, unless there are unsaved changes to be dealt with.

If you want to close all of the currently open windows—for example, when moving on from one project to another—you can issue the File Close All command. The program will check each window for changes and close each one in turn, prompting you to save work if you have not done so already. When you close all windows you are left with an abbreviated Quattro PRO menu that shows just one item: File. When you select File and there are no worksheets open you have five choices:

New	To open a new worksheet window
Open	To read a file from disk into a new worksheet window
Workspace	To restore a stored workspace
Utilities	To use the File Manager (from which you can open files) or the DOS Shell
Exit	To quit Quattro PRO

The first time that you see this reduced menu you may wonder what has happened, but as soon as you open a worksheet window the full menu will be restored.

Arranging Windows

When you have several windows open at once you have a lot of options when it comes to arranging them on the screen. When a window is first opened it occupies the whole screen. You can use the Stack command from the Windows menu, shown in Figure 7-16, to tell Quattro PRO to arrange all open windows one on top of another with the name of each worksheet displayed. The current window is displayed above the rest. Windows are numbered consecutively based on the order in which they are opened.

You can move from window to window with the Next Window key (SHIFT-F6). To move to a window based on the number of the window, use ALT plus the window number. Thus you can move to window [3] by pressing ALT-3. The current window is indicated by a double border line as opposed to a single. As you move from one window to another the cell selector jumps to a particular cell of the worksheet you are moving to. This is the cell that was active when last you left that window. You can zoom to full screen size any window that has been reduced in size by commands like Windows Stack. Move to that window and press the Zoom key (ALT-F6). To reduce the window to its previous state, press Zoom again.

An alternative to stacking windows is to tile them by issuing the Windows Tile command. This tells Quattro PRO to arrange all of the open windows on the screen at once, automatically adjusting their size to fit the available space. In Figure 7-17 the windows that were stacked in Figure 7-16 have been tiled. The current window is marked by the double-line border. You move from window to window with the Next Window key and you can enlarge any window to full screen size by pressing the Zoom key. Press Zoom again to return the screen to its tiled size. The allocation of available display space is determined by the number of windows to be tiled. Several arrangements are shown in the diagram in Figure 7-18.

Mouse users can move between windows by clicking the mouse on any part of the window they want to move to. To zoom a window with the mouse, just click on the pair of arrows in the top right of the screen. These will zoom the current window, or unzoom it if it is already zoomed.

When you are working with a large number of windows you can use the Windows Pick command to select a specific window from a list of open

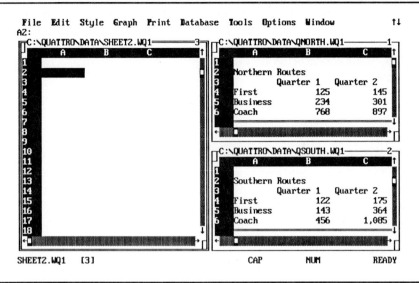

Figure 7-17. *Tiled worksheets*

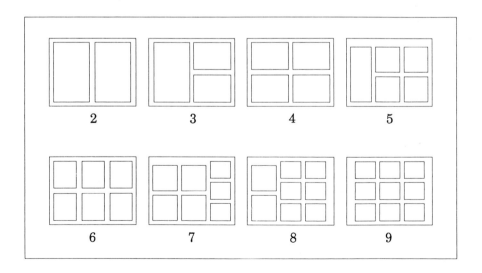

Figure 7-18. *Diagram of tile arrangements*

windows. Figure 7-19 shows a list of windows displayed by the Windows Pick command. You can highlight the one to which you want to move and press ENTER. You can also use the Pick key (ALT-0) instead of the Windows Pick command to bring up this list. SHIFT-F5 will also display a pick list of windows.

Sizing Windows

For some work with multiple windows you may want an arrangement other than the tiled or stacked look. You may want to overlap certain parts of windows and obscure others. For mouse users this is very easy. To alter the size of a window using a mouse simply place the mouse pointer on the move/size box in the lower right of the window, and then press the mouse button and drag. The window frame will change shape as you drag the mouse. When you are satisfied with the shape, release the mouse button.

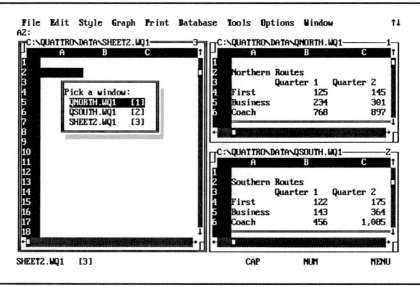

Figure 7-19. *The window pick list (SHIFT-F5)*

To move a window with the mouse, place the mouse pointer on the title of the window and then press the mouse button. The MOVE message will appear in the window and you can drag it to a new location. Release the mouse button when you reach the new location.

To move or size windows from the keyboard you use the Windows Move/Size command. For example, suppose that you want to arrange the windows shown in Figure 7-19 so that they are viewed as wide horizontal strips, as shown in Figure 7-20. The first step is to make window [1] the active window. Then select Window Move/Size. A box called MOVE appears on the screen to let you know that you are in MOVE mode, as shown in Figure 7-21. Use the arrow keys to move the box within the Quattro PRO Desktop. Press ENTER when the new location is reached. To change the size and shape of the window, press SCROLL LOCK after you have selected Move/Size and the MOVE box will change to SIZE, as shown in Figure 7-22. You can switch back and forth between MOVE and SIZE by using the SCROLL LOCK key.

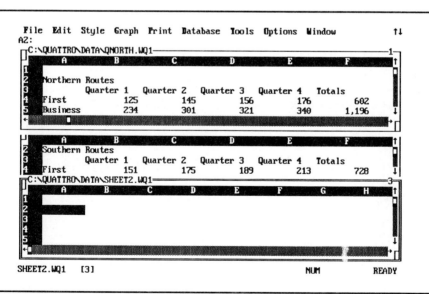

Figure 7-20. *Three worksheets arranged*

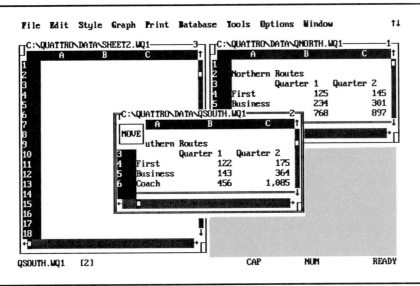

Figure 7-21. Window Move command

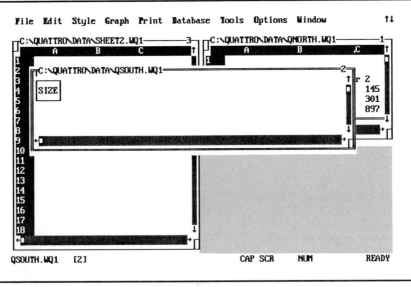

Figure 7-22. Window Size command

Using Workspaces

When you have gone to a lot of trouble to set up the right arrangement of windows for your work you may well want to preserve the arrangement. As discussed earlier in this chapter, Quattro PRO has a special type of file, called a workspace file, that will store information about a window arrangement, including the position of the windows and the names of the files that occupy them. To store the current arrangement of windows you issue the File Workspace command and pick the Save option. There is a default workspace file called RESTART.WSP. You can use this name or create other workspace files with the WSP extension. These files do not save the data in worksheet files, but only the arrangement of files. When you issue the Files Workspace Restore command all of the windows and the files that were occupying them will be opened.

Odd Shapes and Sizes

You cannot do much work with multiple windows without realizing that Quattro PRO stores the size and shape of a worksheet, as well as the data it contains, when you perform a File Save or File Save As. Just as the location of the cell selector is the same when a stored worksheet is opened as when it was last saved, so it is with the worksheet's desktop location and size. Sometimes this can be disconcerting. For example, if you have tiled a number of windows and then saved the worksheets in them, each one will be stored rather small. When you open one of these files in a later session you may not recognize it at first. There is an easy way to fix this: zoom the window to full size. In fact, you might want to make a practice of zooming windows to full size before saving them.

Linking Worksheet Files

Beyond the advantages of just viewing several worksheets at once, Quattro PRO provides the ability to link those worksheets, making data in one dependent upon data from another. This ability opens up a new realm of spreadsheet design possibilities. In some cases you will want to use this feature to split large and cumbersome worksheets into more manageable, interrelated units. Since you can copy or move data from one worksheet window to another it is easy to disassemble a large worksheet into more manageable parts. Knowing that Quattro PRO supports linked formulas between files allows you to approach new projects in a different way, following more closely the traditional accounting model of consolidated sheets and supporting sheets.

You can link Quattro PRO worksheets to files produced by other programs such as 1-2-3. You can pull data from several files into one graph. As mentioned in Chapter 3, when working with databases you can use multiple spreadsheets to establish multiple criteria and output ranges.

Creating a Linked File Model

Earlier in this chapter you saw two worksheets containing passenger volume figures for an airline. The figures are divided into northern and southern routes because the airline has two centers of operation, one in the north and one in the south. Suppose that you want to consolidate the figures from these two worksheets, called QNORTH.WQ1 and QSOUTH.WQ1 respectively. You could copy figures from both worksheets into a new one, perhaps called QTOTALS.WQ1. You would then have three worksheets. However, if there were changes to the figures you would have to alter two worksheets. For example, if the northern office corrected the First Class number for the fourth quarter you would need to alter the regional and the total worksheets. A better approach is to link the two regional worksheets to the totals worksheet.

To do this you first need to create the totals worksheet. This is easy to do as you can copy labels and formatting from one of the existing worksheets. To begin you open the two regional worksheets, and then use the File New command. The new window is where you will build the total worksheet. Use the Windows Tile command to show all three windows at once and the effect will look like Figure 7-17. In the newly opened window you issue the Edit Copy command. When you are prompted for the Source Block of cells, press SHIFT-F6 to move to one of the regional worksheets in either window [2] or window [3]. Note that the Source Block prompt changes to the coordinates of the cell that was active the last time you used this worksheet, as shown in Figure 7-23. Also note that the full file name of the worksheet in the current window is shown in the Source Block

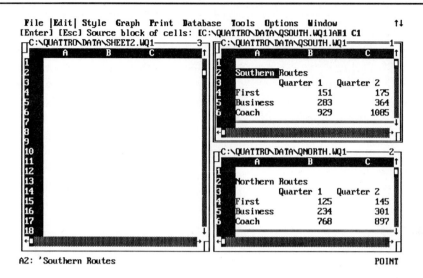

Figure 7-23. *Copying between windows*

prompt. Now you can enlarge the Source Block to cover the cells that you want to copy, in this case all of the occupied cells of the model, A2..F7. Press ENTER to confirm the Edit Copy command and the cells are copied from one window into the window that was current when you issued the command. You can see the results in Figure 7-24, where the new worksheet is being edited to become the totals worksheet. Note that the column widths settings are not copied from one worksheet to another, but the line drawing style is.

Once you have changed the label in cell A2 and adjusted the column widths to 12 with the Style Block Widths command, you are ready to establish the links between this worksheet and the other two. As a precaution, you might want to use the File Save As command to store the work on the totals model so far. The links you create are actually formulas, so that, for example, cell B4 in the totals worksheet is equal to cell B4 of the southern worksheet plus cell B4 of the northern worksheet. The completed formula looks like this:

+[QSOUTH]B4+[QNORTH]B4

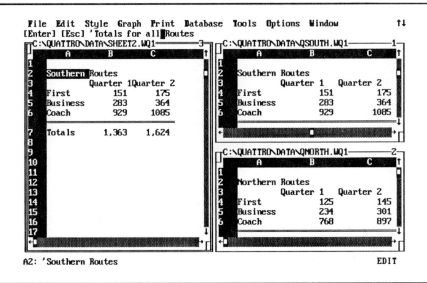

Figure 7-24.   *Creating the totals worksheet*

You can build the formula quite easily using the pointing method. With the cell selector in B4 of the totals worksheet, type + and then press the Next Window key. This will take you to the next window where you can point to cell B4 and type another +. You will be returned to the totals worksheet where the formula so far on the input line will read

+[C:\QUATTRO\DATA\QSOUTH.WQ1]B4+

This looks a little intimidating because Quattro PRO gives the full worksheet name and path of the cells you are working with. These will be abbreviated when the formula is completed. Now press Windows twice to move to the third window where you again point to B4. Press ENTER to complete the formula, which is shown in place in Figure 7-25.

Like other Quattro PRO formulas, this one can be copied. You want every cell from B4 through E6 to reflect the addition of the corresponding cells in the other two worksheets. To achieve this you simply copy the formula

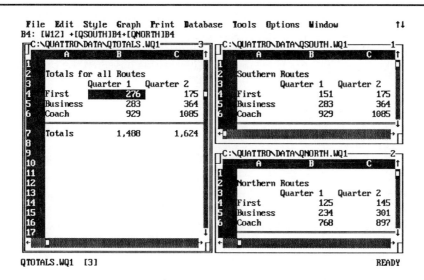

Figure 7-25. *Completed link formula*

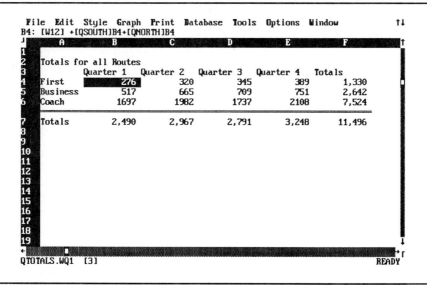

Figure 7-26. *Totals worksheet zoomed*

from B4 of the totals worksheet to the block B4..E6. The results are shown in Figure 7-26, where the totals worksheet has been zoomed to full screen size. Note that there was no need to adjust the formulas in column F or those in row 7 because they are @SUM formulas based on the columns and rows of the model.

Working with Linked Files

Obviously, the preceding is a fairly simple example of what can be done with linked worksheets, but the principles are the same even with much larger models. Formulas that refer to cells outside of the current worksheet are called *dependent formulas*. Values that are supplied to another worksheet are called *supporting values*. Worksheets that depend upon other worksheets for values, like the one just created in this model, are called *dependent* worksheets. A worksheet that supplies values to a dependent worksheet is called a *supporting worksheet*.

When you establish a link with a supporting Quattro PRO worksheet that is stored in the same directory as the dependent worksheet, then the formula you need to use is the name of the supporting worksheet enclosed in square brackets, as in [BUDGET], rather than the full path, as in [C:\NEWYORK\BUDGET.WQ1]. You can also establish links to foreign files, such as 1-2-3 worksheets. However, if the file you are linking to is not a Quattro PRO file with the default extension of WQ1, then your link reference will need to include the extension. For example, suppose that you want to create a link with cell B4 in a 1-2-3 file called WEST.WK1. Entering [WEST]B4 will not work since Quattro PRO will be looking for a file called WEST.WQ1. If you do enter an invalid reference in a link formula Quattro PRO returns the error value NA in the cell. However, this is difficult to do because when you attempt to link to a file that Quattro PRO cannot find you will be presented with an error message and a file name box, as shown in Figure 7-27. This gives you an opportunity to look up the correct file. The problem may be that the file is not in the current directory, or that the file does not have the default extension as in this case. If you press ESCAPE at the prompt in Figure 7-27 you are shown a file list that you can browse until you find the correct name, as shown in Figure 7-28. Highlight the correct name and press ENTER to complete the link.

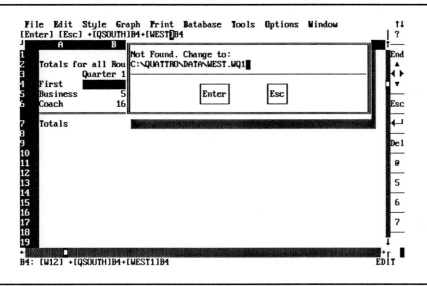

Figure 7-27.   *Correcting the link file name*

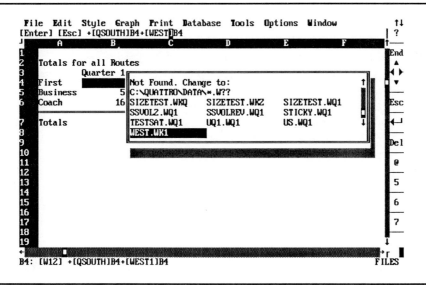

Figure 7-28.   *Selecting the correct link file name*

Saving and Loading Linked Files

When you have established a linked formula you should close the dependent file (the one containing the link formula) before closing the supporting worksheets. This is because Quattro PRO links are active only when the supporting files are open. If you colse the dependent worksheet before the supporting worksheets, the link formula cells will return the error value NA. This NA will change to a proper value if you then open the supporting worksheets. Note that the normal procedure for saving worksheets, as opposed to closing them, is least dependent to most dependent.

When you open linked worksheets you might want to open the least dependent first, and the most dependent last. This is because, when you open a dependent worksheet, Quattro PRO checks to see if the supporting worksheets are open. If they are not open, the dependent worksheet cannot function correctly. However, Quattro PRO knows this and will prompt you to open the supporting files, as shown in Figure 7-29.

The first option, Load-supporting, will open all worksheets referred to in formulas in the worksheet that is currently being loaded. This is a great

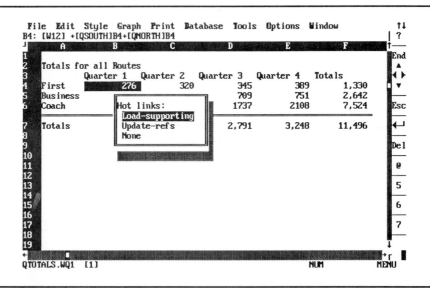

Figure 7-29.   *Hot links menu*

time saver as it circumvents the need to open supporting files first. You can simply have Quattro PRO do the loading for you.

The second Hot links option, Update-refs, is used to update references to unopened supporting documents. When you issue the Update-refs command, Quattro PRO reads the values referred to in any link formulas in the current worksheet. The supporting worksheets do not need to be open for this command to work. This means that you can work on a dependent worksheet without opening the supporting worksheets.

Refreshing Links

After you open a dependent worksheet and decide not to open the supporting sheets—using the Update-refs command instead to read the supporting values from files on disk—you normally do not need to issue this command again. However, there is the possibility that the supporting files will be altered. For example, a colleague might give you an updated copy of a worksheet that is used to support the dependent worksheet you have loaded. If you are using Quattro PRO on a network, another user might update a supporting file. If the supporting worksheet on disk is altered— perhaps by copying—Quattro PRO will not necessarily know this immediately. To be sure that you are using the most recent figures in the dependent worksheet, you can use the Tools Update Links command shown here to refresh data links:

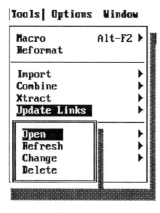

The Open command is the same as the Load-supporting option when you are retrieving a dependent worksheet. The Refresh command allows you to read linked values from a supporting worksheet, by selecting the worksheet from a list. When the list of supporting files is displayed you can select one name by highlighting it and pressing ENTER. To select more than one name from the list, highlight each name in turn and press the Extend key (SHIFT-F7). This places a checkmark by the name. You can then select other names. When all the files that you want to refresh from are checked, press ENTER. (Mouse users can simply click each file name to select it and then click the Enter button in the mouse palette.)

The Change option on the Update Links menu allows you to substitute a new supporting file for an existing one, by automatically performing a global search and replace to change the old name to a new one that you supply. The Delete option allows you to remove supporting links.

Out-of-Space Problems

When you are building a large worksheet, it is surprising how fast it can grow in size. The Edit Copy command in particular quickly generates a lot of data. This can result in space problems, both on disk and in memory.

Disk Space

When you attempt to save a file that is too large to fit in the remaining free space on your disk, Quattro PRO displays a "disk full" error message. You can respond to this in several ways.

Save to a Floppy Disk   If you have been saving to a floppy disk and the current disk cannot accommodate the worksheet you are trying to save, you can retry the save after inserting a disk with more free space on it. You can use the DOS Shell command on the File Utilities menu to temporarily exit to DOS and format a fresh floppy disk if you need one. The DOS Shell command, which is described in more detail later in this chapter, does not affect your unsaved work. If you have been saving to a hard disk that has now filled up, you might consider saving to a floppy disk as a temporary measure. Remember that some floppy disks can now store over a megabyte of information.

Clean Up Your Hard Disk   If you are trying to save to a hard disk that has run out of space, you can either use DOS via the DOS Shell command or the File Manager to erase unwanted files from your hard disk. This will make more room available and help to accommodate the worksheet you are trying to save.

Convert Values   The amount of space required by formulas in a worksheet is greater than that taken up by values. If you convert numbers that are generated by formulas into their values, using the Edit Values command, then the worksheet can be stored in less space.

SQZ! the Worksheet   If saving a worksheet in the regular WQ1 format results in a "disk full" message, you might want to try the SQZ! option, described later in this chapter. You do this by using the file extension WQ! instead of WQ1. This causes Quattro PRO to compress the worksheet, sometimes by as much as 75%, and thus store it in a smaller file.

Divide the Worksheet   When you attempt to save a worksheet and get a "disk full" message you may want to consider splitting the worksheet into separate, smaller worksheets. To do this you can open a new window and use the Edit Move command to move data from the current worksheet to the new one.

Memory Space

Quattro PRO displays the message "memory full" when you attempt to retrieve a file that is too large to fit in currently available memory. You get a similar message when you expand the current worksheet beyond the limits of available memory. If you want to check on the amount of memory you have available, use the Options Hardware command and read the current memory status from the Hardware menu. If you have a worksheet loaded when you read the Hardware menu, you can see how much room there is for expansion. If you have a blank worksheet, you can tell how large a file you can retrieve. Quattro PRO needs enough free memory to read in the file from disk and to manipulate the data within the worksheet. Thus, if you had 82,944 bytes available, you would be unwise to try and retrieve anything larger than 80,000 bytes.

When you use a command that results in the "memory full" message you should save parts of the worksheet to separate files using the Tools Xtract command. This will allow you to store the data safely so that you can redesign the worksheet, perhaps free more memory, or add more memory to the system. You can free memory by saving the current worksheet, exiting Quattro PRO, and removing any memory-resident programs you might have loaded.

If it was an Edit Copy command that caused the "memory full" message, you will probably find that only part of the block was copied. However, the data you had before the copy operation should still be intact. Likewise, if you tried to retrieve a file that was too large, only part of the file will be in your worksheet, but the entire file will still be safely stored on disk.

Password Protection

To prevent unauthorized access to a worksheet stored on disk, you can assign a password to the worksheet while you are saving it. Select File Save As and then type in the file name followed by a space and the letter **P**. When you press ENTER Quattro PRO prompts you for a password. Actually, this can be several words, numbers, and spaces up to a total length of 15 characters. Pick a password that you can remember. Neither Borland nor anyone else can retrieve the data if you forget the word. No one can see the letters of the password as you type, because Quattro PRO displays only a blank rectangle for each letter as shown here:

```
Enter password: ████████
```

When you have typed the password, press ENTER. You are then asked to verify the word by typing it again. The theory is that if you can type the word twice, you know what it is and did not make a mistake the first time you entered it. After typing the word a second time, press ENTER. The file-saving process continues as usual.

When you attempt to retrieve or open the password-protected file, you are prompted for the password. This time you need only type the password once and then press ENTER to access the file. If you type an incorrect password, Quattro PRO beeps and gives you the message "Invalid password." When you save a file with password protection Quattro PRO *encrypts* the file; that is, it scrambles the data to make it unintelligible, even to a sophisticated, well-trained programmer. Do not expect to be able to get the data back if you forget the password. Trying to get around the password by using the partial file retrieval command, Tools Combine, does not work either. You should leave a copy of the password in a secure place such as a locked desk drawer or in another password-protected Quattro PRO file.

When you want to remove password protection from a file, you first open the file, and then use the File Save As command. Quattro PRO will remind you that the file is password protected as shown here:

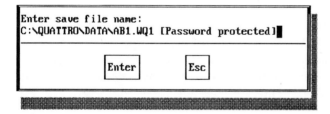

You can press BACKSPACE to remove the protection message. Press ENTER to complete the file save and the file is no longer protected. Unless you remove the password protection with File Save As, the file will continue to be password protected.

If you are using Quattro PRO to read 1-2-3 files, as described later in this chapter, and those files are protected by 1-2-3 password protection, Quattro PRO will be able to decode the files, provided you supply the correct password. If you are sharing Quattro PRO data with a 1-2-3 user, however, be sure to save your Quattro PRO file as a WK1 file rather than a WQ1 file. 1-2-3 cannot read DES-encrypted files.

Using passwords can be a nuisance and so you should decide if the need for security is real. If it is, then you will want to make sure you use proper passwords. A password is of little use if it is a useless password such as *password, pass, your first name, the filename,* and so on. Believe it or not, you can buy lists of common passwords and the serious data thief is likely to guess most words that do not have the following features:

- at least eight characters
- a mixture of text and numbers
- some odd characters, like @, spaces, and commas
- a mixture of uppercase and lowercase
- a lack of logic

While some applications are not sensitive to upper- and lowercase distinctions, Quattro PRO is, which is an important point to remember when recording your passwords. The password *Fred's File* will not be accepted if it is supplied as *FRED'S FILE* and even *Fred's file* will be rejected. To use the last feature—a lack of logical connection between the content of the file and the password protecting it—you need to be imaginative. For example, a banker might use the names of birds to protect a series of salary recommendation files. Combined with the other features, something like this would be difficult to guess:

Robin@5769

Since such a name would also be difficult to remember you must also make proper provision for recording and securing passwords. A sheet of paper locked in a drawer is usually a good technique. You can use a spreadsheet or word processor to list files and their passwords. The more paranoid might want to code the passwords on the printed listing.

Data Loss and Recovery

The best approach to prevent data loss is the same one you can use for steady monetary accumulation: save on a regular basis. This means saving every 15 minutes. You should also save your files before you do any of the following:

■ perform a file retrieve

■ exit Quattro

■ leave your PC unattended

■ move or copy a large block

■ sort data or perform an extract or block fill operation

■ combine files

However, even if you try to live by these rules, there is always a possibility that something will go wrong. Quattro PRO has a built-in method of helping out.

Using Transcript

If you have lost data, you can rely on the Quattro PRO *keystroke log*. This is a transcript of your recent activity that is created by a built-in feature of Quattro PRO called Transcript, which automatically keeps track of your keystrokes on disk. The keystrokes are saved to a special log file with the name QUATTRO.LOG. If your machine malfunctions or you accidentally delete data, you can recall this data by replaying your actions from the Transcript log. Several thousand actions can be recorded in one log before Quattro PRO copies the log to a backup file called QUATTRO.BAK and continues with a new QUATTRO.LOG. This means that between QUAT-TRO.BAK and QUATTRO.LOG you can keep an extensive record of what has been done during your Quattro PRO sessions.

To gain access to the Transcript log file and review or restore keystrokes from it, use the Tools Macro command and select Transcript. You can use the Macro key, (ALT-F2) to display the Macros menu shown here:

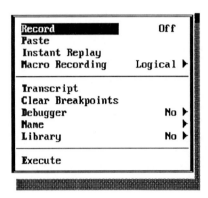

When you select Transcript you will see a screen similar to that shown in Figure 7-30. You can browse through this list with the highlight bar, which you move by means of the UP and DOWN ARROW keys. You can view up to 14 lines of commands at once. Use the PAGE UP and PAGE DOWN keys to move 14 lines at a time through this list. The line on the left side of the log groups commands that occurred since the current session started.

To use the recorded keystrokes, type / and you will see the Transcript menu shown in Figure 7-31. You use this menu to mark blocks or sections of commands for playback. Alternatively, you can have Transcript play back the commands up to the point marked by the highlight bar.

Suppose you start working with Quattro PRO and have loaded Transcript. The first piece of work you do is retrieve a budget file. You are busy updating the budget numbers when there is a power outage. You have lost the changes to the budget file; however, the original file is still on the disk. When power returns you simply reload Quattro PRO and run Transcript. The log file will then come up and the commands from it may be replayed. These will include the retrieval of the budget file and the changes you made. If you have lost data because of an inadvertent command, such as Edit Copy, you can run the log up to, but not including, that command. Of course, if you have enabled Undo, as described in the next section, then you can reverse the consequences of many typical spreadsheet

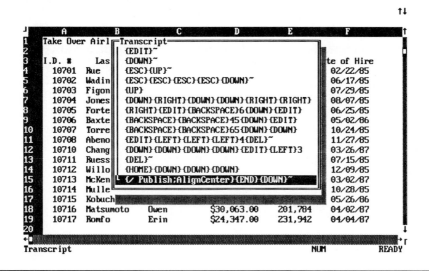

Figure 7-30. *Transcript log*

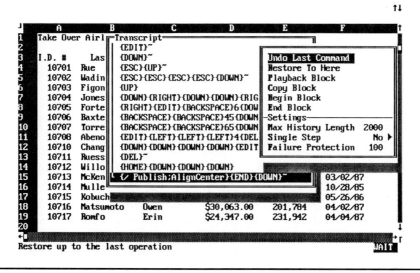

Figure 7-31. *Transcript menu*

actions. However, Transcript allows you to undo a whole series of actions, which Undo cannot.

Note the Settings part of the Transcript menu. The Max History Length determines how many lines of recorded actions will be held in the log file before is backed up and a new one created. The Single Step option allows you to play back your Transcript commands one at a time. The Failure Protection feature determines how many keystrokes Quattro PRO should wait before recording them to disk. The smaller you set this number the more complete your recovery from disaster will be. However, lower numbers also mean more frequent disk writing. For more on Transcript commands, see Chapter 12.

Activating Undo

Sometimes you can overcome errors and accidents without resorting to Transcript. If you activate Quattro PRO's Undo feature you can press ALT-F5 after a command to reverse its effects. This is very handy after a mistaken Edit Erase Block, or a disastrous Data Sort. To activate Undo, you use the Option Other command and select Undo. Select Enable and be sure to use the Options Update command to record this change if you want it to be in effect in the next session. You may notice a slight slowing of Quattro PRO's reaction time when Undo is in effect. This is due to the extra work that the program is doing to keep track of your actions, but it is a small price to pay for the ability to reverse critical actions. Table 7-3 lists actions that cannot be reversed with Undo.

Special Files

Quattro PRO can read and write not only its own worksheets but also data files created by several other popular programs. If you have 1-2-3 or Symphony files on your directory, they will automatically be listed by Quattro PRO because the *.W?? pattern includes WRK and WK1 files. You do not have to do anything special to retrieve one of these files. Highlight the name, press ENTER, and the file is read into Quattro PRO. When you

Commands that make settings such as Sort Block (but Sort Go and Data Query Extract can be undone)

Print commands that send a document to the printer (use CTRL-BREAK to stop printing)

File menu commands

Copy, move, and delete operations in the File Manager

Format commands from the Style or Options menu

Note: To undo some commands you need to return to READY mode from the menu first. Repeat the Undo key to reverse an Undo operation.

Table 7-3. *Actions That Cannot Be Undone*

go to save the file, Quattro PRO will assume that you want to store it in the original format, using the same extension. For example, if you open SALES.WK1 and then use the File Save As command, the suggested name will be the same, SALES.WK1, and the file will be stored as a 1-2-3 worksheet. However, when you use the File Save As command you can alter the save file name to WQ1 to match the 1-2-3 format you require.

You can read other types of files with the File Retrieve or File Open command if you enter the full file name or alter the *.W?? prompt to *.* to list them. Files that can be read in this manner are listed in Table 7-4.

Extracting from Foreign Files

You can also read selected data from foreign database files by using the Database Query command. When you specify the Block needed in the Database Query menu you can specify a file name as shown in Figure 7-32. The results can be seen in Figure 7-33.

Ext.	Type of File
WKQ	Worksheets from Quattro 1.0
WKZ	Worksheet from Quattro 1.0 compressed with SQZ!
WK1	1-2-3 Release 2 worksheet
WK!	1-2-3 Release 2 worksheet compressed with SQZ!
WKS	1-2-3 Release 1 worksheet
WRK	Symphony worksheet
RXD	Reflex database
DB	Paradox database
DBF	dBASE II or III database, dBASE IV database without memo fields
SLK	Symbolic Link worksheet (Multiplan or Excel)
DIF	Data Interchange Format

Table 7-4. *Files That Can Be Retrieved by Quattro PRO*

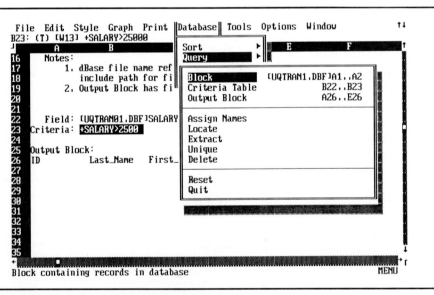

Figure 7-32. *Data Query from a dBASE file*

```
       File  Edit  Style  Graph  Print  Database  Tools  Options  Window        ↑↓
       B22: [W13] '[UQTRANO1.DBF]SALARY
      ┘        A         B          C         D         E         F             ↑
      16    Notes:
      17        1. dBase file name refers to a file in the current directory:
      18           include path for files stored elsewhere.
      19        2. Output Block has field names to match dBase file.
      20
      21
      22    Field:  [UQTRANO1.DBF]SALARY
      23  Criteria: +SALARY>2500                                                 ▓
      24
      25  Output Block:
      26  ID         Last_Name   First_Name   Salary    Sales    Hire Date
      27     10701 Rue          Mick         24234.00  301793.00
      28     10702 Wading       Les          27357.00  331960.00
      29     10703 Figone       Fred         22238.00  241263.00
      30     10704 Jones        Karen        18141.00  321607.00
      31     10705 Forte        Steve        33282.00  200935.00
      32     10706 Baxter       Andrew A.    26469.00  210937.00
      33     10707 Torres       Lisa         23453.00  251404.00
      34     10708 Abenojar     Bill         29036.00  221265.00
      35     10710 Chang        Charly       24489.00  330152.00             ↓
      ←▓▓▓▓▓▓░░▓▓▓▓▓▓▓▓▓▓▓▓▓▓▓▓▓▓▓▓▓▓▓▓▓▓▓▓▓▓▓▓▓▓▓▓▓▓▓▓▓▓▓▓▓▓▓▓▓▓▓▓→ r
       TOACRIT2.WQ1 [1]                                        NUM        READY
```

Figure 7-33. *Completed query*

Writing to Foreign Files

You can save data into some foreign file formats simply by changing the file extension. For example, to save a file in the SYLK format that can be read by Excel, you use the File Save As command to change the worksheet extension to SLK and proceed with the save. If you want to save data from a Quattro PRO worksheet to a database format such as dBASE or Paradox, you need to consider the location of the data that you are going to save. You can only save fields and records to a database format. For this reason you will probably want to use the Tools Xtract command to perform the save and specify only those cells that contain records and field names.

The Tools Xtract command allows you to save just part of a worksheet, rather than the whole thing. For example, in Figure 7-34 the cells to be exported to dBASE are A3 through F19. When you use the Tools Xtract command you must specify whether you want to save values or formulas and values. When you are storing to other worksheet formats you can save formulas, but when you are saving to a database format you will want to

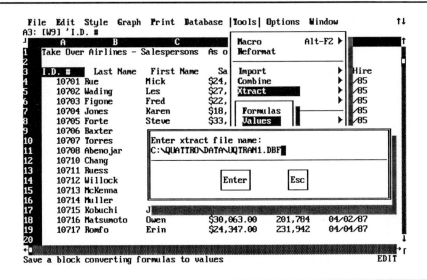

Figure 7-34. *File Xtract to dBASE format*

save values. In the figure, the Tools Xtract command was issued and the file name was entered with the DBF extension. The block of cells to be saved was then pointed out. When you have pressed ENTER to confirm the selection of cells, Quattro PRO knows you are exporting data to dBASE because of the DBF extension, and you get the opportunity to check the structure that Quattro PRO has assigned to your data. You can see this from the specific format review menu displayed in Figure 7-35.

The first option on this menu, View Structure, shows the Field-name, Type, Width, and Decimals settings:

Field-name	Type	Width	Decimals
A	Numeric	9	0
LAST_NAME	Text	9	
FIRST_NAME	Text	9	
SALARY	Numeric	11	2
SALES	Numeric	13	2
DATE_OF_HI	Date		

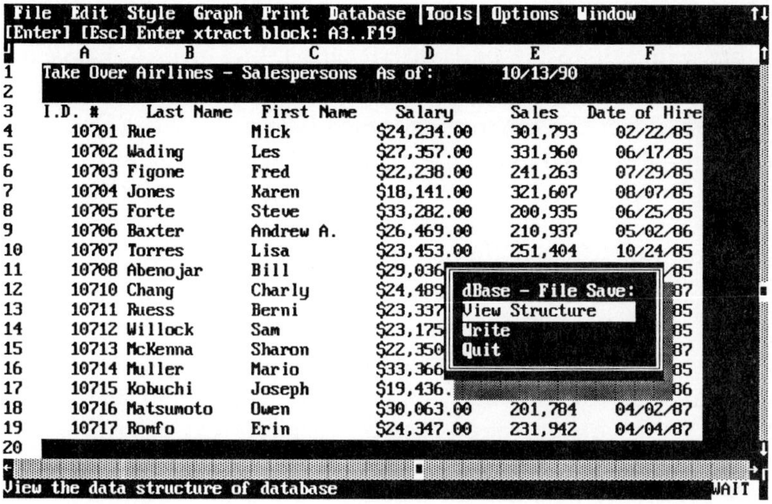

```
 File  Edit  Style  Graph  Print  Database |Tools| Options  Window        ↑↓
[Enter] [Esc] Enter xtract block: A3..F19
      A           B            C            D          E         F         ↑
 1 Take Over Airlines - Salespersons  As of:        10/13/90
 2
 3  I.D. #    Last Name    First Name    Salary      Sales   Date of Hire
 4   10701 Rue           Mick          $24,234.00   301,793   02/22/85
 5   10702 Wading        Les           $27,357.00   331,960   06/17/85
 6   10703 Figone        Fred          $22,238.00   241,263   07/29/85
 7   10704 Jones         Karen         $18,141.00   321,607   08/07/85
 8   10705 Forte         Steve         $33,282.00   200,935   06/25/85
 9   10706 Baxter        Andrew A.     $26,469.00   210,937   05/02/86
10   10707 Torres        Lisa          $23,453.00   251,404   10/24/85
11   10708 Abenojar      Bill          $29,036.       ┌────────────┐/85
12   10710 Chang         Charly        $24,489 dBase - File Save: 87  ■
13   10711 Ruess         Berni         $23,337 View Structure      85
14   10712 Willock       Sam           $23,175 Write               85
15   10713 McKenna       Sharon        $22,350 Quit                87
16   10714 Muller        Mario         $33,366└────────────┘       85
17   10715 Kobuchi       Joseph        $19,436.                    86
18   10716 Matsumoto     Owen          $30,063.00   201,784   04/02/87
19   10717 Romfo         Erin          $24,347.00   231,942   04/04/87
20
View the data structure of database                              WAIT
```

Figure 7-35. *dBASE File Save menu*

Note that the field names have been altered to match the limits of field naming in dBASE. Every name has been capitalized and underlines are used in place of spaces. The name *I.D. #* contained a punctuation character not acceptable to dBASE, and so the letter *A* was used instead.

To alter settings for a particular field, you highlight the field and ENTER. For example, you might want to change the generic name A to something better. A small menu appears from which you can select Name to change the name of the exported field, or Type to alter the type of the field. When you select Name you are prompted to edit the current name and enter the results. The Type option lists four possibilities for field types in dBASE: Text, Numeric, Logical, and Date. Note that the fifth type of data in dBASE, the Memo field, is not supported either when writing or reading from the DBF format. If you pick Numeric you are prompted for a decimal place setting. When the structure is acceptable, press ESCAPE to return to the dBASE File Save menu, shown in Figure 7-35, and select Write. This creates the dBASE file on disk.

When you are performing extracts to another database format, such as Paradox or Reflex, a menu tailored to the structural requirements of that database is presented.

Autoload Files

You may find that your work with Quattro PRO involves heavy use of one particular worksheet. You can have Quattro PRO retrieve a file automatically whenever the program is loaded by means of the Options Startup command (described in the previous chapter). Autoload File is the second item on the Startup menu. When you select it, Quattro PRO asks you to enter the name of the worksheet that you want to have loaded whenever you start the program. When you enter the name of the file, you will immediately see the file listed on the menu. However, you *must* use the Update option from the Options menu to record this change and have the autoload feature effective the next time the program is loaded.

The autoload feature is always active. Whenever you load Quattro PRO, it looks for the file name recorded from the Startup menu. As you can see from Figure 7-36, the default name is QUATTRO.WQ1. If Quattro PRO finds that file in the default directory when the program is loading, it retrieves the file. You can use the autoload feature either by changing the file name as was shown here, or you can save the file you want to autoload as QUATTRO.WQ1.

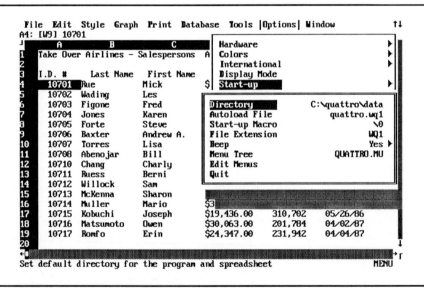

Figure 7-36. *Autoload File on the Start-up menu*

The File Manager

Quattro PRO's File Manager works as a shell between you and DOS to give you easy access to your files. You can use it to work with Quattro PRO spreadsheet files or any other files located on either your hard disk or floppies. With the File Manager, you can display a list of files in any directory or disk drive and open a file by choosing its name. You can use wildcards to filter the file list, for example, *.WQ1 to display only Quattro PRO spreadsheet files. You can turn this around to apply a negative filter, creating a list that shows all files except those specified in the filter. Thus, the filter [*.WQ1] shows all files except Quattro PRO spreadsheet files.

File Manager also lets you sort file lists by name, extension, size, original order, or timestamp. You can display a directory tree that reveals the structure of all directories on your disk. You can move in and out of directories in the tree and use the GoTo key (F5) to search through the tree for a specific file. You can move or copy a file from one directory to another, rename files, and delete them from disk.

The File Manager Window

Quattro PRO's File Manager works within a File Manager window. This is like a worksheet window except that it displays only file names and subdirectories. To open a File Manager window, choose File Manager from the File Utilities menu. Quattro PRO displays a window, as shown in Figure 7-37. Note that the choices in the menu bar change slightly when a File Manager window is active. The choices are now File, Edit, Sort, Tree, Print, Options, and Window (as opposed to File, Edit, Style, Graph, Print, Database, Tools, Options, and Window).

If you have not used the File Manager during the current session, the window displays information about files in the current directory. Otherwise, the directory displayed in the File Manager window is the one that was there the last time you used File Manager in the current session. Similarly, the screen position of this window is taken from the last open File Manager window.

The File Manager window shown in Figure 7-37 is actually divided into two sections. These are called *panes.* The top pane, called the *control pane,*

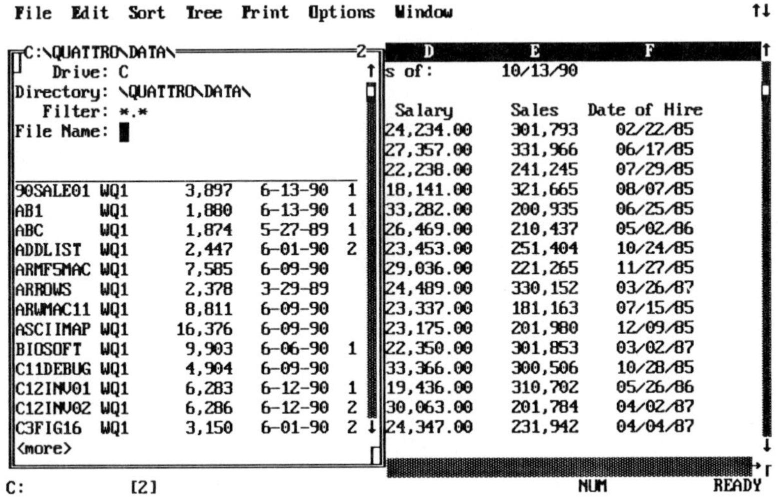

```
 File  Edit  Sort  Tree  Print  Options  Window                      ↑↓

┌C:\QUATTRO\DATA\═══════════════2┐┌ D        E         F              ↑
││    Drive: C                  ↑││s of:      10/13/90                █
│Directory: \QUATTRO\DATA\       ││                                   █
│    Filter: *.*                 ││ Salary     Sales   Date of Hire   █
│File Name: █                    ││24,234.00   301,793    02/22/85     █
│                                ││27,357.00   331,966    06/17/85     █
│                                ││22,238.00   241,245    07/29/85     █
│90SALE01 WQ1    3,897  6-13-90  1│18,141.00   321,665    08/07/85     █
│AB1      WQ1    1,880  6-13-90  1│33,282.00   200,935    06/25/85     █
│ABC      WQ1    1,874  5-27-89  1│26,469.00   210,437    05/02/86     █
│ADDLIST  WQ1    2,447  6-01-90  2│23,453.00   251,404    10/24/85     █
│ARMF5MAC WQ1    7,585  6-09-90   │29,036.00   221,265    11/27/85     █
│ARROWS   WQ1    2,378  3-29-89   │24,489.00   330,152    03/26/87     █
│ARWMAC11 WQ1    8,811  6-09-90   │23,337.00   181,163    07/15/85     █
│ASCIIMAP WQ1   16,376  6-09-90   │23,175.00   201,980    12/09/85     █
│BIOSOFT  WQ1    9,903  6-06-90  1│22,350.00   301,853    03/02/87     █
│C11DEBUG WQ1    4,904  6-09-90   │33,366.00   300,506    10/28/85     █
│C12INV01 WQ1    6,283  6-12-90  1│19,436.00   310,702    05/26/86     █
│C12INV02 WQ1    6,286  6-12-90  2│30,063.00   201,784    04/02/87     █
│C3FIG16  WQ1    3,150  6-01-90  2↓│24,347.00   231,942    04/04/87    ↓
│<more>                          ││                                    →┌
 C:          [2]                              NUM           READY
```

Figure 7-37. *File Manager window*

displays prompts that allow you to make changes in four areas: drive, directory, filter, and file name. In Figure 7-37 the settings are

```
     Drive:  C
 Directory:  \QUATTRO\DATA\
    Filter:  *.*
 File Name:  _
```

You move between these items with the UP and DOWN ARROW keys. The cursor will mark which one is active. You can change the active item by pressing ESCAPE to erase the entire entry, or by pressing BACKSPACE to erase one character at a time. You can then type the new setting and press ENTER to confirm it. When you press ENTER, Quattro PRO immediately reads in a new list based on your changes. When you are entering new subdirectories, be sure to precede the subdirectory in the path name with a backslash (\). For example, to view the files in D:\SALES\REPORTS you would change Drive to D and then change Directory to \SALES\REPORTS. There is no need to enter the final backslash as Quattro PRO will do that for you, changing \SALES\REPORTS to \SALES\REPORTS\.

Underneath the control pane is the *file list pane*. This is the list of files and subdirectories in the specified directory. You can browse this list with the UP and DOWN ARROW keys as well as PAGE UP and PAGE DOWN. You can also change the directory being displayed in the File Manager window by selecting another directory from within the file list pane. If you want to see one of the subdirectories included on the list, just highlight it and press ENTER. You will find subdirectories listed below file names in the file list. If you want to see the parent directory of the current subdirectory, select the double dots (..), which are shorthand for the parent directory.

A third pane, called the *tree pane,* is created when you use the Tree Open command. Figure 7-38 shows a File Manager window with a tree displayed by the Tree Open command. The tree pane now gives a visual representation of part of the directory system on the currently specified drive (C). The section of the directory tree shown includes the current directory and subdirectory.

Before you can work in a particular pane of the File Manager window you must activate that pane. To activate a different pane, press the Pane

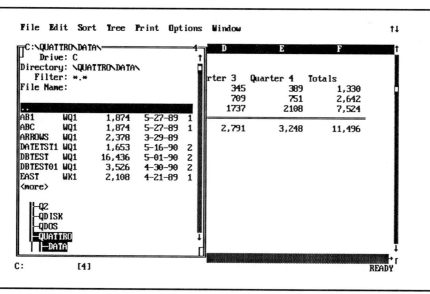

Figure 7-38. *File Manager tree*

key (F6) or the TAB key. As you can see from Figure 7-37, the File Manager window takes up half the screen when it is first displayed. You can expand the File Manager window to fill the screen by pressing the Zoom key (ALT-F6) or choosing the Zoom command from the Window menu. Repeat the zoom command to unzoom the window. File Manager windows are numbered in the same sequence as worksheet windows. You can have two or more File Manager windows open at the same time. Opening a second File Manager window is simply a matter of repeating the File Utilities File Manager command. The second File Manager window takes up the other half of the screen but any more File Manager windows you open will cover up the existing ones. To move between File Manager windows, use the Next Window key (SHIFT-F6). Alternatively, you can move from window to window with the ALT-*number* technique, for example use ALT-5 to move to window [5]. You can use the Move/Size command from the Windows menu to alter the size or position of File Manager windows.

To close the active File Manager window, use the File Close command. If you want to return to the worksheet you were using but do not want to close the File Manager window, press the Next Window key (SHIFT-F6). Quattro PRO temporarily removes the directories from display. You can return to the File Manager window at any time with the Next Window key. Special key combinations make it easy to move around in a File Manager window or switch from one window to another. A complete list of the special File Manager keys is provided in Table 7-5.

The File Manager Menus

When you are in a File Manager window, you have access to a set of menus by typing / or pressing F3. Quattro PRO activates a variation of the main menu as shown in Figure 7-37. This menu contains a subset of the usual menu commands with some new ones added.

With the File command you can create a new window or close the active one; print the file list or directory tree; update the directory display; create a directory; save a particular configuration of open windows; and temporarily exit to DOS.

The Edit command lets you copy, move, rename, duplicate, or erase files from the displayed directory. The Sort command lets you reorder the list of files by name, extension, timestamp, size, or DOS order. With the Tree command you can display the directory tree in a pane below or to the right of the file list, as well as resize the tree pane and close the tree pane.

The Print command displays a menu for printing selected files. This menu works much the same as the standard Print menu. The Options command lets you switch the file list display between names only and names and file status. You can also specify which directory is displayed initially in a File Manager window and reset many system options such as text printer and screen colors. Finally, the Window command allows you to adjust the size and position of the windows, expand the current window, or move to a different window.

Working with the Control Pane

Suppose that you want to view all 1-2-3 worksheet files in the LOTUS directory of drive E. First, make sure that the control pane of the File Manager window is active. This means that the cursor will be flashing in one of the top four fields (press F6 or TAB to change active windows). In the drive field type **E** and press ENTER. In the directory field type **\LOTUS**. Now move to the filter prompt. The filter lets you restrict the files shown in the file list pane. This setting accepts DOS wildcards: * to take the place of any number of characters, and ? to take the place of one character. The default filter setting, *.*, displays all file names with any extension. To narrow down the files listed, you change the filter to exclude files you do not want to see. In this example, you can enter ***.WK?** to list all files with *WK* as the first two letters of their extension. This includes *WKS* and *WK1*. To be more specific, for example to find all files beginning with *SALES*, you would enter **SALES*.***. You can also specify a negative filter to display all files except those that meet the filter specifications. To indicate a negative filter you enclose the wildcard specification in square brackets. For example, to display a list of all files except those beginning with *SALES,* enter the following specification:

[SALES*.*]

You can also combine filter specifications to create one filter. Just separate the specifications with commas. For example,

.WK?,[SALES.*]

General Windowing Keys

SHIFT-F5	Pick Window; accesses other windows
ALT-0	Pick Window; accesses other windows
F6 or TAB	Pane; activates the next File Manager window pane in the following order: control pane, file list pane, directory tree pane.
SHIFT-F6	Next Window; activates the next open File Manager window.
ALT-F6	Zoom Window; zooms an open window to full screen and back again. If the window is already expanded, this key shrinks it again, as with Window Zoom.
ALT-n	Jumps to window number n. The window number appears on the top edge of each frame.

Keys for the Control Pane

F2	Rename; prompts for a new file name, and renames the current file list selection to the file name you specify (same as Edit Rename).
F5	GoTo; finds the file name (or combination of wildcard characters) typed at the file name prompt.
ESCAPE	Clears the entry at the prompt. When you move the highlight bar away from the prompt and make no new entry, restores the original entry.
DELETE	Deletes the character under the cursor.
ENTER	Moves the cursor to the blank file name prompt or, if the cursor is at the file name prompt, opens the file or subdirectory highlighted on the file list.
HOME	Moves the cursor to the beginning of the prompt entry.

Table 7-5.   File Manager Keys

Keys for the File List Pane

F2	Rename; renames the current (highlighted) file (same as Edit Rename).
SHIFT-F7	Select; selects the current (highlighted) file in the list so you can open, move, copy, or delete it. If the file is already selected, this key deselects it.
ALT-F7	All Select; selects all files on the list for moving, copying, or deleting. If some files on the list are already selected, deselects those files.
SHIFT-F8	Move; moves the selected files into the paste buffer, removing them from the list.
ALT-F8	Delete; erase the selected files or the highlighted file from the disk.
F9	Calc; reads the disk and refreshes the file list pane (same as File Read Dir).
SHIFT-F9	Copy; copies the selected files into the paste buffer for copying to another directory or disk, keeping them on the list.
SHIFT-F10	Paste; inserts the files in the paste buffer at the cursor position in the current directory's file list.
ESCAPE	Escape; returns all selected files to normal. Activates the control pane and moves the cursor to the file name prompt.
ENTER	Opens selected files or the file at the cursor. If the highlight bar is on the .., opens the parent directory. If the highlight bar is on a subdirectory, moves to the subdirectory.
HOME	Moves the highlight bar to the .. parent directory item.
END	Moves the highlight bar to the end of the file list.
PAGE UP	Moves the file list display up one screen.
PAGE DOWN	Moves the file list display down one screen.

In the Tree Panel

ESCAPE	Returns all selected files to normal; then activates the control pane and moves the cursor to the file name prompt.
DELETE	Deletes all selected files or the highlighted file in the file list.
F9	Calc; rereads the current disk/directory.

Table 7-5. *File Manager Keys* (continued)

displays all 1-2-3 spreadsheet files except for those beginning with *SALES*. The filter limits the files displayed in the File Manager window, but you can always type in the name of any file at the file name prompt to see whether it is in the current directory, regardless of whether it is shown in the list. The directory filter remains in effect until you change it, even if you change directories. To erase the current filter and return to the default of *.*, highlight the filter prompt and press ESCAPE and then ENTER.

Selecting Files

When you open the File Manager window the file name prompt is blank. At the same time, the control pane is active and the file name prompt is highlighted. You can use this prompt to open a worksheet file or look for a specific file on your disk. To open a worksheet file you type the name at the file name prompt and press ENTER. If Quattro PRO finds the file, the File Manager window disappears and the worksheet is displayed. Note that if Quattro PRO does not find the file you have named in the current directory, it creates a new spreadsheet with that name and displays it. For this reason you may want to locate the file in the file list, as described in a moment, rather than risk a mismatched file name entry.

If you do not know where on a disk a particular file is located you can type in the file name at the file name prompt and press the GoTo key (F5). Quattro PRO searches through every directory on the disk until it finds a file with that name. It then changes the file list to show the directory containing the file you specified, with the file name highlighted and marked by a check. If there are other files with the same name, press F5 again to move to the next. If you do not know the exact name of the file, you can use wildcards to search for near matches. For example, to find a worksheet file with a name that begins with *FRED* you can start typing **FRED∗.WQ1** in the file name field. As you type, Quattro PRO begins looking for the file, highlighting the first file beginning with *F*, then the first one beginning with *FR,* and so on. When you have finished typing you can highlight the next matching file name by pressing F5. When the file you want is highlighted, press ENTER to open it. Table 7-5 provides a list of the special keys you can use in the control pane and their functions.

The File List Pane

The file list pane catalogs all files and subdirectories that pass through the given filter in the specified drive and directory. File names are listed first, followed by subdirectory names, in alphabetical order. Figure 7-39 shows a file list in a File Manager window that has been zoomed to full screen size (with ALT-F6). The first column shows file names, the second shows file name extensions, and the third shows file size measured in bytes. The last two columns show the date and time the file was last altered. If there are more files in the directory than will fit in the pane, Quattro PRO displays "<more>"at the bottom of the screen. You can press PAGE DOWN to display the next page of names or END to move to the end of the list.

Moving to the end of the list is useful since there you can find a directory status that shows the number of files in the current directory and the number of files displayed in the file list, which may be less if you have used a filter. This status line also shows how many bytes of the disk have been

```
  File   Edit   Sort   Tree   Print   Options   Window                    ↑↓

      Drive:  C
  Directory:  \QUATTRO\DATA\                                                ▯
     Filter:  *.*
  File Name:  ▮

   90SALE01 WQ1      3,897    6-13-90   10:11:00
   AB1      WQ1      1,880    6-13-90   11:03:01
   ABC      WQ1      1,874    5-27-89   12:10:13
   ADDLIST  WQ1      2,447    6-01-90   23:23:13
   ARMF5MAC WQ1      7,585    6-09-90    0:12:18
   ARROWS   WQ1      2,378    3-29-89    0:02:00
   ARWMAC11 WQ1      8,811    6-09-90    0:58:10
   ASCIIMAP WQ1     16,376    6-09-90    1:58:25
   BIOSOFT  WQ1      9,903    6-06-90   12:45:01
   C11DEBUG WQ1      4,904    6-09-90    8:36:14
   C12INV01 WQ1      6,283    6-12-90   18:59:20
   C12INV02 WQ1      6,286    6-12-90   23:06:17
   C3FIG16  WQ1      3,150    6-01-90   23:10:22
   C4CTERM  WQ1      2,551    6-06-90   12:07:14
   C4FVAL   WQ1      1,712    6-06-90   12:10:13
   <more>
   C:           [2]                              NUM         READY
```

Figure 7-39. *Full screen file list*

used together with the total number of bytes available on the disk. If you do not need datestamp and file size information you can use the Options File List Wide View command to allow room for more file names in the list, as shown in Figure 7-40. Table 7-5 lists the special keys you can use in the file list pane.

Sorting File Lists

By default, Quattro PRO lists all files and subdirectories in the file list in alphabetical order. This is the Sort Name option. To change the order of the file list you choose Sort from the File Manager menu then select the sort order you want from the list. When you choose Name or DOS Order, Quattro PRO also sorts subdirectories listed in the tree pane. You can sort by Timestamp which lists file names and subdirectories chronologically according to their timestamp, which shows when the file was last modified. The oldest file is listed first. This command sorts by time, even when the Options File List command is set to Wide View. There is an Extension

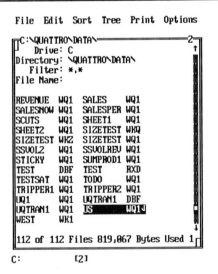

Figure 7-40. *Wide view of files*

option that sorts the file list alphabetically, first by extension, then by file name. The Size option sorts file names and subdirectories by size (in bytes). The smallest file appears first in the list. This command sorts by size, even when you have suppressed size display from the file list (with Options File List Wide View). The DOS Order option sorts file names in the same order that the DOS command DIR would list them (usually in the order of original creation). A wide view list sorted by Extension is shown in Figure 7-41.

Navigating with the File List

The Options Startup Directory setting determines which directory is displayed when you first open a File Manager window. To change the directory displayed at startup you choose Options Startup Directory, and then select either Previous (the default) to display the last directory you looked at in your last Quattro PRO session, or Current to show the directory you were in when you loaded Quattro PRO.

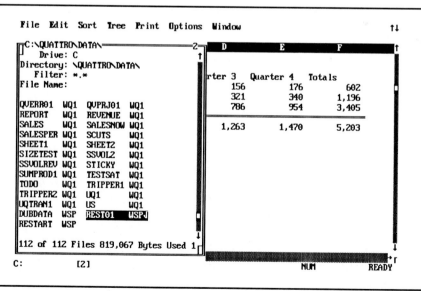

Figure 7-41. *File list sorted by extension*

If the file you want is not in the directory shown in the file list, you can access different directories by choosing subdirectories. These are normally found at the bottom of the alphabetical file list and distinguished by a backslash after the directory name. You can also move up in the directory system by using the item denoted by two dots (..), which is the parent directory of the current directory. To display files in one of the subdirectories listed in the file pane, just move the highlight bar to the directory's name and press ENTER. The directory prompt changes to show the subdirectory name, and the file pane changes to list files in that subdirectory. To move out of the current directory and into its parent directory press HOME to highlight the double dots denoting the parent directory at the top of the file list pane, and then press ENTER. Quattro PRO takes you back one level in the directory and displays file names and subdirectories in the parent directory. Table 7-4 lists the keystrokes you can use in the control pane of a File Manager window.

The Directory Tree

By choosing subdirectories or the parent directory (..) item in the file list you can get to any file stored on your disk. But if you expect to traverse many directories, or if you are not sure what files are in your directories, you may want to use the directory tree, which Quattro PRO can display in a third directory pane. The directory tree lists all directories and subdirectories on your disk in alphabetical order. You can move the cursor around the tree to display different directory contents in the file list pane. Figure 7-42 shows a directory tree in a full screen File Manager window. When you want to use a directory tree, choose Tree from the File Manager window.

To display the directory tree just choose the Tree Open command. Quattro PRO opens a tree pane below or to the right of the file pane in the File Manager window. The root directory is at the top on the far left. Subdirectories branch to the right and down. Quattro PRO highlights the current directory on the tree. If there are more directories on your disk than will fit in the tree pane you can use the direction keys to scroll the list. When you use the cursor keys to move the highlight bar, Quattro PRO displays files in a different directory. As you move the bar the directory prompt changes to show the name of the highlighted directory, and the file list changes to display the files in that directory.

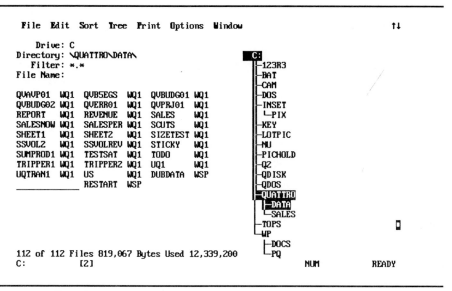

Figure 7-42. *Tree display*

Sizing the Tree

The first time you display a directory tree, Quattro PRO divides the available File Manager window space equally between the file pane and the tree pane. You may want to give more or less space to the tree pane. To change the size of the tree pane, select Tree Resize from the File Manager menu. Quattro PRO prompts you for a percentage. Figure 7-43 shows a zoomed File Manager window with a tree pane sized at 80%. The file list display has been set to Wide View to show as many file names as possible. Enter the percentage you want when prompted by the Tree Resize command. In future, when you display the tree pane, it will be the size you last specified. Table 7-5 lists some keystrokes that let you select, delete, open, and refresh the display of file and directory information in the directory tree pane. If most of your work is in one directory, you can give more space to the file list by closing the directory tree pane. To do this use Tree Close. Quattro PRO removes the directory tree and expands the file list pane to fill its space.

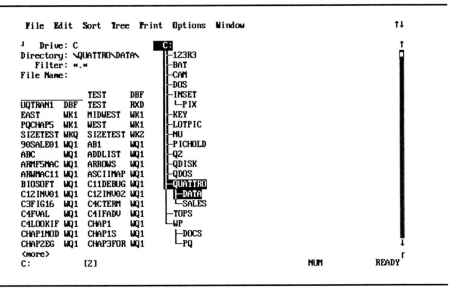

| File | Edit | Sort | Tree | Print | Options | Window | ↑↓ |

```
⌐   Drive: C                       C:                              ↑
Directory: \QUATTRO\DATA\          ├─123R3                         □
    Filter: *.*                    ├─BAT
 File Name:                        ├─CAM
                                   ├─DOS
               TEST      DBF       ├─INSET
UQTRAN1  DBF   TEST      RXD       └─PIX
EAST     WK1   MIDWEST   WK1       ├─KEY
PQCHAP5  WK1   WEST      WK1       ├─LOTPIC
SIZETEST WKQ   SIZETEST  WKZ       ├─NU
90SALE01 WQ1   AB1       WQ1       ├─PICHOLD
ABC      WQ1   ADDLIST   WQ1       ├─Q2
ARMF5MAC WQ1   ARROWS    WQ1       ├─QDISK
ARWMAC11 WQ1   ASCIIMAP  WQ1       ├─QDOS
BIOSOFT  WQ1   C11DEBUG  WQ1       ├─QUATTRO
C12INV01 WQ1   C12INV02  WQ1       │ ├─DATA
C3FIG16  WQ1   C4CTERM   WQ1       │ └─SALES
C4FVAL   WQ1   C4IFADV   WQ1       ├─TOPS
C4LOOKIF WQ1   CHAP1     WQ1       └─WP
CHAP1MOD WQ1   CHAP1S    WQ1         ├─DOCS
CHAP2EG  WQ1   CHAP3FOR  WQ1         └─PQ
<more>                                                             ⌐
C:             [2]                              NUM       READY └
```

Figure 7-43. *Tree display at 80%*

Printing File Information

The File Manager menu bar contains a print option. You can use this specialized Print menu to print parts of the File Manager window. The Print Block command gives you three options instead of a cell block prompt. The default option is Files, which prints a list of all files in the file List pane, even those you have to scroll to display. To print the directory tree, choose Tree. To print the file list followed by the directory tree, choose Both. You can send the output to a printer or to a file.

Managing and Loading Files

With the File Manager, you can move, copy, rename, or delete files on your disk without accessing DOS. You perform these actions from the File Manager Edit menu.

Selecting and Pasting Files

The first option on the File Manager Edit menu, shown in Figure 7-44, is Select File. This marks the highlighted file on the file list so that it stays highlighted even when you move the highlight bar away. You can use this command when you want to select a group of file names. The All Select option highlights all files on the file list, or if some files are already selected, it deselects all files.

The Copy option stores a copy of the selected files in the paste buffer. You can then paste the copy into any other directory. The Move option moves the selected files into the paste buffer and from there you can paste them into another directory. The Erase option deletes the selected files from the disk. The Paste option inserts the files in the paste buffer in whatever directory you select.

The Duplicate option performs double duty, copying and renaming a file, and then storing the copy in the same or a different directory. The Rename option allows you to change the name of a file. Table 7-5 lists the special keys used in the file list pane for moving around, as well as for renaming, moving, copying, opening, and deleting files.

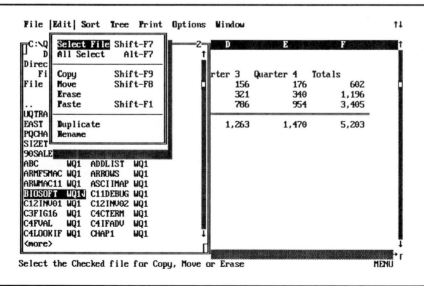

Figure 7-44. *Edit menu*

The first step to moving, copying, or deleting files is to select the files you want to work on. You do this with the Select and All Select keys (SHIFT-F7 and ALT-F7) or the Edit Select File and Edit All Select commands. You then use the Edit command you want, for example, Copy. Then use the file list or the directory tree to select the destination of the files you are copying. Use the Edit Paste command to place the files in this directory.

Opening Files

You can use the File Manager to open a spreadsheet file and display it in a new spreadsheet window. Just select the file name on the file list and press ENTER. Quattro PRO removes the File Manager window from view and displays the spreadsheet, overlaying any existing spreadsheet windows. To open a file using a mouse, move the pointer to the file name and click the button to highlight the name; then click again to open the file.

To open several spreadsheet files at once, use the Edit Select command or SHIFT-F7 key to select each file on the file list, and then press ENTER. Quattro PRO opens a new spreadsheet window for each and loads the file. Remember that you can also open a file from within the File Manager window by entering a name at the control pane's file name prompt and pressing ENTER. The name you enter does not have to be one of those displayed in the list, but it does have to be in the displayed directory.

Managing Directories

The File menu that you access from within a File Manager window contains a New command that opens a new worksheet window, and a Close command that closes the current window. The Read Dir command reads and redisplays the files on the current directory. The Make Dir command creates a new directory or subdirectory with the name and location you supply at the prompt shown in Figure 7-45. As in a worksheet window, the Workspace command lets you save the current setup of windows in a file or retrieve a saved workspace setup. The Utilities command allows you to open another File Manager window or access DOS without leaving Quattro PRO, as with the DOS Shell command on the regular File Utilities menu. The Exit command puts away Quattro PRO and returns you to DOS.

The File Read command rereads the files on the specified directory and updates the file list accordingly. A typical use for this command would be

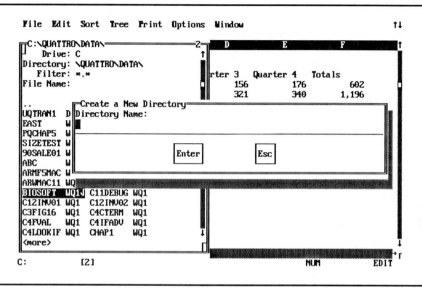

Figure 7-45. *Creating a new directory*

when you have inserted a new disk in a floppy drive. The Calc key, (F9) performs the same function as File Read, by "recalculating" the directory display.

File Manager Options

Selecting Options from the File Manager menu displays an adjusted Options menu. This menu, shown in Figure 7-46, lists some of the same system options available within a worksheet window and two options that deal directly with File Manager windows. The Hardware, Colors, Beep, Display Mode, and Update choices are the same as when you are in a worksheet window. The Start-up option contains the Menu Tree and Edit Menus commands plus a special command called Directory. This allows you to choose between a File Manager display of the directory you were in when you last used Quattro PRO, and the directory from which you just loaded Quattro PRO. The File List command on the Options menu in File Manager displays just the file names in the file list—in several columns, or in a single column that includes size, date, and time information for each file.

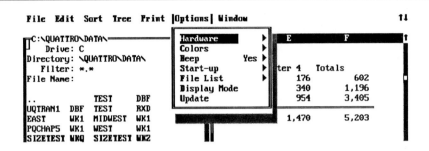

Figure 7-46. *File Manager Options*

Using SQZ!

A very useful file management feature that is built into Quattro PRO is the ability to compress files when storing them on disk. This conserves valuable disk space. To use this feature you simply employ the file name extension WQ!. When storing files with WQ! extension, Quattro PRO uses a piece of software called SQZ! to pack the data tightly. When you retrieve a file with the WQ! extension the SQZ! program, which is contained within the main Quattro PRO program, automatically unpacks the data. You can still use password protection with SQZ! files. What you lose by compressing files is the ability to search for text strings with such file management products as Norton Utilities.

With Quattro PRO you can read compressed 1-2-3 Release 2 worksheet files that have the extention WK!, as well as compressed files from earlier versions of Quattro that have the extension WKZ. For more on using SQZ! see the SQZ! macro in Chapter 13.

8 *Graphing*

Quattro PRO offers exceptional graphics features. You can design a graph that is automatically updated when you change the numbers in the underlying spreadsheet. You can quickly create graphs with just a few keystrokes by using the Fast Graph option shown in Figure 8-1. You can place graphs within spreadsheets and create charts using data from multiple worksheets. But that is only the beginning. Quattro PRO also offers a wide range of graphing options to produce well-designed, professional-quality graphs. In this chapter you will learn how to generate graphs from your data and apply the graphing options to improve and enhance those graphs.

Since Quattro PRO provides so many options for customizing your graphs, illustrating every possible combination is beyond the scope of this book. The main options will be described, however, with suggestions for their application to your specific graphing needs.

Fast Graphs

Quattro PRO can automatically generate graphs from spreadsheet numbers. This provides a quick way to make a graph; you can enter with one command the main settings from which you can develop a variety of customized graphs.

Using the Fast Graph Feature

Consider the spreadsheet in Figure 8-2. This is a record of year-to-date sales by the three agents at the Van Ness office of Quattro Vadis Travel. To make a graph of this data will take only one command. However, before issuing the command, place the cell selector in the top-left corner of the set of data to be graphed. In the case of Figure 8-2, the correct location is D3. With D3 selected you can simply press CTRL-G, the default Shortcut for the Fast Graph feature. Alternatively, you can select Graph from the main menu and then select Fast Graph. You can see the Graph menu in Figure 8-3.

When you issue the Fast Graph command, either as a Shortcut or as a menu command, you are prompted for a Fast Graph block. This is a block of cells that includes the numbers to be graphed. Do not include totals for rows or columns of numbers being graphed—the graph commands compute totals automatically. In the case of the spreadsheet in Figure 8-2, the correct cells to include in the Fast Graph block are D3..G7, as shown in Figure 8-4. When you press ENTER to confirm this block, you are immediately presented with a graph. This can be a little alarming at first, since

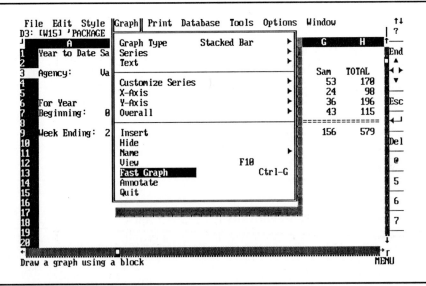

Figure 8-1.   *The Fast Graph option*

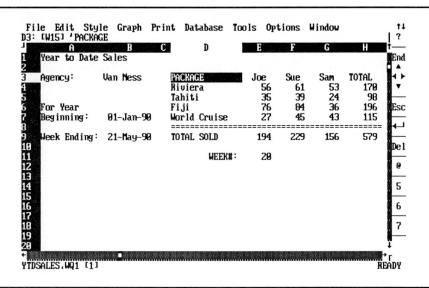

Figure 8-2. *Spreadsheet with cell selector at D3*

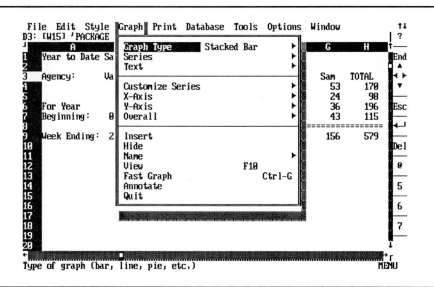

Figure 8-3. *The Graph menu*

Quattro PRO automatically goes into graphics display mode to draw the graph.

In Figure 8-5 you can see the graph drawn by Fast Graph from the highlighted spreadsheet cells in Figure 8-4. This type of chart is called stacked-bar and it is the default graph type in Quattro PRO. The graph in Figure 8-5 has been annotated so that you can see the terms used by Quattro PRO for the component parts of a graph. Note that the program automatically figures out how large to make the y-axis, the scale going up the left side of the graph.

The total number of products in each of the four categories of product are graphed as bars. The portion of the total sold by each agent is indicated by the three different shadings. If you have a color monitor you will see the agents differentiated by color as well. The legend box outside the main body of the graph explains which bar represents each agent. In Figure 8-5 and other figures in this chapter, the shading of the legend may not exactly match that of the main graph. This is due to the process used to reproduce the graph screen for purposes of illustration; the legend will be accurate in graphs printed and displayed by Quattro PRO.

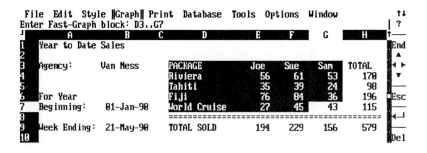

Figure 8-4.   *Spreadsheet with D3..G7 Fast Graph block*

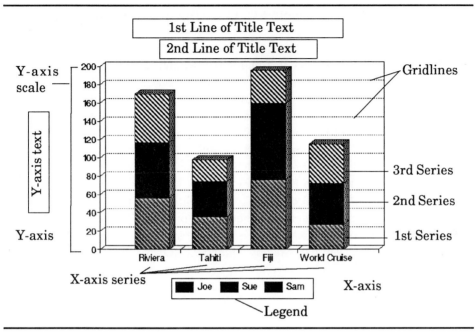

Figure 8-5. *Stacked bar graph drawn by Fast Graph*

To return to the spreadsheet you can press ESCAPE, or the SPACEBAR. In fact, most keys will take you from the graph view back to the worksheet, but typing / while viewing a graph takes you to the *graph annotation screen*. To leave the graph annotation screen, which will be described in detail later, you type / again and then **Q** for Quit. You will be back at the graph view. You can use CTRL-BREAK to go from the annotation screen to the regular graph view, and once again to go from the regular graph view to READY mode.

Working with a Graph

As you review this first graph, note that in graph terminology the numbers for each agent constitute a series. These are measured on the y-axis, which is sometimes called the *value axis*. Each category of product is listed across the x-axis, which is sometimes called the *category axis*. Each value in the cells E4..G7 is represented by a different bar segment, which is referred to as a *data point*. The box that explains the shading is called a *legend*. Quattro PRO allows you to remove the legend if it is not required (for example, when only one series of data is defined). In fact, there are many changes and embellishments you can make to this basic graph and they will be dealt with in the course of this chapter. Bear in mind, however, that making this first graph took just one command, and the results are very respectable. Furthermore, the graph you have made is dynamically linked to the data in the spreadsheet. For example, suppose that Sam actually sold 63 trips to Fiji rather than 36. You exit the graph view and change cell G6 from 36 to 63. To immediately see the difference in the graph you do not even need the menu; just press the Graph key F10. This displays the current graph, which is the graph that the current settings generate. (Later you will see how Quattro PRO stores a variety of graphs in one spreadsheet, but there is only ever one current graph.)

The graph of the corrected figures is shown in Figure 8-6. Notice how the y-axis has been altered to account for the increase in the size of the largest bar being graphed. If you have a printer that is capable of printing

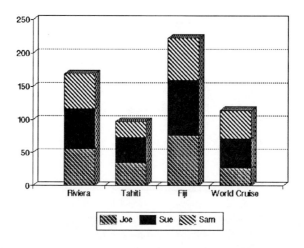

Figure 8-6.   *Corrected stacked bar graph*

graphs you can easily print this graph. In READY mode, select Print from the main menu and then pick Graph Print. Select Destination and choose Graph Printer. Then select Go. Quattro PRO should print out the graph, using the default values for size and layout. Graph printing can take several minutes, so do not be alarmed if your printer does not react for a while.

Inserting a Graph

With Quattro PRO you can insert the graph you have made into the spreadsheet that generated it. If you have either an EGA or a VGA display system, you can actually view the graph and worksheet together. On other display systems, you can insert graphs into worksheets in order to print them together on the same page, but you cannot view them together on the screen.

To insert a graph, select Insert from the Graph menu. You will be asked to specify a graph to be placed into the spreadsheet, as shown in Figure 8-7. Unless you have already defined other graphs, there will be only one graph in the list, the one that is current and appears when you press F10.

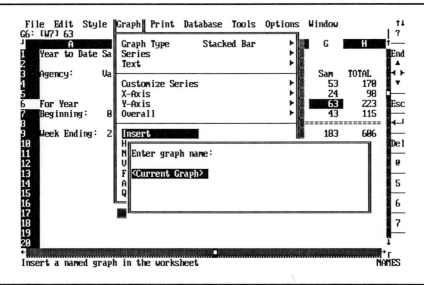

Figure 8-7. *The Insert option*

This is listed as <Current Graph>. Highlight this and press ENTER. You will then be prompted for the location at which the graph is to be inserted. Place the cell selector in a cell below the numbers that generate the graph. In fact, you can insert the graph over the numbers without affecting them, but that is not what is required here; in this case, cell B11 will work nicely. Anchor the block coordinates by typing a period, and then press the RIGHT and DOWN ARROW keys to move the highlighting through to cell G28. This is the area that the graph will occupy. Press ENTER to complete the Graph Insert command.

Unless you have an EGA or a VGA display system and are using the graphics mode, you will not see much of a result from this command. A section of the worksheet will simply be blocked out to show the area occupied by the graph. If you have an EGA/VGA system and you want to see the graph displayed in the spreadsheet, use the Options Display mode command to select Graphics Mode. The graph will be draw as the screen is rewritten. You can see the results in Figure 8-8. Notice the increased number of rows visible in graphics mode, and the improved appearance of the mouse palette and pointer. Also notice the second line of the screen, where cell B11 is especially marked as containing the current graph. In

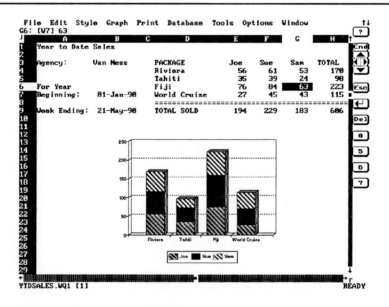

Figure 8-8.   *Graph displayed in spreadsheet*

fact, this notation appears in all the cells of the block that you highlighted for the Graph Insert command. Data in any of these cells is not damaged, but it is obscured by the graph.

When you insert a graph into a spreadsheet it is dynamically linked to the data in the spreadsheet. Any changes you make to the spreadsheet entries that generated the graph are reflected in the graph. For example, suppose that the name of the World Cruise is changed to Mega-Cruise and that Joe realizes his Tahiti figure should be 53. Making these changes updates the graph, as you can see in Figure 8-9.

Working with Inserted Graphs

Displaying a graph in graphics mode can be quite a test of your computer's processing ability. Quattro PRO's response time slows down considerably when you are working in graphics mode on a spreadsheet that contains an inserted graph. Movement of the cell selector and cell editing will be slower because of the constant need to redraw the graph. You will probably want

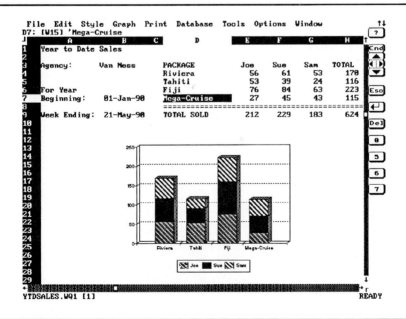

Figure 8-9. *Updated graph in spreadsheet*

to insert graphs toward the end of the design process and switch to character mode when you need to make a lot of changes to a worksheet that contains inserted graphs.

Note that you can insert more than one graph. Later in this chapter the procedure for naming graphs will be reviewed. When you have named a graph you can insert the named graph as well as the current graph, and the graphs will all be updated to reflect changes in the worksheet.

To remove a graph that you have inserted in your worksheet you use the Graph Hide command. This shows a list of all the inserted graphs for you to select the one you want to remove. Highlight the graph name and press ENTER and the graph will be removed. The graph will still be available for display.

To print a worksheet together with a graph you use the Spreadsheet Print command from the Print menu, but with the Print Destination set to Graph Printer. You must include the graph cells (B11..G28) in the Print Block. An example of the combined output is shown in Figure 8-10. Obviously, the results of the combined print operation will depend on your printer and its capabilities; indeed, the graph-making side of spreadsheet work depends heavily on your choice of equipment. The next section reviews some of the hardware considerations in making graphs.

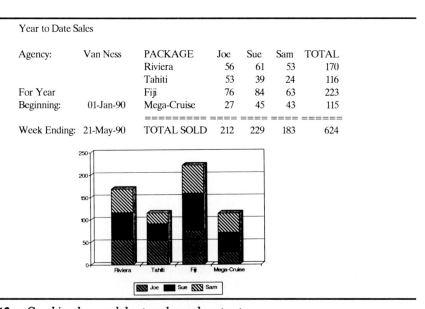

Year to Date Sales						
Agency:	Van Ness	PACKAGE	Joe	Sue	Sam	TOTAL
		Riviera	56	61	53	170
		Tahiti	53	39	24	116
For Year		Fiji	76	84	63	223
Beginning:	01-Jan-90	Mega-Cruise	27	45	43	115
		=========	====	====	====	======
Week Ending:	21-May-90	TOTAL SOLD	212	229	183	624

Figure 8-10.   *Combined spreadsheet and graph output*

Graphics Equipment

Displaying and printing graphs imposes more demands on your hardware than printing spreadsheet text. As was discussed in Chapter 6, there are two different ways of displaying and printing information: character mode and graphics mode. The type of display adapter and printer that you have will affect your ability to produce graphs with Quattro PRO.

Graphics Display

In the character mode of display, each screen you view is made up of 2000 characters arranged in 25 lines of 80 characters each. This is the default mode used by Quattro PRO and the one shown in most of the screens in this book. The alternative is a graphics mode, where the screen is composed of a series of dots that draw shapes, including numbers, text, circles, and so on. Quattro PRO switches between different modes of display. This means that typical spreadsheet operations such as data entry and calculation can take place in the faster environment of character mode. However, when you want to design a high-quality report or a graph, Quattro PRO can switch you to graphics mode.

If you have an IBM Color Graphics Adapter, a Hercules graphics card, an IBM Enhanced Graphics Adapter, or a VGA system, you will be able to display Quattro PRO graphs on your screen when you press the F10 key. The graphs shown in Figures 8-5 and 8-6 were displayed by a VGA system. If your system does not support graphics displays, you can still create a Quattro PRO graph; however, you will not be able to see the results until they are printed.

If you have an EGA or aVGA display you can also use the Options Display Mode command to activate a special high-resolution mode that can display additional columns and rows in the workspace, as well as graphs that have been inserted within worksheets using the Graph Insert command (discussed in a moment). When you use the graphics mode, display systems such as EGA and VGA allow you to adjust the display resolution; that is, how sharply the graphics images are formed. You do this in Quattro PRO with the Hardware Screen Resolution command. However, you must set the resolution before switching to graphics mode. Quattro PRO cannot change resolution while you are in graphics mode. You can record your desired resolution and mode as the new defaults for Quattro PRO by selecting the Update command on the Options menu.

Graphics Printing

To print a Quattro PRO graph, you need a graphics *output device*; that is, a printer or plotter capable of reproducing graphics images. Most dot-matrix, laser, ink-jet, and thermal printers can produce graphs; however, daisy-wheel printers cannot produce Quattro PRO graphs. Quattro PRO graphs can be reproduced in color with a color printer or plotter. You initially tell Quattro PRO about your graphics output device through the installation program. If you did not specify a printer then or you need to change printers, use the Hardware command on the Options menu, as discussed in Chapter 6. When you select Printers from the Hardware menu you will see that Quattro PRO allows you to define two printers, 1st Printer and 2nd Printer.

You define one of these two printers as the default; this is the one that is used when you issue a print command from the Print menu. As you saw from the Graph menu in Figure 8-3 there is no Print option. In Quattro PRO you print graphs from the Print menu shown in Figure 8-11. As you can see, the Print menu has a Destination option. However, this affects only the direction of spreadsheet output sent to the printer with the Spreadsheet Print command, not the printing of graphs. The Graph Print command has its own Destination option, as shown in Figure 8-12.

The three options on the Graph Print Destination menu are File, Graph Printer, and Screen Preview. You can see that Graph Printer is the default selection; this is the option to use when you are sending a graph to the printer on its own, as opposed to being part of a combined spreadsheet/graph print job.

To clarify the printing procedure, consider the following example. Suppose that your printer is an HP LaserJet. This printer is capable of printing text and graphics. Using the Options Hardware menu, you have chosen the correct model of LaserJet as 1st Printer and made sure that 1st Printer is the Default Printer. You have used Fast Graph to create a graph. You have made sure that the numbers are correct. You pressed F9 in READY mode to make sure that the spreadsheet is calculated up to date. You have pressed F10 to view the graph. The graph looks good and you want to print it. Back in READY mode you select Print from the main menu, and then Graph Print. You make sure that Graph Printer is chosen as the Destination. You check that the Layout settings are correct. You then pick Go. Quattro PRO sends the graph to the Default Printer—your 1st Printer, which Quattro PRO knows is a LaserJet.

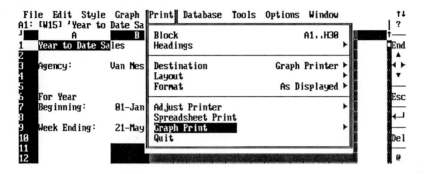

Figure 8-11. *The Print menu*

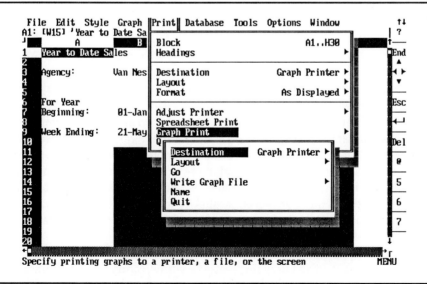

Figure 8-12. *The Destination option*

Now suppose that the graph came out nicely and you want to print a quick draft of the spreadsheet that generated the graph. You pick Print from the main menu and define the Block. You check that the Destination setting on the Print menu is Printer. You check the Layout settings and then pick Spreadsheet Print. You decide you would like a presentation-quality print of the same area of the spreadsheet. You select Destination from the Print menu, change it to Graph Printer, and then select Spreadsheet Print.

Suppose that you decide to insert the graph in the spreadsheet as described earlier. You complete the Graph Insert command, define an area of cells in the spreadsheet that includes numbers, labels, and the inserted graph. You select Print from the main menu, make sure that the Destination setting is Graph Printer and select Spreadsheet Print. Both the spreadsheet cells and the inserted graph are printed on the same page. Details of the other graph printing commands, Layout and Write Graph File, are described in the section on "Finer Points of Graph Printing" later in this chapter.

Manual Graph Commands

Although the Fast Graph feature is a powerful one, you will probably want to learn more about the different commands that you can use to create a graph. This will enable you to use the commands to create graphs from scratch and also to customize graphs that you have started with the Fast Graph feature.

To see how you use Quattro PRO to build a graph from scratch, a typical scenario will be presented here. As the manager of Take Over Airlines you are called upon by the owner to review the year's performance. Immediately, you turn to the worksheet in which you have been accumulating the passenger volume figures in each of three classes: First, Business, and Coach. This worksheet is shown in Figure 8-13. The number of passengers in each class in each of the four quarters can be easily transformed into a graph.

An example of what the numbers might look like as a graph is shown in Figure 8-14. In the following sections you will find the basic elements of building graphs described in the order in which they arise in the building process. As you have already seen in the section on Fast Graph, Quattro

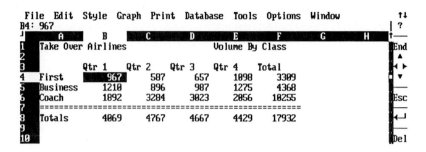

File Edit Style Graph Print Database Tools Options Window

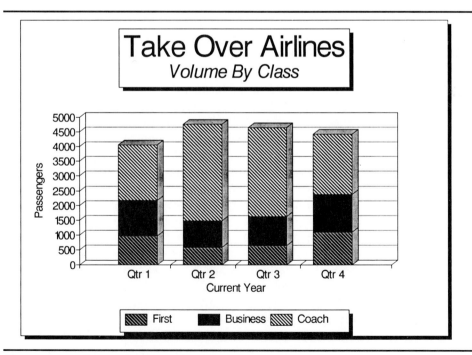

Figure 8-13. *Passenger volume by class as spreadsheet*

Figure 8-14. *Passenger volume by class as graph*

PRO requires very little information to build a very presentable graph. However, since most elements of a graph can be customized to enhance the graph's appearance and accommodate unusual types of data, many of the menus you will use contain several options. Not all of these options will be examined as the graph is built, but they will be presented later.

Preparing to Graph

The basic procedure for creating a graph with Quattro PRO is to indicate the spreadsheet coordinates of the data to be graphed. Usually this data is readily available in your spreadsheet, as in the case of the sales statistics shown earlier in Figure 8-4, or the passenger statistics shown in Figure 8-13. In both cases, the numbers are in consecutive columns that form a block. In fact, Quattro PRO requires that each set of values for your graph be in consecutive cells in the worksheet. Occasionally, prior to building a graph, you will need to rearrange data to comply with this requirement. You can use either the Edit Copy or Edit Move command to accomplish this, or you can develop a new spreadsheet that references the cells from the main model in a compact block suitable for graphing. In most cases, however, you will probably be graphing data that is already arranged in suitable blocks of cells.

Although the position of your cell selector prior to entering the Graph menu is not critical, you should place it near the data that is to be graphed, in this case, in cell B3 or B4. To build a graph from the spreadsheet in Figure 8-13, you first select Graph from the main menu. The Graph menu, shown earlier in Figure 8-3, shows you the main options involved in graphing. The first option, Graph Type, refers to the kind of graph that you want Quattro PRO to produce. The default type is the stacked bar shown in all of the graphs so far in this chapter. When you select Graph Type, you will see a list of the ten available types, as shown in Figure 8-15. If you are using the graphics display mode you will not see the list of types, but a diagram illustrating the different possibilities with the current selection shown highlighted. In Figure 8-16 you can see the Graph Type diagram with stacked bar selected. Use the arrow keys to move the highlighting to the graph type you want and press ENTER to select it.

You do not have to make your final selection of graph type before creating the graph, as the type can be changed later. Unless you have a specific type of graph in mind, leave the setting at the default stacked bar. Next,

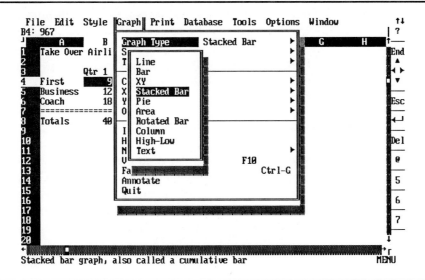

Figure 8-15. *The Graph Type option*

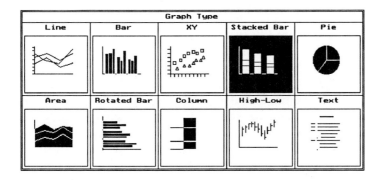

Figure 8-16. *The Graph Type option in display mode*

you need to tell Quattro PRO the various pieces of information it needs to build the graph. Refer to Figure 8-5 for some of the basic terminology used.

Series Values

The numbers you are charting in the graph are called the *series values*. The series values must be values; they *cannot* be labels. You can graph as many as six sets of values at once. In this example, the three series values to be graphed are the volume figures for First, Business, and Coach class. When you select Series from the Graph menu, the Series menu lists 1st Series, 2nd Series, and so on. There is also a command on this menu to specify the x-axis cells; that is, the numbers or labels displayed along the x-axis to identify the different series. The Group option is used to specify more than one set of values at a time, as described in the next section.

When you select 1st Series, you are prompted to enter the cell coordinates of the first set of values. You can highlight, or paint, the cells as you do with other blocks of cells in Quattro PRO. First move the cell selector to make sure it is on the first value in the series, in this case, B4. Then enter a period to anchor the beginning coordinate. The screen will respond with B4 ..B4. Now you can select 2nd Series and use the cursor-movement keys to move to the second coordinate and highlight the column or row of values. Since values for a series must all be in consecutive cells, the END key may work well to highlight the cells you want. However, you do not need to include the total for the column or row that is being specified as a series, since Quattro PRO will calculate the total of the values in the block for you. Thus, the example uses B4..E4 as the 1st Series.

If you want to change the coordinates as you are highlighting them, the ESCAPE key will unlock the coordinates so that you can begin again from the first coordinate. The BACKSPACE key unlocks the coordinates and returns the cell selector to the cell it occupied when you entered the menu system. Of course, if you know the cell coordinates, you can just type them, instead of pointing to the cells. When you press ENTER to confirm the coordinates, you are returned to the Series menu where you can indicate the next series. After you have entered all three of the series values, press ESCAPE to return to the Graph menu.

Note that the menu shows the settings for the series as you establish them, as shown in Figure 8-17. If you need to change the spreadsheet coordinates of the series values, you select Series and pick the number of

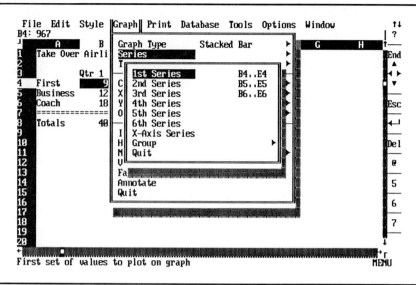

Figure 8-17. *The Series option*

the series you want to check. You will see the currently recorded block of cells highlighted. Press ENTER to confirm this block, or press ESCAPE or BACKSPACE to unlock the coordinates and redefine them. If you want to remove a series, you must use the Reset option, which is described later in this chapter.

Reading and Grouping Series Values

You may wonder why it is necessary to use the Series command when the Fast Graph command reads all of the series for you, including the x-axis. Unfortunately, the Fast Graph command does not know that it should avoid empty cells in a block. For example, Fast Graph applied to the worksheet in Figure 8-18 would produce the graph shown in Figure 8-19. You can see that there are gaps between the data points in each series, leading to greater separation between the bars. Other odd effects will occur if there are labels filling some of the empty cells, such as a line of equal signs (in row 12 in the Figure).

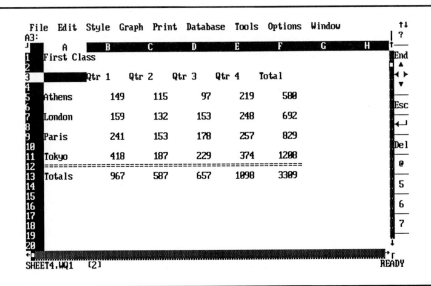

File Edit Style Graph Print Database Tools Options Window

	A	B	C	D	E	F	G	H
1	First Class							
2								
3		Qtr 1	Qtr 2	Qtr 3	Qtr 4	Total		
4								
5	Athens	149	115	97	219	580		
6								
7	London	159	132	153	248	692		
8								
9	Paris	241	153	178	257	829		
10								
11	Tokyo	418	187	229	374	1208		
12	==
13	Totals	967	587	657	1098	3309		

SHEET4.WQ1   [2]   READY

Figure 8-18.   *Spreadsheet with gaps*

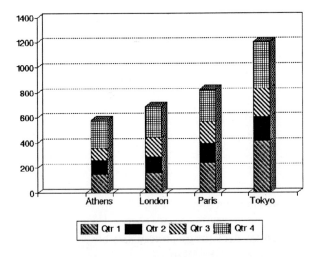

Figure 8-19.   *Fast Graph applied to the worksheet in Figure 8-18*

Another aspect of the Fast Graph command that is not immediately apparent is the way it interprets the block of data to be graphed. The series values in a block can either be read column-wise or row-wise. For example, in the first example in this chapter the three agents, Joe, Sam, and Sue, were read as the series, and the four different packages they sold were read as the x-axis. That is, the data was interpreted column-wise because the series was read from the columns. However, you might have wanted the agents to be the x-axis and the packages the series. You can see the two different graphs in Figure 8-20. The one on the left is the Fast Graph; the one on the right is a manually constructed graph of the same data, reading the series from the rows rather than the columns. (This graph illustrates another feature of Quattro PRO graphs--the ability to include more than one graph in the same spreadsheet.)

The individual selection of series is also a necessity when the data being graphed is not tightly arranged. This is the case when you are graphing data from multiple worksheets. For example, suppose that the data for the graph was not combined into one worksheet, as in Figure 8-13, but spread across several. You might have three separate worksheets, each one storing figures for a single class, as shown in Figure 8-21. In a fourth

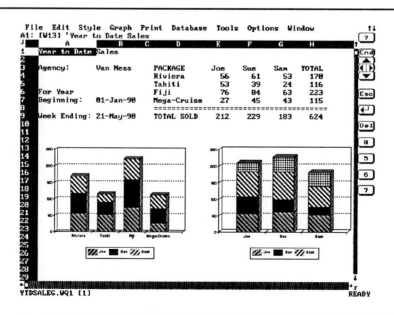

Figure 8-20. *Graphs with different axes on one spreadsheet*

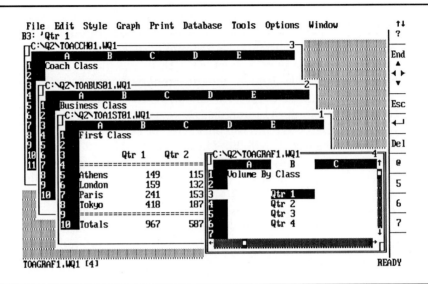

Figure 8-21.   *Three spreadsheets compiled by class*

worksheet you could graph the total figures from the other three, without having to copy the data into the fourth worksheet. Indeed, as you can see from Figure 8-21, the fourth worksheet is relatively small and simply contains the x-axis headings.

To create a graph that refers to data in other worksheets, you simply use the Graph Series command and for each series move to the appropriate worksheet to make the cell selection for the series values. Clearly, you need to specify each series separately for which you cannot use the Fast Graph command. Note that the current graph is the one that is displayed when F10 is pressed. In Figure 8-21 the TOAGRAF1.WQ1 worksheet is current. Also note that you can have the x-axis read from a column of values even though the series values are in rows.

There are times when you have your data series arranged conveniently but separate from the x-axis. In such cases, you can speed up series entry by choosing the Series Group option. When you choose this option you have a choice between Columns and Rows, as shown in Figure 8-22. This worksheet contains quarterly passenger numbers for First Class travelers according to destination city. You can assign each column of values in the block to a series, or each row. In this case, to create a quarterly graph you

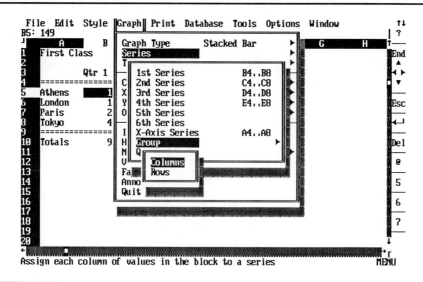

Figure 8-22.   *The Group option*

would use the Rows option. When you select either Columns or Rows you
are prompted for a block of data (as with the Fast Graph option). However,
you do not include the x-axis or labels in this block—just series values.
When you have selected the block you press ENTER. No graph is automatically drawn for you, but you have accomplished in one command the
equivalent of setting four series, one for each city. All you need do now to
get a basic graph is to set the x-axis.

X-Axis

As soon as you have provided at least one series of values, you can actually
view the graph. In this case, Quattro PRO will show three bars, because
there are three parallel observations made about each series of data.
However, until you specify the x-axis values to be displayed along the
bottom of the graph, Quattro PRO cannot tell you what these bars represent. The x-axis values can be numeric values or labels and should be
entered before viewing the graph. This enables Quattro PRO to identify
the observation points along the x-axis. In the case of the First Class

statistics seen in Figure 8-22, or the overall statistics shown in Figure 8-23, the x-axis values are Qtr1, Qtr2, and so on.

To define the x-axis you select Series from the Graph menu and then select x-Axis Series, which is one of the last options on the menu. You are prompted to enter the values as coordinates, as shown in Figure 8-23. You highlight the cells containing the x-axis data (cells B3 through E3 in this case) or type the coordinates, just as you did with the 1st Series command. When you press ENTER to confirm the x-axis coordinates, you are returned to the Graph menu. The coordinates are shown on the menu for reference purposes.

You can have from 1 to 8192 separate data points on the x-axis, if they are stored in a column; or from 1 to 256, if they are stored in a row. However, you will encounter limitations of display space, which may make more than 30 data points difficult to see. In such cases, you do not need to enter any x-axis coordinates. Quattro PRO will simply show a check mark for each set of data.

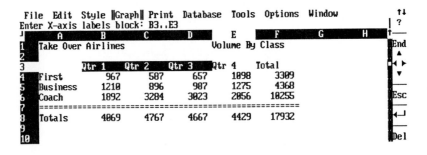

Figure 8-23. *Quarters selected as x-axis*

Viewing the Graph

To produce a basic graph, all Quattro PRO needs is at least one series of values. A set of x-axis values helps only to clarify the chart. When you have entered the values for the volume spreadsheet, you can go ahead and view the graph. The Graph menu contains the View option. When you select View, your screen switches to graphics mode and displays the latest version of the graph you are working on. You cannot change the figures represented in the graph while you are viewing it. After you have viewed a graph, press ENTER or ESCAPE or SPACEBAR to return to the menu you left. The graph view of the volume statistics graph at this point is shown in Figure 8-24.

Although this graph still needs a title to describe what the bars represent, it is important to see how much work has been done so far. Quattro PRO has totaled the figures for each quarter and represented the total as a large bar. It has proportionately divided the bar according to each class of traveler. The scale on the left has been selected to accommodate the

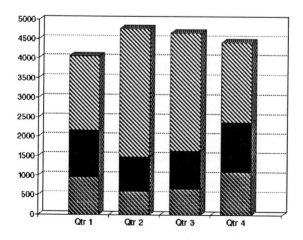

Figure 8-24. *Quarter volume graph*

largest quarterly volume total. The x-axis values—in this case, the labels Qtr1, Qtr2, and so on—are shown along the bottom. At this point the graph also lacks a legend. You create a legend by naming the series values. The Fast Graph command does this automatically by using the labels next to the series value cells. When you are constructing a graph manually, any legend text that you want displayed has to be entered one series at a time. You may also want to enter text for titles and to describe the x- and y-axes.

Adding Text

As you can see from Figure 8-25, there are several areas of the graph to which you can add text. These were diagrammed in Figure 8-5. These pieces of text are fixed to specific points of the graph and should not be confused with the free-floating text that can be added with the Annotate feature, which is described towards the end of this chapter.

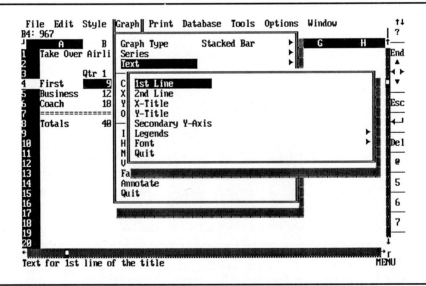

Figure 8-25.   *The Text option*

Text Sources

All of the text added to a Quattro PRO graph can be supplied by worksheet cells. This capability was used by the Fast Graph feature to label the first graph. Using a cell reference for text, rather than simply typing the text, has the advantage of being easy to update. As you saw in Figure 8-9, altering the name from World Cruise to Mega-Cruise automatically updated the graph.

To manually enter text for the graph you select the appropriate item on the Text menu and then type the text you want displayed in the graph, or type the coordinates of the cell containing the label you want used as text in the graph, preceded by a backslash (\ ). Thus, to supply the title Take Over Airlines as the 1st Line of the graph title, you would enter **\A1**. Note that there is no facility for pointing to cells to enter their coordinates in the Text menu. Furthermore, the cell references are not dynamic. If you move the label from A1 to B1, Quattro PRO will not know, and the label will essentially disappear from the graph.

Title Text

Most graphs need a title. To supply one you first select Text from the Graph menu. The item called 1st Line is the one that heads the graph. Select 1st Line from the Text menu and type the text you want, such as **Take Over Airlines**, in the box provided, as shown in Figure 8-26. Alternatively, since this same text has been entered as a label in worksheet cell A1, you can type **\A1**. The title can be 39 characters long. You can use BACKSPACE to correct any errors as you type. If you want to edit the title, the LEFT and RIGHT ARROW keys move the cursor through the text of the title. You can insert new characters to the left of the cursor just by typing them. Pressing ESCAPE while you are typing a title removes the text you have entered. Pressing ESCAPE with nothing on the title edit line returns you to the Text menu. When you have typed the title correctly, press ENTER to confirm it. Quattro PRO returns you to the Text menu, where all or part of the text of the title is visible. This helps you to keep track of text you have entered. Note that when you use a cell reference for text, the cell reference and not the text itself is visible on the Text menu.

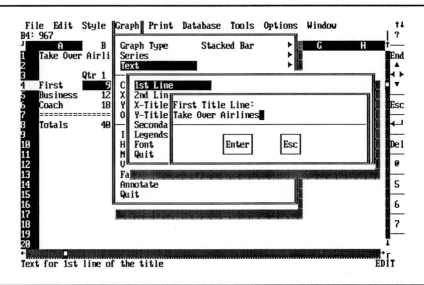

Figure 8-26. *The 1st Line option*

You can add a 2nd Line title, such as Volume by Class, or type **\E1** to use the text from the worksheet. Text to label the x-axis is called the X-Title. In the case of the graph in Figure 8-24 this could be Current Year. The Y-Title labels the y-axis, and the graph in Figure 8-24 should include text that explains what units of measurement are displayed, in this case Passengers. While the x-axis title may sometimes be omitted, a y-axis title is often essential to properly document the graph. Note that if you use a second y-axis, as described later in this chapter, then you can label it with the Secondary Y-axis option.

All of these pieces of text are limited to 39 characters. You can see the graph from Figure 8-24 labeled in Figure 8-27. Note that this figure was produced by using a screen print program, and not the Graph Print option on the Print menu. Since the clarity and dimensions of displayed graphs vary according to display types, this graph may not be an exact replication of what you will see on your screen. Also note that the style of lettering used is the default—the font options for your lettering may be different.

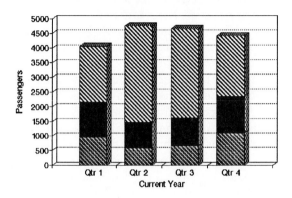

Figure 8-27. *Labeled graph*

The Legend

The one element still lacking in the graph in Figure 8-27 is an explanation of what the different data values represent. You cannot tell from the graph which shading represents which class. The key to a graph is its legend, which you set through the Text Legend option. The legend text for each series consists of either manually entered text, or a reference to a cell where the text can be found. When you select Legends from the Text menu you will be shown a list of six series, one for each of the maximum six sets of values. You enter text here as you do with the other text items. To label the first series, the First Class passengers, you pick 1st Series, and either type the text **First Class** or use the cell reference **\A4**. Remember that the first series appears at the bottom of a stacked bar graph.

The Text Legend menu also includes the Position option, which lets you decide between displaying the legend at the Bottom of the graph, to the

Right of it, or not at all. The default setting is at the Bottom, so that as soon as you enter some legend text a legend will be displayed below the actual graph. You select None from the Position menu to turn off the legend display without erasing the text that you have entered in the legend series. By switching between None and one of the other two choices for Position you can turn the legend on and off. Note that the Annotate feature, described later in this chapter, allows you complete freedom to place the legend wherever you like on the graph.

The maximum number of characters you can enter as the legend text for a series is 19. The number of characters of legend text displayed by the graph will vary according to the dimensions and proportions of the graph. Tall, narrow graphs can accommodate only nine or ten characters in the legend, while wide graphs can show the full 19. After typing the legend text and pressing ENTER, you can proceed to the other series and name them accordingly. After setting up the legends, you can view the results by pressing the F10 key. The resulting graph will look like the one pictured in Figure 8-28. You can see that First Class, the legend for the first series, was truncated in the graph in Figure 8-28. To correct this problem, the font of the legend text could be altered to make it smaller relative to the size of the graph.

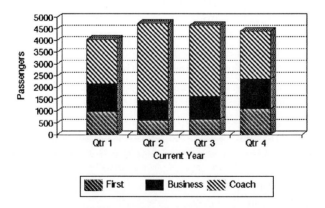

Figure 8-28. *Graph titles in different fonts*

Fonts

You may notice that the text of your titles is displayed in a different typeface, or font, from that seen in Figure 8-28. There are many different fonts available for graphing, including all of those available for enhanced spreadsheet printing (described in Chapter 5). You can adjust the font settings for each piece of text in the chart by using the Font option on the Text menu. When you select Font from the Text menu you see these choices:

Text in each of these areas of the graph can be individually adjusted to achieve the best visual effect. All of the options are the same as in the Text menu, except for Data & Tick Labels. These are the numbers that Quattro PRO adds to the y-axis to document the scale of the graph.

When you select any of the options on the Font menu you are shown a menu of four characteristics that can be adjusted to alter the displayed and printed appearance of your graph, as follows:

Note that selecting the Color option, which leads to a list of colors that can be assigned to the text, does not affect the printed version of your graph unless you have a color printer.

The Typeface option on the Font Characteristics menu leads to a list of available typefaces, with the current selection already highlighted. The list includes the Bitstream fonts, plus the Hershey fonts listed here:

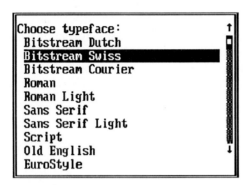

```
Choose typeface:                    ↑
 Bitstream Dutch
 Bitstream Swiss
 Bitstream Courier
 Roman
 Roman Light
 Sans Serif
 Sans Serif Light
 Script
 Old English                        ↓
 EuroStyle
```

In addition, there may be typefaces for specific printers such as those available to LaserJet users. To see the full range of typefaces, scroll down the list. To assign a typeface you highlight your choice and press ENTER. To leave the list without altering the current typeface setting you press ESCAPE.

When you have chosen a typeface you will also want to assign a point size. The Point Size option leads to a list that goes from 8 point to 72 point. To give you an idea of the relative size of these measurements, take a look at Figure 8-28. The 1st Line title is in 16 point and the 2nd Line is in 12 point. The x-axis title is in 8 point.

The Style option allows you to select from the following list of font styles:

```
 Bold
 Italic
 Underlined
 Reset
 Quit
```

The first three items may have the word "On" next to them, indicating that the style has been chosen for the current piece of text. You can turn on one or more of the first three items by highlighting and pressing ENTER, or by typing the first letter.

The Bold option is useful for adding emphasis to a piece of text. The 2nd Line title in Figure 8-28 is shown in Italic. The Underline option causes the text to be displayed with a line below it. The Reset option allows you to turn off all of the attributes.

You can see the effects of font choices while you are still in the menu structure just by pressing F10. While it may take you a while to get used to the effect of different sizes on the text of your graph, you will find that an appropriate choice of font will enhance your graph's appearance and effectiveness.

Graph Keys

When you have designed a graph and returned to READY mode, any changes you make to the cells that make up the x-axis values or the series values will be reflected in the graph and visible the next time you view it. You can try this now by leaving the Graph menu, either with ESCAPE or the Quit option, and typing a new number, 833, for First Class passengers in the third quarter. To see the change that this new number has made to the graph, you can either choose View from the Graph menu, or from READY mode press the Graph key (F10), which displays the current graph. You can have only one graph at a time in memory, and this graph is referred to as the current graph. The next key you press will return you to the Graph menu if you used the Graph View command, or to READY mode if you viewed the graph from READY mode with F10.

The F10 key works either in READY mode or MENU mode, whether or not you are using the Graph menu. Bear in mind that when you have no graphs defined in a worksheet, pressing F10 will cause Quattro PRO to display a blank screen with the message "No series defined." The one exception to this is if you select Text as the Graph type but define no series values. In this case you get a blank graph screen on which to place text with the Annotate feature.

There is one special key to use while viewing a graph and that is the /
key. This activates Quattro PRO's Annotate feature, which is a complete
drawing program built into the Graph feature. With this feature,
described later in the chapter, you can enhance your graphs with a
virtually unlimited range of images. You can even use Annotate to create
pictures that are not graphs but shapes and symbols, like the ones in
Figure 8-29, that can be printed from Quattro PRO or inserted into
spreadsheets. However, before exploring these exciting possibilities it is
important to learn the mundane but vital commands needed to save and
organize your work with graphs.

Naming and Storing Graphs

Having viewed your graph and decided that it is acceptable, you might be
tempted to rush to print the graph. But before proceeding, you should take

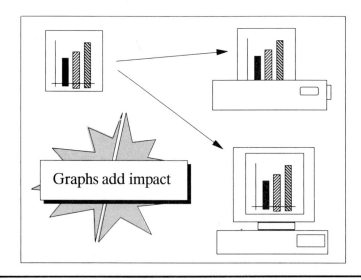

Figure 8-29.   *Pictures created by using Annotate*

a moment to save your work. So far, none of your graphing work has been stored by Quattro PRO. The settings for the x- and y-axes, your titles, the choice of font, and so forth are still only in memory. You must issue the File Save or File Save As command to save the worksheet and the graph settings.

Storing Graph Names

If you design a graph and then store your worksheet, you will be able to see the graph the next time you retrieve the file simply by pressing F10, or by using the Graph View command. Having built one graph, however, you may wish to go on to create another. Since Quattro PRO can have only one graph in memory at a time, changing the graph settings at this point would alter the graph you just designed. To store the collection of settings that together produce the graph you have just viewed so that you can recall them later, you assign a name to the graph, much the same as you do when naming a block of cells. Select Name from the Graph menu and you will see the five options shown here:

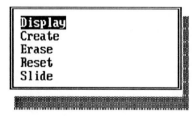

Select Create and you will see a list of any previously stored graphs. Whether or not there are any previously stored graphs, you will be prompted with "Enter graph name:". You can highlight one of the existing names and press ENTER to replace that graph with the current one, or you can simply type a new name and press ENTER. Here you can see that a couple of graphs have already been named:

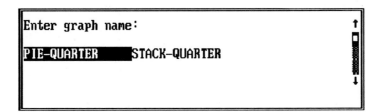

When you have entered a name, you are returned to the Graph menu. If you want to see a previously named graph, select Name again, and then select Display. Finally, select a name from the list. You can remove names from the list with Erase or completely remove all graph names with Reset. The Reset command requires that you answer Yes or No to the question "Delete all named graphs?", since the command is a destructive one, wiping out all named graph settings.

The last option on the Graph Name menu is Slide. Using this option you can create a *slide show* with Quattro PRO. This consists of a series of graphs displayed one after the other. See the section on "Making Slide Shows" in Chapter 13 for more on this command.

Remember, even though you have assigned a name to a graph you still must save the worksheet file to store the graph names on disk.

Storing Graph Files

There may be times when you want to store a graph as a *picture file*, which contains the necessary data for other programs to read the graph as an image and display it, edit it, or print it. To save a graph in this type of file, you print it to a file with the Graph Print option on the Print menu. You then use the Write Graph File option, which is described in the next section.

Finer Points of Graph Printing

When you have stored the worksheet containing the current graph settings, you can proceed to print the graph. You do not have to store before printing, but it is advisable. The Graph Print option on the Print menu prints out the latest version of the current graph if the Destination setting is Graph Printer. You should press F10 once more before printing to make sure that the graph you are about to print is the correct one.

Telling Quattro PRO About Printers

When you select Graph Print from the Print menu you will see a menu like the following:

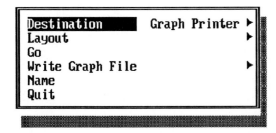

You can see that the default Destination setting is Graph Printer. The Layout option leads to a submenu of settings that describe how you want the graph sized and placed on the page. The Write Graph File option is for creating files from graphic output.

Destination

When you select Destination from the Print menu, you can choose to send the graphic output to one of three places: File, Graph Printer, or Screen Preview. The last option, Screen Preview, shows you what the graph will look like when printed, including the dimensions and placement on the page. The preview system for graphs works in the same way as that for spreadsheets (described at the end of Chapter 5).

If you want to store a Quattro PRO graph as a text file that can be printed later or used by another program, select File as the destination of the print operation. Quattro PRO prompts you to enter a file name of up to eight letters for the graph. When you enter the file name, Quattro PRO sets the destination to which a PRN file containing a data image of the current graph would be written. To create this graph, execute the Graph Print Go command. An alternative file format for storing graphic images is the EPS type, which you can create by using the Write Graph File option on the Graph Print menu.

Write Graph File

To store your graph in a special file that can be read by other programs, you select Write Graph File from the Graph Print menu. The options are EPS and PIC. The EPS format is Encapsulated PostScript. This can be read by a number of other programs, and can be printed on a printer that understands the PostScript page description language, such as the Apple Laser-Writer. For example, when you are using the TOPS network to connect IBM PCs to Apple Macintoshes and LaserWriters you can use the TOPS command TPRINT or the TOPS NetPrint program to send your EPS file to a LaserWriter on the network. The EPS format preserves all of the graph's visual qualities; however, none of the graph file formats are dynamic. This means that once a graph is written to a file it does not automatically change when the worksheet that generated the graph is updated.

The PIC format is compatible with Lotus 1-2-3, which enables 1-2-3 to print Quattro PRO graphs. However, 1-2-3 graphs are limited in scope. Thus, features unique to Quattro PRO—such as special fonts, free-floating text, and drawn objects—are lost when a file is stored in the PIC format.

To create a specialized file of either of the two types, you select the correct type from the list. For example, to create an EPS file you select EPS from the Write Graph File menu and then enter a file name of up to eight letters. Quattro PRO will add the EPS extension. When you press ENTER the file is created on disk.

Layout

When you have selected Graph Printer as the Destination on the Graph Print menu and picked Go, Quattro PRO prints the current graph with the current page layout. The default page layout produces a graph that covers the width of a regular sheet of paper and is positioned halfway between the top and bottom of the paper. The results for the Take Over Airlines example are shown in Figure 8-30. Quattro PRO assumes you are using 8 1/2– × 11-inch paper. This is the graph that was shown as a screen in Figure 8-28.

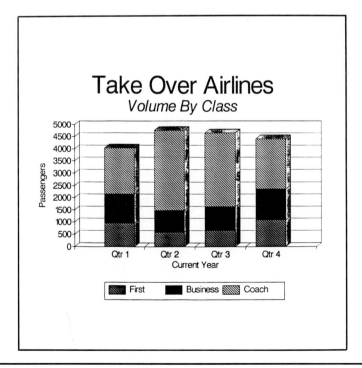

Figure 8-30. *Graph printed with default page layout*

While the default setting is acceptable in many cases, there will probably be times when you want to alter the size and shape of the finished graph. You do this with the Layout option of the Graph Print menu. As shown in the following illustration, the Layout menu lets you define the dimensions of the printed graph in either inches, which is the default, or centimeters:

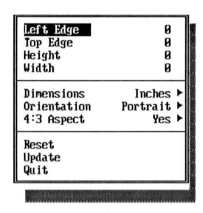

The Left Edge setting indicates the graph's left margin, the number of inches or centimeters from the left edge of the paper. The Top Edge setting indicates the top margin, where Quattro PRO should start printing the graph.

In this illustration you can see that the dimensions of the graph are defined as 4 inches high and 4 inches wide. You might expect that the resulting graph will be square. However, Quattro PRO gives you the option of either preserving a standard ratio of width to height (4:3) or allowing the actual ratio of height to width measurements to determine the proportions of the finished graph. If you select Yes for the 4:3 Aspect option on the Layout menu Quattro PRO will not print the graph as a square. Instead the rectangular shape of the graph is preserved within the space you have allotted. For example, a graph that is laid out as 4 inches by 4 inches will have an x-axis side that is 4 inches long, but the y-axis side will be about 3 inches. However, if you select No for the 4:3 Aspect option, Quattro PRO will scale the graph to the dimensions you have specified, and in this example, you will get a graph that is literally square.

You will find that some printers take a long time to produce full-page graphs, particularly at high resolution. Consequently, you may want to limit their size when printing the first few versions until you have the design ready for a final printing. Note that in their standard configuration, the HP LaserJet II and some other laser printers cannot accept a full graphics image at 300 dots per inch. They must print full-page graphs at 150 dpi or print half-size graphs at 300 dpi. (A LaserJet requires 1MB of memory to print a full-page graph at 300 dpi.)

The Orientation setting on the Layout menu is where you choose between the default (the Landscape placement of the image at right angles to the print path) and the alternative, which is Portrait, or vertical placement. In Figure 8-31 you can see a diagram—drawn with Quattro PRO—of the difference between Landscape and Portrait. If you print the graph in Portrait orientation, the height measurement is the y-axis of a stacked bar graph and the width measurement is the x-axis. In Landscape orientation the height measurement is the x-axis and the width is the y-axis.

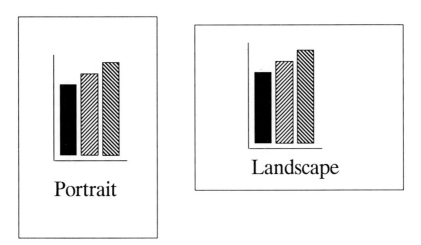

Figure 8-31. *Choices of graph orientation*

Go

With the Destination and Layout information recorded, you can initiate printing with the Go command on the Print menu. Since your printer or plotter has to translate the screen image into a series of dots or pen strokes, some time can pass before the image of the graph appears. The "Now Printing" message appears along with the message "Ctrl-Break to stop". Quattro PRO will stop printing the graph if you press CTRL-BREAK. Do so if you realize you have made a mistake and do not want to complete the printing.

There is one menu item that affects printing of graphs that is not found within the Graph menus. The Options Hardware Printers menu has an item called Plotter Speed. This lets you adjust the speed of your plotter. You may need to do this because some surfaces you plot onto, such as plastic overheads, accept ink better at lower speeds. When you select Plotter Speed, you can enter a value from 0 to 9, with 0 being the fastest, or current speed.

Changing Graph Types

The examples so far in this chapter have featured the default graph type, Stacked Bar. There are nine more types of graph available in Quattro PRO and you can mix types within a graph. The type of graph is easily changed and does not require that you select the values to be graphed all over again. Once you have selected appropriate values, you can see them graphed in each of the different graph types. The main types of graph were shown earlier in Figure 8-16.

Bar Types

Four of the Quattro PRO graph types are variations of a bar graph. The stacked bar graph you have seen so far is a good way to show relative performance across the x-axis for cumulative values. For example, you can clearly see in Figure 8-30 that total volume varied from quarter to quarter.

To see the plain bar graph, select Graph Type from the Graph menu and then select Bar. This version of the graph can then be displayed with the View option or the F10 key. It will look like the graph shown in Figure 8-32. Each piece of data is represented by a separate bar. This graph makes gauging the overall performance in each quarter more difficult, but it makes comparing the relative performance per quarter in each class somewhat easier. Notice that the scale for a bar graph does not need to be as large as that of the stacked bar graph shown earlier. Quattro PRO automatically adjusts the Y-scale.

The third type of bar graph produced by Quattro PRO is the Rotated Bar, shown in Figure 8-33. This chart is very effective when you want to highlight the performance of different categories. The viewer's eye is immediately drawn to the longest bar. If you graph a single series of values this graph is quite effective, as shown later in Figure 8-46 where the use of data labels is demonstrated. Note that the x-axis is the vertical axis in a rotated bar graph.

The fourth type of bar graph is called Column, which is also known as the 100% bar. As you can see from the example on the left of Figure 8-34, this graph type displays a single column that gives a percentage

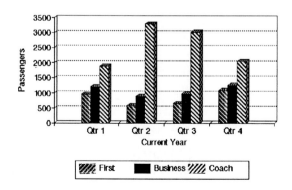

Figure 8-32. *Plain bar graph*

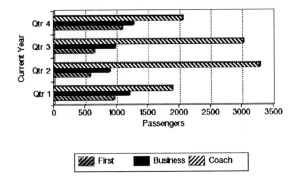

Figure 8 -33.   *Rotated bar graph*

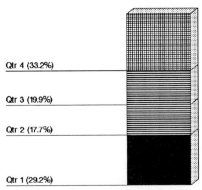

Figure 8 -34.   *Column graph*

breakdown of a single series of values. If you select Column for the same series used in Figure 8-33, you will get a breakdown of the first series—the volume of First class passengers—by quarter, as shown in Figure 8-34. Seeing a chart of the percentage of annual volume attained in each quarter is probably not that useful. The percentage breakdown that you would probably like to see is the total volume for the year according to class. For this task the column graph is ideal, although the series needs to be redefined. The first series would be cells F4..F6 of the worksheet. There would be no other y-axis series. Column charts do not use legend text. Instead, you use the x-axis series to label the data. Thus, the x-axis series would be cells A4..A6. When the graph is drawn, the percentage break-down of the total will be provided next to the names, as you can see from the resulting graph on the left of Figure 8-35. Notice the similarity of a column graph to a pie chart. A column graph is essentially a rectangular pie chart.

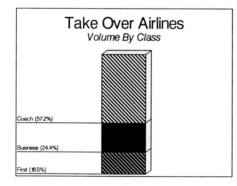 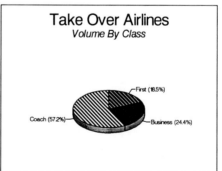

Figure 8-35. *Column graph and pie chart*

Pie Charts

The pie chart is an effective image when you want to display the proportional distribution of values within a single whole. Like a column graph, the pie chart is a one-dimensional graph; it uses only one series of values. If you were to select Pie as the Graph Type for the series graphed in Figure 8-32 or 8-33, you would see the breakdown of the first data series; that is, the First class volume broken down between quarters. What you probably prefer is to show the total volume for the year broken down by class. This is done by redefining the first series as cells F4..F6 of the worksheet. There would be no other y-axis series. You would use the x-axis series to label the data. Thus the x-axis series would be A4..A6. As you can see from the results on the right of Figure 8-35, the percentage breakdown of the total is provided next to the names. This is one of the many elements of a pie chart that can be changed, as described in the following section, "Customizing Graphs."

Line Graphs

When you want data values to appear as points, and lines to be drawn connecting the points, then you need the line graph type. This is used effectively for showing changes in data over time, as in the chart seen in Figure 8-36, which graphs the volume figures. You can use different symbols for the *markers* that represent data points, or you can turn them off and just use lines to connect the points. Alternatively, you can turn off the lines and just use markers for the data. You make these changes through the Customize series command.

Area Graphs

When you want to represent data as an expanse of space rather than as a line or bar, then you can use the area graph, an example of which is shown in Figure 8-37. Note that this type of chart does not allow accurate comparison of relative series values but does give a strong visual impact.

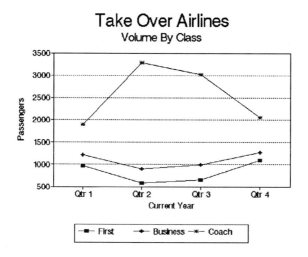

Figure 8 -36. *Line graph*

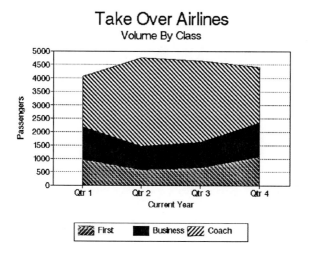

Figure 8 -37. *Area graph*

Hi-Low Graphs

To graph stock price and trading in other commodities in the classic format of hi-low charts, you select the Hi-low option. In its basic form this graph uses two series, one for the highest price during each trading period and the other for the lowest. Each pair of prices is represented by a vertical line from the high number down to the low number. Two further series can be added for the closing price and opening price of the period. These are represented by small horizontal lines, as shown on the graph in Figure 8-38.

Text Graphs

The diagrams in Figures 8-29 and 8-31 were created with the feature in Quattro PRO known as the Graph Annotator. This allows you to place free-floating text, arrows, shapes, and symbols on a graph. You can actually choose a type of graph, Text, that does not require a data series. This allows you to use a blank graph area for designs created entirely by

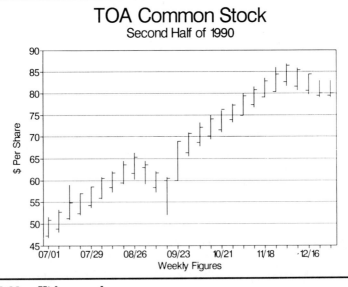

Figure 8-38.   *Hi-low graph*

the Graph Annotator. The Annotate feature is described in greater detail at the end of this chapter.

XY Graphs

The XY graph is mainly used to show the distribution of values, and thus it is helpful when you are analyzing statistical data. XY graphs are described in the context of other Quattro PRO statistical features in Chapter 9.

Customizing Graphs

Quattro PRO is so rich in features for customizing graphs that an entire book could be devoted to the subject. Just about every aspect of a chart can be fine tuned to your personal whim. There are two main approaches to customizing graphs with Quattro PRO. You can use the Annotate feature, described later in this chapter, and you can use the Graph menu, as described in this section. You have already seen that text can be presented in a variety of typefaces, styles, and sizes. The four items in the second section of the Graph menu are used to customize other aspects of a graph: Customize Series, X-axis, Y-axis, and Overall.

Customize Series

In Figure 8-39 you can see the Customize Series menu displayed. The first option allows you to select the colors for each of the six series on the graph. When you select Colors you are shown a list of the series with their current color settings. When you select a specific series, a range of possible colors appears from which to choose. This appears as a palette, as shown in Figure 8-40, if you are using graphics mode. The current choice is outlined and you can use your mouse or the arrow keys to move the selection box to another color. Click the mouse button or press ENTER to select the color

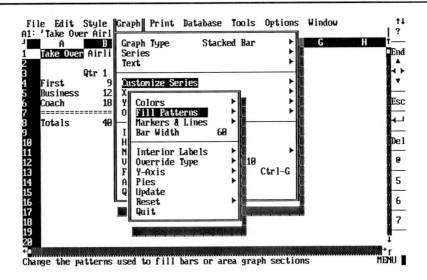

Figure 8 -39. *The Customize Series option*

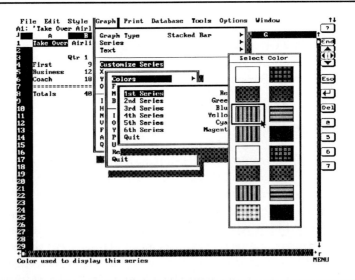

Figure 8 -40. *The color palette in graphics mode*

of your choice. If you are not using graphics mode the color choices appear as a list, as shown in Figure 8-41.

The Fill Patterns option lets you pick a pattern to be used in the bars of bar graphs, the areas of area graphs, and the slices of pie charts. There are 16 different patterns to choose from and they appear as a palette, as shown in Figure 8-42, if you are using graphics mode. Otherwise, the choices are listed as shown in Figure 8-43.

The Markers & Lines option allows you to control the appearance of line and XY graphs by varying three elements for each of the six series. You can vary Line Styles, Markers, and Formats. The eight choices for lines are: Solid, Dotted, Centered, Dashed, Heavy Solid, Heavy Dotted, Heavy Centered, and Heavy Dashed. The ten choices for Markers are: Filled Square, Plus sign, Asterisk, Empty Square, an X, Filled Triangle, Hourglass, Square with X, Vertical Line, and Horizontal Line. The four possibilities for the Formats in a line or XY chart are Lines, Symbols, Both (lines and symbols), or Neither (no lines or symbols). Given so many options you do not have to be a great mathematician to figure out that the total number of design combinations for line graphs is astronomical.

Figure 8-41. *The Colors menu*

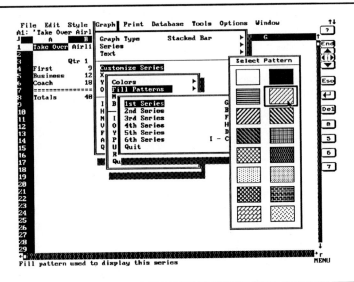

Figure 8-42.   *The Fill Patterns palette in graphics mode*

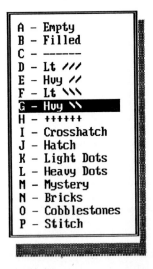

Figure 8-43.   *The Fill Patterns menu*

When you are creating a bar graph, the spacing between bars may not be to your liking. You can use the Bar Width option on the Customize Series menu to alter the spacing. You can make the thickness of the bars anything from 20%, which is really skinny, to 90%, which leaves virtually no gap between the bars. When you select Bar Width, just type in the desired number and press ENTER.

Y-Axis Customizing

There are times when the automatic scale applied to the axes by Quattro PRO does not give the desired effect. On the right side of Figure 8-44 you can see the effect of graphing First class volume figures with an upper limit on the y-axis of 2000 and a base line number of 500. This makes the performance look pretty poor compared to the graph on the left. Both graphs use the same numbers, but the graph on the left uses the automatic scaling of the y-axis whereas the one on the right has had the y-axis customized. This was done because the company goal is 2000 First class passengers per quarter, and the minimum required to make a profit is 500. This adjustment puts the performance into a different perspective.

You adjust the y-axis by selecting Y-axis from the Graph menu and using the options shown here:

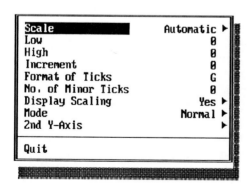

The Scale setting is either Automatic, which is the default, or Manual. When you alter the other settings on the Y-axis menu to create a customized scale you can turn this scale on by selecting Automatic, or turn it off by using Manual.

First Class Volume

First Class Volume

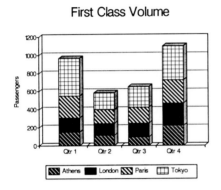
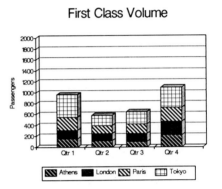

Figure 8 -44.   *Relative y-axis scales*

The Low and High settings determine the boundaries of the scale, normally from 0 to a round number larger than the largest number you want to graph. However, as you can see from Figure 8-43, the use of other starting and ending points can be effective, if these are properly documented in the graph. A typical example of setting the graph's *origin*, (the beginning point of the y-axis), is seen in weekly charts of average stock prices. These are often shown with an origin larger than 0 so as to emphasize the day-to-day variation of the figures.

The Increment affects the numeric gap between the values on the y-axis scale. For example, for the numbers graphed in Figure 8-44 the automatically selected values for the y-axis were 0 to 1200 in 200-unit increments. The manually adjusted graph on the right of Figure 8-44 also uses 200-unit increments.

The Format of Ticks is a rather strange sounding option that is in fact very important. The numbers on the y-axis can be formatted using any of the worksheet formats, such as Currency, Fixed, and so on. For example, in Figure 8-43, the Comma format is used to place commas as thousands separators. This format will also put negative numbers in parentheses.

The No. of Minor Ticks option allows you to create small lines on the y-axis scale instead of numbers. For example, if you set the increment to 50 you will have this series of numbers: 0, 50, 100, 150, 200, and so on. If you request a No. of Minor Ticks setting of 1, then Quattro PRO will skip every other number, showing 100, 200, and so on, and placing tick marks at 50, 150, and so on. Every third scale number is displayed by using a setting of 2.

When Quattro PRO graphs large numbers that run into the thousands or millions, those units are displayed as text on the axis and the actual axis numbers are adjusted accordingly. You can turn off the display of this text if you want, by selecting No for Display Scaling. Although some graphs may appear to need no explanation of the scale, you should use this option to avoid graphs that are deceptive or hard to read.

When you are dealing with large numbers or scientific data you may want to use a logarithmic scale rather than a normal scale. To turn the y-axis scale to log mode, select Mode and then Log. Select Normal to go back to a regular scale. Be sure to document the use of a logarithmic scale on the graph to avoid confusion.

Quattro PRO allows you to set a second y-axis for mixing graph data. When you do this you can completely customize the second axis by choosing the 2nd Y-axis option. You can also use this option to turn off the display of scaling for the second y-axis. An example of a graph with dual y-axes is given later in this chapter.

X-Axis Customizing

There are times when you also want to customize the x-axis. In Figure 8-38 you saw a graph of stock prices. The x-axis consists of a series of dates from column B in the worksheet that generated the graph shown in Figure 8-44. These dates are all seven days apart. If every date was displayed on the x-axis, then they would be unreadable. There are two approaches to clarifying the x-axis when it is crowded. You can have the x-axis series represented on two rows instead of one, and you can skip some of the values. The latter approach was taken in Figure 8-38 where only every fourth date was shown.

You typically use the X-axis option on the Graph menu to adjust the x-axis when it consists of numbers and the graph type is XY. Customizing the x-axis may be redundant when the x-axis series is labels, as is the case when graphing quarterly volume. You can see that the X-axis options closely match those on the Y-axis menu:

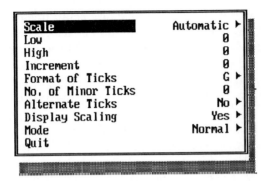

The Scale can be set to Automatic to have Quattro PRO design the x-axis or you can turn on your own design by setting the Scale to Manual and using the other menu options. The Alternate Ticks option is set to Yes when you need to use two rows for your x-axis data. The No. of Minor Ticks option is adjusted to replace labels in the x-axis with minor tick marks. In the example in Figure 8-38, this was set at 3 to produce a date every fourth label.

Overall Customizing

The options for Overall customizing are Grid, Outlines, Background Color, Three-D, and Color/B&W, as shown here:

The last of these options was used in all of the graphs in this chapter to print them in black and white as opposed to color. The nice part of the Color/B&W command is that after you have used B&W you can turn the color back on and Quattro PRO will reinstate all of the default color choices. Do not select B&W if you have customized colors that you want to save.

The Grid option allows you to place lines on your graph. You can use Horizontal, Vertical, or Both. Use the Clear option to remove the lines. The grids you create can be customized by choosing Grid Color, Line Style, and Fill Color.

The Outlines option is used to put boxes and other demarcation around three elements of the graph: Titles, Legend, and Graph (the entire chart, including text and legend). Each of these elements can be outlined with the following: Box, Double-line, Thick-line, Shadow, 3D, or Round Rectangle. The last choice for an outline is None, to turn off the outline. The 3D option draws a perspective box behind an object to give it an appearance of depth. The Shadow option is rather effective for text and was used in Figure 8-14.

The Background Color option on the Overall menu simply lets you choose the color used for the background of the graph, while the Three-D option adds perspective lines to the chart box to give an impression of depth. You can see the effect of Three-D on a pie chart in Figure 8-35 and again in Figure 8-45.

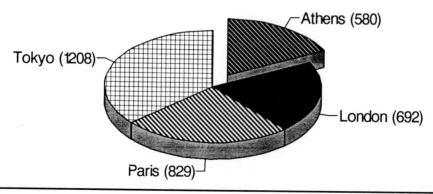

Figure 8-45. *Pie chart in 3-D*

Customizing Pies

There is a whole series of settings that you can use to customize pie charts like the one shown in Figure 8-45. This chart has the Overall option called Three-D set to Yes. The first slice of the pie is exploded from the rest, and the labels show the data values. To adjust a pie chart you first select Customize Series from the Graph menu and then Pies. The Pies menu shows you the various aspects of pie charts that can be altered to fit your preferences, as follows:

In addition to Explode, you can select Patterns to fill the pie slices, Colors to change the color displays of the pie chart, and the Label Format, which will be discussed shortly. You can also add or remove lines called Tick Marks between labels and slices.

When you select Explode from the Pies menu, you are shown a menu of slices 1 through 9. The 1st slice is the leftmost or topmost value in the 1st Series; in Figure 8-45, this is Athens. If you select 1st Slice, you can see the way Quattro PRO records your explosion preference. The Explode choice is normally set to Don't Explode. To change this setting, highlight Explode and press ENTER or type **E**. This tells Quattro PRO to display the first slice offset from the rest, as is the case in Figure 8-45.

When you select Label Format from the Pies menu, you have four options: Value, %, $, and None. The Value option is the one used in Figure 8-45. The % option, which is the default setting, was used in Figure 8-35. If the values are dollars you can use the $ option, which displays the actual values preceded by a dollar sign. Alternatively, you can suppress any value display by selecting None.

Remember that the title for a pie chart will probably be different from that used for other graphs of related data. You can use the Text option from the Graph menu to enter a correct title.

Updating and Resetting Custom Features

If many of the aspects of the graph you are designing are different from the previous one, you can selectively reset those aspects through the Reset option on the Customize Series menu shown in Figure 8-39. Selecting Graph will completely erase the graph settings, so use it with care.

Interior Labels

The graph in Figure 8-46 shows the First class volume figures in a rotated bar graph. The actual volume figures for each city are displayed on the graph by means of the Interior Labels option. Such a display of numbers

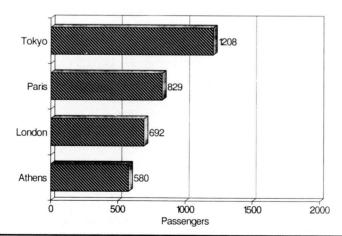

Figure 8 -46. *Rotated bar graph with interior labels*

can be helpful when the graph needs to be used for accurate reporting and also enhances the graph's visual effect.

When you select Interior Labels from the Series menu, you can select each series in turn and specify the spreadsheet coordinates of the data to be used to identify points of the series on the graph. The Interior Labels menu is shown in Figure 8-47. In the example in Figure 8-46, the label cells are the same as the first series cells. However, the labels for your graph do not need to be the values in the chart; they can be any set of numbers or labels. For example, you could use the city names to label the bars by using the cells that are the X-axis series. Alternatively, you could enter into the worksheet a series of remarks about the values represented in the chart and then display them as interior labels. You can see that this was done in Figure 8-47. The labels in column G have been selected as labels for the graph. The results are shown in Figure 8-48. Note that you do not have to label every data point. If you erased cells G5, G7, and G8, but still used the block G5..G8 for the interior labels setting, the graph would only show the comment for London.

When you have entered the cell coordinates for interior labels, you are prompted for the position of the labels on the graph. Your choices are Center, Left, Above, Right, Below, or None. The None option suppresses

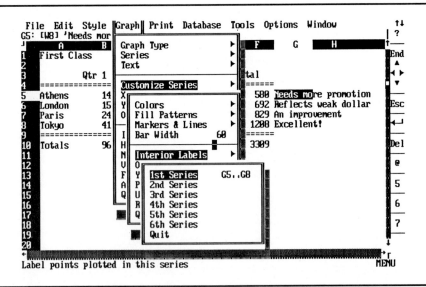

Figure 8-47.   *The Interior Labels option*

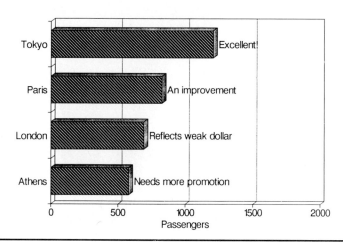

Figure 8-48. *Remarks as interior labels*

display of that set of labels. When you have chosen an appropriate position, you are returned to the Interior Labels menu to work on the next series. The labels in Figures 8-46 and 8-48 are shown with a position setting of Right. Also note that the graph has customized y-axis settings that elongate the graph to make room for the labels.

Multiple Graph Types and Y-Axes

In Figure 8-44 you saw two graphs of passenger volume. The one on the right was customized to show that the passenger volume was not as great as it might appear in the graph on the left, relative to expectations. You might want to create a graph that shows the expectations or goals relative to performance. You can see an example of this in Figure 8-49. The total volume for each quarter is shown as a bar, while the goal for the quarter is shown as a line.

To create this graph from the worksheet in Figure 8-50 you need to establish the totals in cells B10..E10 as the first series and the goal figures in B13..E13 as the second series. The x-axis series is cells B3..E3. If you

First Class Volume

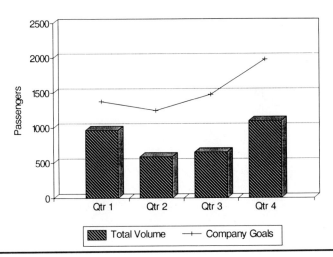

Figure 8-49.   *Combined bar and line graph*

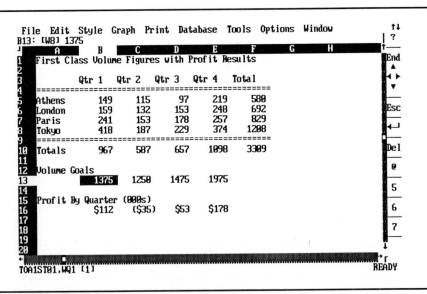

Figure 8-50.   *Spreadsheet of unrelated numbers*

already have data series established you can use the Graph Customize
Reset command to delete the previous series settings, as shown here:

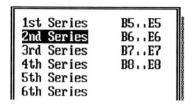

You highlight the series you want to reset and press ENTER. In the
illustration the user is about to remove the 2nd Series coordinates. Bear
in mind that this action cancels the series coordinates but does not change
such items as graph type and graph text. Also bear in mind that the Graph
option on this menu removes all graph settings including text.

Having established the correct data series you can select Bar as the
Graph Type. This will show both series of data as bars. In order to show
the first series as bars but the second as a line you need to use the
Customize Override Type menu shown here:

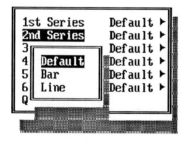

This menu shows each of the six series and the current type setting for the
series. At first these are all the defaults, meaning whatever you have
selected as the current graph type. If you select one of the series you can
then choose between Default, Bar, and Line. In this case, Line will be
chosen for the second series. The results are shown in Figure 8-49.

While the ability to mix graph types increases your options for making a clear presentation of the facts, it does have limitations. You cannot mix stacked bar, pie, column, or area graphs. You can mix only line, mix marker, and bar graphs. Mixing graph types does not get around the problem posed by mixing numbers of completely different types. For example, what if you wanted to add the profit figures to the graph in Figure 8-49? These numbers, in row 16 of the worksheet in Figure 8-50, are in dollars and bear little relation to the other numbers. To help you graph such unrelated numbers, Quattro PRO provides the ability to add a second y-axis.

To graph the profit numbers on a second y-axis you first add cells B16..E16 as the third series. Then you select the Y-Axis option on the Customize Series menu. This allows you to assign each series to either the Primary or the Secondary axis, as shown here:

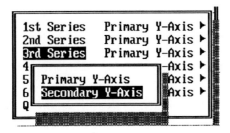

The third series is assigned to the second axis. Since the current graph type is bar, the profit will initially appear as a bar. To change this to a more suitable line type you use the Override Type command on the Customize menu, selecting Line for the third series. The results are shown in Figure 8-51.

Note that the graph in Figure 8-51 has been customized slightly from the default settings. The Fill Patterns option on the Graph Customize menu was used to clarify the bars for the first series. The Marker and Lines option on the Customize Series menu was used to alter the third series display. First, the Line Styles command was used to alter the style of line for the series, in order to distinguish it from the goal line. Then the Markers option was used to make asterisks the symbol for the profit line. The Text Secondary Y-axis command was used to add the words Dollars

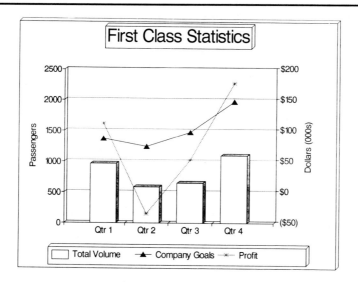

Figure 8-51. *Using a second Y-axis*

(000s) to the graph. The actual scale of the secondary axis was set automatically by Quattro PRO but the 2nd Y-axis command from the Customize Y-axis menu was used to change the format of the numbers to Currency with zero decimal places. Finally, the Overall command was used to add boxes around the legend, the title, and the entire graph. The box style was set to 3D as was the overall style of the graph.

By the careful mixing of features as shown in this example it is possible to use Quattro PRO to graph most information in an attractive and effective manner. When you want to go further in your customization, you can use the Annotate feature described next.

Annotation—The Finishing Touch

The Graph Annotate feature in Quattro PRO is really a full-featured built-in drawing program. You can use it to turn ordinary worksheet-generated graphs into stunning visuals, or even to create drawings that are not related to figures in the spreadsheet. In this area of Quattro PRO, a mouse—while not mandatory—is certainly a great plus, making quick work of drawing and coloring shapes and lines, as well as moving elements of the graph and performing cut-and-paste operations.

The Annotate Screen

You can see the Annotate feature at work in Figure 8-52, where a piece of text is being added to a stacked bar graph. Note that this level of customizing goes beyond the use of interior labels. The text that has been added here can be floated to any point on the graph, resized, or even enclosed in a variety of box styles. The elements of the graph that you have created with the other graph commands can also be moved about. The legend can be moved to a new location, as can any graph text.

There are two ways to get to the Annotate feature. When you view a graph you can press the / key. You can also use the Annotate option from the Graph menu. In both cases the current graph is placed into a window

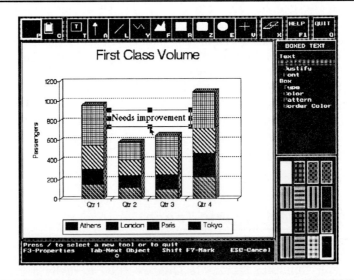

Figure 8-52.   *Text added by using Annotate*

and a panel of tools is provided. If you have used paint or draw programs with a mouse before, then the operation of the Annotate feature will be familiar. Basically, you click on the pointer box labeled P in the top-left corner of the screen to make your mouse or cursor keys act as the selector. Then you click on objects in the graph to select them, or press the TAB key to move from one item to another.

You click on the various tools in the top menu bar to select them and draw lines, polygons, rectangles, and circles by the click-and-drag method. Each object in the graph has a set of handles on it (the small boxes around the boxed text in Figure 8-52). If you point to one of these boxes and then click and drag you can alter the size and shape of the object. If you click within the selected object you can move it to another location on the screen. The menus and palettes on the right side of the screen are used for editing the colors, patterns, and other attributes of the objects you select. You click on the clipboard, the second box, to get into EDIT mode where you can copy and paste elements of the graph and move them to the front or back of the picture. You can click on the Text tool to type free-floating text for the graph.

In the lower part of the screen a very helpful set of instructions guides you through the appropriate actions and provides keystroke alternatives to the mouse commands. In Figure 8-53 you can see the way that the Annotate feature transforms a good but basic graph into a stunning visual. The legend was moved to the top of the chart; the title was moved to the bottom. A piece of boxed text was added, along with two arrows. Then a polygon in the shape of an aircraft was drawn and placed below the main graph area using the clipboard. In Chapter 13 you will find further discussion of this feature and how it can be applied.

Annotated Text Charts

When you want to use the Annotate feature to create a chart like the one in Figure 8-29 that is not based on any numbers in a worksheet you simply open a new worksheet and select Text as the graph type. You can then select Annotate and a fresh canvas appears, ready for you to add text, shapes, or whatever you desire. The capability to perform these actions from within what is ostensibly a spreadsheet program makes Quattro PRO one of the most versatile software packages around. In Figure 8-54 you can see an example of a text chart, which shows that the term really does not do justice to the results. This graphic can even be inserted into a spreadsheet to make very interesting effects.

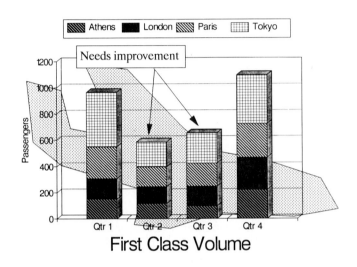

Figure 8-53.   *Graphics created by using Annotate*

Figure 8-54.   *A text chart*

Graph Tips

Given the flexibility of Quattro PRO there are some basic graphics design guidelines you should consider when you need to present data to others. In the rush to add visual interest to everything that passes for information in today's office, the words of Aristotle about painting should be heeded by those who produce presentation graphics: "The most brilliant colors, spread at random and without design, will give far less pleasure than the simplest outline of a figure." Quattro PRO is not as hampered by its relative lack of color as some would suggest. Do not go to great lengths to produce color charts unless there is a real need for them to be in color.

With Quattro PRO you can produce excellent graphs as long as you follow the golden rule of graphics: Keep it simple. Use several separate graphs instead of placing too much on one graph. Remember that the key elements of a good graph are unity, balance, contrast, and meaning. If your graphs contain all four elements, they will be an effective means of communicating information.

In some situations, there is no substitute for a number chart or data table. This is essentially a printed report with the numbers in the spreadsheet arranged in columns and rows with titles and totals (such as the one in Chapter 5). When you need to provide extensive detail as well as summary information, then a spreadsheet printout is the best type of report to use.

There are several techniques that enable you to make charts with Quattro PRO without using the graph commands. Particularly when it comes to word charts, Quattro PRO's publishing features allow it to organize your words and print them out in attractive designs like the one shown in Chapter 1, Figure 1-12. The techniques for making word charts are discussed in Chapter 13.

When you have a lot of graphs to display you can use the slide show feature in Quattro PRO to make presentations with your PC. The techniques for making slide shows are discussed in Chapter 13.

9 Dates and Advanced Commands

Quattro PRO can treat dates mathematically, allowing you to quantify time-related information and manipulate it for spreadsheet and database applications. This chapter begins by explaining how the program manipulates dates. After that, several of Quattro PRO's advanced commands will be presented: Regression, Frequency, What-if, and Matrix Arithmetic. Since these commands facilitate the analysis of spreadsheet data, the chapter closes with a look at an XY graph, which is used for visual data analysis.

Dates as Numbers

Several of the examples in earlier chapters used dates produced by Quattro PRO's date arithmetic feature. The program is designed to perform math with dates and times. To read a date (such as April 1, 1990) as something that has value, the date must be converted to a number. Quattro PRO performs this conversion by calculating the number of days between the date involved and the end of the last century. This is the date's *serial number*. Thus, January 1, 1900 is date number 1. Move ahead 1000 days and you have September 27, 1902. Man first walked on the moon on day number 25, 404, otherwise known as July 20, 1969.

When dates are converted to numbers, two dates can be compared and their difference calculated. Chapter 2 provided a calculation for how many days you have been alive. More typical applications are scheduling projects, dating and sorting records, and calculating loans. Date arithmetic is also useful for producing a series of dates, such as a row with the names of the months or a column of payment due dates.

Entering Dates

How do you tell Quattro PRO to convert a date to a number? After all, if you type April 1, 1990 and press ENTER you create a label, since the letter *A* is a label indicator. There are several ways to enter a date as a number in Quattro PRO.

Entering Dates with CTRL-D

The easiest way to enter a date into a spreadsheet is to press CTRL-D before typing the date and then enter the date in one of the standard formats. In Figure 9-1, CTRL-D was pressed at cell A3 before **4/1/90** was typed.

The mode indicator in the lower right of the screen indicates DATE to let you know that you have pressed CTRL-D. All you need to do is type the date and press ENTER. The effect of CTRL-D is seen when the date is entered. You will see **04/01/90** on the worksheet:

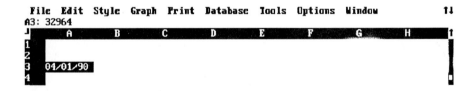

If you were to type **4/1/90** without pressing CTRL-D, Quattro PRO would divide the number 4 by 1 and then divide the result by 90, producing 0.044 in the cell (assuming a format with three decimal places). The CTRL-D approach to entering dates works very well. You can enter the date in any of the standard formats:

01-Apr-90	DD-MMM-YY
01-Apr	DD-MMM (assumes current year)
Apr-90	MMM-YY (assumes first day of the month)
04/01/90	MM/DD/YY
04/01	MM/DD (assumes current year)

For example, if you press CTRL-D and then type **Apr-90**, **Apr-90** will display. The assumptions that Quattro PRO makes when part of the date is missing are current year and first of the month. The current year is read from your computer's system clock. You can type month names in any mixture of capitals and lowercase and you do not need to type leading zeroes for date numbers. The CTRL-D method can also be used with the @NOW function described later.

While the CTRL-D method produces a date in a readable form in the worksheet cell, the cell content displayed on the status line is simply a serial number. In Figure 9-2 **32964** is displayed, which corresponds to 04/01/90. This is one of the standard date formats. The formats can be reviewed on the Style Numeric Format Date menu, which is also displayed in Figure 9-2.

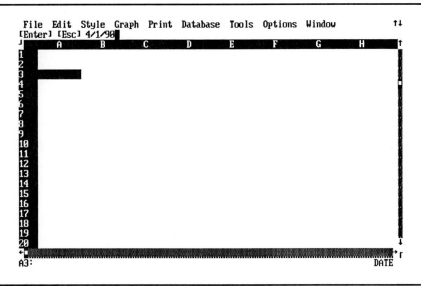

Figure 9-1. *Entering date*

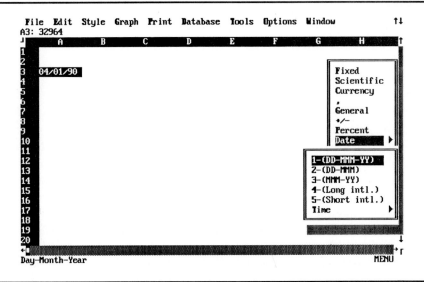

Figure 9-2. *Date and Numeric Format screen*

You can change the format of the cell to one of the other formats by using the Style Numeric Format command and selecting Date. However, bear in mind that the first format, DD-MMM-YY, produces a date too wide for the default column width of 9 characters.

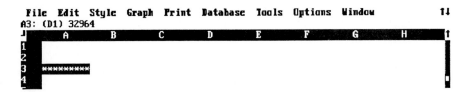

In this example, Quattro PRO is attempting to display **01-Apr-90**, which is nine characters. Since the date is a value, and Quattro PRO allows only eight digits of a value to be displayed in a 9-character column, the result is the series of asterisks that tell you to change the format or column width.

You need only enlarge the column by one character to see the full date. If much of your work includes dates, you can change the default column width to 10 by using the Defaults Formats Width command.

Entering Dates with Functions

In addition to the CTRL-D method, there are several other ways to create a date. One that parallels the approach used in 1-2-3 is the @DATE function. This function has the syntax

@DATE(YY,MM,DD)

where YY is a numeric value between 0 and 199, MM is a numeric value between 1 and 12, and DD is a numeric value between 1 and 31.

The @DATE function returns the serial number of the date specified with year, month, and day arguments. Thus, @DATE(90,12,25) returns the value 33232, or 25-Dec-90. Since Quattro PRO can handle dates well into the next century, the year 2000 is referred to as 100, 2001 is 101, and so on. The highest date available is December 31, 2099, referred to as @DATE(199,12,31).

The number created by @DATE can be a whole number of days plus a fraction of a day expressed as a decimal. The whole number (to the left of the decimal point) in a date serial number is the number of days from January 1, 1900 up to the date referenced in the formula. The fractional portion of a date serial number is used for the time functions, which are discussed later in this chapter.

To display a date's serial number in a date format, you use the Style Numeric Format command and select one of the date formats. This command suppresses the numeric display, showing instead the date in its more common form (1-Jan-87 instead of 31778). Any illegal dates—for example, @DATE(87,2,29)—return ERR as their value. This date corresponds to February 29, 1987, which is invalid since 1987 was not a leap year.

Another method you can use to enter dates in Quattro PRO is the @DATEVALUE function. You may sometimes work with spreadsheets that contain dates entered as labels. This often happens when data is transferred to Quattro PRO from another program and the date values are converted to text in the process. The @DATEVALUE function produces a serial date value from a string of text or labels. This function has the syntax

@DATEVALUE(DateString)

where DateString is a string value in any valid date form. An example would be the label '25-Dec-90.

If the value in DateString is not in the correct format, an ERR value is returned. There are five valid formats for labels to be read as values with the @DATEVALUE function:

- DD-MMM-YY (25-Dec-90)

- DD-MMM (25-Dec) (assumes the current year)

- MMM-YY (Dec-90) (assumes the first day of the month)

- MM/DD/YY (12/25/90) Long International, the system default

- MM/DD (12/25) Short International, the system default (assumes the current year)

Provided they are written in these formats, dates entered as labels can be converted to values. You can display the resulting date values in standard date formats with the Style Numeric Format Date command. If you want to include the string in the function statement directly, you must enclose it in quotes. Thus, @DATEVALUE("25-Dec-90") returns the value 33232, which can be formatted to 12/25/90 using the D4 date format. The statement @DATEVALUE(A1) returns the same value if A1 contains the label 12-Dec-90. For further discussion of strings and their conversion to values, see Chapter 10.

Date Arithmetic

When dates are stored as values, you can perform arithmetic with them. A typical application of this is tracking accounts receivable. Figure 9-3 shows an accounts receivable list for Take Over Airlines. The names of companies, how much they owe, and when their payment was last due are displayed. Note that in cell F1 the @TODAY function has been used to keep

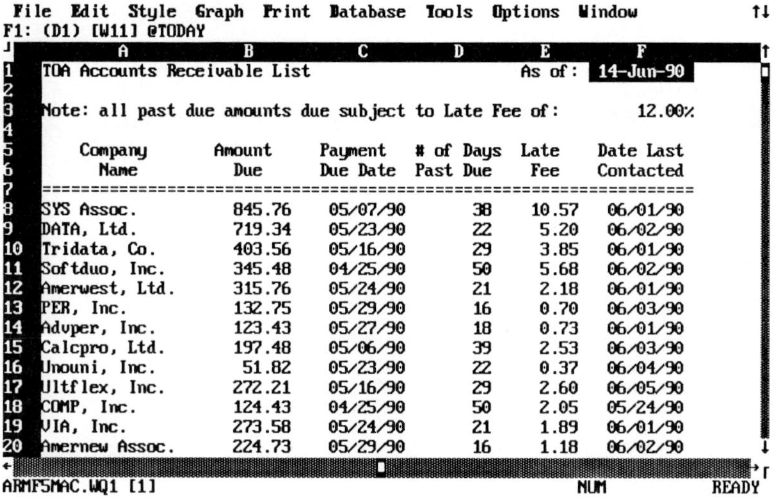

File Edit Style Graph Print Database Tools Options Window   ↑↓
F1: (D1) [W11] @TODAY

	A	B	C	D	E	F	
1	TOA Accounts Receivable List				As of :	14-Jun-90	
2							
3	Note: all past due amounts due subject to Late Fee of:					12.00%	
4							
5	Company	Amount	Payment	# of Days	Late	Date Last	
6	Name	Due	Due Date	Past Due	Fee	Contacted	
7	==						
8	SYS Assoc.	845.76	05/07/90	38	10.57	06/01/90	
9	DATA, Ltd.	719.34	05/23/90	22	5.20	06/02/90	
10	Tridata, Co.	403.56	05/16/90	29	3.85	06/01/90	
11	Softduo, Inc.	345.48	04/25/90	50	5.68	06/02/90	
12	Amerwest, Ltd.	315.76	05/24/90	21	2.18	06/01/90	
13	PER, Inc.	132.75	05/29/90	16	0.70	06/03/90	
14	Aduper, Inc.	123.43	05/27/90	18	0.73	06/01/90	
15	Calcpro, Ltd.	197.48	05/06/90	39	2.53	06/03/90	
16	Unouni, Inc.	51.82	05/23/90	22	0.37	06/04/90	
17	Ultflex, Inc.	272.21	05/16/90	29	2.60	06/05/90	
18	COMP, Inc.	124.43	04/25/90	50	2.05	05/24/90	
19	VIA, Inc.	273.58	05/24/90	21	1.89	06/01/90	
20	Amernew Assoc.	224.73	05/29/90	16	1.18	06/02/90	

ARMF5MAC.WQ1 [1]   NUM   READY

Figure 9-3.   *TOA Accounts Receivable*

the worksheet up to date, as shown by the cell identifier at the top of the screen. The @TODAY function reads your computer system's date from DOS and, if you have the system clock set correctly, will always show the current date.

The number of days that have elapsed between the date the payment was supposed to have been made and the current date is calculated in column D, # of Days Past Due. The figure in D8 is produced by the formula +$F$1−C8, which subtracts the due date in column C from the current date in cell F1, as shown in Figure 9-4. The cell reference to the current date in F1 was made absolute so that the formula could be copied to the other cells in column D.

The practical value of knowing exactly how many days late a payment is can be seen in column E, where the late fee is calculated. This figure represents interest on the amount due. The late fee is calculated by multiplying the number of days past due by 1/365th of the annual percentage rate shown in F3 in Figure 9-5. Thus, when a client is contacted about paying the amount owing, the accrued late fee can be stated.

```
 File  Edit  Style  Graph  Print  Database  Tools  Options  Window            ↑↓
D8: (F0) +$F$1-C8
 ┌────────────A─────────B─────────C─────────D─────────E─────────F──────────────┐
 1 TOA Accounts Receivable List                      As of:  14-Jun-90
 2
 3 Note: all past due amounts due subject to Late Fee of:        12.00%
 4
 5   Company        Amount      Payment    # of Days  Late     Date Last
 6     Name           Due      Due Date   Past Due    Fee      Contacted
 7 ==============================================================================
 8 SYS Assoc.        845.76    05/07/90       38     10.57    06/01/90
 9 DATA, Ltd.        719.34    05/23/90       22      5.20    06/02/90
10 Iridata, Co.      403.56    05/16/90       29      3.85    06/01/90
11 Softduo, Inc.     345.48    04/25/90       50      5.68    06/02/90
12 Amerwest, Ltd.    315.76    05/24/90       21      2.18    06/01/90
13 PEH, Inc.         132.75    05/29/90       16      0.70    06/03/90
14 Aduper, Inc.      123.43    05/27/90       18      0.73    06/01/90
15 Calcpro, Ltd.     197.48    05/06/90       39      2.53    06/03/90
16 Unouni, Inc.       51.82    05/23/90       22      0.37    06/04/90
17 Ultflex, Inc.     272.21    05/16/90       29      2.60    06/05/90
18 COMP, Inc.        124.43    04/25/90       50      2.05    05/24/90
19 VIA, Inc.         273.58    05/24/90       21      1.89    06/01/90
20 Amernew Assoc.    224.73    05/29/90       16      1.18    06/02/90
 └──────────────────────────────────────────────────────────────────────────────┘
ARMFSMAC.WQ1 [1]                                             NUM          READY
```

Figure 9-4.   *Days past due*

```
 File  Edit  Style  Graph  Print  Database  Tools  Options  Window            ↑↓
E8: (,2) +B8*D8*$F$3/365
 ┌────────────A─────────B─────────C─────────D─────────E─────────F──────────────┐
 1 TOA Accounts Receivable List                      As of:  14-Jun-90
 2
 3 Note: all past due amounts due subject to Late Fee of:        12.00%
 4
 5   Company        Amount      Payment    # of Days  Late     Date Last
 6     Name           Due      Due Date   Past Due    Fee      Contacted
 7 ==============================================================================
 8 SYS Assoc.        845.76    05/07/90       38     10.57    06/01/90
 9 DATA, Ltd.        719.34    05/23/90       22      5.20    06/02/90
10 Iridata, Co.      403.56    05/16/90       29      3.85    06/01/90
11 Softduo, Inc.     345.48    04/25/90       50      5.68    06/02/90
12 Amerwest, Ltd.    315.76    05/24/90       21      2.18    06/01/90
13 PEH, Inc.         132.75    05/29/90       16      0.70    06/03/90
14 Aduper, Inc.      123.43    05/27/90       18      0.73    06/01/90
15 Calcpro, Ltd.     197.48    05/06/90       39      2.53    06/03/90
16 Unouni, Inc.       51.82    05/23/90       22      0.37    06/04/90
17 Ultflex, Inc.     272.21    05/16/90       29      2.60    06/05/90
18 COMP, Inc.        124.43    04/25/90       50      2.05    05/24/90
19 VIA, Inc.         273.58    05/24/90       21      1.89    06/01/90
20 Amernew Assoc.    224.73    05/29/90       16      1.18    06/02/90
 └──────────────────────────────────────────────────────────────────────────────┘
ARMFSMAC.WQ1 [1]                                             NUM          READY
```

Figure 9-5.   *Interest calculation*

Date Series

You can use date arithmetic to create a series of dates. Consider the budget worksheet shown in Figure 9-6. This worksheet was developed in Chapter 5. At that time the names of the months in row 6 were simply typed as labels. However, the same data could be created more quickly by using date values. As values, the dates could be easily updated for next year's budget. To create a series of the names of the months with date values, you enter the date as the first day of the first month of the series. Since you can format dates with the MMM-YY format, entering **1/1/90** and changing the format to MMM-YY produces **Jan-90**. You can then add 31 days to this date to produce the first of the next month, **Feb-90**, and so on.

As you can see from Figure 9-6, the label JAN is about to be replaced by a date, January 1, 1990, entered as **@DATE(90,1,1)**. When this is entered, the value of the date is first shown as a date value. This will be changed to a readable date in a moment.

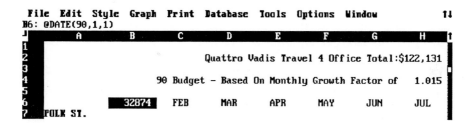

In cell C6 the formula 31+B6 is entered to create a serial date that is 31 days greater than that in the cell to the left.

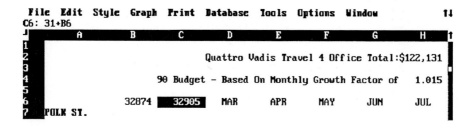

File Edit Style Graph Print Database Tools Options Window   ↑↓
[Enter] [Esc] @DATE(90,1,1)

	A	B	C	D	E	F	G	H
1								
2				Quattro Vadis Travel 4 Office Total:$122,131				
3								
4			90 Budget – Based On Monthly Growth Factor of				1.015	
5								
6		JAN	FEB	MAR	APR	MAY	JUN	JUL
7	POLK ST.							
8	Lease	350	355	361	366	371	377	383
9	Phones	230	233	237	241	244	248	251
10	Telex	110	112	113	115	117	119	120
11	Electric	120	122	124	125	127	129	131
12	Res. Rent	1,100	1,117	1,133	1,150	1,167	1,185	1,203
13	VAN NESS							
14	Lease	500	507	515	523	531	539	547
15	Phones	250	254	258	261	265	269	273
16	Telex	150	152	155	157	159	162	164
17	Electric	225	228	232	235	239	242	246
18	Res. Rent	1,200	1,218	1,236	1,255	1,274	1,293	1,312
19	UNION SQ.							
20	Lease	1,200	1,218	1,236	1,255	1,274	1,293	1,312

B6: ^JAN   VALUE

Figure 9-6.   *Budget worksheet*

In a moment this formula will be copied to the rest of the cells in row 6. However, since all of the date cells need to be formatted, and formats are duplicated by the copy process, the two date cells created so far will be formatted prior to the formula being copied. In Figure 9-7 you can see the third date format being selected. The resulting display of the dates is shown here:

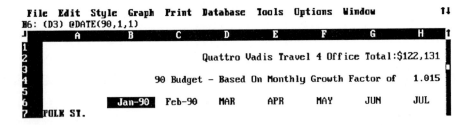

File Edit Style Graph Print Database Tools Options Window   ↑↓
B6: (D3) @DATE(90,1,1)

	A	B	C	D	E	F	G	H
1								
2				Quattro Vadis Travel 4 Office Total:$122,131				
3								
4			90 Budget – Based On Monthly Growth Factor of				1.015	
5								
6		Jan-90	Feb-90	MAR	APR	MAY	JUN	JUL
7	POLK ST.							

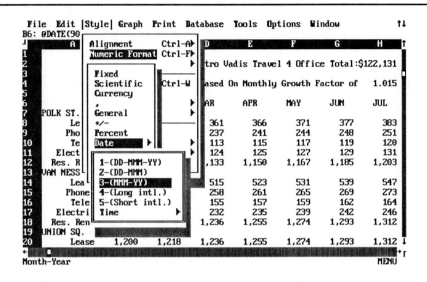

Figure 9-7. *Formatting the date cells*

All that remains to complete the date series for all months is to copy the formula in cell C6 to cells D6..M6, as shown here:

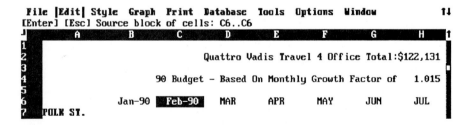

The result is a series of month headings for the budget model. While the actual dates created by repeatedly adding 31 to the first of January are not the first of every month, because of the differing number of days in a month, the D3 format ignores the day of the month to give the date series just created an acceptable appearance.

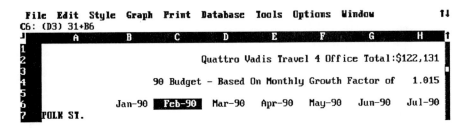

Of course, the major advantage of entering dates in this manner is the ease with which they can be updated for next year's budget. By simply highlighting the starting date of the series in cell B6, pressing F2 to edit it, and changing @DATE(90,1,1) to @DATE(91,1,1), you can update the entire series to the months of 1991.

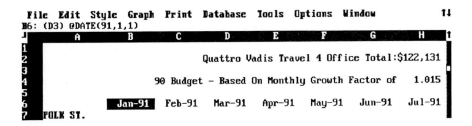

The technique of repeatedly adding 31 days to a beginning date of January 1 will produce acceptable consecutive MMM-YY dates for about 54 months.

When the date series you want to create has to be more exact, showing the complete dates, you can proceed in several ways. Take the case of a payment schedule where you need a list of payment dates. Suppose that the schedule calls for 12 payments, one due every 30 days. In the following illustration the first date of the series has been entered as April 1, 1990, with the statement @DATE(90,4,1) in cell A3. Cell A3 has been formatted to the D1 format. In Figure 9-8 you can see that the value in cell A4 is being created as 30 is added to the starting date in A3.

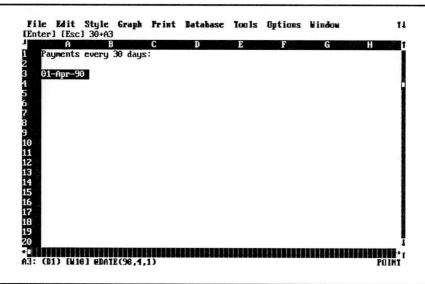

Figure 9-8. *+30 series*

This formula is then copied down the column to produce the results shown in Figure 9-9. This type of formula works well for such applications as a series of weekly meeting dates or biweekly pay days, where the interval between dates is a set number of days. Remember that a cell format is copied with the cell, so formatting before you perform the copy operation will save time. Alternatively, you can wait to format the entire date series until after it has been created; however, working with unformatted dates such as 32964, 32994, 33024, and so on is not always easy.

An alternative method of creating a regular series of dates is to use the Edit Fill command. To use this method, you enter the first date of the series as a function, as in @DATE(90,4,1). This function will display the number 32964 if you do not apply a date format to the cell. With the cell selector on the number 32964, use the Edit Fill command and highlight a block with the number of cells you need. Then use 32964 as the start value and the number of days between dates as the step value. You can use the number 73050, the largest valid date number, as the stop value. The resulting numbers can then be formatted as dates. Note that a date series created with the Edit Fill command is not interactive and will not update when the first date in the series is changed.

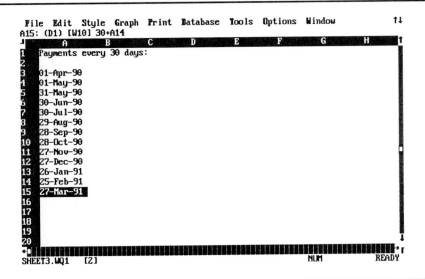

File Edit Style Graph Print Database Tools Options Window   ↑↓
A15: (D1) [W10] 30+A14

```
 ┌───────A─────────B──────────C──────────D──────────E──────────F──────────G──────────H───┐
 1  Payments every 30 days:
 2
 3  01-Apr-90
 4  01-May-90
 5  31-May-90
 6  30-Jun-90
 7  30-Jul-90
 8  29-Aug-90
 9  28-Sep-90
10  28-Oct-90
11  27-Nov-90
12  27-Dec-90
13  26-Jan-91
14  25-Feb-91
15  27-Mar-91
16
17
18
19
20
```

SHEET3.WQ1   [2]   NUM   READY

Figure 9-9. *The complete series of dates*

These methods of creating date series—adding a fixed number of days to the previous date, either by copying formulas or filling a block—work in situations where the interval between dates is fixed. Thus, in the previous example, you assume that the payment schedule works on a fixed cycle of 30 days. When the cycle is based on calendar months, the calculations become more complex because of the differing number of days per month. An example of how to work with this is given in the section "Date Part Functions."

Date Functions

In addition to simple addition and subtraction, there are a number of other ways to manipulate dates. You have already seen how the @TODAY, @DATE, and @DATEVALUE functions are used to create dates and convert labels to dates. There are also date functions that allow you to extract parts of a date value for specialized calculations.

Date Part Functions

Several Quattro PRO functions are designed to extract part of a date from a date value. The @DAY function extracts the day of the month. It has the syntax

@DAY(DateNumber)

where DateNumber is a number under 73050.06249. This number represents the highest date possible, December 31, 2099.

The @DAY function converts the date serial number you supply as DateNumber into the number (1 through 31) associated with that day. Thus, the formula @DAY(A1) would return the answer 25, if A1 contained the number 33232, regardless of whether it is formatted as a date, or the formula @DATE(90,12,25).

The @MONTH function, which has the syntax

@MONTH(DateNumber)

returns the number (1 through 12) corresponding to the month of the year represented by the DateNumber. Thus @MONTH(A1) returns 12 if the number in A1 is 33232 or A1 contains @DATE(90,12,25).

The @YEAR function returns the year of a date value and has the syntax

@YEAR(DateNumber)

The formula @YEAR(A1) would produce the answer 90, if A1 was any serial number or date within 90.

The date part functions can be used with cell references or in combination with other date functions. Thus, the formula @MONTH(@DATE(90,12,25)) returns the answer 12. You can combine date functions with other functions for some useful formulas, such as the one shown here in cell D44:

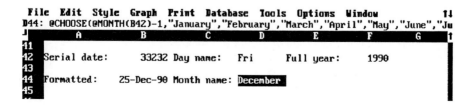

This formula lets you display the full name of the month represented by the date serial number in cell B42. None of the built-in date formats produce the full name of the month. This formula uses the @CHOOSE function (described in Chapter 4) to pick a name from the list of names that are typed as labels in the formula. As you may recall, the syntax of the @CHOOSE function is

@CHOOSE(X,Case0,Case1,Case2,Case$n$)

where X is the number of the case to be selected from the list of cases, and Case0, Case1, and so on are either numbers or labels.

Thus, the formula has the 12 months entered as the cases. Because they are labels, they are entered in quotes. The @MONTH(A1)-1 calculation returns a number from 0 through 11 for the case number, which the @CHOOSE function then reads into the cell.

A similar formula is shown here, where the name of the day of the week for the date number in A1 is returned by dividing the number by 7 and looking up the remainder (0-6) in a list of seven cases:

```
 File  Edit  Style  Graph  Print  Database  Tools  Options  Window                    1↓
[Enter] [Esc] @CHOOSE(@MOD(@DATE(87,9,25),7),"Sat","Sun","Mon","Tue","Wed","Thu"
,"Fri")█
41
42  Serial date:      33232 Day name:    Fri        Full year:      1990
43
44  Formatted:    25-Dec-90 Month name: December
45
```

The @YEAR function is shown to the right of the day formula.

Another example of the date part functions is shown in Figure 9-10. This figure shows a date series for a loan repayment schedule that requires payment on the first day of every month. This series cannot use the +30 method used earlier, because of the varying number of days in a month. Instead, it uses the @CHOOSE function to pick the appropriate number of days of the month from a list. An @IF function statement is used for the second month number to determine if the year in question is a leap year and adjusts the number of days for February accordingly.

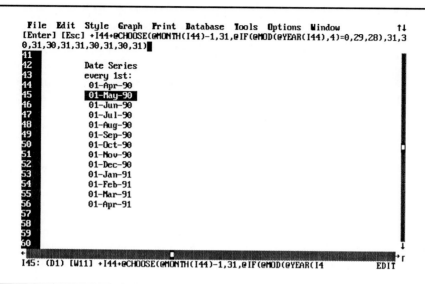

Figure 9-10. *Payments on the first*

Time Functions

In addition to measuring calendar time, Quattro PRO can calculate hours, minutes, and seconds. Calculating clock time can be done with the @NOW function, which is a more precise version of the @TODAY function. In the example shown in Figure 9-11, taken from the TOA Lost Baggage File, the date in cell E1 is created by the @NOW function formatted with the D4 format.

The number in cell G1 is the actual number created by the @NOW function. To read @NOW as a time and not a date, you simply format the cell containing @NOW with a time format, as is about to happen in Figure 9-12, where you can see the four time formats. They are reached from the Date Format menu you see when you use the Style Numeric Format Date Time command. There are two International formats, long and short, and

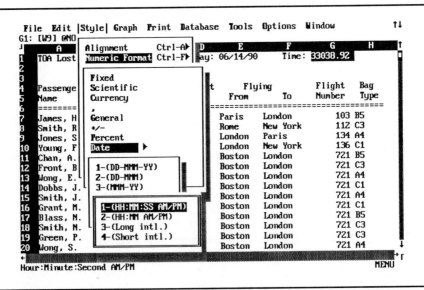

```
File  Edit  Style  Graph  Print  Database  Tools  Options  Window          ↑↓
G1: [W9] @NOW
 ┌─────A──────────B──────────C──────────D─────────E─────────F──────────G──────────H──┐
1 │TOA Lost Baggage File               Today: 06/14/90     Time: 33038.91 │
2 │
3 │
4 │Passenger    Loss      Reported   Shift    Flying            Flight   Bag
5 │Name         Date      Time       Duty   From      To        Number   Type
6 │==================================================================================
7 │James, H.    06/13/88  08:34 AM  Day    Paris     London       103 B5
8 │Smith, R.    06/14/88  09:56 AM  Day    Rome      New York     112 C3
9 │Jones, S.    06/14/88  01:23 PM  Night  London    Paris        134 A4
10│Young, F.    06/14/88  11:35 PM  Night  London    New York     136 C1
```

Figure 9-11.   *@NOW function*

these correspond to your selection from the Options International menu.
The first time format produces a display that is too wide for the default
column width of 9. (It actually requires a column 12 characters wide
because it displays not only hours, minutes, and seconds, but also the AM
or PM indicator). The second time format only requires a column of 9
characters.

```
File  Edit |Style| Graph  Print  Database  Tools  Options  Window          ↑↓
G1: [W9] @NO
 ┌─────A──────────B────┌───────────────────────┐──D─────────E─────────F──────────G──────────H──┐
1 │TOA Lost             │Alignment       Ctrl-A▶│ay: 06/14/90     Time: 33038.92 │
2 │                     │Numeric Format  Ctrl-F▶ │
3 │                     ├───────────────────────┤
4 │Passenge             │Fixed                  │      Flying           Flight   Bag
5 │Name                 │Scientific             │    From      To       Number   Type
6 │=======              │Currency               │=====================================
7 │James, H             │,                      │Paris     London          103 B5
8 │Smith, R             │General                │Rome      New York        112 C3
9 │Jones, S             │+/-                    │London    Paris           134 A4
10│Young, F             │Percent                │London    New York        136 C1
11│Chan, A.             │Date          ▶        │Boston    London          721 B5
12│Front, B             └─────────────┐         │Boston    London          721 C3
13│Wong, E.              │1-(DD-MMM-YY)│         │Boston    London          721 A4
14│Dobbs, J.             │2-(DD-MMM)   │         │Boston    London          721 C1
15│Smith, J.             │3-(MMM-YY)   │         │Boston    London          721 A4
16│Grant, M.            ┌───────────────────┐   │Boston    London          721 C1
17│Blass, N.            │1-(HH:MM:SS AM/PM)│    │Boston    London          721 B5
18│Smith, N.            │2-(HH:MM AM/PM)    │    │Boston    London          721 C3
19│Green, P.            │3-(Long intl.)     │    │Boston    London          721 C3
20│Wong, S.             │4-(Short intl.)    │    │Boston    London          721 A4
                        └───────────────────┘
Hour:Minute:Second AM/PM                                                   MENU
```

Figure 9-12.   *Time formats*

The result of formatting cell G1 with the second time format is shown in Figure 9-13, where more of the Lost Baggage File is shown. Notice the AM indicator and the leading zero used in the time display.

You can also see that a time value is about to be entered into the worksheet in cell C10. This is an application of the @TIME function. Like the @DATE function, the @TIME function can be used to enter a time value so that Quattro PRO can perform arithmetic with it. The syntax of the function is

@TIME(HH,MM,SS)

where HH is the hours (from 0 to 24), MM is the minutes (from 0 to 59), and SS is the seconds (from 0 to 59.99999).

Because the @TIME function works on a 24-hour clock, the time 11:35:00 PM is expressed as @TIME(23,35,00). However, if you want to use the shorter time format that was applied to cell G1—shown in column C—you need to add 30 seconds to the time as it is being entered. Otherwise, Quattro PRO will round down the display to the previous minute. Thus, the entry in cell C10 is @TIME(23,35,30), which is displayed as **11:35 PM**.

Time values are used in such applications as recording customer loss reports or identifying losses not recovered within 12 hours. To add 12 hours to a time, you must bear in mind that the basic unit is a day, and that one day equals 24 hours. Thus, 12 hours is represented by 0.5, and 1 hour is represented by 0.04166 recurring.

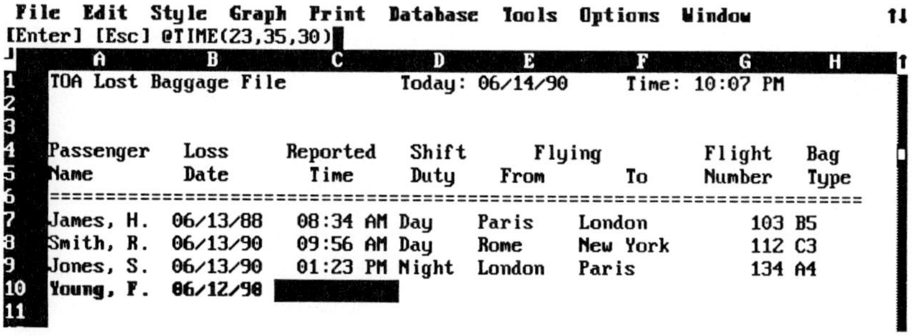

```
 File  Edit  Style  Graph  Print  Database  Tools  Options  Window          ↑↓
[Enter] [Esc] @TIME(23,35,30)█
┌───────A──────────B──────────C──────────D─────────E────────F────────G───────H───┐
1 TOA Lost Baggage File            Today: 06/14/90       Time: 10:07 PM
2
3
4 Passenger    Loss      Reported   Shift     Flying             Flight    Bag
5 Name         Date      Time       Duty      From      To       Number    Type
6 ================================================================================
7 James, H.    06/13/88  08:34 AM Day    Paris     London        103 B5
8 Smith, R.    06/13/90  09:56 AM Day    Rome      New York      112 C3
9 Jones, S.    06/13/90  01:23 PM Night  London    Paris         134 A4
10 Young, F.   06/12/90  ████████
11
```

Figure 9-13. *Formatted time display*

If you have times that are currently entered as labels, you can convert them to time values with the @TIMEVALUE function. Like the @DATEVALUE function, this process converts a string to a value if the string conforms to the standard time formats. The syntax of the function is

@TIMEVALUE(TimeString)

where TimeString is a label in one of the following formats:

HH:MM:SS
HH:MM
Long International
Short International

The International formats are specified with the Options International command. The string must be enclosed in quotes if it is included in the function statement directly. Thus, @STRING("21:39:52") returns the value 0.902685, which is 9:39 PM when formatted with the T2 time format. The statement @TIMEVALUE(A1) returns the same value if A1 contains the label 21:39:52.

Time Part Functions

Just as Quattro PRO can extract parts of the date from a date value, so it can extract the elements of a time value. The time part functions are

@HOUR
@MINUTE
@SECOND

Thus, @HOUR(@TIME(10,30,00)) produces 10 and @MINUTE(A1) produces 30, if A1 contains the value @TIME(10,30,00) or the number 0.4375, which is the serial number of 10:30 AM.

Suppose you want to indicate the shift during which the lost baggage report was made. You could calculate this with a time part function.

Suppose that there are two shifts, the day shift from midnight to noon, and the night shift from noon to midnight. There is a column for this information just to the right of the time record. The worksheet in Figure 9-14 shows a formula that uses the @HOUR function to evaluate the time in the cell to the left. The formula then uses the @IF function to return the label Night if the hour is less than 12 or the label Day if the hour is greater than 12.

Advanced Tools

There are four Quattro PRO features grouped together on the bottom part of the Tools menu: Advanced Math (Regression, Invert, Multiply, and Optimization), Parse, What-if, and Frequency. These are not necessarily

```
 File  Edit  Style  Graph  Print  Database  Tools  Options  Window          1↓
D7: [W7] @IF(@HOUR(C7)>12,"Night","Day")
J        A          B          C          D          E         F        G      H        1
1   TOA Lost Baggage File            Today: 06/14/90      Time: 10:09 PM
2
3
4   Passenger   Loss      Reported   Shift    Flying             Flight   Bag
5   Name        Date      Time       Duty     From      To       Number   Type
6   ==================================================================================
7   James, H.   06/13/88  08:34 AM   Day      Paris     London     103    B5
8   Smith, R.   06/13/90  09:56 AM   Day      Rome      New York   112    C3
9   Jones, S.   06/13/90  01:23 PM   Night    London    Paris      134    A4
10  Young, F.   06/12/90  11:35 PM   Night    London    New York   136    B4
11  Chan, A.    06/11/90  03:05 AM   Day      Boston    London     721    B5
12  Front, B.   06/11/90  03:07 AM   Day      Boston    London     721    C3
13  Wong, E.    06/11/90  03:10 AM   Day      Boston    London     721    A4
14  Dobbs, J.   06/11/90  03:13 AM   Day      Boston    London     721    C1
15  Smith, J.   06/11/90  03:16 AM   Day      Boston    London     721    A4
16  Grant, M.   06/11/90  03:19 AM   Day      Boston    London     721    C1
17  Blass, M.   06/11/90  03:22 AM   Day      Boston    London     721    B5
18  Smith, M.   06/11/90  03:25 AM   Day      Boston    London     721    C3
19  Green, F.   06/11/90  03:28 AM   Day      Boston    London     721    C3
20  Wong, S.    06/11/90  03:30 AM   Day      Boston    London     721    A4
LOSTBAG1.WQ1 [2]                                         NUM            READY
```

Figure 9-14. *@IF function used with @HOUR*

more complicated or less used than other aspects of Quattro PRO, but they have specialized uses, particularly the Advanced Math options shown here:

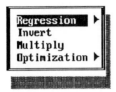

The rest of this chapter reviews these specialized features, with the exception of Parse, which is covered in the next chapter.

Relating with Regression

When you have a large collection of related facts you may want to see how strong the relationship is between them. For example, you may want to evaluate the relationship between goods sold and the amount of money spent on advertising them, or see the connection between earnings and levels of education, and so on. One method of analyzing the connection between such facts is called *linear regression*. Quattro PRO provides a built-in method for performing this through the Regression option on the Advanced Math menu. The subject of regression analysis is complex, and a complete discussion is beyond the scope of this book. A reference such as *Modern Business Statistics* by Ronald L. Iman and W. J. Conover (New York: John Wiley & Sons, 1983) provides complete coverage of all aspects of the field as they relate to typical business situations.

A Regression Example Regression is a measurement of how different factors relate to each other. For example, how does the amount of advertising done by a company relate to its sales? Standard business philosophy states that the amount of advertising a company does is related to the sales level it achieves. Regression can help you determine the strength of this relationship in the case of your company.

Suppose you have compiled the marketing data shown in Figure 9-15. Column B is the number of full-page newspaper advertisements placed by TOA in 1989 listed by month. The numbers in column C represent sales,

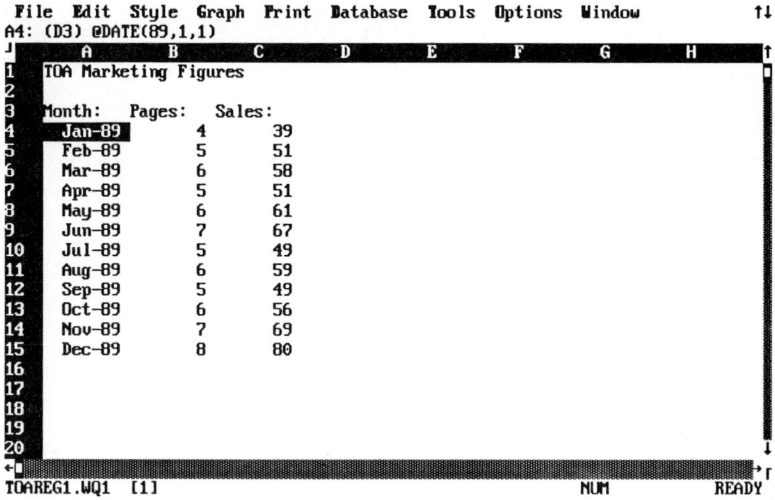

```
   File  Edit  Style  Graph  Print  Database  Tools  Options  Window         ↑↓
   A4: (D3) @DATE(89,1,1)
  ┘       A        B        C        D       E      F      G      H          ↑
  1  TOA Marketing Figures                                                   ▯
  2
  3  Month:   Pages:   Sales:
  4    Jan-89        4        39
  5    Feb-89        5        51
  6    Mar-89        6        58
  7    Apr-89        5        51
  8    May-89        6        61
  9    Jun-89        7        67
  10   Jul-89        5        49
  11   Aug-89        6        59
  12   Sep-89        5        49
  13   Oct-89        6        56
  14   Nov-89        7        69
  15   Dec-89        8        80
  16
  17
  18
  19
  20                                                                         ↓
  ←▮▮▮▮▮▮▮▮▮▮▮▮▮▮▮▮▮▮▮▮▮▮▮▮▮▮▮▮▮▮▮▮▮▮▮▮▮▮▮▮▮▮▮▮▮▮▮▮▮▮▮▮▮▮▮▮▮▮▮▮→ r
   TOAREG1.WQ1  [1]                                        NUM        READY
```

Figure 9-15.   *TOA Marketing Figures*

in thousands, for those same months. You may want to know how these two sets of numbers relate. Once you measure the relationship, you can use that measure to predict future sales based on different levels of future advertising. In the figure, the months were produced by adding 31 days to the first month and formatting the cells with the D3 format.

Setting Up Regression   When you select Regression from the Advanced Math menu, you see the menu shown in Figure 9-16. Note that before this menu was selected, the cell selector was placed in E3. This was done because the Regression command produces a table of results that occupies an area of the worksheet. It should be a block of blank cells set apart from the data being analyzed.

The first two items on the Regression menu refer to the variable factors in the regression calculation. The effect of the independent variable on the dependent variable is being calculated. In this case, Pages, in cells B4..B15, is the independent variable. Its effect on Sales, in cells C4..C15, the dependent variable, is what is to be calculated. Both variables must be situated in matching columns and rows of the worksheet and must contain an equal number of pieces of data, as is the case in this example. When you

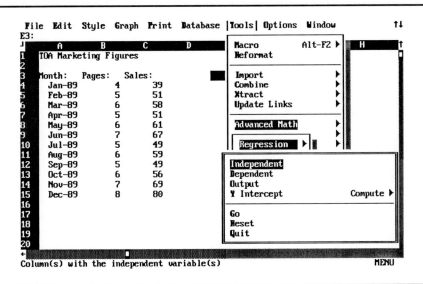

Figure 9-16.   *Regression menu*

select Independent and Dependent, you can enter the cell coordinates either by typing them or by pointing to them. (There can be more than one independent variable, as will be shown in a later example.)

Figure 9-17 shows the completed entries for the regression calculation in the expanded form of the menu. The independent and dependent variables have been defined. The Output block is referred to as E3..E3, although the results of the calculation will occupy four columns and nine rows. You need only define the top-left corner of the cells of the Output block. As you can see from Figure 9-17, the Go option is highlighted to tell Quattro PRO to complete the regression calculation. The results are shown in Figure 9-18.

Regression Results   The result of a regression calculation is a column of numbers that represent the numeric relationships between the variables, and columns of labels describing these numbers. The heading Regression Output will appear more centered if you output to wider columns than the default width of 9. Note that outputting to columns any narrower than 9 will make the data difficult to read.

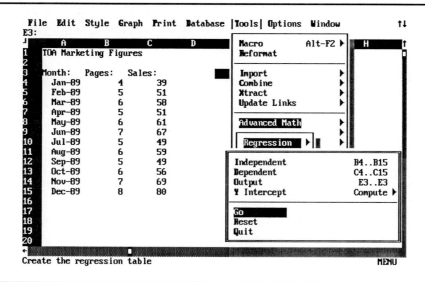

Figure 9-17. *Completed menu*

```
  File   Edit   Style   Graph   Print   Database   Tools   Options   Window        ↑↓
E3:
J     A         B        C        D         E        F        G        H
1 TOA Marketing Figures
2
3 Month:    Pages:   Sales:                      ███████Regression Output:
4    Jan-89      4       39            Constant                    0.719512
5    Feb-89      5       51            Std Err of Y Est            1.607528
6    Mar-89      6       58            R Squared                   0.980377
7    Apr-89      5       51            No. of Observations               12
8    May-89      6       61            Degrees of Freedom                10
9    Jun-89      7       67
10   Jul-89      5       49            X Coefficient(s)   9.719512
11   Aug-89      6       59            Std Err of Coef.   0.434838
12   Sep-89      5       49
13   Oct-89      6       56
14   Nov-89      7       69
15   Dec-89      8       80
16
17
18
19
20
←                          ■                                              →
TOAREG1.WQ1   [1]                                              NUM         READY
```

Figure 9-18. *Results of regression*

Interpreting these results involves understanding numerous concepts from statistics. The No. of Observations is how many data points were observed for the variables, in this case 12, one for each month. Degrees of Freedom represents the number of observations minus one for each variable observed, in this case 10. The value R Squared is sometimes referred to as the coefficient of determination, a measure of the extent to which the variables are related, with 1 being the optimal value. In this example, where the sales are clearly very closely related to the pages, the value of R Squared is nearly 1.

The Std Err of Y Est is the estimated standard error of the Y values. With this you measure the certainty with which the independent variables predict the dependent variables. In general, the larger this measure, the less reliable the relationship between the independent and the dependent variables. This measure, like R Squared, is useful when deciding between different independent variables as predictors of the dependent variables. The Std Err of Coef gives an error measurement of the coefficients. The larger this measurement, relative to the X coefficient, the less certain the relationship between the variables. This measurement will often be smaller when more observations are included in the calculation.

Probably the most useful numbers in the regression output are the constant and the X coefficient. The constant can be described as the y-axis intercept of the regression line that describes the relationship between pages and sales. The X coefficient tells how much the dependent variable, sales, will change for a single unit increase in the independent variable, pages. As you can see in the output in Figure 9-18, this is close to 10, and most of the sales figures are, in fact, about ten times the pages figures.

Using Regression Results The constant and X coefficient readings can be used to predict the value of sales based on different numbers of pages. In Figure 9-19 a calculation has been entered in column D, representing the formula Constant+X coefficient × Independent variable; in this case, cell D4 is **$H$4+$G$10*B4**. This formula was copied down the column to produce the predicted results, which are fairly close to the real results. The value of this calculation can be seen when the pages are changed to the figures shown in Figure 9-20 and the sales for 1990 are predicted. Remember that the prediction shown here is only a statistical inference, not a guaranteed basis for a business decision. However, it is a suggestion that more advertising will produce more sales.

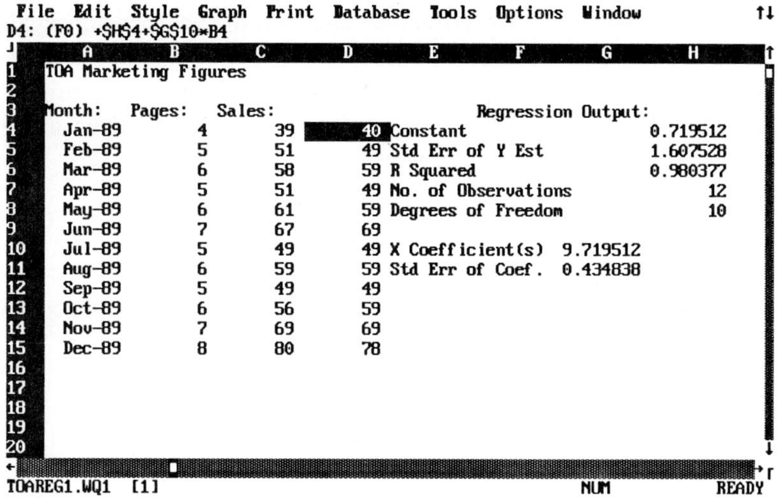

File Edit Style Graph Print Database Tools Options Window   ↑↓
D4: (F0) +$H$4+$G$10*B4

```
J         A         B         C         D         E         F         G         H        ↑
1   TOA Marketing Figures
2
3  Month:    Pages:    Sales:                      Regression Output:
4     Jan-89        4        39        40 Constant                        0.719512
5     Feb-89        5        51        49 Std Err of Y Est                1.607528
6     Mar-89        6        58        59 R Squared                       0.980377
7     Apr-89        5        51        49 No. of Observations                   12
8     May-89        6        61        59 Degrees of Freedom                    10
9     Jun-89        7        67        69
10    Jul-89        5        49        49 X Coefficient(s)  9.719512
11    Aug-89        6        59        59 Std Err of Coef.  0.434838
12    Sep-89        5        49        49
13    Oct-89        6        56        59
14    Nov-89        7        69        69
15    Dec-89        8        80        78
16
17
18
19
20                                                                                 ↓
```
TOAREG1.WQ1 [1]   NUM   READY

Figure 9-19. *Adding predictions*

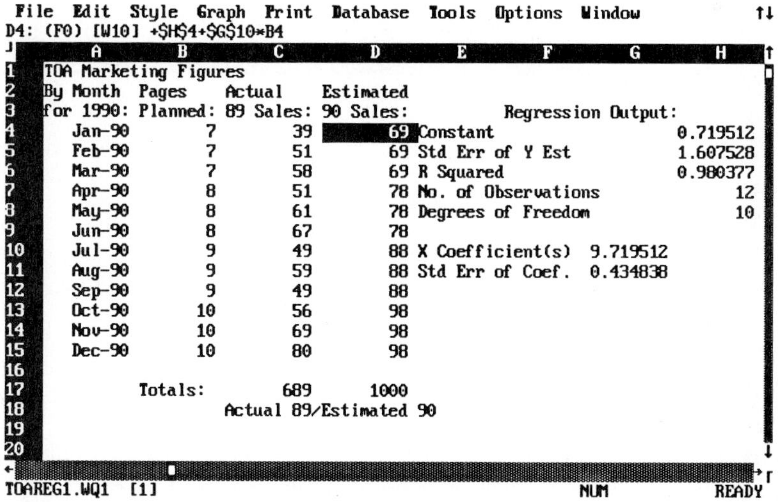

File Edit Style Graph Print Database Tools Options Window   ↑↓
D4: (F0) [W10] +$H$4+$G$10*B4

```
J         A         B         C         D         E         F         G         H        ↑
1   TOA Marketing Figures
2  By Month  Pages     Actual    Estimated
3  for 1990: Planned:  89 Sales: 90 Sales:                Regression Output:
4     Jan-90        7        39        69 Constant                        0.719512
5     Feb-90        7        51        69 Std Err of Y Est                1.607528
6     Mar-90        7        58        69 R Squared                       0.980377
7     Apr-90        8        51        78 No. of Observations                   12
8     May-90        8        61        78 Degrees of Freedom                    10
9     Jun-90        8        67        78
10    Jul-90        9        49        88 X Coefficient(s)  9.719512
11    Aug-90        9        59        88 Std Err of Coef.  0.434838
12    Sep-90        9        49        88
13    Oct-90       10        56        98
14    Nov-90       10        69        98
15    Dec-90       10        80        98
16
17            Totals:         689      1000
18            Actual 89/Estimated 90
19
20                                                                                 ↓
```
TOAREG1.WQ1 [1]   NUM   READY

Figure 9-20. *Making predictions for 1990*

Multiple Variables   You can include more than one independent variable in the regression calculation. An example of this is the analysis of the survey questionnaire shown in Figure 9-21. This set of questions was sent to all of TOA's corporate accounts. The worksheet shows a sample set of responses. The results of the survey were entered into the worksheet in tabulated columns, as shown here:

```
 File  Edit  Style  Graph  Print  Database  Tools  Options  Window              ↑↓
A22: [W17] 'PC  Assoc.
⌐          A          B       C         D          E       F          G         ↑
21  Company Name   Employees  Code   Class       Europe  Europe 86Europe 87
22  PC  Assoc.         22 B          Business    y            4          5
23  Quadkilo, Inc.    420 C          Business    y           40         42
24  Multiper          167 B          Coach       n            8          8
```

The company names are in column A. Column B shows the number of employees at the company. The letters entered in column C refer to a code for the company's type of business. There are just over a hundred responses to the survey. The analyst wants to know if there is a significant

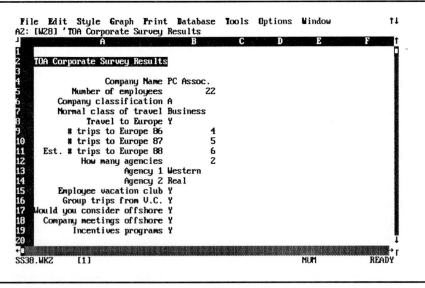

Figure 9-21.   *Questionnaire*

relationship between the size of the company, as measured by the number of its employees; the type of business the company is in, as signified by the code; and the number of flights made to Europe in 1990, listed in column H. This means that the independent variables are columns B and C, and column H is the dependent variable. Before the Code data can be used in a regression calculation, however, it must be converted to its numeric values. This is done by adding a column to the left of the current column C and entering into that column a formula that converts the letter codes A through E into the numbers 1 through 5. A series of @IF statements can accomplish this, as shown here:

```
File  Edit  Style  Graph  Print  Database  Tools  Options  Window          1↓
C22: [W9] @IF(D22="A",1,@IF(D22="B",2,@IF(D22="C",3,@IF(D22="D",4,@IF(D22="E",5,
↓           A              B       C     D       E        F       ↑
21  Company Name       Employees  Code #  Code   Class   Europe
22  PC Assoc.             22        2 B    Businessy
23  Quadkilo, Inc.       420        3 C    Businessy
24  Multiper             167        2 H    Coach   n
```

The new column C now contains numeric data. It is also adjacent to the other column that is used as an independent variable. This is a requirement when there is more than one independent variable. Here you can see the settings made on the Regression menu. Select Go to perform the calculation.

```
Independent      B22..C124
Dependent        I22..I124
Output           P2..P2
Y Intercept      Compute ▶

Go
Reset
Quit
```

The result of this regression example, seen in Figure 9-22, shows two X coefficients, one for each of the independent variables. The measure of R Squared is 0.65642, which shows a moderate relationship between the two independent variables and the dependent one.

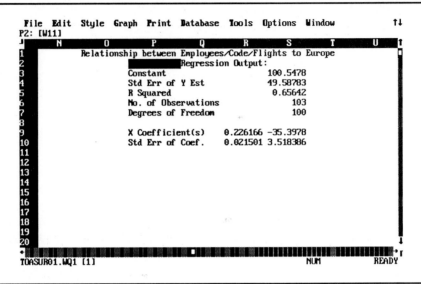

```
 File  Edit  Style  Graph  Print  Database  Tools  Options  Window              ↑↓
P2: [W11]
┘        N        O        P        Q        R        S        T        U       ↑
1            Relationship between Employees/Code/Flights to Europe
2                                   Regression Output:
3                     Constant                      100.5478
4                     Std Err of Y Est              49.58783
5                     R Squared                      0.65642
6                     No. of Observations                103
7                     Degrees of Freedom                 100
8
9                     X Coefficient(s)     0.226166 -35.3978
10                    Std Err of Coef.     0.021501 3.518386
11
12
13
14
15
16
17
18
19
20
 TOASUR01.WQ1 [1]                                        NUM          READY
```

Figure 9-22. *Multiple regression results*

Frequency Distribution

When you are handling large quantities of data, such as that shown in the last example, you often need to analyze the distribution of the data. For example, someone might ask "How big are the companies who responded?" Measured in terms of employees, you could say that they range from 5 to 500, and you could see this from simply browsing column B. But this response would be rather vague. If you were to categorize the companies based on number of employees and count how many fell into each category, you would get a better understanding of the survey's respondents. This is the role of the Frequency command on the Tools menu.

Performing a Distribution   To perform a frequency distribution with Quattro PRO, you need to supply two pieces of information. The first is the block of values that are to be categorized. The second is the column of numbers representing the range over which the values are to be distributed—the categories, as it were. The group of cells containing these category numbers is called the *bins block*, as though each number in the values block was tossed into the appropriate bin for counting. The result of the Tools Frequency command is a list of the totals of that count placed in the column to the right of the bin numbers.

To see this in action, consider the response to the TOA survey, which you want to analyze according to the number of employees at each company. First, a series of numbers for the bins block must be entered. The first number will represent from 0 to the number, so that 100 would represent from 0 to 100. For the employee numbers you could use 100 through 1000 in intervals of 100. This series of numbers can easily be entered with the Edit Fill command, as shown in Figure 9-23.

Be sure that the cells you use for the bins block have empty cells immediately to the right of them. When you select Frequency, you are first prompted for the values block, in this case, cells B22..B124. As soon as you enter this, you are prompted for the bins block, as shown in Figure 9-24. Here you can see that the bin numbers range from 100 to 1000, and are being defined. When you enter the bins block, Quattro PRO immediately responds with the count of numbers shown in Figure 9-25. From this result you can see that 35 of the companies responding to the survey had from 0 to 100 employees. There were 14 companies with 101 to 200 employees. These results provide a valuable picture of the survey data. Frequency

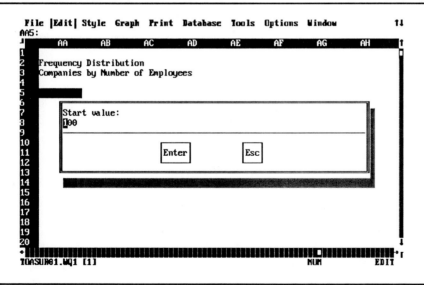

Figure 9-23. *Edit Fill*

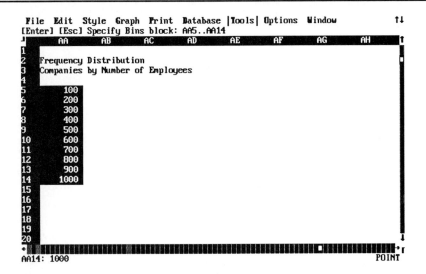

Figure 9-24. *The Bins block*

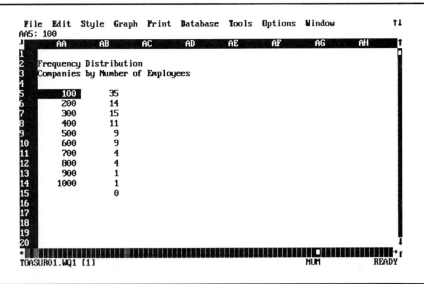

Figure 9-25. *The completed distribution*

distributions are a good basis for many graphs, an example of which is shown in Figure 9-26.

Improving the Distribution   Since the bin numbers are somewhat difficult to interpret, you can add a second column as shown in the worksheet in Figure 9-27. This is a list of sales figures for travel agents. The sales from column C are distributed in column H. The bin numbers are shown in column G. The numbers in column F are there to show the range of numbers implied by the distribution performed by the Frequency command.

What-if Analysis

When making projections, you will want to experiment with values to see what different actions will result in. This is called *what-if analysis.* After you have established the formulas that relate the different cells in a worksheet, you can change the numbers upon which the formulas are based. For example, you can set up a worksheet to calculate sales for the

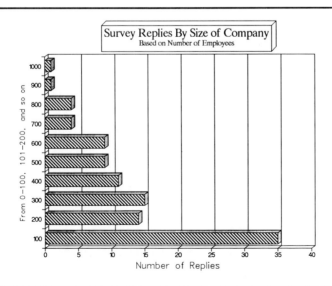

Figure 9-26.   *Distribution graph*

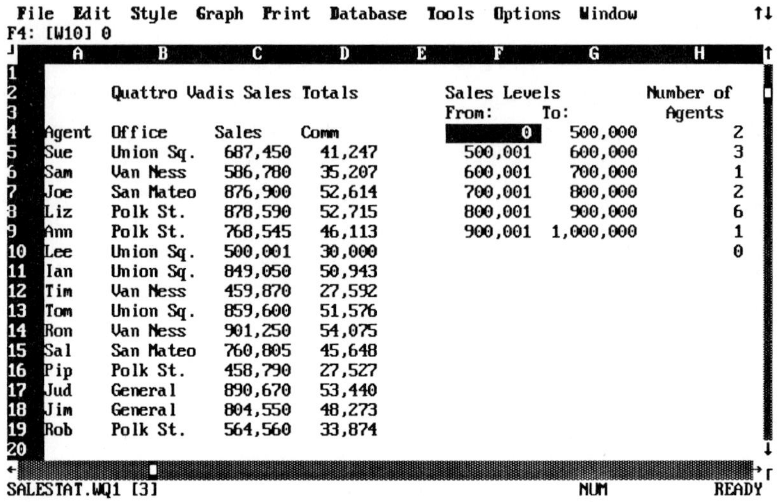

```
 File  Edit  Style  Graph  Print  Database  Tools  Options  Window          ↑↓
F4: [W10] 0
J      A       B        C       D      E      F         G            H        ↑
1
2           Quattro Vadis Sales Totals        Sales Levels        Number of
3                                             From:     To:         Agents
4   Agent  Office    Sales   Comm               0     500,000         2
5   Sue    Union Sq.  687,450  41,247      500,001   600,000         3
6   Sam    Van Ness   586,780  35,207      600,001   700,000         1
7   Joe    San Mateo  876,900  52,614      700,001   800,000         2
8   Liz    Polk St.   878,590  52,715      800,001   900,000         6
9   Ann    Polk St.   768,545  46,113      900,001  1,000,000        1
10  Lee    Union Sq.  500,001  30,000                                0
11  Ian    Union Sq.  849,050  50,943
12  Tim    Van Ness   459,870  27,592
13  Tom    Union Sq.  859,600  51,576
14  Ron    Van Ness   901,250  54,075
15  Sal    San Mateo  760,805  45,648
16  Pip    Polk St.   458,790  27,527
17  Jud    General    890,670  53,440
18  Jim    General    804,550  48,273
19  Rob    Polk St.   564,560  33,874
20
SALESTAT.WQ1 [3]                                      NUM            READY
```

Figure 9-27.   *Improved bin numbers*

next 12 months based on a starting volume of 2000 units increasing at 5% per month. By adding up the sales for the year, you can see what kinds of sales are possible with a 9% growth rate starting at 2000 units. By changing the starting figure, you can calculate sales beginning at 2500 instead of 2000. Then, you might want to create a table of total sales achieved by different starting numbers. Such a table is sometimes referred to as a *one-way data table* because it lists the results obtained from varying one factor in a calculation. You could create a *two-way data table* by varying both the beginning figure and the rate of growth. This kind of what-if analysis can be automated to a certain extent by the What-if selection on the Advanced menu.

A One-Way What-if Example   Suppose you are thinking of buying a car. The spreadsheet shown in Figure 9-28 includes some of the calculations involved. The cells are shown in the text format to reveal the formulas they contain. The total price of the car is calculated and the down payment subtracted to show the amount you would need to finance.

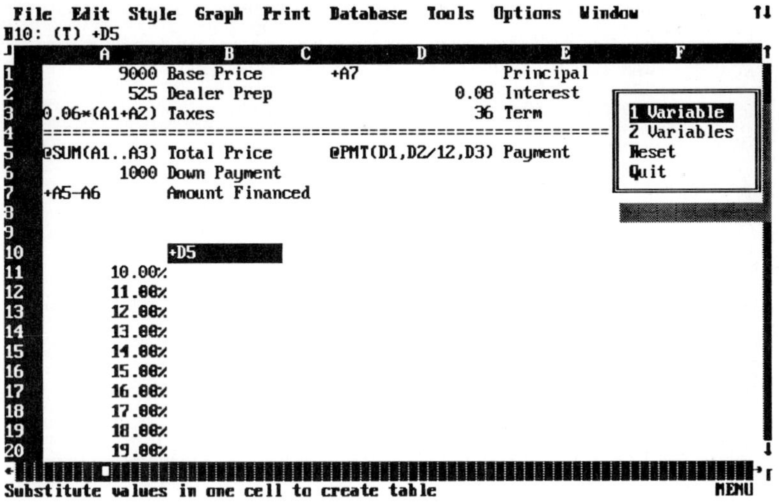

```
  File  Edit  Style  Graph  Print  Database  Tools  Options  Window          1↓
B10: (T) +D5
╔═══════A═══════════B═════════C══════════D═══════════E════════════F═══════════╗
│1          9000 Base Price     +A7               Principal                     │
│2           525 Dealer Prep             0.08 Interest        ┌────────────────┐│
│3     0.06*(A1+A2) Taxes                 36 Term             │1 Variable      ││
│4     ═══════════════════════════════════════════════════   │2 Variables     ││
│5     @SUM(A1..A3) Total Price  @PMT(D1,D2/12,D3) Payment    │Reset           ││
│6          1000 Down Payment                                 │Quit            ││
│7     +A5-A6        Amount Financed                          └────────────────┘│
│8                                                            ▓▓▓▓▓▓▓▓▓▓▓▓▓▓▓▓▓▓│
│9                                                                               │
│10               +D5                                                           │
│11    10.00%                                                                   │
│12    11.00%                                                                   │
│13    12.00%                                                                   │
│14    13.00%                                                                   │
│15    14.00%                                                                   │
│16    15.00%                                                                   │
│17    16.00%                                                                   │
│18    17.00%                                                                   │
│19    18.00%                                                                   │
│20    19.00%                                                                   │
Substitute values in one cell to create table                             MENU
```

Figure 9-28.   *Calculation formulas*

The figures in D1, D2, and D3 show the principal, interest, and term of the loan. You may want to know how large the payments on the loan will be at different rates of interest. For example, the list of rates that begins at 10% in cell A11 could be extended all the way to 19% by the Edit Fill command, filling cells A11 through A20 with values starting at 0.1, incremented by 0.01 to stop at 0.19. The Percent format could then be applied to the cells. The formula in cell B10 simply refers to the loan payment calculation cell. This is the cell whose answers you want to see in the completed table.

You can see from Figure 9-28 that the What-if option has been chosen from the Tools menu. You can actually vary two items with the What-if selection by choosing 2 Variables. The Reset option simply clears any previous settings. The action performed by the first item on the menu, 1 Variable, is to replace one cell with cells from the left edge. This is what is needed to see the loan payment calculated for each rate of interest.

When you select 1 Variable, you are prompted for the block of cells to be used as the data table. In this case the block is cells A10 through B20, as shown in Figure 9-29.

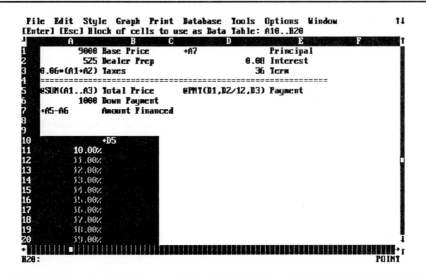

Figure 9-29. *Marking the block*

The table is all of the numbers to be fed into the formula, plus the formula, represented in this case by +D5. When you have entered the data table block, the program prompts "Input Cell from column," meaning "Into which cell do you want to read the values from the left column of the data table?" In this case, the interest cell, D2, is the input cell, as shown in Figure 9-30.

When you have entered the input cell, the results are then tabulated. Quattro PRO feeds each of the values from column A into cell D2 and reads the resulting answer in D5 into the table, creating the output shown in Figure 9-31. This output consists of numbers, not formulas, and so it is not interactive. Changing the terms of the loan on the spreadsheet would not cause any change in the cells of the data table. You must repeat the What-if command to take into account changes in the model. The data table is a quick way to perform a repetitive series of calculations, and pressing Table (F8) repeats the last table command.

Two-Way What-if Calculations The next step is a two-way data table, shown in Figure 9-32. This table shows the payments on the loan based on a variety of interest rates and five different payment terms. The table

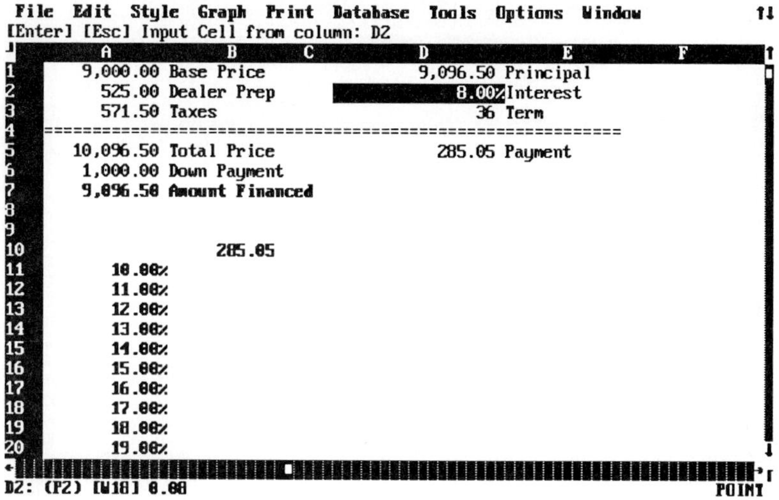

```
 File  Edit  Style  Graph  Print  Database  Tools  Options  Window        ↑↓
[Enter] [Esc] Input Cell from column: D2
┌        A          B          C          D            E          F      ┐↑
1    9,000.00 Base Price              9,096.50 Principal                  █
2     525.00 Dealer Prep                 8.00%Interest
3     571.50 Taxes                         36 Term
4  ================================================================
5   10,096.50 Total Price             285.05 Payment
6    1,000.00 Down Payment
7    9,096.50 Amount Financed
8
9
10                 285.05
11      10.00%
12      11.00%
13      12.00%
14      13.00%
15      14.00%
16      15.00%
17      16.00%
18      17.00%
19      18.00%
20      19.00%                                                          ↓
←                       ■                                              →r
D2: (P2) [W18] 0.08                                              POINT
```

Figure 9-30. *Setting input cell*

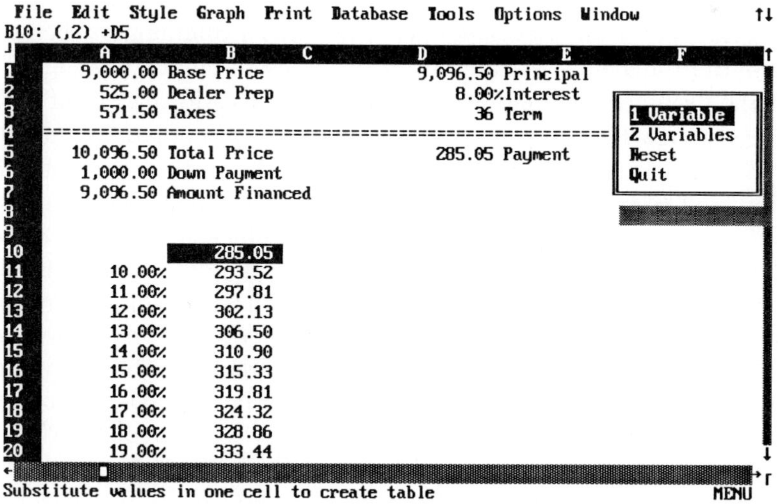

```
 File  Edit  Style  Graph  Print  Database  Tools  Options  Window        ↑↓
B10: (,2) +D5
┌        A          B          C          D            E          F      ┐↑
1    9,000.00 Base Price              9,096.50 Principal
2     525.00 Dealer Prep                 8.00%Interest        ┌──────────┐
3     571.50 Taxes                         36 Term            │1 Variable│
4  ==========================================================│2 Variables
5   10,096.50 Total Price             285.05 Payment          │Reset     │
6    1,000.00 Down Payment                                    │Quit      │
7    9,096.50 Amount Financed                                 └──────────┘
8
9
10                 285.05
11      10.00%    293.52
12      11.00%    297.81
13      12.00%    302.13
14      13.00%    306.50
15      14.00%    310.90
16      15.00%    315.33
17      16.00%    319.81
18      17.00%    324.32
19      18.00%    328.86
20      19.00%    333.44                                                ↓
←          ■                                                          →r
Substitute values in one cell to create table                    MENU
```

Figure 9-31. *A What-if loan*

```
 File  Edit  Style  Graph  Print  Database  Tools  Options  Window          ↑↓
A10: (T) [W13] +D5
⌐          A              B          C          D          E          F        ↑
1      10,000.00 Base Price                    10,156.50 Principal
2        525.00 Dealer Prep                        9.00% Interest
3        631.50 Taxes                                36 Term
4    =======================================================================
5      11,156.50 Total Price                      322.97 Payment
6       1,000.00 Down Payment                                              ■
7      10,156.50 Amount Financed
8
9
10   +D5                    12        24        36        48        60
11           10.00%      892.92    468.67    327.72    257.60    215.80
12           11.00%      897.65    473.37    332.51    262.50    220.83
13           12.00%      902.39    478.10    337.34    267.46    225.93
14           13.00%      907.15    482.86    342.21    272.47    231.09
15           14.00%      911.92    487.64    347.13    277.54    236.32
16           15.00%      916.71    492.45    352.08    282.66    241.62
17           16.00%      921.51    497.29    357.07    287.84    246.99
18           17.00%      926.32    502.16    362.11    293.07    252.42
19           18.00%      931.15    507.05    367.18    298.35    257.91
20           19.00%      935.99    511.98    372.30    303.68    263.47     ↓
←                                                                        →
DT2WAY.WQ1    [3]                                        NUM         READY
```

Figure 9-32.   *Two-way data table*

varies both the interest in D2 and the term in D3. The operation is performed by first setting the interest rates down the side of the worksheet and then the terms across the top. The What-if command is then selected from the Tools menu, and 2 Variables is chosen. The data table is defined, as the block formed by the column of variables and the row of variables, A10 through F20, in this case. You are then prompted "input cell from Column," which is the interest in D2. Finally, you are prompted for the input cell from the top row, the term in cell D3, as entered in Figure 9-33.

The results are then created by Quattro PRO as shown in Figure 9-32. You can use this table to decide what terms are best suited to your budget. You could easily produce a different table with various prices and interest rates to see how expensive a car you could afford to finance. Use the Reset command to clear out the current settings for the data table and input cells. Remember that the data table is not interactive and will not be updated when you change other factors in the model. You must reissue the What-if command to update the table, or press F8, the Table key.

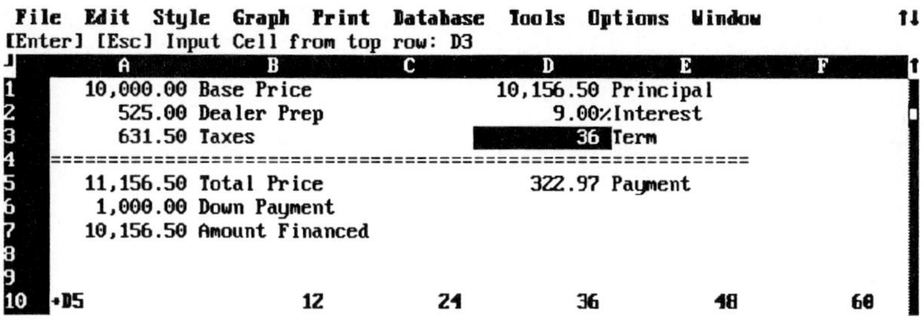

```
 File  Edit  Style  Graph  Print  Database  Tools  Options  Window            1↓
 [Enter] [Esc] Input Cell from top row: D3
 ↓        A           B            C         D          E          F        ↑↑
 1     10,000.00 Base Price            10,156.50 Principal
 2        525.00 Dealer Prep               9.00%Interest
 3        631.50 Taxes                        36 Term
 4  ==================================================================
 5     11,156.50 Total Price             322.97 Payment
 6      1,000.00 Down Payment
 7     10,156.50 Amount Financed
 8
 9
 10 +D5                   12        24        36        48        68
```

Figure 9-33. *Input cell*

Matrix Arithmetic

Two items on the Advanced Math menu, Invert and Multiply, provide you with tools for performing matrix arithmetic. If you know what the inverse of a matrix is and need to perform matrix arithmetic in your work, the following account of the Invert and Multiply commands will get you started applying Quattro PRO to the task. If you are not familiar with inverting matrices, the following example will give you an idea of how they are used to solve practical problems.

Matrix arithmetic is used in linear programming, a technique for determining the optimal allocation of limited resources. This has practical application in many areas, notably economics, which has been defined as "the science that studies human behavior as a relationship between ends and scarce means which have alternative uses." Although a discussion of economic theory and linear programming concepts is clearly beyond the scope of this book, you can get an idea of how matrix commands work and how linear programming is applied with Quattro PRO from a relatively simple example.

At Take Over Airlines, management needs to determine the optimal mix of cargo on a plane, choosing between packages and people. The data from which this mix must be calculated is the amount of fuel needed to fly each package and each person, plus the amount of handling time involved for each package and each person. This data is laid out in the worksheet shown in Figure 9-34.

```
 File  Edit  Style  Graph  Print  Database  Tools  Options  Window          ↑↓
H4: (,0) 2750
↲          A            B        C         D        E       F              ↑
1 TOA Cargo/Passenger Analysis
2
3               Package    Person    Resources            Matrix Output
4 Fuel (gallons)    2,750    9,250    80,000
5 Handling (hours)      3        2        40
6 Profit Per Unit      50       25
7
8 Optimum Mix Calculation
9
```

Figure 9-34.   *The cargo worksheet*

The profit per package and person is also listed in the worksheet. The numbers are pure data, not formulas. You can, however, set up a similar worksheet very easily by setting the width of column A to 16 and the rest to 10. Enter the numbers as values. In cell F3, the words **Matrix Output** have been entered to label the results of the first set of calculations, which will be created by Quattro PRO's Invert command. The calculation that must be performed to determine the optimal mix of packages and persons involves the following equations:

$2750*Packages+9250*Persons=80,000$ Gallons
$3*Packages+2*Persons=40$ Hours

These equations will yield the number of packages and persons you should load to optimize allocation of the given resources. Once you have entered the data in the worksheet, as shown in Figure 9-34, you can have Quattro PRO calculate an inverse of the matrix of numbers in B4..C5.

Matrix Invert   When you select Invert from the Advanced Math menu, you are prompted for the source block of cells. In this case the block is B4..C5. The cell coordinates can be pointed out or typed in, just as you do at other Quattro PRO block prompts. The matrix to be inverted must be square; that is, it must have the same number of columns as rows. When you have entered the Source Block coordinates, you are prompted for a Destination Block. In this case F4 will be used. The Destination Block will be the same size as the Source Block, so you must use an adequate area of your spreadsheet for this. However, you need only point out the top-left corner of the Destination Block. When you enter the Destination Block coordinates, the inverse matrix is produced, as shown in Figure 9-35.

This example shows how Quattro PRO's default General format displays long numbers. The number in cell F4 is –0.000076294277929. But since the column is only ten characters wide, the number is shown in scientific notation, standing for -7.63×10^5. Unless you need to observe the details of the inverse matrix results, you will probably want to leave the output cells in General format. Otherwise, you may have to use a format with a large number of decimal places and a wide column width to see the numbers.

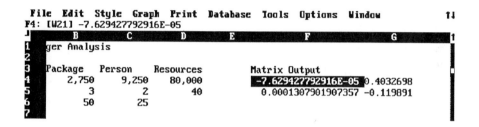

Matrix Multiply   Having calculated the inverse matrix of the numbers, you can use the Advanced Math Multiply command to multiply the original resources of 80,000 gallons and 40 hours by the inverse matrix. The resources, which were the constants in the equations, constitute a matrix. The Multiply command allows you to multiply two matrices together. In this case the results will be the number of packages and persons that make the most efficient use of your limited resources. When you select Multiply from the Matrix menu, you are prompted to "Specify 1st Matrix," which will be the output of the inverse matrix, cells F4..G5.

When you enter these coordinates, you are prompted to "Specify 2nd Matrix," which will be the resources in D4..D5. After entering the second matrix coordinates you are prompted for a "Destination for cells." In this example cell B10 is named, as shown in Figure 9-36, where some additional labels have been added to identify the results. When you enter the destination coordinates, the results of the calculations are seen. In this case a mix of 10.03 packages and 5.67 persons is the most efficient use of the resources available.

Note that cells B10 and B11 in Figure 9-36 have been formatted to two decimal places with the Comma format. Since you cannot have 5.67 persons, you might want to display the result without any decimal places.

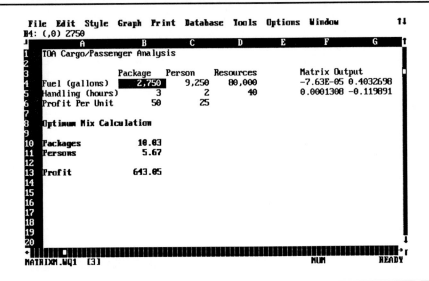

Figure 9-35.   *The inverse matrix*

However, if you are going to use the result in another calculation, you may want to use the @ROUND function to eliminate the decimal places.

In Figure 9-36 there is one additional calculation in the worksheet. This figure shows the amount of profit made by the mix determined in B10 and B11, using the profit figures from row 6. The formula +B6*B10+C6*B11 is used to multiply the per-unit profit by the optimal number of units. You might modify the formula as follows, in order to use whole units of packages and persons:

+B6*@ROUND(B10,0)+C6*@ROUND(B11,0)

XY Graphs

Since this chapter has discussed some advanced features of Quattro PRO for analyzing and determining relationships between collections of data,

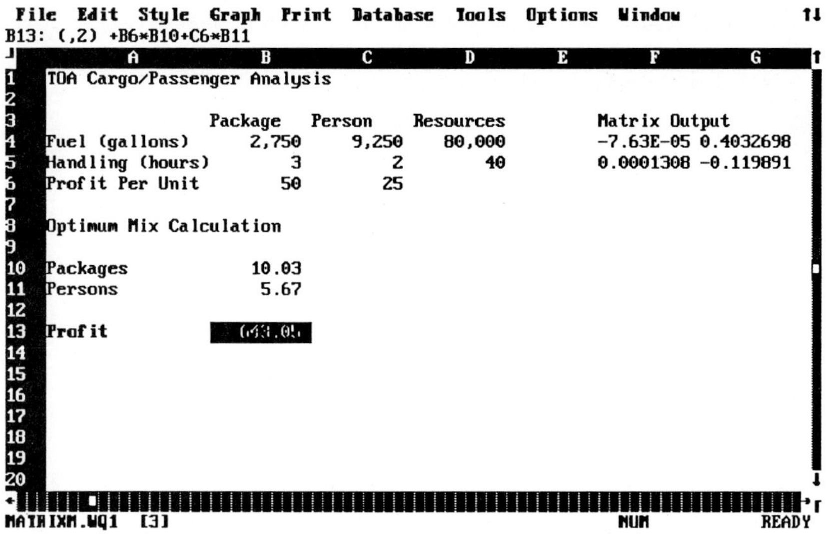

```
 File  Edit  Style  Graph  Print  Database  Tools  Options  Window              ↑↓
B13: (,2) +B6*B10+C6*B11
⌐         A          B        C        D       E       F         G            ↑
1  TOA Cargo/Passenger Analysis
2
3                  Package   Person   Resources        Matrix Output
4  Fuel (gallons)    2,750    9,250    80,000        -7.63E-05 0.4032698
5  Handling (hours)      3        2        40        0.0001308 -0.119891
6  Profit Per Unit      50       25
7
8  Optimum Mix Calculation
9
10 Packages          10.03
11 Persons            5.67
12
13 Profit           [643.05]
14
15
16
17
18
19
20
MATRIXM.WQ1  [3]                                        NUM          READY
```

Figure 9-36.   *Profit calculation*

this is an appropriate place to address the subject of XY graphs. This type of graph was not included with the other graphs in Chapter 8 because it is a specialized type. Used to plot the relationship between data points that have two coordinates, XY graphing can be used for such tasks as analyzing measurements and displaying regression lines.

Making an XY Graph

Figure 9-37 shows a worksheet of size and weight measurements for a number of packages. The weight is in kilos and the size is the sum of the length plus the circumference of the package in centimeters. These packages were picked at random from the airport loading dock in an effort to learn more about the relationship between package size and weight. You decide to graph the size of these packages relative to their weight.

If you set the weight figures in B2..B14 as the x-axis and the sizes in C2..C14 as the 1st Series Value, and use the Marker graph type, you get

File Edit Style Graph Print Database Tools Options Window   ↑↓
A1:
J   A   B   C   D   E   F   G   H   ↑
1   Weight   Size
2   5.8   34.8 0.967132
3   4.8   27.0 0.929585
4   Parcel   7.0   43.5 0.768732
5   Size   6.3   35.0 0.714262
6   To   9.9   59.4 0.656791
7   Weight   4.7   28.2 0.651435
8   Sample   6.7   40.2 0.592239
9   3.5   22.5 0.438103
10   2.5   16.2   0.34214
11   8.9   53.4 0.117351
12   1.6   19.0 0.045641
13   8.0   47.8 0.039306
14   9.3   55.8 0.004667

Figure 9-37.   *Parcel data*

a graph like the one in Figure 9-38. Each measurement is displayed as a point on the graph, a square box in this case. The x-axis numbers are displayed in the order in which they exist in the worksheet. Although each package is graphed, the graph does not tell you much about the relationship between the two axes. However, if you change the graph type from Marker to XY, the graph is much more informative, as you can see in Figure 9-39. This is because the XY graph sorts the data on the x-axis into order of magnitude. You can see a fairly strong relationship between the size and weight. As size increases, so does weight. If you were told a package weighed 6.5 kilos, you could guess that the size is probably 60 centimeters.

Graphing Regression

There is a close relationship between the display of data in an XY graph and the calculations in regression analysis. If you look at the revised TOA marketing figures shown in Figure 9-40, you will see the monthly advertising page count next to the sales for the month (in thousands) and the projected sales based on the regression analysis on the right. If the pages

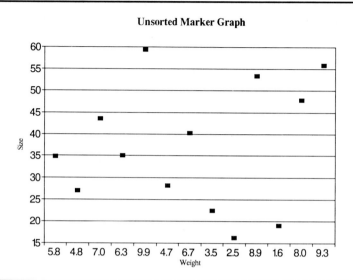

Figure 9-38. *Unsorted Marker graph*

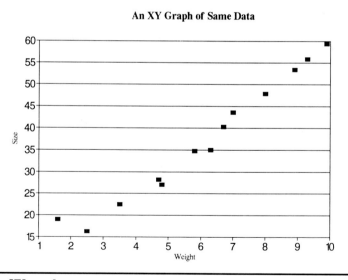

Figure 9-39. *XY graph*

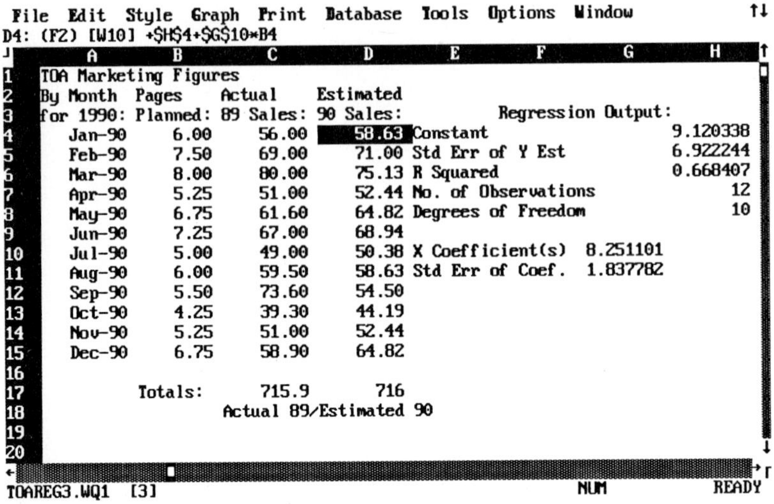

File Edit Style Graph Print Database Tools Options Window   ↑↓
D4: (F2) [W10] +$H$4+$G$10*B4
```
     A            B        C         D         E        F        G        H
1  TOA Marketing Figures
2  By Month    Pages    Actual    Estimated
3  for 1990: Planned: 89 Sales: 90 Sales:            Regression Output:
4     Jan-90     6.00    56.00     58.63 Constant                      9.120338
5     Feb-90     7.50    69.00     71.00 Std Err of Y Est              6.922244
6     Mar-90     8.00    80.00     75.13 R Squared                     0.668407
7     Apr-90     5.25    51.00     52.44 No. of Observations                 12
8     May-90     6.75    61.60     64.82 Degrees of Freedom                  10
9     Jun-90     7.25    67.00     68.94
10    Jul-90     5.00    49.00     50.38 X Coefficient(s)   8.251101
11    Aug-90     6.00    59.50     58.63 Std Err of Coef.   1.837782
12    Sep-90     5.50    73.60     54.50
13    Oct-90     4.25    39.30     44.19
14    Nov-90     5.25    51.00     52.44
15    Dec-90     6.75    58.90     64.82
16
17           Totals:    715.9       716
18                    Actual 89/Estimated 90
19
20
```
TOAREG3.WQ1 [3]   NUM   READY

Figure 9-40. *The updated marketing figures*

were graphed as the x-axis in an XY graph, and if the sales were graphed as the 1st Series value, you could see the relationship between them.

Figure 9-41 shows how this has been done. The actual sales are seen as boxes. The projected sales calculated from the regression figures are also graphed, as the 2nd Series value, and displayed as a line rather than as data points. You can see that the data points produced by the regression calculation represent a straight line drawn to fit as closely as possible to the relationship between sales and pages.

Optimization

The Tools Advanced Math menu provides another tool for analyzing data in the context of a linear model. This is the Optimization command. This command, which actually performs sophisticated linear programming for

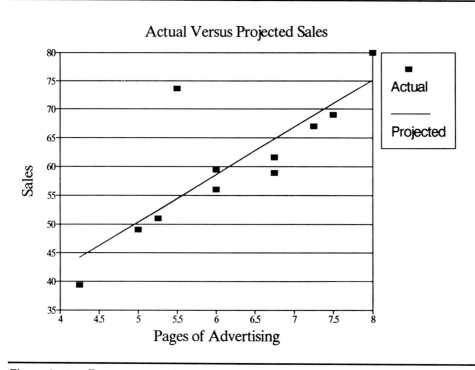

Figure 9-41. *Regression graph*

you, is used to minimize or maximize a combination of variables, subject to various constraints. The calculations are based on data in your spreadsheet that you specify through a series of settings. In the context of Optimization, *constraints* are the limitations placed on your variables. The ability to deal with constraints makes optimization particularly useful in analyzing economic problems, since economics is based on the relationship between ends and scarce means that have alternative uses. Suppose you want to optimize a manufacturing operation. The resources available are a constraint, since you do not have endless supplies nor an infinite number of person-hours per month. Plant capacity is also a constraint since you cannot make an unlimited number of products.

The Scenario

For example, suppose you are a blacksmith running a smithy that makes knives, rapiers, daggers, and swords. To supply the royal army you need to make a minimum number of each item per month and this minimum is a constraint. You know that it takes so many ingots of steel to make each item: knives take 3, rapiers 4, daggers 2.5, and swords 6. If steel is in limited supply, then the maximum amount of steel available each month is also a constraint. For example, the smithy currently has an allocation of 600 ingots per month. Since person-hours are limited by the number of employees and how many hours they can each work per month, the time that can be allotted to making the weapons is a further constraint. For example, the smithy employs 12 people and they each work 40 hours per week, so 1920 hours are the most that can be applied to production. To begin to determine the total profit that can be made in this operation you might want to start with regular math and Quattro PRO's What-if capability. You might set up a model like the one shown in Figure 9-42, which analyzes making an equal number of each weapon.

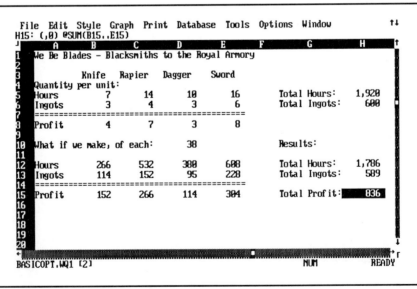

Figure 9-42. *Simple problem analysis*

You can see from row 5 in Figure 9-42 that to make a knife it takes 7 hours; a rapier takes 14, a dagger 10, and a sword 16. The amount of profit per item is listed on row 8. In cell D10 is a guess at the number of units of each item that will yield the greatest profit. This number is used in the multiplication formulas shown in Figure 9-43, where cells are displayed in text format. By simply entering a different number in D10, the blacksmith can see the effect on profit, as well as the total number of hours and ingots consumed. If the numbers exceed the constraints, as they do in Figure 9-43, then a lower number must be used. While this model is helpful in coming to grips with the problem, it cannot address all of the issues facing the blacksmith. For example, this approach does not recognize constraints and therefore cannot adjust all of the factors that can be adjusted to reach an optimal set of figures.

The Optimization Tool

As you can see from Figure 9-44, the Optimization menu is divided into three sections. (The menu is shown in the figure in the narrow form to

```
  File  Edit  Style  Graph  Print  Database  Tools  Options  Window          ↑↓
D10: (T) [W10] 38
┌──────────────────────────────────────────────────────────────────────────┐
│    A          B        C         D        E      F   G          H          │
│1  We Be Blades - Blacksmiths to the Royal Armory                           │
│2                                                                           │
│3             Knife    Rapier    Dagger   Sword                             │
│4  Quantity per unit:                                                       │
│5  Hours         7        14        10       16    Total          1920      │
│6  Ingots        3         4       2.5        6    Total           600      │
│7  ================================================                         │
│8  Profit        4         7         3        8                             │
│9                                                                           │
│10 What if we make, of each:   ▓▓▓▓▓38       Results:                       │
│11                                                                          │
│12 Hours     +$D$10*B5 +$D$10*C5 +$D$10*D5 +$D$10*E5  Total @SUM(B12..E12)   │
│13 Ingots    +$D$10*B6 +$D$10*C6 +$D$10*D6 +$D$10*E6  Total @SUM(B13..E13)   │
│14 ================================================                         │
│15 Profit    +$D$10*B8 +$D$10*C8 +$D$10*D8 +$D$10*E8  Total @SUM(B15..E15)   │
│16                                                                          │
│17                                                                          │
│18                                                                          │
│19                                                                          │
│20                                                                          │
└──────────────────────────────────────────────────────────────────────────┘
BASICOPT.WQ1 [2]                                        NUM        READY
```

Figure 9-43. *Worksheet showing formulas*

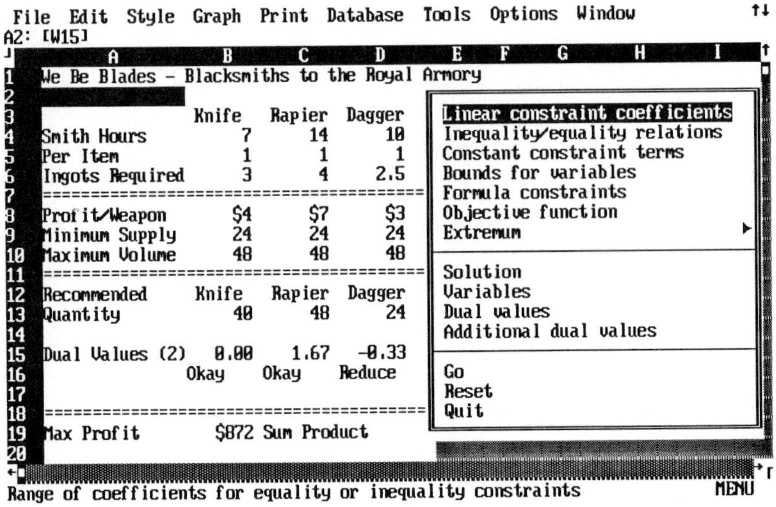

```
     File  Edit  Style  Graph  Print  Database  Tools  Options  Window          ↑↓
   A2: [W15]
   ┌─────────A──────────B────────C────────D────E────F────G────H─────────I─────┐
   1  We Be Blades - Blacksmiths to the Royal Armory
   2
   3                    Knife   Rapier   Dagger   ┌─────────────────────────────┐
   4  Smith Hours          7       14       10    │ Linear constraint coefficients│
   5  Per Item             1        1        1    │ Inequality/equality relations│
   6  Ingots Required      3        4      2.5    │ Constant constraint terms   │
   7  =================================           │ Bounds for variables        │
   8  Profit/Weapon       $4       $7       $3    │ Formula constraints         │
   9  Minimum Supply      24       24       24    │ Objective function          │
  10  Maximum Volume      48       48       48    │ Extremum                  ▶ │
  11  =================================           ├─────────────────────────────┤
  12  Recommended      Knife   Rapier   Dagger    │ Solution                    │
  13  Quantity            40       48       24    │ Variables                   │
  14                                              │ Dual values                 │
  15  Dual Values (2)   0.00     1.67    -0.33    │ Additional dual values      │
  16                    Okay     Okay   Reduce    ├─────────────────────────────┤
  17                                              │ Go                          │
  18  =================================           │ Reset                       │
  19  Max Profit            $872 Sum Product      │ Quit                        │
  20                                              └─────────────────────────────┘
   └──────────────────────────────────────────────────────────────────────────┘
   Range of coefficients for equality or inequality constraints          MENU
```

Figure 9-44.   *The Optimization menu*

make it more readable.) The first section of the menu is called Input Values, the second is Output Values, and the third is Commands. The Input Values section is where you specify cells or blocks of cells as input. These are the cells on which Quattro PRO performs the linear programming operation. In the Output Values section you specify the cells and cell blocks where Quattro PRO is to place the results of the optimization, just as it outputs the results of regression. The third section consists of three commands. The Go command starts the search for the optimal solution. You must define the input value blocks and output value blocks before choosing this command. The Reset command clears all settings in the Input and Output Values sections of the Optimization menu so you can work on a different set of values or completely redefine your model. Note that the cell coordinates defined in the Input and Output Values sections remain defined in the current worksheet for future use. The Quit command returns you to READY mode.

Before running Optimization you need to designate certain cells of data in your spreadsheet. You do this with the items in the Input Values section of the Optimization menu. The variables in your model can be any real numbers that satisfy certain constraints or realistic limitations. The variables must also come within certain bounds. Figure 9-45 shows an optimization model designed for the smithy. The various parts of the model are annotated so that you can see where they fit in. The location of the various input and output items can vary from this arrangement. Each item will be explained as the model and the basic principles of optimization are described.

What Are Constraints?

With the first item on the Optimization menu, Linear Constraint Coefficients, you define the cells that contain the linear constraints on your model's variables. This matrix consists of one row for each constraint and one column for each variable. Constraints are limitations placed on the variables in your model; these limitations can be expressed as algebraic statements. In the blacksmith scenario you might be under royal decree to

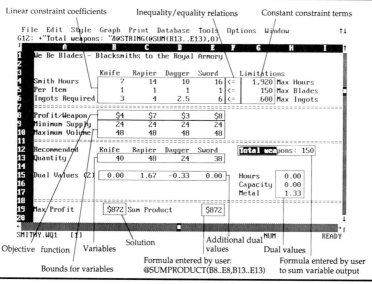

Figure 9-45. *Annotated optimization example*

produce no more than 150 weapons per month, of whatever kind. This is a constraint, which you can describe as

knives + rapiers + daggers + swords <= 150

The smithy must produce at least 60 weapons per month to satisfy the basic needs of the armory. This is another constraint, which can be expressed as

knives + rapiers + daggers + swords >= 60

Remember that it takes so many ingots of steel to make each item: knives take 3, rapiers 4, daggers 2.5, and swords 6. But the smithy can obtain only 600 ingots of steel per month. This is also a constraint, which can be expressed as

(knives*3)+(rapiers*4)+(daggers*2.5)+(swords*6) <= 600

Since person-hours are limited by the number of employees and how many hours they can each work per month, the time that can be allotted to making the weapons is a fourth constraint. With 12 persons working 160 hours per month, this limitation can be expressed as

(knives*7)+(rapiers*14)+(daggers*10)+(swords*16) <= 1920

where 7, 14, 10, and 16 are the hours required to make the respective weapons.

Constraints are said to be linear when their algebraic statements express relationships in which variables are being added or subtracted in various combinations. This is the case in the previous statements.

k	+ r	+ d	+ s	<=	150
k	+ r	+ d	+ s	>=	60
k3	+ r4	+ d2.5	+ s6	<=	600
k7	+ r14	+ d10	+ s16	<=	1920

In Figure 9-45 you can see linear constraint coefficients in cells B4..E6. The columns of this block represent the model's variables, while the rows represent the linear constraints.

Equality and Inequality of Constraints

The constraints on your model are said to be *equality constraints* when an exact figure must be attained. This would be the case if the smithy was ordered to produce exactly 72 blades a month, no more or less. Constraints can also be *inequality constraints,* as in the previous formulas where a minimum or maximum applies.

Each of the linear constraints within the model states that some combination of the variables is equal to (or greater than or less than) some constant value. With the Constant Constraint Terms menu item, you define a column with x number of entries, where x is the number of constraints in the model, that is, the number of rows in the matrix of coefficients. Each of the entries in this column is the constant term for one of the linear constraints in the model. In the model in Figure 9-45 you can see that this setting should be cells G4..G6.

If your model incorporates inequality constraints you must set up a column of labels that describe these constraints, such as >=. Then you enter the coordinates of the labels and the values in the Inequality/Equality Relations setting. You can use the symbols <, >, >=, <=, and <> to express inequality. Just type the label and press ENTER for a left-aligned label. You can also center or right-align these labels without affecting their functionality. You can even precede the symbol with spaces, and you can place any character after it for aesthetic purposes. Thus, the label entry

" < less than

is an acceptable right-aligned label for indicating "less than." If you do not specify a column of Inequality/Equality Relations labels, Quattro assumes all your model's constraints to be equality constraints, using the values in the Constant Constraint Terms setting.

Bounds for Variables

Just as the variables that represent the best solution to your model must satisfy certain constraints, they might also be required to fall within certain upper and lower bounds. For example, as the blacksmith running the smithy you are under royal decree not to produce more than 48 weapons per month of each kind. This is an upper bound for the variables knives, rapiers, daggers, and swords. However, the smithy is required to produce a minimum number of each weapon per month to satisfy the basic needs of the armory, say, 24 weapons. This is a lower bound for the variables knives, rapiers, daggers, and swords.

You specify the bounds by selecting a block with two rows, the first row being the lower bound and the second being the upper. The number of columns is the same as the number of variables. In the case of the smithy, new armory commitments require production of at least 24 of each weapon per month, but royal decree limits output to no more than 48 of each item. To represent these bounds, you would select a block of cells with the following values:

```
24   24   24   24
48   48   48   48
```

Your variables do not have to be bounded. For instance, the only restriction on a particular variable might be that it must be non-negative. This means that the variable's lower bound is 0, but it has no upper bound. If the smithy had no armory commitments, the only lower bound would be zero; it can produce none of a particular item, but it cannot produce a negative number of weapons.

You specify non-negative bounds by putting 0 in the lower-bound cell and leaving the upper-bound cell blank (or putting a label in it). Likewise, a blank or a label in a lower-bound cell means that the corresponding variable has no lower bound. If you do not specify any bounds for variables, Quattro PRO restricts all your variables to non-negative real numbers.

Formula Constraints

Instead of specifying your model's constraints as a matrix of coefficients, you can specify them as formulas, which are required to be non-negative. For example, the constraint

$$3 * A + 4 * B <= 18$$

is essentially equivalent to the formula

$$18 - (3 * A + 4 * B)$$

To use the Formula Constraints menu item, you specify a block of cells that includes all of the formulas you want treated as constraints. Quattro must then find values for the variables such that the formula, when evaluated, is non-negative. The formulas must all be linear in the unknown variables.

Objective Function

In a model where there are more variables than constraints, there is usually more than one set of variable values that satisfies all the constraints. The objective of linear programing is to find the best solution among these sets. Generally, the best solution is one that yields some optimal value when plugged into a specific function. This specific function is called the *objective function,* and it is this function that Quattro PRO optimizes when you choose Go on the Advanced Math Optimization menu.

For example, there might be three or four different combinations of knives, rapiers, daggers, and swords produced in the smithy that meet the monthly production constraints (more than 24, less than 48) and yet do not exhaust the monthly resources (600 ingots of steel, 1920 person-hours). However, the blacksmith is really motivated by another factor: the total profit per month. This profit is a linear function of the number of weapons produced each month:

Total Profit = (knife profit)+(rapier profit)+(dagger profit)+(sword profit)

(number of knives produced)	= W	(profit per knife)	= \$4
(number of rapiers produced)	= X	(profit per rapier)	= \$7
(number of daggers produced)	= Y	(profit per dagger)	= \$3
(number of swords produced)	= Z	(profit per sword)	= \$8

Objective Function = $4(W) + 7(X) + 3(Y) + 8(Z)$

With the Objective Function menu item, you specify a single row of cells containing the coefficients for the variables of your objective function. Use Objective Function to mark the profit function: a single row that contains one cell for each variable in your model. (In this case, there are four variables—knives, rapiers, daggers, and swords.) This row must have x entries, where x is the number of variables in your model. In the example, the Objective Function row is row 8. You can omit the Objective Function block of cells if a suitable formula is in the Solution cell. To be suitable, the formula must be linear in the variables. In this case, the formula would be

@SUMPRODUCT(Objective Function Row, Variables Row)

Setting the Extremum

This item leads to a small menu, from which you select either Largest or Smallest for the optimal value for the objective function. In other words, you specify whether you want to maximize the objective function, such as the profit (choose Largest), or to minimize it, such as the cost of goods (choose Smallest). If you do not specify a value with this item, Quattro PRO automatically chooses Smallest, minimizing the objective function.

Output Settings

Once you have specified the input data for the optimization, you need to designate the blocks where Quattro PRO will place the output values, the results of the optimization. You do this with the items in the Output Values section of the Optimization menu. The row that you specify with the Variables command is where Quattro PRO places the set of variable values that represents the best solution. This row must have N entries, where N is the number of variables in your model. These output values, when plugged into the objective function, yield the optimal value for that function.

With the Solution command, you specify a single cell where Quattro PRO will place the calculated value of the objective function. This optimal value is either a maximum or minimum, as with the Input Values Extremum menu item. You can also obtain the optimal value by leaving the Objective Function range unspecified and entering this formula in the solution cell:

@SUMPRODUCT(Objective Function, Variables Row)

In this case, Objective Function is the row you have specified with Objective Function in the Input Values section of the Optimization menu. If an objective function formula is in the Solution cell, Quattro PRO will use it instead of the Objective Function row. Variables Row is the row of output variable values you have specified with Variables in the Output Values section of the Optimization menu.

Dual values allow you to determine how much the optimal value depends on the individual linear constraints and on the bounds for the variables. A *dual value* is the amount by which the optimal value of the objective function would be increased or decreased if one constant term or one bound is relaxed or tightened by one unit. Dual values are used for sensitivity analysis, for such tasks as determining how much a constraint or bound is restricting your profit or adding to your total cost.

In the Output Settings section of the Optimization menu you can specify two types of dual values, either for constraints or bounds. Dual Values is a column combining as many entries as there are constant terms in your model. Additional Dual Values, on the other hand, is a row combining as many entries as there are variables in your model. If you do not specify any Dual Values blocks, Quattro PRO omits these calculations.

A small change in the constant term multiplied by the dual value for that constraint gives the resultant small change in the optimal value of the objective function. If the dual value corresponding to a constraint is 0, a small change in the constant term of that constraint will cause no change in the optimal value. If the dual value for a given constraint is 1.5, changing the constant term by 1 will change the optimal value by 1.5.

Interpreting bounds for dual values specified by the Additional Dual Values setting can be a little tricky. While only one dual value is associated with each variable, each variable can have two bounds. You need to be able to tell which bound of a variable, upper or lower, is affecting the optimal value of the objective function. If a variable's value is equal to one of its bounds, that bound is said to be active, and the dual value relates to that active bound. A small change in the active bound multiplied by the corresponding dual value gives the resultant small change in the optimal value. If a variable's dual value is 3, changing the active bound by 1 will change the optimal value of the objective function by 3. If, on the other hand, the variable's value does not equal either of its bounds, its bounds' dual value will be 0, and a small change in the bounds for that variable will not affect the optimal value.

Bear in mind that, as with the other Advanced Math operations, Quattro PRO does not automatically recalculate the dual value results. If you change any of the input data, you will have to choose Tools Advanced Math Optimization Go again to get the correct solution and its related values.

Going for the Result

As the blacksmith you want to produce the combination of weapons that yields the most profit; satisfies the limitations of time, capacity, and metal; and meets your commitments to supply the armories as well as to obey the king. To review the terminology used here, remember the following:

■ The resource limitations are your constraints.

■ The amounts of each weapon manufactured are your variables.

■ The armory commitments and factory capacity are the lower and upper bounds on your variables.

■ The sum of the individual profits (total profit, which you want to maximize) is your objective function.

■ The unique combination of weapons that yields the largest total profit is the solution.

■ The most profit you can get (in terms of dollars) is the optimal value. This is calculated as the solution times the objective function.

In Figure 9-45 you saw one way to arrange the spreadsheet, using Optimization to find the best solution. Note that the formula in cell G12 is not part of the Optimization output, but merely an enhancement to sum up the number of weapons from the Variables output.

With your spreadsheet set up like the one in Figure 9-45, the next step is to designate the input settings. These are shown in Figure 9-46. Note that no formula constraints or objective functions are specified. After setting the various input and output blocks, you can use the Go command to get the results. You can then change any of the input factors and repeat the Go command to update the results. By combining the optimization command with the What-if command you can create a powerful analytical tool that presents results from a wide range of scenarios.

To test this particular model, consider what happens when peace breaks out, swords are banned, and there is a need for alternative products such as plowshares. The model can be altered to reflect the new constraints, variables, and bounds. The results are shown in Figure 9-47. Note the addition of string formulas that interpret the results of the command. These are @IF statements that respond to the dual values. You can see that cell I17 displays the word **Increase** because the number in cell H17

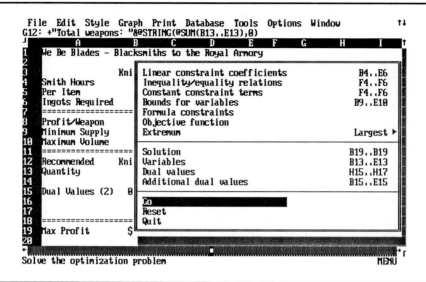

Figure 9-46. *The sample settings*

```
 File  Edit  Style  Graph  Print  Database  Tools  Options  Window        ↑↓
I17: @IF(H17>0.5,"Increase",@IF(H17>0,"Hold"," "))
┌──────────A─────────B───────C───────D───────E────F─────G───────H──────I──┐
│1  We Be Blades - Blacksmiths to the Royal Armory                         │
│2                                                                         │
│3                  Knife  Rapier  Dagger Plowshares Limitations            │
│4  Smith Hours        7      14     10       5 <=   1,920 Max Hours        │
│5  Per Item           1       1      1       1 <=     250 Max Items        │
│6  Ingots Required    3       4    2.5       2 <=     600 Max Ingots       │
│7  ======================================================================= │
│8  Profit/Item       $4      $7     $3      $3                             │
│9  Minimum Supply    24      24     24      36                             │
│10 Maximum Volume    48      48     48     100                             │
│11 ======================================================================= │
│12 Recommended     Knife  Rapier  Dagger Plowshares Total weapons: 222     │
│13 Quantity          48      48     26     100                             │
│14                                                                        │
│15 Dual Values (2) 0.40    2.20   0.00    0.60   Hours     0.00            │
│16                 Okay    Okay   Okay    Okay   Capacity  0.00            │
│17                                              Metal     1.20 Increase    │
│18 ======================================================================= │
│19 Max Profit      $905 Sum Product        $905                            │
│20                                                                       ↓ │
└──────────────────────────────────■──────────────────────────────────────┘
SMITH@PC.WQ1 [3]                                     NUM              READY
```

Figure 9-47. *The new scenario*

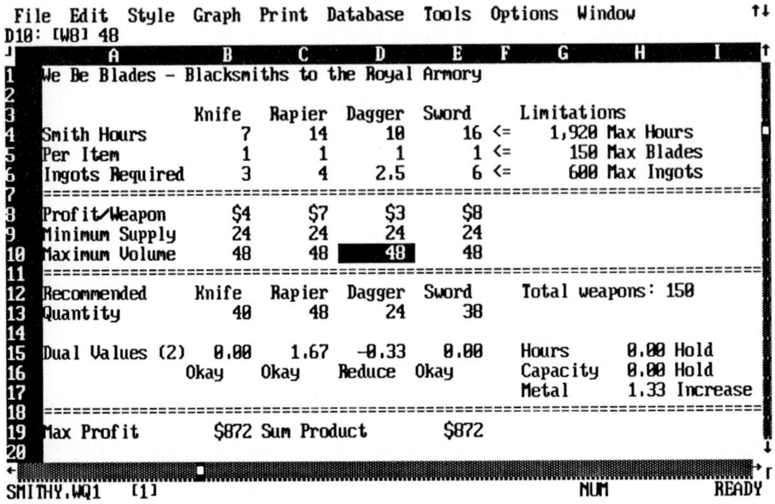

```
 File  Edit  Style  Graph  Print  Database  Tools  Options  Window          ↑↓
D10: [W8] 48
┌─────────────┬───────────────────────────────────────────────────────────────┐
│        A          B       C       D      E     F     G        H        I      │
│1 We Be Blades - Blacksmiths to the Royal Armory                               │
│2                                                                              │
│3              Knife  Rapier  Dagger  Sword    Limitations                     │
│4 Smith Hours     7      14      10     16 <=    1,920 Max Hours               │
│5 Per Item        1       1       1      1 <=      150 Max Blades              │
│6 Ingots Required 3       4     2.5      6 <=      600 Max Ingots              │
│7 =============================================================================│
│8 Profit/Weapon  $4      $7      $3     $8                                     │
│9 Minimum Supply 24      24      24     24                                     │
│10 Maximum Volume 48     48    [48]     48                                     │
│11 =============================================================================│
│12 Recommended  Knife  Rapier  Dagger  Sword   Total weapons: 150             │
│13 Quantity       40      48      24     38                                    │
│14                                                                             │
│15 Dual Values (2) 0.00    1.67   -0.33   0.00   Hours     0.00 Hold          │
│16                Okay    Okay   Reduce  Okay   Capacity  0.00 Hold           │
│17                                              Metal     1.33 Increase        │
│18 =============================================================================│
│19 Max Profit       $872 Sum Product         $872                             │
│20                                                                            │
└─────────────────────────────────────────────────────────────────────────────┘
SMITHY.WQ1  [1]                                          NUM          READY
```

Figure 9-48. *Initial example with strings added*

is greater than 0.5. A value significantly greater than 0 in a dual value result means that an increase in the constraint (in this case, the 600 ingots) would increase the optimized figure (the profit). The formulas in B16..E16 analyze the additional dual values, letting the blacksmith know that the suggested output levels are acceptable. In Figure 9-48 you can see how the results of the first scenario appear when text formulas are added and some of the variables changed. For more on text formulas, see the next chapter.

10 *Managing Text*

Although spreadsheets are designed primarily to manipulate numbers, in some situations you can use them to manipulate text as well. In this chapter several Quattro PRO commands that apply to text will be examined, and Quattro PRO will be used to produce paragraphs of text. Quattro PRO can convert spreadsheet data to text files that can be read by word processors and can also read text files from other programs. This process of data exchange will be examined. Finally, the string commands that manipulate labels will be discussed.

Quattro PRO as a Text Editor

Most spreadsheets require that you enter at least some text—words or phrases that describe the values in the model. Sometimes these pieces of text can be fairly lengthy. Consider the spreadsheet of projected expenses shown in Figure 10-1. The designer of this model felt that it was necessary to explain several of the assumptions at work in the calculations. This is a good practice to adopt, especially if the spreadsheet is going to be used or read by others.

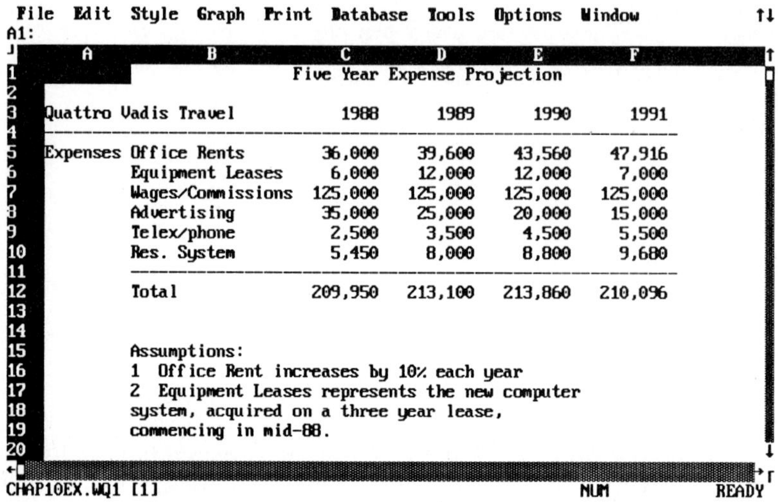

| File | Edit | Style | Graph | Print | Database | Tools | Options | Window | ↑↓ |

A1:

	A	B	C	D	E	F	
1			Five Year Expense Projection				
2							
3	Quattro Vadis Travel		1988	1989	1990	1991	
4			—————	—————	—————	—————	
5	Expenses	Office Rents	36,000	39,600	43,560	47,916	
6		Equipment Leases	6,000	12,000	12,000	7,000	
7		Wages/Commissions	125,000	125,000	125,000	125,000	
8		Advertising	35,000	25,000	20,000	15,000	
9		Telex/phone	2,500	3,500	4,500	5,500	
10		Res. System	5,450	8,000	8,800	9,680	
11			—————	—————	—————	—————	
12		Total	209,950	213,100	213,860	210,096	
13							
14							
15		Assumptions:					
16		1 Office Rent increases by 10% each year					
17		2 Equipment Leases represents the new computer					
18		system, acquired on a three year lease,					
19		commencing in mid-88.					
20							

CHAP10EX.WQ1 [1]   NUM   READY

Figure 10-1.   *Annotated expenses*

Entering Blocks of Text

Entering a piece of text, like assumption 1 in Figure 10-1, is simply a matter of typing a long label. You type the text and then press ENTER. Once you have entered the text, you may need to edit it, for which you use the F2 key, as described in Chapter 2. Remember that you can move your cursor through a long label by using the CTRL-RIGHT or CTRL-LEFT ARROW key combinations, which move the cursor five character positions to the right or left. Use CTRL-\ to delete to the end of the entry.

Text like that in assumption 2 is handled a little differently. It begins as a long label. When you type a label longer than 66 characters, Quattro PRO actually moves the worksheet display down a line to make the text visible as you type it. This is shown in Figure 10-2. The program does not know that you are typing a series of words. Notice that the word *on* is split between two lines because the sixty-sixth character on the first line of the label is the *o* in *on*. Quattro PRO does not perform the word processing function known as word wrap while you enter a long label. When you complete the label and enter it, the label initially spreads across the columns of the worksheet in a long, somewhat hard-to-read line of words.

```
 File  Edit  Style  Graph  Print  Database  Tools  Options  Window            ↑↓
[Enter] [Esc] 2  Equipment Leases represents the new computer system, acquired o
n a three year lease, commencing in mid-88.█
3█Quattro Vadis Travel        1988       1989       1990       1991             █
4                                                                               █
5 Expenses Office Rents      36,000     39,600     43,560     47,916            █
6         Equipment Leases    6,000     12,000     12,000      7,000            █
7         Wages/Commissions 125,000    125,000    125,000    125,000            █
8         Advertising        35,000     25,000     20,000     15,000            █
9         Telex/phone         2,500      3,500      4,500      5,500            █
10        Res. System         5,450      8,000      8,800      9,680            █
11        —————————————————————————————————————————————————————————            █
12        Total             209,950    213,100    213,860    210,096            ■
13                                                                              █
14                                                                             █
15        Assumptions:                                                          █
16        1  Office Rent increases by 10% each year                            █
17        ████████████████                                                     █
18                                                                             █
19                                                                              █
20                                                                              █
21                                                                              █
22                                                                             ↓
←▓█▓▓▓▓▓▓▓▓▓▓▓▓▓▓▓▓▓▓▓▓▓▓▓▓▓▓▓▓▓▓▓▓▓▓▓▓▓▓▓▓▓▓▓▓▓▓▓▓▓▓▓▓▓▓▓▓▓▓▓▓▓▓▓▓▓▓▓▓→┌
B17: [W17]                                                              VALUE
```

Figure 10 -2. *Typing a long label*

You will usually want to format a long label like this into a paragraph.
Quattro PRO does this by breaking the long label into several shorter labels
in a process called *block reformatting.* You perform this process with the
Tools Reformat command, which wraps the text within an area of the
spreadsheet that you designate. Place your cell selector on the cell containing the long label that you want to adjust to a more compact size, in this
case B17. Select Reformat from the Tools menu and, when you are
prompted for the block to be modified, point out the area into which you
want the long label rearranged. In this case, the block of cells B17..E19 is
highlighted, as shown in Figure 10-3.

The highlighted area should be empty except for the cell being reformatted. It should be as wide as you would like the paragraph to be and
should stretch several rows below the original cell, so that there is room
for the formatted text. When you press ENTER, the long label is divided into
a series of shorter labels as wide as the block you highlighted. Notice that
the label is divided without breaking the words. The results can be seen in
Figure 10-1 and in Figure 10-4, where the second line of the second
assumption is highlighted to show that it is indeed a label formed in the
cell below the original label.

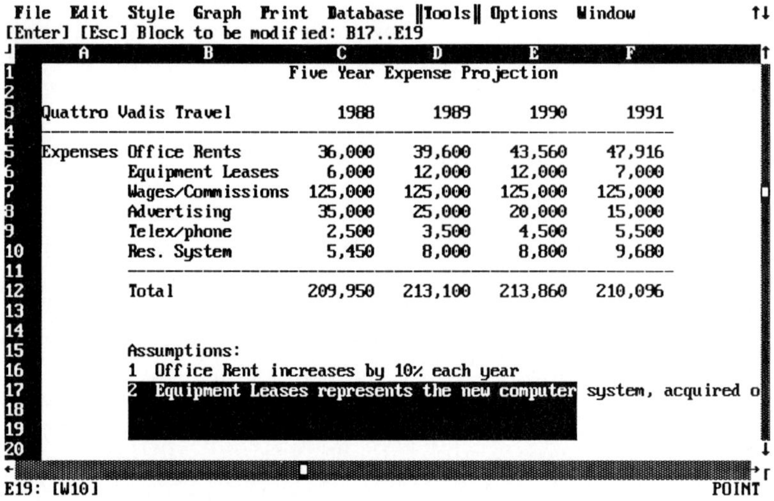

```
 File  Edit  Style  Graph  Print  Database ‖Tools‖ Options  Window                ↑↓
[Enter] [Esc] Block to be modified: B17..E19
⌐      A          B         C        D        E        F                            ↑
1                      Five Year Expense Projection
2
3  Quattro Vadis Travel           1988     1989     1990     1991
4  ─────────────────────────────────────────────────────────────
5  Expenses Office Rents        36,000   39,600   43,560   47,916
6           Equipment Leases     6,000   12,000   12,000    7,000
7           Wages/Commissions  125,000  125,000  125,000  125,000     ■
8           Advertising         35,000   25,000   20,000   15,000
9           Telex/phone          2,500    3,500    4,500    5,500
10          Res. System          5,450    8,000    8,800    9,680
11         ────────────────────────────────────────────────
12          Total              209,950  213,100  213,860  210,096
13
14
15          Assumptions:
16          1  Office Rent increases by 10% each year
17          2  Equipment Leases represents the new computer system, acquired o
18
19
20                                                                              ↓
←░░░░░░░░░░░░░░░░░░░░░░░░░░░░░░░░░ ■ ░░░░░░░░░░░░░░░░░░░░░░░░░░░░░░░░░░░░░░→ ⌐
E19: [W10]                                                                  POINT
```

Figure 10-3. *Reformat block*

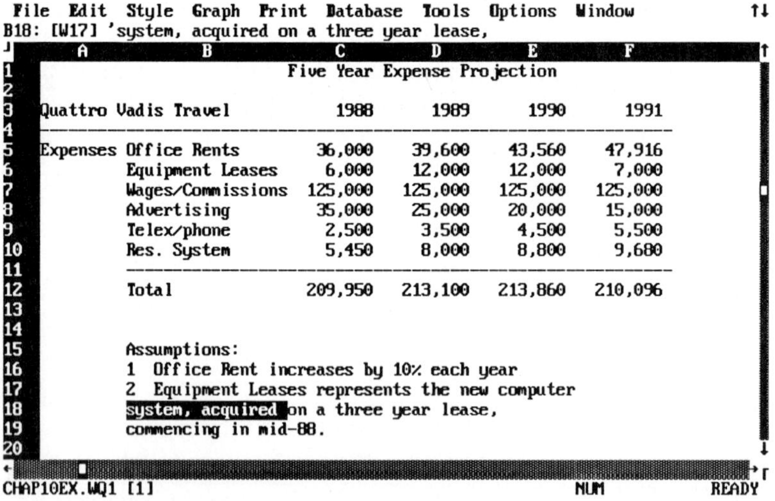

```
 File  Edit  Style  Graph  Print  Database  Tools  Options  Window                ↑↓
B18: [W17] 'system, acquired on a three year lease,
⌐      A          B         C        D        E        F                            ↑
1                      Five Year Expense Projection
2
3  Quattro Vadis Travel           1988     1989     1990     1991
4  ─────────────────────────────────────────────────────────────
5  Expenses Office Rents        36,000   39,600   43,560   47,916
6           Equipment Leases     6,000   12,000   12,000    7,000
7           Wages/Commissions  125,000  125,000  125,000  125,000     ■
8           Advertising         35,000   25,000   20,000   15,000
9           Telex/phone          2,500    3,500    4,500    5,500
10          Res. System          5,450    8,000    8,800    9,680
11         ────────────────────────────────────────────────
12          Total              209,950  213,100  213,860  210,096
13
14
15          Assumptions:
16          1  Office Rent increases by 10% each year
17          2  Equipment Leases represents the new computer
18          system, acquired on a three year lease,
19          commencing in mid-88.
20                                                                              ↓
←░░ ■ ░░░░░░░░░░░░░░░░░░░░░░░░░░░░░░░░░░░░░░░░░░░░░░░░░░░░░░░░░░░░░░░░░░░░░→ ⌐
CHAP10EX.WQ1 [1]                                                   NUM      READY
```

Figure 10-4. *Reformatted label*

If you need to edit the text that you have reformatted into shorter labels, you highlight the cell containing the text to be edited and press F2. However, you should not make any line in the middle of a paragraph (such as line 18 in this example) much shorter or longer than it was before editing. Quattro PRO will not automatically rearrange a paragraph of text after part of it has been shortened or lengthened, so you should keep editing to a minimum after reformatting. Nevertheless, you can compose short documents, letters, and memos from a series of long labels using the reformatting command. You can use a number of macros to simplify successive reformatting of text. Macros will be described in Chapter 11.

Figure 10-4 illustrates one small problem with reformatting: The numbers of the assumption are not set off from the text when the assumption is longer than one line. The Tools Reformat command cannot perform a paragraph indentation. However, you can solve this problem by approaching the text layout a little differently. By putting the assumption numbers in a separate column, either as values or right-aligned labels, you can set off the numbers from the text. This is shown in Figure 10-5. However adept you become with Quattro PRO, you cannot duplicate all of the editing features of a word processor. Fortunately, you can easily transfer information from Quattro PRO to a word processing program.

```
 File  Edit  Style  Graph  Print  Database  Tools  Options  Window          ↑↓
A1:
J     A          B          C        D        E        F                      ↑
1                    Five Year Expense Projection
2
3  Quattro Vadis Travel      1988     1989     1990     1991
4
5  Expenses Office Rents     36,000   39,600   43,560   47,916
6           Equipment Leases  6,000   12,000   12,000    7,000
7           Wages/Commissions 125,000 125,000 125,000  125,000
8           Advertising      35,000   25,000   20,000   15,000
9           Telex/phone       2,500    3,500    4,500    5,500
10          Res. System       5,450    8,000    8,800    9,680
11                           --------------------------------------
12          Total           209,950  213,100  213,860  210,096
13
14
15          Assumptions:
16        1 Office Rent increases by 10% each year
17        2 Equipment Leases represents the new computer
18          system, acquired on a three year lease,
19          commencing in mid-88.
20                                                                            ↓
CHAP10EX.WQ1 [1]                                      NUM            READY
```

Figure 10-5.   *Indented text*

Printing to a File

The basic process for transferring words and numbers from Quattro PRO to a word processing program is to create a special file that the word processor can read. Different word processing programs store their documents in different file formats. That is, the way in which the actual letters are stored on disk varies from program to program. However, all popular word processing programs can read files that are stored in ASCII, the American Standard Code for Information Interchange. One reason word processing programs can read information stored this way is that they communicate with printers in ASCII. Printers receive the letters and numbers of your documents as ASCII characters. In fact, that is how Quattro PRO sends your spreadsheet cells to the printer. By diverting data intended for the printer to a file on disk, you can create an *ASCII file,* or *print file,* of the spreadsheet data. Quattro PRO creates this file through the Print Destination command, which changes the target of the print block from the printer to a file. The file name usually has the extension PRN to distinguish it from other files. The data in the file is simply strings of letters, numbers, and spaces. Formulas are converted to their values and the values become text, including any formatting such as the dollar signs of the Currency format. The resulting file is sometimes called a *text file.*

Suppose that you have prepared projected revenue figures using Quattro PRO and you want to include them in a memo that you have been writing with your word processing program. Retyping the numbers from Quattro PRO into a word processing document would be a chore, and errors could arise from inaccurate typing. Instead, you decide to export the figures as an ASCII file. To do so, you use the Print Block command to tell Quattro PRO which cells of the worksheet are to be placed in the file.

Preparing for Printing

In order to make the data coming from Quattro PRO easier for your word processor to read, you may want to use the Print Layout command to change some of the options prior to printing to disk. By selecting Margins options from the Layout menu, you can change the left margin from 4 to 0 characters. This number will prevent Quattro PRO from adding four spaces to the left of the data in the file. Similarly, entering 0 for a top margin will stop Quattro PRO from adding lines to the top of the print block. The right margin setting needs particular attention, since the data in the file will be split into sections if you have set the right margin narrower than the width of the print block. In general, you will not want to use a right margin wider than 80 for a text file that will be read by a word processor that is using a normal 8 1/2- by-11-inch page. Otherwise, your text file will contain more data than will fit between the word processor's margins.

Completing the Print

Having selected the Print options you want to use, you can proceed to indicate the print block, the cells whose contents will be placed in the print file. With the settings indicated in Figure 10-6, the print block would be

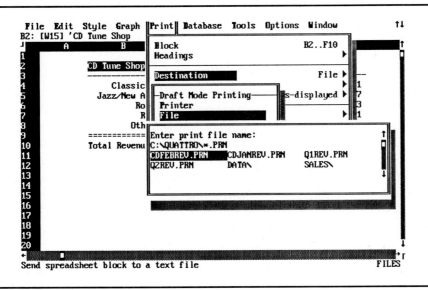

Figure 10 - 6. *The print block*

B2..F10. You do not want to include any extra columns and rows in the print block, since they will only add empty space to the word processing document.

In Figure 10-6 you can see that Destination has been selected from the Print menu and File is being chosen. As soon as you select File, Quattro PRO displays a list of existing PRN files. You can choose one of these names as the destination of the print block. If you select an existing name, the program asks if you want to replace the data in an existing print file with new data or if it should append the new data to the old. Appending new data is useful for accumulating data from various parts of a spreadsheet or from different spreadsheets into one text file. You can also choose to cancel the overwriting of an existing file or to back up the data already in it to a file with the BAQ extension.

To create a new file in the current directory, you type the file name. If you want the extension PRN, you leave the extension blank and Quattro PRO supplies it. Otherwise, you can enter a file name with an extension of your choice. Once you have selected or typed a name, that file name is written to the disk and space is set up to receive the print data. When you select Spreadsheet Print from the Print menu, the data is actually written into the file.

Editing the Results

Once you have created the print file, you can edit it with a word processor. Make sure that you have saved any necessary changes to your worksheet; then quit Quattro PRO and load your word processing program. You can type text as you normally would, up to the point where the print file is to be included. Before issuing the command to read in the print file, you may want to set the margins wide enough to accommodate the incoming data. How word processors read in ASCII text varies. The following list shows how to approach reading text with four popular word processors:

WordStar	Use Nondocument mode
WordPerfect	CTRL-F5, DOS Text, Retrieve
Displaywrite	CTRL-F6, Get File
Microsoft Word	ESCAPE, Transfer Load

Figure 10-7 shows the screen that WordPerfect users see when they use the CTRL-F5 command. Item 2, Retrieve, has been selected. The name of the document to be retrieved has been entered at the bottom of the screen. The results of this command are shown in Figure 10-8, where the data has been imported from Quattro PRO. You can now manipulate the text with traditional word processing tools like underlining, boldfacing, and so on. Bear in mind that the columns of numbers and labels are not set up with tab stops at this point; they are simply arranged with spaces. For this reason, you may want to avoid extensive rearranging of the data you have imported. Some word processors can convert such text into columns, which might be a good step to take if you want to rearrange the imported data extensively.

One category of data that is treated differently by word processing programs is the names and addresses used for *mail merging,* the customizing of a form letter with names and other information from a list. Some word processing programs—WordPerfect, for example—can read a name-and- address list from a spreadsheet file for mail merging if the file is saved in the DIF format. Accomplishing this is a specialized word processing function, and you should consult the word processor program manual or a

---

```
                        Memorandum

To:       Fred

From:     Sue

Subject:  CD Tune Performance

Fred:

     Here are the figures that you asked me to pull together for
the new investment property called the CD Tune Shop.
```

```
1 Save; 2 Retrieve (CR/LF to [HRt]); 3 Retrieve (CR/LF to [SRt] in HZone): 0
```

Figure 10 -7. *WordPerfect Text menu*

```
                             Memorandum

To:       Fred

From:     Sue

Subject:  CD Tune Performance

Fred:

          Here are the figures that you asked me to pull together for
      the new investment property called the CD Tune Shop.

      CD Tune Shop     Jan-90    Feb-90    Mar-90    Qtr Total
      ------------------------------------------------------------
          Classical    1,002      676       443        2,121
      Jazz/New Age       497      385       145        1,027
             Rock        997      892       524        2,413
              R&B        267      567      1657        2,491
            Other        315      311       517        1,143
      ============================================================
      Total Revenue    $3,078    $2,831    $3,286      $9,195


C:\WP\DOCS\MEMO2F                              Doc 1 Pg 1 Ln 3.17" Pos 1"
```

Figure 10 - 8.   *The memorandum*

detailed text about that program. Although Quattro PRO may not be mentioned in the documentation, remember that a Quattro PRO spreadsheet can be saved as a 1-2-3 worksheet by using the extension WKS for Release 1A or WK1 for Release 2.

Text into Quattro PRO

Having seen how Quattro PRO creates a text file that can be read by word processing programs, you will see next how Quattro PRO reads text files into a spreadsheet. At times you may have useful information stored in files created by another program, but Quattro PRO cannot read the format of those files. You might like to bring this information into a Quattro PRO spreadsheet. One way of doing this is to convert the data into a text file by using the other program's equivalent of Quattro PRO's Print Destination File command.

Importing ASCII Text Files

Suppose your company has an accounting program for accounts receivable. You would like to take a spreadsheet of the accounts receivable with you when making calls. The accounting program should be able to print a text file to disk. In Figure 10-9 you can see the command in Quattro PRO that you need to use, the Tools Import command, about to be issued with the cell selector in A1 of a blank worksheet.

You will probably want to try your first experiments with importing text files using a blank spreadsheet, since the data that is brought in can have unexpected effects on existing data in the spreadsheet. Your choices when importing files are between ASCII Text File and Comma & "" Delimited File. The Delimited File option is used for bringing in data from programs that create files in which the pieces of information are separated by either commas, quotes, or both. The ASCII Text option is for importing a file name that consists simply of lines of data separated by spaces, not punctuation.

When you issue the Tools Import ASCII Text File command, you must specify the name of the file. That file is then read into the worksheet at the current position of the cell selector, as shown in Figure 10-10.

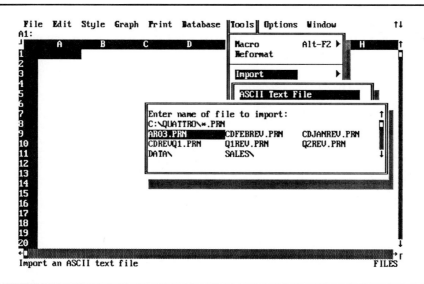

Figure 10-9.   *Tools Import*

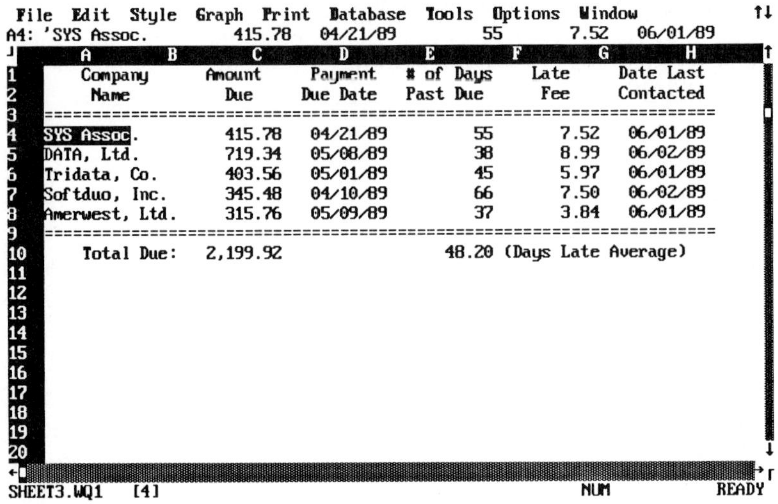

```
 File  Edit  Style   Graph  Print  Database  Tools  Options  Window                ↑↓
A4: 'SYS Assoc.            415.78   04/21/89          55       7.52    06/01/89
  ┌────A──────B───────C────────D──────E───────F───────G────────H─────┐
 1│   Company        Amount    Payment   # of Days   Late     Date Last        │
 2│   Name           Due       Due Date  Past Due    Fee      Contacted        │
 3│===================================================================│
 4│ SYS Assoc.        415.78   04/21/89      55       7.52    06/01/89          │
 5│ DATA, Ltd.        719.34   05/08/89      38       8.99    06/02/89          │
 6│ Tridata, Co.      403.56   05/01/89      45       5.97    06/01/89          │
 7│ Softduo, Inc.     345.48   04/10/89      66       7.50    06/02/89          │
 8│ Amerwest, Ltd.    315.76   05/09/89      37       3.84    06/01/89          │
 9│===================================================================│
10│   Total Due:     2,199.92               48.20 (Days Late Average)          │
11│                                                                            │
12│                                                                            │
13│                                                                            │
14│                                                                            │
15│                                                                            │
16│                                                                            │
17│                                                                            │
18│                                                                            │
19│                                                                            │
20│                                                                            │
  └────────────────────────────────────────────────────────────────┘
SHEET3.WQ1   [4]                                             NUM        READY
```

Figure 10-10.   *Imported file*

This looks a lot like a spreadsheet, but if you carefully observe the contents of cell A4, you will see that it is one long label. There is no data in columns B, C, D, and so on. There are two techniques you can use to help Quattro PRO make sense of data like this. The first is called *parsing,* which involves breaking up the lines of data according to a set of interpretation rules. The second approach is to use the string functions, described later in this chapter.

Using the Tools Parse Command

To give Quattro PRO a set of rules by which to break up the long labels of data into separate cells of information, you place your cell selector on the first cell containing a label to be parsed. You then issue the Tools Parse command, which displays the menu shown in Figure 10-11. Next, select the third option, Create. This option inserts a new row into the worksheet above the current row. Quattro PRO places a line of symbols, called the *parse line,* into this row, as shown in Figure 10-12.

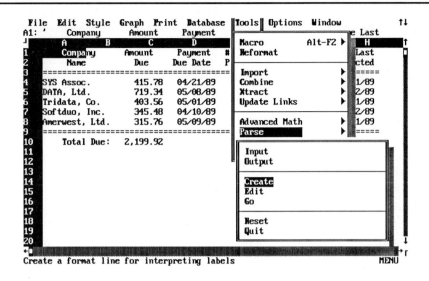

Figure 10-11. *Parse menu*

```
 File  Edit  Style  Graph  Print  Database ‖Tools‖ Options  Window                      ↑↓
A1: │*****L>>>>>>>*******L>>>>>******L>>>>>>***L*L>*L>>>****L>>>*****L>>>*L>>>
 ┌   A       B       C       D        E        F        G       H                        ┐↑
 1 *****L>>>>>>>*******L>>>>>******L>>>>>>***L*L>*L>>>****L>>>*****L>>>*L>>>
 2   Company        Amount    Payment    # of Days    Late      Date Last
 3   Name           Due       Due Date   Past Due     Fee       Contacted
 4 ==========================================================================
 5 SYS Assoc.        415.78    04/21/89       55        7.52     06/01/89
 6 DATA, Ltd.        719.34    05/08/89       38        8.99     06/02/89
 7 Tridata, Co.      403.56    05/01/89       45        5.97     06/01/89
 8 Softduo, Inc.     345.48    04/10/89       66        7.50     06/02/89
 9 Amerwest, Ltd.    315.76    05/09/89       37        3.84     06/01/89
10 ==========================================================================
11    Total Due:    2,199.92                 48.20 (Days Late Average)
12
13
14
15
16
17
18
19
20
 └                                                                                       ┘↓
SHEET3.WQ1  [4]                                              NUM OVR              FRMT
```

Figure 10-12. *Parse line*

The symbols begin with the | character, which tells Quattro PRO not to print this line. Several asterisks follow, indicating spaces in the label in the new row 2. The letter *L* stands for labels, and each of the labels on row 2 have been identified as such. The greater-than sign (>) stands for the number of characters in the labels.

Parse Editing

If you look closely at the way this parse line reads, you can see that the text *# of Days* has been read as three labels. However, these characters should be read as one label. This is why the Parse menu has the Edit option. There are many situations in which the parse line created by Quattro PRO does not interpret the text as you would like it to. After all, it is a complex logical task to determine what parts of this long label should be placed in which cells.

When you are still at the Parse menu, you can select Edit immediately after issuing the Create command, and the menu will disappear so that you can make changes to the symbols. Notice that you are automatically placed into OVERSTRIKE mode, as indicated by the bottom status line message, OVR. The reason for this mode is that, although the symbols on the parse line may be wrong, there are just the right number of them to describe the line. Instead of adding and deleting symbols, you type the ones you want over the top of the incorrect ones. For example, suppose two sets of labels need to be changed because they have been erroneously read as multiple columns (and note the edited line in Figure 10-13). When you have edited the line, press ENTER to return to the Parse menu. You can also edit a parse line from READY mode by using the F2 key, since the parse line is simply a label.

Although the parse line in Figure 10-13 looks fairly good for the column heading labels, clearly the data on row 5 is significantly different from the top three lines. Consequently, the Parse command must be issued again to create a second parse line for the number rows. You do this by quitting the Parse menu and placing the cell selector in column A of row 5. This time when you select the Tools Parse Create command, the parse line will contain the letters *V* for value and *D* for date. If you had time data, you would see *T* for time. Note that dates and times are only read as such by the Parse command if they conform to the date and time formats shown in the last chapter. The greater-than sign (>) is used for the number of digits in the values and dates. By looking closely, you can see that the *V* and *L*

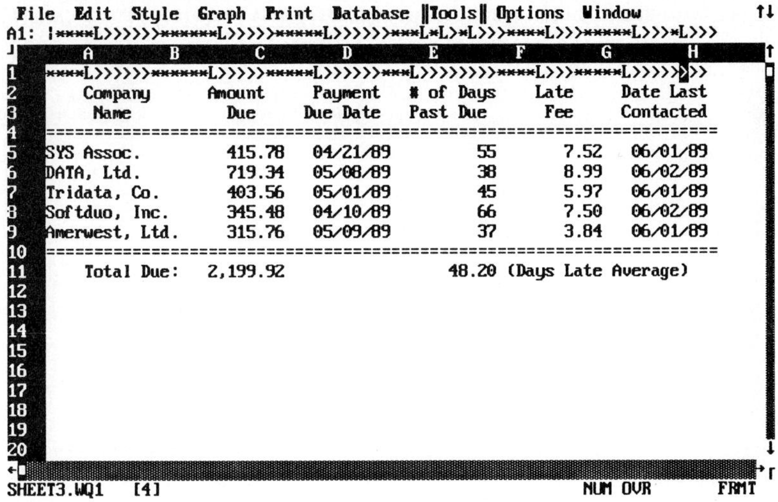

```
    File  Edit  Style  Graph  Print  Database ‖Tools‖ Options  Window            ↑↓
  A1: |*****L>>>>>*****L>>>>>*****L>>>>>***L*L>*L>>>****L>>>*****L>>>*L>>>
 ⌐       A       B       C       D       E       F       G       H            t
 1 *****L>>>>>*****L>>>>>*****L>>>>>***L>>>>>>>>*****L>>>*****L>>>>> >>          ▯
 2     Company       Amount  Payment  # of Days   Late   Date Last
 3      Name          Due    Due Date Past Due    Fee    Contacted
 4    =====================================================================
 5 SYS Assoc.        415.78  04/21/89     55      7.52   06/01/89
 6 DATA, Ltd.        719.34  05/08/89     38      8.99   06/02/89
 7 Tridata, Co.      403.56  05/01/89     45      5.97   06/01/89
 8 Softduo, Inc.     345.48  04/10/89     66      7.50   06/02/89
 9 Amerwest, Ltd.    315.76  05/09/89     37      3.84   06/01/89
10    =====================================================================
11    Total Due:    2,199.92            48.20 (Days Late Average)
12
13
14
15
16
17
18
19
20                                                                            ↓
 ◄■                                                                        ►  r
  SHEET3.WQ1    [4]                                     NUM OVR          FRMT
```

Figure 10-13.   *Edited parse line*

are themselves counted in the numbering of the characters. Thus, the first value in Figure 10-14 is being read as six digits long. In fact, the line you see on row 5 of Figure 10-14 has been edited to conform more closely to the data. The company name *SYS Assoc.* was originally read as two labels, which were changed to one label with the Parse Edit command.

Parse Completion

When the parse lines are acceptable (and it may take several attempts to perfect them) you must identify the input and output cells. The *input cells* are those that contain the data to be parsed including the parse lines, in this case cells A1..H12. The *output cell* is the top-left corner of the area of the spreadsheet you want the parsed data to occupy, in this case, cell A14. When you have specified the input and output cells, you can issue the Go command. The results are shown in Figure 10-15, where both of the parse lines used are completely visible. Although not all of the company names are readable because the column widths are currently set at the default of 9, you can see that the numbers were read as numbers and the dates as

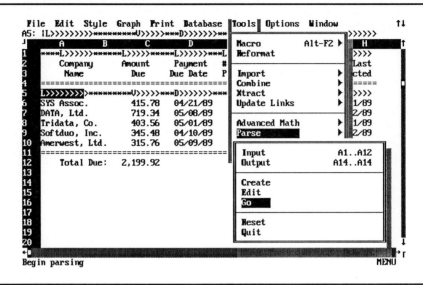

Figure 10-14. *Parse Go command*

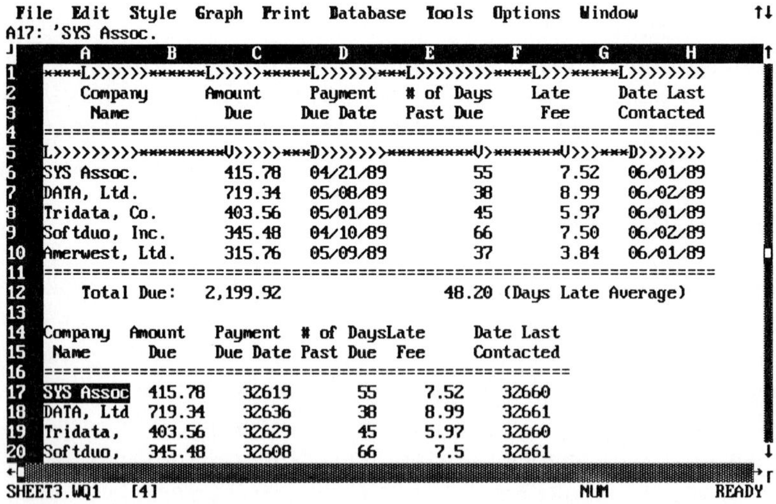

Figure 10-15. *Parse results*

serial numbers. You can format the dates as described in Chapter 9. The labels appear to be fine, although widening the columns will show that there are not enough equal signs. The == labels can be replaced with \=.

The one item that is likely to be problematic in parsing is the total line. It is not worth a separate parse line, since the formulas for the totals will need to be recreated anyway. A formula and the formatting of dates can be added later to complete the process.

Parsing text is not a particularly common operation for most spreadsheet users, but it can be a great time-saver when you need to work with data from other programs.

Text in Formulas

Text entered into a cell in Quattro PRO is a label and has no numeric value. However, the program can still use labels in many formulas. This means that you can handle a variety of data in your spreadsheet. Text formulas are particularly useful when you are developing macro commands, as described in Chapter 12.

Labels in Logical Functions

You can use text in several of the @functions. As you saw in Chapter 9, Quattro PRO can enter a label in a cell by means of an @IF formula. The formula

@IF(A1>1000,"Expensive","Cheap")

returns the answer "Expensive" if the contents of A1 are greater than 1000, or "Cheap" if not.

You can use text in the @CHOOSE function to supply a label for a number. Thus, the formula for typing the day of the week, described in the last chapter, used @CHOOSE to look up the words Saturday, Sunday, and so on. As with the @IF function, text in a @CHOOSE statement must be enclosed in quotes.

The @VLOOKUP function can turn a number into a label or vice versa. This function is useful for such applications as evaluating survey responses that are recorded as letters. A simple table, entered into a spreadsheet and named TABLE with the Edit Name Create command, can convert the letters *A* through *E* to the numbers 1 through 5:

A   1
B   2
C   3
D   4
E   5

The formula to return a number corresponding to the value in cell B5 would read @VLOOKUP(B5,TABLE,1).

The company names used in the survey example in Chapter 9 were imaginary names, created by looking up numbers in a table of typical names. In fact, the formula combined parts of names in the table to form new names. Combining text from separate cells is described in the next section.

Combining Labels

Quattro PRO formulas can reference labels in other cells as well as values, as you can see in Figure 10-16.

The formula +B16 has been placed in cell B19. This formula cross references the name Emma from the list of names into the Availability Report. There are a number of situations where it is useful to relate label cells in this manner. Using the formula +C16 in cell C19, you could bring the last name into the cell next to B19.

If you are preparing an information report from a spreadsheet, you may want to connect the two names with just one space between them, as in Emma Wong. You might be tempted to use the formula +B16+C16 to do this, but that formula results in 0 because Quattro PRO thinks you are trying to add two labels together, and labels have a value of 0. However, you can combine labels with the & sign. The formula +B16&B16 produces Emma Wong.

The & sign adds labels together. This process is called concatenation. Unfortunately, the two parts of the name have been completely concatenated without a space between them. You can add a space and other text such as words and punctuation to a concatenated formula by enclosing

```
 File  Edit  Style  Graph  Print  Database  Tools  Options  Window          ↑↓
B19: +B16
      A         B        C     D     E        F        G        H
1
2              TOA On-Call Roster                    As of: 07-May-90
3
4              First     Last  Rank  Based    Standby  Notice  Last Call
5              Joe       Smith   3   Rio      Yes        2     04/06/90
6              Alan      Chan    1   London   Yes        6     04/26/90
7              Sue       Wong    1   Paris    No         4     04/08/90
8              Jane      Folsom  2   Rio      Yes        3     04/23/90
9              Nancy     Blass   3   Paris    Yes        1     05/06/90
10             Peter     Green   6   Paris    No        10     05/04/90
11             Will      Right   2   London   No         2     04/14/90
12             Bill      Front   4   Paris    No         3     04/17/90
13             Jane      Dobbs   7   Rome     No         1     05/03/90
14             Mary      Grant   2   Tokyo    Yes        4     05/05/90
15             Nina      Smith   7   Paris    Yes        6     04/15/90
16             Emma      Wong    2   Rome     Yes        3     04/24/90
17
18             Availability Report:
19             Emma
20
DBPRESRT.WQ1 [3]                                      NUM              READY
```

Figure 10-16. *Referencing text*

it in quotes ("). You must add the text in quotes to the formula with an &
sign. Thus,

+B16&" "&C16

produces the desired result, shown in Figure 10-17.

The & sign is not acceptable as the first character in a formula, but you
can use it between cell references and strings of text in a formula. The
previous formula is simply three pieces of information: a cell reference,
B16; text placed in quotes, in this case, a space " "; and another cell
reference, C16. The formula begins with a + sign to let Quattro PRO know
this a formula. The & sign simply works as an addition sign for text data.
You can create some useful formulas by using these elements for cell
referencing (the & sign and the quoted text preceded by a + sign). In Figure
10-18 you can see that the Availability Report can take on the appearance
of a written statement; using the last two cells of the staff list. If the list is
sorted by the Standby column, in ascending order, then the employees with
"Yes" in this column will be at the bottom.

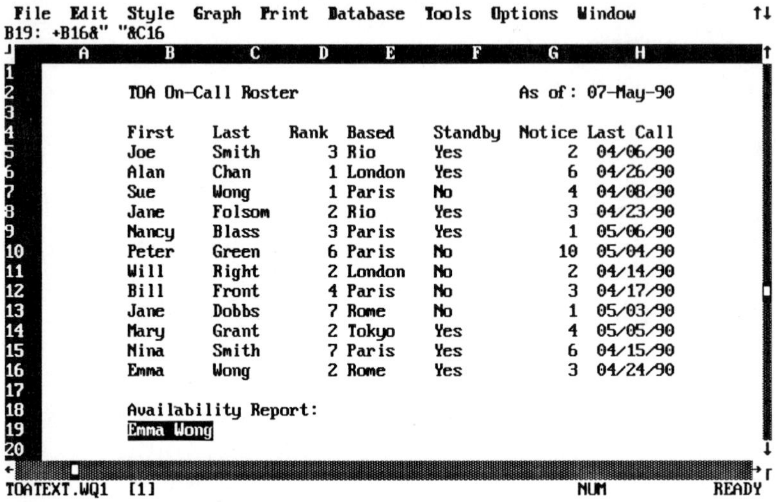

```
 File  Edit  Style  Graph  Print  Database  Tools  Options  Window          ↑↓
B19: +B16&" "&C16
┘      A        B        C      D      E        F     G        H            ↑
1┌──────────────────────────────────────────────────────────────────────┐
2│        TOA On-Call Roster                        As of: 07-May-90      │
3│                                                                        │
4│        First    Last     Rank  Based    Standby  Notice Last Call      │
5│        Joe      Smith      3 Rio        Yes         2  04/06/90         │
6│        Alan     Chan       1 London     Yes         6  04/26/90         │
7│        Sue      Wong       1 Paris      No          4  04/08/90         │
8│        Jane     Folsom     2 Rio        Yes         3  04/23/90         │
9│        Nancy    Blass      3 Paris      Yes         1  05/06/90         │
10│       Peter    Green      6 Paris      No         10  05/04/90         │
11│       Will     Right      2 London     No          2  04/14/90         │
12│       Bill     Front      4 Paris      No          3  04/17/90         │
13│       Jane     Dobbs      7 Rome       No          1  05/03/90         │
14│       Mary     Grant      2 Tokyo      Yes         4  05/05/90         │
15│       Nina     Smith      7 Paris      Yes         6  04/15/90         │
16│       Emma     Wong       2 Rome       Yes         3  04/24/90         │
17│                                                                        │
18│       Availability Report:                                            │
19│       ▮Emma Wong▮                                                      │
20└──────────────────────────────────────────────────────────────────────┘↓
←░░░░░░░░░░░░░░░░░░░░░░░░░░░░░░░░░░░░░░░░░░░░░░░░░░░░░░░░░░░░░░░░░░░░░░░→ ┌
TOATEXT.WQ1   [1]                                        NUM        READY
```

Figure 10-17. *Improved concatenation*

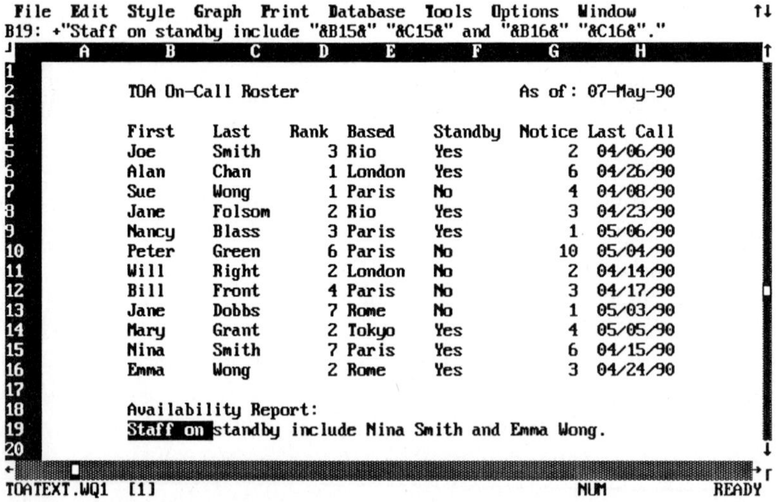

```
 File  Edit  Style  Graph  Print  Database  Tools  Options  Window          ↑↓
B19: +"Staff on standby include "&B15&" "&C15&" and "&B16&" "&C16"."
┘      A        B        C      D      E        F     G        H            ↑
1┌──────────────────────────────────────────────────────────────────────┐
2│        TOA On-Call Roster                        As of: 07-May-90      │
3│                                                                        │
4│        First    Last     Rank  Based    Standby  Notice Last Call      │
5│        Joe      Smith      3 Rio        Yes         2  04/06/90         │
6│        Alan     Chan       1 London     Yes         6  04/26/90         │
7│        Sue      Wong       1 Paris      No          4  04/08/90         │
8│        Jane     Folsom     2 Rio        Yes         3  04/23/90         │
9│        Nancy    Blass      3 Paris      Yes         1  05/06/90         │
10│       Peter    Green      6 Paris      No         10  05/04/90         │
11│       Will     Right      2 London     No          2  04/14/90         │
12│       Bill     Front      4 Paris      No          3  04/17/90         │
13│       Jane     Dobbs      7 Rome       No          1  05/03/90         │
14│       Mary     Grant      2 Tokyo      Yes         4  05/05/90         │
15│       Nina     Smith      7 Paris      Yes         6  04/15/90         │
16│       Emma     Wong       2 Rome       Yes         3  04/24/90         │
17│                                                                        │
18│       Availability Report:                                            │
19│       ▮Staff on▮ standby include Nina Smith and Emma Wong.            │
20└──────────────────────────────────────────────────────────────────────┘↓
←░░░░░░░░░░░░░░░░░░░░░░░░░░░░░░░░░░░░░░░░░░░░░░░░░░░░░░░░░░░░░░░░░░░░░░░→ ┌
TOATEXT.WQ1   [1]                                        NUM        READY
```

Figure 10-18. *Lengthy string formula*

The benefit of using a formula like this, rather than simply typing a statement, is that the cell references in the formula are dynamic. When members of the available staff change, the text is updated. When new names appear in B15 through C16, then they will also appear in the formula.

This means that you can create invoices, letters, and other documents that have the appearance of static text but are, in fact, dynamically related to the contents of the spreadsheet.

A simple example of this is shown in Figure 10-19, which is a list of travel agents and their sales figures. The list is sorted by sales, and the formula in cell A3 states that the two top agents are those whose names appear in cells A6 and A7. If the figures in the Sales column change and the list is re-sorted, the statement will still be correct. This occurred when it was discovered that Liz's sales figures were incorrect. The correct figure now places her at the top of the re-sorted list, as shown in Figure 10-20.

```
 File  Edit  Style  Graph  Print  Database  Tools  Options  Window          ↑↓
A3: [W9] +"The top two agents are "&A6&" and "&A7&"!"
 J        A        B          C           D        E      F      G          ↑
1                     Quattro Vadis Sales Totals
2
3  The top two agents are Ron and Jud!
4
5       Agent      Office      Sales    Commissions
6        Ron    Van Ness     $901,250     $54,075
7        Jud    General      $890,670     $53,440
8        Liz    Polk St.     $878,590     $52,715
9        Joe    San Mateo    $876,900     $52,614
10       Tom    Union Sq.    $859,600     $51,576
11       Ian    Union Sq.    $849,050     $50,943
12       Jim    General      $804,550     $48,273
13       Ann    Polk St.     $768,545     $46,113
14       Sal    San Mateo    $760,805     $45,648
15       Sue    Union Sq.    $687,450     $41,247
16       Sam    Van Ness     $586,780     $35,207
17       Rob    Polk St.     $564,560     $33,874
18       Lee    Union Sq.    $500,001     $30,000
19       Tim    Van Ness     $459,870     $27,592
20       Pip    Polk St.     $458,790     $27,527
SALESTAT.WQ1 [1]                              NUM        READY
```

Figure 10-19. *The top agents*

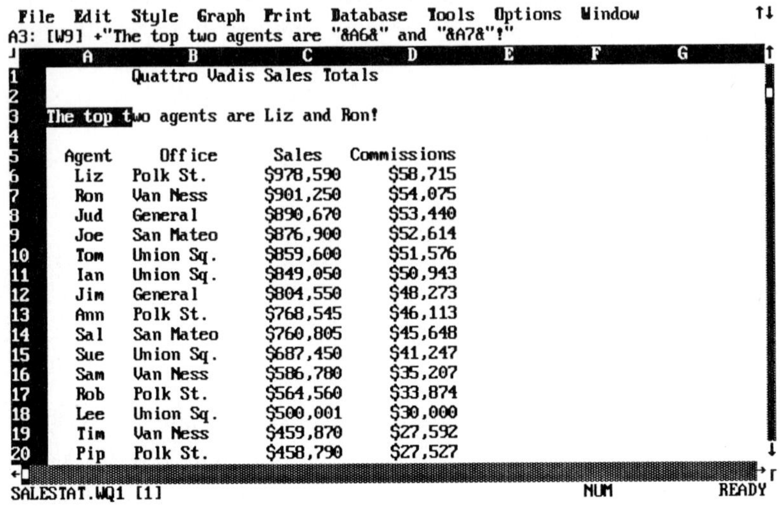

```
 File  Edit  Style  Graph  Print  Database  Tools  Options  Window        ↑↓
A3: [W9] +"The top two agents are "&A6&" and "&A7&"!"
↓       A         B          C         D         E      F       G        ↑
1                    Quattro Vadis Sales Totals
2
3   The top two agents are Liz and Ron!
4
5     Agent       Office      Sales    Commissions
6      Liz      Polk St.    $978,590     $58,715
7      Ron      Van Ness    $901,250     $54,075
8      Jud      General     $890,670     $53,440
9      Joe      San Mateo   $876,900     $52,614
10     Tom      Union Sq.   $859,600     $51,576
11     Ian      Union Sq.   $849,050     $50,943
12     Jim      General     $804,550     $48,273
13     Ann      Polk St.    $768,545     $46,113
14     Sal      San Mateo   $760,805     $45,648
15     Sue      Union Sq.   $687,450     $41,247
16     Sam      Van Ness    $586,780     $35,207
17     Rob      Polk St.    $564,560     $33,874
18     Lee      Union Sq.   $500,001     $30,000
19     Tim      Van Ness    $459,870     $27,592
20     Pip      Polk St.    $458,790     $27,527
SALESTAT.WQ1 [1]                                    NUM        READY
```

Figure 10-20. *The re-sorted sales*

Label Formulas to Labels

If you ever want to change a formula that results in a label to the label produced by that formula, you can use the Edit Values command. This command requires that you indicate the cell or block of cells that is being converted to values and a destination. The destination can be a separate area of the worksheet, if you want to preserve the original formulas; or the original cells themselves, if you want to convert them permanently to their result.

Numeric Formulas to Labels

In several situations you will find it useful to convert a numeric formula to a label. Suppose you have developed a lengthy formula containing numerous relative references to cell locations. The formula is correct but located in the wrong cell. When you copy or move a formula with the Edit commands, the relative cell references change relative to the new location of seen the formula. To prevent this from happening, you first convert the formula to a label and then copy or move it. Finally, you convert it back to a formula. The easiest way to do this is to highlight the formula in question, press F2 to edit the cell, press HOME to move the cursor to the beginning of the formula, and then type an apostrophe ('). When you press ENTER, the formula will appear as a left-justified label. To return the formula to active status, you reverse the procedure: edit the cell, press HOME, and delete the apostrophe.

This procedure is particularly useful when you enter a formula to which Quattro PRO objects, that is, one containing a syntax error. If the formula is lengthy, the error might not be immediately apparent and you might need time to find it. If the formula contains a reference to a named block that has not yet been created, you will not be able to enter the formula, and you might think that you have to abandon the typing that it took to create the formula. This loss can be avoided if you press HOME to go to the beginning of the formula, type an apostrophe ('), and press ENTER to store the formula as a label. Then you can examine the formula, find the problem, and create any necessary block names before converting the label back to a formula.

String Functions

A specialized means of working with labels in formulas in Quattro PRO is through the use of @functions specifically designed for manipulating text. These functions are called the *string functions* because a string in Quattro PRO is a series of characters that results in a label and not a value. String functions are very valuable when working with data imported from other programs in the form of text files. They can also be used effectively with some advanced macro commands, as described in Chapter 12.

@CHAR

Earlier you saw that many programs can share information by using ASCII characters. There are 256 ASCII characters, numbered from 0 to 255. Many of them are symbols not found on the keyboard, such as graphics characters. The @CHAR function can display these codes in Quattro PRO.

@CHAR returns the ASCII character corresponding to a given ASCII code. Its syntax is

@CHAR(*code*)

where *code* is a numeric value between 0 and 255. Since Quattro PRO will truncate any values entered as *code* to an integer, you should always enter the *code* argument as an integer.

While you can refer to a standard ASCII table for numbers corresponding to the ASCII codes for each character, you can use the @CHAR function instead to create such a table within Quattro PRO. In Figure 10-21, the numbers 80 through 255 have been entered in alternating columns. The @CHAR function has been used to show the character corresponding to that code number. For example, the pounds sterling sign is code 156. You can print this as a reference for the codes, although some printers will not print all of the characters.

The usefulness of the @CHAR function depends on how much of your programming requires looking up ASCII codes, or on how much imagination you want to use in designing your spreadsheets. For example, the box around the assumptions in the Expense Projection shown in Figure 10-22

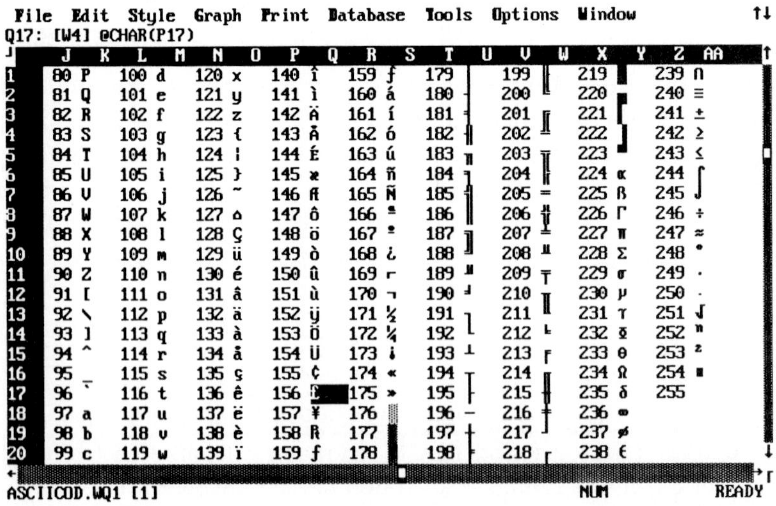

Figure 10-21.   *ASCII table*

was created with the @CHAR command and another string function, @REPEAT. Of course, you can use the Line Drawing and Shading commands on the Style menu to create boxes and other designs without using the @CHAR function.

@REPEAT

The @REPEAT function repeats a string of characters a specified number of times. Its syntax is

@REPEAT(*string,number*)

where *string* is a string value and *number* is a numeric value greater than or equal to 0. @REPEAT returns as many copies of the *string* as you specify with *number*. The result is a label.

While this function is somewhat similar to the repeating label prefix (\) that is used to produce dashed lines in a cell, the main difference is that with @REPEAT you can specify exactly how many times you want the string to be repeated. Also, the label prefix adjusts the number of repeated

```
 File  Edit  Style  Graph  Print  Database  Tools  Options  Window          ↑↓
B14: [W17] @REPEAT(@CHAR(205),17)
J      A         B           C        D        E        F                    ↑
1                       Five Year Expense Projection
2
3  Quattro Vadis Travel        1988     1989     1990     1991
4
5  Expenses Office Rents      36,000   39,600   43,560   47,916
6           Equipment Leases   6,000   12,000   12,000    7,000
7           Wages/Commissions 125,000 125,000  125,000  125,000
8           Advertising       35,000   25,000   20,000   15,000
9           Telex/phone        2,500    3,500    4,500    5,500        ■
10          Res. System        5,450    8,000    8,800    9,680
11
12          Total            209,950  213,100  213,860  210,096
13
14
15          Assumptions:
16          1  Office Rent increases by 10% each year
17          2  Equipment Leases represents the new computer
18             system, to be acquired on a 3 year lease,
19             commencing in mid-88.
20                                                                           ↓
LINETXT.WQ1  [1]                                         NUM         READY
```

Figure 10 -22. *Boxed assumptions*

characters to fit the column, even when the width is changed. The @REPEAT function can display a fixed number of characters that does not change. When you specify a text string with @REPEAT, you must surround it by double quotes (").

The *number* argument in the @REPEAT statement can be a formula or a cell reference. This argument can be used to repeat a character or characters according to a variable factor. An application of this ability is shown in the formula used to produce a dashed line that is one character shorter than the width of the column. For example, when you have a column that is seven characters wide you can obtain this effect:

```
May-88 Jun-88 Jul-88
====== ====== ======
```

Compare this with the effect of using the Cell Fill command (in this case, \=) to produce a continuous row of equal signs, as shown here:

```
May-88 Jun-88 Jul-88
=====================
```

The formula that creates the short line uses the @CELL function to measure the width of the current column, as in

```
@REPEAT("=",@CELL("width", X)-1)
```

where X is the cell above the one in which the formula is placed. Note that although the @CELL function will read the current column width when you enter the formula, it does not respond to changes as quickly as the Cell Fill (\) command. If you alter the column width after entering the @CELL formula you will need to press the Calc key (F9) to update the @CELL reading, even if you have Background or Automatic calculation in effect.

Whether you will like the appearance of this short line will depend on the width of the column and the length of the data in the column. Remember that you can use the Style Alignment command to center the results of string formulas. This enables you to produce an effect like this:

```
May-88   Jun-88   Jul-88
======   ======   ======
```

In this case the column widths were set to 10 and the formula was modified to take four characters away from the column width:

@REPEAT("=",@CELL("width", X)-4)

Center alignment was then applied to both rows.

One important difference between using and the @REPEAT function is that you can use @REPEAT with the @CHAR function. In this way you can repeat any of the ASCII characters. These include the line characters with which you can build shapes from the ASCII codes. An example is the box shown in Figure 10-12. Thus, the formula

@REPEAT(@CHAR(205),17)

creates a label by repeating the character represented by ASCII code 205 (a double horizontal line) 17 times, as shown in Figure 10-22.

By copying this formula to C14..E14 and adjusting the number by which the character is repeated so that it matches each column width, you can build a double line. The block B14..E14 can be copied in its entirety to line 20, columns B through E. The labels in columns A and F are combinations of characters. Here you can see that F15 is the blank character (255) repeated four times plus the double vertical line (186):

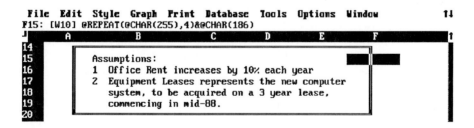

The formula to make the corner in E14 is the same as the one that makes the vertical line, except that the blank (255) is replaced by the double line (205), and the vertical line (186) is replaced by the character for an upper-right, double vertical line corner (187). This might seem like a lot of work to build a box, but remember that copying and editing the formulas makes it easy to duplicate and enhance the basic box. You can also perform a Tools Xtract operation to save the box into a separate file for later use in other spreadsheets. You may want to change the box or any other @CHAR creation from a formula to a series of characters. Like other formulas that produce labels on screen, the Edit Values command converts the @CHAR result into a label. Remember that you can also create lines and shading with commands from the Style menu, which may be easier to use if you are not confident with string functions.

@CODE

A reverse of the @CHAR function, the @CODE function tells you the ASCII code of a special character. Why would you want to know this? Sometimes data that you import from another program is corrupted by odd characters. Identifying them with the @CODE function could help you determine their origin. Its syntax is

@CODE(*string*)

where *string* is a string value, and the first letter is evaluated by @CODE to return the ASCII code.

As you have seen, converting results of the @CHAR function allows you to produce unusual characters yourself in a Quattro PRO spreadsheet. You can determine the character's ASCII number by applying the @CODE function to it. Another way of producing special characters in Quattro PRO is to type them and then press ENTER. You type them by using the ALT key together with the numeric keypad. The worksheet in Figure 10-23 shows the characters produced by holding down ALT and typing the numbers 155 through 196. You cannot use this method of making special characters for ASCII codes 0 through 28. This is because these codes are nonprinting characters that are used for control functions. In Figure 10-23, you can see that the @CODE function is being applied to cell B5. This tells you that the yen symbol is ASCII code 157.

You can use ASCII characters for making simple pictograms. A pictogram is a chart that represents numbers as pictures. In a pictogram one picture usually equals one unit of measure. For example, you can use the

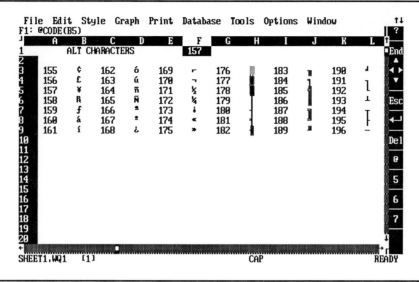

Figure 10-23. *Control characters*

@REPEAT function to repeat the male symbol, @CHAR(11), as shown in Figure 10-24.

The upper bar shows the number 28 by repeating the male symbol 28 times. The lower bar shows the number 21 as the female symbol, which is @CHAR(12).

This method of making a chart is an alternative to selecting the +/– bar chart format from the Style Numeric Format menu. You can see the numbers 28 and 21 formatted with this style in the lower pair of pictograms in Figure 10-24.

@FIND

The @FIND function uses three arguments to find characters within a string. Its syntax is

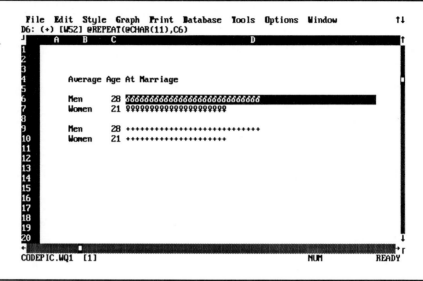

Figure 10-24.   *Pictograms*

@FIND(*substring,string,startnumber*)

where *substring* is a string value representing the target value to search for, *string* is a valid string value representing the source value to search within, and *startnumber* is a numeric value of 0 or greater representing the character position to begin searching with. The @FIND function returns the character position at which the first occurrence of the target was found.

The number 0 represents the first character in the string, the second is 1, and so on. Thus, @FIND("t",A1,0) returns the value 3 if A1 contains the label *Quattro PRO,* because the letter *t* first occurs at position 3. Note that the *startnumber* value tells the program to begin the search at that number of characters into the string. You will receive an error if the value of *startnumber* is more than the number of characters in *string* minus 1. You will also get an error if @FIND fails to find any occurrences of the *substring.*

Consider the spreadsheet in Figure 10-25, prepared by the Union Square office of Quattro PRO Vadis Travel. The users in this office are new to spreadsheets and enter the agent name and office name as one long label, rather than as separate facts in separate cells. You need to convert the data to a more useful format.

This example will be used several times in the following sections to demonstrate string functions. The most likely source of problem entries like this is either a new user or a set of data imported from another program. The first three names of agents are exactly the same length, and all of the labels have a hyphen in them. The hyphen might help break the labels into their separate parts. You can use the @FIND function to measure the position of the hyphen, as shown in Figure 10-26.

While this is not exactly vital data, it shows how the function can be used to compare labels, a function that might prove useful with larger collections of labels.

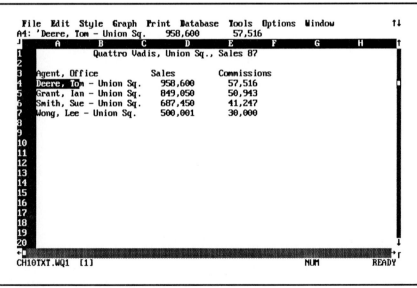

Figure 10-25. *Entries as long labels*

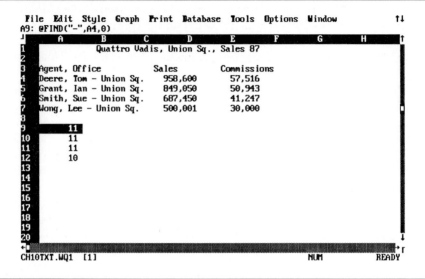

File Edit Style Graph Print Database Tools Options Window   ↑↓
A9: @FIND("-",A4,0)

	A	B	C	D	E	F	G	H
1			Quattro Vadis, Union Sq., Sales 87					
2								
3	Agent, Office			Sales		Commissions		
4	Deere, Tom – Union Sq.			958,600		57,516		
5	Grant, Ian – Union Sq.			849,050		50,943		
6	Smith, Sue – Union Sq.			687,450		41,247		
7	Wong, Lee – Union Sq.			500,001		30,000		
8								
9		11						
10		11						
11		11						
12		10						
13								
14								
15								
16								
17								
18								
19								
20								

CH10TXT.WQ1 [1]   NUM   READY

Figure 10-26.   *@FIND results*

@EXACT

Another way to compare labels is to use the @EXACT function. This function has the syntax

@EXACT(*string1,string2*)

where *string1* is a string value or a reference to a cell containing a string, and *string2* is a second string value or cell reference.

The @EXACT function compares the values of *string1* and *string2*. If the values are exactly identical, including capitalization, it returns a value of 1. If there are any differences, it returns a 0 value. As you can see in Figure 10-27, the text in strings that you are comparing must be surrounded by double quotes.

Since @EXACT returns a value of 1, you can use it to activate mathematical calculations. Thus, agents who have not answered Yes in this

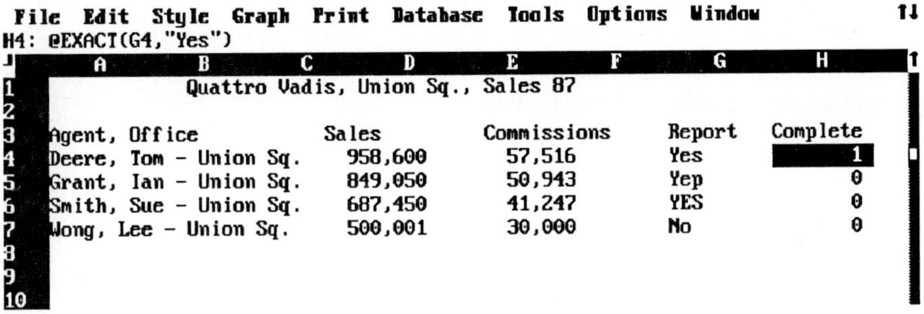

```
 File  Edit  Style  Graph  Print  Database  Tools  Options  Window              1↓
H4: @EXACT(G4,"Yes")
↓        A         B          C         D          E          F          G          H         1
1                      Quattro Vadis, Union Sq., Sales 87
2
3   Agent, Office              Sales            Commissions       Report    Complete
4   Deere, Tom - Union Sq.    958,600          57,516            Yes            1
5   Grant, Ian - Union Sq.    849,050          50,943            Yep            0
6   Smith, Sue - Union Sq.    687,450          41,247            YES            0
7   Wong, Lee - Union Sq.     500,001          30,000            No             0
8
9
10
```

Figure 10-27.   *The @EXACT function*

example could be paid commissions times the value in column E. You can compare only the contents of label cells with @EXACT. If you attempt to compare one or more numbers or empty cells, the result is ERR. Label prefixes are ignored.

To compare strings or cell contents without regard for capitalization, you can use the @IF function. The @IF function is not case-sensitive. For example, @IF(A1=A2,1,0) will return a 1 value, meaning true, if the contents of the cells are the same but capitalized differently (for example, if A1 contained **YES** and A2 contained **Yes**). Another formula that you can use to check for a spelling match that disregards capitalization in a string is shown in the +D4="Yes", which returns 1 for both Yes and YES.

@REPLACE

You can use the @REPLACE function with four arguments to replace a string of characters within a label. The syntax is

@REPLACE(*string,startnumber,num,newstring*)

where *string* is a string value, the label to be worked on; *startnumber* is the character position to begin with; *num* is the number of characters to delete; and *newstring* is a string value, the characters to insert at the position marked by *num*. In Figure 10-28 you can see @REPLACE used to update the spelling of *Sq.* to *Square:*

This formula would not work for Mr. Wong since the twentieth character in his label is a period, not *q*. Thus, the result for him would be *Union Sqquare*. The @FIND function works well with @REPLACE to locate the first occurrence of *Sq* in order to replace it with *Square*. This can be seen in Figure 10-29, where the string *Sq* is being used as the place to make the replacement. The only time this would cause a problem is when an agent has a last name like Squib, since @FIND is looking for the first occurrence of *Sq* and would replace *Squib* with *Square* rather than *Sq* with *Square*. Other uses of @REPLACE are to add one string to the end of another. You do so by specifying as the *startnumber* a number that is one greater than the number of characters in String. To delete part or all of a string, specify " " as *newstring*. Remember that you can also use the Edit Search & Replace command to perform search-and-replace operations instead of @FIND and @REPLACE.

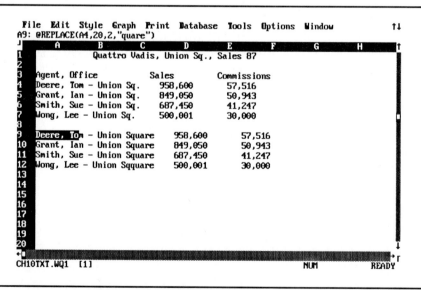

Figure 10 -28. *The @REPLACE function*

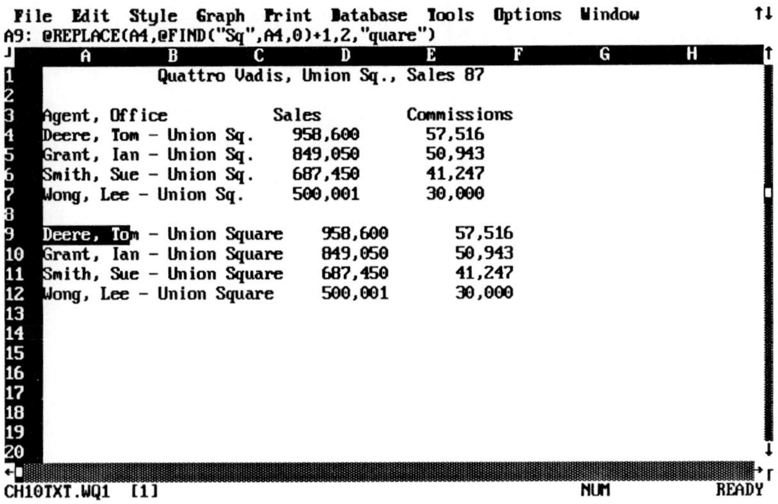

```
   File  Edit  Style  Graph  Print  Database  Tools  Options  Window        ↑↓
A9: @REPLACE(A4,@FIND("Sq",A4,0)+1,2,"quare")
 ┌───────A────────B────────C────────D────────E──────F──────G──────H──────┐
 1              Quattro Vadis, Union Sq., Sales 87
 2
 3  Agent, Office          Sales        Commissions
 4  Deere, Tom – Union Sq.     958,600       57,516
 5  Grant, Ian – Union Sq.     849,050       50,943
 6  Smith, Sue – Union Sq.     687,450       41,247
 7  Wong, Lee – Union Sq.      500,001       30,000
 8
 9  Deere, Tom – Union Square   958,600       57,516
10  Grant, Ian – Union Square   849,050       50,943
11  Smith, Sue – Union Square   687,450       41,247
12  Wong, Lee – Union Square    500,001       30,000
13
14
15
16
17
18
19
20
 CH10TXT.WQ1  [1]                               NUM           READY
```

Figure 10-29.   *@FIND with @REPLACE*

@LEFT, @RIGHT, and @MID

The @LEFT, @RIGHT, and @MID functions are used to find strings of characters within labels based on the position of those characters. These functions follow the same basic syntax

@LEFT(*string,number*)

where *string* is a string value and *number* is a numeric value of 0 or greater.

The @LEFT function returns the leftmost characters of String, the number of characters returned being that specified by the Number argument. In Figure 10-30, @LEFT returns the characters *Deere* from cell A4 since they are the five leftmost characters.

This function can be used to extract the agent names from the label where the agent name and office are mixed. However, the problem of varying label lengths appears once again due to cell A7. You can solve this problem by using the @FIND function. You use it to specify how far the reading of the leftmost characters must go. In this case, that is as far as the comma.

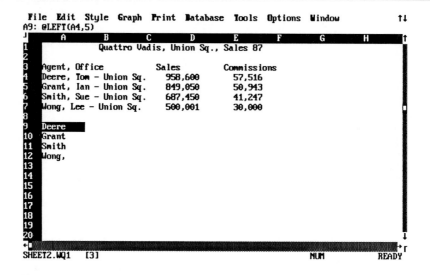

Figure 10-30. *The @LEFT function*

In Figure 10-31 the comma is being found by the @FIND function. The @RIGHT function is sometimes easier to apply, as is the case when you want to extract the commission figure from the labels.

The formula in C9 uses the function statement @RIGHT(C4,6) to extract the last six characters of the label, which is the commission figure in every case.

@TRIM and @LENGTH

The @TRIM function has the syntax

@TRIM(*string*)

It is used to remove any extra spaces from *string*. These extra spaces include the trailing spaces following the last nonspace character. It can also mean spaces preceding the first nonspace character plus duplicate spaces between words. Normal strings are not affected. If *string* is empty or contains a numeric value, the @TRIM function returns ERR. This

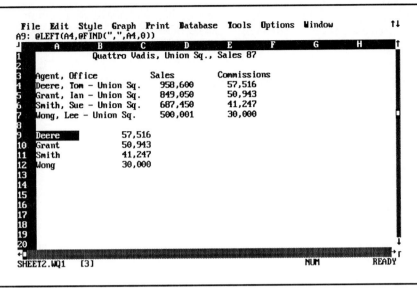

```
  File  Edit  Style  Graph  Print  Database  Tools  Options  Window        ↑↓
A9: @LEFT(A4,@FIND(",",A4,0))
       A        B        C        D        E        F        G        H
1                    Quattro Vadis, Union Sq., Sales 87
2
3  Agent, Office              Sales           Commissions
4  Deere, Tom - Union Sq.     958,600          57,516
5  Grant, Ian - Union Sq.     849,050          50,943
6  Smith, Sue - Union Sq.     687,450          41,247
7  Wong, Lee - Union Sq.      500,001          30,000
8
9  Deere           57,516
10 Grant           50,943
11 Smith           41,247
12 Wong            30,000
13
14
15
16
17
18
19
20
SHEET2.WQ1    [3]                                          NUM        READY
```

Figure 10-31. *@FIND with @LEFT*

function is particularly useful when you are working with data from other programs that pad some data to equal lengths by using trailing spaces.

The @LENGTH function is used to measure the length of a label. It uses the syntax

@LENGTH(*string*)

Thus, @LENGTH(A1) returns 20 if A1 contains the words *Quattro PRO*.

@LOWER, @UPPER, and @PROPER

These three functions change the case of a string. Their syntax is as follows:

@LOWER(*string*)
@UPPER(*string*)
@PROPER(*string*)

You can use @LOWER to turn a string into all lowercase characters. The @UPPER function returns all uppercase characters; that is, it capitalizes the string. The formula @UPPER(B4) returns YES if B4 contains either yes or YES.

To make the change permanent, you can use the Edit Values command to copy over the original label with the value of the formula. A more typical use of these three functions is to change an entire block of labels, which can save you some extensive editing.

The @PROPER function converts the first letter of every word in the string to uppercase and the rest of the characters to lowercase. In Quattro PRO a word is defined as an unbroken string of alphabetic characters. The @PROPER function considers any blank spaces, punctuation symbols, or numbers as marking the end of a word. You can use @PROPER to produce better looking text from heavily capitalized text entries. Thus @PROPER(B4) text from heavily capitalized text entries. Thus @PROPER(B4) returns "William Shakespeare" if B4 contains WILLIAM SHAKESPEARE.

In all three functions, numbers and symbols within the string are unaffected by the function. If the string is blank or is a numeric or date value, the result is ERR.

@STRING

Used to convert numbers to labels, the @STRING function has the syntax

@STRING(*x,decplaces*)

where x is a numeric value and *decplaces* is a numeric value between 0 and 15 representing the number of decimal places to the right of the decimal point. Thus, for example, @STRING(A1,0) converts 20.01 to a label, rounding it and then returning the decimal precision indicated by the *decplaces* argument. The label returned is 20.

You can use @STRING to convert a ZIP code entered as a number into a piece of text that can be concatenated with the rest of the address. This can be seen in Figure 10-32.

```
     File  Edit  Style  Graph  Print  Database  Tools  Options  Window        ↑↓
   C26: [W25] +E20&", "&F20&"  "&@STRING(G20,0)
   ┘        C              D                    E            F    G  ↑
   1 Company            Address                  City          ST  Zip
   9 Control Systems, Inc   3150 Holcomb Bridge Road Norcross    GA  30071
  10 Cricchio Studio    2701 Gulfway Drive       Port Arthur   TX  77640
  11 Fingerhut Corporation  440 Baker Road       Minnetonka    MN  55343
  12 Good Samaritan Hospital 1111 E. McDowell Rd. Phoenix      AZ  85006
  13 Green River Comp Care  416 West 3rd Street  Owensboro     KY  42301
  14 Itron Inc.         E. 15616 Euclid Ave.     Spokane       WA  99215
  15 Larry D Noe, Attorney  PO Box 15            Campbell      KY  42718
  16 Leon & Bayless     500 Lexington            San Antonio   TX  78215
  17 Marine Midland Bank  360 S. Warren St.      Syracuse      NY  13202
  18 Martin V. Smith Assoc.  300 Esplanade DR. #2100 Oxnard    CA  93031
  19 Maryknoll Fathers  224 SW 40th Street       Gainesville   FL  32607
  20 Mt. Sinai Med. Center  Box 1000             New York      NY  10029
  21
  22 Label:
  23 Linda Coates
  24 Mt. Sinai Med. Center
  25 Box 1000
  26 New York, NY  10029
  27                                                                     ↓
   ←                                                                  →
   ADDRESS1.WQ1 [4]                                  NUM             READY
```

Figure 10-32. *The @STRING function*

@VALUE

The @VALUE function converts a label to a numeric value. The syntax is

@VALUE(*string*)

where *string* is a string value that can contain any of the arithmetic operators, but must not contain dollar signs, commas, or embedded spaces. One period, interpreted as the decimal place, is permitted, and leading and trailing spaces are ignored.

The @VALUE function—together with @DATEVALUE and @TIME-VALUE—is useful for converting data that was imported as text with the Tools Import command but was not automatically converted into values. You can also use this function to return values for numbers that have been turned into labels.

More Text Formulas

The possibilities for text manipulation with Quattro PRO are extensive. Using the string functions and text in formulas, you can handle many tasks beyond the traditional number crunching for which spreadsheets were originally designed. As a final example, consider the Quattro PRO Business Name Generator shown in Figure 10-33. The plausible-looking company name in F4 was produced by the formula at the top of the screen. The @VLOOKUP function was used to look up a random number in the table of name parts from A1..D46. The table consists of a column of numbers roughly spaced across the possible value of @RAND, from 0 to 1.

Columns B and C are typical business names. Column D contains several types of companies repeated down the list. The @PROPER function is used to turn the actual business name into a capitalized word. The & sign is used to connect the three @VLOOKUP statements, and the comma and space separate the name from the type. By repeatedly pressing F2 to edit the cell containing the formula and then pressing ENTER, you can cause

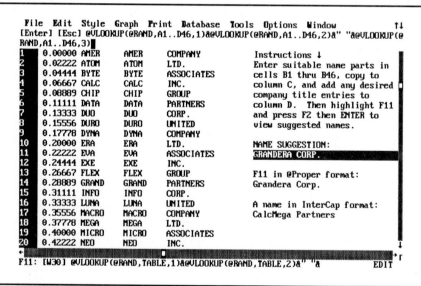

Figure 10-33.   *Name generator*

```
  File  Edit  Style  Graph  Print  Database  Tools  Options  Window        ↑↓
F14: [W30] @PROPER(F11)
 ┘        A        B        C        D        E              F                 ↑
 1  0.00000 AMER     AMER     COMPANY       Instructions ↓
 2  0.02222 ATOM     ATOM     LTD.          Enter suitable name parts in
 3  0.04444 BYTE     BYTE     ASSOCIATES    cells B1 thru B46, copy to
 4  0.06667 CALC     CALC     INC.          column C, and add any desired
 5  0.08889 CHIP     CHIP     GROUP         company title entries to
 6  0.11111 DATA     DATA     PARTNERS      column D.  Then highlight F11
 7  0.13333 DUO      DUO      CORP.         and press F2 then ENTER to
 8  0.15556 DURO     DURO     UNITED        view suggested names.
 9  0.17778 DYNA     DYNA     COMPANY
10  0.20000 ERA      ERA      LTD.          NAME SUGGESTION:
11  0.22222 EVA      EVA      ASSOCIATES    SUPERSTAR ASSOCIATES
12  0.24444 EXE      EXE      INC.
13  0.26667 FLEX     FLEX     GROUP         F11 in @Proper format:
14  0.28889 GRAND    GRAND    PARTNERS      Superstar Associates
15  0.31111 INFO     INFO     CORP.
16  0.33333 LUNA     LUNA     UNITED        A name in InterCap format:
17  0.35556 MACRO    MACRO    COMPANY       TeraSync Corp.
18  0.37778 MEGA     MEGA     LTD.
19  0.40000 MICRO    MICRO    ASSOCIATES
20  0.42222 NEO      NEO      INC.                                            ↓
←                                                                           →
NAMER.WQ1    [4]                                        NUM        READY
```

Figure 10-34. *The @PROPER function*

Quattro PRO to reselect the random numbers and keep producing new combinations of names.

If you make the lookup table references absolute in the formula, you can copy the formula to many cells in a column to produce a list of possible names. By extending the table with phrases that fit the kind of business for which you are trying to create a name, you can produce some very interesting results. The list of company names shown in the survey in Chapter 9 was produced by a formula of this kind. You can use @PROPER to alter the capitalization of the name, as shown in Figure 10-34. You can also use *string* formulas to simulate intercapitalization, the style so favored in the computer business by companies such as the WordPerfect corporation.

11 *Shortcuts and Macros*

As you become familiar with Quattro PRO and apply it to more tasks, you will want to take advantage of several shortcuts to frequently used menu items, and to use macros to reduce repetitive typing. In this chapter you will read how to use, modify, and create Quattro PRO Shortcuts; and how to record and use basic macros.

You may be somewhat in awe of the term macros, since macros have traditionally been in the realm of power users and spreadsheet aficionados. However, with Quattro PRO it is easy to create and use macros. Macros are no more complex than other spreadsheet tasks, and they do not require you to be highly proficient with everything else in the book to this point. If you plan on using more than a few macros, you should have a good grasp of naming blocks, described in Chapter 2. Perhaps the most important requirement for using macros is that you are already using Quattro PRO for a task that you want to simplify or speed up.

In the Quattro PRO menu system, the most commonly used commands are grouped in a logical way, making them easily accessible. The size of menus is kept manageable. Because different types of spreadsheet work require different sets of commands, however, you may often use commands that are several layers down in the menu structure. Quattro PRO addresses this problem in two ways. First, you can create Shortcuts. A Shortcut allows you to use a single keystroke to select any menu item. The second approach, described in the next chapter, is to redesign the menu system. Quattro PRO allows you to regroup and rename menu items to match your pattern of work with a feature called the Menu Builder.

Shortcuts

You may have noticed that several of the Quattro PRO menus have notations on the right, such as the CTRL-S and CTRL-X on the File menu shown in Figure 11-1. These represent Shortcuts or *hot keys* that are already incorporated into Quattro PRO. A hot-key Shortcut allows you to access a menu item with a single keystoke, bypassing the menu system. Little mention has been made of these keys so far in order to concentrate on the purpose of the menu items rather than quick ways of selecting them. However, once you are familiar with what a particular menu item does you may want to start selecting it with the assigned Shortcut. You can see all of the preassigned Shortcuts listed in Table 11-1. Perhaps the most useful is CTRL-C for the Edit Copy command. This takes you directly to the Source Block prompt, ready to perform a copy operation. Another very convenient Shortcut when building worksheets is CTRL-W for Style Column Width. One Shortcut, CTRL-D, is rather special since it does not represent any single menu item, but is used to enter dates, as described in Chapter 9.

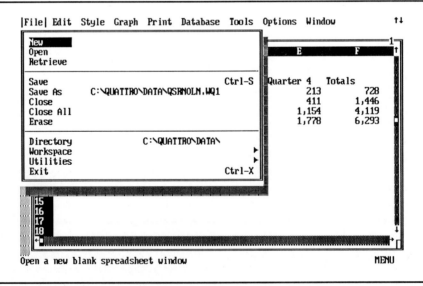

Figure 11-1.   *File menu Shortcuts*

Shortcut	Command
CTRL-A	Style Alignment
CTRL-C	Edit Command
CTRL-D	Date Prefix
CTRL-E	Edit Erase Block
CTRL-F	Style Numeric Format
CRTL-G	Fast Graph
CTRL-I	Edit Insert
CTRL-M	Edit Move
CTRL-N	Edit Search & Replace Next
CTRL-P	Edit Search & Replace Previous
CTRL-R	Window Move/Size
CTRL-S	File Save
CTRL-T	Window Tile
CTRL-W	Style Column Width
CTRL-X	File Exit

Table 11-1. *Default Shortcuts*

Creating Shortcuts

The more spreadsheet work you do, the more you will appreciate an opportunity to reduce keystrokes and Shortcuts do just that. However, you may not like or use all of the preassigned Shortcuts. Fortunately, Quattro PRO allows you to reassign or eliminate them. Suppose you are designing a large spreadsheet. You find you are repeatedly using the Window Options Locked Titles Both command to set titles in the worksheet. (Recall that this command freezes the cells above and to the left of the cell selector, so that row titles and column headings do not scroll off the screen when you move around the worksheet.)

While you are working on your design you often need to use the Window Options Locked Titles Clear command to make changes to the titles area. Using Quattro PRO's Shortcuts feature, you can execute the Window Options Locked Titles Both command with a single keystroke, such as CTRL-L. The same feature can be applied to the Window Options Locked Titles Clear command, assigning it to CTRL plus a different letter. This will enable you to set and remove titles with just two keystrokes instead of eight.

To make a shortcut for a menu item, you first highlight the menu item you want, as shown in Figure 11-2 where the Locked Titles Both command is highlighted. You then press CTRL-ENTER, and Quattro PRO prompts you at the bottom of the screen for the keystroke combination to which you want this menu item assigned:

Here you can see that CTRL-ENTER has been pressed and that the prompt for a CTRL-letter key combination has appeared. Press CTRL-L and the prompt disappears. The menu remains on the screen. The menu item you assigned to CTRL-L has not been selected, but the menu now shows the name of the assigned Shortcut:

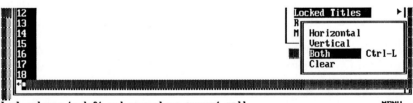

You do not have to select the menu item just to assign it to a CRTL-letter key combination. If you do not need the menu item at this time, press ESCAPE or CTRL-BREAK to leave the menu. Whenever you are ready to set titles in the worksheet, press CTRL-L. The command is instantly executed.

Reassigning Shortcuts

To match the Locked Titles Both Shortcut you might want to assign Locked Titles Clear to a different CTRL-letter key combination, for example, CTRL-C.

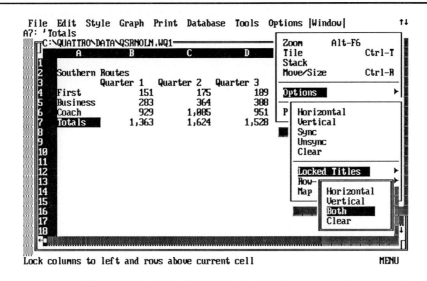

Figure 11-2.   *Setting locked titles*

You do this by highlighting the Clear command on the Locked Titles menu and pressing CTRL-ENTER followed by CTRL-C. You can then clear titles simply by pressing CTRL-C. However, this new Shortcut conflicts with the preassigned use of CTRL-C for Edit Copy. You must first remove the current assignment of the CTRL-C shortcut. To remove CTRL-C from Edit Copy you simply highlight Copy on the Edit menu and press CTRL-ENTER followed by DELETE.

Managing Shortcuts

After taking these steps to eliminate the existing CTRL-C shortcut, you will be prompted to press DELETE again to confirm the action. If you press ESCAPE at this point, the Shortcut is not affected. If you press DELETE a second time, then the Shortcut is eliminated. If you try to reassign an existing Shortcut without first deleting the current assignment, Quattro PRO will warn you "Shortcut key is already in use."

Quattro PRO has no built-in means of displaying a list of current Shortcut assignments. However, you can see the Shortcuts on the menus from which they operate. You can use the Help system to find a list of the default or preassigned Shortcuts. Just highlight a menu item, press CTRL-ENTER, and then press F1. This will take you to Help for Shortcuts and a list of Preset Shortcuts. You might want to keep track of active Shortcuts by noting them on a piece of paper or in a worksheet file. If you share a PC system and Quattro PRO with other users, you should inform them of the Shortcuts you have set up. This will help prevent problems that arise from accidental activation of a Shortcut. Quattro PRO automatically records Shortcuts in the current configuration file. See Appendix A for more about configuration files.

Macros

When you find yourself repeating the same keystrokes over and over, but they are not simply menu items you can assign to Shortcuts, then you need the power of macros. Originally developed for word processing programs as a way to record and play back frequently used phrases, macros store multiple keystrokes under a single key or name.

Macros in Quattro PRO

The macros you create in Quattro PRO enable you to record and play back any series of keystrokes, including labels, numbers, formulas, menu choices, and even Shortcuts. For example, you could create a macro for setting titles in your worksheet. In addition to simply picking the Locked Titles Both command from the menu, the macro could move the cell selector to the correct cell prior to issuing the command, thus eliminating the need for you to position the cell selector yourself. If you have to format a lot of separate cells to Percent format you could create a macro to perform that action. You might have noticed that the Numeric Format option on the Style menu already has a Shortcut, CTRL-F. But this only takes you to the list of formats. If you assigned a Shortcut to the Percent format, you would still need to specify decimal places and select the block to be formatted. A macro can complete the whole command, including selection of decimal places, without having to go through the menus every time.

A Quattro PRO macro can be defined as a set of keystrokes or instructions stored as labels. Numbers and letters are stored as numbers and letters; commands are stored as special symbols or words within brackets. For example, you can have a macro that consists of the label **Quattro PRO~.** This macro tells Quattro PRO to type the letters **Q-u-a-t-t-r-o P-R-O** and then press ENTER (represented by the tilde symbol, ~). You can use this macro to enter the words "Quattro PRO" into a cell. In fact, you can easily create this macro in a blank worksheet, as follows:

1. Place the cell selector in A1, type **Quattro PRO~**, and then press ENTER. The cell identifier will show **'Quattro PRO ~** as the contents of the cell.

2. Move the cell selector to A3, where the words "Quattro PRO" will be typed by the macro.

3. Press ALT-F2 for the Macro menu shown in Figure 11-3. Select Execute from the Macro menu. You will be prompted for the cell coordinates of the block of macro commands that you want to execute.

4. Type or point to A1 and press ENTER. The words "Quattro PRO" are entered in cell A3. You have just created and used your first macro.

Obviously, this is a simple example; the macro is of limited use and sophistication. Macros can consist of much longer instructions. When a macro contains many instructions, the instructions are placed on successive rows of the same column. A macro that consists of more than one line of instructions is executed by indicating the first cell in the macro. Quattro PRO reads the instructions in that cell, then the instructions in the next cell down, and so on until a blank cell is encountered. One problem with the simple macro just described is that it is not particularly easy to use. Executing it involves several steps, including entering the location of the macro. You can make a macro easier to execute by using the Macro Name command to name the cell containing the macro. You can use several types of macro names.

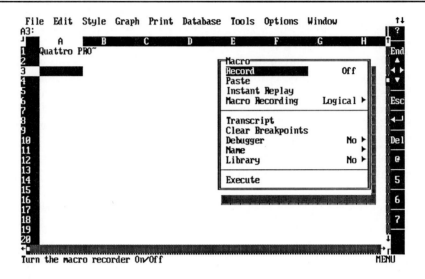

Figure 11-3.   *Macro menu*

Macros by Name

When you have attached a name to a cell containing a macro, you can use F3 to execute that macro. For example, if cell A1 were named QP with the Macro Name command, the macro could be executed more easily. To name a macro and use the name to execute the macro, follow these steps:

1. Place the cell selector in the cell that contains the first line of the macro, in this case A1.

2. Press ALT-F2 for the Macro menu (you can also use the Macro command from the Tools menu). Select Name and then Create and type the name **QP**, as shown in Figure 11-4. Press ENTER.

3. Quattro PRO prompts you to specify coordinates for the block, but it assumes the current cell, in this case A1..A1, as the block. This is correct, so press ENTER.

4. To execute the newly named macro, move to a blank cell into which you will enter the words "Quattro PRO" and press ALT-F2. Select Execute and then press F3. You will see QP in the list of named blocks, as shown in Figure 11-5. Highlight QP and press ENTER. The macro in the cell named QP will execute.

Macro Shortcuts

One Shortcut you can use to improve the macro-execution process is to assign the Macro Execute command to CTRL-E. To do this you must first delete CTRL-E as the Edit Erase Block Shortcut. To do this, highlight Erase Block on the Edit menu, then press CTRL-ENTER, followed by DELETE, and DELETE again. Now bring up the Macro menu from the Tools menu. Then highlight Execute and press CTRL-ENTER. Now press CTRL-E and the Execute command is assigned to CTRL-E.

You might wonder if it is not better to keep Edit Erase Block as CTRL-E, but in fact Edit Erase Block is a somewhat redundant command when you are familiar with Quattro PRO. An easier way to erase a block is to use the Extend key, (SHIFT-F7) to select the block of cells and then press the DELETE key. This performs a block erase without using the menu system at all.

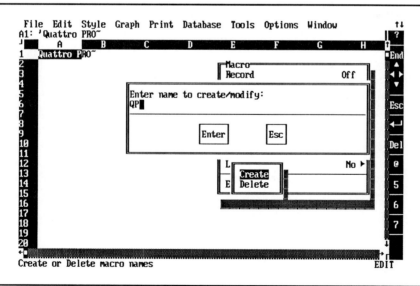

Figure 11-4. *Naming a macro*

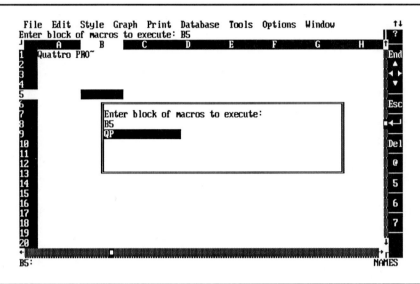

Figure 11-5.   *Named macro list*

With CTRL-E as the macro-execute key you can run your named macros very efficiently. Simply press CTRL-E followed by F3 and then select the macro name from this list.

If you want instant access to a macro, you should name the macro with a special combination of characters: the backslash (\) together with a letter. You can then execute the macro by holding down the ALT key and pressing the letter you used in the name. To make an instant macro, use the following steps, which describe the procedure in the case of the Quattro PRO macro. This macro can be called \Q, so that it can be executed with ALT-Q.

1. Place the cell selector in the cell that contains the first line of the macro, in this case A1.

2. Select Name from the Macro menu, pick Create, and type the name **\Q**. Press ENTER.

3. Quattro PRO prompts you to specify coordinates for the block but it will assume the current cell, in this case A1..A1, as the block. This is correct, so press ENTER.

4. To execute the newly named macro, move to a blank cell and press ALT-Q. The macro will execute.

Note that block names can overlap, as in this case, where the names QP and \Q were both assigned to cell A1. Since \Q is a block name, you can execute this macro with the Macro Execute command as well as with the ALT key. You can create 26 instant macros named from \A to \Z. These names are usually reserved for frequently used macros. The letter used in the macro name should have some mnemonic relationship to the action of the macro, such as \Q for the Quattro PRO macro.

Applying Macros

In practical applications, macros are used for common operations and repetitive tasks, particularly ones that involve many settings. Good examples are database operations and printing. You will recall that Quattro PRO can remember only one Sort Block and one set of sort keys at a time. Similarly, the Print command can remember only one Print Block at a time. Sorting two different databases on the same spreadsheet or printing two different blocks of the spreadsheet involves changing a lot of settings. You can use macros to specify all of the details about two different sort or print jobs, reducing many keystrokes and many chances for error to just one accurate set of instructions.

You can even create macros that contain conditional statements. Such statements as If-Then-Else enable you to have a macro choose among several different actions based on user input or spreadsheet conditions. The ability to include special command language statements in macros transforms macros into the equivalent of a programming language. With this capability you can create custom menus, data input forms, and specialized applications. The Quattro PRO command language and its use in macros is explained in greater detail in the next chapter.

Ways to Create Macros

When you consider creating practical macros you will quickly face the question of how to tell Quattro PRO to perform typical actions such as Edit or END, or UP ARROW. You have seen that a macro is essentially a label or series of labels stored in a worksheet cell. When you created the macro to enter "Quattro PRO" into a cell you used the tilde (~) to represent pressing ENTER. This is because you cannot type "ENTER" as a label. In fact, if you are typing a label and you press ENTER, what you are typing is simply entered into the cell. Consequently, there is a whole system of codes for those actions that cannot simply be typed as labels. They are listed in Table 11-2.

There are also special ways of describing menu actions in macros. If you wanted a macro to execute the Spreadsheet Print command you could use the characters "/PS" but Quattro PRO has a better way than this, as you will see as you examine the different ways to create macros. The method you use for a particular macro will depend on the purpose of the macro, its level of complexity, and your level of familiarity with the macro process. You can combine all three methods of making macros when you are creating large macros.

Macro Recording

The simplest method of creating useful macros is to record them. Even novice users can make macros in this way to simplify commonly used tasks. Recording a macro simply means telling Quattro PRO to keep a record of your actions while you use the program. This is done by placing the program in RECORD mode, and then typing the necessary keystrokes to perform the actions that are to be part of the macro. Quattro PRO holds a record of the actions you carry out in memory, until you either paste the macro into a worksheet or record a new macro. You do not have to paste the recorded macro into a worksheet in order to use it. However, if you do paste the recording into a worksheet you can examine it, edit it, and add to it. For example, suppose you have recorded the following actions:

■ move the cell selector to B4 with the GoTo key (F5)
■ set both vertical and horizontal locked titles

Macro Equivalent	Key Represented	Macro Equivalent	Key Represented

Function Keys

{ABS}	F4
{CALC}	F9
{CHOOSE}	SHIFT-F5
{COPY}	SHIFT-F9
{EDIT}	F2
{FUNCTIONS}	ALT-F3
{GOTO}	F5
{GRAPH}	F10
{MACROS}	SHIFT-F3
{MARK}	SHIFT-F7
{MARKALL}	ALT-F7
{MOVE}	SHIFT-F8
{NAME}	F3
{NEXTWIN}	SHIFT-F6
{PASTE}	SHIFT-F10
{QUERY}	F7
{STEP}	SHIFT-F2
{TABLE}	F8
{UNDO}	ALT-F5
{WINDOW}	F6
{ZOOM}	ALT-F6

Movement Keys

{HOME}	HOME
{END}	END
{LEFT} or {L}	LEFT ARROW
{RIGHT} or {R}	RIGHT ARROW
{UP} or {U}	UP ARROW
{DOWN} or {D}	DOWN ARROW
{PGUP}	PAGE UP
{PGDN}	PAGE DOWN
{BIGLEFT}	CTRL-LEFT
{BACKTAB}	SHIFT-TAB
{BIGRIGHT}	CTRL-RIGHT
{TAB}	TAB
{WINDOWn}	Selects window n

Status Keys

{NUMON}	NUM LOCK
{SCROLLOFF}	SCROLL LOCK on
{SCROLLON}	SCROLL LOCK off
{CAPOFF}	CAPS LOCK on
{CAPON}	CAPS LOCK on
{INS}	INSERT
{INSOFF}	INSERT off
{INSON}	INSERT on

Other Keys

{BREAK}	CTRL-BREAK
{BACKSPACE} or {BS}	BACKSPACE
{DATE}	CTRL-D
{DEL}	DELETE
{DELEOL}	CTRL-\ (delete to end of line)
{ESC}	ESCAPE
{CLEAR}	ESCAPE
{CR} or ~	ENTER
{?}	PAUSE (for user input)
/ or {MENU}	Displays menu

Table 11-2. *Macro Equivalents and Keys*

The recorded macro would look like this:

{GOTO}B4~
{/ Titles;Both}

From this macro code you can see what the macro is supposed to do, and you can see that Quattro PRO has provided the codes for special keys and menu items. In the next section a complete macro recording example will be presented.

Macro Writing

The sample macro that enters the words "Quattro PRO" was created by simply writing it into a cell. When you become familiar with how macros work, you can use this method to write macros. Use Table 11-2 to find the equivalents that Quattro PRO uses for common commands when you are writing macros. Remember to use a label prefix before such entries as @SUM when writing macros.

Macros from Transcript

The record of your keystrokes maintained by Transcript (the feature described in Chapter 7) is compatible with Quattro PRO's macro terminology. Thus, you can call up the Transcript log and copy sections of the keystroke record to your spreadsheet. An example of the Transcript log is shown in Figure 11-6. The actions since the last file retrieve operation are linked by a line in the left margin of the keystroke records. You can see that the line-drawing command was used in two instances since the file was retrieved. You could use this code to create line-drawing macros. You call up the Transcript log by using the Macro Transcript command. When the log is on screen, you can type / for the Transcript menu and mark a block for copying to the spreadsheet. This process is described in detail in Chapter 12.

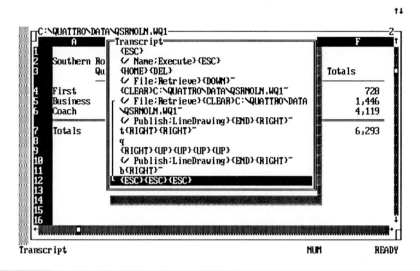

Figure 11-6. *Transcript log*

Recording a Macro

To see the macro-recording process in action and to get a better understanding for the potential of macros, try the example in the following section. This macro enters the current date in the worksheet.

Macro Design

Whenever you create a macro, you need to give some thought to what the role of the macro will be. You can use macros to enter values and labels, to select menu items, and to activate function keys. You can execute macros in READY mode, in EDIT mode, and from within the menu system. Of course, if you make a macro that works from READY mode, you must execute it in READY mode and not in the middle of a menu. Also, you need to be careful about the action of the macro and the cells it will affect. Keep in mind that there is a possibility of losing data through any of these actions: Copy, Move, Fill, Transpose, Output, Erase, or Delete. For example, if the macro is designed to perform a particular action on a cell, you must remember to move your cell selector to a suitable cell before executing the macro.

Suppose you need to enter today's date at several different places in a spreadsheet used for recording sales calls. If the choice of date format is not important, you can press CTRL-D, type **@NOW**, and press ENTER. This action enters the current date in the D4 format.

To enter the current date with the D1 format, you would type **@NOW**, press ENTER, and then format the cell using Style Numeric Format Date 1. Doing so requires a dozen keystrokes, and it is a tedious operation if you have to repeat it often. To make a macro to perform this task, you simply perform the steps once while Quattro PRO is in RECORD mode. This operation is presented here in a sales call worksheet used by salespersons, and shown in the following illustrations. Of course, you can try this operation in any practice worksheet.

1. Select any empty cell on a spreadsheet into which you want to enter the date. You may want to make sure that the column is at least ten characters wide, so that the date you are about to create can be seen properly.

2. To begin recording the macro, press the Macro key (ALT-F2) and select Record. This command begins and ends the macro-recording process. After you select Record, the Macro menu disappears and you are returned to the READY mode with the REC message in the status line, as shown in Figure 11-7.

3. Type **@NOW** and press ENTER. Then select Style Numeric Format Date. Select the D1 format and press ENTER to confirm that the current cell is the one you want to format. The result is shown in Figure 11-8. The current date has been read from the system clock and formatted with the D1 format. The REC message is still displayed as the recording mode is still active.

4. Press ALT-F2 and select Record to end the recording. The REC message will disappear. Your macro is ready to use.

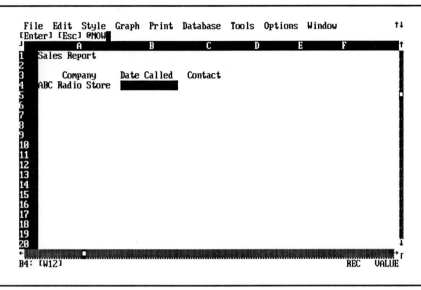

Figure 11-7. *Macro recording*

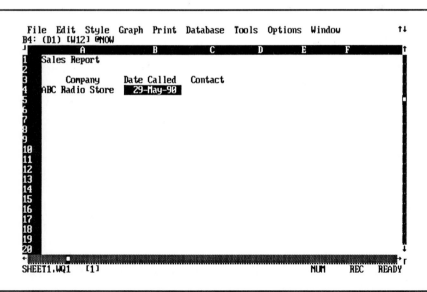

Figure 11-8. *Actions completed*

There are two ways to stop the macro recorder other than using the ALT-F2 key. You can select Paste from the Macro menu, or you can select Instant Replay. These options will be described next.

Instant Replay

As soon as you are back in READY mode you can use the macro that you have just recorded. Move the cell selector to an empty cell, press ALT-F2, and then select Instant Replay. The macro instructions are carried out, and the date is entered and formatted. Instant Replay plays back the most recently recorded macro. Quattro PRO stores what you record in a small area of memory called a *buffer.* When you begin a new recording the contents of the buffer are cleared out to be replaced by the new recording. For this reason Instant Replay is best used for one-shot macros that you will not need again. Using Instant Replay saves you the trouble of naming a macro if you will need it only for a short while. If you like you can assign a Shortcut to Instant Replay and so execute the recorded macro with a single keystroke.

Macro Paste

Another way to stop macro recording is to use ALT-F2 followed by Paste. This command allows you to paste the recorded macro into a worksheet where you can examine, name, and store it. In fact, before doing more work with the @NOW macro you have just created, you might want to take a look at the way it has been recorded by Quattro PRO. You can do this by selecting Paste from the Macro menu. You will be prompted for a name to create or modify, as shown in Figure 11-9. This is the name of the macro and the block of cells it will occupy. In this case, use the backslash and the letter *T* (for Today). Now press ENTER to confirm the name. Next, you will be prompted for the coordinates of the block of cells in which to store the keystrokes that make up the macro. Quattro PRO assumes you want to use the current location of the cell selector. This location is not correct, since the current position of the cell selector is the cell in which you actually want to enter the date. You change the cell coordinates by first unlocking them with ESCAPE.

Move the cell selector to an empty cell away from the rest of the worksheet—one that has at least two empty cells directly beneath it. For

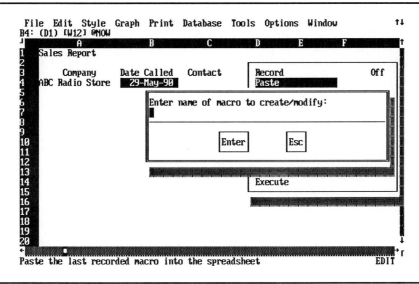

Figure 11-9. *Naming a recorded macro*

example, you could press HOME and then TAB. Using these keys is a quick way to move to a position away from the main work area with only two keystrokes. Press ENTER to confirm the location. You have now named the macro so that it can be executed with ALT-T. Before you use the macro, you might want to examine it.

An easy way to move to the cell you named to store the macro is to press the GoTo key (F5) and then the Name key (F3). You should see \T on the name list along with the names of any other blocks of cells that have been named in the spreadsheet. Highlight \T and press ENTER. Your cell selector will be placed in the top cell of the block you named \T. In Figure 11-10 you can see the record that Quattro made of your keystrokes while in RECORD mode. The first cell is the function @NOW, as you typed it, followed by the tilde (~), which is macro language for ENTER. Below this is a record of the menu items you chose. These are stated in terms that Quattro calls menu equivalents. Instead of simply saying /SND1, which were the actual letters for the menu items you selected, Quattro shows you the nature of the menu commands you chose.

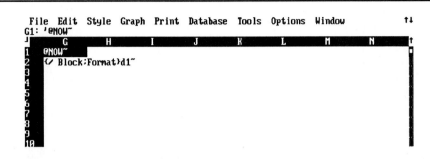

Figure 11-10.   *Macro code*

To use the \T macro you have created, first place the cell selector on the cell into which you want to enter the date. Then press ALT-T and the date will be entered and formatted for you.

Macro-Naming Strategies

If you had named the macro using the word DATE instead of \T you could execute it by first using the Macro Execute command and then pressing F3 for a list of named blocks. Selecting DATE by highlighting it and pressing ENTER would execute the macro commands stored in that block. As was mentioned earlier, you can create as many as 26 instant macros named with ALT plus a letter *A* through *Z*. While this method limits you to 26 macros, you can use any valid block name for a macro and thus create an unlimited number of macros. The chances are that as your applications become more complex and your procedures more streamlined, you will use both macro-naming methods, together with Shortcuts. Thus, you could have 26 menu items assigned to CTRL-A/Z, 26 common operations assigned to ALT-A/Z, and then a selection of macros accessible with Macro Execute.

Expanding Macros

Recall that in the previous example, only cell G1 was named as \T. The macro record occupied more than one cell, however, so Quattro split the record of your keystrokes to prevent the creation of very long labels that are hard to read and edit. Since Quattro reads macros from the first cell, then from the next cell below that, and so on until it reaches an empty cell, you can easily add steps to the end of an existing macro. For example, when entering the date with the @NOW function, which was the purpose of the ALT-T macro described previously, you may want to add a step to convert the date in a function statement to a fixed date value.

The @NOW function returns the current date from your system clock. If you load the same spreadsheet the next day, the @NOW date changes. What you would probably want in a record of sales calls is a permanent date that does not change. You can set this with the Edit Values command. To add another set of instructions to the existing macro in G1 and G2 using the record method, follow these steps:

1. Place the cell selector in the cell that contains the @NOW function (B4 in this example). This location is where the actions to be recorded will be carried out.

2. Press ALT-F2 and pick Record to initiate the record feature.

3. You are now in RECORD mode. Use the Edit Values command and press ENTER to confirm that the cell containing the @NOW function is the one you want to transform into a value. Press ENTER again to copy the value to the same cell.

4. Press ALT-F2 and select Paste to terminate RECORD mode. Quattro PRO prompts for the "name of macro to create/modify" and displays a list, as shown in Figure 11-11. Do not pick \T, but press ESCAPE once and then press ENTER. This will result in a prompt for a paste location.

5. Press ESCAPE to unlock the prompted coordinates, move the cell selector down to G3, and press ENTER. The recorded action is now pasted into the worksheet below the existing macro code.

If you look at cells G3 and G4 now, you will see the action you just performed recorded as

{/ Block;Values}~~

Since this instruction is directly below the last cell of the \T macro, it will be read as part of the \T macro. You can now move to the cell into which you need to enter today's date and press ALT-T; the date will be entered and

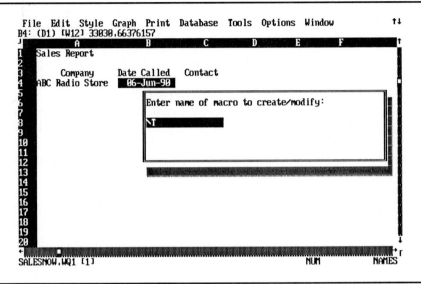

File Edit Style Graph Print Database Tools Options Window   ↑↓
B4: (D1) [W12] 33030.66376157

	A	B	C	D	E	F	
Sales Report

    Company   Date Called   Contact
ABC Radio Store   06-Jun-90

Enter name of macro to create/modify:

\T

SALESNOW.WQ1 [1]   NUM   NAMES

Figure 11-11. *Name macro prompt*

converted to a value that will not change when the worksheet is reloaded at a later date.

Note that you could have replied to the prompt in Figure 11-11 by typing a new name, such as **VALUE** or **\V**, which would then have been attached to the recorded code even as it became a part of the other macro. However, placing macros within macros is not recommended. If you want to use the code in G3 and G4 in a separate macro, the best approach is to copy it to another location, which brings up the question of macro management.

Macro Management

Since macros are such powerful and useful tools for spreadsheet users, once you start to develop them you will probably begin to accumulate many of them. Placement of macros within a worksheet, conventions used for assigning names, and sharing macros between worksheets are important factors to consider when organizing your macros.

Macro Placement

If you want to store additional macros close to the ones already entered into the worksheet, but you do not want them to become part of the existing macros, you should make sure that at least one blank cell separates each macro. In Figure 11-12 you can see that several more macros have been added in the same area of the worksheet as the \T macro. The macro in G7 is the Edit Values macro that turns a formula in a cell into a value. In cell G10 is a macro that widens the current column by one character, while the macro in G14 narrows the current column by one character. Because each of these macros are separate from the others, they are not activated by another macro.

Where you place macros on your spreadsheet not only affects how they relate to other macro instructions but also the rest of your work. Consider

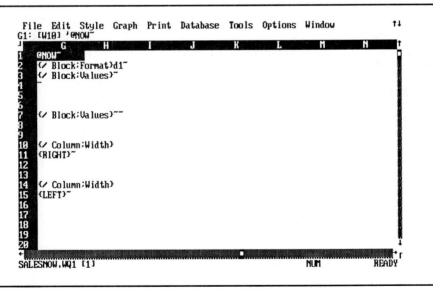

Figure 11-12. *Additional macros*

the location of the macros in the previous example, that is, to the right of the work area. This location is acceptable until you decide to delete a row from the work area. Since the macros and the work area are probably not going to be in view at the same time, it is all too easy to delete a row from the work area and accidentally delete a row of macro code. Since macros run until they encounter a blank row, even deleting a blank row or inserting a new row can cause problems for macros stored to the right of the work area. One way to avoid damaging these macros is to use the full movement of the cursor when you use the Row Delete or Row Insert command. You can press not only the DOWN ARROW key when deleting or inserting rows but also the RIGHT ARROW and the TAB keys. Doing so allows you to move to the right of your work area to check for macros before deleting or inserting the rows.

Another way to avoid problems for macros caused by deleting rows is to store the macros below the work area. In this way you are less likely to delete columns, and adding columns is less likely to disrupt a macro, since the instructions are stored in single columns. Some users like to place their macros above the main work area and to the left of the spreadsheet, that is, around the home position. Here they are safe from row deletion and easy to find, but still susceptible to column deletion. Such considerations are a part of worksheet aesthetics or spreadsheet design. The three different arrangements—on the right, below, and to the left and above—are shown in Figure 11-13. You will probably develop your own style of organizing your spreadsheets.

Organizing Macros

If you want to rearrange your macros within a worksheet, keep in mind that you can easily move a macro without affecting its operation by using the Edit Move command. This command retains the integrity of block names, so that Quattro PRO knows where a named block is, even after it has been moved.

When you are designing macros, remember that you can use the TAB and PAGE DOWN keys to quickly move your cell selector a number of columns and rows at a time. By using HOME before TAB and PAGE DOWN, you can consistently move to the same location from anywhere on the worksheet. Thus, you can set up a macro area at cell A61 that you can reach from anywhere on the worksheet with just four keystrokes: HOME, PAGE DOWN, PAGE DOWN, PAGE DOWN. But keep in mind that while this method is convenient, it is unreliable if you have to add or delete many columns or

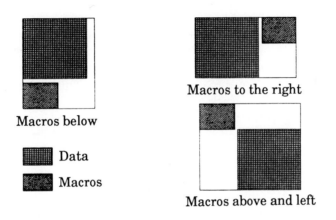

Macros below

Macros to the right

Macros above and left

▓ Data

▓ Macros

Figure 11-13. *Macro layout diagram*

rows. The series of cursor keystrokes you have been using to get to a specific area may no longer be accurate.

An alternative way of moving to a specific area is to name the area with the Edit Names Create command. In this example, to make moving directly to the area where you have stored the macros easier, you could assign the name MACROS to the entire macro storage area. Then you can move to the named block by pressing GoTo (F5), typing **MACROS,** and pressing ENTER. You could also use GoTo, followed by F3 to list the names and then select the name from the list. (One way to move quickly to an important block is to name it with a block name, such as AAA, that is alphabetically prior to any other names you have used. In this way the name becomes the top name on the F3 list. Then you can move to the block with GoTo, F3, and ENTER.)

Using cursor-movement keys to move to a specific location can be a problem in macros themselves. When designing cursor movement into a macro the best approach to locating a specific area is first to name the cell in the top-left corner of the area you want to get to and then, in the macro instruction, to use {GoTo} and the block name. Subsequent changes to the location or size of the block will not affect the macro instruction.

Macro Layout

In addition to the possible danger to the macros in Figure 11-12 from deleting rows, there are other problems with the layout of these macros. You cannot see what their names are from looking at them. One way of finding out the names and locations of all named blocks in a worksheet is to use the Edit Names Make Table command. This command produces a 2-column list of the block names and their corresponding coordinates, as shown in Figure 11-14.

In the figure, the Edit Names Make Table command was issued with the cell selector in K1. The table occupies columns K and L and as many rows as are needed to list all the current block names. You should always issue this command with enough room for the resulting table to appear; otherwise, the table will overwrite the contents of existing cells. Note that the table is not dynamic; that is, it is not linked to the Edit Names Create command and will not be automatically updated when new names are created.

As useful as the Make Table command is in many situations, particularly when you have many block names to keep track of, it does not really tell

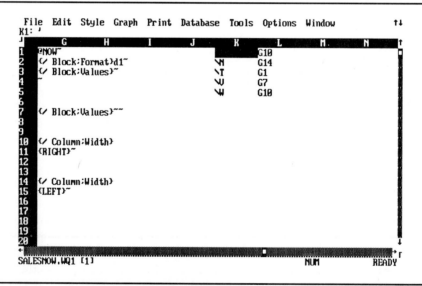

Figure 11-14. *Edit Names Make Table results*

you what you want to know about the macros in the worksheet. Consider the layout of the macros shown in Figure 11-15. These macros were moved to an area of the spreadsheet below the main work area. This arrangement follows the 3-column convention that has been widely adopted by many spreadsheet users. The first column contains the block names of the macros. The second column contains the actual lines of macro instructions. The third column contains a series of labels briefly describing what each macro does. (Note that entering \T as a label requires a label prefix character.)

One reason for the popularity of this arrangement is that it works well with the Edit Names Labels command that assigns names to blocks based on labels in adjacent cells. For example, with the @NOW macro in cell B22 and the label \T in cell A22, as in Figure 11-15, you can use the Edit Names Labels Right command to name cell B22 as T. Similarly, you could use the Edit Names Labels Down command to attach the names Name, Code, and Action, to cells A21, B21, and C21. When you use the Labels command to assign names, you must include all the cells on the row or in the column that contain the names you want to use. Blank cells do not create blank names, they are simply ignored.

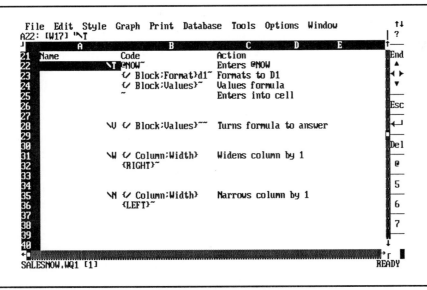

Figure 11-15. *Three-column layout*

Macro Libraries

Macros stored in a regular spreadsheet are specific to that spreadsheet. Unlike Shortcuts, which can be recorded as part of the program settings with the Options Update command, macros initially consist of labels stored in the cells of a single worksheet. Macros are saved with that worksheet and are not immediately available when you move to a new worksheet. However, the chances are that you will want to use some macros in many different worksheets. You can easily copy macros from one worksheet to another by using the Edit Copy command, but when you copy a named block from one worksheet to another the block name does not go with it. This means that to make a macro active in the worksheet to which it has been copied, you must issue the Edit Names command. If you use the 3-column layout you can use the Labels Right method described in the previous section.

Creating a Macro Library

You may want to collect macros from several worksheets into a single worksheet file called a macro library. A macro library is a very useful file to maintain in an office with several users developing Quattro PRO macros. You can share macros and avoid duplication of effort if a common macro library is maintained. A prerequisite to this is adherence to some basic standards of layout such as the 3-column method. In Quattro PRO a macro library is not just a useful collecting place for macros. You can open macro libraries so that the macros they contain can be used in other worksheets.

A macro library is a document that typically consists of nothing but macros. Whenever you execute a macro Quattro PRO looks for the name of the macro in the current worksheet. If the macro you have called on is not there, the program looks to see if there are any open macro libraries. These are worksheets that are specially designated as libraries with the Macro Library command. Any worksheet can be designated as a macro library. To make a macro library out of a worksheet you must load the worksheet and make it current, and then execute the Macro Library command. This command gives you a Yes/No choice, as shown in Figure 11-16. Choose Yes and then save the worksheet. From now on, whenever

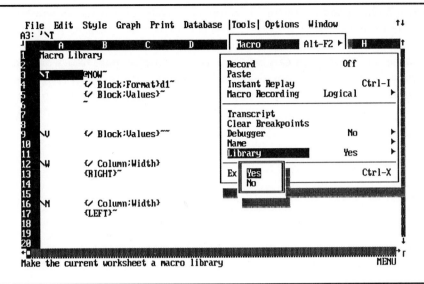

Figure 11-16. *Macro library command*

this worksheet is loaded Quattro PRO will look to it for macros that are not in the current worksheet.

There is no special name for a macro library document; you can use any worksheet name. When more than one macro library is open, Quattro PRO will look into them in the order in which they were opened. Remember, Quattro PRO only looks outside of the current worksheet for a macro if the current worksheet does not contains the macro you have asked to execute.

Applying Macro Libraries

There are numerous advantages to placing most of your macros into one or more macro libraries. Earlier, the question of protecting and preserving macros was discussed. From an organizational point of view, macros are much safer from accidental corruption when they are stored separately in a macro library, and they are generally easier to keep track of.

Since Quattro PRO allows you to have more than one macro library, you can develop libraries for specific types of work. A macro library for spreadsheet design work could contain 26 instant macros plus many others that you have developed to speed design work. When it comes time to move on to data entry you can close the design macro library and open the data entry macro library, containing 26 different instant macros plus other macro routines. You can save a macro library as part of a workspace so that it is available immediately when you get down to work. You can use some special macros, described later in this chapter, in a macro library to initiate a whole chain of events and provide real power over your Quattro PRO environment.

Macro Control

Quattro PRO contains numerous features for controlling macro execution. You can use these features to determine why a macro does not work the way you expect it to.

Stopping Macros

If you give the command to execute a macro and the effects immediately appear to be different from what you expect, you may want to stop the macro. You do this with CTRL-BREAK (CTRL-SCROLL LOCK on some keyboards). When you press CTRL-BREAK during macro execution, Quattro responds with "Macro Error at Location." *Location* is the cell containing the macro instruction that was interrupted. This message appears at the bottom of the screen. To remove the error message and return to READY mode, just press ESCAPE. You can pause a macro by pressing CTRL-NUM-LOCK. Press any key to then resume macro execution.

Debugging Macros

Since Quattro macros execute quickly, it may be hard to tell what goes wrong when a macro misbehaves and it may be hard to stop the macro before it is completed. For this reason, Quattro PRO provides a DEBUG mode of macro execution. This mode is both a sophisticated tool for identifying errors in advanced macro programming and a simple way of seeing your macro run one step at a time. Using the Macro Debugging menu, you can set *breakpoints* in the macro—points at which Quattro PRO will pause during playback. These breakpoints allow you to see sections of the macro at a time.

As an example of how the macro debug feature can help in a relatively simple macro, consider the worksheet in Figure 11-17. This worksheet is a monthly expense projection. The expenses are listed in columns by month. The columns are being summed on row 11 using an @SUM formula like the one in B11. Two macros are visible on the worksheet. The first one, \C, is used to copy the contents of a cell across the model to the last column. The second macro, \S, is designed to sum a column. The macro is supposed to do this by first typing the @SUM function and the opening parenthesis. The macro then moves the cell selector to the top of the column, anchors the block to be summed at that point with a period, and includes all the cells down to the bottom of the column. Finally, a closing parenthesis is added and the formula is entered in the cell with a tilde.

The idea behind the \S macro is that the user will place the cell selector in C10 and press ALT-S to activate the macro and sum the column. But as you can see from Figure 11-18, the results are not as expected. Cell C11

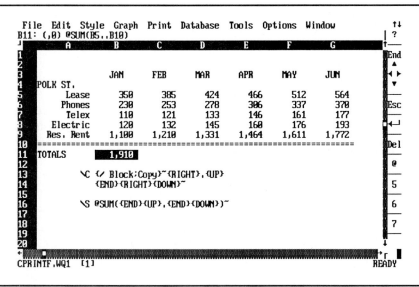

Figure 11-17. *The \C and \S macros*

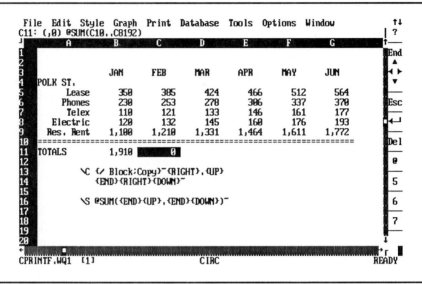

File Edit Style Graph Print Database Tools Options Window
C11: (,0) @SUM(C10..C8192)

	A	B	C	D	E	F	G
1							
2							
3		JAN	FEB	MAR	APR	MAY	JUN
4	POLK ST.						
5	Lease	350	385	424	466	512	564
6	Phones	230	253	278	306	337	370
7	Telex	110	121	133	146	161	177
8	Electric	120	132	145	160	176	193
9	Res. Rent	1,100	1,210	1,331	1,464	1,611	1,772
10	===
11	TOTALS	1,910	0				
12							
13	\C (/ Block;Copy)~{RIGHT}.{UP}						
14	{END}{RIGHT}{DOWN}~						
15							
16	\S @SUM({END}{UP}.{END}{DOWN})~						
17							
18							
19							
20							

CPRINTF.WQ1 [1]   CIRC   READY

Figure 11-18. *The CIRC error*

contains the formula @SUM(C10..C8192), which is not only incorrect but also a circular formula, as noted by the message CIRC at the bottom of the screen. The debug feature should help show where the problem lies.

To activate DEBUG mode, press the Step key (SHIFT-F2). The message DEBUG appears at the bottom of the screen. From this point until you reissue the SHIFT-F2 command, any macro you execute will cause the debug windows to appear. Before executing the macro you want to debug, however, you should make sure that the conditions are correct. For example, in the case of the worksheet in Figure 11-18, the incorrect formula needs to be deleted from cell C11 before the macro is retried. If you then issue the command to run the sample macro \S that needs to be debugged, Quattro opens up two windows in the lower half of the screen, as shown in Figure 11-19. In the upper window, called the *debug window*, Quattro shows the location of the macro you are executing and places the cursor on the first instruction. (The apostrophe is not an instruction, merely the label indicator.) The lower window, the trace window, shows you any trace cells

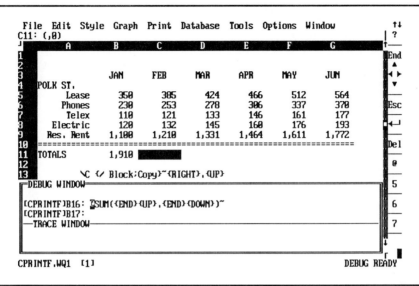

Figure 11-19. *The DEBUG screen*

that you have specified. This feature is used in advanced debugging, which is described in Chapter 12.

The SPACEBAR is used to play back the macro one step at a time. Pressing the ENTER key tells Quattro PRO to run the macro until the next breakpoint. For a simple investigation of a malfunctioning macro you will not need to set breakpoints; you can use the SPACEBAR to play back the macro one step at a time. (Breakpoints are discussed further in Chapter 12.)

In Figure 11-20 you can see that the problem with this macro has become apparent. The END, UP ARROW combination took the cell selector only to cell C10, and the END, DOWN ARROW combination is about to take the cell selector to the bottom of the worksheet. You can abort the macro at this point by typing / for the Macro Debugging menu shown in Figure 11-21. Select the Abort option from the menu to return to READY mode. Note that this action does not reverse the effect of SHIFT-F2, which will continue to cause macros to be executed in DEBUG mode until you press it again. The other options on the Macro Debugging menu will be examined in Chapter 12, which explores more advanced macro applications.

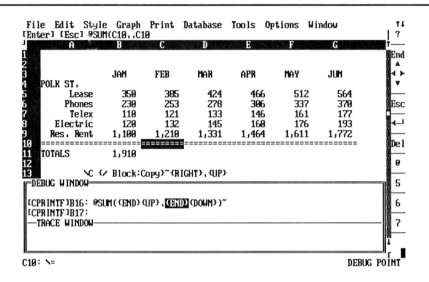

Figure 11-20. *The problem revealed by DEBUG*

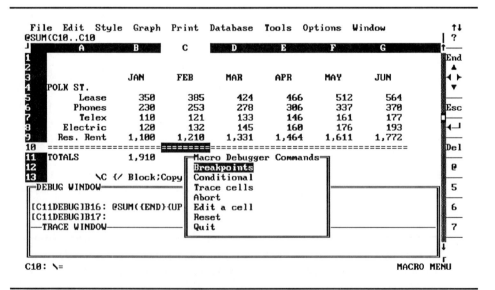

Figure 11-21. *The DEBUG menu*

Special Macros

A macro consists of instructions stored in a series of spreadsheet cells. You enter the instructions as labels, using either the exact keys you press to enter a command, as in **/FR** for the File Retrieve menu command; or menu equivalents, as in {/File;Retrieve}. The menu equivalents are used by Quattro PRO when it records your commands, both in the macro RECORD mode and the Transcript log. You execute macros instructions with the Macro Execute command, either by pointing at the first cell in the macro or by looking up its name with the F3 key. You can create an unlimited number of named macros that you can select with ALT-F2 and F3. You can create 26 instant macros named \A through \Z. You activate these macros by pressing the ALT key and the letter. In addition to these, there are several special types of macros that you can use.

Automatic Macros

You can have Quattro activate a macro as soon as the file in which it is stored is retrieved. This *Startup macro* is normally called \0, but you can use a different name, such as FIRST, as long as you record your choice with the Options Startup and Options Update commands. The Startup macro works well with the autoload file, which is a worksheet file that is retrieved from disk as soon as you load Quattro PRO. The name of the file that the program looks for when it is loaded is normally called QUATTRO.WQ1, but you can change it to another name (such as FIRST.WQ1) by using the Options Startup menu. If you create a Startup macro in a worksheet named as the autoload file, you can initiate any series of events that macros can control.

A simple application of the Startup macro feature is to have Quattro PRO display a list of files every time you load the program. To do this, enter the label **'/FR** or

{/ File;Retrieve}

into an empty worksheet and name the cell as the Startup macro, \0. Then save the file using the name QUATTRO.WQ1 or whatever name you have selected as your autoload file. When you next start up Quattro, the first thing you will see is a list of files from which to select. Note that the label '/FR is the exact key equivalent of the command, while the words in braces are the menu equivalent of the command.

Command-Line Macros

If you want to load Quattro and then a particular spreadsheet, you can do so without using the autoload feature. Type the name of the file after the name of the program when you are loading from the DOS prompt or the command line. For example, suppose you have to respond to an urgent request for a price quote. Your pricing calculations are in a file called PRICING.WQ1. You have turned on your PC and are at the DOS prompt ready to load Quattro PRO. Simply type

Q PRICING

and press ENTER. The program will load and immediately retrieve the pricing worksheet.

You can go one step beyond this by naming a macro on the command line as well. Thus, if you have a macro in the PRICING worksheet called QUOTE that is a series of steps to produce a price quote, you could type

Q PRICING QUOTE

at the DOS prompt and press ENTER. The program would then load itself, the worksheet, and the macro. This level of flexibility, together with the speed with which Quattro loads, opens a wide range of possibilities for your applications. For example, you could set up several different DOS batch files to load Quattro PRO together with different worksheets. (DOS batch files are described in Appendix A.) The automatic and command-line macro-loading options take on particular significance when you work with the Macro commands described in the next chapter.

You can also load a workspace from the command line. You do this by specifying the full name of the workspace file, as in

Q PRICING.WSP

which loads a workspace called PRICING.WSP. If this workspace includes a worksheet that has been designated as a macro library, and includes an autoexecute macro, then you can initiate a whole series of events from the command line.

A Macro-Executing Macro

When you have created a number of named macros and want a quick way to execute them, you can develop a macro that will help you select one macro from a macro list. You could create this macro-executing macro by entering the label

{/ Name;Execute}{NAME}

into a blank cell. If you use the Edit Names Create command to name this cell with an instant macro, possibly \M for macro executing, the next time that you need to execute a named macro, you can simply press ALT-M. The macro uses the Macro Execute command and the F3 function {NAME} to display a list of named macros from which you can choose.

Macro Writing and Editing

As you have seen, there are several ways to create macros in Quattro PRO. You can record your keystrokes. You can use sections of the log of your keystrokes recorded by Transcript, as described in the next chapter. You can also write the macro yourself, using your knowledge of Quattro PRO to compose a set of keystrokes. You can combine sections of macros that you have written with sections produced by the other methods. Writing or editing macros becomes more important as your macros become more complex. The chances are that you will need to edit lengthy macros to improve their performance, streamline their arrangement in the worksheet, or correct bugs in their operation.

Composing Macros

Before composing a macro, it is helpful to make notes of the operations you want the macro to perform and sketch out the required steps. When you enter the macro instructions into the worksheet, remember that you can use either direct keystrokes for menu selections or the menu equivalents. Thus, you could enter a macro to convert the current cell into a value as **/EV** or

{/ Block;Values}~~

While the first approach might seem quicker, it is more difficult to read. The second approach does not require that you memorize all of the menu equivalents. You can look these up by using ALT-F3 and selecting /Commands from the menu. The commands are logically grouped together and easy to find.

Often you will be able to put together a macro from several sources. For example, you can use the record method to capture the keystrokes for part of an operation and then add those recorded keystrokes to the rest of the macro with the Edit Move command. When you are combining macro instructions, you may want to use several of the techniques described here.

Repeating and Abbreviating

When you use the record method to capture keystrokes, you sometimes get rather cumbersome lines of instructions like this one:

{/Block;Copy}{DOWN}{DOWN}{DOWN}{DOWN}{DOWN}{RIGHT}{RIGHT}

Quattro PRO records each cursor movement as a separate keystroke, repeating the keystroke representation over and over. However, you can refer to a series of repeated keystrokes by the name of the key representation and a number. That is, the key representation takes a numeric argument enclosed within braces, as in {DOWN 5}. You can use this system with any of the macro key representations listed in Table 11-2 except for {CR} and {MENU}.

The number used as the argument can be a number you type in or a number in a cell referenced by the cell coordinate or a block name. Thus, {DOWN A1} causes the DOWN ARROW action to be repeated five times if A1 contains the number 5 or a formula that results in 5. Likewise, the instruction {DOWN TIMES} causes the action to be repeated five times if the block TIMES contains the number 5 or a formula that results in 5.

You can further shorten your macros if you refer to the arrow keys as follows: DOWN as {D}, UP as {U}, LEFT as {L}, and RIGHT as {R}. Also, you can use {ESC} instead of {ESCAPE} and {BS} instead of {BACKSPACE}. Thus, {DOWN 5} becomes {D 5} and the lengthy instruction just given can be reduced to this:

{/ Block;Copy}{D 5}{R 2}

This abbreviated version is easy to read and much more compact. However, you will probably want to look carefully at the use of multiple cursor-movement keystrokes in your macros. In general, you will find macros more reliable if you use block names wherever possible, instead of the pointing method of identifying cell coordinates.

Splitting Macro Lines

At times you may not be able to reduce the length of recorded macro instructions by using the abbreviation method. However, you may still want to split the macro line into more manageable sections. One way to do this is to copy the line that needs to be split and then edit both versions. For example, you might want to split the following line:

{/ Sort;block}{BS}.{END}{RIGHT}{END}{DOWN}

To split this line of instructions, first copy the line from its current cell to the one below it (assuming that the cell you are copying to is empty or contains expendable data). Then highlight the original instruction and press F2 to edit it. Use the BACKSPACE key to erase all the text to the right of the period. Then press ENTER to return the edited line to the cell. Move your cell selector to the copy of the original line and press F2 to edit it. Press

HOME and then press DELETE to remove all of the text up to and including the period. Press ENTER to return the edited contents to the cell. The resulting cells will look like this:

{/ Sort;block}{BS}.

{END}{RIGHT}{END}{DOWN}

You now have the macro instruction in two short labels rather than one long one. This technique often helps to make macro instructions more manageable.

There may also be times when it is prudent to combine lines of macro code. For example, earlier in Figure 11-12 you saw that Quattro PRO recorded a single tilde on one line at the end of a macro. This was later added to the line above to make the macro easier to copy and keep together.

12 *Advanced Macros and Custom Menus*

This chapter explores the more advanced aspects of creating Quattro PRO macros, including automatic macros and the use of Transcript. You will learn about the macro commands that allow you to create menu-driven applications with Quattro PRO. You will see examples of macros that prompt for user input. At the end of this chapter, you will learn how to customize the actual program menus of Quattro PRO, using the Menu Builder add-in program. You will see how to cut and paste menu items to arrange them the way you want, thus developing a unique program interface.

Transcript Macros

The Transcript feature keeps track of all your keystrokes while you are using Quattro PRO. It saves the keystrokes to a log file on disk so that you can reconstruct your work after a power outage or a serious operator error. The format in which Transcript records your keystrokes is the same as that used in macro recording. You can actually copy sections of the Transcript log to your worksheet for use in macros.

Using the Transcript Log for Macros

If you have loaded Quattro PRO and have performed an operation that you would like to incorporate into a macro, you can access the Transcript log of your actions by using the Tools Macro command or by pressing the Macro key (ALT-F2). From the Macro menu, select Transcript. A window showing the Transcript log will open in the middle of the screen. You can see this window in Figure 12-1, which shows an accounts receivable worksheet in which a new column for Total Amount Now Owed is being added. The most recent actions are at the bottom of the list. You use the UP ARROW key to scroll through the log. The line in the left margin of the Transcript window marks the activity since the last File Retrieve, Open, Save, or New command. Transcript remembers changes incrementally since the last time a disk file was read, using the stored file as a basis for the recreation of your work in the event of data loss. You can see the File Retrieve command in Figure 12-2, where the log has been scrolled and the menu activated by typing /.

Suppose that you copy the new formula created in cell G9 of the accounts receivable worksheet down to the bottom of the model, using the END key.

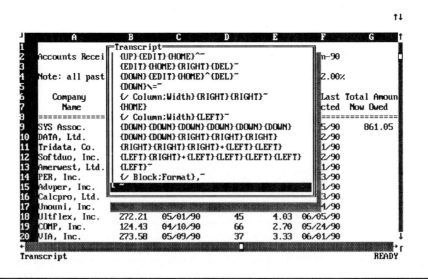

Figure 12-1. *Transcript window*

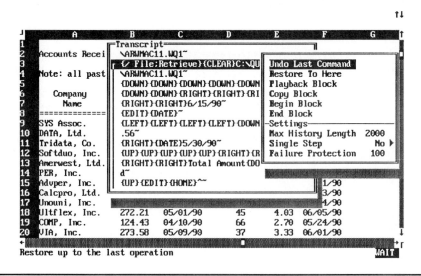

Figure 12-2. *The Transcript menu*

You would like to make a macro out of this action. Press ALT-F2, select Transcript, and you will see that the action has been recorded, as shown in Figure 12-3, where it occupies the last two lines of the log. To copy a section of the log to your worksheet, first place the highlight bar on the first line of instructions you want to copy, as was done in Figure 12-3. Then type / for the Transcript menu. Select Begin Block from the menu. The menu will disappear and leave a triangle marking the beginning point of the block. You can move the highlight bar to the last line of the section you want to copy. Type / and select End Block as shown in Figure 12-4. This marks the end of the block with a triangle.

Having marked the block of Transcript code, type / again and select Copy Block from the Transcript menu. You will be returned to the worksheet and prompted for a macro name to create or modify, as shown in Figure 12-5. This allows you to name the worksheet cell into which you are about to paste the Transcript code. You can enter a name if you have one picked out already, or just press ENTER to continue with the copy operation without naming the destination cell. When you press ENTER or enter a name you will be prompted for a cell location, just as you are when you use the Macro Paste command. You can paste the code into the current

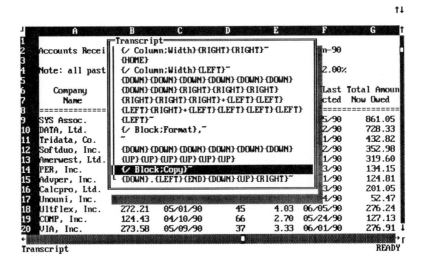

Figure 12-3. *Action recorded*

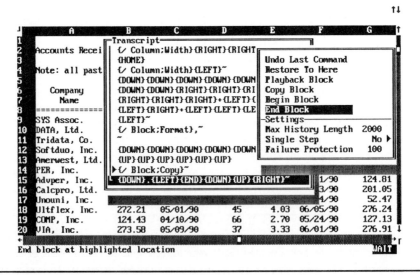

Figure 12-4. *Marking a block*

worksheet or into a macro sheet by entering the worksheet name in brackets before the address. After specifying the first cell of the block to which you want the instructions copied, press ENTER and the copy is completed. You can now use the instructions—which are simply long labels—in macros. As you can see from cells I1 and I2, the copied instructions are simply long labels. These can be rearranged as seen in cells I9 through I14.

Bear in mind that the destination cell must be above enough empty cells to accommodate the number of lines you are copying into the worksheet. The Transcript log records the copy action as a Macro Paste and remembers the block markers. You can move these to other parts of the Transcript log with the Begin Block and End Block commands.

Other Transcript Commands

The Undo Last Command option at the top of the Transcript menu is useful when you do not have the regular Undo feature activated. The important factor in the successful use of this command and the Restore To Here command is to maintain your position in the spreadsheet before issuing the command. When you tell Quattro PRO to restore to here it carries out

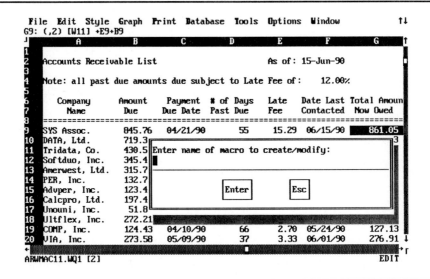

Figure 12-5.   *The Name prompt*

all of the actions since the last file save or retrieval. If you make an error and then move all over your worksheet trying to fix it before remembering Transcript and selecting Restore To Here, you can get unexpected and chaotic results. It is best to use this command as soon as you realize you have made a mistake.

You might wonder how far back you can go to get code for macros from the Transcript log. Notice the Settings section of the Transcript menu in Figure 12-2. The Max History Length option is currently set at 2000 lines. This is how many lines of instructions Transcript will record before discarding line 1. You can increase this setting to store more of your actions, resulting in larger Transcript log files on disk, or you can shorten the setting to conserve space. The maximum setting is 25,000 lines. To change this setting, simply highlight the menu option and press ENTER. Note that adding to History Length increases the memory area used by Transcript.

In Figure 12-2 you can see that the option called Single Step is currently set to No, meaning that if you use the Playback Block command the code in the log will be played back one step at a time, as in the DEBUG mode of macro execution. Setting this option to Yes provides a greater level of control when playing back Transcript with the Restore To Here or Playback Block commands.

Under the Transcript settings, the Failure Protection option refers to the number of lines recorded before Transcript saves the log to disk. Currently this is set to 100. If you decrease this number you will notice more disk activity, but recovering from a disaster will likely be more complete. Bear in mind that the Undo feature will reverse some actions if you use it immediately, providing a front line of defense ahead of Transcript.

Macro Commands

In addition to using macros for a fixed set of instructions that replicate keystrokes as if they were entered manually from the keyboard, you can use special macro commands to access features and functions that are not available from the keyboard. The following sections discuss the theory of macro commands and provide examples of how you can use these commands. Most of the rest of this chapter is devoted to a review of the individual commands. These range from {BEEP}—which sounds your computer's beep to alert the user—to {GETLABEL}—which prompts for user input—to {MENUBRANCH}, which branches to the data for a custom menu.

The Role of Macro Commands

The basic purpose of macro commands is to add logic to macros, thus enabling you to create macros that evaluate conditions and choose between different courses of action based on parameters you specify. For this reason the macro commands are a lot like programming statements. This does *not* mean that macro commands are just for programmers. Typical power users are quite capable of taking advantage of this facility, either to simplify their own work or to prepare Quattro PRO applications for others. However, the macro commands do permit you to develop macros to such a high level of sophistication that complete texts have been devoted to programming in macro command languages.

Since the Quattro PRO macro commands closely follow the syntax and format of the 1-2-3 macro command language you will find that texts on that subject are generally applicable to Quattro PRO. You should bear in mind that there are some commands in Quattro PRO that do not exist in 1-2-3 Release 2, and that the design of Quattro PRO has alleviated the need for some of the programming steps necessary in 1-2-3. These differences will be pointed out as the commands are described in this chapter.

Using the {BRANCH} Command

A simple, yet typical situation where a macro command can be very effectively applied is the need to repeat a series of operations. Suppose you have a column of values that need to be rounded to two decimal places. You edit the first cell and place **@ROUND(** in front of the value. Then you place **,2)** at the end of the value and enter the new information into the cell. You could use a macro called \R to do this:

\R   {EDIT}{HOME}@ROUND({END},2)~

After performing this action on one value you would move down to the next. Alternatively, you can add this movement to the macro. Since the DOWN ARROW key enters data from EDIT mode you could amend the macro to read:

\R   {EDIT}{HOME}@ROUND({END},2){DOWN}

If the column of values is long, you will need to repeat the macro many times. Instead of repeatedly executing the same macro, you can incorporate this repetition into the macro by means of the macro command {BRANCH}. The {BRANCH} command tells Quattro PRO to go to a new cell and read the instructions from there. Like @functions, many of the macro commands require arguments. Include these within the braces, separated from the name of the command by a space. Connect multiple arguments with commas, just as you do in @functions.

The following \R macro tells Quattro PRO to go back and repeat the macro. When the first line of code is read the second line tells Quattro PRO to return to the first, the actual cell named \R:

\R   {EDIT}{HOME}@ROUND({END},2){DOWN} {BRANCH \R}

Once you execute \R the macro will loop continuously until you stop it. You can stop the macro with CTRL-BREAK or pause it with CTRL-NUM LOCK. While this is a fairly crude way of controlling macro execution it is simple to implement.

Using the @CELL Command

The @CELL command—and its companions, @CELLPOINTER and @CELLINDEX—is very useful in macros when you need to get information about a cell. For example, suppose you want to know whether a cell is a blank. There are several methods to determine this but the simplest is @CELL("type",A1). This returns **b** if the cell is blank (also **v** if it contains a value, **l** if a label). The codes you can use in the @CELL commands are listed in Appendix A, and the function is described in more detail in Chapter 2. The information returned by the @CELL function covers address, row, column, contents, type, prefix, protection status, width, and format.

Bear in mind that the @CELL response itself may be a label, so an {IF} or @IF statement using @CELL may need to refer to the result as a string in quotes, like the "b" in this formula, which returns VACANT if A1 is blank:

@IF(@CELL("type",A1)="b","VACANT","OCCUPIED")

Using the {INPUT} Command

Many macros are designed to make a worksheet easier for novices to use. Often, you would like a macro to prompt the user for the required pieces of data. An example of this is shown in Figure 12-6 where an automobile loan is being calculated. Cells E8 through E19 are formatted with text format to show the calculations that they perform. The calculations all stem from the price of the automobile. A macro has been designed to ask the customer the price on which they want to base the loan. In Figure 12-7 you can see some of the macro code. The first line of the macro places the price of the automobile into the cell named PR, using the {GETNUMBER} command.

A {GETNUMBER} statement needs two pieces of information: the text of the prompt or question, enclosed in quotes; and the location into which

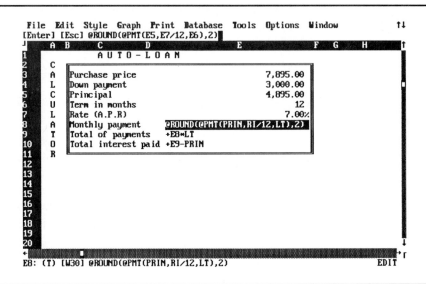

Figure 12-6. *Auto loan calculator*

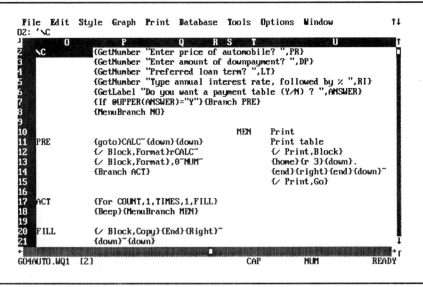

Figure 12-7. *Macro code*

to place the response. This location can be a cell coordinate or a block name. Block names are preferable since they are more constant than cell references. When you activate this macro you are prompted with

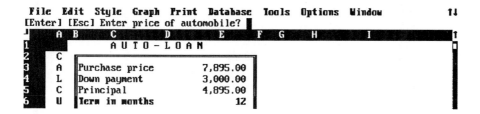

When you type a number and press ENTER, the number is placed into the designated cell, E3. If you enter something other than a number, you get an ERR message.

Finding Commands

You can use Quattro PRO to look up macro commands as you are writing macros. The Macro key (SHIFT-F3) shows a list of different types of macro commands, as shown in Figure 12-8. The commands that prompt for user input are called the *interactive commands.* If you select Interactive from the SHIFT-F3 list, you will see the possibilities shown in Figure 12-9. Highlight the one you want to use in your macro and press ENTER to place it on the edit line. In the case of user-input commands, you can use a whole series one after the other to prompt for all of the variables in the loan calculation. The {GETLABEL} command you see in Figure 12-9 handles label input in a continuation of the \C macro. This command has been set up to place the response in a location stated as a named block, ANSWER.

Using the {IF} Command

The example is designed so that the responses to the price, down payment, and term questions of the loan calculation are placed in their respective cells. The {GETLABEL} command asks the user if he or she wants to see a payment table, and places the response in a cell named ANSWER. The next line of the macro, on row 7 of the worksheet, evaluates the contents of the ANSWER cell, using the very powerful {IF} command.

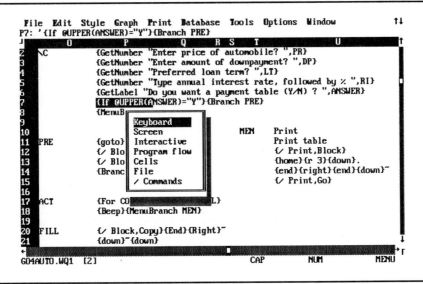

Figure 12-8.   *Macro commands*

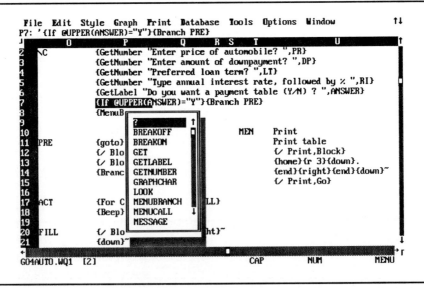

Figure 12-9.   *Interactive commands*

This command is used to make the macro evaluate a specific condition before proceeding. Like the @IF function, it is followed by a condition statement. If the cell named ANSWER contains the label **Y**, then the macro branches to a macro cell called PRE. The {BRANCH} command moves the flow of the macro to the cell specified in its argument. If the condition is not True, then the macro continues with the next line, which is a {MENUBRANCH} command.

Another Branch Macro

The PRE macro in Figure 12-7 is activated if you type **Y** in response to the prompt in line 6 for a payment table. The instructions in PRE create a payment table. This is done by first exposing a block of cells called CALC (whose contents were previously disguised with the Hide format) as shown in Figure 12-10. These are the titles and first two lines of calculations in the payment table. After resetting the format of those cells so that they can be seen, the macro branches to ACT.

Using the {FOR} Command

The macro called ACT, shown in Figure 12-11, uses the {FOR} command to control repetition of a task. In this case the task it repeats is a macro called FILL, which copies a line of the payment table once. The {FOR}

```
 File  Edit  Style  Graph  Print  Database  Tools  Options  Window        ↑↓
G3: (,2) [W5] "#
┌──────────────────────────────────────────────────────────────────────────┐
│   A B      C        D       E    F  G     H          I          J        ↑│
│1  C               A U T O - L O A N                                       │
│2  C          ┌─────────────────────┐                                    ■│
│3  A          │Purchase price   7,895.00│  ■■■# Payment  Interest   Balance │
│4  L          │Down payment     3,000.00│  1.00 423.55      28.55   4,500.00│
│5  C          │Principal        4,895.00│  2.00 423.55      26.25   4,102.70│
│6  U          │Term in months        12│                                  │
│7  L          │Rate (A.P.R)        7.00%│                                  │
│8  A          │Monthly payment    423.55│                                  │
│9  T          │Total of payments 5,082.60│                                  │
│10 O          │Total interest paid 187.60│                                  │
│11 R          └─────────────────────┘                                    │
│12                                                                        │
└──────────────────────────────────────────────────────────────────────────┘
```

Figure 12-10. *Exposed cells*

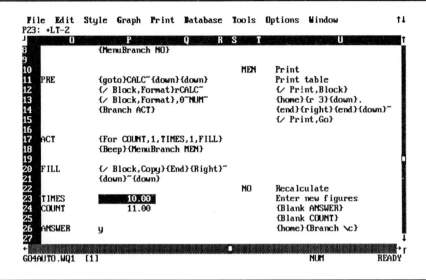

Figure 12-11.   *The {FOR} command*

command has several arguments. The first is the location of the counter, in this case a cell named COUNT. The second argument is the starting number to be placed in the counter. The next argument is the step, the amount to increment the counter after each iteration. The total number of times the command repeats is determined by the fourth argument, in this case the cell called TIMES. Located at P23, this cell is the number of periods in the term of the loan, minus two because of the lines already entered and hidden in the worksheet. The result of a complete execution of the \C macro, in which the user responded **Y** to the payment table question, is shown in Figure 12-12.

Evaluating Input

When you are designing applications to be used by others there are many factors to consider that do not arise when you are simply creating macros for you own use. For example, the macro command used to prompt for the payment table in the loan calculation model might have been written as

```
 File  Edit  Style  Graph  Print  Database  Tools  Options  Window        ↑↓
A1: [W4]
  ┌─────────────────────────────────────────────────────────────────────────┐
  │    A B    C         D        E     F  G     H        I         J        ↑│
 1│    C              A U T O - L O A N                                       │
 2│    A    ┌──────────────────────────┐                                     │
 3│    L    │Purchase price    7,895.00│   # Payment  Interest  Balance      │
 4│    C    │Down payment      3,000.00│   1 423.55     28.55   4,500.00     │
 5│    U    │Principal         4,895.00│   2 423.55     26.25   4,102.70     │
 6│    L    │Term in months          12│   3 423.55     23.93   3,703.09     │
 7│    A    │Rate (A.P.R)         7.00%│   4 423.55     21.60   3,301.14     │
 8│    T    │Monthly payment     423.55│   5 423.55     19.26   2,896.84     │
 9│    O    │Total of payments 5,082.60│   6 423.55     16.90   2,490.19     │
10│    R    │Total interest paid 187.60│   7 423.55     14.53   2,081.17     │
11│         └──────────────────────────┘   8 423.55     12.14   1,669.76     │
12│                                         9 423.55      9.74   1,255.95     │
13│                                        10 423.55      7.33     839.73     │
14│                                        11 423.55      4.90     421.07     │
15│                                        12 423.55      2.46       0.00     │
16│                                                                           │
17│                                                                           │
18│                                                                           │
19│                                                                           │
20│                                                                          ↓│
  └───────────────────────────────────────────────────────────────────────── 
GO4AUTO.WQ1  [1]                                        NUM           READY
```

Figure 12-12. *Completed command*

{If ANSWER="Yes"}{Branch PRE}

This would require that the user enter three characters, thus increasing the chance of mistakes. The {IF} command is not case-sensitive, so **YES** and **yes** will be accepted as well as **Yes**. The decision to make the response requirement a single letter simplifies the user's role. There is actually a redundant function in the statement

{If @UPPER(ANSWER)="Y"}{Branch PRE}

The @UPPER function, which turns the contents of ANSWER into capitals, is not required since {IF} evaluates **y** and **Y** as the same response. However, there may be situations where you would like to maintain tight control of the input to ensure accuracy. You can demand an exact response by using @EXACT, as in

{If @EXACT(ANSWER,"Yes")}{Branch PRE}

Here, the user would have to type **Yes** to proceed. Entering **YES** would not be acceptable.

Providing Feedback

In Figure 12-10, the {BEEP} command is used in the ACT macro. This sounds the beep when the payment table is completed. Tasks that take more than a few seconds to complete and keep the user waiting can benefit from a {BEEP} to alert them to the task's completion.

Menus Created by Macros

Following the completion of the ACT macro in the loan payment example, the macro branches to a menu by using the {MENUBRANCH} command. One of the most popular uses of the macro commands is to create customized menus within a spreadsheet to simplify its operation, either for yourself or for other users. You can place macro menus in macro libraries to make them available in any worksheet. Figure 12-13 shows the menu named MEN that is called from within the loan calculation macro. This menu offers the user three choices: printing the loan table, changing the figures in the loan calculation, or saving the worksheet.

Writing Macro Menus

Macro-generated menus follow the same format as regular Quattro PRO menus, with a vertical list of the options, descriptions of the options at top of the screen, and the first letter method of selection. Quattro PRO automatically places the menu on the screen in a suitable location, based on the position of the cell selector when the menu is invoked, as well as the size of the menu. To let you know that you are still in the middle of a macro, and not in a Quattro PRO menu, the program automatically displays the MACRO message at the bottom of the screen.

When the user selects one of the items on the menu in Figure 12-13, macro commands are activated to carry out the menu item. You can easily

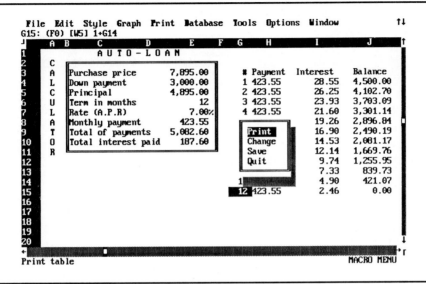

File Edit Style Graph Print Database Tools Options Window   ↑↓
G15: (F0) [W5] 1+G14

A B	C	D	E	F	G	H	I	J	

```
            A U T O - L O A N
 C
 A   Purchase price       7,895.00      # Payment   Interest   Balance
 L   Down payment         3,000.00      1 423.55      28.55    4,500.00
 C   Principal            4,895.00      2 423.55      26.25    4,102.70
 U   Term in months             12      3 423.55      23.93    3,703.09
 L   Rate (A.P.R)            7.00%      4 423.55      21.60    3,301.14
 A   Monthly payment        423.55                    19.26    2,896.84
 T   Total of payments    5,082.60        Print       16.90    2,490.19
 O   Total interest paid    187.60        Change      14.53    2,081.17
 R                                        Save        12.14    1,669.76
                                          Quit         9.74    1,255.95
                                                       7.33      839.73
                                        1              4.90      421.07
                                       12 423.55       2.46        0.00
```

Print table   MACRO MENU

Figure 12-13. *The MEN menu*

create such a menu to operate macros in your worksheets. However, remember that this menu is part of this worksheet, not a part of the overall Quattro PRO menu system. You can use the Menu Builder to splice macros into the system menu, as described later in this chapter, but the macros remain specific to one spreadsheet. You can place macro menus in a macro library if you would like to access them from any spreadsheet.

All of the instructions that make up the menu macro in Figure 12-13 are shown in Figure 12-14. Each menu item is in a separate but contiguous column, listing the parts of the macro on consecutive rows. The first row is the name of the item as it is to appear on the menu. Quattro PRO can normally display about 12 menu items in a single level of a menu macro out of a total of 256. The actual number of menu items displayed depends on the position of the cell pointer when the macro is called. Quattro PRO dynamically adjusts the menu size to fit the available space on the screen and to avoid obscuring your work.

You can create multiple-level menus just as in the Quattro PRO menu system itself. Each menu item at the same level should begin with a different first letter if you want to be able to use the first-letter method of picking them. The second line is the explanation of the item that appears

File Edit Style Graph Print Database Tools Options Window   ↑↓
X11: [W10] 'Leave the menu

```
 J    T         U                  V               W           X       ↑
10   MEN   Print              Change          Save        Quit
11         Print table        Change figures  Store file   Leave the
12         {/ Print,Block}    {Blank ANSWER}  /FS{?}       {Quit}
13         {home}{r 3}{down}. {Blank COUNT}   ~r{esc}
14         {end}{right}{end}{down}~  {Goto TABLE}
15         {/ Print,Go}       {/ Block,Reformat}h
16                            {end}{right}{d 2}~
17                            {d 3}{/ Block,Erase}
18                            {end}{right}{end}{down}~
19                            {home}{Branch \C}
20
21
22   NO    Recalculate        Quit
23         Enter new figures  Leave the program
24         {Blank ANSWER}     {/ Basics,Quit}
25         {Blank COUNT}
26         {home}{Branch \c}
27
28
29                                                                        ↓
GO4AUTO.WQ1  [1]                                    NUM         READY
```

Figure 12-14.   *Menu macro code*

at the top of screen when the item is highlighted. While menu item names can be up to 55 characters long, the explanation line can be up to 72 characters long. (In normal practice, make the menu name brief and the explanation lengthier.) Below the explanation text are the macro commands that are executed when an item is chosen. To refer to a menu like this in a {MENUBRANCH} command the top-left cell of the menu is named, in this case I30.

Note that in cell U13 of Figure 12-14 the command {r 3} is used instead of {right}{right}{right}. This is an abbreviation that you can use with all of the direction commands. It helps to shorten the macro and makes it easier to change should the number of repetitions be incorrect.

You can see from Figure 12-14 that the placement of macros in adjacent columns stipulated by the menu macro command syntax could make it difficult to see all of the commands on a given line, particularly if you could not widen the columns. However, this is not a problem for the execution of the macro since Quattro PRO does not care if the entire command is visible.

Macro Menu Control

When the user selects any one of the menu items in the example in the last two figures, the commands beneath that item are executed and Quattro PRO returns to the READY mode. Alternatively, you could refer the macro back to the menu for more choices. You would accomplish this with the command

{MENUBRANCH MEN}

at the bottom of each item. If you take this approach you will probably want to include an option to quit the menu.

Another example of a menu macro is shown in Figure 12-15, where an employee database has been set up with a four-item menu offering: Enter, Sort, Print, and Quit. The Quit option takes the user out of the menu and back to the READY mode. Most of the menu macro cells are shown in Figure 12-16. Notice that each menu item except Quit leads the user to a second menu. For example, the Sort option leads to SORTMENU. The sort macro uses block names instead of cell references when identifying the sort blocks. This makes the macro easier to read and minimizes its length.

Menu Types

There are two types of menus in Quattro PRO. There are the menus you create with macros and there are the system menus that you access with the / key. It is this system menu structure that you modify with the Menu Builder feature described in detail later in this chapter. While this system or program menu structure can be modified it remains constant between worksheets. That is, the program menu structure is not worksheet-dependent. This is an important difference from the macro menus you create with the {MENUBRANCH} and {MENUCALL} commands, such as the one shown in Figure 12-15. These macro menus, which consist of a series of macros in consecutive columns, are created in one worksheet. While they can be shared by making the worksheet that contains them into a macro library, the library must be open for them to work and so they are still

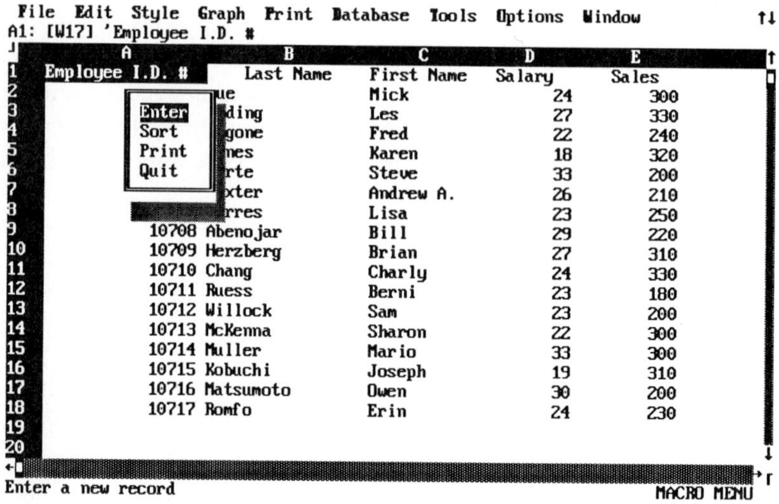

```
    File  Edit  Style  Graph  Print  Database  Tools  Options  Window        ↑↓
    A1: [W17] 'Employee I.D. #
  ╷          A              B            C           D           E          ↑
  1  Employee I.D. #    Last Name    First Name   Salary      Sales        ▯
  2              ┌────────┐ue         Mick            24          300
  3              │ Enter  │ding       Les             27          330
  4              │ Sort   │gone       Fred            22          240
  5              │ Print  │nes        Karen           18          320
  6              │ Quit   │rte        Steve           33          200
  7              └────────┘xter       Andrew A.       26          210
  8                  ▄▄▄▄▄▄ rres      Lisa            23          250
  9            10708 Abenojar         Bill            29          220
 10            10709 Herzberg         Brian           27          310
 11            10710 Chang            Charly          24          330
 12            10711 Ruess            Berni           23          180
 13            10712 Willock          Sam             23          200
 14            10713 McKenna          Sharon          22          300
 15            10714 Muller           Mario           33          300
 16            10715 Kobuchi          Joseph          19          310
 17            10716 Matsumoto        Owen            30          200
 18            10717 Romfo            Erin            24          230
 19
 20
  Enter a new record                                        MACRO MENU
```

Figure 12-15. *Menu macro*

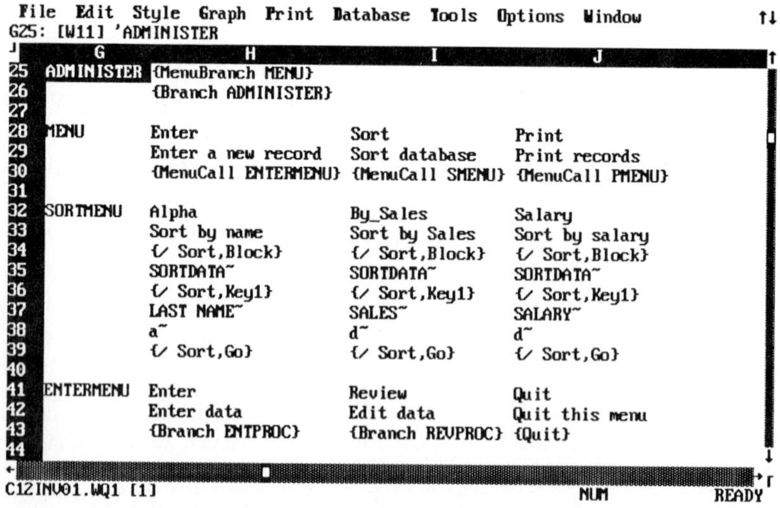

```
    File  Edit  Style  Graph  Print  Database  Tools  Options  Window        ↑↓
    G25: [W11] 'ADMINISTER
  ╷        G          H                I                 J                  ↑
 25  ADMINISTER {MenuBranch MENU}
 26             {Branch ADMINISTER}
 27
 28  MENU       Enter             Sort              Print
 29             Enter a new record Sort database    Print records
 30             {MenuCall ENTERMENU} {MenuCall SMENU} {MenuCall PMENU}
 31
 32  SORTMENU   Alpha             By_Sales          Salary
 33             Sort by name      Sort by Sales     Sort by salary
 34             {/ Sort,Block}    {/ Sort,Block}    {/ Sort,Block}
 35             SORTDATA~         SORTDATA~         SORTDATA~
 36             {/ Sort,Key1}     {/ Sort,Key1}     {/ Sort,Key1}
 37             LAST NAME~        SALES~            SALARY~
 38             a~                d~                d~
 39             {/ Sort,Go}       {/ Sort,Go}       {/ Sort,Go}
 40
 41  ENTERMENU  Enter             Review            Quit
 42             Enter data        Edit data         Quit this menu
 43             {Branch ENTPROC}  {Branch REVPROC}  {Quit}
 44
  C12INV01.WQ1 [1]                                      NUM        READY
```

Figure 12-16. *More macro code*

worksheet-dependent. By using the autoload file and the \0 macro you can have Quattro PRO load directly to a macro library and a macro menu. However, this menu is still specific to a worksheet, unlike items that are part of the program menu system tree that you can customize with the Menu Builder.

Flow Control

On row 28 of Figure 12-16 you can see the beginning of the set of instructions called MENU. These are the menu item names. Below them are the descriptions of the items and the actions each one performs. Notice that the first three items lead to further menus by means of the {MENUCALL} command. This differs from the {MENUBRANCH} command in that the flow of the macro returns to the macro stated as the {MENUCALL} argument after the actions in the menu have been completed. This serves to keep the user within the menu structure. The fourth item on the MENU menu is Quit. This provides a direct (and easy to pick) route out of the menu and back to the READY mode. The menu created by the MENU macro was shown earlier in Figure 12-15. Most of the contents of SORTMENU, called by the second option on the menu, are shown in Figure 12-16. As you can see, SORTMENU is a series of database sort actions to rearrange the data according to LAST NAME, SALES, and so on. The cells in the database have been named SORTDATA.

The ENTERMENU code can be seen in Figures 12-16 and 12-17. The first option, Enter, is the most important. It leads to the ENTPROC macro, a series of prompts for data. The data is placed in a vertical set of cells named ENT1, ENT2, and so on, located elsewhere in the worksheet. The entry of data is followed by a move with the {GOTO} command to view the cells where the data has been placed. The user is prompted to respond **Y** or **N** to the question "Is the data correct?" The response is placed in a cell called DYN.

You can see in Figure 12-17 that the {IF} command is employed to check the user's response. The @CELL function is used to determine the contents of DYN. If the response is **Y**, then the macro proceeds with the {BRANCH} command following the {IF} statement. This leads to the PUT macro, which places the user input from ENT1, ENT2, and so on into the database. The combined data entry cells ENT1 through ENT5 are called ENTRY. The PUT macro inserts a blank row into the database called SORTDATA, and then transposes the vertical list of entered data from ENTRY into the

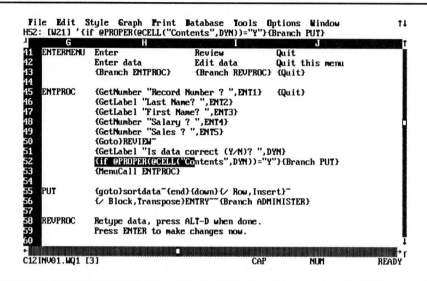

```
 File  Edit  Style  Graph  Print  Database  Tools  Options  Window          ↑↓
H52: [W21] '{if @PROPER(@CELL("Contents",DYN))="Y"}{Branch PUT}
⌐     G            H                   I               J                       ↑
41 ENTERMENU    Enter                Review          Quit
42             Enter data           Edit data       Quit this menu
43             {Branch ENTPROC}     {Branch REVPROC} {Quit}
44
45 ENTPROC     {GetNumber "Record Number ? ",ENT1}   {Quit}
46             {GetLabel "Last Name? ",ENT2}
47             {GetLabel "First Name? ",ENT3}
48             {GetNumber "Salary ? ",ENT4}
49             {GetNumber "Sales ? ",ENT5}
50             {Goto}REVIEW~
51             {GetLabel "Is data correct (Y/N)? ",DYN}
52             {if @PROPER(@CELL("Contents",DYN))="Y"}{Branch PUT}
53             {MenuCall ENTPROC}
54
55 PUT         {goto}sortdata~{end}{down}{/ Row,Insert}~
56             {/ Block,Transpose}ENTRY~~{Branch ADMINISTER}
57
58 REVPROC     Retype data, press ALT-D when done.
59             Press ENTER to make changes now.
60                                                                            ↓
←▓▓▓▓▓▓▓▓▓▓▓▓▓▓▓▓▓▓▓▓▓▓█▓▓▓▓▓▓▓▓▓▓▓▓▓▓▓▓▓▓▓▓▓▓▓▓▓▓▓▓▓▓▓▓▓▓▓▓→ r
C12INV01.WQ1 [3]                        CAP          NUM          READY
```

Figure 12-17. *The ENTERMENU code*

SORTDATA block. After new data has been entered the macro loops back
to the first menu, ADMINISTER, where the user can choose to sort the
expanded database or add more data.

You can see that menu instructions like those in Figure 12-17 can
become crowded. In fact, the instructions for the Review option in column
I were curtailed so that all of the Enter option could be seen. There is
certainly not room to annotate the steps in the menu macro when it is
arranged this way. Furthermore, you may already have several macros in
a worksheet and want to add a menu to access them, yet you do not want
to move the macros around. One solution is to place most of the menu item
code in a separate area and direct flow to it from the third line of the menu
macro. The following arrangement provides menu access to macros called
PD and SD:

Print	Sort	Quit
Print data	Sort data	Leave menu
{BRANCH PD}	{BRANCH SD}	{QUIT}

If the user picks Print, the PD macro is executed.

Subroutines

An alternative to this approach is to call on macros with a subroutine command. In its simplest form, this is the name of the macro in braces, as in {PD}, entered on a line by itself. When Quattro PRO encounters this statement in a macro it looks for the macro called PD and executes it. The difference between a subroutine and a branch is that the macro flow after a subroutine is back to the place from which the subroutine was called, whereas flow after a branch does not return but continues in the new direction. The subroutine is normally referred to as {subroutine} in lower-case to indicate that the only argument is a variable. You can actually add data to a subroutine, a technique described later under the heading "The {subroutine} Command."

In the case of {BRANCH PD}, the flow is directed to PD when the user picks Print and it terminates there (unless the menu itself was generated with {MENUCALL}, which essentially runs menu choices as subroutines; or unless the PD macro redirects the flow). In the following example the selection of List runs the SORT DATA macro and then the PRINT DATA macro. The SORT DATA macro does not have to contain any statements directing macro flow. Quattro PRO automatically returns to the line after the SORT DATA call in the macro.

{PRINT DATA}   List
                     Sort and print list
                     {SORT DATA}

Notice that Quattro PRO's ability to refer to macros by full block names makes it easy to read and write macro statements, particularly as they begin to approach a programming language in their complexity of flow control. However, you may want to avoid names that are too similar, such as the block name SORTDATA and the routine called SORT DATA.

One of the main appeals of the {subroutine} command is that it provides the ability to assemble macros from reusable parts. Thus, the SORT DATA macro might be a sorting operation that is used in several other macros. Instead of repeating the same code each time sorting is required, the SORT DATA macro can simply be referenced as a subroutine. A simple subroutine can store commonly used commands such as the standard steps for printing:

{CALC}	Recalculate spreadsheet
{/ Print; Align}	Align printer
{/ Print;ResetAll}	Reset printer settings

Placing this macro in a subroutine called PRE-PRINT would enable you to insert these commands into any print macro in the spreadsheet with the simple statement {PRE-PRINT}.

Links and Flow

When you are designing and running more complex macros you need to consider the question of current cell location. The macro command {GOTO}B52~ directs Quattro PRO to make B52 of the current worksheet the current cell. This means that the next action will affect cell B52 of the worksheet. This is radically different from the command {BRANCH B52} which directs macro flow to cell B52 of the worksheet. You might want to think of macros as establishing two movable pointers, one being the regular cell selector, the other being a macro cell selector. As the macro executes, both pointers are moved. The regular cell selector goes from one cell to another based on the macro commands, while the special macro pointer goes from cell to cell of macro code, based on the rules of flow and any subroutine or branching commands.

This concept of two independent pointers is particularly important in multiple spreadsheets. Before the advent of linked spreadsheets and macro libraries, a subroutine could only call macros from the current spreadsheet. However, when you are running macros from a macro library file, additional questions about macro flow need to be addressed. A standard method of operation with Quattro PRO is to keep macros in a library file—one that has been saved with a Tools Macro Library setting of Yes, as described in the last chapter. With the library file open, any open worksheet can call macros from the library. If you press ALT-M while SALES.WQ1 is the current worksheet and there is a macro named \M in an open library file called MACLIB.WQ1, that macro is run. (If there is a macro called \M in the SALES.WQ1 worksheet, that macro will run first, giving you an opportunity to preempt your library macros on special occasions.)

When the \M macro in MACLIB.WQ1 is running, the flow of command moves the macro pointer through the library worksheet. The regular cell pointer is maneuvered in the regular worksheet. However, there is nothing to stop the macro from using links, either for worksheet actions or macro flow. The command {GOTO}B52~ tells Quattro PRO to make cell B52 the current cell of the current worksheet, whereas {GOTO}[BUDGET]B52~ makes cell B52 of the open worksheet BUDGET.WQ1 the current cell. The macro command {BRANCH [MACLIB1]B52} directs macro flow from the current macro library to the worksheet called MACLIB1. You can even direct flow to the worksheet that called up the macro to begin with. This is done by referring to the worksheet with empty square brackets. For example, if you execute \M while SALES.WQ1 is current and \M runs from a macro library, but you want to direct flow to a section of code at cell B100 of SALES.WQ1, you use {BRANCH []B100}.

If you bear in mind the difference between the active cell of the worksheet and the current location of the macro pointer, you can keep track of macro action even while crossing several worksheets. However, you will probably find it easier to put most subroutines in one place, rather than skip from worksheet to worksheet. One advantage of running macros from a macro library is that you can copy to your favorite library subroutines that you have developed in other worksheets. You can name these and then pull them into new macros whenever you need them with the {*subroutine*} command.

Syntax of Macro Commands

Having explored the way in which some of the more popular macro commands are used, it is time to review all of the commands. Quattro PRO's macro commands can be categorized in several ways. There are those that do not have arguments, and those that do. Both types include a keyword in braces. Subroutine calls are an exception since they invoke another macro, making the name of the called macro (rather than a keyword) the item that is placed in the braces. The format of the nonargument commands is simply a keyword enclosed in braces, { }. These braces are recognized as label indicators by Quattro PRO. A subroutine call also follows this pattern except that the characters inside the braces represent a macro name instead of a keyword.

The format of the argument type of command consists of the keyword followed by a blank space and a list of arguments separated by commas.

As with @function arguments, no spaces are allowed between or within arguments. The entire statement complete with arguments is enclosed in the braces.

Screen and Response Commands

You can use macro commands to control updating of the display screen and the Quattro PRO control panel. If you leave such commands turned on, you can follow the progress of the macro on-screen; when you turn them off, the screen does not change. The macro commands in this group also allow you to customize the mode indicator and to give audible feedback to the user.

The {BEEP} Command

The {BEEP} command produces a sound from your computer's speaker, somewhat like the one Quattro PRO makes when you press an invalid key (such as BACKSPACE in the READY mode). The format for the {BEEP} command is {BEEP *number*}, where *number* is an optional argument that you can use to affect the tone of the sound. The *number* argument can have any value from 1 to 4; 1 is the default value when no number is specified.

You can use the beep to alert the operator to an error, indicate that you expect input, periodically show that a macro is still functioning during a lengthy set of instructions, or signify the conclusion of a step. Try using several beeps of different tones to really grab attention, and to distinguish between actions. Since each PC seems to make a different sound in response to the {BEEP} command, you may want to test your system's beeper. This is easy to do in a blank spreadsheet with the value **1** entered in A1 and the following formula entered in B1:

+"{BEEP "&@STRING(A1,0)&"}"

This formula produces the result {BEEP 1} in B1 and is an excellent example of how string functions can be used to generate dynamic macros, that is, macros that depend on the contents of other cells. Now enter the numbers **2**, **3**, and **4** in cells A2, A3, and A4. Copy the formula from B1 to B2..B4. Your spreadsheet should look like this:

	A		B
1	1		{BEEP 1}
2	2		{BEEP 2}
3	3		{BEEP 3}
4	4		{BEEP 4}

Now use the ALT-F2 key or Tools Macro menu to select Macro Execute and then point to B1 as the cell to execute. You will hear all four tones from your computer's speaker. By varying the number in column A you can compose short jingles that add a personal touch to your macros. (Try the sequence 1,1,2,2,3,3,2, which sounds like "Twinkle Twinkle Little Star" on some systems.)

The {INDICATE} Command

The {INDICATE} command allows you to customize the mode indicator in the lower-right corner of the screen, which normally says READY. The format of the {INDICATE} command is

{INDICATE *string*}

where *string* is any character string. Actually, the screen can show only five characters and thus {INDICATE} will use only the first five characters of the string. You can blank out the indicator by using an empty string (that is, {INDICATE ""}). You can return the indicator to READY mode by omitting the string argument (that is, {INDICATE}). Another way of blanking out the mode indicator is to adjust the colors of the status line so that the text is not visible.

The indicator you establish with {INDICATE} remains in effect until you use the command again, either to establish a new setting or to return it to the default, READY. In fact, the {INDICATE} setting continues beyond the completion of a macro. Setting the indicator to PAUSE in a macro causes the word PAUSE to remain on the screen even if you are back to the READY mode. Use {INDICATE} without any argument to restore Quattro PRO's normal indicator display at the conclusion of the macro.

The {INDICATE} command is useful if you have a series of menu selections. You can use it to supply a string that reflects the menu selection, providing positive feedback as to the user's selection. Thus, the command {INDICATE "SORT"} can be inserted near the beginning of a macro that performs a sort operation. The user can then see that Sort has been selected.

The {PANELOFF} and {PANELON} Commands

These two commands control redrawing the control panel, the upper and lower areas of the screen that normally show you the progress of an action or command. The format for the {PANELOFF} command is simply {PANELOFF}. The {PANELON} command restores the default setting, instructing Quattro PRO to update the control panel with each instruction executed. The format for the {PANELON} command is {PANELON}. These commands have no arguments.

You can use these commands to temporarily obscure the details of a macro's execution. After a macro reads the {PANELOFF} command, the entries on the input line are not visible as they are typed by the macro. When the macro reads {PANELON} the normal display is restored. One reason for these commands was to control the annoying screen jitters that occurred when 1-2-3 executed macro instructions, particularly those involving menu choices. This is less of a problem in Quattro PRO since the menu equivalents bypass menu selection. The commands are still useful if you do not want the operator to be aware of the macro code being run. Even if a user invokes DEBUG to slow down the operation of the macro so that the instructions can be read, the control panel will not be updated while {PANELOFF} is in effect.

The {WINDOWSOFF} and {WINDOWSON} Commands

The {WINDOWSOFF} command freezes the entire screen, except for the control panel. The format for the {WINDOWSOFF} command is {WINDOWSOFF}. The {WINDOWSON} instruction returns the normal mode of screen updating. The format of the {WINDOWSON} command is {WINDOWSON}. Neither command uses an argument. Like the panel commands, the window commands reduce the flicker that occurs on the screen with some macro instructions. They can also speed execution of long macros, since Quattro PRO does not have to redraw the screen every time the macro moves the cursor or changes data. You can use {PANELOFF} and {WINDOWSOFF} together with {INDICATE "WAIT"} to flash the WAIT message and simply suspend further screen change until a macro is complete. Of course, you should use {WINDOWSON} near the end of a macro to have the screen updated with the current results.

Interactive Macro Commands

When you want user input during a macro's execution, you need to use the interactive macro commands. These commands can streamline data entry and add flexibility to macro designs.

The {?} Command

The {?} command is one of the most convenient and powerful of the macro commands, and it is often the first macro command that users learn beyond simple replaying of keystrokes. Its purpose is to allow the operator to enter information from the keyboard. This command has no arguments and uses the simple format {?}. Place this at any point in a macro where you need to obtain information from the user. After a macro encounters a {?} command, program control is handed to the user who can type a label or number, make a menu selection, or highlight an area of the spreadsheet. However, as soon as the user presses ENTER, the macro resumes control. For this reason, the {?} is followed by an ENTER (~ or {cr}) to actually enter or confirm the user input.

If you want to prompt for input of values or labels, then {GETNUMBER} and {GETLABEL} are more useful. These commands provide prompts as a part of the instruction to clarify the exact information you want. {GET-NUMBER} tests the response to see if it is indeed a number. If you use the {?} instruction, you can use an instruction before it to place a prompt message in the current cell. For example, this instruction places the cell selector in the cell called AGE, enters the message "Type Age and Press Enter," and then replaces that message with the number when the user types it and presses ENTER:

{GOTO}AGE~Type Age and Press Enter~{?}~

One disadvantage of such a macro is that the user is free to access the menu system (and potentially destructive options) as long as they don't press ENTER. Some power users would say that {?} is better suited to your own macros than to applications for beginning users.

The {GET} Command

The {GET} command is designed to accept the entry of a single character from the keyboard. The format of the {GET} command is {GET *location*} where *location* is the storage location for the single character you enter from the keyboard. Thus, you could use {GET ANSWER} to place the response letter **Y** or **N** into the cell named ANSWER. The response to {GET} can be any key, letter, number, or function key. This command is yet another option to consider when you need to incorporate keyboard input in a macro. For example, you could use the following to prompt for a single-letter piece of information:

Type Y/N
{GET ANSWER}
{ESC}

The text **Type Y/N** will appear on the input line. The next character typed will be placed in ANSWER. The input line will be cleared.

The {GETLABEL} Command

You use the {GETLABEL} command to handle entering a label from the keyboard in response to a prompt message. The format for the {GET-LABEL} command is {GETLABEL *prompt message, location*}. The *prompt message* argument is a word or words. The *location* is the cell into which the label is placed when the user presses ENTER. You must enclose the prompt text in double quotation marks if you use a comma or a semicolon because these characters are used as argument separators (as in {GET-LABEL "Enter Name: ",D1}). You must include a space at the end of the prompt text if you want a space to appear between the text and the cursor on the input line.

The length of text in the prompt is limited by the space at the top of the screen, which is used by the macro when it displays the {GETLABEL} instruction. If you use a string longer than 76 characters, the text will wrap to the next screen line and may be difficult to read since Quattro PRO will not wrap the text of the prompt according to complete words. However, you can use spaces after the 76th character to push text onto the next line, and you can use up to three lines at the top of the screen for the prompt. This makes for some interesting prompts, as you can see from the following example.

```
  File  Edit  Style  Graph  Print  Database  Tools  Options  Window          ↑↓
[Enter] [Esc] Enter employee record number,
Note: this can be found on the white registration card
in the Employee Folder:█
2                                                                             ▐
3                                                                             ▐
4 Employee I.D. #      Last Name     First Name    Salary        Sales        ▐
5             10701 Rue            Rick               24          300          ▐
```

The prompt text string can be stored in a separate cell and referenced if you construct the macro as a formula. Thus

+"{GETLABEL "&C3&"? ,E3}"

will give you the prompt "Last Name?" if cell C3 contains the label **Last Name**. This is very convenient when you have a series of field names and want to provide prompts for each one.

The *location* argument in {GETLABEL} is a reference to the cell, block, or block name where the information entered from the keyboard will be stored. Up to 80 characters will be accepted as input. If a named block is supplied for the argument, the character string entered will be stored in the upper-left cell of the block. The {GETLABEL} command stores your entry as a left-justified label in the specified location. This is true regardless of the current default label alignment setting. If the entry is a number it is still stored as a label.

The {GETNUMBER} Command

The {GETNUMBER} command is very similar to the {GETLABEL} command and is used to elicit numeric information from the user in response to a prompt message. The format for the {GETNUMBER} command is {GETNUMBER *prompt message, location*}. The rules for the *prompt message* argument are the same as for {GETLABEL}. The elements of the prompt text string can be stored in a separate cell and referenced by constructing the macro as a formula. When you use a whole series of data cells, your formula can even determine whether to use the {GETLABEL} or {GETNUMBER} command. Thus, the formula

+"{GET"&@IF(@CELL("type",D3)="v","NUMBER","LABEL")&'} "

returns {GETNUMBER} if cell D3 contains a value, or {GETLABEL} if it contains a label. You can combine that result with a formula to produce the prompt message from a label in cell C3:

+"{GET"&@IF(@CELL("type",D3)="v","NUMBER","LABEL)"&'"&C3&"?
,D3)"

This formula will give you the {GETLABEL} prompt "Last Name?" if cell C3 contains the label **Last Name** and D3 contains a label. The formula gives you a {GETNUMBER} prompt "Age?" if C3 contains the label **age** and D3 contains a value. This is very convenient when you have a series of labels for a column of mixed number and label data and you want data entry macro prompts for each.

The {GETNUMBER} rules for the location argument are the same as for {GETLABEL}. However, if the user enters a label in response to a {GETNUMBER} prompt the response in the location cell is ERR, produced by the @ERR function. This makes for a convenient method of trapping entry errors. If you follow a {GETNUMBER} command with an {IF} command you can direct the flow of the macro to an instruction in another cell if the user does not enter a number. For example, in

{GETNUMBER Age? ,ANSWER}

{IF @ISERR(ANSWER)}{BEEP}{BRANCH MESSAGE}

the macro flow goes to MESSAGE when the content of ANSWER is @ERR. Of course, MESSAGE could be a loop back to the {GETNUMBER} command but it could also be an error-message display routine. For more on @ISERR and related functions, see the next chapter.

The {LOOK} Command

The {LOOK} command is similar to {GET}, except that if a macro uses {LOOK} the user can type the entry ahead and the macro will still find it. This is because {LOOK} checks the keyboard buffer for data and places the first character from this buffer into the location defined in the command. The format of the {LOOK} command is {LOOK *location*}. The *location* argument refers to a cell used to store the character from the keyboard's typeahead buffer. If {LOOK} finds the buffer blank, it blanks the location cell. Whereas the {GET} instruction suspends macro execution while waiting for a response, {LOOK} does not. This makes {LOOK} suitable for use in a loop where you want to give the user some time to respond before the application is aborted.

The {MENUBRANCH} Command

As you saw earlier in this chapter, the {MENUBRANCH} command diverts macro flow to a set of cells into which you have placed the data required to build a custom menu. The format of the {MENUBRANCH} command is {MENUBRANCH *location*} where *location* is the upper-left cell of the area used for menu storage. Information for the customized menu must be organized according to certain rules.

The top row of the menu area must contain the words used for the menu items, entered one per cell, in contiguous columns. Each of these words should begin with a different character, just as in Quattro PRO's menus, if you want to be able to pick from the menu by pressing the first letter of an item as well as using the point and ENTER method. (If you use menu items with the same first letters Quattro PRO will pick the first of the similar items when you press the duplicated letter: from a menu consisting of Erase and Extract the letter *E* will pick Erase). Menu-selection words can be up to 55 characters long but remember that the longer the word, the wider the menu, and thus the more obtrusive it will be. You can have up to 256 items in a menu although you will only be able to see 13 different items in the menu box (the rest can be scrolled into view).

The second row of the menu area contains the expanded description for each menu choice that will display at the top of the screen when you highlight the menu selection. Since these are explanations they are likely to exceed the width of the column into which they are entered, particularly as they will occupy contiguous columns. Unsightly as this is, it will not affect macro performance.

The third row of the menu instructions contains the actual macro instructions for each choice in the column with the menu item and description. These instructions begin in the cell immediately under the description. They can extend down the column or branch to a subroutine. The subroutine approach makes for cleaner design since macro instructions in contiguous columns can be hard to read, edit, and annotate.

The {MENUCALL} Command

The {MENUCALL} command works like {MENUBRANCH}, but whereas a macro using {MENUBRANCH} ends when the code for the selected option completes, {MENUCALL} returns control to the statement following {MENUCALL} in the main code for the macro, and execution begins again at that location. This has the effect of locking the user into the menu system, returning them to a menu rather than dumping them when the action they chose from the menu is complete. The format of the {MENUCALL} command is {MENUCALL *location*} where *location* is a cell address or block name that represents the upper-left cell in the area for menu storage. The rules for the menu building are the same as those for {MENUBRANCH}.

The {WAIT} Command

The {WAIT} command is the "hold-up" command. With {WAIT} you can stay the execution of a macro until a stated time. The format of the command is {WAIT *time serial number*} where *time serial number* is a decimal value that represents the serial number for the time of day when you want execution to resume. Suppose you want users to read a lengthy instruction on the screen. You need to pause the macro long enough for this information to be read, say 45 seconds. This can be accomplished by the following instruction:

{WAIT @NOW+@TIME(0,0,45)}

The wait value is computed by adding a time value to the value returned by @NOW. This results in a measured delay. The instruction adds the desired 45 seconds to the current time and waits until that time is reached before continuing execution. The mode indicator will say WAIT while Quattro PRO is waiting.

Program-Flow Macros

Normally, a macro is read line by line, proceeding down a column from the cell that bears the macro name. However, you can redirect flow in many different ways, branching to other locations or calling subroutines, controlled by the program-flow macro commands.

The {BRANCH} Command

The {BRANCH} command transfers the flow of a macro to a new location. The format of the {BRANCH} command is {BRANCH *location*} where *location* is a cell address or block name that tells Quattro PRO where the next instruction to be executed by the macro is stored. The {BRANCH} command is often combined with the {IF} command to change the flow of execution based on a test condition. The classic example of this combination is the loop controller, shown here in a macro called CENTER that turns a column of values into a centered label:

{EDIT}{HOME}^~{DOWN}
{IF @CELLPOINTER("type")="b"}{QUIT}
{BRANCH CENTER}

After the edit is performed the macro moves the cell selector down one cell. The {IF} command tells Quattro PRO to check the cell currently occupied by the cell selector and return the cell's type. If this is *b* for blank (as opposed to *v* for value or *l* for label) the macro will quit. If the cell is not blank the macro will branch, or loop, back to its beginning, the macro called CENTER.

Remember that {BRANCH} controls macro flow, not cell selector positioning. Do not confuse {BRANCH} with {GOTO} since {GOTO} repositions the cell selector without affecting the execution of the macro. {BRANCH} moves the macro's execution flow but does not move the cell selector.

The {QUIT} Command

The {QUIT} command, used to terminate a macro, has no argument. You simply include {QUIT} as the last line of the macro you want to terminate. Although it can be said that macros automatically stop when they get to a blank cell, this is not strictly true. If a macro has been called by {subroutine} or {MENUCALL}, then Quattro PRO returns to the calling point when it gets to a blank line. Placing a Quit option that uses {QUIT} in a {MENUCALL} menu thus provides the user with a way out of the menu. Placing a {QUIT} command at the end of a macro called by a subroutine ends both the subroutine macro and the one that called it. You will also find {QUIT} useful as a value at the end of an {IF} command. When the {IF} condition evaluates as True, the macro—including all subroutines—terminates.

The {RESTART} Command

The {RESTART} command cancels the execution of the current subroutine. This command also cancels all pointers or calls in the macro that reference the subroutine to prevent return. The {RESTART} command has no arguments. Placing this command anywhere within a called subroutine will immediately cancel the call, complete the routine, and continue executing from that point downward. In the process, any upward pointers to higher-level routines are cancelled.

The {RETURN} Command

The {RETURN} command is used to return from a subroutine to the calling routine. Used in conjunction with {MENUCALL} and {subroutine} this command has the same effect on macro flow as a blank cell. This command has no arguments. When Quattro PRO reads {RETURN} in a called subroutine it returns the flow of control back to the instruction beneath the one that called the subroutine. The difference between {RESTART} and {RETURN} is that the latter does not cancel upward pointers. The difference between {QUIT} and {RETURN} is that {RETURN} continues processing after returning to the call point, whereas {QUIT} actually ends the macro at the point where it is encountered.

The {subroutine} Command

This is the command that calls a specific macro subroutine. The format is: {subroutine argument1,argument2,argumentN}. The subroutine is a macro name. The arguments, and there may be many of them, are values or strings to be passed to the *subroutine*. These arguments must have corresponding entries in a {DEFINE} statement.

The {subroutine} is a great way to reuse common sections of macro code in a spreadsheet and to spread out macro sections for clarity. Remember that unless the macro called by the {subroutine} ends in {QUIT}, program flow returns to the line below the one on which the {subroutine} command was placed.

The {BREAKOFF} and {BREAKON} Commands

The {BREAKOFF} command is used to disable the CTRL-BREAK key function, thereby preventing the interruption of a macro. The format of the command is simply {BREAKOFF} with no arguments. The {BREAKON} command reinstates the CTRL-BREAK key's function so that you can press CTRL-BREAK to interrupt a macro. The format of the command is {BREAKON} with no arguments.

Normally, CTRL-BREAK can be used to stop a macro. It will display ERROR as a mode indicator. When you press ESCAPE, you can proceed to make changes in the worksheet from the READY mode. However, when you have designed an automated application and want to ensure its integrity by maintaining control throughout the use of the worksheet, you will want to disable the Break function by placing {BREAKOFF} in your macro. Be sure you have tested the macro before dong this; the only way to stop a macro that contains an infinite loop and {BREAKOFF} is by turning off the computer.

You may choose to disable the Break function during part of a macro and then restore its operation for a later section, such as printing or data entry. In any case, the Break function is automatically restored at the end of a macro.

The /X Macro Commands

In early versions of 1-2-3 the original concept of macros as a typing alternative was augmented by special macro commands that all began with /X. The earliest form of the macro-command language, these commands provided limited logic and program-flow control for macro execution. Still functional in 1-2-3 Release 2 and in Quattro PRO, each one now has a macro language equivalent. Refer to that equivalent for a full explanation of the /X commands. Unlike the macro language commands, the /X commands are preceded by a slash (/) and are not enclosed in braces. There is no space between the command and its arguments.

The /XC Command

The /XC or "call" command corresponds to the {*subroutine*} command. The format for the /XC command is /XC*location~* where *location* is the address or block name of a cell containing the subroutine that you are calling. After /XC executes the routine or when it encounters the /XR or {RETURN} statement at the end of the routine, control will return to the macro line following the /XC instruction.

The /XG Command

The /XG command is the {BRANCH} command, directing the flow of a macro by branching to a new location containing the commands that will be entered next. The format of the /XG command is /XG*location*~ where *location* is the address containing the commands that you want executed next.

The /XI Command

The /XI command is the equivalent of the {IF} command. The format for the /XI command is: /XI*condition*~true. The *condition* argument is a comparison of two values in cells or a formula. If the condition evaluates as True, the macro will execute the instructions on the same macro line as the /X1 statement. If the condition is False, the next instructions executed will be on the macro line that follows the condition. The argument True is any valid macro instruction.

The /XL Command

The /XL command is equivalent to {GETLABEL}. It causes Quattro PRO to wait for the operator to input a character string from the keyboard and then to store the entry in a specified location. The format for the /XL command is /XL*prompt message*~location~. The *prompt message* argument is a message of up to 39 characters that prompts the user for label input.

The /XM Command

This is the equivalent of the {MENUBRANCH} command, directing flow of the macro to a set of cells that form a custom menu. The rules for the custom menu are the same as for the {MENUBRANCH} command.

The /XN Command

The equivalent of the {GETNUMBER} command, /XN uses the format /XN*prompt message~location~* to prompt the user for numeric input and enter it in the cell specified as *location*. If the user enters a label instead of a number the *location* cell will return ERR.

The /XQ Command

Used to terminate a macro, the /XQ command is the same as {QUIT} and is normally used at the end of a macro to ensure that it terminates correctly.

The /XR Command

The equivalent of the {RETURN} command, the /XR command returns the flow of a macro to the point at which it was called as a subroutine. There are no arguments to this command.

The Cells Commands

Quattro PRO groups the following macro commands as cells commands because they let you manipulate values and strings stored in spreadsheet cells. You can use these commands to blank out a section of the spreadsheet or to store a value or a string in a cell. These are also the commands that you can use to recalculate the worksheet in row or column order.

The {BLANK} Command

A macro command alternative to the Block Erase menu option, {BLANK} erases a block of cells on the worksheet. It has the format {BLANK *location*} in which *location* is the address of a block of cells or a block name. Generally used to clean out a data entry area ready for new data, you will find {BLANK} effective when a macro has to reuse an area of the worksheet.

Use a block name rather than the call coordinates as the argument for better control and remember that {BLANK} does not reset cell formatting information; it just removes the contents.

The {CONTENTS} Command

The {CONTENTS} command copies the contents of one cell into another, converting to a label of specified format and width in the process. The syntax of the {CONTENTS} command is {CONTENTS *destination,source,width,format*}. The *destination* argument is the location where you wish the resulting label to be stored, stated as a cell address or a block name. The *source* argument is the cell address or block name of the value entry you want copied into *destination* as a label. The *width* and *format* arguments are optional. Thus, the command

{CONTENTS A1,B1}

would take the number 2001 from the fixed-format (0 decimal places) cell A1 and copy it into B1 as the left-aligned label 2001.

The *width* argument is only required if you want to control width or specify format. It determines the width of the resulting label, so omitting it lets Quattro PRO use the width of the source location. The *format* argument provides control over the appearance of the value copied into the *destination.* Thus, the command

{CONTENTS A1,B1,12,34}

copies the same 2001 into B1 as $2,001.00 with three leading spaces. This is because 12 is the specified cell width and 34 is the code for currency format with two decimal places. The codes used for the different formats in the {CONTENTS} command are listed in Appendix A.

The {LET} Command

The {LET} command assigns a value to a location in the spreadsheet using the format {LET *location,value: type*}. This saves a macro from having to move the cell selector to a location to enter data. The *location* argument is the address or block name of the cell where you wish to store the value or label. (Specifying *location* as a multcell block means that the upper-left cell in the block will be used.) The *value* is the data you want assigned to the *location*. Quattro PRO will try to assign a numeric value but if it cannot it will assign a string. Use the optional *type* argument to control how the value is handled. Thus, the command

{LET A1,101}

places the number 101 in cell A1. The command

{LET A1,101:string}

places the left-aligned label 101 in cell A1. Of course, you can use cell references for the value argument.

The {PUT} Command

Unlike {LET}, which accepts only a cell address, {PUT} allows you to place a value in a location by selecting a row and column offset within a block. The format for the {PUT} command is thus {PUT *locaion,column, row,value: type*}. The block of cells, identified by cell addresses or a block name, into which you want to place the data are stated in the *location* argument. The *column* argument is the column number of the cell within the block you want to use for the data (as in other Quattro PRO commands, such as @VLOOKUP, the first column in the block is column 0). The *row* argument works the same way, the first row being 0. Thus the command

{PUT A1..C5,0,0,20:string}

places the left-aligned label 20 in cell A1. The command

{PUT A1..C5,1,1,Help}

places the label **Help** in cell B2.

The {RECALC} Command

The {RECALC} command recalculates the formulas within a block you specify, proceeding rowwise within the block. The format for the {RECALC} command is {RECALC *location,condition,iteration*}. The block to be recalculated is specified as *location*. The *condition* is an optional argument, specifying a condition that must be evaluated as True before the block is no longer recalculated. While the *condition* evaluates to False, Quattro PRO will continue to recalculate the worksheet (used in conjunction with *iteration,* which specifies a maximum number of iterations, the *condition* stops recalculation short of the maximum number of iterations if it returns True).

The point of this command, and the companion command {RECALCCOL}, is to avoid unnecessary delays in processing data. When a worksheet gets large it is normal to make recalculation manual as opposed to automatic. New entries do not cause dependent data in the rest of the spreadsheet to be updated. Instead, this is done by returning to automatic calculation or pressing the Calc key (F9). While this key recalculates the entire worksheet, the {RECALC} and {RECALCCOL} commands evaluate just a portion, which takes far less time. Use {RECALC} when the area you are recalculating is below and to the left of the cells referenced by the formulas in the area. Use {RECALCCOL} when the area you are recalculating is above and to the right of the cells referenced by the formulas in this area. Use these commands prior to printing a report to ensure that the reported data is correct, but avoid lengthy delays in updating the entire spreadsheet. (Note that if the formula to be calculated is both above and to the left of cells with new values, you must use the Calc key.

The {RECALCCOL} Command

The {RECALCCOL} command recalculates the formulas within the specified block, just like {RECALC}, except that it proceeds column by column. The format is {RECALCCOL *location,condition,iteration*} using the same argument definitions as {RECALC}.

The File I/O Macro Commands

The file I/O macro commands provide you with a means of manipulating data in a disk file, somewhat like the sequential file-handling capabilities you get in the BASIC programming language. In your macros, these commands allow you to read and write data in ASCII files. An example of the file I/O commands is provided in the next chapter.

Utility Commands

There are a couple of commands that make it easier for the macro writer to handle the chores of documentation and design.

The {;} Command

When you want to place a comment in a macro you can do so with the {;} command. Entering **{; This line is a comment}** in a macro allows the comment to appear in the spreadsheet but not to affect the way the macro runs. The macro skips this line during execution. This is useful for documenting macros, particularly where space considerations prevent the use of comments to the right of the code cells.

The {} Command

To skip a cell completely during macro execution you can use { }, which lets a macro come as close as possible to containing a blank cell without stopping. This is sometimes useful when you want to have two macros arranged so that comparable commands are in adjacent cells but one macro is not as complex as the other. For example:

Enter	List
Enter data	Sort and print list
{ENTER}	{SORT DATA}
{ }	{PRINT DATA}
{QUIT}	{QUIT}

System Menu Building

The Quattro PRO command language is not the only way you can develop a custom menu system with Quattro PRO. The entire Quattro PRO menu structure is designed so that it can be redesigned. This means that you can make custom menus that are not specific to just one worksheet or macro library.

The MU Files

The Quattro PRO menu system is stored in a file called QUATTRO.MU. You can copy and modify this file. For example, you do not need to have the same set of items on the main menu bar as the program comes with. In fact, two complete sets of menus different from the standard Quattro PRO menus are provided along with the program. There is a set in the file 123.MU, which is a menu system that will be familiar to users of 1-2-3. The file Q1.MU contains menus that are similar to those in the original Quattro PRO.

As you can see in Figure 12-18, which shows the main menu displayed by the 123.MU menu system, the menu still has the look of the regular Quattro PRO menu. Some items are named differently and the commands are grouped differently, however. For example, the Edit Erase command is found on the Range menu shown in Figure 12-19. This command is functionally equivalent to the 1-2-3 Range Erase command. To change from one menu system to another, you can use the Options Startup command and select Menu Tree. As you can see here, QUATTRO.MU is the current main menu file selected:

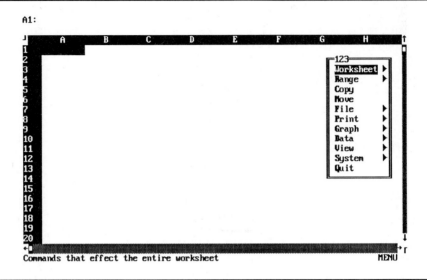

Figure 12-18.   *The 1-2-3 menu*

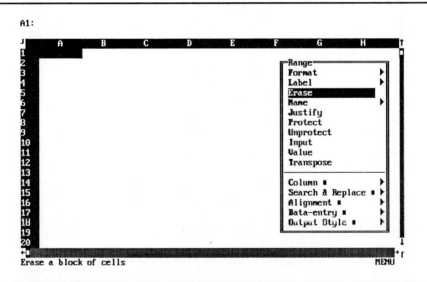

Figure 12-19.   *Edit Erase as Range Erase*

You can select the file menu you want by highlighting and pressing ENTER. Your choice appears in the Menu Tree setting for you. As soon as you exit the Options menu, the new menu tree will be in place. If you select Update from the Options menu, your choice of menu system will be written to the configuration file. When you exit from Quattro PRO and reload the program, the new menu system you selected will be in effect. In addition to the 123.MU file that comes with Quattro PRO, you can create your own MU file containing your personalized menu system.

Customizing Menus

Quattro PRO is written so that the actions it performs can be requested by several different methods, not simply by a specific set of keystrokes. This allows you to use menu equivalents in macros. The same design feature allows you to choose your own names for the program's actions and then access them from a menu that is arranged to suit the way you work. You define menu items and cut and paste menus by using the Menu Builder feature.

The Menu Builder Windows

To use the Quattro PRO Menu Builder, select the Options Startup command and pick Edit Menus. Quattro PRO reads the current menu file into memory and you get a screen like the one that appears in Figure 12-20. In the center of the screen, in the Menu Tree window, you see the top level of your current menu system. The one that is shown in Figure 12-20 is the default Quattro PRO menu. The middle window is the current window, so designated by the double-line border. The window above it is the Current Item window, which defines whatever item is highlighted in the Menu Tree window.

The Current Item window displays the six different fields of information by which Quattro PRO defines each menu item. The Desc field stores the

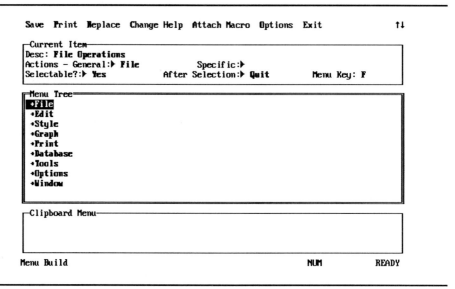

Figure 12-20.   *The Menu Builder*

description of the menu item that appears at the bottom of the screen when you are using the menu tree. There are two forms of Action for each menu item: General and Specific. Items that lead to further menus have no Specific action. Most menu items can be selected and so carry the entry Yes in the Selectable field. However, some items are placed just for show, like the lines dividing the menus into parts, and these are not selectable. All items that can be selected have an action that they perform After Selection. In the case of the File item on the main menu, the After Selection setting is Quit, which is the case for all items that lead to further menus. You can select items on menus by a key letter. The Menu Key field stores this letter, which is *F* in the case of the File menu.

In the Menu Tree window there is a highlight bar that you can move up and down the menu to highlight different items. All items preceded by a plus sign have submenus, or child menus. When an item is highlighted, you can press the numeric plus key to show the corresponding child menu branching to the right. Thus, the Edit option on the top level shows the options on the Edit menu to the right, as seen in Figure 12-21. You can use the RIGHT ARROW key to move to this set of items and then DOWN ARROW to move down the list. In Figure 12-21 you can see that the Copy item has

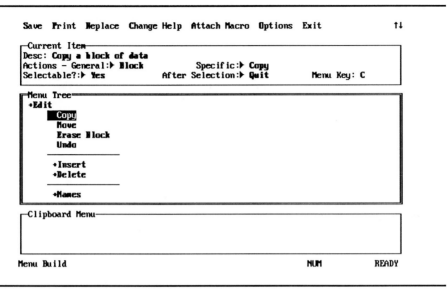

Figure 12-21. *The Edit menu child menus*

both a General action, Block, and a Specific action, Copy. Note that the lines on the menu are separate items. To shrink a set of submenus back under the parent item, press the minus sign (–) on the numeric keypad while the Menu Tree window is active and you are highlighting the parent item. Thus, to put the Edit menu items back under Edit, you highlight Edit and press minus.

The third window in the Menu Builder is the Clipboard menu, which is a place to store items that have been cut from the menu structure. Using the middle and bottom window you can alter the placement of items on the menu tree by performing cut-and-paste operations, rearranging the menu items to suit your taste.

Moving a Menu Item

Suppose that you want to move the Database commands to the Tools menu. You do this with a cut-and-paste operation. The first half of the cut-and-paste involves highlighting in the middle window the menu item you want to move, in this case Database. Then you press the DELETE key to remove the highlighted item from the Current menu to the bottom window, where it is stored, as you can see in Figure 12-22. The paste half of the operation involves first highlighting the item in the bottom window that you want to insert back into the tree. If you move only one item at a time, this item will already be highlighted as seen in Figure 12-22. With the middle window active you move to the new location for the Database item, above Macro in the Tools menu. To do this you highlight Tools, type the numeric +, press RIGHT ARROW to highlight Macro, as shown in Figure 12-23. Now you can press INSERT to insert the item from the Clipboard.

All of the child menus of a command are moved with it, as you can see by expanding the newly placed item as shown in Figure 12-24. Once an item is pasted it disappears from the Clipboard menu. Using this technique, you can rearrange items that are already defined. Items that have been cut are shown in the bottom window to remind you that they have been cut and need to be pasted or they will be lost when you save the new menu tree.

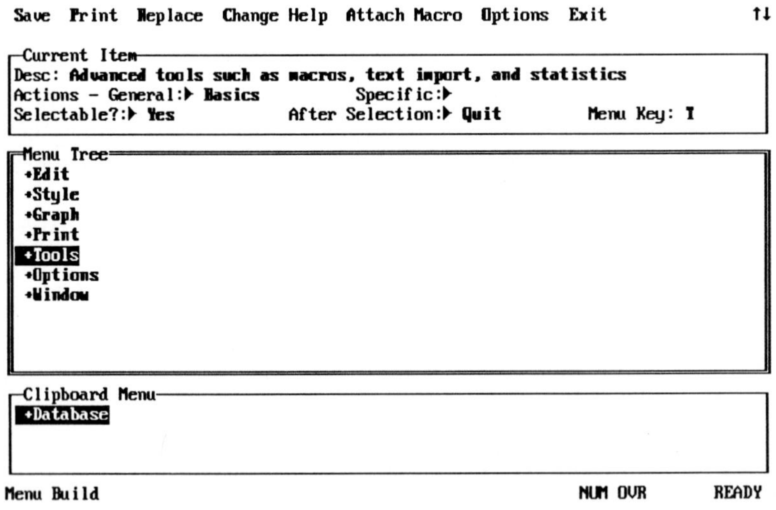

```
 Save  Print  Replace  Change Help  Attach Macro  Options  Exit            ↑↓
┌─Current Item─────────────────────────────────────────────────────────────┐
│Desc: Advanced tools such as macros, text import, and statistics           │
│Actions - General:▶ Basics          Specific:▶                             │
│Selectable?:▶ Yes              After Selection:▶ Quit        Menu Key: T    │
└───────────────────────────────────────────────────────────────────────────┘
┌─Menu Tree─────────────────────────────────────────────────────────────────┐
│+Edit                                                                       │
│+Style                                                                      │
│+Graph                                                                      │
│+Print                                                                      │
│█+Tools█                                                                    │
│+Options                                                                    │
│+Window                                                                     │
│                                                                            │
│                                                                            │
└────────────────────────────────────────────────────────────────────────────┘
┌─Clipboard Menu────────────────────────────────────────────────────────────┐
│█+Database█                                                                 │
│                                                                            │
└────────────────────────────────────────────────────────────────────────────┘
 Menu Build                                          NUM  OVR        READY
```

Figure 12-22. *A menu item clipped*

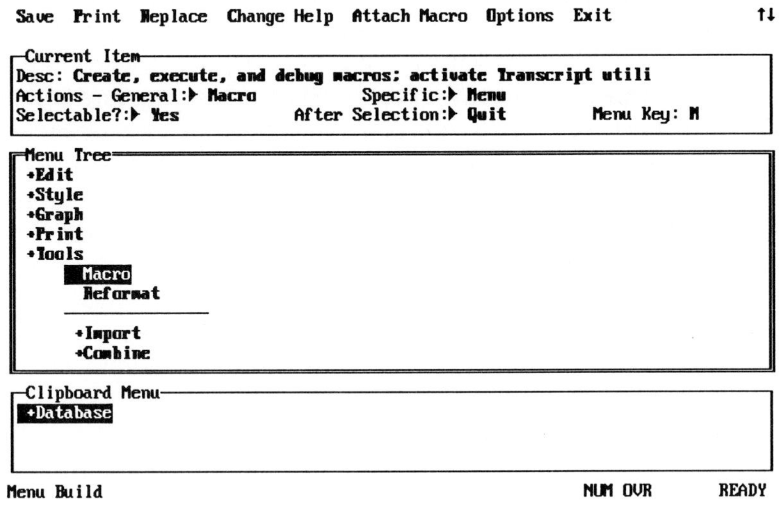

```
     Save  Print  Replace  Change Help  Attach Macro  Options  Exit          ↑↓
    ┌Current Item──────────────────────────────────────────────────────────┐
    │Desc: Create, execute, and debug macros; activate Transcript utili      │
    │Actions - General:▶ Macro          Specific:▶ Menu                      │
    │Selectable?:▶ Yes            After Selection:▶ Quit       Menu Key: M    │
    └────────────────────────────────────────────────────────────────────────┘
    ┌Menu Tree─────────────────────────────────────────────────────────────┐
    │ +Edit                                                                  │
    │ +Style                                                                 │
    │ +Graph                                                                 │
    │ +Print                                                                 │
    │ +Tools                                                                 │
    │      ▐Macro▌                                                           │
    │       Reformat                                                         │
    │      ──────────────────                                                │
    │      +Import                                                           │
    │      +Combine                                                          │
    └────────────────────────────────────────────────────────────────────────┘
    ┌Clipboard Menu────────────────────────────────────────────────────────┐
    │▐+Database▌                                                             │
    │                                                                        │
    └────────────────────────────────────────────────────────────────────────┘
    Menu Build                                      NUM OVR        READY
```

Figure 12-23.   *The Tools menu expanded*

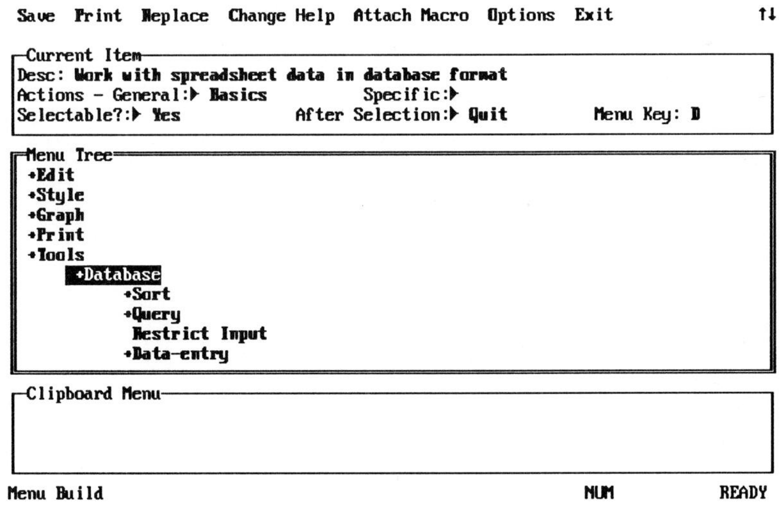

```
     Save  Print  Replace  Change Help  Attach Macro  Options  Exit          ↑↓
    ┌Current Item──────────────────────────────────────────────────────────┐
    │Desc: Work with spreadsheet data in database format                     │
    │Actions - General:▶ Basics          Specific:▶                          │
    │Selectable?:▶ Yes            After Selection:▶ Quit       Menu Key: D    │
    └────────────────────────────────────────────────────────────────────────┘
    ┌Menu Tree─────────────────────────────────────────────────────────────┐
    │ +Edit                                                                  │
    │ +Style                                                                 │
    │ +Graph                                                                 │
    │ +Print                                                                 │
    │ +Tools                                                                 │
    │      ▐+Database▌                                                       │
    │        +Sort                                                           │
    │        +Query                                                          │
    │         Restrict Input                                                 │
    │        +Data-entry                                                     │
    └────────────────────────────────────────────────────────────────────────┘
    ┌Clipboard Menu────────────────────────────────────────────────────────┐
    │                                                                        │
    │                                                                        │
    └────────────────────────────────────────────────────────────────────────┘
    Menu Build                                      NUM            READY
```

Figure 12-24.   *The Database item pasted*

Defining Menu Items

When you are in the top window of the Menu Builder you can edit any of the items. By pressing the SPACEBAR while highlighting any entry except Desc and Menu Key, you get a menu of possible choices. For example, suppose that you want to add an item called Copy on the main menu, right after Tools. First, make the Menu Tree window active, and then place the highlight bar *below* Tools. Press ENTER and a space will appear. Now press F6 to move to the Current Item window to define this new item.

In the first field of the Current Item window, Desc, you could type **Copies a cell or block of cells**. After typing this entry, press ENTER. When you move the cursor to the General field, using the TAB key, you can press the SPACEBAR to see a list of actions, as shown in Figure 12-25. You want to pick Block. Notice that the top of the menu shows a generic menu equivalent for the commands, which is further evidence of the link between Quattro PRO's macro language and the menu structure. When you move to the Specific field, the list that is displayed by pressing the SPACEBAR is more specific, showing a list of Block operations from which you can select Copy, as shown in Figure 12-26. Leave the Selectable field entry as Yes

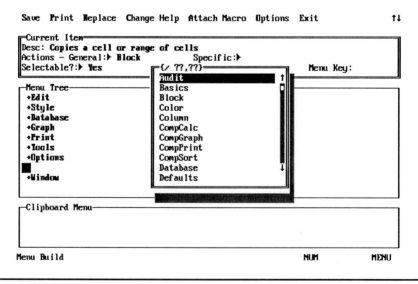

Figure 12-25.   *General action list*

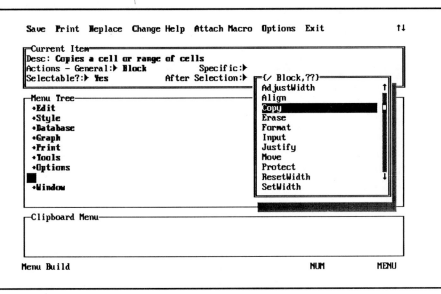

Figure 12-26.   *Specific action list*

and move to After Selection. Pressing the SPACEBAR here lists three options entitled What to do next. The self-explanatory choices are Stay, Quit, and GoTo Parent. The Copy command should Quit after being used. You can then move to the next field and type Ċ for the Menu Key.

The new menu item is almost completed, but it still lacks a name. In fact, as you enter **C** as the Menu Key Quattro PRO will remind you that the letter must refer to a named item on the menu. Press F6 to move to the Menu Tree window, type **Copy** in the empty slot, and press ENTER. The result is shown in Figure 12-27. Do not worry about the plus sign—this command does not get one as it does not lead to a child menu. In the Current Item window Quattro PRO has entered C for the Menu Key.

This is the basic procedure for defining new menu items. There is still a Copy option under Edit on this menu tree. Of course, if you simply want to move Copy from the Edit menu you can use the cut-and-paste procedure just described. Defining new menu items is useful when you want to add a specialized command in several places. You will also use this procedure when you are adding macros to menu trees, as described later in this chapter.

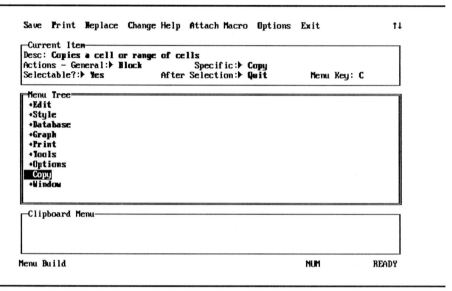

Figure 12-27.   *Defining Copy on the main menu*

Saving Menus

When you have made your changes to the menu structure, type / for the Menu Builder menu. Here you select Save. You will see a submenu requesting a name for your new menu system. When you type a name and press ENTER, Quattro PRO will save the menu, which takes a little while. You are still left in the Menu Builder. Select Exit from the menu to return to the regular worksheet window.

When you are picking a name for a new or modified menu tree, avoid using one of the existing names from the list of MU files unless you are sure you want to replace an existing menu file. Quattro PRO will warn you before replacing an existing menu tree. You do not want to accidentally replace the QUATTRO.MU file with a faulty menu tree menu—one that does not include all of the options you need. If you damage the QUAT-TRO.MU file you can recopy it from the original Quattro PRO disks.

You activate the new menu system with the Options Startup Menu Tree command. As soon as you select your new menu file from the list and quit the Options menu, the new menu tree will be in place, as you can see here:

```
 File  Edit  Style  Database  Graph  Print  Tools  Options  Copy  Window      ↑↓
A1: [W17] 'Employee I.D. #
┌─────────────A─────────────B──────────────C─────────D─────────E──────────────┐
│1   Employee I.D. #     Last Name     First Name   Salary     Sales           │
│2            10701 Rue                Nick             24        300           │
│3            10702 Wading             Les              27        330           │
│4            10703 Figone             Fred             22        240           │
```

For this reason, your menu designs should always include the Startup Menu Tree command as well as the Edit Menus command, even if they are disguised as something else to prevent novice users from getting to them. You will have a hard time changing back to the original menu tree if you do not include these items. However, if you do not pick Update from the Options menu your choice of menu file will not be recorded. This means that you can call up a special simplified menu tree for a novice user, possibly using a macro. When the user is done, Quattro PRO will revert to the original menu tree. If you do get stuck in a menu that has no Menu Tree option, you can get back to square one by recopying the RSC.RF file into your Quattro PRO directory from the original program disk. Indeed, if you are going to do a lot of experimenting with menu designs you might want to place a copy of your RSC.RF file in another directory in readiness for this eventuality.

Adding Macros to the Program Menu

Quattro PRO lets you use the Menu Builder to add the running of a macro to the program menu structure. The ability to call macros from the main menu system adds greatly to your ability to create customized menu-driven applications with Quattro PRO. Users can be prompted to enter and manipulate information by means of a set of specialized program and macro menus.

Figure 12-28 shows a customized program menu that includes the option Administer. This option was inserted into the menu tree with the Menu Builder, but the action it performs is not a normal program action. When Administer is selected, a macro called ADMINISTER is executed. There must be a macro with that name currently loaded, either in the current worksheet or in a macro library. If there is no ADMINISTER macro

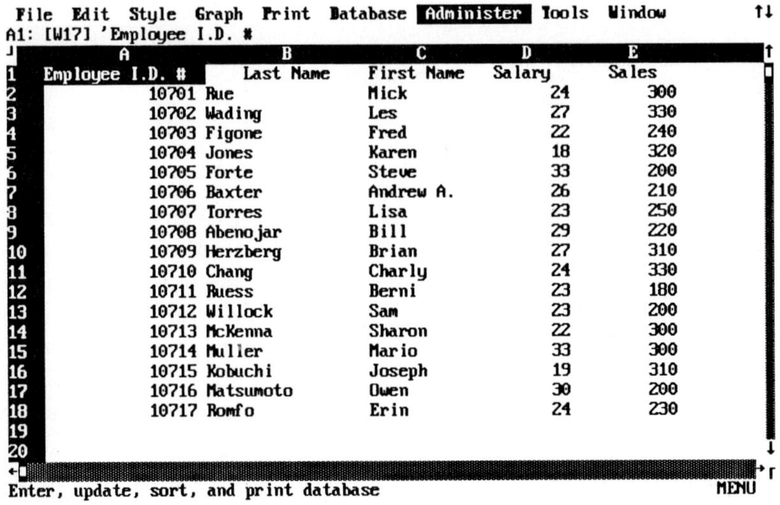

```
 File  Edit  Style  Graph  Print  Database  Administer  Tools  Window        ↑↓
A1: [W17] 'Employee I.D. #
┌       A              B              C          D            E                 ↑
│1   Employee I.D. #     Last Name    First Name   Salary      Sales           
│2        10701 Rue            Nick            24         300
│3        10702 Wading         Les             27         330
│4        10703 Figone         Fred            22         240
│5        10704 Jones          Karen           18         320
│6        10705 Forte          Steve           33         200
│7        10706 Baxter         Andrew A.       26         210
│8        10707 Torres         Lisa            23         250
│9        10708 Abenojar       Bill            29         220
│10       10709 Herzberg       Brian           27         310
│11       10710 Chang          Charly          24         330
│12       10711 Ruess          Berni           23         180
│13       10712 Willock        Sam             23         200
│14       10713 McKenna        Sharon          22         300
│15       10714 Muller         Mario           33         300
│16       10715 Kobuchi        Joseph          19         310
│17       10716 Matsumoto      Owen            30         200
│18       10717 Romfo          Erin            24         230
│19
│20                                                                            ↓
←                                                                            r
 Enter, update, sort, and print database                            MENU
```

Figure 12-28.   *The Administer item on the menu*

available when Administer is selected, nothing happens. The AD-
MINISTER macro was shown in Figure 12-16, where it was used to initiate
a macro menu system.

To create a system menu item that executes a macro command you first
enter the Menu Builder feature by using the Edit Menus option on the
Options Startup menu. Use the cursor keys to move around the Menu Tree
window and locate the menu to which you want to add the macro command.
Insert a new menu item by positioning your cursor on the menu item below
which the new item is to appear. Press ENTER to put in a new line and type
a menu name for the item. This does not have to be the same as the name
of the macro, although using the same name may make it easier to keep
track of the program flow. Press F6 to get to the Current Item pane of the
Menu Builder screen. Enter a description of the menu item. Then type /
for the Menu Builder menu and pick Attach Macro. In the Attach Macro
box, type the name of the macro as it is recorded in the worksheet. You can
see that this has been done in Figure 12-29. Press DOWN ARROW or RIGHT

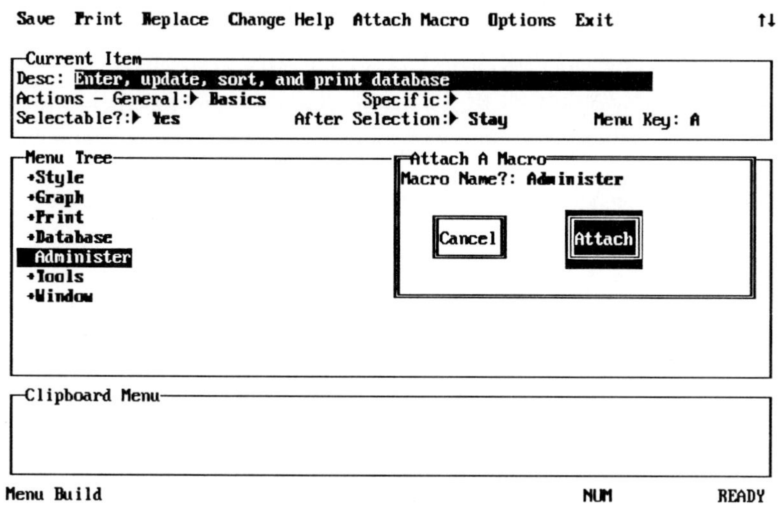

```
     Save  Print  Replace  Change Help  Attach Macro  Options  Exit              ↑↓
    ┌Current Item────────────────────────────────────────────────────────────┐
    │Desc: Enter, update, sort, and print database                            │
    │Actions - General:▸ Basics            Specific:▸                          │
    │Selectable?:▸ Yes        After Selection:▸ Stay        Menu Key: A        │
    └──────────────────────────────────────────────────────────────────────────┘
    ┌Menu Tree──────────────────┐┌Attach A Macro──────────────────────┐
    │ ◆Style                    ││Macro Name?: Administer              │
    │ ◆Graph                    ││                                     │
    │ ◆Print                    ││                                     │
    │ ◆Database                 ││   ┌──────┐        ┌──────┐          │
    │  Administer               ││   │Cancel│        │Attach│          │
    │ ◆Tools                    ││   └──────┘        └──────┘          │
    │ ◆Window                   │└─────────────────────────────────────┘
    │                                                                   │
    │                                                                   │
    └───────────────────────────────────────────────────────────────────┘
    ┌Clipboard Menu─────────────────────────────────────────────────────┐
    │                                                                   │
    │                                                                   │
    └───────────────────────────────────────────────────────────────────┘
     Menu Build                                  NUM            READY
```

Figure 12-29.   *Attaching a macro*

ARROW to highlight Attach and press ENTER to select it. The box will disappear and the General action Name will be attach to the new menu item. The Specific action will be Attach, and the key letter will be selected.

Now that you have added the macro to the system menu you can save the new menu tree. By selecting the new tree with the Options Startup Menu Tree command and then picking Update to record this change in the default or RF file, you can use the new menu in the current session and when you reload Quattro PRO. When you pick the macro item from the new menu, Quattro PRO will look for a macro with the appropriate name in the current worksheet. If it does not find a macro with the correct name in the current worksheet, the program will look for the macro in any open macro library worksheet. When the macro is found, Quattro PRO will execute it. For example, you could have several different worksheets all containing a macro called ADMINISTER. The Administer item on the / menu would activate any one of them, depending upon which worksheet was loaded and current, even if they each contained different commands.

Menu Builder Options

There are several options that you can use when you are designing a menu system—options that affect how the menu will work. If you select Options from the Menu Builder menu you can see these options listed, as shown in Figure 12-30. Each one offers a Yes/No choice to turn the feature on or off. These options are not tied to the menu structure you are designing; they affect all menus. Once you make a change to an option, it stays in effect for the rest of the current session regardless of whether you save the menu tree you have been editing. Changes to the options are stored only by the Update command on the Options menu. When you want to alter one of the options in Figure 12-30, you pick Options Startup Edit Menus, and then type / and pick Options. After making your choice you do not have to save the menu tree before picking Exit to return to the spreadsheet window, unless you have made changes to the tree that you want to keep.

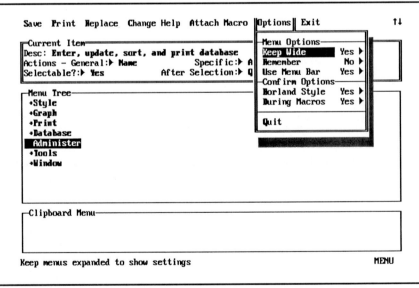

Figure 12-30. *Menu Builder Options*

Keep Wide

The Keep Wide option for your menus enables you to see the settings for menu items such as the coordinates of the block in the Sort or Print commands. Changing this setting to No will display slimmer menus that reveal more of the underlying spreadsheet. You can always expand menus with the numeric plus key or shrink them with the numeric minus key, and thus the Keep Wide option does not prevent you from accessing either wide or narrow views; it merely sets the norm for your menu tree.

Remember

This is a feature that some people love and others hate. When Remember is set to Yes, Quattro PRO remembers the last item you picked from a particular menu. For example, when Remember is in effect and you pick the Edit Insert Columns command, the next time you activate the menu the Edit command will be highlighted. When you pick Edit, the Insert command will be highlighted. When you pick Insert, the Columns command will be highlighted. This means that you can type / and press ENTER ENTER ENTER to repeat the Edit Insert Columns command. This saves you a lot of time, particularly with commands like Style Numeric Format Percent. Instead of having to find Percent on the list of Numeric Formats, Remember will take you there if that was the last format you picked.

Some tricks are useful when the Remember feature is in effect. Do not use the Quit option on a menu to leave the menu. Use CTRL-BREAK, which takes you directly back to the READY mode from just about any menu level. For example, when you pick Go from the Database Sort menu and you want to do more sorting after editing your list, exit the Sort menu with CTRL-BREAK. Then you can type / and press ENTER ENTER ENTER to repeat the Sort command. If you had used Quit to leave the Sort menu, then that would be the remembered choice when you went back there. While some users prefer each menu selection to revert to the default top item, others enjoy the speed of repetition that the Remember feature provides.

Use Menu Bar

This option lets you turn on and off the menu bar across the top of the Quattro PRO screen. When set to No you will find that there is no menu on the screen until you type /, at which point the main menu pops up as a vertical list, as shown in Figure 12-31. Note that the name at the top of the menu tree is the first part of the MU file that is current at the time. If you save a set of menus as STEPHEN.MU, then STEPHEN will be the name of the main menu. You could put your company name there to customize Quattro PRO.

Confirm Options

Quattro PRO normally displays a confirmation menu when you attempt an operation that will result in a loss of data, checking to see what actions you have performed and whether your work is saved. For example, you are

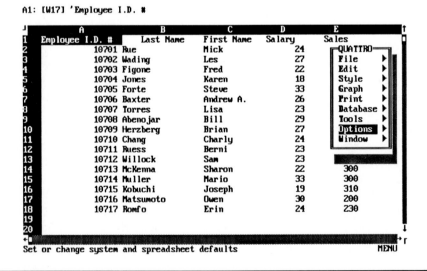

Figure 12-31.   *The pop-up vertical menu*

prompted when you are retrieving a file or resetting block names. You can turn this option to No to be compatible with 1-2-3, which is particularly useful when you are running macros.

The During Macros option is normally set to Yes to prompt for confirmation while macros are being run and recorded. To make macros compatible with 1-2-3, set this option to No. Another command needed to record macros that are compatible with 1-2-3 is Macro Recording on the Macro menu. To record with keystrokes rather than the menu equivalents—using /EC rather than {/ Block;Copy}—change Macro Recording from the default of Logical to Keystroke. When you want to record macros compatible with 1-2-3, first change to the 123.MU menu tree, then set Macro Recording to Keystrokes, and finally alter the Confirm Options to No.

13 *Applying Special Features*

This chapter takes a second look at some of the more interesting features of Quattro PRO. A number of the more powerful commands and functions are reviewed, with examples of how they may be applied. The chapter begins with a look at Quattro PRO's ability to create presentation-quality text.

Word Charts

The ability to line up text in columns is very valuable to workers in many different jobs, from the secretary who is typing up a budget from a rough draft, to the salesperson who has a presentation to make. Word processing programs often make heavy going of columns, requiring mastery of complex commands. Many people have found that spreadsheet programs offer a simple way of typing up lists that maintain a strict column and row format, such as the one shown in Figure 13-1. You can use several of Quattro PRO's special features to dress up such information.

Quattro PRO for Professional Text

The text in Figure 13-1 was simply typed into the worksheet. The figures in column V are summed in cell V51, but otherwise there is no calculation

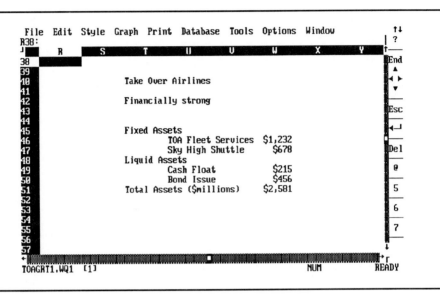

Figure 13-1. *Basic list typed into worksheet*

going on in this collection of information. To dress up the text, perhaps to use it as part of a presentation, you could add bullet characters, as shown in Figure 13-2. The characters in column R are simply the letter "o" centered in the column. The characters in column S are the ASCII character 175, created by holding down ALT and typing **175** from the numeric keypad (not the row of numbers across the top of the keyboard). These characters are centered in the column. While this effect looks better, the bullet characters will simply print as characters when the cells are printed. Even if you use Graph Printer as the Print Destination the results will not be particularly eye-grabbing.

Instead of ordinary characters in your text you might want to use one or more of Quattro PRO's seven special bullet characters. These are shown in Figure 13-3, which was printed directly from a spreadsheet. These bullet characters are graphic symbols that can be placed in spreadsheet cells. The bullets only print as images when you use Graph Printer as the Print Destination for the Print Spreadsheet command.

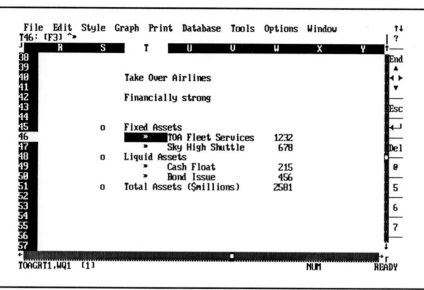

Figure 13-2. *Simple bullets added*

Quattro Professional Bullet Styles:

Bullet Style	0	☐ Empty square
Bullet Style	1	■ Filled square
Bullet Style	2	☑ Checked square
Bullet Style	3	✓ Check mark
Bullet Style	4	☐ Shadow box
Bullet Style	5	☑ Checked shadow
Bullet Style	6	● Filled circle

Figure 13-3. *Special bullet characters printed*

You enter a bullet as a coded label that Quattro PRO translates into an image during printing. For example, a style 1 bullet is created by the code

\bullet 1\

You must enter this preceded by a label prefix (', ", or ^); otherwise, Quattro PRO will assume you are using the cell fill character (\).

You can enter a bullet code into a cell on its own or you can combine it with other text. You can even use a bullet code in a string formula. For example, to combine the word *Present* with the number 5 bullet you can enter

' \bullet 5\ Present

Note that the apostrophe must be typed, and that there is a space between the second backslash and the text that follows. This space is not mandatory, but without one the bullet would print too close to the text.

A string formula using the bullet code was used to make the list of printed codes in Figure 13-3. A column of numbers, from 0 through 6, were entered in column D, beginning at row 21. In column E, string formulas were entered to pick up the numbers from column D and use them in the bullet code. The descriptions of the codes were stored lower down the worksheet in cells B29 through B34. As you can see from Figure 13-4, bullet 0 was created on row 21, with this formula:

+"\bullet "&@STRING(D21,0)&"\"&" "&B29

This formula was copied from E21 to E22 through E27. This produced a list of codes, with descriptions. Notice the use of &" "& to create a space in the resulting label. Also notice the use of the @STRING function. You cannot simply use the contents of cell D21 in the formula, as the formula is creating a label. You need to use @STRING to turn the value 0, which Quattro PRO looks at as 0.000000, into the label *0.* The second argument in the @STRING statement is also 0, for zero decimal places.

There are some minor inconveniences when using bullet codes. As you can see from Figure 13-4, they do not look pretty when you are working on the spreadsheet, but only when you print it out. Bullets are hard to line up with text unless you give them their own column. As you can see from Figure 13-3, the amount of space between the bullet and the following text varies, leaving the text improperly aligned. The solution is an arrangement

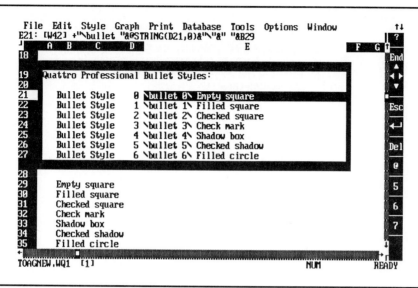

Figure 13-4. *Bullet text formula*

like that shown in Figure 13-5, where you can see bullets applied to the worksheet in Figure 13-2. These bullets are in their own columns, and so can be aligned accurately. You can then vary the printed location of the bullet within the column by using the left, right, and center label prefixes (', ", ^). In Figure 13-6 you can see the text from Figure 13-5 printed. Notice that the second bullet in the first column has been centered. Also notice that a different font has been applied to the first two lines of the text.

Adding Style

In earlier chapters you saw how the Style commands could be used to dress up text in Quattro PRO. You can use Style Line Drawing to add single, double, or thick lines that go over, under, or around labels and numbers. The Style Shading command allows you to add several levels of gray to areas of your printouts. With the Style Font command you can vary the appearance of printed text, as shown in Figure 13-6. By combining these commands you can create impressive text charts and reports.

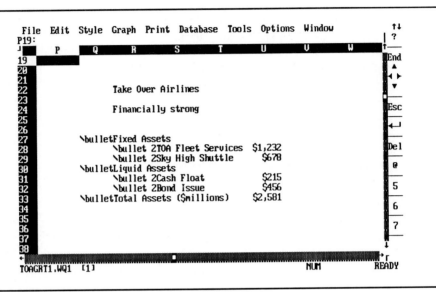

Figure 13-5. *Bullets in separate columns*

Take Over Airlines

Financially strong

☐ Fixed Assets
    ☑   TOA Fleet Services $1,232
    ☑   Sky High Shuttle $678
  ☐ Liquid Assets
    ☑   Cash Float $215
    ☑   Bond Issue $456
☐ Total Assets ($millions) $2,581

Figure 13-6. *Printed version of the worksheet in Figure 13-5*

For example, Figure 13-3 was printed from Quattro PRO, the box around the text being created by the Style Line Drawing command. The thick line option was used. You can see how this line appears in the worksheet itself by looking at Figure 13-4. In Figure 13-7 you can see an example of a text chart printed from Quattro PRO using a combination of bullets, lines, and fonts.

The Joy of Annotating

The Graph Annotate feature in Quattro PRO is a full-featured drawing program. A complete description of what can be done with Annotate could support a whole book, or at least several more chapters than will fit in this book. However, the following examples may give you an idea of what can be accomplished with this feature.

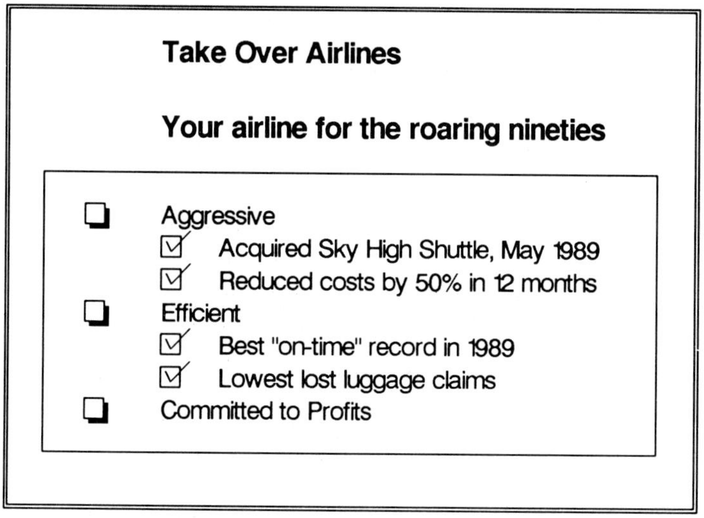

Take Over Airlines

Your airline for the roaring nineties

☐ Aggressive
  ☑ Acquired Sky High Shuttle, May 1989
  ☑ Reduced costs by 50% in 12 months
☐ Efficient
  ☑ Best "on-time" record in 1989
  ☑ Lowest lost luggage claims
☐ Committed to Profits

Figure 13-7.   *Text chart with lines, bullets, and different fonts*

Making a Shape

To create a drawing with Graph Annotate you first use the Graph Type command from the Graph menu to select Text. This type of graph requires no series values to be established. After selecting Text as the Graph Type you can press F10 to view what is basically a blank canvas. You then type / for the Annotate window. When you first enter the Annotate window you can see the large empty rectangle that is your canvas. The menu across the top is not active at first. You type / to activate the menu. This places a thick line around the arrow or Pick icon labeled P in Figure 13-8. Keyboard users can use the arrow keys to move the highlighting across the menu to the item they want, pressing ENTER to select it; or by typing the requisite letter. Mouse users do not need to press / to activate the menu and can select menu items by clicking on them.

The Annotate menu is in several parts. The first two items are Pick and Clipboard. When the Pick option is active you can select items within the canvas area. The Clipboard allows you to copy and cut items that have been

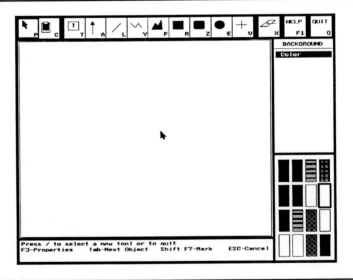

Figure 13-8. *Annotate screen*

selected, and also to move them to the top or bottom when there are overlapping items.

The next nine menu items are the drawing tools for such shapes as lines, arrows, polygons, filled polygons, rectangles, and circles. Beyond that are Link, Help, and Quit. To select a drawing tool, keyboard users first make sure the menu is active by typing /. Suppose you want to draw a free-form object, or a polygon. You highlight the icon marked F and press ENTER (or type **F**). This places a cross on the screen, which is your pointer. To begin the shape, you move the pointer to the place on the screen where you want to begin, using mouse movement or cursor keys. The specific actions of the cursor keys are listed in Table 13-1.

To anchor the beginning point, you click the mouse button or type a period (referred to as *Dot* by the help section at the bottom of the Annotate screen). You can then move the pointer to begin drawing a line from the fixed point in the direction that you are moving the pointer, as shown in Figure 13-9. To fix the next point of the polygon you press ENTER again. You can press ESCAPE to cancel the action or type / to change tools. When you want the polygon to be completed you press ENTER twice and Quattro PRO closes up the object's outline, as shown in Figure 13-10.

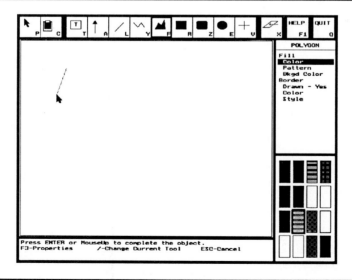

Figure 13-9.   *Beginning a polygon*

Key	Function
ARROW keys	Moves or resizes a selected element or group of elements
TAB	Moves the pointer clockwise around the elements in the drawing area
SHIFT-TAB	Moves the pointer counterclockwise around the elements in the drawing area
SHIFT-F7	Selects elements in the drawing area; use in combination with TAB and SHIFT-TAB to select multiple elements
SHIFT	Used with a mouse, the SHIFT key held down as you click on elements in the drawing area selects multiple elements that are not connected
DELETE	Deletes a selected element or group of elements; if used with a mouse, point and press DELETE to delete one element
PERIOD (.)	With an element or group of elements selected, period anchors the selected area and allows you to resize it. The lower right-hand corner is the default corner, which will extend or contract the element as you press ARROW keys or move the pointer with the mouse. To resize the area using a different corner, press the PERIOD repeatedly to cycle around the corners of the selected area.
HOME, END	Moves the corners of a selected area diagonally
PAGE DOWN, PAGE UP	Moves the corners of a selected area diagonally
F2	With an element selected, enters Move mode so you can reposition the element; for a text element, enters text editing mode
CTRL-ENTER	In text editing mode, wraps inserted text to a new line
BACKSPACE	Used to erase characters and line breaks in text editing mode
SLASH(/)	Activates the Toolbox
F3	Activates the Property sheet
F10	Redraws the Graph Annotator screen
ESCAPE	Returns to the drawing area from the Property Sheet or Toolbox; with a selected element in RESIZE mode, switches to MOVE mode

Table 13-1.   *Keys Used in Graph Annotator*

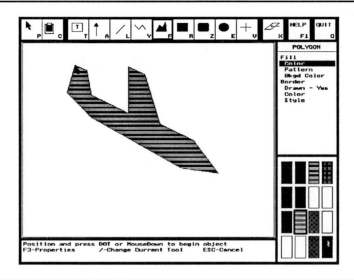

Figure 13-10. Completed polygon

Enhancing the Shape

This object can now be enhanced by changing its attributes. This is done by using the Property Sheet—the menu to the right of the main area that lists Fill, Border, and so on. Before you use the Property Sheet, you need to select the object you have just made. You can do this by typing / to change tools and then selecting Pick, the first item on the left of the menu. This allows you to point and click on the item with the mouse, or to press TAB to select the object. If there is more than one object, pressing TAB selects each one in turn. A selected item is given a set of handles, as you can see in Figure 13-11. These are used to move and size the object.

To alter the attributes of an object you activate the Property Sheet by pressing F3. When you press F3 the box around the Property Sheet becomes a double line and you can highlight an item that you want to alter, such as the Pattern used to fill the polygon object. The items on the menu vary according to which object is current. When you press DOWN ARROW to move the highlight to Pattern and then press ENTER (or click on it with the mouse), the palette below the Property Sheet is activated and you can use the arrow keys to move the highlighting to the attribute you want. The

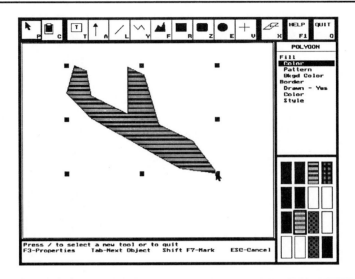

Figure 13-11. *Selected item with handles*

filling of the current object will change as you move from one pattern to another. When you have highlighted the pattern you want, press ENTER or click with the mouse and the current object is filled with the chosen pattern, as shown in Figure 13-12.

You can proceed in this fashion to alter the attributes of the object. You press ESCAPE or click in the main section of the window to return to creating new objects. You can move the current object with the cursor-movement keys, or by clicking and dragging with the mouse. You can choose a new tool from the menu to make a new object, such as lines, arrows, rectangles, rounded rectangles, or even text.

You could add the letters *TOA* to the plane in Figure 13-12. When you select the Text tool you can type text at a selected point on the screen. To create a second line of text you press CTRL-ENTER. You press ENTER to complete the text object.

When you enter text, it is initially boxed in a rectangle. You can alter the attributes of this box, adding shading for example, or removing it. As you can see from Figure 13-13, you can alter the font of the text by using a selection process similar to that used when selecting fonts for your spreadsheet entries. To edit text that you have already created, you first

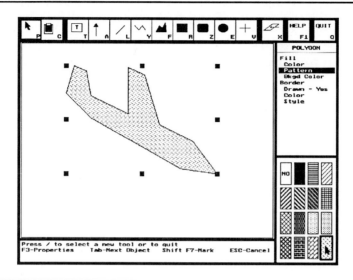

Figure 13-12. *Filling with a pattern*

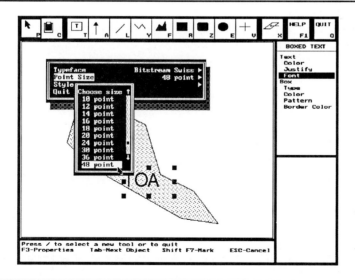

Figure 13-13. *Changing the font*

select the text object and then press F2. This places an edit cursor after the last character of the text. You can use the UP and DOWN ARROW keys to move from line to line in the text. The LEFT and RIGHT ARROW keys move the edit cursor through the text.

Using the Shape

When you want to see the drawing at full size you type / to activate the menu and pick Quit; this takes you to the full-screen graph view mode. From here you can press ENTER to return to the worksheet. There does not need to be any entry in the worksheet to support a text graph or drawing. However, you can use drawings effectively with worksheets that contain text and numbers. For example, you could enhance the presentation of facts about TOA by inserting the drawing into the worksheet. To do this you use the Insert command from the Graph menu. The procedure is the same as for inserting a numeric graph (described in Chapter 8). You can see the Graph Insert command in action in Figure 13-14. The inserted graph cannot be seen in ordinary display mode, but in graphics mode it

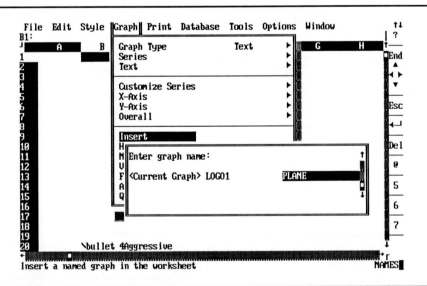

Figure 13-14. *Inserting a paragraph*

appears with impressive effect, as shown in Figure 13-15. Note that a circle and some text were added to the basic filled polygon to make the chart shown. The results of printing from this spreadsheet, including the inserted graph as well as the text with bullet characters, is shown in Figure 13-16. Remember that to print the inserted drawing and text together you must include both in the Print Block.

Bear in mind that when you insert a drawn graph into a spreadsheet, the entire graphic is placed. You cannot place objects smaller than the full graph view screen. While the Graph Insert command reduces the graph to fit the block of cells you define for it, the text in the spreadsheet will need to be placed outside of the insert block to be visible and printable. The graph can be inserted over text or numbers but these will be hidden in the display and in any printout of that section of the worksheet. Note that you must be in graphic display mode to see the graph in your worksheet. In character mode the inserted graph appears as a permanently highlighted blank block of cells.

You may find that Quattro PRO's response time slows down when you are in graphics mode and have inserted one or more graphs into a worksheet. Furthermore, keeping track of cells that contain special formats, lines, and fonts can be cumbersome when you are engaged in writing

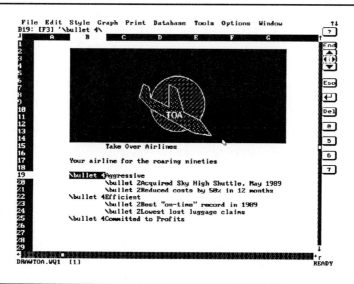

Figure 13-15. *Viewing the inserted graph*

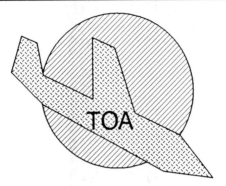

Take Over Airlines

Your airline for the roaring nineties

❏   Aggressive
     ☑   Acquired Sky High Shuttle, May 1989
     ☑   Reduced costs by 50% in 12 months
❏   Efficient
     ☑   Best "on-time" record in 1989
     ☑   Lowest lost luggage claims
❏   Committed to Profits

Figure 13-16.   *Printed results*

formulas and setting up numerical analyses. For this reason you might want to consider placing highly formatted entries in a special worksheet and feeding data to that worksheet from a less intensely formatted worksheet, using linked cell reference formulas. This allows you to work quickly on one worksheet while providing correct numbers to the presentation worksheet.

Other Annotate Examples

You can use the Annotate feature for such projects as organization charts and flow diagrams. Figure 13-17 shows an example of an organization chart. All that you need for such a chart are a few lines and boxed text

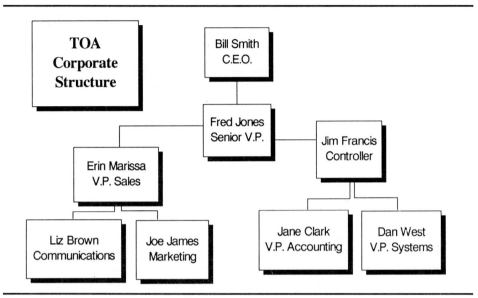

Figure 13-17. *Organization chart printed from Quattro PRO*

entries. The shadow attribute was selected for the boxes and the center attribute was chosen for the text with the Justify option.

Although free-form drawing with Annotate is fun as well as practical, one of the primary uses of the feature is to enhance graphs. Figure 8-53 in Chapter 8 shows an ordinary graph made much more interesting with the addition of objects from Annotate.

Slide Shows

The Graph Name Slide command in Quattro PRO adds a new dimension to spreadsheet graphics, giving you the ability to develop self-running presentations based on your Quattro PRO graphs. A series of graphs are displayed one after another like a slide show. Quattro PRO takes the information about each graph from a list of graphs. You can develop your own slide shows fairly easily or view one put together by another Quattro

PRO user. Included with your copy of Quattro PRO are several sample worksheets, one of which features a slide show. If you have the file PRESENT.WQ1 on your disk you can load it and follow the instructions that appear. The file contains an auto-executing macro that starts the slide show.

Making a Slide Show

A slide show actually consists of two columns of information entered into the worksheet. The first column contains the graph names. The second column contains a list of numbers that indicate the length of time, in seconds, that each graph is to be displayed. In Figure 13-18 you can see a slide show arranged in columns A and B. The first slide, called INTRO, is identified in cell A13 and is to be displayed for ten seconds. The names you use in the first column are those assigned to your graphs with the Graph Name Create command. The graphs must be named in the current worksheet, although you can display graphs from the current worksheet that use data supplied by other worksheets.

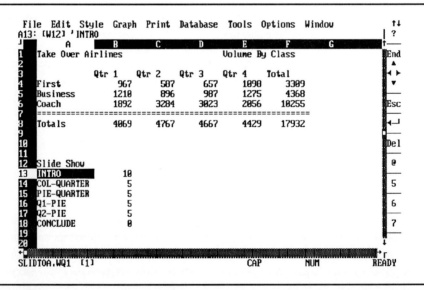

Figure 13-18. *Slide show instructions*

When you issue the Graph Name Slide command you must identify the block of cells containing the slide show instructions. In Figure 13-18 the block is A13..B18. When you enter the coordinates the show begins. Each slide is displayed in turn, for the specified period of time. You can make the display self-paced by having the user press a key to advance to the next slide. You do this by entering 0 in the second column instead of a number of seconds. When Quattro PRO encounters a graph name with 0 for the display time, such as the CONCLUDE graph in Figure 13-18, it waits until a key is pressed before going on to the next graph.

Suppose you have created a number of Quattro PRO graphs that you want to use to highlight points in a sales presentation. Printed versions of the graphs form part of your handout. However, you would like to display the graphs during your speech for extra impact. You have a large-screen monitor connected to your PC so that the graphs can be seen properly, but you are nervous about having to type a series of instructions every time you want to move to a new graph. This is where the slide show feature comes in. Instead of having to type a series of Graph Name Display commands, and having to pick the correct graph name each time, you can use the slide show list to control your graphs. This avoids the F10 key and the constant need to return to the Graph menu. When a slide show is running you cannot tell that the program is actually a spreadsheet.

If you need to break out of a slide show while it is running, perhaps to resume manual control of graphs, you can always press CTRL-BREAK. If Quattro PRO encounters a graph name that does not exist in the current worksheet, then it goes on to the next graph in the list. To provide complete control over a slide show and automate the process even further you can use macro commands, as described in the next section. Before using a slide show in a live presentation, always do a dry run to make sure the graphs appear as you want them to. This will also ensure that all the fonts required by the graphs have been built; otherwise, the slide show will pause while fonts are built, which detracts from the professional appearance of the show.

Slide Show Macros

The ability to start a slide show with a macro and to make slide displays dependent upon keystrokes gives you the ability to make some very sophisticated presentations with Quattro PRO. Slide shows are activated by the macro command

{/ Graph;NameSlide}

This is followed by the coordinates of the slide show instructions. Typically, you will use a block name for this to simplify matters. The following macro will present a slide show stored in the block named SALES as soon as the worksheet is retrieved:

\0   {/ Graph;NameSlide}SALES~

To make self-paced presentations you can use text graphs that contain instructions together with the {Graphchar} command, which returns user input during graph display. Figure 13-19 shows an instruction graph that was created with the Annotate feature and named INTRO1. The following macro code is used to display it and handle user input:

```
SLIDES       {/ Graph;NameUse}INTRO1~
             {GRAPHCHAR RESPONSE}
             {If RESPONSE="1"}{Branch VOLMAC}
             {If RESPONSE="2"}{Branch REVMAC}
             {Branch NEXT}
```

When the macro SLIDES is executed, the INTRO1 graph is displayed and Quattro PRO waits until the user presses a key. The {Graphchar} command places the user's response in a cell named RESPONSE and the {If} statement evaluates the contents of this cell. If the user presses 1, then the macro branches to code called VOLMAC. If the users presses 2, then the macro branches to code called REVMAC. If the user presses any other key, then the macro continues to the last line, branching to NEXT. The macro VOLMAC looks like this:

```
VOLMAC       {/ Graph;NameSlide}VOLUME~
             {Branch SLIDES}
```

The block named VOLUME contains the data for a slide show. The macro REVMAC is similar and looks like this:

```
REVMAC       {/ Graph;NameSlide}REVENUE~
             {Branch SLIDES}
```

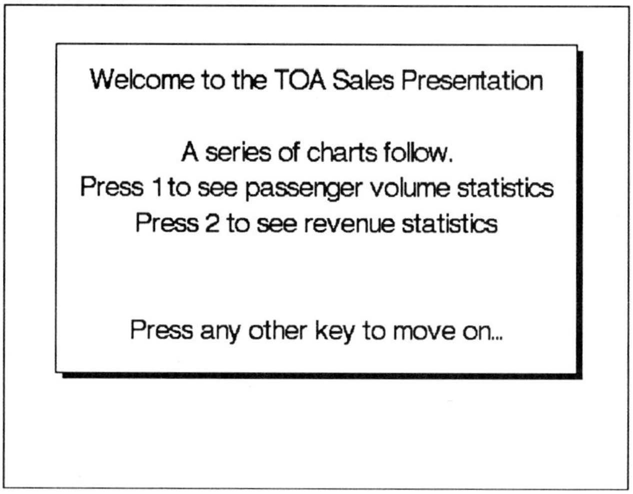

Figure 13-19. *Graph giving instructions*

There has to be a cell named RESPONSE for the macro to work. The code loops the user back to the instruction screen until a key other than 1 or 2 is pressed.

The {Graphchar} command is very useful for displaying graphs that act as menus. You can also use it with the {Message} command to get user response from a screen message. The {Message} command is discussed later in this chapter.

Advanced Functions

As you have seen in previous chapters, a complete set of macro menus to enter, review, sort, and print data is a fairly involved undertaking. The elements that make up such a system were illustrated in the examples in Chapter 12, some of which used a set of advanced Quattro PRO @functions that can be very useful in more complex macros. Sometimes called the miscellaneous functions, these advanced functions allow you to perform such operations as data entry checks and macro control.

The @CELL Functions

The @CELLPOINTER, @CELL, and @CELLINDEX functions return information about a cell. The type of information produced by the function depends on the code specified in the function statement. The cell about which information is returned, in the case of @CELLPOINTER, is the cell that the selector currently occupies. In the case of @CELL, the cell is the one referred to by a cell reference or the one in the top-left corner of a named block referred to by name in the function statement. For the @CELLIN-DEX function, the cell is the one referenced by the specified column and row of a defined block. The syntax is as follows

@CELLPOINTER(Code)
@CELL (Code,Cell)
@CELLINDEX(Block,Col,Row)

The Code argument is a string that determines the information about the cell that the function references. There are nine of these codes, and they are shown in Table 13-2. With careful use of these codes, particularly when combined with the {If} command and @IF function, you can extract valuable information about cells of the worksheet for use in macros. Remember that if you use a block name to refer to the cell required in the @CELL function, the cell addressed will be the one in the top-left corner of the block. Since the cell used by the @CELLPOINTER function is the current cell, this function is useful for controlling looping macros. For example, the following macro, called ROUND, turns a column of formulas into results rounded to one decimal place:

```
{EDIT},1){HOME}@ROUND(
{CALC}{DOWN}
{If @CELLPOINTER("type")="v"{Branch CENTER}
{Quit}
```

The first line of the macro edits a cell and places the @ROUND statements around the existing formula. The second line calculates the formula and

Code	Response
address	The absolute address of a cell
row	The row number of cell (from 1 to 8192)
col	The column number of the cell (from 1 to 256 corresponding to columns A through IV)
contents	The actual contents of the cell
type	The type of data in the cell: b if the cell is blank v if the cell contains a number or any formula l if the cell contains a label
prefix	The label-prefix character of the cell: ' if label is left-aligned ^ if label is centered " if label is right-aligned l if cell starts with that character \ if label is repeating
protect	The protected status of the cell: 0 if the cell is not protected 1 if the cell is protected
width	The width of the column containing the cell: (between 1 and 240)
format	The current display format of the cell: Fn is Fixed *(n=0-15)* En is Exponential *(n=0-15)* Cn is Currency *(n=0-15)* + is +/- (bar graph format) G is General Pn is Percent *(n=0-15)* D1-D5 is Date 1=DD-MMM-YY 2=DD-MMM 3=MMMY 4=MM/DD/YY,DD/MM/YY, DD.MM.YY,YY-MM-DD 5=MM/DD,DD/MM,DD.MM,MM-DD D6-D9 is Time 6=HH:MM:SS AM/PM 7=HH:MM AM/PM 8=HH:MM:SS-24hr, HH.MM.SS-24hr, HH.MM.SS-24hr, HHhMMmSSs 9=HH:MM:-24hr, HH.MM-24hr, HH, MM, HHhMMm T is Show Formulas (Text) H is Hidden , is Commas used to separate thousands

Table 13-2.   *Codes Allowed By the @CELLPOINTER and @CELL Functions*

then moves down to the next cell. The third line of the macro checks whether the next cell is a value and, if it is, the macro loops to the beginning. If the cell is a label or is blank, and therefore not a value, then the macro quits. Note that the response to the function as well as the code must be identified with quotes.

The @@ Function

Another function that responds with information about cells is the @@ function. The @@ function can play a valuable role in more complex macros, since it returns the contents of a cell that is referenced as a label in another cell. Thus, @@(A1) returns the answer 10 if A1 contains a reference to a cell that contains the number 10—either the label A1 or a label that is the name of a block, the top-left cell of which contains 10.

The @COLS and @ROWS Functions

When you need to know how many columns or rows there are in a block of cells, you use the @COLS and @ROWS functions. Thus, @COLS(DATA) returns the response 7 if DATA is the name given to cells A1..G20. The response to @ROWS(DATA) would be 20.

The @N and @S Functions

Some spreadsheet programs cannot work with formulas that include cells containing labels or string values. The labels are not zero values and so can cause an ERR message to result from the formula. The @N function returns the numeric value of the cell or the top-left cell of the block that it references. Thus, @N(DATA) returns the value 5 if the top-left cell of DATA contains a 5 or a formula that results in 5. If the top-left cell of DATA contains a label, the result will be 0.

Since Quattro PRO already considers labels to be zero values, there is not much need to use this function in a Quattro PRO spreadsheet. However, the function is available to provide compatibility with other spreadsheet programs. The companion to @N is @S, which returns the string value of the cell it references. Thus, @S(DATA) will return Name if the top-left cell of the block DATA contains the label Name or a string formula that results in Name. If the same cell contains 5, @S will return the empty label " ", which appears as an empty cell.

The Utility Functions

When you need to know the amount of regular and expanded memory available, you can use the Options Hardware command and read the screen. However, you can retrieve the same data into a spreadsheet cell with the @MEMAVAIL and @MEMEMSAVAIL functions. These functions are useful in macros when you need to check whether there is enough room for an operation to be performed or simply check that free memory is not getting too low. For example, the statement

{If @MEMAVAIL /146389>.20}{/ Block;Copy}DATA~NEW~

would cause the macro to execute the Copy command only if there was more than 20% of the total memory free. The number 146389 is the total amount of memory, as you can read from the Options Hardware menu using @CURVALUE. Of course, if you have expanded memory installed, you will need to include that information in the equation (you can use @MEMAVAIL+@MEMEMSAVAIL). If you have no expanded memory in your system, the @MEMEMSAVAIL function responds with NA.

True and False Tests

In some spreadsheet designs you may need to test whether a statement or condition is true or false. Quattro PRO represents a true statement as 1 and a false statement as 0. Thus, A1>99 results in 1 if A1 contains any number larger than 99, or 0 if A1 contains a number less than 99 or a label (labels have a 0 value). The more likely place to find true/false tests is in an @IF statement, such as @IF(A1>99,1,0). Since this statement is somewhat difficult to read, you can use

@IF(A1>99,@TRUE,@FALSE)

The @TRUE and @FALSE functions return the responses 1 and 0 respectively and require no arguments.

The @IS Functions

@ISERR and @ISNA are true/false functions that give you the means to check whether a formula or cell entry results in either the ERR or NA response, respectively. These functions take the form @ISERR(Value) and @ISNA(Value), where Value is a cell reference or a formula. The @ISERR function returns the response 1, meaning true, if Value results in ERR, as is the case with @ISERR(1/0) or @ISERR(A1/A2), where A2 contains the value 0.

A typical application of the @ISERR function is shown in Figure 13-20, where a formula avoids the problem of dividing one column of numbers by another when some of the cells in the columns might be empty or contain zeroes. Thus, the division of total sales by the number of agents would result in an ERR message in cell D8 if the formula was simply C8/B8. The added @IF function uses @ISERR to turn the ERR result into the string of text "Not Available."

Another application of the @ISERR function is shown in Figure 13-21, where it is used in a data entry macro that completes the simple order form in the upper half of the screen. The command {GetNumber} places ERR in

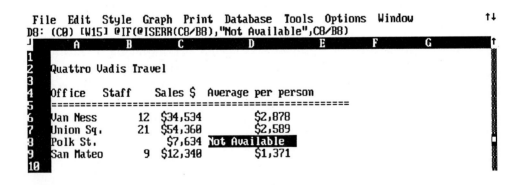

Figure 13-20. *An @ISERR formula*

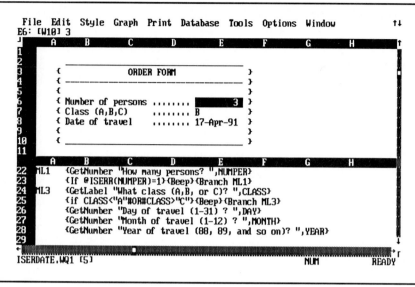

Figure 13-21. *Using @ISERR in data entry*

the destination cell if the user enters a label instead of the requested number. The macro code at B23 causes Quattro PRO to beep and repeat the {GetNumber} command if the user accidentally enters a label.

Notice the other test in this macro in cell B25. The {If} statement causes a beep and a repeat of the preceding {GetLabel} prompt if the user enters a label less than A or greater than C. This statement restricts valid responses to the A, B, or C requested in the {GetLabel} prompt. This line is an example of the # sign being used to join two conditions. The statement

CLASS>"A"#OR#CLASS<"C"

evaluates as true if the contents of the cell named CLASS are either less than A or greater than C. You can also use #AND# to join two conditions. In this way, both conditions must be met for the result to prove true. The operator #NOT# can be used to preface a condition to negate it. Thus, #NOT#CLASS>"C" would work just as well in cell B25.

The @ISNA function is used in the same manner as @ISERR. However, @ISNA is used less frequently. The value NA is less common than ERR, since few formulas give this result unless you design them that way.

However, an example would be the statement @ISNA(@MEMEMSAVAIL), which returns 1 if you have no expanded memory in your system.

The statements @ISNUMBER(Value) and @ISSTRING(Value) are used in Quattro PRO to test whether the referenced value is a number or a string. An example of these functions at work is shown in Figure 13-22, where a set of highlighted cells in column B is being used to receive data about a piece of lost baggage. The first piece of data, Passenger Name, has been entered in B5 and the Note in column C states "Okay." This method of data entry and prompting uses formulas next to the data entry cells to flag entries as they are made. You can see the formulas revealed in text format in Figure 13-23. Cell C5 evaluates to "Okay" because the statement @ISSTRING(B5) results in 1. In cell B6 there is a blank label, a simple apostrophe. This causes the message "Enter a number" to be displayed as the result of the formula in C6 because @ISNUMBER produces 0 when it is applied to a cell containing a label. Of course, all the user sees is a note that the information for Date Lost must be a number rather than a label.

Note that the blank entry form should start with no entries in cell B6 or in cells B8 through B11. There should be blank labels in B6 and B7 to create the "Enter" prompts.

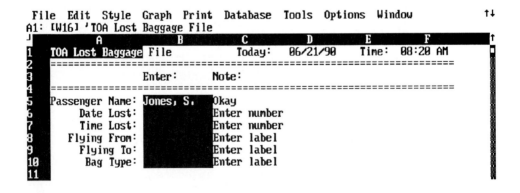

Figure 13-22. *Data entry check*

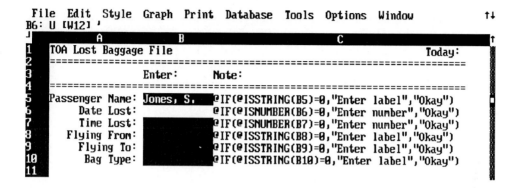

Figure 13-23.   *Data entry formulas*

Protection and Input

The worksheets in Figures 13-21 and 13-22 are typical examples of a spreadsheet used for data entry. If there is much data to be entered, the person doing the entry may be accomplished at the keyboard but inexperienced with spreadsheet operation. To prevent accidental deletion or overwriting of important cells in a worksheet, you may want to take steps to protect your worksheet.

Complete Protection

To completely protect a worksheet, you use the Options Protection Enable command. This command prevents any cell of the worksheet from being changed. You use this feature in a number of situations. For example, when you share your PC with others, you may worry that someone will accidentally retrieve one of your worksheets and damage it before realizing they have the wrong file. Of course, password protection (described in Chapter

7) will prevent such file retrieval, but a less drastic step is to enable protection prior to saving the worksheet. The only way someone can alter your data is by turning off protection. Removing protection is done for the entire spreadsheet with Options Protection Disable. However, you can use Style Protection Unprotect to allow access to specific cells or groups of cells. When you enable protection for the entire worksheet, you will see the code PR in the cell descriptor of all cells, except those that have been unprotected by the Style Protection Unprotect command. Unprotected cells will show the code U.

Partial Protection

To turn on default protection and then remove it for specific blocks of cells is exactly what you need when turning over a spreadsheet to an inexperienced user. Quattro PRO highlights the unprotected cells to make it easier to see which cells can accept data. For this reason the data entry area in Figure 13-22 is shaded. The formulas and macros that run the worksheet are safe from damage while the data cells are clearly displayed. (If you try default protection and then block unprotect on your system and cannot see a different shading, try adjusting your monitor's contrast control and check the settings under Options Colors Spreadsheet.)

If you want to do more to restrict a user's access to a spreadsheet, you can use the Database Restrict Input command to define an area of the spreadsheet beyond which the cell selector cannot be moved. This area must coincide with a block of unprotected cells in an otherwise completely protected worksheet. When the Database Restrict Input command is issued, the top-left cell of the Input Block is placed in the top left of the screen and the cell selector is placed in the first cell that is unprotected. At this point the cursor keys will not move the cell selector beyond the bounds of this block. However, pressing ESCAPE will remove this movement restriction, so you should keep in mind that an input area will not keep prying eyes away from confidential areas of a spreadsheet.

Advanced Macro Notes

You can see that complete use of the macro commands and advanced functions in Quattro PRO can take you into areas that are not mere spreadsheet usage but applications development and programming—areas that are beyond the scope of this book. However, the macro-building methods that you have seen here and in the previous chapter contain the basic principles on which you can build complete customized systems. If you bear in mind some basic rules, you will be able to assemble sophisticated systems of commands as your confidence with macros increases.

One Step at a Time

Probably the biggest mistake in developing complex macros is to start big. When you have an idea for a complex macro or series of macros, try developing the ideas in a fresh worksheet with test data, rather than in the large worksheet in which they will eventually be applied. Testing helps ensure against accidental data loss as well as making the success of the macro logic easier to assess. Once you are comfortable with the basic structure, you can apply it to large sets of real data.

You should also avoid making any single macro too large. This is particularly true in the case of menu macros. Just because the {MenuCall} and {MenuBranch} commands require the menu options to be in consecutive columns does not mean that the entire macro for each menu option needs to be below the menu. You can use a {Branch} command as the first line of macro code for each menu item, directing flow from the menu macro to code for each item that is stored in a separate area of the worksheet. An example of this is shown in Figure 13-24.

One Line at a Time

One simple feature of Quattro PRO's macro environment is that you can execute a macro without naming it. All you need to do is simply point at it. To test the last three lines of a 10-line macro, you can use Tools Macro Execute, place your selector on the third to the last line of the macro, and press ENTER. This avoids the need to create temporary macro names just to test certain steps. If you assign the Shortcut CTRL-E to the Tools Macro Execute menu item you can execute macro code very quickly.

To check only one line of a macro, you can temporarily insert a blank row below the line you want to check to prevent the macro from continuing.

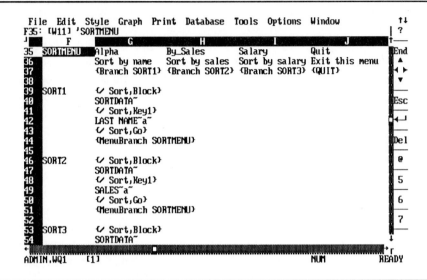

Figure 13-24.   *Organization of menu with branches*

Debug   Do not forget the DEBUG command (SHIFT-F2), which will, at the very least, provide you with single-step macro execution. To see the macro execute in single-step mode, you repeatedly press the SPACEBAR. While you are executing a macro in DEBUG mode, you can type / to get the Macro Debugger menu shown in Figure 13-25. The Edit a cell option allows you to edit the cells of the macro and thus avoid errors that you have noticed during execution. You select Quit from the Debugger menu to return to macro execution in DEBUG mode. If the macro appears fine during DEBUG playback, you can let it run to completion by pressing ENTER. To assist in problem-solving when a macro is not running properly, you can use the tools provided on the Debugger menu.

Breakpoints   In addition to the single-step feature, you can set breakpoints to control macro execution. These are blocks or cells of macro code at which the macro should pause during execution. Breakpoints are an easier way of testing sections of larger macros than inserting blank cells after the last line you want to execute. By pressing ENTER during DEBUG playback, you can run the macro to the next breakpoint. As many as four

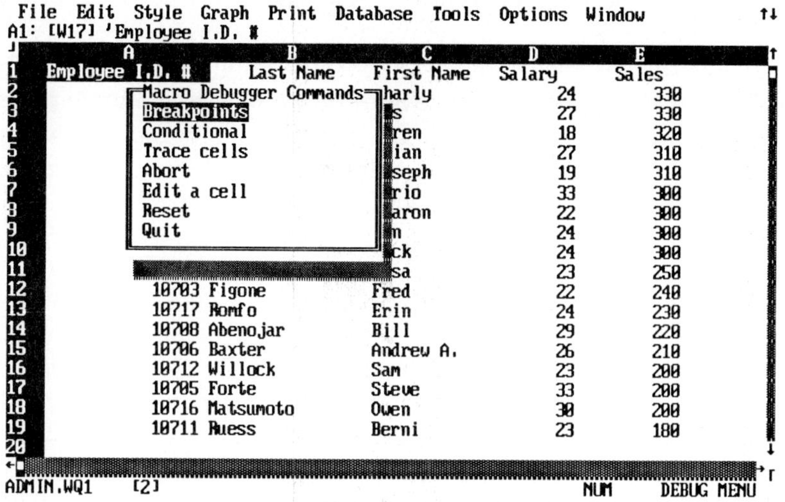

```
 File  Edit  Style  Graph  Print  Database  Tools  Options  Window        ↑↓
A1: [W17] 'Employee I.D. #
J          A              B             C            D           E           ↑
1  Employee I.D. #      Last Name    First Name    Salary      Sales
2       ┌─Macro Debugger Commands─┐ harly         24          330
3       │ Breakpoints             │ s             27          330
4       │ Conditional             │ ren           18          320
5       │ Trace cells             │ ian           27          310
6       │ Abort                   │ seph          19          310
7       │ Edit a cell             │ rio           33          300
8       │ Reset                   │ aron          22          300
9       │ Quit                    │ m             24          300
10      │                         │ ck            24          300
11      └─────────────────────────┘ sa            23          250
12          10703 Figone          Fred           22          240
13          10717 Romfo           Erin           24          230
14          10708 Abenojar        Bill           29          220
15          10706 Baxter          Andrew A.      26          210
16          10712 Willock         Sam            23          200
17          10705 Forte           Steve          33          200
18          10716 Matsumoto       Owen           30          200
19          10711 Ruess           Berni          23          180
20
ADMIN.WQ1     [2]                                    NUM      DEBUG MENU
```

Figure 13-25. *Macro Debugger menu*

breakpoints can be set from the Macro Debugger menu. If you want the breakpoint to be effective only on a repetition of the macro, you can set a pass count for the breakpoint. Use Reset from the Macro Debugger menu to clear the breakpoints.

Conditional If you want a macro to run until a particular condition is met, you can use the Conditional option on the Macro Debugger menu to point to a cell in which you have entered a logical formula. An appropriate logical formula would be one that returns 1 for true and 0 for false. Thus, a cell containing the formula A1>99 could be used to make the macro playback pause if it caused A1 to exceed 99.

Trace Cells If you are concerned with the macro's effect on particular cells of the spreadsheet, you can identify four trace cells that will be monitored in the Trace Window during macro execution in DEBUG mode. This method is very helpful for running a large macro that affects diverse areas of the worksheet.

Save Your Spreadsheet

While the DEBUG mode provides a controlled environment in which to run your macros, you should still save files frequently as a basic precaution before running a complex macro for the first time. Numerous actions can accidentally erase data or, worse, an entire spreadsheet, during a macro's trial run. The Transcript feature is a great asset here, since it helps you restore the spreadsheet if disaster does strike. Bear in mind that Transcript will not be recording while you record a macro.

When you are involved in critical operations, you may want to adjust the Transcript Failure Protection setting to reduce the number of keystrokes between saves from 100 to a smaller number. Use the Tools Macro Transcript command to display the Transcript log and then type / for the Transcript menu. Select Failure Protection and enter the number you want. Press ENTER and then ESCAPE to clear the menu. A very small number, such as 5, will mean that Quattro PRO slows down, saving to disk every five keystrokes. But a number like 25 is a good compromise between slow response and maximum recall in the event of a mistake or an equipment problem.

A Collection of Macros

The macros described here have proved useful for designing and developing worksheets. You can see several of them in Figure 13-26. The macro names are in column A so that the Edit Names Labels Right command can be used to attach the names to the corresponding cells in B. Column B is the macro code. There are no comments on these macros, partly so that they can be spread across the screen for purposes of display, and partly because these macros are self-explanatory for the most part. A power user setting up fairly simple macros for personal use may not want to go to the trouble of documenting each one. This is a situation where Quattro PRO's full-length macro names offer an advantage over 1-2-3's single-letter names, which have limited mnemonic value. Of course, you might want to substitute instant macro names (\A through \Z) for some of these macros if you are going to make frequent use of them.

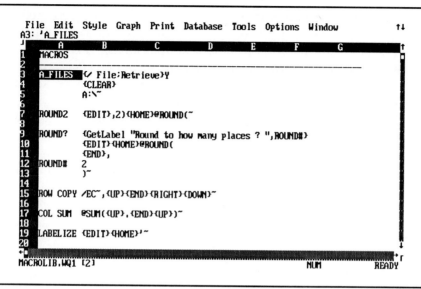

Figure 13-26.   *Collection of macros*

A_FILES   This macro helps you retrieve a file from drive A without having to change the directory. It is often assigned the instant macro name \A. Thus, numerous keystrokes are condensed into one. You can alter this macro slightly for use with any drive or directory.

ROUND2   Some spreadsheets require extensive application of the @ROUND function in order to work correctly. Quattro PRO's ability to format cells can produce apparent errors such as those shown here:

The ROUND2 macro adds the @ROUND function to the current cell, using 2 for the decimal places. Obviously, you can use any number from 0 through 14 instead of 2. If you need to vary decimal places in your use of the @ROUND function, then the next macro may be more appropriate.

ROUND? The {GetLabel} command is used in this macro to solicit the number of decimal places to be used. When the number has been entered it is placed in the cell named ROUND# (B13 in this case). Since this cell is in direct line with the rest of the macro, the macro reads the result directly from the cell and then completes the action with the closing parentheses and tilde in the next cell. This is a very useful technique for direct incorporation of user response in a macro. Macros using this feature are sometimes called self-modifying. Note that the {GetLabel} command was used instead of {GetNumber}, despite the fact that the user is supposed to type a number. The reason for this is that macros terminate whenever they reach a line that contains a numeric value. Remember that macros began as, and still are in essence, keystrokes stored as labels. After all, a macro to enter the number 101 into a cell is '101~. If you simply type **101~** you will get a beep and Quattro PRO will place the input line cursor at the front of the entry, ready for you to type an apostrophe or one of the other label prefixes. Quattro PRO always disregards the label prefixes of macro cells.

ROW COPY This macro copies the current cell to the end of a typical mode that is being built row by row, like the one shown here, where the formula for telephone expense is about to be copied from 1990 to the other years:

```
 File  Edit  Style  Graph  Print  Database  Tools  Options  Window        ↑↓
C5: (C0) +B5*1,1                                                            | ?
                                                                           ↵——
        A              B        C       D       E       F       G      ┃End
1  CD Tune Shop     1990     1991    1992    1993    1994    1995     ┃ ▲
2  ───────────────────────────────────────────────────────────────  ┃◀ ▶
3  Rent           $2,343   $2,577  $2,835  $3,119  $3,430  $3,773     ┃ ▼
4  Electric       $4,321   $4,753  $5,228  $5,751  $6,326  $6,959     ┃
5  Telephone        $345    $380                                      ┃
6                                                                     ┃Esc
```

Note that the ROW COPY macro uses /EC instead of the menu equivalent {/ Block,Copy}. While this method of macro writing (required in 1-2-3

Releases 1 and 2) may look more convenient or more abbreviated, it is less easy to read as menu-equivalent macro code. Furthermore, because Quattro PRO reads menu equivalents as direct program calls, using them in your macro code makes for faster execution, particularly as macros get more complex.

COL SUM   In a typical model, such as the one shown in Figure 13-27, this macro writes a sum formula that provides a column total such as you might place in cell B10. Note that this macro should be modified if the column heading is a value. For example, if the entry in B4 was still a date serial number, that number would be added to the total revenue. In this case it would be safer to use the following macro:

@SUM({UP}.{END}{UP}{DOWN})~

Note that you could use the COL SUM formula followed immediately by ROW COPY to total all of the columns in the model in Figure 13-27.

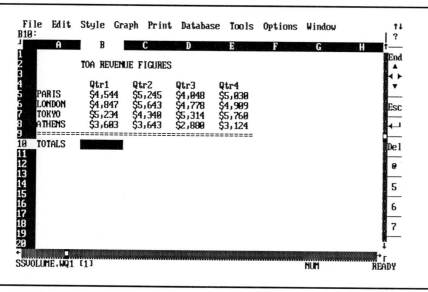

Figure 13-27.   *More macros*

LABELIZE   When you are developing complex formulas it is sometimes desirable to copy them from one location to another while avoiding the normal effect of the Copy command: relative translation of cell references. One way to achieve this is to convert the formula to a label. This is done by the LABELIZE macro, which simply places an apostrophe in front of the formula and re-enters it into the current cell. A companion formula might well be called BACK2NUM and look like this:

{EDIT}{HOME}{DEL}~

MONTHS   Figure 13-28 shows six more macros, the first of which is MONTHS. Some spreadsheets require a series of months as headings for columns or rows. If you are working with this kind of spreadsheet, a macro can save a lot of repetitive typing each time a set of month labels is needed. One approach is to store the month names in a macro and copy them into the desired location as a series of labels. This macro takes a slightly different approach and makes months from the D3 format (Jan-89, Feb-89, and so on). The year used with the month is the current year, which is read

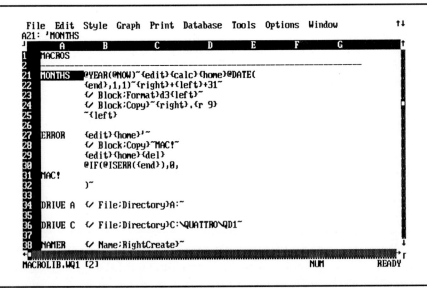

Figure 13-28.   *Further macros*

from the system clock by the @NOW function and extracted from that with the @YEAR function.

A more traditional "copy the date labels macro" might take the form

January{RIGHT}
February{RIGHT}
March{RIGHT}
April{RIGHT}
May{RIGHT}

and so on. You could further enhance both macros by giving the operator a choice between copying across the worksheet or down.

ERROR   Quattro PRO uses the ERR message in cells to warn you that a formula cannot be calculated. There are several reasons why this condition might arise. The formula may reference a cell that was removed by a column or row deletion. The formula might also be a mathematical impossibility, such as dividing by zero. An example is shown here, where the missing entry for Number of Clerks causes the ERR result from the formula +C4/B4:

```
 File  Edit  Style  Graph  Print  Database  Tools  Options  Window          ↑↓
D4: (,2) +C4/B4                                                            | ?
 ⌐              A                  B             C          D          E   |─────
 1   Store            Number of Clerks  Total Sales  Average sales per clerk ▓End
 2   ----------------------------------------------------------------      ▓ ▲
 3   San Francisco            243       $342,150  1,408.02                 ▓ ◄ ►
 4   San Mateo                          $343,216       ERR                 ▓ ▼
 5   San Jose                    0       $23,426       ERR                 ▓─────
 6   San Ramon                   0      $234,238       ERR                 ▓ Esc
 7   San Rafael                 98       $56,455    576.07                 ▓
```

This particular condition frequently arises when data is missing, or is currently represented by a 0, as is the case here in cells B5 and B6. Since such situations often arise in spreadsheets you are designing for others to fill out, the ERR message can become annoying. You certainly do not want it to appear in printed reports. This is where the @ISERR function comes in handy in combination with @IF, providing a way to control the display of a formula result. This is somewhat the same theory as was used in applying @ROUND to an existing formula. However, unlike @ROUND,

@ISERR is not that easily added to a formula cell. Adding @ISERR to the formula in the example would produce a new formula like this:

@IF(@ISERR(C4/B4),0,C4/B4)

If the formula evaluates to ERR, then a 0 is displayed; otherwise, the formula result is shown. Note that the original formula is used twice in the @IF statement. The macro ERROR in Figure 13-28 shows one approach to the problem of qualifying a formula with the @ISERR function.

The first step in applying @ISERR is to turn the original formula into a label. A copy of the formula is then placed into a separate cell to be used later in the macro. In this case the cell is called MAC! (B31). The macro then removes the apostrophe that made the formula a label, adds the @IF/@ISERR test and then completes the macro with the copy of the original formula in MAC!. You do not have to use a 0 as the formula response to the ERR condition. Using text can be effective, as in this example:

```
 File  Edit  Style  Graph  Print  Database  Tools  Options  Window        ↑↓
D4: (,2) @IF(@ISERR(C4/B4),"Not Available",C4/B4)                           | ?
┘          A            B            C          D              E          ┬───
█ Store            Number of Clerks  Total Sales  Average sales per clerk ▓End
2                                                                          ░ ▲
3 San Francisco         243       $342,150 1,408.02                        ▓◄ ►
4 San Mateo                       $343,216 Not Available                   ░ ▼
5 San Jose               0        $23,426 Not Available
6 San Ramon              0        $234,238 Not Available                   ▓Esc
7 San Rafael             98        $56,455   576.07                        ░───
```

Here, the formula uses "Not Available" instead of 0. Note that successful use of this type of macro technique, where a copy of a piece of data is stored in a named cell within the macro, requires some planning. If the ERROR macro in Figure 13-28 was to be executed in a worksheet other than the one containing the macro, the block name MAC! in B28 would need to refer to the worksheet name as well as the cell, as in

{/ Block;Copy}~[MACROLIB]MAC!~

This ensures that the copy is placed into the macro worksheet. Otherwise, Quattro PRO would look in the current worksheet for a block named MAC!.

Failing to find such a block, the macro would crash with an invalid block error.

DRIVE A   When you are developing spreadsheets on a hard-disk system it is sometimes convenient to store unfinished worksheets on a disk in drive A so that they can be removed easily, rather than placing them on the hard disk. The DRIVE A macro performs a simple File Directory command, changing the current drive to A. This does not affect the default setting of the system.

DRIVE C   A natural companion to the DRIVE A macro is this one, which makes C the current drive. A specific directory, \QUATTRO\QD1, is also provided.

NAMER   When you are creating macros that use named cells within the spreadsheet to store data used in the macro, you often need to enter a block name and attach it to the adjacent cell on the right. The NAMER macro streamlines this by performing an Edit Names Labels Right command on the current cell.

SUPERZ!   Figure 13-29 shows four more macros. The first two relate to the SQZ! feature that is built into Quattro PRO. While SQZ! is a great way to maximize disk space, you can actually maximize the effects of SQZ! if you make some adjustments to its settings. The SUPERZ! macro tells SQZ! to do three things: remove blank cells from the stored file, store only approximate values, and use the SQZ! Plus version. Removing blanks does not affect the arrangement of spreadsheet data or any formulas; it simply uses less space. If your spreadsheet does not require the 15 decimal places to which Quattro PRO normally carries calculations, and many financial models do not, then you can have SQZ! retain only seven decimal places. When developing models and seeking maximum file shrinkage you can actually choose Remove for the SQZ! Storage of Values option. This requires Quattro PRO to perform a calculation on the worksheet when it is retrieved, but saves more space.

By running SUPERZ!, or your own variation of it, before saving files in a Quattro PRO session, you can ensure that your work occupies a minimum of disk space. Bear in mind that if you are preparing spreadsheets that are to be run by 1-2-3, the SQZ! extension should be WK$ for WKS files and

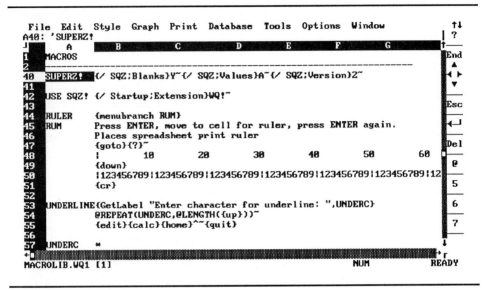

Figure 13-29. *Additional macros*

WK! for WK1 files. Be sure that the recipient of the spreadsheet has the Plus version of SQZ! before using that version to store the spreadsheets.

USE SQZ! Of course, there is not much point in maximizing the SQZ! settings if you do not invoke SQZ! by using the WQ! extension. The USE SQZ! macro makes the necessary change to the default file extension so that files in the current session will be saved in SQZ! format. Since you may be working on a system that does not normally use SQZ!, this macro does not update the defaults to make WQ! the permanent extension.

RULER The RULER macro contains the two labels necessary to make a ruler to measure a spreadsheet Print Block. The macro copies the labels into a cell indicated by the operator. To make the macro clearer to the user, the {MenuBranch} command is used in the single-item menu technique. This technique creates a hard-to-miss message in the middle of the screen. You can see the macro running in Figure 13-30. When the user presses ENTER, the prompt in the top left of the screen will change to "Enter address to go to," which is the F5 (Goto) prompt. Note that the menu is called RUM

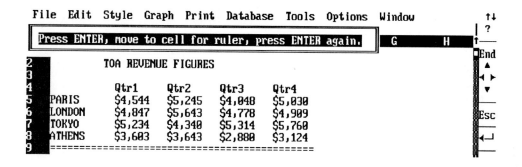

File   Edit   Style   Graph   Print   Database   Tools   Options   Window

```
File  Edit  Style  Graph  Print  Database  Tools  Options  Window        ↑↓
                                                                         | ?
 Press ENTER, move to cell for ruler, press ENTER again.      G      H   ↑──
2                                                                        End
3        TOA REVENUE FIGURES                                            ▲
4                                                                       ◄ ►
5         Qtr1      Qtr2      Qtr3      Qtr4                             ▼
  PARIS   $4,544    $5,245    $4,048    $5,030
6 LONDON  $4,847    $5,643    $4,778    $4,909                          Esc
7 TOKYO   $5,234    $4,340    $5,314    $5,760
8 ATHENS  $3,603    $3,643    $2,880    $3,124                          ◄┘
9 ======================================================
```

Figure 13-30.   *RULER macro in action*

and is placed directly below the {MenuBranch} command. The text of the single menu item is one long label, which can contain up to 55 characters.

Full-Screen Effects

There are several situations in which you may want to present the user with a clear picture of what is required, or with a wide variety of options. You can use the following techniques to present a screen that is easy to read and hard to miss.

A Large Menu of Macros

When you are managing a large number of macros, you may want to set up a menu from which to select groups of macros to be brought into the current worksheet. The menu in Figure 13-31 shows one method of organizing a large number of choices. When the user has highlighted the desired file, ALT-M is pressed to initiate a Tools Combine of that file. The ALT-M macro, shown in Figure 13-32, copies the name to a cell called CHOICE, which forms part of the macro instructions.

Other Large Menus

The large menu design can be used with other macro choice techniques. In Figure 13-33 a large menu offers the user 14 options. Each number on the menu represents a different macro, which is chosen by typing the number of the desired option. A menu like this is effective as a first screen, activated by a Startup macro (\0). Figure 13-34 shows the code that uses this menu. After the cell selector is positioned by a pair of {goto} statements, the user is prompted by a {GetNumber} statement: "Enter the number of your choice:." The response is placed in the cell called TEST. The series of {If} statements branch to the chosen macros—ENTER, REVIEW, and so on.

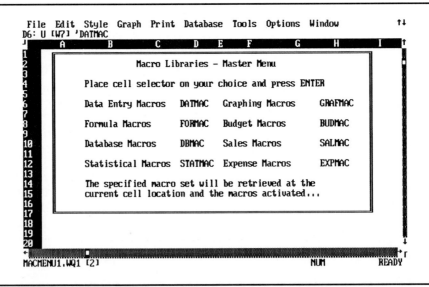

Figure 13-31. *Macro choice menu*

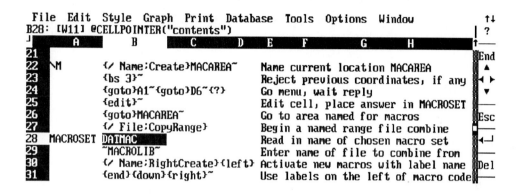

```
 File  Edit  Style  Graph  Print  Database  Tools  Options  Window        ↑↓
B28: [W11] @CELLPOINTER("contents")                                      | ?
┘      A        B          C        D    E      F        G        H      ↑──
21                                                                       End
22  ⌐M     {/ Name;Create}MACAREA~     Name current location MACAREA      ▲
23         {bs 3}~                     Reject previous coordinates, if any ◄ ►
24         {goto}A1~{goto}D6~{?}       Go menu, wait reply                ▼
25         {edit}~                     Edit cell, place answer in MACROSET
26         {goto}MACAREA~              Go to area named for macros       Esc
27         {/ File;CopyRange}          Begin a named range file combine
28  MACROSET DATMAC                    Read in name of chosen macro set  ←┘
29         ~MACROLIB~                  Enter name of file to combine from
30         {/ Name;RightCreate}{left}  Activate new macros with label name Del
31         {end}{down}{right}~         Use labels on the left of macro code ──
```

Figure 13-32.   *The ALT-M macro code*

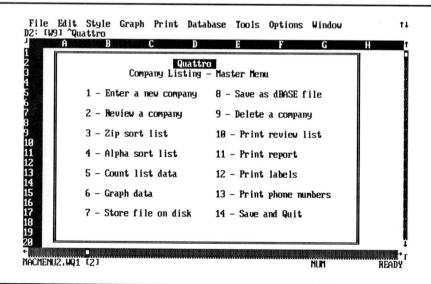

```
 File  Edit  Style  Graph  Print  Database  Tools  Options  Window        ↑↓
D2: [W9] ^Quattro
┘      A        B        C        D      E        F        G        H     ↑
1   ┌──────────────────────────────────────────────────────────────┐
2   │                    ┤ Quattro ├                                │
3   │            Company Listing - Master Menu                       │
4   │                                                                │
5   │     1 - Enter a new company     8 - Save as dBASE file         │
6   │                                                                │
7   │     2 - Review a company        9 - Delete a company           │
8   │                                                                │
9   │     3 - Zip sort list           10 - Print review list         │
10  │                                                                │
11  │     4 - Alpha sort list         11 - Print report              │
12  │                                                                │
13  │     5 - Count list data         12 - Print labels              │
14  │                                                                │
15  │     6 - Graph data              13 - Print phone numbers        │
16  │                                                                │
17  │     7 - Store file on disk      14 - Save and Quit             │
18  │                                                                │
19  │                                                                │
20  └──────────────────────────────────────────────────────────────┘
MACMENU2.WQ1 [2]                                      NUM        READY
```

Figure 13-33.   *Large menu*

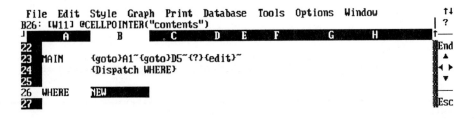

```
     File  Edit  Style  Graph  Print  Database  Tools  Options  Window          ↑↓
   B41: [W9]
   ┌──────A────────B──────────C─────────D──────────E──────F────────G────────H────┐↑
   23  MAIN    {goto}A1~{goto}D2~
   24          {GetNumber "Enter the number of your choice: ",TEST}
   25          {If TEST=1}{Branch ENTER}
   26          {If TEST=2}{Branch REVIEW}
   27          {If TEST=3}{Branch ZIPS}
   28          {If TEST=4}{Branch ALPHAS}
   29          {If TEST=5}{Branch COUNTS}
   30          {If TEST=6}{Branch GRAPHS}
   31          {If TEST=7}{Branch STORES}
   32          {If TEST=8}{Branch SAVES}
   33          {If TEST=9}{Branch DELETES}
   34          {If TEST=10}{Branch PRINTREV}
   35          {If TEST=11}{Branch PRINTREP}
   36          {If TEST=12}{Branch PRINTLAB}
   37          {If TEST=13}{Branch PRINTTEL}
   38          {If TEST=14}{Branch SANDQ}
   39          {Branch MAIN}
   40
   41  TEST    █████████
   42
   └───────────────────────────────────────────────────────────────────────────┘↓
   MACMENU2.WQ1 [2]                                             NUM           READY
```

Figure 13-34.   *Macro code*

This approach can be used in a number of different situations where the choices fit into a normal Quattro PRO menu. (Remember that in a normal {MenuBranch} menu, Quattro PRO allows 13 menu choices to be shown at once, and more can be incorporated into the menu, although the user will have to scroll down the list to see them.)

The slight pause while Quattro PRO evaluates the {If} statements in macros like this might become annoying. An alternative approach that provides faster response and far less code is shown here:

```
     File  Edit  Style  Graph  Print  Database  Tools  Options  Window          ↑↓
   B26: [W11] @CELLPOINTER("contents")                                          | ?
   ┌──────A────────B──────────C─────────D──────E────────F─────────G─────────H───┐↑
   22                                                                            |End
   23  MAIN    {goto}A1~{goto}D5~{?}{edit}~                                      | ▲
   24          {Dispatch WHERE}                                                  |◄ ►
   25                                                                            | ▼
   26  WHERE   NEW                                                               |
   27                                                                            |Esc
```

The {Dispatch} command is used to direct macro flow to the cell called WHERE. This cell contains a formula that reads the contents of the cell currently occupied by the cell selector. This macro employs a menu screen like that shown in Figure 13-35 to present the user with options that are actual subroutine names that can be highlighted. When the user presses ENTER, the contents of the currently highlighted cell are read into WHERE and thus used in the macro.

Notice the {?}, which is the pause for the user to move the cell selector and press ENTER. This command is followed by the code {edit}~. This causes Quattro PRO to update the @CELLPOINTER function in the WHERE cell. If this is omitted, WHERE may retain the cell selector's previous location and the macro will branch improperly.

The macro names on the menu can sometimes be normal names, but in a large model where many names are used up you may be forced to make do with approximate choices, as shown in Figure 13-35. The fact that the names are not proper words is offset by the descriptions that accompany each one on the menu. You might want to elaborate on this menu system by using the Form Input command. When global protection has been turned on and the choice cells (shown in inverse in Figure 13-35) have been

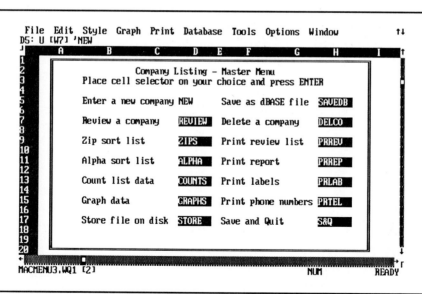

Figure 13-35.   *Menu of subroutines*

unprotected, the area from D5 to H17 becomes a Form Input area to restrict the user's movement to the choice cells.

An Opening Number

When a novice user application begins, it should make the operator comfortable with the program. You can do this by careful use of the Startup macro (\0) and screen positioning. This is an excellent way to use the wide-screen menus shown in Figures 13-33 and 13-35. However, you can accentuate a regular Quattro PRO macro menu to make an effective opening. In Figure 13-36 the user is shown the first menu and told how to use it. This was achieved by the {goto} command, first to the top-left corner of the screen, and then to the highlighted label. The menu was then called. Note that Quattro PRO's menu positioning means some changes for those used to designing for 1-2-3's horizontal menu. Here the designing has positioned the box accordingly. This design could be improved by stating the application's name in the first screen for user reassurance.

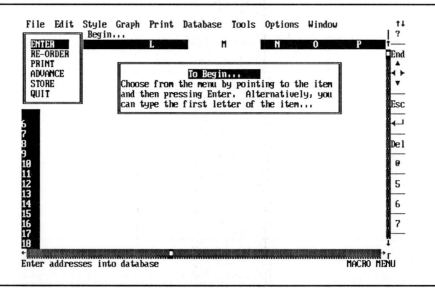

Figure 13-36. *Opening menu*

While You Wait

Power users hate to wait, and one should assume the same for novice users. It is certainly prudent to let users know when they have initiated a procedure that takes time. The screen shown in Figure 13-37 is an example of this. The macro that performs the printing simply moves the cell selector to this screen before issuing the {/ Print;Go} command. Similar screens, such as the one in Figure 13-38, are advisable when the user saves the file. You might want to add an extra warning if the application is written for floppy-disk users, letting them know it is important not to remove the disk until the save process is complete.

A Message System

As an alternative to the previous techniques for displaying messages and menus, you can use graphs as described earlier in the section on slide shows. Graph message screens are not simply for use in presentations. By

Figure 13-37. *Print wait screen*

Figure 13-38. *Save wait screen*

using the {Graphchar} command you can get user input while a graph is displayed and use this to branch to a series of macro instructions. For example, in Figure 13-39 you can see a macro menu created by a graph screen. The Graph Name Display command is used to present the graph and the {Graphchar} command is used to get the user's response.

An alternative to displaying graphs for messages is the {Message} command. This can be used to display boxed message text that appears over the top of your work area, even when you are in the File Manager window. The {Message} command can display the message text for a period of time or until a key is pressed. The {Message} command takes the form

{Message Block,Left,Top,Time}

where Block is the cell or cells occupied by the message text, Left and Top are the screen coordinates for the message box, and Time is the length of time for the message to be displayed. The Block coordinates must be wide enough for the whole piece of text to be displayed. For example, in Figure 13-40 you can see a macro called MESS01. This can be called by another

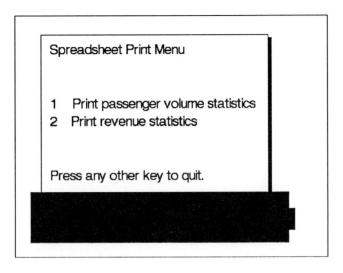

Figure 13-39. *Graphic macro menu*

macro when a message needs to be displayed. The macro refers to a message block called MSGA. This is actually cells B62..G62. If you use a smaller block, the message will be truncated. This means that you cannot simply name MSGA with the Edit Names Labels command. To display the message called MSGB in Figure 13-40, you would have to name cells B64..F65 as MSGB.

The macro MESS01 produces the results shown in Figure 13-41. The boxed message stays on the screen for 15 seconds, as defined by the formula @NOW+@TIME(0,0,15). The macro that calls this routine is suspended for that period of time, as indicated by the WAIT message in the lower right of the screen. If you enter 0 for the time, then the macro pauses until the user presses a key, at which point the macro continues with whatever code is on the next line.

The screen coordinates of the message displayed in Figure 13-40 are ten characters from the left of the screen and ten rows from the top, as defined by the Left and Top arguments. This locates the top left of the box.

By combining {Message} with the {Graphchar} command you can display messages and get user responses. Figure 13-41 shows a macro called MESS02, which displays the message shown in the figure, and waits for

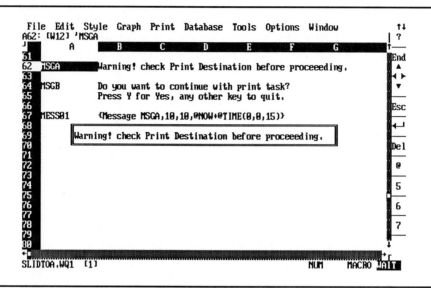

Figure 13-40. *Message macro*

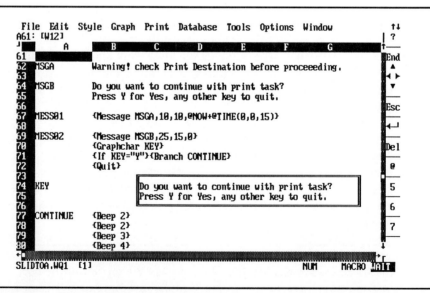

Figure 13-41. *Message macro with question*

user response. When the user types **Y** the macro branches to CONTINUE, which in this case is a test macro of beeps. If the user presses any other key, the macro quits. Note that both lower- and uppercase **Y** are acceptable as a response. Also note the position of the message box, which is further across the screen and lower down than the one in Figure 13-40, as indicated by the screen coordinates of 25,15. The {Message} and {Graphchar} commands make for convenient single-key user input routines. A series of {If} statements can be used to evaluate a whole range of inputs and branch to different macro routines, making this yet another means of providing a menu for users.

Developer Tips

The following are assorted tips that have proved useful when designing spreadsheets that contain a lot of macros. They are presented as suggestions for use when building macro-intensive applications.

Macro Documenting

As you develop macros it is easy to forget just how a particular formula or line of code was designed to work. Make sure that you document lines of macro code and annotate formulas, using the semicolon technique. (Type a semicolon after the formula and then type your comments, which will be stored in the cell with the formula, without affecting its performance.) To keep track of code and formulas that can be reused in other situations, use a macro library system or the simple but effective alternative of paper records. You can document a lot of work by using the PRSC key. Taking a screen shot of a particularly useful piece of macro code is an excellent way to preserve it. Keep a file of these shots, noting on each one the name of the worksheet in which it can be found.

Anonymous Recordings

Quattro PRO's Record feature simplifies the task of entering the necessary keystrokes and menu equivalents for macros by recording your actions as you perform them. You do not have to record a macro in its entirety during a single take. The Record feature is particularly useful for recording small sections of code, as an alternative to looking up menu equivalents with the ALT-F3 key and writing keystroke sequences from memory. However, there is one potential problem when using the Record feature for odd sections of macro code: an overabundance of block names is likely to result if you follow the ALT-F2 Paste prompt to specify a name for each recording.

The normal prompt when you select Paste from the ALT-F2 menu to place recorded code into a worksheet is "Enter name of macro to create/modify." Quattro PRO expects you to enter a block name that will be attached to the cell into which the first line of the text of the recording will be placed. If any block names already exist in the worksheet they will be listed as possible locations to use for the recording. One response to this prompt is not to specify a name. This avoids creating one more block name when all you need is a place to store some keystrokes. If the prompt is listing existing names, you just press ESC and then ENTER to go past the name prompt and paste the recording into an unnamed area. If there are no block names in the worksheet you can just press ENTER to get past the name prompt. If there are previous block names, then the initial cell location prompt in macro record will be the current cell coordinate. Press ESCAPE, move the cell selector to the desired location for the recorded keystrokes, and then press ENTER.

Wholesale Name Changes

When you have used a block name for a macro or other piece of information in the spreadsheet, the name is likely to occur in numerous places, either in macros or within formulas. If you decide to change a name that has already been used extensively, you may find Quattro PRO's Search & Replace feature to be useful. You can specify the old name as the Search String and the new name as the Replace String. This will allow you to update all references to the name that has been changed, even those within formulas. If you want to ensure that the entire worksheet is included in this process, make A1 the starting point of the Search & Replace Block. Use END and then HOME to move the far corner of the block to the end of the spreadsheet area.

Note that Search & Replace does not update the actual record of block names seen in the Edit Names Create option. You will need to delete or reassign the old name and to assign the new one, or else the change will not take effect.

Listing Block Names

When you need hard copy of the list of current block names and their locations, use the Edit Names Make Table command and print out the table that is placed in your worksheet. The following macro can be adapted to make a table and print it out:

{/ Name;Table}
{/ Print;Block}{bs}.{end}{right}{end}{down}
{/ Print;Go}

The table will be two columns wide and as many rows long as you have names.

Removing Errors

Quattro PRO does not have a built-in "errors-be-gone" feature, but you can often use the Search & Replace command to counter large outbreaks of ERR messages. Suppose you have a whole series of formulas that refer to a particular named block. If the block name is deleted, then the formulas will all result in ERR. After you have redefined the erroneously deleted block name you can use Search & Replace to look for ERR in cells and replace it with the block name.

Conclusion

This book has taken you from the basics of spreadsheet operation to the sophistication of graphics, macros, and even custom menus. You should not expect to retain everything you have seen on first reading. In many ways, the tremendous power of a program like Quattro PRO is equivalent to that of an entire programming language, which students may take several semesters to study. You should not expect to learn or use all of Quattro PRO's capabilities right away. Unlike most programming languages, however, Quattro PRO is easily applied to practical tasks almost immediately. You can also have fun with Quattro PRO, designing impressive graphs, charts, and drawings. Many examples of Quattro PRO at work are given throughout the book, but the best way to become familiar with Quattro PRO is to consider the tasks you perform in your own work and try to apply Quattro PRO to them. Through using Quattro PRO you will get to know Quattro PRO, and you will become more productive and creative in the process.

A *Advanced Setups*

Quattro PRO uses sophisticated programming techniques to make startup a simple process despite the wide variety of hardware on which the program runs. Using the commands on the Options menu you can adjust most aspects of the way in which the program runs, as described in Chapter 6. However, to provide maximum flexibility for using Quattro PRO on your system, you may want to employ some of the advanced startup techniques described on the following pages. After completing the initial installation process for Quattro PRO described in the manual, you can take steps to make Quattro PRO more convenient to use. These steps are not essential to the program's operation, but experienced users may want to employ at least some of them if they are setting up Quattro PRO for less-experienced end users.

The Question of Memory

These days your PC can come with several different types of random access memory (RAM). How much RAM and of what kind makes a difference to how efficiently Quattro PRO will run.

Memory Size

To learn how much RAM is in your computer, use the CHKDSK command from the DOS prompt. Simply type **CHKDSK** and press ENTER. The results will look something like this:

Volume TOWER 386   created Jun 16, 1990 8:23a

```
33449984  bytes total disk space
  569344  bytes in 57 hidden files
   69632  bytes in 26 directories
26648576  bytes in 1139 user files
    2048  bytes in bad sectors
 6160384  bytes available on disk

  655360  bytes total memory
  146496  bytes free
```

Most of the information is about the current disk and the files on it, but the last section is about memory. To run Quattro PRO a computer will need at least 512K of normal RAM memory. With 512K of RAM in your PC, Quattro PRO will be able to handle modest spreadsheets. Your capacity to handle larger worksheets increases when you have 640K of RAM. Depending on market conditions, RAM can be a fairly inexpensive commodity and it is definitely worth upgrading to at least 640K. The benefits in speed and capacity will be reflected in your use of other programs as well as Quattro PRO.

Due to the different types of information that go to make up spreadsheets, including values, calculations, and formatting, it is not really possible to give an upper limit to spreadsheet size with Quattro PRO. Basically, Quattro PRO can work better with more memory. The question is how to add more memory to your system in such a way that Quattro PRO can recognize it.

Types of Memory

There are two types of memory in a PC, Read Only Memory (ROM) and Random Access Memory (RAM). (Some people refer to disks as a third type of memory, but it is easier to think of disks as storage rather than memory.) The ROM holds instructions, permanently burned into the chips, that your computer uses immediately after the power is turned on, before even a disk is read. The RAM is where all of the instructions for the programs that the computer is to execute are held prior to being carried out. The RAM is also where data is held before it is stored onto disk. When you turn off the power to your computer you wipe out the contents of RAM.

Consider how memory works in a typical session with a typical piece of application software such as WordPerfect (for the sake of clarity and brevity this tale is simplified somewhat, but basically a true story). First you turn on the computer. Almost immediately instructions are read from ROM. This includes the testing of memory that gives the numeric display in the top left of the screen, as well as the BIOS (Basic Input/Output System) instructions that lay the ground rules for the exchange of information between different parts of the system, such as keyboard, display, disks, and so on.

The ROM instructions tell the computer to look to the drive(s) to find software on disk. When the computer finds a disk with DOS on it, DOS is read into memory. DOS actually consists of several parts, the two most important being the hidden system files and the command processor, COMMAND.COM. After COMMAND.COM is loaded DOS looks for two special files that tell it about the computer, CONFIG.SYS and AUTOEXEC.BAT. The CONFIG.SYS file is a list of settings for DOS to use, plus instructions about any special equipment that is part of the hardware configuration. The AUTOEXEC.BAT file is a list of instructions about what DOS should do first, like set the date and time and display a menu of programs.

As manager of the flow and storage of information, DOS then allows you to issue an instruction that loads a program, such as WordPerfect. Word-

Perfect is read from disk into RAM. DOS remains in RAM as well. You type some text on the keyboard and this is held in RAM. You issue the save instruction and a copy of the text in RAM is stored on disk, but remains on screen as well for further editing. When you are done editing you resave the document, replacing the old version on disk with the new one, and then exit WordPerfect, which removes both text and the program from RAM.

How Much Is Enough?

The preceding story is simple enough, *if* you have enough RAM to hold both DOS and WordPerfect. How much is enough and how much have you got? Like file storage space on disk, RAM is measured in bytes and kilobytes. As you have seen, if you type **CHKDSK** at the DOS prompt and press ENTER you will see a report on memory, such as "655360 bytes total memory, 554688 bytes free." This indicates the total amount of memory recognized by DOS, plus what is left after accounting for the space occupied by such information as the COMMAND.COM file itself.

When the IBM PC was first introduced it came with 65,536 bytes or 64K of RAM. This was considered a lot of RAM at the time. Competing systems such as the Apple II had 48K of RAM in standard configuration and only the hottest CP/M machines had 64K. WordStar, one of the most prevalent applications of the day, was only 32K in size, so 64K was more than enough. Since the power users back then had 64K CP/M machines, the designers of DOS figured that ten times that much would be sufficient "user RAM" for DOS and any future applications; hence the figure of 640K, which is the maximum amount of user RAM that DOS can recognize.

This sounded like a reasonable limit at the time. However, users kept demanding more features from software and each new wave of programs required more RAM. These days, a commonly used word processing program on PCs is WordPerfect, which takes up about 320K. New functions have been added to DOS, which used to occupy less than 30K but now requires some 80K. In addition to DOS and regular application programs a new breed of software, called TSRs or Terminate-and-Stay-Resident programs, gained popularity and consumed RAM. A TSR program, such as the original Borland SideKick, is loaded into memory after DOS but before application software and stays there as you unload one application and then load another. This way, a TSR program can offer the same features, such as a notepad or clipboard, within whatever application you are using.

There is also pressure on memory limits from the thirst for more exotic hardware. The designers of the original PC and DOS could not anticipate every type of storage system, communications equipment, and hardware interface that was to be developed for PCs. Equipment like removable hard disks, FAX boards, and MIDI interfaces simply did not exist then. However, DOS was designed so that someone who designed a new piece of equipment could also write a piece of software that told the PC how to relate to that equipment. This specialized software is called a *device driver*, and many products for the PC come with a device driver. The problem with device drivers is that they are loaded into memory when the computer starts up, right after COMMAND.COM. You cannot use such equipment as Bernoulli boxes without these drivers occupying space in memory. This is how the 640K limit of DOS came to be such a squeeze: bigger and better applications and versions of DOS, plus TSR software and specialized equipment. Then along came networking to really put on the pressure, which has become known as RAM-CRAM.

Memory Architecture

You might wonder why DOS has not been altered to recognize more than 640K. The answer lies in the original design of the PC and what many users have seen as the necessity to keep each new wave of PC designs compatible with the last. Understanding the problem begins with understanding *addresses*. In order for a computer to keep track of the data it handles it needs to know where it is. The location of each byte that is going to be processed needs to be defined. This is done by assigning a unique address to every byte. You can think of a delivery person attempting to make deliveries. If every customer has a unique address the job of locating them is made much easier. In a computer each piece of data that is processed has to pass through memory. Every address in memory has to be coded in binary code. If you have eight digits, or bytes, to work with you can come up with 256 unique addresses. With 16 bits you can create 65,536 combinations, or unique addresses. The 8088 chip used in the first PCs had the capacity to use 20 bits for addressing. This was a function of the physical design of the chip. This results in a maximum potential number of addresses of 1,048,576. This is exactly 1 megabyte worth of addresses or addressable memory. The 8088 chip can be said to have a 1 megabyte address space.

However, not all of this space can be used by programs that you load from disk. Some of the area needs to be reserved for information passing through memory from and to displays. There needs to be room to address the BIOS, which controls how the pieces of hardware communicate with each other. To allow for these factors IBM engineers preallocated 640K for programs and 384K for system overhead. Remember that this 640K is the limit of user RAM. In addition to this user RAM, there is the memory area occupied by ROM. The total amount of ROM and RAM that a PC can work with is limited by the type of chip, the central processing unit, that is running the system. The CPU chip must move data and program code in and out of memory. The Intel 8088 and 8086 chips that powered the first PC can address up to 1024K, or 1 megabyte, of memory. This space is made up of the 640K of RAM, plus 128K reserved for use by video boards, plus 256K reserved for the system ROM (640K + 128K + 256K = 1024K = 1MB).

Therefore, beyond the 640K of user RAM the rest of the PC's 1MB total address space is reserved for system operations, a 384K range of memory locations where the CPU finds data or instructions for its own use. The space from 640K to 768K is for video buffers, the data used to draw and redraw the screen display. Optional or installable ROM modules, such as those used by hard disk controllers and enhanced graphics boards, fit between 768K and 896K. The computer's own built-in ROM that starts the computer running is addressed from 896K to 1024K. Note that this is address space here, not actual memory chips. The 8088/8086 processors can actually see a total memory space no bigger than 1024K, of which no more than 640K can be RAM. Even if you have more than 640K worth of RAM chips, DOS will not recognize it.

However, the address area above 640K is rarely full. An 80-column, 25-line text display uses 4K of video memory. The Monochrome Display Adapter occupies just the area from 704K to 708K. Only the most colorful EGA and VGA modes fill or exceed the 128K assigned to video. Only IBM's PS/2 models, not PCs or ATs, use all the address space above 896K for system ROM. Having vacant space in high memory can come in handy. Having a 64K gap amidst the video buffers and BIOS routines makes possible EMS expanded memory, described in a moment.

Although the 8088 CPU stops at 1MB of RAM, the 80286 found in the PC AT can address 16MB, and the 80386 CPU can address as much as four gigabytes (4096MB). Compared with the mess of addresses below it, RAM above the 1MB boundary is fairly simple. It is known as extended memory and is straightforward additional space for 286 or 386 systems running OS/2, Xenix, or some 386-specific software. Unfortunately, a 286 or 386 using DOS runs in something called real mode. This was designed into the chip for backward compatibility with earlier computers. The 8088-based PCs were around so long that hardware designers built their peripherals to take advantage of the addresses above 640K. Altering the limit would affect your ability to use many popular hard disk controllers, video boards, and so on.

The real mode of 80286 and 80386 chips has the same 1MB address limit as the 8088. There is an alternative mode that can be addressed by operating systems other than DOS. This is called the *protected mode* and it can use large extended memory spaces. Very few DOS programs, a few utilities and disk caches, actually do anything with extended memory. For example, many PC ATs come with 384K of actual RAM memory installed beyond 640K, but DOS cannot use it. An AT with 1MB of built-in RAM gives the same CHKDSK report of available memory as one with 640K. Some 1MB systems use the extra memory as *shadow RAM*, loading a copy (or shadow) of sluggish video and BIOS ROM code into RAM for quicker performance. Shadow RAM makes screen displays more responsive, especially for EGA, but will not stop programs from displaying "Out of memory" messages.

EMS Architecture

Compared with the simple linear addressing of extended RAM, expanded memory relies on a technical trick known as *paging*, or bank-switching; that is, taking a "window" within the region visible to the processor (the 8088's 1MB address space) and swapping different areas, or pages, of expanded memory in and out of that space as needed. What happens is that an unused 64K section of the memory between 640K and 1024K is used as the address for a larger area, like a mail drop that is one stop on the postal route but that has boxes for lots of customers. The CPU is fooled, busily operating within this virtual space on data whose real, or physical, address may be many megabytes away.

Simple bank-switching is nothing new, but EMS is a sophisticated scheme. It involves hardware and software working together—the extra RAM and memory-mapping hardware on an EMS board, combined with a software driver added to your CONFIG.SYS file. This driver, the expanded memory manager (EMM), lets DOS and your applications recognize the paged memory. Given at least 64K of contiguous, vacant address space above 784K (one of the unused gaps, EMS creates a page frame holding at least four 16K pages). The memory manager can map any 16K segment, anywhere within expanded RAM, into any of these pages, fielding CPU requests while preventing collisions among multiple programs and data areas.

The original Expanded Memory Specification, EMS 3.2, supported 8MB of expanded memory, mostly as workspace for spreadsheets and other data files. AST and other firms modified that standard to create the Enhanced Expanded Memory Specification (EEMS), which can swap more pages, including some below the 640K line as well as in the page frame above it. This helps environments such as DESQview shuffle programs in and out of conventional memory. Now EMS 4.0 has surpassed the EEMS standard. With EMS 4.0 you get support for up to 32MB at 8MB per expansion slot. This is swapped into pages almost anywhere below 1MB, and it has many more functions and routines for executing program code as well as handling data.

Understanding the difference between expanded and extended memory can take some effort, but there is a simple rule to follow when installing RAM in your system for use with Quattro PRO: Configure as much memory as possible as *expanded*. Quattro PRO can make use of expanded memory but not extended. Many memory boards can be configured as either extended or expanded. Even if you have an extended memory board you may find software that allows the extended memory to be treated as expanded.

The Memory Crunch

Now that you know why memory is organized the way it is in a PC, you can evaluate some techniques for getting around the limits imposed by this state of affairs. After taking steps to maximize the amount of memory in your system, and configuring as much of it as expanded memory as you can, you may still run into memory problems, typically when you have loaded Quattro PRO and then built a very large worksheet. Quattro PRO's VROOMM feature allows you to keep building very large worksheets by reducing the amount of memory used by the program itself. The Virtual Real-time Object-Oriented Memory Manager is a technology designed by Borland to allow software to perform more efficiently under the 640K limitations of DOS. Programs written to run under VROOMM are composed of small modules that can be quickly loaded into memory as needed, allowing more room for data in memory. However, at some point the amount of disk access that this process requires will slow you down. Moving from one cell to the next will require a disk read and this is the point at which you really need more memory.

You could also run into a memory problem trying to load Quattro PRO after you have just installed and loaded a new piece of memory-resident software such as a network program. Try some of the following techniques to cope with the memory crunch.

Slimming Your CONFIG.SYS

Computer systems that have been around for a while can accumulate a lot of unnecessary additions. You may have noticed this in the disk file department—dozens of files that have been on a hard disk for ages, but nobody is sure why. A similar thing can happen to your CONFIG.SYS. Some applications add information to CONFIG.SYS when they are installed. Some hardware requires that lines be added to CONFIG.SYS. If the application or hardware falls into disuse it can be removed, but the additions to CONFIG.SYS may remain. A good example is the ATALK.SYS driver that was supplied with TOPS network adapters. This is no longer necessary because TOPS now uses a memory-resident program instead of an installed driver. Devices loaded in CONFIG.SYS can take up precious memory, so you should remove ones you no longer need. Make sure you know why what is in your CONFIG.SYS is there.

Mapping Out Your Memory

A valuable tool for checking what you have in memory and where it is located is a utility program called a *memory mapper*. There are several of these available from bulletin boards such as IBMNET on CompuServe. Some of these programs are free once you have downloaded them; others are shareware, which you pay for after if you decide to use them. If you are doing extensive work with memory, for example configuring several different machines, then a program of this kind is very helpful.

Hardware Solutions

If you are using a PC XT or other 8088/8086-based PC, you have limited hardware options when it comes to extra memory. You can add EMS memory for use by programs like Quattro PRO but you cannot access that memory for use with network software and other memory grabbers. However, a company called RYBS Electronics offers a product called HIcard that uses something called Advanced Memory Specification to help out PC XT users. The HIcard is a board that is installed into your PC and is fitted with up to 512K of memory. This can be used to bring 512K machines up to 640K but also provides memory beyond that. By using AMS software, this memory can be incorporated into the system to be put to use. The SYSMAP software that comes with HIcard maps out the memory usage in your PC before and after the card is installed. You are shown how much "HIDOS" memory you have available and how much regular RAM will be freed if you load such things as mouse drivers and network drivers into this HIDOS area. Gains of 100K to 200K in regular RAM required by applications are possible. Note that HIDOS is the term that RYBS uses for memory beyond 640K—memory that can be addressed by using those addresses not needed by BIOS, display adapters, and other equipment.

The software used by HIcard is reliable, taking care of potential conflicts between calls on memory and making operation of the HIDOS transparent to the user. All that you have to do to utilize the extra RAM space is load into it those programs that are best suited to that region, such as your network software.

Another hardware solution is available for users of AT and PS/2 systems that are based on the 80286 chip. The ALL CHARGECARD is a device that adds powerful memory-management capabilities to 80286 machines. Using the chips on the ALL CHARGECARD you can choose to reorganize your memory usage in several different ways, including access to high-memory areas such as those accessed by the HIcard. The ALL CHARGE-CARD does not contain memory itself, but it allows you to reorganize all types of memory in your system: motherboard RAM, EMS, and Extended memory. This can permit you to run TOPS together with applications that would otherwise not be able to fit in memory.

Software Solutions

Since 80386 systems have the capacity to address larger memory areas and have better memory-management functions built into their hardware, you can use software solutions to achieve results on an 80386 that require hardware solutions on earlier systems. Two examples of this are HI386 from RYBS, the makers of HIcard, and 386MAX from Qualitas. With 386MAX you can treat extended memory as expanded, access high DOS memory, and perform other tricks. Using programs of this nature requires that you coordinate several aspects of your computer system: video display, hard disk controllers, and network interface card. There are a lot of optional commands with 386MAX that allow you to alter the way it runs in order to avoid conflict with other programs. In some situations problems with high memory will require extensive analysis to resolve conflicts. For example, there are some VGA cards, such as the FastWrite VGA from Video7, that use up an area of memory often used by memory-swapping routines. If you load the VGA BIOS into RAM as described in the VGA utilities manual you can get around this conflict, but you will need to coordinate memory addresses with your memory expansion software.

DESQview is a multitasking windows environment for DOS-based machines, made by Quarterdeck Office Systems. The current version is 2.2 plus. You can run DESQview on just about any machine running DOS 2.0 or later on an 8088, 8086, 80286, or 80386 microprocessor. On 386-based machines, DESQview is most commonly used in conjunction with Quarterdeck's 386 Expanded Memory Manager, QEMM-386, to form a combination generally referred to as DESQview386. You can run DESQview on a 386 without QEMM-386, but you lose significant memory-management capability, ending up with an environment virtually identical to DESQview on a 286, only faster. Note that DESQview and QEMM-386 are separate products and must be purchased separately; they can be used together or independently. For the reason just stated, it is rare to find someone running DESQview on a 386 without QEMM-386. However, for reasons that will become clear, many people who do not own DESQview buy and use QEMM-386 as their 386 Expanded Memory Manager of choice.

QEMM-386 has two major functions. First, like 386MAX, it can transform extended memory into expanded memory (LIM EMS 4.0 and EEMS 3.2), which can then be accessed by programs designed to take advantage of expanded memory, as well as by DESQview, which can use it to create virtual DOS environments for simultaneous operation of multiple programs. Second, it can map RAM into the unused addresses between 640K and 1MB and allow a user to load TSR modules into it, thus making more conventional RAM available to applications.

Adjusting Expanded Memory Use Within Quattro PRO

The extra work of shuffling data through the DOS memory window into expanded RAM means that EMS RAM responds less quickly than RAM below 640K. For this reason Quattro PRO allows you to make some trade-offs when using expanded memory. The Options Other Expanded Memory command provides these options:

Both
Spreadsheet Data
Format
None

The last of these shuts off EMS so that your worksheet responds faster, although it cannot grow as large as when one of the other three options are used. The Both option allows EMS to be used for all types of worksheet information, permitting the largest possible models. The Spreadsheet Data option is the default setting, which limits EMS use to just formulas and labels, giving faster response than Both. The Format option is the fastest operation you can get while still making some use of EMS. Try changing your selection in this area when you need to increase worksheet capacity or program response times.

Configuration File Enhancement

To efficiently use Quattro PRO on your system you may need to fine tune the way the system, not just Quattro PRO, is configured. One file that greatly affects system performance is CONFIG.SYS.

The Role of CONFIG.SYS

When your computer starts up, it looks to the floppy disk in drive A for DOS. If DOS is found on the disk in drive A, it is loaded into RAM. If not, the system looks to the hard disk, drive C, if you have one installed. If DOS is found on drive C, it is loaded into memory. The disk from which your system loads DOS is called the *boot disk* (harking back to the days when a computer was started by kicking it). DOS is the first piece of software loaded into memory.

One of the first pieces of information DOS looks for when it is loaded is the configuration file. This is a file on the boot disk called CONFIG.SYS. The CONFIG.SYS file contains information about how your system is configured. It is not essential for the boot disk, since DOS assumes certain default conditions if it does not find a CONFIG.SYS file. However, you will need to establish some settings with CONFIG.SYS when running Quattro PRO. In fact, Quattro PRO's install program can update the CONFIG.SYS file for you during initial installation.

The two settings that affect Quattro PRO involve two aspects of the way DOS manages information in RAM: buffers and files. The number of buffers (temporary holding areas into which DOS can put information your programs use) is normally five. The number of open files that DOS can keep track of is normally eight. By increasing these settings with a CONFIG.SYS file, you can improve the speed with which DOS manipulates information in your system. A setting of 20 for buffers and 20 for files is often used. The settings are established by placing the following instructions in the CONFIG.SYS file:

BUFFERS = 20
FILES = 20

The instructions can be upper- or lowercase letters. They are placed one instruction per line. This may have been done to your system when you installed Quattro PRO; however, it is a good idea to check out the CONFIG.SYS file on your system.

Other Settings in CONFIG.SYS

The CONFIG.SYS file may need additional information about your hardware. The CONFIG.SYS file for the author's system looks like this:

Entry	Used To
BUFFERS = 20	Set buffers
FILES = 20	Set files
DEVICE = RCD.SYS	Support Bernoulli drive
DEVICE = EMM.SYS	Support Expanded Memory board
DEVICE = HARDRIVE.SYS	Support hard disk configuration
DEVICE = RAMDRIVE.SYS	Support RAM disk

The instruction DEVICE = RCD.SYS is required to run the Iomega Bernoulli box, a special high-capacity disk drive. The EMM.SYS instruction refers to expanded memory installed in the system. The DEVICE = HARDRIVE.SYS instruction lets the system know that a large-capacity hard disk with the Speedstor program has been installed. The RAMDRIVE.SYS instruction sets up part of the expanded memory to act like an extra disk drive. If you use memory to emulate a disk drive as a RAM disk, you can quickly copy data or programs there since the disk is electronic and not mechanical.

Checking and Changing CONFIG.SYS

You can check whether your system has a CONFIG.SYS file by using the command DIR *.SYS at the DOS prompt while in the root directory of your hard disk or on the floppy disk with which you start your system. If you find a CONFIG.SYS file, you can examine its contents with the TYPE command, as in TYPE CONFIG.SYS. If you plan to change the CONFIG.SYS file or create a new one, you should copy the original file to another file, such as CONFIG.OLD. You do this at the DOS prompt with the command

COPY CONFIG.SYS CONFIG.OLD

A new CONFIG.SYS file can be created with the DOS COPY command. Type the following at the DOS prompt:

COPY CON CONFIG.SYS

After this press ENTER. The ENTER key gives you the first line for an instruction. Type the instruction, for example, FILES = 20, and then press ENTER for another line. After the last line of instruction, press F6 and press ENTER again. The file will be written to the disk. (Pressing F6 produces the CTRL-Z code, which DOS reads as meaning end-of-file.) This CONFIG.SYS file is a pure ASCII file. You can create one with SideKick's Notepad, WordStar in the non-document mode, and many other word processors, such as SPRINT and WordPerfect, that can save text in ASCII format.

Hard Disk Enhancement

Quattro PRO is always installed on a hard disk. The installation program ordinarily places the program files in a subdirectory called QUATTRO. A hard disk directory system for a computer running Quattro PRO and WordPerfect might look like the one shown in Figure A-1, which was drawn with Quattro PRO's Annotate feature. Note that the directory containing Quattro PRO is called QUATTRO, rather than QPRO which is the default directory used by the Quattro PRO installation program. Users of the older version of Quattro who are upgrading may want to use QUATTRO as their directory. Other users may find QPRO too short and cryptic for a directory name.

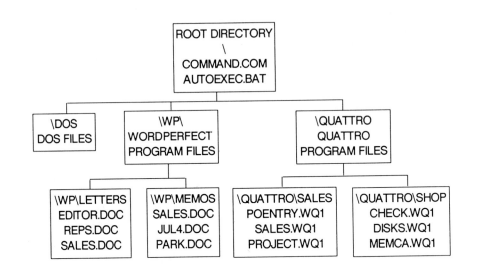

Figure A-1.   *Hard disk drive directory system*

Navigating Directories

For DOS to find either a program file or a data file, you must specify a path for it to follow. For example, the path to the worksheet file called PROJECT.WQ1 in the sales subdirectory of Quattro PRO is \QUAT-TRO\SALES\. To identify files accurately on a hard disk, the path to the file becomes part of the file name. Thus, the full name of the PROJECT.WQ1 file is

C:\QUATTRO\SALES\PROJECT.WQ1

When you use a hard disk you cannot be in two places at once. Normally, you begin working with a hard disk in the root directory. You are said to be in the root directory when you are at the top of the directory tree and the root directory is the one you are currently using. You can always ensure that the root is current by typing **CD** and pressing ENTER.

In order to navigate a hard disk with one or more subdirectories, you might want to change the uninformative C> prompt, which tells you only that you are using drive C, to the C:\> prompt, which shows not only the current drive but also the path and the current subdirectory (in this case the root, or main directory). This more informative prompt will always tell you what subdirectory you are in. If you move into the Quattro PRO subdirectory, the prompt will read

C:\QUATTRO>

If your hard disk is not drive C but drive D or E or any other valid letter, just substitute that letter for *C* in the instructions that follow.

To change the prompt to a more informative version, type **PROMPT PG** at the C> prompt. When you press ENTER you will see the drive letter, the path ($P) to whatever subdirectory you are in, and the greater-than sign ($G). Now change your location to a subdirectory such as the one for Quattro PRO. Type

CD \QUATTRO

and press ENTER. You will see your prompt change. To change your current location back to the root directory, type

CD\

and press ENTER.

Quattro PRO data files should be kept in a separate directory from the program files. To create a subdirectory called QWORK directly below the root directory, type

MD \QWORK

and press ENTER. To create a subdirectory called MYWORK below the Quattro PRO directory, type

MD \QUATTRO\MYWORK

and press ENTER. If you want to copy all the files from a disk in drive A into this new directory, you can move into the subdirectory by typing

CD \QUATTRO\MYWORK

pressing ENTER, and then entering

COPY A:*.*

Alternatively, you could type

COPY A:*.* C:\QUATTRO\MYWORK

from the root directory.

Using Batch Files

Unfortunately, DOS forgets the helpful PROMPT command when you turn off the system. To solve this problem, you resort to batch files, which are collections of instructions to DOS that are delivered in a group or batch. A batch file has the extension BAT and is activated by typing the first part of the file name preceding the period. For example, the file P.BAT might contain the following lines:

PROMPT PG
DIR /W

Typing **P** and pressing ENTER would tell DOS to change the prompt and then list the files in the current directory.

Every system can have a batch file called AUTOEXEC.BAT, which DOS looks for when the system starts up. You might want to go straight to working on Quattro PRO. The following AUTOEXEC.BAT file on the hard disk would accomplish this:

DATE
TIME
PROMPT PG
CD \QUATTRO
Q

To create this batch file, you copy the instructions from the keyboard directly into a file by typing

COPY CON AUTOEXEC. BAT

at the DOS prompt. Pressing ENTER gives you the first line for an instruction. Type the instruction (for example, CD QUATTRO), and press ENTER for another line. After the last line of instruction, press F6 and press ENTER again. The file will be written to the disk. This file is a pure ASCII file. Note that you can add items to the last line of this batch file that cause Quattro PRO to load specific worksheets or configurations, as will be described shortly.

A Batch File Menu System

If you have a hard disk, you can easily move among different programs stored on the hard disk by using a series of small batch files and a message file. A message file is simply an ASCII file that contains text you want DOS to display. If you use the command TYPE together with the name of an ASCII file, DOS reads the text from the file to the screen. By preceding this command with the CLS command, which clears the screen in DOS, you can achieve a display such as this:

```
                Main Menu
=====================================
1   Run Quattro PRO
2   Run WordPerfect
3   Use Backit program
Type the number of your choice and press ENTER.
```

You can display this message any time you return to DOS from another program by writing a batch file called Z.BAT, which changes the directory back to the root (CD \), clears the screen (CLS), and types the message ("TYPE MENU.MSG"). If you write a batch file called 1.BAT that starts Quattro PRO, you can load Quattro PRO simply by pressing 1 and ENTER. If the 1.BAT file that starts Quattro PRO runs the Z.BAT file after Quattro PRO, you have created a loop from the menu to Quattro PRO and back. You could set up other batch files such as 2.BAT and 3.BAT to load other programs such as WordPerfect (2.BAT) and Backit (3.BAT).

You may want to place these batch files in a special subdirectory. Most systems have a subdirectory called DOS, which is used to store the DOS files. If you place your batch files in a subdirectory, make sure that your AUTOEXEC.BAT uses the DOS command PATH to let DOS know where to look for a batch file if it does not find it in the current directory. If you place the Z.BAT file in the \DOS subdirectory, and then place the command

PATH = C:\DOS

in your AUTOEXEC.BAT file, DOS will always be able to find Z.BAT. Thus, you will always be able to return to the root directory and the menu from anywhere on the disk by pressing **Z** and then ENTER at the DOS prompt. You can easily adapt this system to your own needs by substituting the commands for other software programs and expanding the list.

Improving Menus

As you saw in Chapter 10, programs on your PC have the ability to display line and corner characters that can be used to create boxes. Some word processing programs, like WordPerfect and DisplayWrite 4, can perform an operation called Cursor Draw, in which boxes made of lines are easily drawn around text. If saved as ASCII files, these boxes can be displayed with the TYPE command. The boxes help make attractive menus. You can even make such a menu with the @CHAR function in Quattro PRO and then print the worksheet to disk.

Quattro PRO Menus

A command to load Quattro PRO can be given with an accompanying worksheet name, so that as soon as the program is loaded, the worksheet is retrieved from disk. For example, if you enter the following at the DOS prompt in the Quattro PRO directory

Q SALES

then Quattro PRO will load, followed by the worksheet SALES.WQ1, *if* there is a worksheet called SALES in the default directory with the default extension. This ability can be used in batch files to load Quattro PRO in several different ways. You can set up a menu like this to offer a choice between different Quattro PRO configurations:

Quattro PRO Menu

```
=================================
1   Run Quattro PRO for Pricing
2   Run Quattro PRO for Budget Analysis
3   Run Quattro PRO with no file
```

The file 1.BAT used to activate this menu contains the instruction

Q PRICING.WQ1

so that Quattro PRO loads the pricing worksheet as soon as the program loads. The 2.BAT file loads

Q BUDGET.WQ1

and so on. You could use a variation of these instructions to load Quattro PRO for different users. Bear in mind that the file you call needs to be available to Quattro PRO. To help ensure this you can use a more specific request such as

Q C: \DATA\SALES.WQ1

You can set up this menu system in your QUATTRO directory. To use this system the batch file called from the Main Menu to load Quattro PRO contains the command ECHO OFF, followed by

```
CD \QUATTRO
CLS
TYPE Q.MEN
```

The file Q.MEN is the menu of Quattro PRO choices.

Parameter Passing

One further technique that is useful in batch file construction is to add a parameter to the file. This can then be replaced by a value that you provide when you use the batch file. This is similar to the technique used by Quattro PRO. When you enter Q followed by a file name to load 1-2-3 you are passing a parameter, in this case, the file name. If you create a batch file called 3.BAT that looks like this

```
ECHO OFF
CLS
Q %1
Z
```

then you can load Quattro PRO with a worksheet by entering

3 FILENAME

The %1 entry in the batch file is parameter 1. The nice feature of parameters is that they do not need to be entered. Thus, you can enter 3 on its own just to load Quattro PRO, or 3 followed by a space and a file name to load Quattro PRO and a file.

Managing Shortcuts and RF Files

You may want to use batch files to manipulate Quattro PRO configuration files. Quattro uses a special configuration or resource file to store basic definitions that specify the way the program is to be run. The file where the default settings are stored when you use the Options Update command or assign Shortcuts is called RSC.RF. You can create additional configuration files that all contain different sets of defaults. To create a file other than RSC.RF, first copy the current RSC.RF to a new file. For example, use the command

COPY RSC.RF MY.RF

Now load Quattro PRO with the command

Q /dMY.RF

at the DOS prompt. Using /d and the RF file name loads the RF file that
you specify, meaning in this case that changes made to the configuration
will be stored in MY.RF. Now make the changes you want to the Shortcuts
and program options. Use the Options Update command to make sure that
the current default settings are stored in the configuration files. The next
time you load Quattro PRO you can either use the program defaults, by
typing **Q** to start the program, or you can use your own defaults by loading
with the command Q /dMY.RF.

You can specify both a resource file and a worksheet on the command
line, as in

Q /dMY.RF PIE

to load your RF file plus the worksheet PIE.WQ1.

By using batch file language with a parameter you can establish a batch
file to run Quattro PRO that looks like this:

```
ECHO OFF
CLS
Q /d%1.rf %2
```

If you call this file QP.BAT you can load Quattro PRO plus a special RF
file and a worksheet called PIE by simply entering

QP MY PIE

By incorporating batch file code like this into a menu system you can
provide users with a choice between default settings. For example, for
those who like to use Quattro PRO 1-2-3 emulation you can set up a
configuration file to run Quattro PRO in 1-2-3 mode, as discussed in
Appendix B.

About Mice

If you have connected a mouse to your system and installed it correctly, a mouse palette and pointer should appear when you load Quattro PRO. If the mouse palette and pointer do not appear, check the installation instructions for the mouse. For example, mice require that a special program called a device driver be loaded or installed for DOS to recognize the mouse. This means that you either have to enter something like MSMOUSE at the DOS prompt before the mouse is recognized, or add a line to the CONFIG.SYS file, described earlier in this appendix, such as

DEVICE = MSMOUSE.SYS

If you have performed the necessary hardware and software installation of the mouse and Quattro PRO still does not recognize it, check the mouse test program that comes with most mice. You may have a conflict between different devices that is affecting the mouse port or mouse card.

B Quattro PRO and Other Programs

Quattro PRO has exceptional capabilities when it comes to getting along with other programs. This appendix explains how to exchange files between Quattro PRO and 1-2-3 as well as how to make the Quattro PRO user interface consistent with that of 1-2-3.

Relating to 1-2-3 and Other Spreadsheets

Quattro PRO is similar in many respects to other electronic spreadsheet programs such as Lotus 1-2-3 and Microsoft Excel. (In this appendix, references to 1-2-3 are to Release 2.01. There are some references to 1-2-3 Release 3 but they are specifically identified as such.) The actual arrangement of data in Quattro PRO, Excel, and 1-2-3 is very similar, because all three programs use indexed columns and rows for managing data. However, there are some differences in terminology that need to be noted.

Blocks and Ranges

The arrangement of indexed columns and rows in an electronic spreadsheet produces a collection of boxes, or cells. A cell is named or indexed by the column and row forming the cell. Thus, column B, row 3 is named cell B3. When a contiguous group of cells must be acted on collectively, it is called a *block* in Quattro PRO. In 1-2-3 a group of cells is called a *range*.

Excel uses the term range as well but generally refers to selected cells rather than ranges. Commands that affect a group of cells are handled differently by the three programs. Excel and Quattro PRO gather many block-related commands into an Edit menu. Formatting of grouped cells is handled by the Style commands in Quattro PRO, the Format commands in Excel. In 1-2-3 there is a main menu item called Range that covers most commands affecting a group of cells, both formatting and editing. However, two editing commands for ranges, Copy and Move, are presented on the main menu.

Global and Default

When a command affects the entire spreadsheet, 1-2-3 refers to it as *global*. In 1-2-3 the Global commands are a subset of Worksheet commands. Even the program defaults are handled by the /Worksheet Global menu. Quattro PRO refers to commands that affect the whole spreadsheet as Options, as does Excel. Quattro PRO distinguishes between default settings made for a particular worksheet and those written to the configuration file per-manent settings. This is done with the Options Update command. The global commands in 1-2-3 and their equivalent default settings in Quattro PRO are as follows:

1-2-3 Global Commands	**Quattro PRO Settings**
/Worksheet Global Column-Width	/Options Formats Global Width
/Worksheet Global Format	/Options Formats Numeric Format
/Worksheet Global Recalc	/Options Recalculation
/Worksheet Global Protection	/Options Protection

Interfacing

Both Quattro PRO and Excel allow you to use a mouse to select cells and issue commands. Excel does this through the Windows operating environ-ment whereas mouse support is an integral part of Quattro PRO. Both Quattro PRO and Excel allow you to select cells before issuing commands that affect those cells, whereas 1-2-3 requires you to issue a command and then select the cells. In fact, Quattro PRO can operate in both modes. While all three programs use menu bars across the top of the screen, the 1-2-3 menu bar is only present when you press the / key. In Quattro PRO and Excel the main menu bar normally remains on screen and you then pull down vertical menus of additional commands.

Both Quattro PRO and Excel allow you to add or subtract items from the menu system, including macros. In Quattro PRO this is done with the Options Startup Edit Menus command. This command also allows you to alter the style of menu between the normal pull-down style and pop-up menus that only appear when the menu is activated. You can adjust the width of Quattro PRO menus to either display settings or hide them. You can even tell Quattro PRO to remember the last item you picked from the menu, allowing rapid repetition of commands.

File Sharing

To use a 1-2-3 Release 2.01 worksheet in Quattro PRO, all you need to do is select it from the list of worksheet files. Quattro PRO automatically translates the file and the macros it contains into a Quattro PRO worksheet. To save any work you do in Quattro PRO in a 1-2-3 worksheet file, just include the desired extension at the end of the file name. Remember that 1-2-3 Version 1A uses WKS and Version 2.01 uses WK1. For Quattro PRO to use macros in a 1-2-3 worksheet you will need to set up Quattro PRO with the 1-2-3 menu as described in the next section. To share files with users of Excel you can also use the WK1 format, which can be read by both Excel and Quattro PRO. For a complete list of file formats that can be read and written by Quattro PRO, see Table B-1.

Obviously, there are some situations in which Quattro PRO cannot directly store your worksheet as a WK1 file. When you use a Quattro PRO feature that has no equivalent in 1-2-3, such as line drawing, then that feature is lost when the file is saved in 1-2-3 format. This affects those @functions that Quattro PRO supports but 1-2-3 does not. When you save a file containing such functions, Quattro PRO will warn you that it is about to convert an unknown function to a value and you are given a chance to cancel the file save operation and use a Quattro PRO format instead. Table B-2 shows a list of Quattro PRO @functions that should not be used in a worksheet you are saving in 1-2-3 format. When you are exchanging files between Quattro PRO and 1-2-3 you will need to pay particular attention to macros. See the following section on sharing macros for more details.

WKS	Lotus 1-2-3, Release 1A
WK1	Lotus 1-2-3, Release 2.01
WKE	Lotus 1-2-3, Educational Version
WRK	Lotus Symphony, Release 1.2
WR1	Lotus Symphony, Release 2.0
WKQ	Earlier versions of Quattro
WQ1	Quattro PRO
WKP	Surpass
WK$	SQZ (Lotus 1-2-3, Release 1A)
WK!	SQZ (Lotus 1-2-3, Release 2.01)
WR$	SQZ (Lotus Symphony, Release 1.2)
WR!	SQZ (Lotus Symphony, Release 2.0)
WKZ	SQZ (Earlier versions of Quattro)
WQ!	SQZ (Quattro PRO)
DB	Paradox
DB2	dBASE II
DBF	dBASE III, III+, and IV
RXD	Reflex (early versions)
R2D	Reflex (Version 2)

Table B-1.   *File Formats Read / Written by Quattro PRO*

@CELLINDEX	@HEXTONUM	@PAYMT
@CURVALUE	@IPAYMNT	@PPAYMT
@DEGREES	@IRATE	@PVAL
@DSTDS	@MEMAVAIL	@RADIANS
@DVARS	@MEMEMSAVAIL	@STDS
@FILEEXISTS	@NPER	@SUMPRODUCT
@FVAL	@NUMTOHEX	@VARS

Table B-2.   *Quattro PRO @Functions to Avoid When Exporting to 1-2-3*

Quattro PRO and 1-2-3

The differences between Quattro PRO and 1-2-3 can be minimized by using the emulation features that Quattro PRO provides. You may want to do this either to run 1-2-3 macros or to minimize retraining employees who already know how to use 1-2-3. In the long run you will probably find that users of 1-2-3 adjust quite happily to the Quattro PRO menu system without using the 1-2-3 emulation features. However, if you do wish to make Quattro PRO emulate 1-2-3, for example to run 1-2-3 macros, then the following steps should be followed.

The 1-2-3 Menu

Quattro PRO provides a menu tree that will be familiar to users of 1-2-3. Found in the file 123.MU, this menu set appears much like the Quattro PRO menus, but options have names to match the 1-2-3 menu system and the commands are grouped differently. The Quattro PRO Edit Erase command, for example, is found on the 1-2-3 Range menu, as the Range Erase command.

The 1-2-3 menu can be selected for use with Quattro PRO during the installation process. If you did not select the 1-2-3 menu tree during installation you can still run Quattro PRO in 1-2-3 mode by starting the program with this special command:

Q123

This command tells Quattro PRO to use a special configuration file called 123.RF. This file contains settings that cause Quattro PRO to emulate 1-2-3. For more on using RF files with Quattro PRO, see Appendix A.

You can also switch to the 1-2-3 menu tree after loading Quattro PRO with the regular menus. If you would like to switch menu trees during a session, you can use the Options Startup command. You can also use this command if you selected the 1-2-3 menu system during installation and would like to try the regular Quattro PRO menu. When you select Options Startup you will see from the menu the name of the current menu file. Normally, this is QUATTRO.MU, the regular Quattro PRO menu tree. Select Menu Tree from the Startup menu and you will see a list of currently available menu files, including 123.MU. When you highlight 123.MU and press ENTER, you will be returned to READY mode and the 1-2-3 menu will be visible across the top of the screen.

The 1-2-3 menu in Quattro PRO remains on screen at all times, like the regular Quattro PRO menu. However, you still have to press / to activate it. When the 1-2-3 menu is activated, the word *Worksheet* is highlighted, just as in 1-2-3, and you can select items by either the first letter method or the highlight and ENTER method. Take a moment to explore the 1-2-3 menu tree. Some commands look slightly different. For example, the System command in 1-2-3 itself takes you immediately to DOS, whereas in Quattro PRO's 1-2-3 emulation mode the System command requires that you make a further menu selection before reaching DOS. You will also notice that the 1-2-3 menu tree has some items that are not found in 1-2-3 itself. These items are marked by small boxes next to their names in the menu list.

To make your menu tree file selection permanent you need to use the Options Update command. Under the 1-2-3 menu tree this command is Worksheet Global Default Update. When you select Update, Quattro PRO writes your choice of menu system to the configuration file. When you exit from Quattro PRO and reload the program, the new menu system you selected will be in effect.

Comfort Features

If you are using Quattro PRO in 1-2-3 mode you will probably want to make Quattro PRO save files in a 1-2-3 file format. If you install 1-2-3 emulation during installation, load Quattro PRO with the Q123 option, or change from the Quattro PRO menu tree to the menus in 123.MU, then the default file extension is automatically changed to WK1. You can alter this extension, for example to the SQZ version of the 1-2-3 format, by using the Worksheet Global Default Files command in the 1-2-3 menus, or Options Startup from the Quattro PRO menu tree.

Borland designed Quattro PRO so that it does not prompt you to save data before it executes the Erase or Exit command if you have already saved the data. However, because erasing block and graph names can waste hours of work, Quattro PRO always prompts before completing an Edit Names Reset or a Graph Names Reset command. If you are familiar with 1-2-3, then you will know that this approach to name resetting and file saving is different from that used by Lotus. If you are comfortable with the Lotus-style confirmation prompts, you can use them. To make the change while using the Quattro PRO menu tree, use the Options Startup Edit Menus command and select Options. Select Borland Style and change the setting to No. Use the Worksheet Global Default Files Edit Menus command in the 1-2-3 menu tree to switch to Lotus-style save and reset prompts. Select Options, then Borland Style, and change the setting to No. This is done automatically when you switch to 1-2-3 menus.

You will notice that while you are using the Edit Menus command there is another Confirm Options setting on the Options menu called During Macros. Setting this option to Yes preserves the Borland style of confirmation during the recording and execution of macros. Changing this option to No helps you to successfully share macros with 1-2-3. This option is automatically set to No when you invoke the 1-2-3 menus.

Sharing Macros

There are major differences between 1-2-3 and Quattro PRO in the area of macros. When making macros in Quattro PRO you do not have to use lists of actual keystrokes when replicating menu choices. For example, suppose that you want to print the cells you have named TOTAL. In 1-2-3 the macro code would be

/PPRTOTAL~AG

This is compact, but far from obvious to decipher. If you happened to use /PFRTOTAL~AG by mistake, the macro could have unpleasant effects. In the menu equivalent approach used by Quattro PRO the macro would look like this:

{/ + Print;Block}TOTAL~
{/ + Print;Align}{/ + Print;Go}

This is very easy to read and debug. Since Quattro PRO records macros for you it takes no longer to create than the 1-2-3 version. The style of macro recording normally used by Quattro PRO language is called Logical. The 1-2-3 style is called Keystroke.

When it comes to sharing macros, Quattro PRO can run macros made with 1-2-3, but only if you first load Quattro PRO's 1-2-3 menu tree. Quattro PRO can record macros that 1-2-3 can run, but only if you record them with the 1-2-3 menu tree in place and the Keystroke style of macro recording in effect, instead of the usual Logical or menu equivalent style. The style of macro recording is set by the Worksheet Macro Macro Recording command in the 1-2-3 menu tree. This is automatically set to Keystroke when you invoke the 1-2-3 style menus. In the regular Quattro PRO menu tree the command is Tools Macro Macro Recording. Of course, for your macros to be compatible with 1-2-3 you cannot use any of the menu items or macro commands unique to Quattro PRO. These are listed in Table B-3.

Note that Quattro PRO macros recorded with the Logical style will run regardless of the menu tree that is in place. This means that you can be using the 1-2-3 style menu and still run a Quattro PRO macro developed under the normal Quattro PRO menu. Since Quattro PRO allows you to run macros from libraries, this feature gives users of the 1-2-3 menu tree access to macros developed by regular Quattro PRO users. To make a macro library, first open the worksheet containing your collected macros. Use the Macro Library command and set the option to Yes, then save the file. As long as the file is open you can use macros that are in it, even if the library file is not the current worksheet.

Added Features

Several features found in Quattro PRO are not found in 1-2-3 Release 2.01. These features have been incorporated into Quattro PRO's 1-2-3 menu system where appropriate. They include the Worksheet Macro command and such Graph commands as Area and Rotated Bar. Note that saving graphs in worksheets with the WK1 or WKS format removes color information about the graph. Use the regular WQ! format to retain color settings.

There are some Quattro PRO features that are not part of the menu system and that 1-2-3 users need to know. These include the use of the DELETE key for deleting the contents of a cell (the equivalent of /Range Erase ENTER in 1-2-3) and the Undo key (ALT-F5). The CTRL-D date entry method, the rest of the Shortcuts features, and the ability to assign menu items to CTRL keys should also be pointed out to 1-2-3 users switching to Quattro PRO. The use of the Record feature and Transcript for macro making is part of Quattro PRO that experienced 1-2-3 users will want to explore. The function keys are largely used in the same way in Quattro PRO and 1-2-3. Exceptions in Quattro PRO are the following:

Menu Items

Worksheet	Macro
Worksheet	Undo
Range	Column
Range	Alignment
Range	Output Style
Range	Data Entry
Range	Search & Replace
File	New
File	Open
File	Workspace
File	!SQZ!
File	Update Links
Print	All Final Quality options
Graph	Instant Graph
View	All options

Macro Commands

{;}	{GRAPHCHAR}	{NUMON}
{BACKTAB}	{INSOFF}	{PASTE}
{CAPOFF}	{INSON}	{READDIR}
{CAPON}	{MACROS}	{SCROLLOFF}
{CHOOSE}	{MARKALL}	{SCROLLON}
{CLEAR}	{MARK}	{STEPOFF}
{COPY}	{MESSAGE}	{STEPON}
{CR}	{MOVE}	{STEP}
{DATE}	{NAME}	{TAB}
{DELEOL}	{NEXTWIN}	{UNDO}
{FUNCTIONS}	{NUMOFF}	{ZOOM}

Table B-3. *Menu Items and Macro Commands to Avoid When Exporting Macros to 1-2-3*

- ALT-F2 for macro options
- F3 to activate the menu (in addition to /)
- ALT-F3 to list @functions
- SHIFT-F3 to list macro commands
- ALT-F5 to undo your last action
- ALT-F6 to zoom a window

Also note the use of the plus key on the numeric keypad to expand menus, and the use of the minus key to contract them. Expanding menus shows the current settings of items when they exist. Contracting menus makes them less obtrusive. These keys make for more flexible and informative uses of menus than in 1-2-3, where many of the current settings cannot be seen from the menu.

C Support and Printer Tables

Technology as powerful as that used by today's personal computers is not always easy to understand and is bound to give rise to questions. This appendix provides some suggestions for when you run into problems using Quattro PRO. Some common questions are answered and there are tips on using printer setup strings, together with a listing of strings for use with many popular printers.

Getting Support

When you are facing a problem using Quattro PRO, one of the first steps to take is a break. Give yourself a few minutes away from the computer to relax; you can then return to the problem in a better, and often clearer, frame of mind. If that does not help, try asking fellow workers for their suggestions. Describing the problem to someone else can often help you see the solution. Be sure to check relevant sections in the manual. Check the spelling and syntax of any formulas, functions, or macro commands you are using. Refer to the index of this book for the relevant subject. If you still do not have an acceptable answer, consider the following sources of support.

Written Support

Do not underestimate the venerable process of putting the problem into words and putting those words on paper. This process can sometimes solve the problem as you think it through. If you still need help, send the problem, together with any printouts or screen prints, plus the software version and the serial number from the front of the original program disk to

Borland International, Inc.
1800 Green Hills Road
P.O. Box 660001
Scotts Valley, CA 95066-0001

While this is not the fastest way of finding support, it is sometimes the best way, particularly if you feel you need to present printed data from the program.

On-Line Support

If you have a modem and communications software, you should consider subscribing to CompuServe, the on-line information bank. Here you will find the Borland Applications Forum (accessed with GO BORAPP from the CompuServe prompt). The Forum contains answers to many common questions, a few of which are included at the end of this appendix. The Forum also has many useful Quattro PRO worksheet files that you can copy, and a message and discussion system for exchanging views and news with other Quattro PRO users. Many computer stores and bookstores sell sign-up packages for CompuServe, or you can write to

CompuServe Information Service, Inc.
P.O. Box 20212
Columbus, OH 43220

Registration

If you have just bought Quattro PRO, be sure to fill out and return the user registration card in the front of the manual. Registering your software protects your investment in it and ensures that you will hear of upgrades and related product announcements. For information about the latest version of the program, plus complimentary products as they become available, write to Borland at the address just provided.

Printer Setup Strings

To obtain the desired effects when printing, you may need to send certain codes to your printer. Although Quattro PRO has a built-in system for communicating font and layout information to your printer, you may want to send specific print instructions. You can do this with a setup string, a special code that your printer understands. Note that you should only use setup strings in draft mode printing, not when the Print Destination setting is Graphics Printer.

In a setup string you tell the printer to use such features as condensed pitch and italic print. A setup string consists of one or more ASCII character codes, which are translated from the printer control codes listed in your printer's user manual. For example, Hewlett-Packard LaserJet printers understand the code

\027E\027(s16.66H

to mean compressed print (17 pitch). You can enter a setup string with the Print Layout Setup String command, or you can place the string in the worksheet by entering it in a cell in the leftmost column of the Print Block, and preceding it with two of the special label prefix characters, as in

| |\027E\027(s16.66H)

When Quattro PRO encounters this entry it will send the print instruction to the printer. Quattro PRO will not print the line on which the entry occurs, which means that you should not place the code in a row that you want to print. The code does not have to be in the first row of the Print Block and you can use several codes in the same Print Block, for example, to turn on condensed print, and then turn it off again. (Note that you can use the I I code alone to cause a row to be hidden during printing.)

Each printer recognizes its own set of control codes. The following tables list ASCII codes for several different printers. To enter a command for a printer other than those listed, refer to your printer's user manual for the control code or what is sometimes called an *escape code*.

Printer control codes can be sent in several forms. Most begin with the ESCAPE or ESC character, which is entered as \027. This is followed by further codes that are either entered as a \ followed by a number, or as a simple character like *E*. The first 32 ASCII codes do not have keyboard equivalents. Thus, your printer manual might tell you to use ESC,18, which is entered as \027\018. Using the chart in Table C-1 you can check the character equivalent for the codes you are using. For example, the code \027\069 is the same as \027E, which may appear in your printer manual as ESC,E.

You can enter more than one code in a setup string as long as the printer supports it and the entire string does not exceed 254 characters. For example, the EPSON FX-85 can print near-letter-quality, bold, and elite pitch characters, but it cannot print italicized characters in near-letter-quality mode.

Decimal Value	Hexadecimal Value	Control Character	Character
0	00	NUL	Null
1	01	SOH	☺
2	02	STX	☻
3	03	ETX	♥
4	04	EOT	♦
5	05	ENQ	♣
6	06	ACK	♠
7	07	BEL	Beep
8	08	BS	◘
9	09	HT	Tab
10	0A	LF	Line-feed

Table C-1. *ASCII Codes*

Decimal Value	Hexadecimal Value	Control Character	Character
11	0B	VT	Cursor home
12	0C	FF	Form-feed
13	0D	CR	Enter
14	0E	SO	
15	0F	SI	
16	10	DLE	
17	11	DC1	
18	12	DC2	
19	13	DC3	
20	14	DC4	
21	15	NAK	
22	16	SYN	
23	17	ETB	
24	18	CAN	↑
25	19	EM	↓
26	1A	SUB	→
27	1B	ESC	←
28	1C	FS	Cursor right
29	1D	GS	Cursor left
30	1E	RS	Cursor up
31	1F	US	Cursor down
32	20	SP	Space
33	21		!
34	22		"
35	23		#
36	24		$
37	25		%
38	26		&
39	27		'
40	28		(
41	29		)
42	2A		*
43	2B		+
44	2C		,
45	2D		-
46	2E		.
47	2F		/

Table C-1. *ASCII Codes (continued)*

Decimal Value	Hexadecimal Value	Control Character	Character
48	30		0
49	31		1
50	32		2
51	33		3
52	34		4
53	35		5
54	36		6
55	37		7
56	38		8
57	39		9
58	3A		:
59	3B		;
60	3C		<
61	3D		=
62	3E		>
63	3F		?
64	40		@
65	41		A
66	42		B
67	43		C
68	44		D
69	45		E
70	46		F
71	47		G
72	48		H
73	49		I
74	4A		J
75	4B		K
76	4C		L
77	4D		M
78	4E		N
79	4F		O
80	50		P
81	51		Q
82	52		R
83	53		S
84	54		T

Table C-1.   *ASCII Codes (continued)*

Decimal Value	Hexadecimal Value	Control Character	Character
85	55		U
86	56		V
87	57		W
88	58		X
89	59		Y
90	5A		Z
91	5B		[
92	5C		\
93	5D		]
94	5E		^
95	5F		—
96	60		`
97	61		a
98	62		b
99	63		c
100	64		d
101	65		e
102	66		f
103	67		g
104	68		h
105	69		i
106	6A		j
107	6B		k
108	6C		l
109	6D		m
110	6E		n
111	6F		o
112	70		p
113	71		q
114	72		r
115	73		s
116	74		t
117	75		u
118	76		v
119	77		w
120	78		x
121	79		y

Table C-1. *ASCII Codes (continued)*

Decimal Value	Hexadecimal Value	Control Character	Character
122	7A		z
123	7B		{
124	7C		¦
125	7D		}
126	7E		~
127	7F	DEL	⌂
128	80		Ç
129	81		ü
130	82		é
131	83		â
132	84		ä
133	85		à
134	86		å
135	87		ç
136	88		ê
137	89		ë
138	8A		è
139	8B		ï
140	8C		î
141	8D		ì
142	8E		Ä
143	8F		Å
144	90		É
145	91		æ
146	92		Æ
147	93		ô
148	94		ö
149	95		ó
150	96		û
151	97		ù
152	98		ÿ
153	99		Ö
154	9A		Ü
155	9B		¢
156	9C		£
157	9D		¥
158	9E		Pt

Table C-1.   *ASCII Codes (continued)*

Decimal Value	Hexadecimal Value	Control Character	Character
159	9F		*f*
160	A0		á
161	A1		í
162	A2		ó
163	A3		ú
164	A4		ñ
165	A5		Ñ
166	A6		ª
167	A7		º
168	A8		¿
169	A9		⌐
170	AA		¬
171	AB		½
172	AC		¼
173	AD		¡
174	AE		«
175	AF		»
176	B0		░
177	B1		▒
178	B2		▓
179	B3		│
180	B4		┤
181	B5		╡
182	B6		╢
183	B7		╖
184	B8		╕
185	B9		╣
186	BA		║
187	BB		╗
188	BC		╝
189	BD		╜
190	BE		╛
191	BF		┐
192	C0		└
193	C1		┴
194	C2		┬
195	C3		├

Table C-1. *ASCII Codes (continued)*

Decimal Value	Hexadecimal Value	Control Character	Character
196	C4		
197	C5		+
198	C6		╞
199	C7		╟
200	C8		╚
201	C9		╔
202	CA		╩
203	CB		╦
204	CC		╠
205	CD		=
206	CE		╬
207	CF		╧
208	D0		╨
209	D1		╤
210	D2		╥
211	D3		╙
212	D4		╘
213	D5		╒
214	D6		╓
215	D7		╫
216	D8		╪
217	D9		┘
218	DA		┌
219	DB		■
220	DC		▬
221	DD		▌
222	DE		▐
223	DF		▬
224	E0		α
225	E1		β
226	E2		Γ
227	E3		π
228	E4		Σ
229	E5		σ
230	E6		μ
231	E7		τ
232	E8		φ

Table C-1. *ASCII Codes (continued)*

Decimal Value	Hexadecimal Value	Control Character	Character
233	E9		θ
234	EA		Ω
235	EB		δ
236	EC		∞
237	ED		$\emptyset$
238	EE		ε
239	EF		$\cap$
240	F0		$\equiv$
241	F1		$\pm$
242	F2		$\geq$
243	F3		$\leq$
244	F4		$\lceil$
245	F5		$\rfloor$
246	F6		$\div$
247	F7		$\approx$
248	F8		$^{\circ}$
249	F9		$\bullet$
250	FA		$\cdot$
251	FB		$\sqrt{}$
252	FC		n
253	FD		2
254	FE		$\blacksquare$
255	FF		(blank)

Table C-1. *ASCII Codes (continued)*

Setting Up the LaserJet

The HP LaserJet is found in many of today's offices. You can produce excellent reports using a LaserJet with Quattro PRO if you follow a few basic guidelines. For normal 8.5- by- 11-inch paper you should set the page length at 60 lines. For normal 10-pitch printing, use a left margin of 5 and a right margin of 80. Use the following settings in the Print Layout menu (only use the setup strings if you are not using the LaserJet as a Graphics Printer).

Portrait mode, 8.5 x 11, 10 pitch
Page length: 60
Right margin: 80
Setup string: \027E
Portrait mode, 8.5 x 11, 17 pitch
Page length: 60
Right margin: 132
Setup string: \027E\027(s16.66H

Landscape mode, 11 x 8.5, 10 pitch
Page length: 45
Right margin: 106
Setup string: \027E\027&l10
Landscape mode, 11 x 8.5, 17 pitch
Page length: 45
Right margin: 176
Setup string: \027E\027&l10 \0279s16.66H

Always use Print Adjust Printer Align before each print job. You may find that the last page of the printout is not ejected from the printer. You can eject the paper by using the printer's control panel. Press the ON LINE button to take the printer offline; then press FORM FEED, followed by ON LINE.

Alternatively, you can cause a page eject with a setup string in the worksheet. Place either the label | | \012 or | | \027E in a cell of the leftmost column of the Print Block (below the last line of data but within the Print Block) to cause a page eject. This code should be the only item on the row it occupies.

Setups for Other Printer Models

C. Itoh 8510

Mode	String
Compressed	\027Q
10 pitch	\027N
12 pitch	\O27E
Double spacing	\027T48
Standard spacing	\027A
8 lines per inch	\027B
Emphasized	\027!
Cancel emphasized	\027\034
Underlined	\027X
Printer reset	\027Y

DEC LA100

Mode	String
Compressed	\027[4w
10 pitch	\027[0w
12 pitch	\027[2w
Expanded print	\027[5w
Double spacing	\027[3z
Standard spacing	\027[0z
8 lines per inch	\027[2"z
Emphasized	\027[2"z

Epson FX, MX, or RX, and many other printers that have an Epson FX-compatible mode

Mode	String
Compressed	\015
10 pitch	\027P
12 pitch	\027M
Expanded print	\027W1
Double spacing	\027\065\024
Standard spacing	\0272
8 lines per inch	\0270
Emphasized	\027E
Cancel emphasized	\027F
Underlined	\027-1
Cancel underlined	\027-0
Italic	\0274
Cancel italic	\0275
Printer reset	\027@
Near-letter-quality mode	\027X1
Draft mode selection	\027X0
Expanded print (one line)	\014
Cancel expanded print	\020
Double-strike printing	\027G
Cancel double-strike	\027H
Superscript printing	\027S0
Subscript printing	\027S1
Cancel sub/superscript	\027T
Select/cancel underlining	\027-1
Italic mode printing	\0274
Cancel italic mode	\0275
International character set	\027R(n)
Right margin (n no. of chars.)	\027Q(n)
Left margin (n no. of chars.)	\027I(n)
Select skip-over perforation	\027N(n)
Cancel perforation skip	\027O
Double-spaced printing	\027A24

Return to single spacing	\0272
Page length (*n* no. of lines)	\027C(*n*)
Page length (*n* no. of inches)	\027C0(*n*)

Epson LQ1500

Mode	String
Compressed	\027x0\015
10 pitch	\027P
12 pitch	\027M
Expanded print	\027W\001
Double spacing	\027\065\024
Standard spacing	\0272
8 lines per inch	\0270
Letter quality	\027X1
Emphasized	\027E
Underlined	\027-\001
Italic	\0274(s1S
Printer reset	\027@

HP LaserJet

Mode	String
Compressed	\027&k2S
10 pitch	\027&k0S
12 pitch	\027(s12H
Double spacing	\027&l3D
Standard spacing	\027&l6D
8 lines per inch	\027&l8D
Emphasized	\027(s3B
Underlined	\027&dD
Printer reset	\027E

HP Thinkjet

Mode	String
Compressed	\016
Expanded print	\014
8 lines per inch	\0270

Mode	String
Emphasized	\027E
Underlined	\027-1

IBM 5182 Color Printer

Mode	String
Compressed	\015
10 pitch	\018
12 pitch	\027\058
Expanded print	\027\087\001
Standard spacing	\027\050
8 lines per inch	\027\048
Emphasized	\027\069
Cancel emphasized	\027\070
Underlined	\027\045\001
Printer reset	\024

IBM Color Jetprinter

Mode	String
Compressed	\015
10 pitch	\018
Expanded print	\027\081\001
Standard spacing	\027\050
8 lines per inch	\027\048
Letter quality	\027\073\002
Emphasized	\027\069
Cancel emphasized	\027\070
Underlined	\027\045\001
Cancel underlined	\027\045\000

IBM Graphics Printer (5151) and many other printers that can operate in a compatible mode (for example, IBM QuietWriter II and Citizen 120D)

Mode	String
Compressed	\015
10 pitch	\018
12 pitch	\027\058
Expanded print	\027\087\001

Standard spacing	\027\050
8 lines per inch	\027\048
Emphasized	\027\069
Cancel emphasized	\027\070
Underlined	\027\045\001
Cancel underlined	\027\045\000
Expanded print (one line)	\014
Cancel expanded print	\020
Double-strike printing	\027G
Cancel double-strike	\027H
Superscript printing	\027S0
Subscript printing	\027S1
Cancel sub/superscript	\027T
Select/cancel underlining	\027-1
International character set	\0276
Return standard character set	\0277
Set margins (1 left/2 right)	\027X($n1$)($n2$)
Select skip-over perforation	\027N(n)
Cancel perforation skip	\027O
Double-spaced printing	\027A24
Return to single spacing	\0272
Page length (n no. of lines)	\027C(n)
Page length (n no. of inches)	\027C0(n)

IBM Proprinter

Mode	**String**
Compressed	\015
10 pitch	\018
12 pitch	\027\058
Expanded print	\027\087\001
8 lines per inch	\027\048
Letter quality	\027I2
Emphasized	\027E
Underlined	\027\045\001

IBM QuietWriter

Mode	String
Compressed	\015\027\073\000
Expanded print	\027\087\001
Double spacing	\027\065\024\027\050
8 lines per inch	\027\048
Underlined	\027\045\001

IDS Prism 80/132

Mode	String
Compressed	\031
10 pitch	\029
12 pitch	\030
Double spacing	\027,B,16,$
Standard spacing	\027,B,8,$
8 lines per inch	\027,B,6,$

NEC 8023A

Mode	String
Compressed	\027Q
10 pitch	\027N
12 pitch	\027E
Double spacing	\027\,T,48
Standard spacing	\027A
8 lines per inch	\027B
Emphasized	\027!
Cancel emphasized	\027"
Underlined	\027X
Cancel underlined	\027Y

Okidata Microline

Mode	String
Compressed	\029
10 pitch	\030
12 pitch	\028

Expanded print	\030\031
Double spacing	\027\037\057\048
Standard spacing	\027\054
8 lines per inch	\027\056
Letter quality	\027\049
Emphasized	\029\031
Underlined	\027\067
Cancel underlined	\027\068
Printer reset	\027\024

Toshiba P351, P1350

Mode	**String**
Compressed	\027\091
12 pitch	\027*1\027E10
Expanded print	\027!
Double spacing	\027L16
Emphasized	\027K2
Cancel emphasized	\027\077
Italic	\027\018
Cancel italic	\027\020
Printer reset	\027\0261

Star Micronics Gemini

Mode	**String**
Compressed	\015
10 pitch	\018
12 pitch	\027\066\002
Expanded print	\027\087\001
Double spacing	\027\065\024
Standard spacing	\0272
8 lines per inch	\0270
Emphasized	\027\069
Underlined	\027-1
Cancel underlined	\027\045\000
Italic	\027\052
Cancel italic	\027\053
Printer reset	\027\064

Common Quattro Pro Questions

The following are some of the questions most commonly asked by Quattro PRO users. The answers provided should help if you are still having difficulty after referring to the manual, the Help function, and the appropriate section of this book.

Q: I used the /Default Protection command to protect all of the cells in the worksheet. Then I unprotected several cells with /Block Advanced Unprotect, but the cells do not appear any different. Shouldn't unprotected cells be highlighted?

A: In addition to the U message in the cell descriptor, you should see the contents of unprotected cells in a different color or shade. If you are using a monochrome monitor, you might need to adjust the brightness and contrast to see the difference between regular and boldfaced text.

Q: The DELETE key is very convenient for erasing the contents of the current cell, but is there any way to reverse it, an "Oops!" key to get back what I just deleted?

A: You can reverse the action of the DELETE key if you have activated the Undo feature with the Options Other Undo command. To use the Undo feature press ALT-F5. Remember that you can undo Undo simply by pressing ALT-F5 a second time.

Q: What is the difference between BACKSPACE and ESCAPE when changing block settings, such as a /Block Fill Block?

A: When you are looking at a set of block coordinates such as B3..B9, pressing the ESCAPE key simply unlocks the coordinate so that just B3 appears in the prompt. Pressing BACKSPACE when you see B3..B8 unlocks the coordinates and changes the cell coordinate to the cell your cell selector was in before you entered the menu. Thus, if you wanted to fill columns B and C from row 3 to row 8, you would begin with column B, placing the cell selector in B3 and anchoring it there when prompted for the cells to be filled. Having filled cells B3..B8, you would then place the cell selector in C3. When you begin the /Block Fill command, Quattro PRO will assume you want to fill B3..B8 again; but then you press BACKSPACE when prompted for the location of the cells to be filled. Quattro PRO will change the prompt to C3, where you can anchor the cell selector with a period and proceed.

Q: When I am editing a long cell entry is there a way to delete all of the characters from the cursor to the end of the line?

A: Use the Delete-to-end-of-line key, CTRL-\. You can also use CTRL-BACK-SPACE or CTRL-[in EDIT mode to remove the entire contents of the edit line.

Q: When I am checking a large block setting, not all of the selected cells are visible, so how can I look at the different corners of the block?

A: Press the period key and you will move the active corner of the range. You can then move the corner with the cursor keys to see more of the worksheet in that area. For example, suppose that the print range is cells A1..X45. When you select Range from the Print menu you see A1..X45 as the range prompt and the cursor flashes in cell X45. Press period (.) and the prompt changes to X1..A45 with the cursor at A45. Press period (.) again and the prompt becomes X45..A1 with the cursor in A1. A third press of the period moves the cursor to X1 and changes the prompt to A45..X1. A fourth period returns the display to the way it was.

Q: How can I look up the names of @functions and get help with using them?

A: Press ALT-F3 to see a list of functions. Press F1 at this point for the Function Index in the Help system. Highlight the function you are interested in and you will get details of the function arguments. By pressing ALT-F3 in either EDIT mode or READY mode, and then highlighting a function and pressing ENTER, you can enter the function on the edit line complete with @ sign and opening parenthesis.

Q: How can I look up the names of macro commands and get help with using them?

A: Press SHIFT-F3 to see a list of commands. Highlight the appropriate group of commands and press ENTER. Press F1 at this point for details of the command arguments. By pressing SHIFT-F3 in either EDIT mode or READY mode, and then highlighting a command and pressing ENTER, you can enter the command on the edit line complete with braces.

Trademarks

AboveBoard™	Intel Corporation
Apple®, Apple II®	Apple Computer, Inc.
AppleLaserWriter®	Apple Computer, Inc.
AST RAMpage!®	AST Research, Inc.
AT®	International Business Machines Corporation
Bitstream®	Bitstream, Inc.
Borland Graphic Interface™	Borland International, Inc.
C. Itoh ™	C. Itoh and Company, Ltd.
Colorpro®	Hewlett-Packard Company
COMPAQ 386®	COMPAQ Computer Corporation
CompuServe®	CompuServe Information Service, Inc.
CP/M®	Digital Research, Inc.
dBASE®, dBASE II®, dBASE III®, dBASE III Plus®, dBASE IV™	Ashton-Tate
DEC™	Digital Equipment Corporation
DESQview®, QEMM-386®	Quarterdeck Office Systems
DisplayWrite™	International Business Machines Corporation
DOS™	International Business Machines Corporation
Epson®, Epson FX™	Seiko Epson Corporation
Gemini™	Star Micronics
Hercules®	Hercules Computer Technology
HIcard®	RYBS Electronics
HP®, HP LaserJet™, HP ThinkJET®	Hewlett-Packard Company
IBM®, IBM PS/2®, IBM Proprinter™	International Business Machines Corporation
IBM Color Graphics Adapter™	International Business Machines Corporation
InSet™	InSet Systems, Inc.
Lotus ®, 1-2-3 ®, Lotus Symphony®	Lotus Development Corporation
Mace Utilities®	Paul Mace Software, Inc.
MenuBuilder®	Borland International, Inc.
Microline™	Okidata
Microsoft®, Microsoft Mouse™, Microsoft Windows™, MS-DOS®	Microsoft Corporation
The Norton Utilities®	Peter Norton Computing, Inc.
OS/2®	International Business Machines Corporation
Paradox®	Ansa Software, A Borland Company
PostScript®	Adobe Systems, Inc.
Quadram®	Quadram
Quattro®	Borland International, Inc.
Reflex®: The Database Manager	Borland International, Inc.
SideKick®	Borland International, Inc.
SPRINT™: The Professional Word Processor	Borland International, Inc.
SuperCalc®	Computer Associates International, Inc.
TOPS®	Sun Microsystems, Inc.
Toshiba®	Toshiba America, Inc.
VisiCalc®	Lotus Development Corporation
WordPerfect®	WordPerfect Corporation
WordStar®	MicroPro International Corporation
XENIX®	Microsoft Corporation
XT ®	International Business Machines Corporation

Index

FUNCTION KEYS

Key	Name	Action
F1	Help	Displays a help menu
F2	Edit	Activates Edit mode; when lists are displayed, activates search mode in bottom status area
ALT F2	Macro Menu	Displays the Macro menu
SHIFT F2	Debug	Activates macro Debug mode
F3	Choices	Activates main menu from Ready mode, zooms lists, displays block names
SHIFT F3	Macro List	Displays a list of macro commands
ALT F3	Functions	Displays a list of @function commands
F4	Absolute	In Edit or Point mode, makes a cell address absolute; repeat to show absolute options
F5	GoTo	Moves the cell selector to the specified address
ALT F5	Undo	When enabled, reverses the last action
SHIFT F5	Pick Window	Displays a list of open windows
F6	Pane	Activates the next window pane

Key	Name	Action
ALT F6	Zoom	Expands or shrinks the active window
SHIFT F6	Next Window	Activates the next open window
F7	Query	Repeats the last Query command
ALT F7	Select All	Selects all items in a list in File Manager
SHIFT F7	Select	Selects an item in a list in File Manager
F8	Table	Repeats the last What-if command
SHIFT F8	Move	Moves selected files in the File Manager
F9	Calc	Recalculates formulas in the spreadsheet, rereads file list in File Manager
SHIFT F9	Copy	Copies selected files in the File Manager
F10	Graph	Displays the current graph, redraws current graph in the Graph Annotator
SHIFT F10	Paste	Inserts in current directory files stored in the paste buffer in File Manager

OFTEN USED KEYS

Key	Action
	(Backspace, not the left arrow) Deletes one character to the left of the cursor when entering or editing data; in Point mode, unanchors the current cell and moves the cell selector back to the original cell position; in Help mode, displays the previous screen
	When entering data in a cell, type a backslash and subsequent character(s), and they will be repeated as often as needed to fill the cell; also used with a letter to name instant macros
DEL	Erases the contents of the current cell; in Edit mode erases the character at the edit cursor
ESC	Backs out of current action, for example, exits a menu, erases changes to an entry on the input line, or removes a prompt without responding to it; press ESC within the Help system to return directly to the spreadsheet
Caps Lock	Enters Caps mode, in which all letters A through Z are typed as capital letters without shifting; does not affect any other keys; press again to exit Caps mode
Scroll Lock	If pressed in Window Move mode, switches to Size mode so you can adjust window size
-	The gray minus key on the numeric keypad is the Contract key; press it with a menu displayed to remove command settings from the menu and therefore to display narrower menus

Key	Action
+	The gray plus key on the numeric keypad is the Expand key; press it to return display of command settings to the menus
SHIFT	Used to enter the upper character on any key, including capitls A through Z, symbols such as $, and numbers on the numeric keypad; used with some function keys
Num Lock	Locks numeric pad into numbers; locks out cursor movement with those keys
CTRL	Used with some function keys and certain other keys to execute commands, such as CTRL-BREAK, which exits menus and halts macro execution, CTRL-D, which prepares cell for data entry, and CTRL-ENTER, which assigns shortcuts
ALT	Used with selected keys A through Z to execute macros and with some function keys
PrtSc	Prints current screen on some systems; will not print graphs
/	In Ready mode, Debug mode, Graph view, Transcript, and Graph Annotator, activates the menu; also used in formulas for division.
*	Used for multiplication sign

FILE MANAGER KEYS

General Windowing Keys

Key	Action
[SHIFT]–[F5]	Pick Window, to access other windows
[ALT]–[0]	Pick Window, to access other windows
[F6] or [TAB]	Pane, activates the next File Manager window pane in the following order: control pane, file list pane, directory tree pane
[SHIFT]–[F6]	Next Window, activates the next open window
[ALT]–[F6]	Zoom Window, zooms an open window to full screen and back again; if window is already expanded, shrinks it again, as with /Window Zoom
[ALT]–[n]	Jumps to window number *n* (The window number appears on the top edge of each frame.)
[F2]	Rename, prompts for a new file name and renames the current file list selection to the file name specified (same as /Edit Rename)
[F5]	GoTo, finds the file name (or combination of wildcard characters) typed at the File Name prompt
[ESC]	Clears the entry at the prompt; when you move the highlight bar away from the prompt and make no new entry, Quatrro restores the original entry
[DEL]	Deletes the character under the cursor
[ENTER]	Moves the cursor to the blank File Name prompt or, if the cursor is at the File Name prompt, opens the file or subdirectory highlighted on the file list
[HOME]	Moves the cursor to the beginning of the prompt entry
[INS]	Moves the cursor to the end of the prompt entry
[CTRL]–[←]	Activates the control pane and moves the highlight bar to the File Name prompt

FILE MANAGER KEYS

Keys for the File List Pane

Key	Action
F2	Rename, lets you rename the current (highlighted) file (same as /Edit Rename)
SHIFT — F7	Select, selects the current (highlighted) file in the list so you can open, move, copy, or delete it; if the file is already selected, unselects it
ALT — F7	All Select, selects all files on the list for moving, copying, or deleting; if some files on the list are already selected, unselects those files
SHIFT — F8	Move, moves the selected files into the paste buffer, removing them from the list
ALT — F8	Delete, erases the selected files or the highlighted file from the disk
F9	Calc, reads the disk and refreshes the file list pane (same as /File Read Dir)
SHIFT — F9	Copy, copies the selected files into the paste buffer for copying to another directory or disk, keeping them on the list
SHIFT — F10	Paste, inserts the files in the paste buffer at the cursor position in the current directory's file list
ESC	Escape, returns all selected files to normal, then activates the control pane and moves the cursor to the File Name prompt
ENTER	Opens selected files or the file at the cursor; if the highlight bar is on the .., opens parent directory; if the highlight bar is on a subdirectory, moves to the subdirectory
HOME	Moves the highlight bar to the parent directory item
END	Moves the highlight bar to the end of the file list
PG UP	Moves the file list display up one screen
PG DN	Moves the file list display down one screen
ESC	Returns all selected files to normal, then activates the control pane and moves the cursor to the File Name prompt
DEL	Deletes all selected files or the highlighted file in the file list
F9	Calc, rereads the current disk/directory

EDITING KEYS

Key	Action
←	Moves the cursor one space to the left
→	Moves the cursor one space to the right
HOME	Moves the cursor to the first character in the cell
END	Moves the cursor to the last character in the cell
CTRL ← or TAB	Moves the cursor five spaces to the left
CTRL → or CTRL TAB	Moves the cursor five spaces to the right
↑	Enters the data and moves the selector up one cell
↓	Enters the data and moves the selector down one cell
PG DN	Enters the data and moves the selector down 20 lines
PG UP	Enters the data and moves the selector up 20 lines
INS	Press to activate Overstrike mode so that new characters replace old, press again to return to normal Insert mode
F3	Lists named blocks if edit cursor is at suitable place for a block name—for example, after an open parenthesis